KARL MARX
FREDERICK ENGELS
COLLECTED WORKS
VOLUME
13

KARL MARX
FREDERICK ENGELS

COLLECTED
WORKS

INTERNATIONAL PUBLISHERS

NEW YORK

KARL MARX
FREDERICK ENGELS

Volume
13

MARX AND ENGELS: 1854-55

INTERNATIONAL PUBLISHERS

NEW YORK

This volume has been prepared jointly by Lawrence & Wishart Ltd., London, International Publishers Co. Inc., New York, and Progress Publishers, Moscow, in collaboration with the Institute of Marxism-Leninism, Moscow.

Editorial commissions:

GREAT BRITAIN: Jack Cohen, Maurice Cornforth, E. J. Hobsbawm, Nicholas Jacobs, Martin Milligan, Ernst Wangermann.

USA: James S. Allen, Louis Diskin, Philip S. Foner, Dirk J. Struik, William W. Weinstone.

USSR: for Progress Publishers—N. P. Karmanova, V. I. Neznanov, V. N. Sedikh, M. K. Shcheglova; for the Institute of Marxism-Leninism— P. N. Fedoseyev, L. I. Golman, A. I. Malysh, M. P. Mchedlov, A. G. Yegorov.

Copyright © Progress Publishers, Moscow, 1980

Library of Congress Cataloging in Publication Data

Marx, Karl, 1818-1883.
    Karl Marx, Frederick Engels: collected works.
    1. Socialism—Collected works. 2. Economics— Collected works. I. Engels, Friedrich, 1820-1895. Works. English. 1975. II. Title.
HX 39.5.A16 1975 335.4 73-84671
ISBN 0-7178-0513-1 (v. 13)

Printed in the Union of Soviet Socialist Republics in 1979

Contents

FROM THE PREPARATORY MATERIALS

APPENDIX

NOTES AND INDEXES

Contents

ILLUSTRATIONS

TRANSLATORS:

SUSANNE FLATAUER: In Retrospect; The Press and the Military System; The Crisis in Trade and Industry; The Four Points; Sunday Observance and the Publicans.—Clanricarde; Critical Observations on the Siege of Sevastopol; The Aims of the Negotiations.—Polemic against Prussia.—A Snowball Riot

BARRIE SELMAN: The Opening of Parliament; Comments on the Cabinet Crisis; Parliamentary News; From Parliament.—From the Theatre of War; On the Ministerial Crisis; The Defeated Government; The Parties and Cliques; Two Crises

Preface

Volume 13 of the *Collected Works* of Marx and Engels contains articles written by them in the period from February 13, 1854 to February 6, 1855. For the most part these articles were published in the *New-York Daily Tribune,* to which Marx and Engels had begun to contribute in August 1851. Many were also reprinted in the newspaper's special issues, the *New-York Semi-Weekly Tribune* and the *New-York Weekly Tribune;* some of them also appeared in the Chartist *People's Paper.* In January 1855 Marx began to publish his articles in the democratic German newspaper, the *Neue Oder-Zeitung,* using as a rule material intended for the *New-York Daily Tribune.* Marx's and Engels' newspaper articles in this period deal with a broad range of contemporary socio-economic and political problems, as well as with questions of the bourgeois-democratic and working-class movement, and are an important part of their literary legacy.

Marx's and Engels' journalism is an outstanding phenomenon. Their articles written more than a century ago about specific events and in a language not their own, have not lost their importance and interest for later generations. Their analysis of contemporary events showed up their causes and inner connections, explained their sometimes apparently fortuitous succession, and made clear their meaning in terms of contemporary history. Marx and Engels were not content with only superficial current information. Their articles reflect the results of many years of study in economics, politics, history, military science, and language. When circumstances compelled them to turn to subjects with which they did not consider themselves fully conversant, they would undertake special researches. Thus, in 1854, in connection with the beginning of the fourth bourgeois revolution in Spain, Marx embarked upon a study of the country's language and history, in particular, of the three revolutions which had taken place there earlier. His surviving five notebooks with excerpts on the Spanish history bear eloquent witness to the depth and thoroughness of these studies. A great deal of literature on the history of the Slavs, Greeks and other peoples inhabiting the Balkan Peninsula, the history of Turkey and its social structure, the Orthodox Church and other problems was studied by Marx and Engels in 1854 in connection with the events in the Balkans.

At the same time Marx and Engels were not merely academic commentators. They wrote on the basis of very close contacts with their contemporaries, with influential political and public figures, and particularly with the proletarian and democratic émigrés of various nationalities in London. Marx's visits to sessions of the British Parliament and Engels' daily contact with Manchester business circles provide cases in point.

In 1854, their journalism was for Marx and Engels practically the only way to disseminate among the democratically-inclined reading public in general, and the workers in particular, the results of their own studies in various spheres of history, political economy and military science.

All that took place in the international arena or in the domestic life of this or that country was evaluated by Marx and Engels from the point of view of their steady aim to establish and equip a revolutionary working-class party; and the experience and knowledge accumulated by them in this connection has enriched the treasury of working-class revolutionary theory. The contents of the present volume illustrate most clearly Marx's and Engels' ability unfailingly to represent the interests of the proletariat in the process of the not yet completed bourgeois-democratic transformations in Europe, as well as the separation, which had just begun, of the working-class movement from the general democratic movement. In their articles strictly scientific analysis is accompanied by invective against the representatives of the ruling classes: the cupidity and mediocrity of the ruling circles, their hypocrisy, sanctimoniousness and corruption are exposed with mordant wit and sarcasm.

The central political event in Europe in 1854 was the military conflict between Russia and Turkey, which broke out in 1853 and in 1854 developed into a war of Britain, France and Turkey against Russia—the Crimean War. Marx and Engels devote the utmost attention to the history of this conflict, the analysis of its causes, and the policies of the individual states. They approach the analysis of the foreign policy of the European powers in the period of the Crimean War, the diplomatic negotiations in Vienna, and the actual course of the military operations, from the viewpoint of the revolutionary proletariat. In examining the events taking place, they always bear in mind the prospects for the development of the working-class movement in Europe and the future of the national liberation and unification movements.

Proceeding from concrete historical conditions, Marx and Engels saw in Tsarism the bulwark of feudal absolutist reaction in Europe. They regarded Tsarism's collapse and the consequent removal of its reactionary influence on Europe as an essential precondition for the victory of a proletarian revolution in Britain and France and for a democratic settlement of the fundamental questions of the historical development of Germany, Italy, Poland, Hungary and other European countries—questions which remained unsolved during the revolution of 1848-49.

At the same time Marx and Engels saw clearly that, in spite of their political and military rivalry, Tsarist Russia and oligarchical Britain and Bonapartist France, who were fighting against it, as well as the "neutral" reactionary regimes of Austria and Prussia, in fact held the same counter-revolutionary position.

The aim of the Western powers was the removal of Russia as a rival in the struggle for supremacy in the Near East, the consolidation of their own influence in the Balkans and the Black Sea area, the weakening, but by no means the collapse, of the military power of Tsarist Russia, and the pursual, under the pretext of defending Turkey, of a policy aimed at strengthening its colonial dependence on the Western powers. "A feeling of doubt, mistrust and hostility against their western allies is gaining possession of the Turks," Marx writes in April 1854. "They begin to look on France and England as more dangerous enemies than the Czar himself..." (p. 160).

Marx and Engels paid special attention to exposing the foreign policy of the British ruling classes and their parties, the Whigs and the Tories. In articles dealing with debates in the British Parliament in connection with the publication of documents relating to the pre-history of the Eastern conflict—"The Documents on the Partition of Turkey", "The Secret Diplomatic Correspondence" and several others, Marx exposed the "infamy" (p. 466) of British diplomacy, which was allegedly striving to keep intact the Ottoman Empire and the "balance of power ... in Europe", but was in fact defending its own mercenary interests in the Eastern question. Marx shows that if the partition of Turkey had not, in the last analysis, contained the spectre of revolution, "Her Majesty's Government would be as ready to swallow the Grand Turk [i.e., the Sultan] as his Cossack Majesty [i.e., Nicholas I]" (p. 97). Throughout the article runs the idea that the allies were conducting a "mock", "sham" war. Both sides, write Marx and Engels in the article "That Bore of a War", "are ruled more by diplomatical than strategical motives" (p. 336).

Considerable space in this volume is devoted to the domestic and foreign policy of Bonapartist France. Marx and Engels believed that the ruling clique in this country had acted as one of the main instigators of the Crimean War and that it regarded foreign policy adventurism and wars of aggrandisement as a means of strengthening the shaky Bonapartist regime. "Bonaparte," writes Marx in February 1854, "is of course in good earnest in embarking in the war. He has no alternative left but revolution at home or war abroad" (p. 33). The representatives of the Bonapartist clique were, moreover, using the war as a means of helping themselves from public funds, as an excuse, to quote Marx, "to remove the last weak barriers yet standing between themselves and the national treasury" (p. 52).

In a number' of articles Marx and Engels engage in a polemic (directly and indirectly) with the bourgeois and petty-bourgeois émigrés, individual representatives of whom regarded the war against Russia as "a war between liberty and despotism" (p. 228). The fundamental difference between this point of view and the position of Marx and Engels was that the latter advanced the battle-cry of a revolutionary war against Tsarism. Marx's and Engels' tactical position during the Crimean War was essentially a continuation of their tactics in 1848-49 when, in the columns of the *Neue Rheinische Zeitung*, they had called for a revolutionary war against Tsarism. As Lenin pointed out (*Collected Works*, Vol. 21, p. 300), these tactics were dictated by the historical conditions of the whole period 1789-1871, when the task of finally destroying absolutism and feudalism came to the fore.

In outlining the tactics of the proletariat at the time of the Crimean War, Marx and Engels proceeded from the fact that if the war against Tsarism were to assume a European character, it could produce a new revolutionary upsurge in the countries of Europe and lead to the collapse of the anti-popular, despotic regimes in these countries and to the liberation of the oppressed nationalities in Europe; in these conditions the war which had broken out would turn into a revolutionary war of the peoples against Tsarism. This war could hasten the maturing of a revolutionary situation in Russia itself and bring closer a revolution aimed against autocracy and serfdom.

Marx's and Engels' belief in the possibility of a new revolutionary upsurge during the Crimean War was based on their conclusion from the experience of the revolution of 1848-49 that a new revolutionary upsurge was possible only after a new economic crisis. In 1853-54 signs of crisis began to be observed in the economy of the European countries. At this time Marx engaged in a thorough study of the problem in question, compiled the large conspectus "Money, Credit, Crises" (extant in one of the notebooks of excerpts), which he later used for his *Grundrisse der Kritik der Politischen Ökonomie*. He also studied and drew conclusions from information on the state of industry and trade published by the journal *The Economist*. In the articles "British Finances", "The Crisis in Trade and Industry", "The Commercial Crisis in Britain" and certain others, Marx writes about the first symptoms of the approaching economic crisis: a certain degree of overproduction, general stagnation in trade and industry, suspension of payments, bankruptcies, etc. Marx not only records these symptoms, but also notes a number of most important factors. He pays special attention to these phenomena in the economy of Britain where the capitalist mode of production was most highly developed. The crisis in the economy of Britain, which still continued to hold its monopolist position in the world market, was of decisive importance for social and economic development throughout the world. Marx examines these symptoms of crisis as a manifestation of the general laws inherent in the capitalist mode of production with its antagonistic contradictions. "The crisis may be traced to the same source—the fatal working of the English industrial system which leads to overproduction in Great Britain, and to over-speculation in all other countries" (p. 588). In the signs of crisis in 1853-54 Marx detected the approach of the acute economic crisis of 1857.

Marx and Engels believed that the impending economic crisis and the Crimean War were together creating the conditions for a new revolutionary upsurge in the European countries, preparing the downfall of their anti-popular despotic regimes and the liberation of the oppressed nationalities of Europe. Marx and Engels also showed how the future of both the peoples oppressed by the Austrian Empire, and the Slav and other peoples who formed part of the Ottoman Empire, was integrally bound up with the revolutionary-democratic transformations in Europe, and with a revolutionary war which would lead to the collapse of these empires and the formation of independent democratic states in the Balkans.

Contrary to the opinion of many West-European politicians, in particular, the English conservative writer and journalist David Urquhart, who supported the preservation of the reactionary Turkish state, Marx and Engels regarded the feudal Ottoman Empire as a great obstacle to historical progress, and supported the demand for national independence of the Slav and other peoples under the rule of their Turkish conquerors. In the article "The Policy of Austria.—The War Debates in the House of Commons" Marx calls Turkey "that keystone of the antiquated European system" (p. 324).

Many of the articles in the present volume are devoted to the description and analysis of the course of the military operations, the alignment of forces on both sides, the military organisation, and questions of the art of war.

In the military articles published in the *New-York Tribune,* usually in the form of leaders, Engels analyses the strength and organisation of the armies of Russia, Austria, Britain, France and Turkey, and gives a description of their men and officers. He concludes that the allied armies are commanded by "strategical mediocrities and routine generals" (p. 513). In the articles "The Present Condition of the English Army—Tactics, Uniform, Commissariat, &c.", "The Formation of a Special Ministry of War in Britain.—The War on the Danube.—The Economic Situation", "Reorganisation of the British War Administration.—The Austrian Summons.—Britain's Economic Situation.—St. Arnaud", "British Disaster in the Crimea", and a number of others, Marx and Engels criticise the organisation of Britain's war department, and the Coalition Government's conduct of the war.

Engels drew attention to the gross incompetence of the British and French Army and Navy Commands. Their confusion in orders issued, and preservation of an antiquated system of Army and Navy organisation, together with routine and perfunctory training of the lower ranks, led to needless casualties, epidemics and hunger for the ranks, and great loss of life in Gallipoli, Varna and the Crimea. These shortcomings, he writes, "are still aggravated by the oligarchic character of the English Administration, which entrusts the most important offices to men, who, although their parliamentary support may be needed by the set of place-hunters just in power, are altogether destitute even of elementary professional knowledge and fitness" (pp. 212-13).

In the articles "The Siege of Silistria", "That Bore of a War",

"The Battle of the Alma", "The Battle of Inkerman", "The Crimean Campaign", and many others, Engels—while praising the heroism of the Russian soldiers—points to the backwardness of the art of war in the Russia of landowners and serfs, the mediocrity of a considerable section of the officers, and the "parade-drill" of the lower ranks in the Tsarist army.

The military operations in the Danube region and in the Crimea gave Engels the opportunity not only to analyse them from the point of view of the art of war, the comparative merits of the armies and their leaders, but also to develop a number of important questions of military theory, strategy and tactics. Engels' erudition as a military theoretician enabled him, in spite of the extreme scarcity of information and contrary to generally accepted judgments and forecasts, to give a correct assessment of individual episodes in the war and to make a number of assumptions which were later in all respects confirmed. Engels refuted the communiques that boasted of a "formidable" victory over the Russians in the Danube theatre (see "News from the European Contest") or of the capture of Sevastopol by the allies in September 1854 ("The News from the Crimea", "The Sevastopol Hoax", "The Sevastopol Hoax.—General News"). At the very beginning of the war Engels demonstrated the impossibility of Russian troops marching on Constantinople, and explained the landing of Russian troops in the Dobrudja as a strategical manoeuvre aimed at reducing the front line. As early as October 1854 he correctly judged the importance for the outcome of the whole campaign of the battle of Sevastopol, which would remain "unparalleled in military history" (p. 509).

Engels revealed the inner laws of the war, established the dependence of a country's military potential on the extent of its industrial development and the deployment of its economic resources, and showed how the actual conduct of war and the tactical manoeuvrability of the troops corresponds to the level of development of the country's socio-economic and political structure. Thus these articles written by Engels in 1854 constitute an important stage in the development of Marxist military thought. The analysis of military operations was later generalised by him in a number of articles for the *New American Cyclopaedia* (see this edition, Vol. 18).

The exposure of the foreign policy of the British oligarchy was combined in the writings of Marx and Engels with a revelation of the anti-popular nature of the bourgeois-aristocratic system in

Britain. Marx draws attention to the disparity in Britain between the political system and economic and social development, which was brought out particularly clearly by the Crimean War. In the articles "On the Ministerial Crisis", "Fall of the Aberdeen Ministry", "The Defeated Government" Marx speaks of the crisis of the traditional two-party system, and the breaking down of the old aristocratic parties of the Whigs and Tories which was in process. "The old parliamentary parties that had been entrusted with a monopoly of government now exist merely in the form of coteries," Marx writes in the article "The Parties and Cliques" (p. 643), and their internal contradictions are no longer of a party nature, but are "only due to personal whims and vanities" (p. 638).

Many articles ("Debates in Parliament", "The War Debate in Parliament", "The War.—Debate in Parliament", and others) deal with the proceedings of the British Parliament, the analysis of debates on the causes, outbreak and course of the Crimean War, the activity of the war departments, the state of the army, the Budget, and various draft reforms, etc. In this concrete material is revealed the class essence of British parliamentarianism, the limited nature of British bourgeois democracy, the hypocrisy and pretence of the representatives of the main political groupings, their opposition to any reforms which might affect the interests of the ruling oligarchy (for example, electoral reform), and the cumbersome and routine nature of parliamentary procedure itself. "Then why remains Parliament?" Marx asks in the article "The Treaty Between Austria and Prussia.—Parliamentary Debates of May 29", "Old Cobbett has revealed the secret. As a safety-valve for the effervescing passions of the country" (p. 219).

The criticism by Marx and Engels of the position of the bourgeois Free Traders and their ideologists Bright and Cobden is of fundamental importance. These representatives of the so-called Manchester school, which expressed the interests of the British industrial bourgeoisie, opposed the war with Russia, arguing that the two states had interests in common. As in his earlier works, Marx exposes the hypocrisy of these bourgeois ideologists, stressing that behind their feigned love of peace lay the conviction that Britain was capable of establishing its monopoly on the world market without military expenditure. Their "philanthropy", says Marx, disappears as soon as it is a question of the working class; in that case the self-same Free Traders support the uncontrolled exploitation of the workers, opposing the restriction of the working day and the protection of female and child labour by law (p. 576). The latter is one of Marx's first demands for labour legislation. He engages in an open polemic with Cobden and Bright also on the question of crises, refuting the assertion of the Free Traders that the repeal of the Corn Laws and Free Trade are a panacea against economic crises.

Marx continues to denounce the eviction of tenants from land belonging to big landowners in Scotland and Ireland. "The process still continues," he writes, "and with a vigor quite worthy of that virtuous, refined, religious, philanthropic aristocracy of this model country" (p. 197).

As ever, the position of the working class and its struggle with capital remained at the centre of the attention of Marx and Engels. For a number of reasons Marx was able in 1854 to study the position of the working class and observe the working-class movement mainly in Britain, which is why he writes primarily about the British proletariat in his articles of this period.

He speaks of its lack of political rights, its difficult economic position and its resort to strike action ("Debates in Parliament", "British Finances.—The Troubles at Preston" and others). He carefully traces the processes taking place in the working-class movement following structural changes in the capitalist economy and new developments in the socio-economic life of Europe and America, and studies the special features of the growth and spread of the working-class movement itself.

Marx notes with satisfaction the signs of political activity in the British working class, which were particularly significant with the decline of the Chartist movement after 1848. This is why he paid special attention to the opening of the Labour Parliament in Manchester, which was convoked on the initiative of the Chartists led by Ernest Jones with the aim of creating a broad working-class organisation, a "Mass Movement", to unite trade unionists and unorganised workers. Marx and Engels, who had been closely connected with the Chartists for many years and had greatly assisted Ernest Jones in the fifties in his struggle to revive Chartism on a new, socialist basis, welcomed the creation of this organisation. Marx was invited to take part in the Labour Parliament as an honorary delegate. In connection with its convocation he wrote two articles and one address ("Opening of the Labour Parliament.—English War Budget", "The Labour Parliament", "Letter to the Labour Parliament"). In them he maintains that the Labour Parliament, whatever its outcome, was an important milestone in the history of the working class because it was convoked on the initiative of the workers themselves. Marx points out, however, that the success of the movement as a whole depended on whether the British workers could create "organisation of the labouring classes on a national scale" (p. 60).

In the article "Evacuation of the Danubian Principalities.—The Events in Spain.—A New Danish Constitution.—The Chartists" Marx gives a detailed account of a speech by Ernest Jones at a workers' meeting in Bacup (near Rochdale, Lancashire), in which he touched upon the question of the need for the working class to gain political power and implement the People's Charter at the new stage of the working-class movement. Thus, having defined the revolutionary tendency in the development of the mass working-class movement, Marx sees its task as the creation of its own mass political, genuinely revolutionary party. And although Marx's hopes that the convocation of the Labour Parliament would pave the way for the founding of such a party in Britain were not justified, because the British workers in fact turned increasingly to programmes of limited reform and the trade unions grew increasingly indifferent to politics, his deductions were none the less of theoretical and practical value for the subsequent development of the working-class movement. These deductions, important not only for British workers but for the workers of other countries, were later developed in the programme of the First International.

A number of other articles collected in this volume are devoted to an analysis of the policies of the French Government. They reveal the Bonapartist regime as one of adventurism in foreign policy and demagogy, deception and repression at home. Marx and Engels show how the processes of corruption and decay, integral features of the Bonapartist regime, were also affecting its mainstay—the army. In the article "Reorganisation of the British War Administration.—The Austrian Summons.—Britain's Economic Situation.—St. Arnaud" Marx denounces the moral degeneration of the French army command, using the example of War Minister Marshal St. Arnaud who carved out his career in the Foreign Legion at Algiers, the nucleus of which was formed by "notorious desperadoes, adventurers of broken fortune, deserters from all countries, the general offal of the European armies" (p. 232). Napoleon III himself, intoxicated by the theatrical illusion of his own greatness, appears before the reader in the articles of Marx and Engels as the "actual official apery of a great past" (p. 473), i.e., of Napoleon I.

Marx and Engels relentlessly attacked pro-Bonapartist feeling among the bourgeois and petty-bourgeois democrats, both in emigration and in France itself, individual representatives of whom (Barbès, Kossuth, and some of the Polish émigrés) were inclined to believe Napoleon III's demagogic protestations about the defence of the freedom and interests of the oppressed nationalities. In this connection Marx and Engels ridiculed Barbès' belief in "Decembrist civilization" (p. 491). The chauvinist position adopted by Barbès during the Crimean War placed him outside the working-class movement and from then on he "ceased to be one of the revolutionary chiefs of France" (p. 491). In the article "The Sevastopol Hoax.—General News" Marx and Engels contrast Barbès with Auguste Blanqui whom they consider a true revolutionary.

A number of articles in the present volume are devoted to an analysis of the domestic and foreign policy of Prussia and Austria. Marx and Engels associated the participation of these countries in the Crimean War with the settlement of the problem of the revolutionary-democratic unification of Germany, with the possible collapse of the Prussian monarchy and the Austrian Empire, the formation by the enslaved peoples of independent states, and the democratic reorganisation of a number of European countries. They hoped that Prussia's entry into the war against Tsarist Russia would serve as a stimulus for a new upsurge of the revolutionary-democratic movement in which the decisive role would be played by the working class. From this point of view Marx and Engels denounce the policy of reactionary Prussian, and also Austrian ruling circles, for whom the main task was to ensure the inviolability of counter-revolutionary systems, maintain their rule in the captured territories, and enjoy "undisturbed possession of Posen, of Galicia, of Hungary, and of Italy" (p. 216).

Marx and Engels devoted considerable attention to Austria, for in the diplomatic intrigues around the conflict between Russia and Turkey it played the role of armed mediator and held "the post of honor and of advantage" (p. 255). Marx makes a detailed examination of Austria's position, the state of its finances, and its military potential. He shows the internal instability of the Habsburg Empire. An analysis of the Austrian monarchy's budget and the state of its finances in the article "Austrian Bankruptcy" leads Marx to the conclusion that "on the possession of Hungary and Lombardy depends not only the political but the economical existence of the Austrian Empire, and that with their loss the long-delayed bankruptcy of that state becomes inevitable" (p. 49). Marx and Engels believed that Austria was, on the one hand,

interested in preventing the spread of the influence of Tsarist
Russia in the Balkan Peninsula, but, on the other, thought it
impossible to permit any serious weakening of Tsarism "because
in that case the Hapsburgs would be left without a friend to help
them out of the next revolutionary slough" (p. 255). This also
determined Austria's policy of being "treacherouş to either of the
belligerents or to both" for the sake of its own interests, the
interests of the Habsburg dynasty (p. 256), while outwardly acting
as a mediator (the Vienna conferences, the occupation of the
Danubian Principalities by Austrian troops, etc.).

Marx and Engels assumed that the drawing of Austria into the
war would mean the transfer of military operations to Europe,
which would produce an upsurge in the national liberation
movement of the oppressed peoples. "The populations most
immediately interested in the issue of the eastern complications
are, besides the Germans, the Hungarians and Italians" (p. 156),
writes Marx in the article "Reshid Pasha's Note.—An Italian
Newspaper on the Eastern Question".

Denunciation of the anti-democratic policies of the ruling classes
in the European states is accompanied in Marx's and Engels'
articles by sharp criticism of the government and bourgeois press
which acted as the apologist and bearer of these policies. They
castigate the press for its sensationalism, its incorrect and
sometimes deliberately falsified information, its professional incompetence, and its "mean servility" (p. 308) to the powers-that-be.

Considerable space in the present volume is taken up by articles
on Spain. A section of them is devoted to the events of the
revolution of 1854. In addition, a series of articles printed in the
New-York Daily Tribune in the form of leaders from September to
December 1854 is published under the general heading "Revolutionary Spain". This work, which deals with the history of the
three preceding Spanish revolutions of the nineteenth century
(1808-14, 1820-23, 1834-43), was published by the newspaper in
part only; the last three articles in the series have not been
discovered, but one can get an idea of their contents from the
draft contained in the present volume (pp. 654-59). Marx's articles
on Spain, in particular, his work "Revolutionary Spain", not only
provide a key to the explanation of the essential features of the
country's history, but are also important for an understanding of the
general problems of bourgeois revolutions.

On the basis of his study of the most important events in Spain's
earlier political and civic history: the period of the Reconquest,

the creation of the united Spanish kingdom, the establishment of absolutism, the relations of the monarchy with the townspeople, the nobility and the Church, Marx reveals the causes, character and specific features of the Spanish bourgeois revolutions of the nineteenth century.

Marx came to the conclusion that modern Spanish history deserved a very different appreciation from what it had hitherto received (p. 286). He emphasises that in Spain absolutism did not play the role of a centralised state as it did in other large-scale European absolutist regimes. "The absolute monarchy in Spain," he writes, "bearing but a superficial resemblance to the absolute monarchies of Europe in general, is rather to be ranged in a class with Asiatic forms of government. Spain, like Turkey, remained an agglomeration of mismanaged republics with a nominal sovereign at their head" (p. 396). Marx maintains that already in the reign of Charles V Spain "exhibited all those symptoms of inglorious and protracted putrefaction" (p. 395). Describing the pernicious influence of Spanish absolutist rule on the country's history, he remarks that as a consequence of this in Spain "the aristocracy sunk into degradation without losing their worst privilege, the towns lost their medieval power without gaining modern importance" (p. 396).

However, the national liberation struggle of the Spanish people against Napoleon I showed that if the Spanish state was moribund, the popular masses, on the contrary, were possessed of revolutionary energy, a sense of national dignity and the ability to resist. Marx emphasises that the resistance to the Napoleonic invasion in 1808 "originated with the people, while the 'better' classes had quietly submitted to the foreign yoke" (p. 399). He devotes considerable space to the heroic guerrilla struggle of the Spanish people against the Napoleonic invasion and describes the various stages of this national liberation movement.

Marx reveals the inner contradictions of this Spanish national liberation movement; the combination of the spirit of political and social regeneration with the spirit of reaction, a feature of all the wars against Napoleonic France, was particularly characteristic of Spain (p. 403). National in character, the first bourgeois revolution in this country was aimed not only against the foreign yoke, but also against the putrescent regime of the Spanish Bourbons. In this respect its aim was achieved on a national scale. At the same time the national liberation struggle took on superstitious and fanatical forms and was exploited by reactionary ruling circles in order to return Ferdinand VII to the throne and restore the

Inquisition. Marx notes the same phenomenon in the third revolution and the Carlist War, when the struggle between capitalism, which was establishing itself, and feudalism, which had become obsolete—the struggle of two social systems—assumed the form of a struggle of opposing dynastic interests.

Marx sees the root of this contradictory phenomenon in the backwardness of the popular masses, above all the peasantry, and in the weakness of the national bourgeoisie, the interests of which, due to lack of development in industry and the home market and to agricultural backwardness and decline, were linked with the interests of the ruling circles, the bureaucracy, and the preservation of the colonial empire. Marx describes the limitations and weakness of the Spanish bourgeoisie most vividly in his analysis of the Constitution of 1812, in which radical demands were combined with sombre vestiges of the age of clerical domination. He draws attention to the fact that "it was almost the chief principle of that Constitution not to abandon any of the colonies belonging to Spain" (p. 369).

Marx's study of the Spanish revolutions enabled him to reveal a number of features characteristic of bourgeois revolutions, particularly in countries with poorly developed capitalism and a large number of feudal vestiges. He showed the role of the popular masses as the driving force of these revolutions, but at the same time wrote also of their prejudices and ignorance, their political limitations, their belief in "a sudden disappearance of their social sufferings from mere change of Government" (p. 437).

Marx emphasised that in a country with a low level of socio-economic development, the political immaturity of the masses and the weakness of the national bourgeoisie can lead to a situation in which the army becomes the spokesman of national interests and the instrument of insurrection. However, this exceptional position of the army, in cases when it is divorced from the popular masses, contains the danger of its becoming a Pretorian Guard—an instrument in the hands of ambitious generals. Marx's analysis of all four Spanish revolutions bears out this truth.

The events of 1854 in Spain enabled Marx to conclude that pressure must be exerted on the military by the revolutionary masses to make them adhere to a more radical programme. He writes: "It is a fact, then, that the military insurrection has obtained the support of a popular insurrection only by submitting to the conditions of the latter" (p. 310).

In the fighting at the barricades in 1854 in Madrid and other

Spanish towns Marx and Engels recognised a revival of this form of struggle against government troops, which had seemed to have lost its importance after the defeats of 1848. "That prejudice has fallen," we read in the article "That Bore of a War". "We have again seen victorious, unassailable barricades" (p. 338).

Marx repeatedly returns to the idea of the objective prerequisites for a bourgeois-democratic revolution and the impossibility of importing it. At the basis of a bourgeois-democratic revolution lie deep-seated social, economic and political causes, the struggle between the obsolete feudal system and elements of emergent and growing capitalism. A state of "revolutionary crises" (p. 369) has to develop for the success of a revolution in any given country. Marx illustrates this tenet with the example of the second revolution in Spain. It began with an armed uprising by Rafael Riego's detachment of 1,500 men in January 1820. In March Riego was forced to disband the remnants of the detachment, but by then the movement had already enveloped the whole country, and on March 9 Ferdinand VII was compelled to swear in the Constitution. "Notwithstanding its [the military insurrection's] failure," writes Marx, "the revolution proved victorious" (p. 444).

For a revolution to be successful the most decisive action is required from its leaders. "At the outset," writes Marx of the events of 1808, "the Spanish revolution failed by its endeavor to remain legitimate and respectable" (p. 409). Marx stresses the importance of a strong central revolutionary authority, capable of carrying out profound social and political transformations at home, abolishing existing feudal institutions, and renouncing all the debts and financial obligations of the former government. In the surviving preliminary draft from the series of articles "Revolutionary Spain", Marx writes that the alliance of the peasantry with the urban revolutionary masses is of paramount importance (pp. 657, 658). Speaking of the causes of the defeat of the second revolution, Marx emphasises that, by failing to link the interests of the peasantry with the interests of the urban population, the revolutionary party alienated the peasant masses from the revolution, thereby narrowing the social basis of the movement.

Marx demonstrates the negative role of the liberal leaders of the revolution, their limitations, their close link with the ruling circles, their fear of a radical solution of cardinal problems. As can be seen from Marx's letter of October 10, 1854 to Engels, the description which Marx gave of such Spanish leaders as Espartero and O'Donnell was used by him in his broad generalisations, and criticism not only of the Spanish liberals, but also of the leaders in the War of Independence of the North American colonies and the French Revolution at the end of the eighteenth century (Washington, Lafayette, and others) (present edition, Vol. 39).

In his articles on the fourth bourgeois revolution in Spain, the bulk of which are published in this volume (the rest, written at a later date, are in Volume 15 of the present edition), Marx notes the characteristic features of this revolution which distinguish it sharply from the preceding ones. They stem from the development of modern industry in Spain, the formation of a working class, and the greater activity of the peasant masses. Marx notes the participation of the Spanish proletariat in the revolutionary fighting of 1854-56. Although in this revolution the working class did not advance its own social and political programme and was close to the radical wing of the bourgeoisie, its appearance in the political arena had a considerable influence on the revolution, depriving it, unlike preceding ones, of a dynastic and military character. The first three revolutions gave Marx grounds for maintaining that "the social question in the modern sense of the word has no foundation in ... Spain" (p. 376). After the experience of the events of 1854-56 he came to the conclusion that "the next European revolution will find Spain matured for co-operation with it" (present edition, Vol. 15). This forecast of Marx's was proved correct by the events of the fifth bourgeois revolution in Spain of 1868-74. The events of 1854-56 were also one of the first signs of the instability of the reaction which had reigned on the European continent since the defeat of the revolution of 1848-49, and heralded new revolutionary upheavals.

*   *   *

The present volume contains 94 works in all, of which about 40 have not been reproduced in English after their initial publication in the *New-York Tribune*; 16 articles are published in English for the first time (14 articles from the *Neue Oder-Zeitung* and two articles by Engels "The Fortress of Kronstadt" and "The Russian Army", which were not published during his lifetime). The manuscripts contained in the section "From the Preparatory Materials" are published in full in English for the first time.

In the course of work on the present volume the authorship of the articles "The European War", "The Turkish War" and "News from the European Contest" was established for the first time.

Throughout, authorship and dating of the articles have been

carefully checked on the basis of Marx's Notebook in which their despatch to New York was recorded, of Marx's and Engels' correspondence with each other and with third persons, of the sources which they used in writing articles, as well as of other materials. Any changes are indicated in notes to the respective works.

In the case of articles which were published both in the *New-York Daily Tribune* and *The People's Paper*, and in the *New-York Daily Tribune* and the *Neue Oder-Zeitung* all discrepancies of substance are indicated in footnotes.

As is known from letters of Marx and Engels, the editors of the *New-York Daily Tribune* frequently treated the text of their articles in an arbitrary fashion, particularly those which were printed as leaders. This applies in particular to Engels' military reviews. In the present volume all known cases of editorial interference with the texts of Marx and Engels are indicated in the notes.

In studying the historical material quoted in Marx's and Engels' articles, it must be borne in mind that they made use of newspaper information which in a number of cases proved to be inaccurate.

In texts written in English proper names and geographical names have been reproduced on the basis of the nineteenth-century reference books; obvious misprints and errors in figures, dates, etc., discovered in the preparation of the present volume have been silently corrected.

In cases where an article has no title, the editors have provided one which is given in square brackets.

The volume was compiled, the text prepared and the preface and notes written by Valentina Smirnova and edited by Lev Churbanov (Institute of Marxism-Leninism of the CC CPSU). All the indexes were prepared by Galina Voitenkova; the index of periodicals and the glossary of geographical names with the help of Vasily Kuznetsov and Yuri Vasin respectively (Institute of Marxism-Leninism of the CC CPSU). The translations were made by Susanne Flatauer and Barrie Selman and edited by Richard Abraham and Frida Knight (Lawrence and Wishart) and Salo Ryazanskaya, Natalia Karmanova and Margarita Lopukhina (Progress Publishers) and Norire Ter-Akopyan, scientific editor (USSR Academy of Sciences).

The volume was prepared for the press by the editors Natalia Karmanova, Margarita Lopukhina, Mzia Pitskhelauri and the assistant editor Natalia Belskaya (Progress Publishers).

KARL MARX
and
FREDERICK ENGELS

WORKS

February 13, 1854-February 6, 1855

Karl Marx and Frederick Engels

THE WAR QUESTION IN EUROPE[1]

Though the arrival of the *Nashville* puts us in possession of no decisive news from the seat of war, it puts us in possession of a fact of great significance in the present state of affairs. This is that now, at the eleventh hour, when the Russian Embassadors[a] at Paris and London have left, when the British and French Embassadors[b] at St. Petersburg are recalled, when the naval and military strength of France and England is being already concentrated for immediate action—at this very last moment, the two Western Governments are making fresh proposals to negotiate by which they concede almost everything that Russia wants. It will be remembered that the main point claimed by Russia was her right of settling directly with the Porte, and without the interference of the other Powers, a quarrel which, it was pretended, concerned Russia and Turkey only. This point has now been conceded to Russia. The proposals are contained in the letter of Napoleon,[c] which we copy in another place,[2] and are to the effect that Russia shall treat with Turkey direct, while the treaty to be concluded between the two parties shall be guaranteed by the four Powers. This guarantee is a drawback upon the concession, as it gives the Western Powers a ready pretext to interfere in any future quarrel of the kind. But it does not make matters worse for Russia than they are now, when the Emperor Nicholas must see that any attempt of his at a dismemberment of Turkey cannot be

---

[a] N. D. Kiselyev and F. I. Brunnow.— *Ed.*
[b] G. H. Seymour and Castelbajac.— *Ed.*
[c] Letter of Napoleon III to Nicholas I dated January 29, 1854. *Le Moniteur universel*, No. 43, February 14, 1854.— *Ed.*

carried out without the risk of a war with England and France. And then, the actual gain to Russia will depend upon the nature of the treaty which is not yet concluded; and Russia, having seen in how cowardly a manner the Western Powers now shrink from the necessity of war, will but have to keep her armies concentrated, and to continue her system of intimidation in order to gain every point during the negotiations. Besides, Russian diplomacy need hardly be afraid of a contest with those egregious Embassadors who manufactured the famous blundering first Vienna note.[3]

Whether, however, the Czar will accept this proposal, or trust to his army, remains to be seen. He cannot afford to go through such armaments and dislocations of troops over his vast Empire once in every five years. The preparations have been made on such a scale that a very great material gain only can repay their cost. The Russian population are thoroughly roused to warlike enthusiasm. We have seen a copy of a letter from a Russian merchant—not one of the many German, English, or French traders, who have settled in Moscow—but a real old Muscovite, a genuine son of *Sviataia Russ,*[a] who holds some goods on consignment for English account, and had been asked whether in case of war these goods would run the risk of confiscation. The old Russ, quite indignant at the imputation thus cast upon his Government, and perfectly well acquainted with the official phraseology, according to which Russia is the great champion of "order, property, family, and religion," in contrast to the revolutionary and socialist countries of the West, retorts that

"Here in Russia, God be praised, the distinction between *mine* and *thine* is yet in full force, and your property here is as safe as anywhere. I would even advise you to send over as much of your property as you can, for it will perhaps be safer here than where it is now. *As to your countrymen, you may perhaps have reason to fear,* as to your property, not at all."[4]

In the meantime, the armaments prepared in England and France are upon a most extensive scale. The French ocean squadron has been ordered from Brest to Toulon in order to transport troops to the Levant. Forty or sixty thousand, according to different statements, are to be sent, a large portion of them to be drafted from the African army; the expedition will be very strong in riflemen, and be commanded either by Baraguay d'Hilliers or by St. Arnaud. The British Government will send

---

[a] Holy Russia.— *Ed.*

about 18,000 men (22 regiments of 850 each) and at the date of our last advices,[a] a portion of them had already embarked for Malta, where the general rendezvous is to be. The infantry go in steamers, and sailing vessels are employed for the conveyance of cavalry. The Baltic fleet, which is to be concentrated off Sheerness, in the Thames, by the 6th of March, will consist of fifteen ships of the line, eight frigates, and seventeen smaller vessels. It is the largest fleet the British have got together since the last war; and as one half of it will consist of paddle or screw steamers, and as the rating and weight of metal is at present about 50 per cent. higher than fifty years ago, this Baltic fleet may prove to be the strongest armament ever turned out by any country. Sir Charles Napier is to command it; if there is to be war, he is the man to bring his guns to bear at once upon the decisive point.

On the Danube, the battle of Chetatea[b] has evidently had the effect of delaying the Russian attack upon Kalafat. The Russians have been convinced by that five days' struggle that it will be no easy matter to take an intrenched camp which can send out such sallies. It seems that even the positive command of the Autocrat himself is not sufficient, after such a foretaste, to drive his troops to a rash attempt. The presence of Gen. Schilder, Chief of the Engineers, who was sent from Warsaw on purpose, seems even to have had a result contrary to the Imperial order, for instead of hurrying on the attack, an inspection of the fortifications from a distance was sufficient to convince him that more troops and more heavy guns were needed than could at once be brought up. Accordingly the Russians have been concentrating whatever forces they could around Kalafat, and bringing up their siege guns, of which, it seems, they brought seventy-two into Wallachia. *The London Times* estimates their forces at 65,000 men, which is rather high, if we consider the strength of the whole Russian army in the Principalities.[c] This army now consists of six divisions of infantry, three divisions of cavalry, and about three hundred field-guns, besides Cossacks, riflemen, and other special corps, of a total nominal strength before the beginning of the war, of 120,000 men. Assuming their losses, by sickness and on the battle-field, to be 30,000 men, there remain about 90,000 combatants. Of these, at least 35,000 are required to guard the line of the Danube, to

---

[a] i.e. February 10, 1854, when Marx's article "Russian Diplomacy.—Blue Book on the Eastern Question.—Montenegro" (see present edition, Vol. 12) was sent off.— *Ed.*

[b] See present edition, Vol. 12, pp. 579-82.— *Ed.*

[c] Moldavia and Wallachia.— *Ed.*

garrison the principal towns, and to maintain the communications. There would remain, then, at the very outside, 55,000 men for an attack upon Kalafat.

Now look at the respective positions of the two armies. The Russians neglecting the whole line of the Danube, disregarding the position of Omer Pasha at Shumla, direct their main body, and even their heavy artillery, to a point on their extreme right where they are further from Bucharest, their immediate base of operations, than the Turks are. Their rear is therefore as much exposed as it possibly can be. What is worse still is that, in order to get some slight protection for their rear, they are obliged to divide their forces, and to appear before Kalafat with a force which by no means has that evident superiority which, by insuring success, might justify such a maneuver. They leave from thirty to forty per cent. of their army scattered behind the main body, and these troops are certainly not capable of repelling a resolute attack. Thus, neither is the conquest of Kalafat assured, nor the communications of the besieging army placed out of the reach of danger. The blunder is so evident, so colossal, that nothing short of absolute certainty of the fact can make a military man believe that it has been committed.

If Omer Pasha, who still has a superior force disposable, passes the Danube at any point between Rustchuk and Hirsova, with say seventy thousand men, the Russian army must either be annihilated to the last man or take refuge in Austria. He has had a full month for concentrating such a mass. Why does he not cross a river which is now no longer obstructed by floating ice? Why does he not even retake his *tête-de-pont* at Oltenitza, in order to be able to move at any moment? That Omer Pasha is ignorant of the chances the Russians have given him by their unheard-of blunder is impossible. He must, it would seem, be tied by diplomatic action. His inactivity must be intended to form an offset against the naval promenade of the combined fleets in the Black Sea. The Russian army must not be annihilated or driven to take refuge in Austria, because then peace would be endangered by fresh complications. And in order to suit the intrigues and the sham-action of diplomatic jobbers, Omer Pasha must allow the Russians to bombard Kalafat, to place their whole army, all their siege artillery at his mercy, without his being allowed to profit by the occasion. It would indeed seem that if the Russian commander[a] had not had a material, positive guarantee that his flanks and rear would not be

---

[a] M. D. Gorchakov.— *Ed.*

attacked, he would never have attempted to march upon Kalafat. Otherwise, in spite of all stringent instructions, he would deserve to be tried at the drum-head and shot. And unless, by the steamer now due here, or at furthest within a few days, we hear that Omer Pasha has crossed the Danube and marched upon Bucharest, it will be scarcely possible to avoid the conclusion that a formal agreement of the Western Powers has been made to the effect that in order to satisfy the military point of honor of Russia, Kalafat is to be sacrificed without the Turks being allowed to defend it by the only way it can be effectually defended—by an offensive movement lower down the Danube.[5]

Written on February 13-14, 1854

First published in the *New-York Daily Tribune*, No. 4019, March 6, 1854 as a leader

Reproduced from the newspaper

Karl Marx

[DECLARATION OF THE PRUSSIAN CABINET.— NAPOLEON'S PLANS.—PRUSSIA'S POLICY][6]

The following information, which, if true, is of the highest importance, and a portion only of which has appeared in the European journals, and that in a partial and disguised form, we have received from a most trustworthy source[7] at London:

I. On the 3d of February the following declaration on the part of the Prussian Cabinet was dispatched to Paris and London:

"1. The explanations of Count Orloff leaving no doubt whatever as to the uselessness of any further attempt at mediation with the St. Petersburg Cabinet, Prussia hereby withdraws her mediation, the opportunity for which can no longer be said to exist.

"2. Count Orloff's proposals of a *formal* and binding treaty of neutrality have met with an absolute refusal, communicated to him in a note, Prussia being decided upon observing even without the concurrence of Austria, the most strict neutrality on her part, which she is determined to enforce by *suitable armaments*, as soon as the proper moment shall have arrived.

"3. Whether Prussia shall propose, in common with Austria, a general arming of the German Confederation,[8] will depend on the conduct of the maritime powers toward Germany."

II. Louis Napoleon has sent a confidential agent (Mr. Brenier) to Turin, with the following message for the King of Piedmont[a] and Mr. Cavour: At a given time insurrectionary movements are to break out in Parma, Piacenza, Guastalla, and Modena. Sardinia must then occupy those countries, from which the now reigning princes are to be expelled. Napoleon is to guarantee to the King the incorporation with Sardinia of the three former principalities, and perhaps of Modena, also, in compensation for which territories the County of Savoy is to be ceded to France.[9] This

---

[a] Victor Emmanuel II.— *Ed.*

arrangement England may be said to have as good as agreed to, although reluctantly and with very bad grace. Mr. Brenier then proceeded further on his tour through Italy till he reached Naples, where his arrival evoked the "most painful sensation." His mission is that of preparing an Italian insurrection, as Napoleon is seriously convinced that he is the man, not only to set Italy on fire, but also to draw the exact line which the flame shall be forbidden to cross. He proposes to concentrate the following armies:

1—100,000 men on the frontier of Savoy.
2— 60,000 men at Metz.
3— 80,000 men at Strassburg.

III. Prussia does not object to the assembling of a French army of 100,000 men on the frontier of Savoy, but she considers the concentration of an army at Metz, and of another at Strassburg, to be a direct menace against herself. She already fancies Baden, Hesse, Württemberg, etc., in full insurrection and some 100,000 peasants marching from the south of Germany on her own frontiers. She has, therefore, protested against these two measures, and it is this eventuality which is alluded to in section 3 of the Prussian declaration. At all events, Prussia will put her army on a war footing *by,* and perhaps *before,* the end of March. She intends calling out a force of 200,000 to 300,000 men, according to circumstances. But if Napoleon insists on concentrating the two armies at Metz and Strassburg, the Prussian Government *has* already resolved to augment its force to 500,000 men. In the Berlin Cabinet, where the King,[a] with the great majority of his Ministers, had chosen to side with Russia, and Manteuffel alone, backed by the Prince of Prussia,[b] carried the declaration of neutrality (Manteuffel originally proposed a formal alliance with England), fear and confusion are asserted to reign supreme. There exists already a formal resolution of the Cabinet (Cabinets-Beschluss) according to which, under certain circumstances, all the more notorious democrats of the monarchy, and, above all, of Rhenish Prussia, are to be arrested on the same night, and to be transported to the eastern fortresses, in order to prevent them from favoring the subversive plans of Napoleon, (*die Umsturzpläne Napoleon's!!*) or from getting up popular movements generally. This measure, it is proposed, shall be executed instantly in the case of 'talian disorders breaking out, or if Napoleon concentrates

---

[a] Frederick William IV.— *Ed.*
[b] Future King of Prussia, William I.— *Ed.*

the two armies at Metz and Strassburg. This resolution, we are
assured, has been taken *unanimously,* although *all* the eventualities
are not provided for under which the Cabinet might think fit to
put it into execution.

Written on February 17, 1854   Reproduced from the newspaper

First published in the *New-York Daily
Tribune*, No. 4022, March 9, 1854 as a
leader

Karl Marx

DEBATES IN PARLIAMENT[10]

London, Tuesday, Feb. 21, 1854

The military and naval estimates have been laid before Parliament. In the army, the total number of men asked for the current year is 112,977, an increase upon last year of 10,694. The total cost of the land forces for service at home and abroad, for the year ending on the 31st of March, 1855, exclusively of the Australian colonies, and of the charge transferred to the East India Company,[11] is £3,923,288. The gross total amount is £4,877,925, which will provide for 5,719 officers, 9,956 non-commissioned officers, 126,925 rank and file. The naval estimates for the year ending March 31, 1855, show a total for the effective service of £5,979,866, an increase upon last year of £1,172,446. The charge for the conveyance of troops and ordnance stands at £225,050, an increase of £72,100. The grand total for the year amounts to £7,487,948. The force will consist of 41,000 seamen, 2,000 boys, 15,500 marines; the total, including 116 men in the picking service, 58,616.[a]

Mr. Layard had given notice that he should call attention to the Eastern question on last Friday evening, and he seized upon the very moment when the Speaker[b] was to leave the Chair, in order that the House might consider the navy estimates.[12] Shortly after 4 o'clock all the galleries were overcrowded, and at 5 o'clock the House was full. Two long hours, to the visible mortification of the members and the public, were killed with indifferent conversation

---

[a] Marx took these figures from the leading articles in *The Times*, Nos. 21668 and 21669, February 18 and 20, 1854.— *Ed.*

[b] Charles Shaw-Lefevre.— *Ed.*

on minor topics. So intensely excited was the curiosity of the honorables themselves that they delayed dinner till 8 o'clock, to assist at the opening of the great debate [a]—a rare occurrence, this, in the parliamentary life of the Commoners.

Mr. Layard, whose speech was continually interrupted by cheers, began by stating that the government had placed them in so extraordinary a position that they were at a loss to know how they really stood. Before they could vote the demanded advances, it was the duty of the government to state *what their intentions were.* But before asking [the] government what they were about to do, he wished to know *what they had already done.* He had said last year that if the government had adopted a tone more worthy of this country, they would not have been plunged into war; nor, after a careful perusal of the voluminous Blue Books lately issued,[b] had he found cause to change his opinions. Comparing the contents of various dispatches on various sides, he argued that the Ministry had overlooked the most obvious facts, had misunderstood the most unmistakeable tendencies, and trusted to the most evidently fallacious assurances. Declaring that the tragedy of Sinope[c] impeached the honor of England and required ample explanation, he drew evidence from the published documents to show that the Admirals of the united fleets might have prevented the catastrophe, or that the Turks by themselves [might] have averted it, if it had not been for the timorous and vacillating instructions sent out by the British government. He inferred from their recent language that they would still treat on the basis of the *status quo ante bellum,*[d] which presumed step he condemned. He called upon the government to do their duty, in the certainty that the people of England would do theirs.

Sir James Graham, with his notorious effrontery, answered him that they must either put their confidence in Ministers or turn them out. But "meanwhile don't let us *potter* over Blue Books." They had been deceived by Russia, who was an old and faithful

---

[a] The debates in the House of Commons on February 17 and 20, 1854 are reported according to *The Times,* Nos. 21668 and 21670, February 18 and 21, 1854.— *Ed.*

[b] The reference is to *Correspondence Respecting the Rights and Privileges of the Latin and Greek Churches in Turkey,* the first issues of which appeared at the beginning of 1854.— *Ed.*

[c] This refers to the naval battle of Sinope (Black Sea) on November 30 (18), 1853 between Russian and Turkish squadrons during the Crimean War. The Turks were defeated.— *Ed.*

[d] The state before the war.— *Ed.*

ally of Great Britain, but "dark, malignant suspicions did not easily take root in generous minds." This old fox, Sir Robert Peel's "dirty little boy," the murderer of the Bandieras,[13] was quite charming with his "generous mind" and his "slowness to suspect."

Then came Lord Jocelyn and Lord Dudley Stuart, whose speeches filled the papers the next day, but emptied the House on this evening. Mr. Roebuck next commenced by defending the ministers for their conduct in a delicate situation, but ended by declaring that it was now time for the ministry to *declare clearly what they intended to do.* Lord John Russell, on the plea of answering this question, rose, gave an apologetic recapitulation of the history of the late differences, and when he had convinced himself that this would not do, feigned to be willing to tell them "what they intended to do;" a thing he himself may not have been quite sure of. According to his statement they had entered into some vague sort of alliance with France, not by means of a treaty concluded, but of notes interchanged. England and France were now proposing to Turkey also a sort of treaty, by virtue of which the Porte should not sue for peace without their consent. They had been cruelly overcome by the incredible perfidy of the Czar. He (Russell) despaired of peace being preserved. They were likely to enter on war. He consequently wanted some £3,000,000 more than last year. Secrecy was the condition of success in war and therefore he could not tell them just now what they were to do in that war. As the latter, or theatrical part of his speech was performed with great force and with much moral indignation at the Czar "the butcher," the applause was immense, and the House, in their enthusiasm, were on the point of voting the estimates, when Mr. Disraeli interceded and succeeded in adjourning the discussion to Monday evening.

The debates were resumed yesterday evening[a] and only concluded at 2 o'clock, a.m.

First rose Mr. Cobden, promising to confine himself strictly to the practical question in hand. He took great pains to prove from the Blue Books, what was denied by nobody, that the French Government had originated "this melancholy dispute," by the mission of Mr. Lavalette respecting the Holy Places and the concessions it wrung from the Porte.[14] The French President, who, at that time, had some expectation of becoming Emperor, might have had some wish to make a little political capital by making these demands upon Turkey on behalf of the Latin Christians.

---

[a] February 20, 1854.— *Ed.*

The first movement of Russia, therefore, was traceable to the proceedings of France, in this matter. The non-signature of the Vienna note had been the fault of the allies, not of the Turkish government, because, if it had been threatened with the withdrawal of the fleet from Besika Bay, the Porte would immediately have signed it. We were going to war because we insisted upon Turkey refusing to do that by a note to Russia which we intended to ask her to do for ourselves, viz: to give us a guarantee for the better treatment of the Christians. The vast majority of the population in the Ottoman Empire was looking with eagerness to the success of that very policy which Russia was now prosecuting (as now exemplified in Moldo-Wallachia). From the Blue Books themselves he could show that the evils and oppressions under which that Christian population lived, could not be tolerated — referring principally to dispatches of Lord Clarendon, ostensibly written with the view to make out a case for the Czar. In one of these dispatches Lord Clarendon writes:

"The Porte must decide between the maintenance of an erroneous religious principle, and the loss of the sympathy and support of its allies."[a]

Mr. Cobden was therefore enabled to ask:

"Whether the House did think it possible that a population like the fanatical Mussulman population of Turkey would abandon its religion? And without total abandonment of the law of the *Koran*, it was absolutely impossible to put the Christians of Turkey upon an equality with the Turks."

We may as well ask Mr. Cobden whether with the existing State Church and laws of England, it is possible to put her working-men upon equality with the Cobdens and the Brights? Mr. Cobden proceeded then with a view to show from the letters of Lord Stratford de Redcliffe and the British Consular agents, that there reigns a general dissatisfaction through the Christian population in Turkey threatening to end in a general insurrection. Now, let us again ask Mr. Cobden whether there does not exist a general dissatisfaction with their governments and their ruling classes, among all peoples of Europe, which discontent soon threatens to terminate with a general revolution? If Germany, Italy, France or even Great Britain had been invaded, like Turkey, by a foreign army, hostile to their governments and appealing to their insurrectionary passions, would any of these countries have as long remained quiet as the Christian population of Turkey have done?

---

[a] The Earl of Clarendon to Stratford de Redcliffe, June 24, 1853, *The Times*, No. 21670, February 21, 1854.— *Ed.*

In entering upon a war in defense of Turkey, Mr. Cobden concludes, England would be fighting for the domination of the Ottoman population of Turkey and against the interest of the great body of the people of that country. This is merely a religious question between the Russian army on the one side and the Turkish on the other. The British interests were all on the side of Russia. The extent of their trade with Russia was enormous. If the export trade to Russia amounted to only £2,000,000, this was but the transitory result from Russia still laboring under the Protectionist delusion. However their imports from Russia amounted to £13,000,000. With the exception of the United States, there was no one foreign country with which their trade was so important as with Russia. If England was going to war, why were they sending land forces to Turkey, instead of exclusively using their navy? If the time had come for the contest between Cossackism and Republicanism, why were Prussia, Austria, the rest of the German States, Belgium, Holland, Sweden, and Denmark remaining neutral, while France and England had to fight single-handed? If this were a question of European importance, was it not to be supposed that those who were nearest to the danger would be the first to fight? Mr. Cobden concluded by declaring that "he was opposed to the war with Russia." He thought "the best thing was to fall back upon the Vienna note."

Lord John Manners considered that the Government were to blame for their supineness and false security. The communications originally made by Lord Clarendon to the governments of Russia, France and Turkey, in which, instead of acting in accordance with France, Lord Clarendon persisted in refusing so to cooperate, and made known to the government of Russia that England would not cooperate with France, had induced the Emperor of Russia to give Prince Menchikoff the orders which led to the whole catastrophe.[a] It was no wonder that when England at last announced her intention to interfere actually at Constantinople, the government of France should entertain some doubt as to the sincerity of Her Majesty's Government. It was not England that advised the Porte to reject Prince Menchikoff's *ultimatum,* but, on the contrary, the Ministers of the Sultan[b] acted upon their own responsibility, and without any hope of the assistance of England. After the occupation of the Principalities by the Russians, the prolonged

---

[a] On Menshikov's mission see Marx's article "Affairs in Holland.—Denmark.—Conversion of the British Debt.—India, Turkey and Russia" (present edition, Vol. 12).— *Ed.*

[b] Abdul Mejid.— *Ed.*

diplomatic negotiations of the British government had been very prejudicial to the interests of Turkey, and very serviceable to those of Russia. Russia had taken possession of the Principalities without a declaration of war, in order to prevent those treaties which were her real instruments of oppression toward Turkey from falling to the ground. Consequently, after Turkey had declared war, it was not wise to insist upon the renewal of these treaties as a basis of negotiation. The main question really in hand now was, what were the objects which the Government contemplated in entering upon this tremendous struggle? It was generally announced that the honor and the independence of Turkey were to be maintained; but it was essential that there should be some understanding of a far more specific nature as to what was meant by this announcement.

Mr. Horsman endeavored to refute the fallacies propounded by Mr. Cobden. The real question was not what Turkey is, but what Russia would become with Turkey absorbed in her dominions—a question whether the Emperor was to be Emperor also of Turkey? With Russia there was but one object recognized, the advancement of the political power by war. Her aim was territorial aggrandizement. From the monstrous mendacity of the first step taken in this matter by the Russian Autocrat, down to the atrocious massacre of Sinope, his course had been one of ferocity and fraud, of crimes that would be conspicuous even in the annals of Russia, a country whose history was all crime, and which were rendered still more fearful by that blasphemy which dared to invoke the Christianity whose laws it so flagrantly violated. On the other hand, the conduct of the intended victim had been admirable. Mr. Horsman then took great pains to excuse the oscillating course of the government by the difficulties which they found their position surrounded with. Hence their diplomatic hesitation. If all the Cabinets of Europe, if the most experienced diplomatists had been engaged in opposition to the Autocrat, it would have been impossible to place him in a position of greater difficulty and embarrassment and from which he could not extricate himself without difficulty and loss, than that in which either by the blunders of our own Ministers or the adroitness of his own, he was now placed. Six months ago the Emperor Nicholas was the chief supporter of the order and legitimacy of Europe; now he stood forward, unmasked as the greatest revolutionist. Foiled in his political intrigues, unsuccessful in the war in Asia, and well thrashed by the Turks on the Danube, the Czar had really shown an alacrity in sinking which was quite refreshing. It was now the duty of the government, if hostilities should commence, to take care not to secure peace except upon such terms as would involve ample and certain security against any future repetition of similar aggression. He trusted that one of the conditions for the restoration of peace would be that Russia should indemnify Turkey for the expenses to which she had been put, and that Turkey should receive, as a material guarantee, the restoration of territories of which she had been deprived.

Mr. Drummond believed that we are going to engage in a religious war, and are about to enter into another crusade for the tomb of Godfrey of Bouillon, which is already so broken that it cannot be sat upon. It appears that the author of the mischief from the very beginning has been the Pope.[a] England had not the least interest in the Turkish question, and a war between this country and Russia could not be brought to a successful termination, because they will fight each other for ever and never do each other any harm.

"All that you will gain in the present war will be hard knocks."

Mr. Cobden had some time ago offered to crumple Russia up, and if he would do so now it would save them a world of trouble. In fact, the present dispute was, whether the milliners should come from Paris or from St. Petersburg to dress the idols of the Holy Sepulchre. They had now found out that Turkey was their ancient ally, and quite necessary to the balance of power of Europe. How in the world did it happen that they never found that out before they took the whole kingdom of Greece from her, and before they fought the battle of Navarino,[15] which he remembered Lord St. Helens having described as a capital battle, only that they knocked down the wrong men. How came they not to think of this when the Russians passed the Balkans and when they might have given Turkey effectual aid by their fleet? But now, after they had reduced the Ottoman Empire to the last stage of decrepitude, they thought to be able to uphold this tottering power on the pretense of the balance of power. After some sarcastic remarks on the sudden enthusiasm for Bonaparte, Mr. Drummond asked who was to be Minister of War? All of them had seen enough to show them that there was a feeble hand at the helm. He did not believe that the character of any general or of any admiral was safe in the hands of the present Administration. They were capable of sacrificing either to please any faction in the

[a] Pius IX.— *Ed.*

House. If they were determined to go to war, they must strike their blow at the heart of Russia, and not go wasting their shots in the Black Sea. They must begin by proclaiming the reestablishment of the kingdom of Poland. Above all, he wanted to be informed what the government was about.

"The head of the government,"[a] said Mr. Drummond, "prides himself on his powers of concealment, and stated in another place that he should like to see any one extract information from him which he was not inclined to afford. That statement reminded him of a story which he heard once in Scotland—a Highlandman had gone to India, and on his return to England brought home a parrot as a present to his wife, which talked remarkably well. A neighbor, not wishing to be outdone, went to Edinburgh and brought his wife home a large owl. On its being remarked to him that the owl could never be taught to speak: 'Very true,' he replied; 'but consider the power o' thocht he has in him.'"

Mr. Butt stated that this was the first time since the revolution that a Ministry had come down to the House and asked for a war supply without stating distinctly and fully the grounds for such a proposition. In the legal sense of the word, they were not yet at war, and the House had a right to know, on voting these supplies, what was delaying the declaration of war against Russia? In what an equivocal position was their fleet at the Black Sea put! Admiral Dundas had orders to send back Russian vessels to a Russian port, and if, in the execution of these orders, he destroyed a Russian ship, while being at peace with Russia, were Ministers prepared to justify such a state of things? He hoped it would be explained whether assistance was to be given upon those humiliating terms—that Turkey was to place herself in the hands òf England and France in making peace with Russia? If that was to be the policy of England, then Parliament was now called upon to vote an additional force, not for the independence of Turkey, but for her subjugation. Mr. Butt betrayed some doubt whether Ministers were not merely making a parade of those military preparations for the purpose of arriving at a dishonorable peace.

Mr. S. Herbert, the Minister of War, made the most vulgar and silly speech that could possibly be expected even from a Coalition [16] Minister at such a momentous crisis. The government was placed between two fires, and they could not find any means of ascertaining what opinion the House itself really entertained upon the question. The honorable gentlemen opposite had the advantage of coming to facts; they were criticising the past; but the Government had no facts to deal with—they had only to

[a] Lord Aberdeen.— *Ed.*

speculate as to the future. They were inclined to embark in this war not so much for the purpose of defending Turkey as of opposing Russia. This was all the information the House could get from poor Mr. Herbert, "as to the future." But no; he told them something very new.

"Mr. Cobden is," according to Mr. Herbert, "the representative of the feeling of the largest class of the people of this country."

This assertion being denied in all parts of the House, Mr. Herbert proceeds to state:

"If not the largest class, the honorable member was a representative, at any rate, of *a great portion of the working classes* of this country."

Poor Mr. Herbert. It was quite refreshing to see Mr. Disraeli rise after him, and thus to have the babbler supplanted by a real debater.

Mr. Disraeli, alluding to the theatrical declamations with which Lord John Russell had terminated his speech on Friday evening, commenced with this statement:

"I have always been of opinion that any nation, and this one in particular, would be much more prepared and much more willing to bear the burdens which a state of warfare must induce and occasion, if they really knew for what they were going to war; than if they should be hurried into a contest by inflammatory appeals to the passions, and be carried away by an excitement which at the first moment might be convenient to a Minister, but which in a few months after would be followed by the inevitable reaction of ignorance, or perhaps ignorance and disaster combined."

Thus it had been with the war of 1828-29, when they took part on the side of Russia and not on that of Turkey. The present perplexed position and the recent prostrate condition of Turkey, were entirely to be ascribed to the events of that war, in which England and France were united against Turkey. At that time there was not a member of the House who really had any idea why they went to war, or what was the object they intended to accomplish, when they leveled a blow at the power of Turkey. Therefore they must clearly comprehend the cause and the object of the present war. This knowledge was only to be obtained from the Blue Books. What had been the origin of the present state of affairs they must learn from the words written in these very dispatches lying on the table. The policy there developed was preparing that future which, according to Ministers, alone was to absorb their attention. He protested, therefore, against the doctrine of Sir James Graham. Mr. Herbert had just protested against the reading of isolated pages from those dispatches. He however could not promise to read these Blue Books through to the House; yet if they admitted the validity of the right honorable gentleman's objection, this would seem to be the only course open to him. It was the received opinion of all that were well acquainted with the Eastern question, and his own opinion, that Russia had no intention whatever of forcibly conquering the Ottoman Empire; but that, by adroit policy and by improved means, she intended to obtain and to exercise such an influence over the Christian population of the Turkish Empire, that she would obtain all that authority which would have been the result of her possessing, perhaps, the seat of the Sultan's empire. At the outset of these negotiations Count Nesselrode himself, in his dispatches dated January, 1853, and June, 1853, distinctly and explicitly described the policy of Russia.[a] Ascendancy to be obtained over the Turkish Empire by exercising a peculiar influence over 12,000,000, who compose the large majority of the Sultan's subjects. By the Russian dispatches addressed to the British Government, not merely is that policy defined, but the British Government is no less candidly informed of the mode by which it is to be accomplished—not by conquest, but by maintaining treaties that exist, and by extending the spirit of those treaties. Thus, from the very beginning of this important controversy, the base of the diplomatic campaign was found in a treaty—the treaty of Kainardji.[17] By that treaty the Christian subjects of the Porte are placed under the especial protection of the Sultan; and Russia, in interpreting that treaty, states that the Christian subjects of the Sultan are placed specially under the protection of the Czar. Under the same treaty representations may be made by Russia in favor of her new church—a building in the street called Bey Oglu—the Russian interpretation of that article of the treaty is, that Russia has the power of interfering in favor of every church of the Greek denomination, and, of course, in favor of all the communities of that faith in the Sultan's dominions, who happen to be the large majority of his subjects. This was the avowed Russian interpretation of the treaty of Kainardji. On the other hand they might see, from a dispatch of the 8th of January, 1853,

---

[a] The reference is to the dispatches of Count Nesselrode to the Russian envoy in England Baron Brunnow dated January 14 and June 1, 1853; they were communicated to the British Foreign Secretaries: Russell on January 24, and Clarendon, his successor, on June 8, 1853. The text of the dispatches was published in *Correspondence...*, Part I, pp. 61-65 and 238-45.— *Ed.*

from Sir Hamilton Seymour, that Count Nesselrode informed Sir Hamilton, who informed Lord Clarendon,

"that it was necessary that the diplomacy of Russia should be supported by a demonstration of force."[a]

According to this same dispatch, Count Nesselrode's belief that this question would be brought to a satisfactory conclusion, rested upon the

"exertions which were to be made by Her Majesty's Ministers at Paris and Constantinople."

Russia, then, at once declared that the demonstration of force was only a demonstration; but that the object was to be peaceably attained by the exertions of the English Ministers at Paris and Constantinople.[b]

"Now, Sir," continued Mr. Disraeli, "I want to know, with that object expressed, with those means detailed, and with that diplomacy to deal with, how the Ministers encountered such a combination?"

It was unnecessary to touch on the question of the Holy Places. That was, in fact, soon settled at Constantinople. Even Count Nesselrode, at a very early period of these negotiations, expressed his surprise and satisfaction, and stated his acknowledgment of the conciliatory spirit of France. But all that time the forces of Russia were accumulating on the Turkish frontiers, and all that time Count Nesselrode was telling Lord Clarendon that his Government would ask an equivalent for the privileges which the Greek Church had lost at Jerusalem, but in the settlement of which his Government had not been disturbed. Even the mission of Prince Menchikoff was mentioned at that time, as proved by various dispatches from Sir Hamilton Seymour. Lord John Russell had told them the other night that the conduct of Count Nesselrode was fraudulent. On the other hand Lord John Russell confessed himself that Count Nesselrode kept saying that his Imperial master would ask an equivalent for the Greek Church; but on the other he complained that Count Nesselrode never told them what he wanted.

---

[a] Here and below Marx quotes from Sir Hamilton Seymour's dispatch of January 8, 1853 according to Disraeli's speech published in *The Times*, No. 21670, February 21, 1854 which greatly differs from the text in *Correspondence...*, Part I, p. 57.— *Ed.*

[b] Lord Cowley and Stratford de Redcliffe.— *Ed.*

"Wicked Count Nesselrode! (Laughter.) Fraudulent duplicity of Russian statesmen! (Laughter.) Why could the noble Lord not find the information he wanted? Why is Sir Hamilton Seymour at St. Petersburg, if he is not to ask for the information that is desired?"

If Count Nesselrode never told him what he wanted, it was because the noble Lord never dared to ask. At this stage of the proceedings it was the duty of the Ministers to put categorical questions to the Cabinet of St. Petersburg. If they could not define what they wanted, then it was time to declare that the friendly offices of the British Government at Paris and Constantinople were to cease. When Lord John Russell had relinquished the seals of office, and was followed by Lord Clarendon, there was a different character in the diplomatic proceedings—a bias in favor of Russia. When Lord Clarendon was made Minister of Foreign Affairs he had to draw up instructions for Lord Stratford de Redcliffe, the Queen's Embassador, repairing to the seat of action. Now what were these instructions? At the moment of her utmost need and her utmost exigency, Turkey is lectured about internal reform and commercial reform. It is intimated to her that the conduct of the Porte must be distinguished by the utmost moderation and prudence, viz: that it must comply with the demands of Russia. Meanwhile the government continued not to demand an explicit explanation of what was meant on the part of Russia. Prince Menchikoff arrived at Constantinople. After having received most agitating missives from Col. Rose, and warning dispatches from Sir Hamilton Seymour, Lord Clarendon in a letter to Lord Cowley, the British Embassador at Paris, denounced Colonel Rose's order in calling up the British fleet, regretted the order given to the French Admiral[a] to sail to the Greek waters, favoring France with contemptuous dogma,

"that a policy of suspicion is neither wise nor safe,"

and declared he placed full reliance on the Emperor of Russia's solemn assurances that he would uphold the Turkish Empire.[b] Then Lord Clarendon writes to his Embassador at Constantinople,[c] that he feels quite sure that the objects of Prince Menchikoff's mission,

---

[a] Hamelin.— *Ed.*

[b] The Earl of Clarendon to Lord Cowley. March 22, 1853.— *Ed.*

[c] This is obviously a mistake; the reference is to the letter of Lord Clarendon to the British Ambassador at St. Petersburg, Sir Hamilton Seymour, dated March 23, 1853.— *Ed.*

"whatever they may be, do not expose to danger the authority of the Sultan, or the integrity of his dominions."

Aye! Lord Clarendon went out of his way to accuse their solitary ally in Europe, and stated that their only grounds for now apprehending embarrassment in the East, was the position for some time occupied by France with respect to the Holy Places. Accordingly Count Nesselrode complimented Lord Aberdeen upon the *beau rôle*[a] (translated in the Blue Book "*important role*,")[b] that he had played, by having left France "*isolée.*" On the 1st of April, Colonel Rose informed this country of the *secret* convention which Russia demanded from Turkey.[18] Only ten days after Lord Stratford arrived at Constantinople and confirmed everything that Colonel Rose had stated. After all this, on the 16th of May, Lord Clarendon writes to Sir H. Seymour,

"that the explanations offered by the Emperor of Russia," explanations not contained in the Blue Books, "had enabled them to disregard, instead of sharing, in the apprehensions which the proceedings of Prince Menchikoff, coupled with the military preparations in the south of Russia, had not unnaturally produced throughout Europe."

After this Count Nesselrode felt free to announce to Lord Clarendon, on the 20th of June, that they had occupied the Principalities. In that document Count Nesselrode states

"that the Emperor will occupy the Provinces as a deposit until satisfaction; that in acting as he has done, he has remained faithful to his declarations to the English Government; that in communicating with the Cabinet of London as to the military preparations coincident with the opening of negotiations, he did not conceal from it that the time might yet come when he should be obliged to have recourse to them, complimenting the English Government on the friendly intentions it had shown; contrasting its conduct with that of France, and laying all the blame of Prince Menchikoff's subsequent failures on Lord Stratford."[19]

After all this, on the 4th of July, Lord Clarendon writes a circular, in which he still hopes in the justice and moderation of the Emperor, referring to the Emperor's repeated declaration that he would respect the integrity of the Turkish Empire. On the 18th of July he writes to Lord Stratford, that

"France and England, if they set to work in earnest, might certainly cripple Russia, but Turkey meanwhile might be irretrievably ruined, and peaceful negotiations are the only course to pursue."[20]

---

[a] Honourable role.— *Ed.*

[b] Count Nesselrode's dispatch to Brunnow dated April 7, 1853; its content was communicated to Lord Clarendon on April 15, 1853.— *Ed.*

Why? If that was a good argument then, it is a good argument now. Either the Government were influenced by a degree of confidence which assumed a morbid character of credulity, or they were influenced by connivance. The cause of the war had been the conduct of the negotiations during the last seven months upon the part of her Majesty's Government. If they had been influenced by credulity, Russia, by her perfidious conduct, may have precipitated a struggle which, perhaps, will be inevitable, and a struggle which might secure the independence of Europe, the safety of England, and the safety of civilization. If their conduct had been suggested by connivance, a timorous war, a vacillating war, a war with no results, or rather with the exact results which were originally intended. On the 25th of April Lord Clarendon had made the false statement in the House of Lords that the Menchikoff mission was to arrange disputes with respect to the Holy Places, although he knew the contrary to be true. Mr. Disraeli next briefly traced the history of the Vienna note to show the utter imbecility of the Ministry or their connivance with the Court of St. Petersburg. He came then to the third period, the period of the interval that took place between the failure of the Vienna note and the battle of Sinope. At that time Mr. Gladstone, the Chancellor of the Exchequer, spoke in a public assembly in the most depreciating tone with respect to Turkey. And so did the semi-official papers. What changed the aspect and fortunes of Turkey, and gave a new tone to the Cabinet, was the energies of the Turks themselves. But no sooner was the battle of Oltenitza[21] fought than the policy of credulity, or the policy of connivance, was at its dirty work again. However, the slaughter of Sinope operated again in the favor of the Turks. The fleets were ordered to enter the Black Sea. But what did they do? Return to the Bosphorus! As to the future, Lord John Russell had been very vague in the description of the conditions of their alliance with France. Mr. Disraeli disclaimed confounding the maintenance of the balance of power with the maintenance of the present territorial distribution of Europe. The future of Italy mainly depended upon the appreciation of that truth.

After Mr. Disraeli's splendid speech, of which I have, of course, only given the outlines, Lord Palmerston rose and made a complete failure. He repeated part of the speech he had made at the close of the last session,[a] defended in a very inconclusive

---

[a] Lord Palmerston's speech in the House of Commons on August 20, 1853. *The Times*, No. 21513, August 22, 1853.— *Ed.*

manner the ministerial policy, and was anxiously cautious not to drop one word of new information.

On the motion of Sir J. Graham certain votes for the Navy estimates were then agreed to without discussion.

After all, the most curious feature of these agitated debates is, that the House completely failed in wresting from the Ministers either a formal declaration of war with Russia, or a description of the objects for which they are to plunge into war. The House and the public know no more than they knew already. They have got no new information at all.

Written on February 21, 1854

First published in the *New-York Daily Tribune*, No. 4022, March 9; reprinted in the *New-York Semi-Weekly Tribune*, No. 917, March 10, 1854

Signed: *Karl Marx*

Reproduced from the *New-York Daily Tribune*

Karl Marx

[PARLIAMENTARY DEBATES OF FEBRUARY 22.—POZZO DI BORGO'S DISPATCH.—THE POLICY OF THE WESTERN POWERS][22]

London, Friday, Feb. 24, 1854

A good deal of idle talk about Kossuth's "warlike preparations" and probable "movements" has infested the public press. Now I happen to know from a Polish officer, who is setting out for Constantinople, and consulted the ex-Governor about the course he should take, that Kossuth dissuaded him from leaving London, and expressed himself by no means favorable to the participation of Hungarian and Polish officers in the present Turkish war, because they must either enlist themselves under the banner of Czartoryski or abjure their Christian faith, the one step being contradictory to his policy and the other to his principles.[23]

So deep was the impression produced by Mr. Disraeli's masterly exposure of the Ministerial policy[a] that the Cabinet of all the talents[24] thought fit to make a posthumous attempt to burke him in a little comedy arranged between themselves and Mr. Hume, and performed in Wednesday morning's sitting of the Commons.[b] Lord Palmerston had concluded his lame reply to Mr. Disraeli's epigrammatic alternative of a morbid "credulity" or a treacherous "connivance" by appealing from faction to the impartial judgment of the country, and Mr. Hume was the man chosen to answer in the name of the country, just as Snug, the joiner, was chosen to play the lion's part in "the most cruel death of Pyramus and Thisbe."[c] Mr. Hume's whole Parliamentary life has been spent in making opposition pleasant, moving amendments, in order to withdraw

---

[a] See this volume, pp. 19-25.— Ed.

[b] February 22, 1854. Speeches in the House of Commons were reported in The Times, No. 21672, February 23, 1854.— Ed.

[c] Shakespeare, A Midsummer Night's Dream, Act I, Scene 2.— Ed.

them afterward—constituting, in fact, the so-called independent opposition, the rear-guard of every Whig Ministry, sure of coming forward to rescue it from danger whenever its own registered partisans may show any signs of vacillation. He is the great Parliamentary "extinguisher" par excellence. He is not only the oldest member of Parliament, but an independent member; and not only an independent, but a radical; and not only a radical, but the pedantic and notorious Cerberus of the public purse, with the mission of making pounds slip unnoticed by while picking quarrels about the fractional part of a farthing.

For the first time in his Parliamentary life, as he himself emphatically stated, Mr. Hume rose not to condemn, but to express his approval of the "Estimates." This extraordinary event, as he did not fail to remark himself, was the most incontestable proof that the Ministry had not in vain appealed to the sound judgment of the country from the unmerited slanders of faction, but had received a solemn acquittal from the charge of credulity and connivance. His arguments were characteristic. In order to rescue the Ministers from the alternative of credulity or connivance, he proved the credulity of the Ministers in their transactions with Russia. He had, then, understood the true sense of Lord Palmerston's appeal. All the Ministry asked for was the discharge from intentional treason. As to credulity, had not that excellent Sir James Graham already declared that "a generous mind is slow to suspect"?[a] Because the impending war was brought about by the Ministry's own diplomatic mismanagement, certainly it was a war of their own, and they, therefore, were, of all men, as Mr. Hume thought, the very men to carry it cunningly. The relative littleness of the proposed war estimates was, in Mr. Hume's opinion the most convincing proof of the greatness of the war intended. Lord Palmerston, of course, thanked Mr. Hume for the sentence Mr. Hume had pronounced in the name of the country, and, in compensation, favored his audience with his own doctrine of state papers, which papers, according to him, must never be laid before the House and the country, until matters are sufficiently embroiled to deprive their publication of any use whatever. Such was all the after-wit the coalition had to dispose of after due deliberation. Lord Palmerston, their manager, had not only to weaken the impression of their antagonist's speech, but to annihilate also his own theatrical appeal from the House to the country.

---

[a] See this volume, pp. 12-13.—*Ed.*

On Tuesday night,[a] Mr. Horsfall, the Member for Liverpool, asked the question:

"Whether the treaties with foreign nations or the steps which Her Majesty's Government were prepared to take in the event of war were such as would effectually prevent privateers being fitted out in neutral ports to interfere with British shipping?"

The answer given by Lord Palmerston was:

"That the honorable gentleman and the House must feel that this was a question to which, in the present state of things, no explanatory answer could be given."

In quoting this answer of its master, *The Morning Post*, Palmerston's private *Moniteur*,[b] remarks:

"The noble Lord could have given no other answer (whatever knowledge the Government may possess on the subject) without entering upon the discussion of a most delicate and difficult topic, which may, at the present moment, form the subject of negotiations, and which, to be brought to a satisfactory issue, should be left to the spontaneous sense of justice of those powers who have no desire to revive in this civilized age a system of legalized piracy."[c]

On the one hand, the Palmerston organ declares the "difficult topic" to form the subject of pending negotiations, and on the other, the necessity of leaving it to the "spontaneous sense of justice" of the interested powers. If the much boasted treaty of neutrality with Denmark and Sweden[25] was not dictated by the St. Petersburg Cabinet, it must, of course, have forbidden privateers being fitted out in their ports; but, in fact, the whole question can only be understood to refer to the United States of America, as the Baltic is to be occupied by English line-of-battle ships, and Holland, Belgium, Spain, Portugal, and the Italian ports on the Mediterranean, are completely in the hands of England and France. Now, what is the opinion of the St. Petersburg Cabinet as to the part to be performed by the United States in the case the Turkish war should lead to a war between England and Russia? We may answer this question authentically from a dispatch addressed by Pozzo di Borgo to Count Nesselrode in the autumn of 1825.[26] At that time Russia had resolved upon invading Turkey. As now she proposed to begin by a pacific occupation of the Principalities.

---

[a] February 21, 1854. Mr. Horsfall's question and Lord Palmerston's reply are quoted according to *The Times*, No. 21671, February 22, 1854.— *Ed.*

[b] Official organ.— *Ed.*

[c] *The Morning Post*, No. 25016, February 23, 1854, leader.— *Ed.*

"In supposing the adoption of this plan," says Pozzo di Borgo, "it would be requisite to enter into explanations with the Porte in the most measured terms, and to assure it that if it did not wish to precipitate itself into a war, the Emperor was willing to terminate these differences by conciliation."

After having enumerated all the steps they would be obliged to take, Pozzo di Borgo continues as follows:

"It would be advisable to communicate all these acts to the United States of America as an evidence of the regard of the Imperial Cabinet, and of the importance which it attaches to enlightening its opinion and even obtaining its suffrage."

In case of England's siding with Turkey and undertaking a war with Russia, Pozzo di Borgo remarks that

"in blockading our ports they (England) would exercise *their pretended maritime rights in respect to neutrals. This the United States would not suffer! thence would arise bitter dissensions and dangerous situations.*"

Now, as the Russian historian Karamzin justly remarks that "nothing changes in our (Russian) external policy",[27] we are justified in presuming that, at the present moment, and perhaps as long ago as February, 1853, Russia has "communicated all her acts to the United States," and done her best to cajole the Washington Cabinet into at least a neutral attitude. At the same time, in the case of a war with England, she bases her hopes upon eventual quarrels about the "maritime rights of the neutrals" producing "bitter dissensions and dangerous situations", and involving the United States in a more or less avowed alliance with St. Petersburg.

As I am quoting the most celebrated of Pozzo di Borgo's dispatches, I may as well cite the passage respecting Austria, the contents of which have certainly lost nothing of their actuality by the events that have passed since 1825, in Galicia, Italy, and Hungary.

"Our policy," says Pozzo, "commands that we shall show ourselves to this State under a terrible aspect, and by our preparations persuade it that, if it makes movements against us, *the fiercest of storms that it has yet to bear, will burst upon its head*.... Either Prince Metternich will declare to the Turks that our entry into the Principalities is a resolution that they themselves have provoked, or he will throw himself *on other provinces of the Ottoman Empire* more to his convenience. In the first case we will be agreed, *in the second we will become so*. The only chance that we have to run is that of an open declaration against us.... If Prince Metternich is wise he will avoid war; if he is violent, *he will be punished*. With a ministry placed in a situation such as his, a cabinet such as ours, will find in events a thousand ways of terminating differences."

Lord John's stump-oratory, the beating of big drums about
English honor, the show of great moral indignation at Russian
perfidy, the vision of England's floating batteries defiling along
the walls of Sevastopol and Kronstadt, the tumult of arms and the
ostentatious embarkation of troops, all these dramatic incidents
quite bewilder the public understanding, and raise a mist before
its eyes, which allowed it to see nothing save its own delusions.
Can there exist a greater delusion than believing this Ministry,
after the revelations made by the Blue Books, to have been
all at once transformed not only into a warlike Ministry, but
into a Ministry that could undertake any war against Russia
except a simulated one, or one carried on in the very interest
of the enemy against whom it is ostensibly directed? Let us
look at the circumstances under which the warlike preparations
are made.

No formal declaration of war is made against Russia. The very
object of the war the Ministry is not able to avow. Troops are
embarked without the place of their destination being distinctly
described. The estimates asked for are too small for a great war
and too great for a small one. The coalition, who have grown
notorious for ingenuity displayed in hatching pretexts for not
keeping their most solemn promises and reasons for delaying the
most urgent reforms, all at once feel themselves bound by
overscrupulous adherence to pledges rashly given to complicate
this momentous crisis by surprising the country with a new reform
bill, deemed inopportune by the most ardent reformers, imposed
by no pressure from without, and received on all sides with the
utmost indifference and suspicion. What then can be their plan
but to divert public attention from their external policy by getting
up a subject of overwhelming domestic interest?

Transparent efforts are now made to misguide the public as to
the situation of England in respect to foreign States. No binding
treaty has yet been concluded with France, but a substitute has
been provided by "notes exchanged." Now, such notes were
exchanged in 1839, with the cabinet of Louis Philippe, by virtue of
which the allied fleets were to enter the Dardanelles, and to arrest
the intervention of Russia in the affairs of the East, either singly
or collectively with other powers, and we all know what came out
of the notes exchanged then—a Holy Alliance against France and
the Treaty of the Dardanelles.[28] The sincerity and the earnestness
of the Anglo-French alliance may be inferred from a Parliamentary incident in yesterday's sitting of the Commons. Bonaparte, as
you have seen in the *Moniteur*, threatens the Greek insurrection-

ists,[a] and has sent a similar remonstrance to the Government of King Otto. Sir J. Walsh having interrogated the Ministry on this point, Lord John Russell declared that

"he was aware of no understanding between the French and English Governments in the matter alluded to, and had not been able to see the Minister of Foreign Affairs on the subject. His impression was, however, that no such remonstrance had been sent by the Government of France, and certainly not with the consent of, or in concert with, the Government of this country."[b]

If the British Government intend a real war with Russia why do they anxiously eschew the international forms of declaring war? If they intend a real alliance with France, why do they studiously shun the legalized forms of international alliances? As to the German powers, Sir James Graham declares that they have entered an alliance with England, and Lord John Russell on the same evening contradicts him, stating that the relations with those powers are in fact the same as at the beginning of the Eastern complication.[29] According to the very statement of the ministers, they are just now about coming to terms with Turkey and proposing a treaty with her. They are embarking troops, with a view to occupying Constantinople, without having beforehand concluded a treaty with Turkey. We are, then, not to be surprised at learning from a Constantinople letter that a secret agent of the Porte has been sent from Vienna to St. Petersburg to propose to the Czar a private settlement.

"It would be rational," says the correspondent, "that the Turks, after discovering the treachery and folly of their pretended friends, should seek to avenge themselves by contracting an alliance with a wise enemy. The terms of settlement, the former are endeavoring to settle on Turkey, are ten times more ruinous than the Menchikoff claims."[30]

The prospect of what the embarked troops are intended to do, at least in the opinion of the English Ministry, may be justly inferred from what the united squadrons have done and are doing at the present moment. Twenty days after having entered the Black Sea they return to the Bosphorus. A few days previous, we are informed,

"the Ministers of the Porte, out of deference for the remonstrances of the British Embassador, had to put in prison the editor of the Greek journal, *The Telegraph of the Bosphorus*,[c] for having said in his paper that both the English and

---

[a] Review of Current Events. February 21. *Le Moniteur universel*, No. 53, February 22, 1854.— *Ed.*

[b] Lord John Russell's speech in the House of Commons of February 23, 1854. *The Times*, No. 21673, February 24, 1854.— *Ed.*

[c] *Télégraphe du Bosphore.— Ed.*

French fleets would shortly return from the Euxine to the Bosphorus. The Editor of the *Journal de Constantinople* was authorized to declare that both fleets were to continue their stay in the Euxine."

In order to show his deference for the intimation received from the British and French Admirals,[a] the Russian Admiral on the 19th ult. sent out two steamers to bombard the Turks at Shefketil, and Russian steamers cruise in sight of Trebizond, while no vessels belonging to the united squadrons are in the Black Sea, except an English and a French steamer, off Sevastopol; Sinope, then, and the bombardment of Shefketil by Russian steamers, are the only feats the united squadrons have to boast of. The quarrel between the Embassadors and the Admirals all relations between whom have come to a dead stand—Lord Stratford de Redcliffe refusing to receive Admiral Dundas and Baraguay d'Hilliers excluding from a state ball the French Admiral and his officers—this quarrel is of minor importance, as the diplomatic triflers being compromised by the publication of their dispatches at London and Paris, may strive to rescue, at any risk of ships and crews, their lost reputation.

But the serious side of the question is, that the public instructions given to the Embassadors were countermanded by a set of secret instructions forwarded to the Admirals, and that the latter are really incapable of executing instructions which are self-contradictory—and how could they be otherwise, no declaration of war having preceded them? On the one hand they are ordered to attack Russian ships in order to enforce their withdrawal from the Euxine to Sevastopol, and on the other, not to swerve from the mere *defensive*. Lastly, if a serious war be intended, how could the British Embassador at Constantinople have regarded it as an important triumph to have got the leader of the war party in the Turkish ministry—Mehemet Ali Pasha—turned out of his office as war Minister, having him replaced by the peace-mongering Riza Pasha, while he intrusted Mehemet Pasha, a creature of Reshid Pasha, with the office of Grand Admiral?

Now look at another most important point. The embarkation of the British and French troops is only proceeded with after the news of a Greek insurrection having broken out in Albania, and being spread over Thessaly and Macedonia,[31] has reached London and Paris. This insurrection was from the first anxiously waited for on the part of the English Cabinet, as is proved by the

---

[a] Dundas and Hamelin.— *Ed.*

dispatches of Russell, Clarendon and Lord Stratford de Redcliffe.[32] It gives them the best occasion to interfere between the Sultan and his own Christian subjects on the plea of interfering between the Russians and the Turks. From the moment that the
Latins interfere with the Greeks (I use this word here only in the
religious sense) you may be sure of a concert becoming established
between 11,000,000 inhabitants of European Turkey and the Czar,
who will then really appear as their religious protector. There
exists no polemical schism between the Mussulmans and their
Greek subjects, but the religious animosity against the Latins may
be said to form the only common bond between the different
races inhabiting Turkey and professing the Greek creed. In this
respect things have not changed since the period when Mohammed II laid siege to Constantinople, when the Greek Admiral
Lucas Notaras, the most influential man in the Byzantine Empire,
publicly declared that he would prefer seeing the Turkish turban
triumphant in the capital rather than the Latin hat, while on the
other hand there was a Hungarian prophecy afloat that the
Christians would never be fortunate till the damned heretical
Greeks should be extirpated and Constantinople destroyed by the
Turks. Any interference, then, on the part of the Western powers,
between the Sultan and his Greek subjects, must favor the plans of
the Czar. A similar result will be brought about should Austria, as
she did in 1791,[33] undertake to occupy Servia on the pretext of
thwarting the treasonable designs of the Russian party in that
Principality. Let me add that it is rumored at London that the
insurged Epirates were supported and joined by Greeks from the
Ionian Islands, who had not been checked by the English
authorities, and that the news of the Greek insurrection was
announced by *The Times*, the coalition organ, in Saturday's
number, as a most opportune event.[a]

I, for my part, have no doubt at all that treachery lurks behind
the clamorous war preparations of the coalition. Bonaparte is of
course in good earnest in embarking in the war. He has no
alternative left but revolution at home or war abroad. He cannot
any longer continue, as he does, to couple the cruel despotism of
Napoleon I with the corrupt peace policy of Louis Philippe. He
must stop sending new batches of prisoners to Cayenne, if he
dare not simultaneously send French armies beyond the frontiers.
But the conflict between the avowed intentions of Bonaparte and
the secret plans of the coalition can only contribute to further

---

[a] *The Times*, No. 21668, February 18, 1854, leader.— *Ed.*

embroil matters. What I conclude from all this is, not that there will be no war, but, on the contrary, that it will assume such terrible and revolutionary dimensions as are not even suspected by the little men of the coalition. Their very perfidy is the means of transforming a local conflict into a European conflagration.

Even if the British Ministry were as sincere as they are false, their intervention could not but accelerate the downfall of the Ottoman Empire. They cannot interfere without demanding pledges for the Christian subjects of the Porte, and these pledges they cannot wrest from it without dooming it to ruin. Even the Constantinople correspondent I quoted before, and who is an avowed Turkophile, cannot but own that

"the proposal of the Western Powers to put all the subjects of the Porte on a perfect footing of civil and religious equality, will lead at once to anarchy, intestine warfare, and a final and speedy overthrow of the empire."

Written on February 24, 1854

First published in the *New-York Daily Tribune*, No. 4025, March 13; reprinted in the *New-York Semi-Weekly Tribune*, No. 918, March 14 and the *New-York Weekly Tribune*, No. 653, March 18, 1854

Signed: *Karl Marx*

Reproduced from the *New-York Daily Tribune*

Karl Marx

[ENGLISH AND FRENCH WAR PLANS.—GREEK INSURRECTION.—SPAIN.—CHINA] [34]

London, Friday, March 3, 1854

In my last letter I mentioned that Sir Charles Napier owed his appointment as Commander-in-Chief of the Baltic fleet to his public expression of mistrust in the French alliance; to his accusing France of having betrayed England in 1840, while in fact the English Government at that time conspired with Nicholas against Louis Philippe.[35] I ought to have added that the second Admiral in the Black Sea, Sir Edmund Lyons, during his stay in Greece as English Minister, showed himself the avowed enemy of France, and was removed from that office on the representations of Lord Stratford de Redcliffe. Thus in the ministerial appointments the greatest possible care is taken to insure a crop of misintelligence, not only between the French and English commanders, but also between the Admirals and the English Embassador at Constantinople.

These facts are not denied and certainly not refuted by Bonaparte's congratulating himself, in the opening speech he addressed to his own representatives, upon his close alliance with England. The *entente cordiale* is certainly somewhat older than the restoration of the Imperial etiquette.[a] The most remarkable passage in Bonaparte's speech is neither this reminiscence from Louis Philippe's harangues, nor his denunciation of the Czar's ambitious plans, but rather his proclaiming himself the protector of Germany, and especially of Austria, against the foe from without and the enemy from within.[36]

---

[a] The reference is to the restoration of the Empire in France on December 2, 1852.— Ed.

The ratifications of the treaty entered into by the Porte with
the Western Powers, containing the clause that it was not to
conclude peace with Russia without their concurrence,[37] had
hardly been exchanged at Constantinople on the 5th inst., when
negotiations relative to the future position of the Christians in
Turkey were also opened between the representatives of the four
Powers and the Porte. The real end aimed at in these negotiations
is betrayed in the following passage from Wednesday's *Times*:

"The condition of several parts of the Turkish Empire which have already
obtained by firmans and treaties the complete internal administration of their
affairs, while they continue to recognize the sovereignty of the Porte, is a precedent
which may be extended without prejudice to either side, and which would perhaps
afford the best means of providing for the Provinces in their present state."[a]

In other words the Coalition Cabinet intends securing the
integrity of the Turkish Empire in Europe by the transformation
of Bosnia, Croatia, Herzegovina, Bulgaria, Albania, Rumelia and
Thessaly into so many Danubian Principalities. The acceptance on
the part of the Porte of these conditions must infallibly lead, if the
Turkish armies prove victorious, to a civil war among the Turks
themselves.

It is now ascertained that the discovery of the conspiracy at
Vidin[38] only hastened the Greek explosion, which at Bucharest
was considered as an accomplished fact before it had broken out.
The Pasha of Scutari is concentrating all his troops with a view to
prevent the Montenegrins from joining the insurgent Greeks.

The Anglo-French expedition may be set down, as far as the
present intentions of the British Government go, as another piece
of humbug. The landing places are fixed for the French at
Rodosto, for the British at Enos. This latter town lies on a small
peninsula at the entrance of a marshy bay, at the rear of which the
extensive marshes of the valley of the Maritza, will no doubt
greatly contribute to the salubrity of the camp. It lies *outside* not
only of the Bosphorus, but of the Dardanelles also, and the troops,
in order to get to the Black Sea, would have either to reembark
and enjoy 250 miles round-about sail against the currents of the
Straits, or to march through a roadless country for the distance of
160 miles, a march which no doubt could be completed in a
fortnight. The French are at Rodosto, at least on the sea of
Marmora, and only a week's march from Constantinople.

But what are the troops to do in this inexplicable position?
Why, they are either to march upon Adrianople, there to cover

---

[a] *The Times*, No. 21677, March 1, 1854, leader.— *Ed.*

the capital, or in the worst case, to unite at the neck of the Thracian Chersonesus, to defend the Dardanelles. So says *The Times,* "by authority," and even quotes Marshal Marmont's strategic observations in support of the wisdom of the plan.[a]

One hundred thousand French and English troops to defend a capital which is not menaced, which cannot possibly be menaced for the next twelvemonth! Why, they might as well have stopped at home.

This plan, if it is to be carried out, is decidedly the worst that can be devised. It is based upon the very worst sort of defensive warfare, viz: that which seeks strength in absolute inactivity. Supposing the expedition was to be of a mainly defensive character, it is evident that this object would be best obtained by enabling the Turks, based upon such a reserve, to pass into the offensive, or else, by taking up a position in which a casual and partial offensive, where opportunities offer, could be taken. But at Enos and Rodosto the French and British troops are entirely useless.

The worst of it is, that an army of 100,000 men, with plenty of steam transports, and supported by a fleet of twenty sail of the line, is in itself a force competent to take the most decided offensive action in any part of the Black Sea. Such a force must either take the Crimea and Sevastopol, Odessa and Kherson, close the Sea of Azov, destroy the Russian forts on the Caucasian coasts, and bring the Russian fleet safe into the Bosphorus, or it has no idea of its strength and its duty as an active army. It is affirmed on the part of the Ministerial partisans that, when the 100,000 men are once concentrated in Turkey, such operations may be undertaken, and that the landing of the first divisions at Enos and Rodosto is merely contrived to deceive the enemy. But even in this case it is an unnecessary loss of time and expense not to land the troops at once on some point on the Black Sea. The enemy cannot be misled. As soon as the Emperor Nicholas hears of this pompously announced expedition of 100,000 men, he is bound to send every soldier he can spare to Sevastopol, Kaffa, Perekop and Yenicale. You cannot first frighten your enemy by enormous armaments, and then try to make him believe that they are not intended to do any harm. The trick would be too shallow; and if it is expected to mislead the Russians by such paltry pretexts, British diplomacy has made another egregious blunder.

---

[a] *The Times,* No. 21673, February 24, 1854, leader.— *Ed.*

I, therefore, believe that those who have planned the
expedition intend betraying the Sultan[a] directly, and, on the plea
of frightening Russia as much as possible, will take good care to
do her by all means the least possible harm.

England and France occupying Constantinople and part of
Rumelia; Austria occupying Servia, and perhaps Bosnia and
Montenegro, and Russia being allowed to reenforce herself in
Moldo-Wallachia,—this looks like an eventual partition of Turkey
in Europe rather than anything else. Turkey is placed in worse
circumstances than in 1772, when the King of Prussia,[b] in order to
induce the Empress Catherine to retire from the Danubian
Principalities, the occupation of which threatened to lead to a
European conflict, proposed the first partition of Poland, which
was to defray the expenses of the Russo-Turkish war. Be it
remembered that, at that time, the Porte originally rushed into the
war with Catherine with the view of defending Poland from
Prussian aggression, and that, at the end, Poland was sacrificed at
the shrine of the "independence and integrity" of the Ottoman
Empire.

The treacherous policy of procrastination pursued by the
Coalition Cabinet has given the Muscovite emissaries the opportunity for planning and maturing the Greek insurrection, so
anxiously expected by Lord Clarendon. The insurrection had
commenced on the 28th January and according to the last
dispatches from Vienna assumed more threatening dimensions on
the 13th inst. The districts of Acarnania and Aetolia, and circles
of Ilussa and Delonia are said to be in a state of revolt. An
insurrection is stated to have broken out at Egrippo, the capital of
Euböa, equal in gravity to that in Albania. The fact of the towns of
Arta and Yannina being quitted by the Turks and occupied by the
Greeks is of smaller importance, as the domineering citadels
remain in the hand of Ottoman troops and as we know, from the
numerous wars carried on between the Christians and the Turks
in Albania, the final possession of these towns depended always on
the possession of the citadels. The Gulfs of Contessa and Salonica
and the coasts of Albania will be declared in a state of siege. I
stated in my last letter[c] that one of the results of the Greek
insurrection the most to be apprehended on the part of the Porte,

---

[a] Abdul Mejid.— *Ed.*
[b] Frederick II.— *Ed.*
[c] See this volume, p. 33.— *Ed.*

would be the opportunity it afforded the Western Powers for interfering between the Sultan and his subjects, instead of fighting the Russians, and thus driving the Greek Christians into alliance with the Czar. How eager these Powers are to grasp at this opportunity may be inferred from the fact of the same post bringing the news of the Porte having accepted the convention proposed by England and France, and of the French and English Embassadors having sent two steamers to the assistance of the Turks, while the British minister at Athens[a] had informed the Cabinet of King Otto that England would interfere in the insurged districts. The immediate result of the insurrection, from a military point of view, is clearly described by the Vienna correspondent[b] of to-day's *Times*, as follows:

"During the last few days a certain discouragement has been observable in headquarters at Vidin, the reenforcements which had been announced having received counter-orders, and being on their way to the south-western districts of Turkey. The news of the insurrection of the Christians in Epirus had produced an alarming effect on the Arnauts and Albanians on the Danube, who loudly demanded permission to return home. The Generals of Brigade, Hussein Bey and Soliman Pasha, had lost all their influence over their wild troops, and it was feared that if an attempt was made to detain them by force there would be an open mutiny; while if they were permitted to return, they would ravage the Christian districts on their way home. If the hostile movement of the Christian population in the West should assume more formidable dimensions, the west wing of the Turkish army would be obliged to make a retrograde movement, which would more than counterbalance the check which the Russians had received by the entry of the allied fleets into the Black Sea."[c]

These are some of the first results of that policy of procrastination so rhetorically praised by Graham, Russell, Clarendon and Palmerston in vindication of the ministerial management of Eastern affairs. As they were informed, late on last Friday night,[d] that the Czar, without having waited for the recall of Sir Hamilton Seymour, from England, had ordered him off, in the most abrupt and unceremonious manner, they held two Cabinet Councils, one on Saturday and the other on Sunday afternoon—the result of their consultations being to allow the Czar once more a delay of three or four weeks, which delay is to be granted under the form of a summons,

---

[a] Thomas Wyse.— *Ed.*
[b] T. O'M. Bird.— *Ed.*
[c] Report from the Vienna correspondent of February 22. *The Times*, No. 21676, February 28, 1854.— *Ed.*
[d] February 24, 1854.— *Ed.*

"calling upon the Czar to give within six days from the receipt of that communication a solemn pledge and engagement that he will cause his troops to evacuate the Principalities of the Danube on or before the 30th of April."[a]

But mark that this summons is *not* followed with the menace of a *declaration of war* in case of a refusal on the part of the Czar. It may be said, and it is said, by *The Times*, that, notwithstanding this new delay granted, war preparations are actively pursued; but you will observe that on the one hand all decisive action of the Porte on the Danube is prevented by the prospect held out of the Western Powers being resolved upon directly participating in the war—and every day of delay in that quarter puts the Turks in a worse position, as it allows the Russians to reenforce themselves in the front, and the Greek rebels to grow more dangerous in the rear of the Danubian army; while, on the other hand, the embarkation of troops for Enos and Rodosto may embarrass the Sultan but will certainly not stop the Russians.

It has been settled that the British expeditionary force shall consist of about 30,000 and the French of about 80,000 men. Should it happen to appear, in the course of events, that Austria, while apparently joining the Western Powers, only proposed to mask her understanding with Russia, Bonaparte would have much to regret this most injudicious dispersion of his troops.

There is another insurrection which may be considered as a diversion made in favor of Russia—the insurrection in *Spain.* Any movement in Spain is sure to produce dissension between France and England. In 1823, the French intervention in Spain was, as we know from Chateaubriand's *Congress of Verona,*[b] instigated by Russia. That the Anglo-French intervention in 1834,[39] which finally broke up the *entente cordiale* between the two states, proceeded from the same source, we may infer from Palmerston having been its author. The "Spanish marriages"[40] prepared the way for the downfall of the Orleans dynasty. At the present moment, a dethronement of the "innocent" Isabella would allow a son of Louis Philippe, the Duke of Montpensier, to bring forward his claims on the throne of Spain; while, on the other hand, Bonaparte would be reminded of one of his uncles[c] having once resided at Madrid. The Orleans would be supported by the Coburgs, and resisted by the Bonapartes. A Spanish insurrection,

---

[a] *The Times*, No. 21676, February 28, 1854, leader.— *Ed.*

[b] Chateaubriand, *Congrès de Vérone. Guerre d'Espagne. Négociations. Colonies espagnoles.— Ed.*

[c] Joseph Bonaparte.— *Ed.*

then, which is far from meaning a popular revolution, must prove a most powerful agency in dissolving so superficial a combination as what is termed the Anglo-French alliance.

A treaty of alliance is said to have been concluded between Russia, Khiva, Bokhara and Cabul.[a]

As to Dost Mohammed, the Ameer of Cabul, it would be quite natural that after having proposed in 1838 to England to place forever a *feud of blood* between himself and Russia, if the English Government required it, by causing the agent dispatched to him by the Czar to be killed, and being renewed in 1839 on the part of England by the Afghan expedition, by his expulsion from the throne and by the most cruel and unscrupulous devastation of his country [41]—that Dost Mohammed should now endeavor to avenge himself upon his faithless ally. However, as the population of Khiva, Bokhara and Cabul, belong to the orthodox Mussulman faith of the Sunni, while the Persians adhere to the schismatic tenets of the Schii, it is not to be supposed that they will ally themselves with Russia, being the ally of the Persians, whom they detest and hate, against England, the ostensible ally of the Padishah[b], whom they regard as the supreme commander of the faithful.

There is some probability of Russia having an ally in Thibet and the Tartar[c] Emperor of China,[d] if the latter be forced to retire into Manchuria and to resign the sceptre of China proper. The Chinese rebels, as you know, have undertaken a regular crusade against Buddhism, destroying its temples and slaying its Banzes.[42] But the religion of the Tartars is Buddhism and Thibet, the seat of the great Lama, and recognizing the suzeraineté of China, is the sanctuary of the Buddhist faith. Tae-ping-wang,[e] if he succeed in driving the Mandshu dynasty out of China, will, therefore, have to enter a religious war with the Buddhist powers of Tartary. Now, as on both sides of the Himalayas Buddhism is confessed and as England cannot but support the new Chinese dynasty, the Czar is sure to side with the Tartar tribes, put them in motion against England and awake religious revolts in Nepal itself. By the last Oriental mails we are informed that

---

[a] "India and China", *The Times,* No. 21676, February 28, 1854.— *Ed.*

[b] Here Abdul Mejid.— *Ed.*

[c] Here Marx uses the term "Tartar", which in nineteenth-century West-European literature denoted Mongols, Manchurians and other Turkic tribes in Eastern Asia.— *Ed.*

[d] Hsien Fêng.— *Ed.*

[e] Hung Hsiu-ch'üan.— *Ed.*

"the Emperor of China, in anticipation of the loss of Pekin, had directed the governors of the various provinces to send the Imperial revenue to Getol, their old family seat and present summer residence in Manchuria, about 80 miles north-east of the Great Wall."[a]

The great religious war between the Chinese and the Tartars, which will spread over the Indian frontiers, may consequently be regarded as near at hand.

Written on February 28 and
March 3, 1854

First published in the *New-York Daily Tribune*, No. 4030, March 18; reprinted in the *New-York Semi-Weekly Tribune*, No. 920, March 21, 1854

Signed: *Karl Marx*

Reproduced from the *New-York Daily Tribune*

---

[a] "India and China", *The Times*, No. 21676, February 28, 1854.— *Ed.*

Karl Marx

AUSTRIAN BANKRUPTCY[43]

Notwithstanding the imminence of war and their pressing needs, the French and the Austrian Governments have not yet succeeded in strengthening the *nervus belli*,[a] namely, the money-power. Notwithstanding the Lucullian magnificence displayed in the dinners given by the French Minister of Finance[b] to the Receivers-General, the *Crédit Mobilier*,[44] and the principal bankers of Paris, those capitalists prove stubborn and cling to that discreet sort of patriotism, which, by exacting the greatest possible interest from the state, is wont to indemnify its private interests with the public ones. Thus the terms of the proposed French loan of two hundred million francs remain still unsettled.

As to Austria there can exist no doubt that one of principal motives which induce her to profess friendly feelings toward the Western Powers is the hope of thus reviving the confidence of moneyed men and getting out of her financial difficulties. Indeed, the official gazette at Vienna[c] had hardly uttered a few words about Austrian neutrality and good understanding with France, when it surprised the public with the announcement of an intended sale of a considerable portion of the six million acres of crown lands, and with a financial rescript, dated Feb. 23, 1854, to the effect that the whole of the State paper-money, 150,000,000 florins, now in circulation, and of compulsory currency, was to be transferred to the National Bank, and successively converted into

---

[a] *Nervus belli*—the nerve of the war.— *Ed.*
[b] Bineau.— *Ed.*
[c] *Wiener Zeitung.*— *Ed.*

bank-notes,[a] at the expiration of which change all the paper issued by the treasury will be withdrawn from circulation, and no more State paper-money of a forced currency be issued. In making this change the Imperial Government is guarantee to the Bank for the paper-money transferred to it, and pledges itself to indemnify it for the expenses connected with that conversion; to pay, in extinction of the debt thus created, a yearly installment of at least 10,000,000 florins; to mortgage the customs' revenue as security for the regular payment of these installments, and to pay the Bank in specie in proportion as those duties are received. At the same time the Government is bound to do its best to enable the Bank to fulfill its obligations and resume specie payments. Meanwhile, in order to give the holders of bank-notes the means of changing their notes at pleasure into a debt bearing interest, payable in specie, the Bank undertakes to issue bonds bearing interest, to be in all respects on the same footing as State bonds or obligations. The Government will also call in what are known as Redemption notes and Anticipation notes, and put them entirely out of circulation.

The conversion of State paper of a forced course into inconvertible bank-notes will not reduce the amount nor ameliorate the quality, but only simplify the denominations of the paper-money issued. As the State is in the possession of the same means which it grants the Bank for the redemption of the paper-money, it would itself have made use of them if not fully aware that the want of confidence in itself was such as not to allow credit to be restored save by the help of a bank, which is not the property of the State. Thus the dependence of the Emperor[b] on the Jews of the Vienna Bank grows at the same pace as the military character of his Government. In January 1852, he mortgaged to them the salt-works of Gmünden, Aussee and Stallein. In February 1854, they obtain a lien on the customs' revenue of the whole monarchy. Step by step the Bank becomes the real and the Government merely the nominal owner of the Empire. The more Austria has resisted the demands of participation in political power on the part of the middle classes, the more she is forced to undergo the unmitigated despotism of one fraction of those classes—the money lenders.

The decree, of which we have above given the substance, disguises an attempt at a new loan under the form of aid tendered

---

[a] Report from Vienna. *L'Indépendance belge*, No. 60, March 1, 1854.— *Ed.*
[b] Francis Joseph I.— *Ed.*

to the holders of bank-notes, in changing them into a debt bearing interest; the latter to be paid in specie. In 1852 the Government also pledged itself to meet in specie various minor payments and obligations, but as it received the taxes only in State paper-money or in bank-notes the Administration was forced to contract a loan of thirty-five million florins at London and Frankfort. The new loans, of course, augment the old deficits and the augmented deficits lead to new issues of paper-money, the superabundance and consequent depreciation of which they were intended to prevent. The broad distinction drawn on the part of the Government between payments in specie and payments in bank-notes is as good a means of rescuing the notes from their discredit as the augmentation of the circulating medium of the Bank by 150 millions is a means of enabling it to fulfill its engagements and resume cash payments. The Government will pay the Bank in specie in proportion as the customs duties are paid in the same, but it is well known that not only the Austrian peasants but even the citizens in the larger towns are as fond of hoarding as the Chinese and the Indians; that in 1850 sums were hoarded even in copper, and that in 1854 they are paying all taxes in paper, although it is only accepted with a discount of full seventeen per cent.

Those conversant with the past history of the Austrian Exchequer will fail in discovering any novelty either in respect to the promises held out in the new decree, or the financial devices resorted to. The first issue of Austrian paper-money took place under the Empress Maria Theresa, toward the end of the Seven Years' War. It consisted originally of Bank bills exchangeable by the State authorities for silver. In 1797, in consequence of the pecuniary difficulties of the Government in the wars against France, the convertibility into silver was abolished. The first issue under the Empress Maria Theresa having amounted to twelve million florins, the total sum of Bank bills issued in 1809 amounted to 1,060,793,653 florins, their reduction in value having at the same time reached its maximum. On the 20th of February, 1811, the Government published a patent[45] by which the Bank bills were altogether withdrawn from circulation and redeemed (hence the name Redemption notes) at the rate of 20 for 100 for a new paper called *Wiener Währung*.[a] The Government declared this to be the real money of the country, and promised that this new paper should never be increased beyond the amount necessary for

---

[a] Vienna currency.— *Ed.*

exchanging the Bank bills. In May 1811 the *Wiener Währung* was already at a discount of 8 per cent., and Anticipation notes were issued, so called because the proceeds of a part of the taxes for twelve years were anticipated by them. The first issue of Anticipation notes really amounted to only forty-five million florins, and for their redemption within twelve years an annual sum of 3,750,000 florins was destined to be taken from the land taxes.

But in consequence of the war, new issues of Anticipation notes quietly followed each other, each new issue being attended by a reduction of their value. In 1815 the premium for silver reached the hight of 400 per cent. against the *Wiener Währung.* On the first of June, 1816, an imperial patent appeared declaring that the State would in future never again have recourse to an inconvertible paper currency; that the paper-money in circulation should be gradually withdrawn and specie be restored as the standard medium of circulation. In order to fulfill these promises, the privileged National Bank was constituted definitively, January 18th, 1818, the State having made an arrangement with the Bank by which it pledged itself to redeem the inconvertible paper-money. As late as June, 1852, however, we find again the Finance Minister[a] announcing in the official gazette that, in future, compulsory loans, extraordinary taxation, depreciation of the value of money, would be absolutely excluded; if not exactly at present, yet in future, Austrian paper would be converted into coin without loss, and that the loan now contemplated would be applied to withdraw the State paper-money and for the payment of the State debts to the Bank. There can be no better proof of the hollowness of such promises than their periodical occurrence.

At the time of Maria Theresa the Austrian Government was powerful enough to issue its own Bank bills, exchangeable for specie, and even at a premium over silver. In 1818 the State, in order to redeem its paper-money, was obliged to recur to the establishment of a privileged bank, the property of private capitalists, who received advantages very burdensome to the State, but who were pledged to the issue of convertible notes. In 1854 the Government appeals to the help of a bank, whose own paper has become as depreciated and inconvertible as that of the State itself.

Although from 1815 to 1846 Austria enjoyed a period of almost uninterrupted peace and internal tranquility, the first shock after

---

[a] Baumgartner.— *Ed.*

that long period found her altogether unprepared. The insurrection at Cracow, and the disturbances in Galicia, at the end of February, 1846,[46] augmented the public expenditures by more than 10,000,000 compared with 1845. The army expenses were the principal cause of this increased outlay. They amounted to 50,624,120 florins, in 1845, but in 1846 rose 7,000,000 more, while the administrative expenses of the provinces rose 2,000,000. In 1847 the commercial crisis and the bad harvest produced a great diminution in the excise revenue, while the army [budget] rose to 64,000,000, chiefly in consequence of troubles in Italy. The deficit of that year was 7,000,000. In 1848-9 the revenue of whole provinces was lost, besides the war expenses in Italy and Hungary. In 1848 the deficit was 45,000,000 florins, and in 1849, 121,000,000. State paper of compulsory currency, to the sum of 76,000,000, Three-per-Cents, was issued in 1849. Long before this, the Bank had stopped specie payments, and its issues were declared by the Government to be inconvertible. In 1850 there was a deficit of 54,000,000, and the chances of a war with Prussia brought down the paper-money to a discount of 60 per cent. The total amount of State paper-money issued in the years 1849, '50 and '51 was 219,000,000. In 1852 the deficit was 8,000,000 more than in '49, and 46,000,000 more than in '47. In 1851 the war budget was 126,000,000, fully double what it was in '47. In '52 the police expenses were 9,000,000, fourfold greater than those of '48. Both police and war expenses also increased in 1853.

The real question, however, is not how Austria got into her financial *cul-de-sac*, but how, when thus immersed in bank paper and debt, she has avoided open bankruptcy. In 1850 her revenue amounted to one hundred and ninety-six millions more than in 1848; and to forty-two millions more than in 1849. In 1851 the receipts were two hundred and nineteen millions over those of 1850. In 1852 they reached two hundred and twenty-six millions, an increase of six millions over those of 1851. Thus there has been a continual increase of revenue although not in the same proportion in 1852 as in 1851, and in 1851 not in the same proportion as in 1850.

Whence this increase of revenue? Putting aside the extraordinary receipts from the Sardinian war indemnity and the Lombardo-Venetian confiscations, the transformation of the Austrian peasant into a landholder [47] has of course increased the tax-paying power of the country and the revenue derived from the land tax. At the same time the abolition of the patrimonial courts brought the income, which the aristocracy had formerly enjoyed from their

private administration of justice, into the coffers of the State, and
this branch of revenue has been constantly increasing since 1849.
Then a considerable increase arose from the income-tax, introduced by the patent of October 29, 1849. This tax has proved
particularly productive in the Italian provinces of Austria. In
1852, for instance, the increase of the income-tax in the German
and Slavonic provinces together amounted to six hundred and one
million florins, while in the Italian provinces alone it was six
hundred and thirty-nine. The principal cause, however, which has
saved the Austrian Empire from a formal bankruptcy, is the
subjugation of Hungary and her assimilation with the other
provinces in respect to taxation.

The basis of the whole Austrian system of taxation may be said
to be the land-tax. On the 23d Dec. 1817, appeared an imperial
patent, in which the Emperor Francis announced his resolution to
establish uniformity in the land-tax system all over his German,
Slavonic and Italian provinces. In one paragraph of this patent it
is ordered that no exemptions from the land-tax should in future
"be made according to the personal quality of the possessors of
estates or houses", and as a whole this view was acted upon. In the
Archduchy of Austria, the new survey was introduced in 1834,
and this was the first hereditary domain in which the new system
was brought into operation. Austrian-Lombardy possessed an
excellent survey from the time of Charles VI, the *Censimento
Milanese*. Hungary and Transylvania, however, by no means
contributed to the land-tax and other taxes, in the same degree
with the other provinces of the Empire. According to the
Hungarian Constitution, the Hungarian possessors of by far the
greatest part of all the land were subject to no kind of direct tax,
and even several of the indirect taxes imposed upon the other
provinces pressed neither upon Hungary nor upon Transylvania.
The population of Hungary, Transylvania and the Military
Frontier[48] together amounted, in 1846, to 14,549,958; those of the
other provinces of the Monarchy, to 24,901,675, so that the
former should have contributed seven-eighteenths of the whole
revenue. But Hungary and Transylvania in 1846 only contributed
twenty-three millions, which, as the whole revenue in that year
amounted to one hundred and sixty-four millions was only
somewhat less than one-seventh of the revenue. The Hungarian
provinces occupy 5,855 of the 12,123 German square miles, which
form the area of the Austrian Monarchy; consequently one-half of
its superficial extent.

The Emperor Joseph II, whose great aim was the centralization and complete Germanization of the Austrian Monarchy, had arbitrarily introduced innovations in Hungary intended to place her on the same footing with the other provinces. But this produced such an effect on the public mind in that country that Joseph II, at the close of his life, feared that the Hungarians would rebel as the Netherlands had done.[49] The Emperors Leopold II, Francis I, and Ferdinand I did not dare to repeat the hazardous experiment. This cause—the impediments to an equalization of taxes existing in the Hungarian Constitution— ceased to work after the Hungarian revolution was quelled by Russian assistance. The Emperor Francis Joseph having never sworn to the Hungarian Constitution, and being made Emperor in the place of Ferdinand because he had never sworn to it, at once introduced the land-tax on the same footing with the other crown lands. Besides, by the abolition of the frontier of Hungary on the 1st of October, 1850, the Austrian Monarchy came to form one single territory with respect to customs as well as taxes. The Excise and the tobacco monopoly were also introduced there on March 1, 1851. The increase of the direct taxes alone in the Hungarian provinces amounted to 11,500,000 florins in 1851, and to about 8,000,000 florins in 1852.

We arrive then at the irrefragable conclusion that on the possession of Hungary and Lombardy depends not only the political but the economical existence of the Austrian Empire, and that with their loss the long-delayed bankruptcy of that State becomes inevitable.

Written on March 3, 1854

First published in the *New-York Daily Tribune*, No. 4033, March 22; reprinted in the *New-York Weekly Tribune*, No. 655, April 1, 1854 as a leader

Reproduced from the *New-York Daily Tribune*

Karl Marx

[OPENING OF THE LABOUR PARLIAMENT —
ENGLISH WAR BUDGET][50]

London, Tuesday, March 7, 1854

The delegates to the Labor Parliament[51] met yesterday at the People's Institution, Manchester, at 10 o'clock in the forenoon. The first sitting was, of course, applied to preliminary business. It was moved by James Williams of Stockport, seconded by James Bligh of London, and supported by Ernest Jones, that Dr. Marx be invited to sit as honorary delegate at the Labor Parliament, which motion was carried unanimously. Similar resolutions were passed with respect to Messrs. Blanc and Nadaud. Whatever may be its immediate results, the mere assembling of such a Parliament marks a new epoch in the history of labor. The meeting at the Palais du Luxembourg at Paris, after the revolution of February,[52] might perhaps be considered a precedent in a similar direction, but at first sight there appears this great difference, that the Luxembourg was initiated by the Government, while the Labor Parliament is initiated by the people themselves; that the Luxembourg was invented with a view to removing the Socialist members of the Provisional Government from the center of action and any serious participation in the real business of the country; and lastly, that the delegates to the Luxembourg only consisted of members of the various so-called *corps d'états*, corporations more or less corresponding to the medieval guilds and the present trades-unions, while the Labor Parliament is a true representation of all branches and divisions of labor on a national scale. The success of the Labor Parliament will principally, if not exclusively, depend on its acting upon the principle that it is not the so-called organization of labor,[53] but the organization of the laboring classes they have at present to deal with.

The privileges of the now governing classes, and the slavery of the working classes, are equally based on the *existing* organization of labor, which, of course, will be defended and maintained on the part of the former by all means in their hands, one of these means being the present State machinery. To alter, then, the existing organization of labor, and to supplant it by a new one, you want power—social and political power—power not only of resisting, but also of attacking; and to acquire that power you want to organize yourselves as an army possessed of that moral and physical strength which will enable it to meet the fiendly hosts. If the Labor Parliament allows its time to be absorbed by mere theoretical propositions, instead of preparing the way for the actual formation of a national party, it will prove a failure as the Luxembourg did.

A new election of the Chartist Executive having taken place, according to the statutes of the National Charter Association,[54] Ernest Jones, James Finlen (London), and John Shaw (Leeds), were declared duly elected to serve on the Executive of the N.C.A. for the next six months.

As Bonaparte's intention of contracting a loan at the Bourse was frustrated by the passive resistance of the Paris capitalists, his Minister of Finance[a] has presented to the Senate a Budget containing the following article:

"The Minister of Finance is authorized to create, for the service of the Treasury and the negotiations with the Bank of France, Treasury bonds, bearing interest and payable at fixed periods. The Treasury bonds circulation shall not exceed 250,000,000 francs (£10,000,000); but the bonds delivered to the sinking fund are not included within this limit, by virtue of the law of June 10, 1833, nor are the bonds deposited as a guarantee at the Bank of France and the discount establishments."[55]

In an additional clause it is provided that

"the Emperor reserves to himself the right of issuing supplementary emissions by virtue of mere decrees,"

to be registered afterward by the Senate. I am informed by a Paris letter that this proposal has struck with horror the whole of the middle classes, as on the one hand the Treasury bonds shall not exceed the sum of 250,000,000 and on the other exceed that identical sum by whatever amount the Emperor may think fit to decree, the bonds thus issued being not even to be deposed as a guarantee at the Bank of France and the other discount

---

[a] Bineau.—*Ed.*

establishments. You know that on the like amount taken from the *Caisse des Dépôts et Consignations*[a] 60,000,000 have been already advanced by the bank on Treasury bonds. The mere appearance of war is eagerly grasped at by the Decembrists[56] to remove the last weak barriers yet standing between themselves and the national treasury. While this prospect of an imminent disorganization of the public credit, already much shaken, perplexes the middle classes, the bulk of the people will be exasperated at the proposed increase of the salt tax and similar most unpopular imposts. Thus, this war which is sure to gain for Bonaparte a sort of popularity in foreign countries, may, nevertheless, accelerate his downfall in France.

That I was right in presuming the present Spanish troubles as likely to afford the occasion for serious misunderstandings between France and England,[b] one may infer from the following intelligence of a London paper:

"The French Emperor has made inquiries of Lord Clarendon, through Mr. Walewski, whether the British Government would be disposed to aid him in placing the Carlist Pretender to the Crown of Spain[c] upon the throne, in the event of Queen Isabella being dethroned. Lord Clarendon is said to have declared that, happily, Queen Isabella was firmly seated on her throne, and that a revolution was but a remote contingency in a country so devoted to monarchical institutions; but that even if a revolution should break out in Spain and the Queen be dethroned, the British Cabinet must decline to enter into any engagements.

"The Emperor's proposal to place the Comte de Montemolin upon the throne is inspired by his very natural desire to prevent the Duchess of Montpensier[d] from inheriting her sister's diadem; for he thinks it would be inconvenient that he should have for a neighbor a son of Louis Philippe as husband of the Queen of Spain."

In Friday's sitting of the Commons Lord John Russell stated[e] that he was forced to withdraw his Reform bill for the moment, which, however, would be proceeded with on the 27th of April if, in the meantime, in consequence of the new proposal made to the Emperor of Russia[f] being accepted, the Eastern question was settled. It is true that after the publication of the Czar's manifesto to his subjects and his letter addressed to Bonaparte,[57] such a settlement has become more improbable than ever before, but, nevertheless, the ministerial declaration proves the Reform bill to

---

[a] Deposit Bank.— *Ed.*

[b] See this volume, p. 40.— *Ed.*

[c] Montemolin.— *Ed.*

[d] Maria Luisa Fernanda.— *Ed.*

[e] Lord John Russell's speech in the House of Commons on March 3. *The Times*, No. 21680, March 4, 1854.— *Ed.*

[f] See this volume, pp. 39-40.— *Ed.*

have been brought forward only with a view to absorb and appease public opinion in case the coalition diplomacy should succeed in reestablishing the Russian *status quo ante bellum*.[a] The eminent part taken by Lord Palmerston in his ministerial intrigue is thus described by *The Morning Advertiser*, one of his most ardent partisans:

"Lord Aberdeen is the nominal, but not the real Prime Minister. Lord Palmerston is practically the first Minister of the Crown. He is the master spirit of the Cabinet. Ever since his return to office, his colleagues have been in constant fear of his again flying off from them at a tangent, and are consequently afraid to thwart any of those views to which he is known to attach importance. He has consequently everything his own way. A striking instance of his Lordship's ascendency in her Majesty's Councils was afforded last week. The new Reform bill was then brought formally under the consideration of the Cabinet, and the question came to be whether it should be proceeded with this session or abandoned. Lord Aberdeen, Lord John Russell, Sir James Graham, and Sir William Molesworth, were for proceeding with the measure. Lord Palmerston proposed that it should be abandoned, and intimated, in plain terms—as we stated some days ago, that he would vote for its abandonment in the House should he be defeated in the Cabinet. The result of the discussion or conversation, which took place, was, that Lord Palmerston carried his point. Those opposed to him—among whom were the ministerial leader in the Lords and the ministerial leader in the Commons[b]—eventually succumbed. Another triumph of Lord Palmerston, within the last eight days, has been the appointment of Sir Charles Napier to the command of the Baltic fleet. It is no secret that both Lord John Russell and Sir James Graham were opposed to that appointment; but Lord Palmerston was for it and therefore it took place. Nothing, therefore, could be more appropriate than that the noble Lord should this evening occupy the chair at the banquet to be given in the Reform Club to the gallant Admiral."

Mr. Gladstone presented last night to the House a novelty unknown to the present generation—a war budget. It was evident from his speech[c] that the reason why the Government took this early opportunity of submitting his financial measures to the House was that of giving a preliminary record of the most disagreeable effects produced by war on private purses, thus to cool down the warlike energies of the country. Another main feature of his speech was his only asking for the sum which would be required to *bring back* the 25,000 men about to leave the British shores, should the war now be brought to a close.

He commenced by explaining the actual state of the income and expenditure of the last financial year. This not having yet closed, he observed that one month of the amount of the revenue could

---

[a] The situation previous to the war.— *Ed.*
[b] Lord John Russell and Sir James Graham.— *Ed.*
[c] Mr. Gladstone's speech in the House of Commons on March 6, 1854. *The Times*, No. 21682, March 7, 1854.— *Ed.*

be only an estimate. The total estimate of the income of the year
on the 18th of April last had been £52,990,000, while the actual
receipts of the year had reached to no less a sum than
£54,025,000; thus showing an increase in the actual income over
the presumed expenditure of £1,035,000. On the other hand
there had been a saving in the expenditure beyond the estimate of
£1,012,000. He therefore calculated, that but for the peculiar
circumstances in which the country was at present placed, there
would this year be a surplus over the expenditure amounting to
£2,854,000.

Mr. Gladstone then adverted to the results of the *reductions of
duty* introduced by him. The receipts of the Custom duties,
notwithstanding these reductions, had been £20,600,000 in
1853-54, while in 1852-53 they had only realized £20,396,000,
showing an increase in the Custom duties of £204,000. The
reduction made in the duty upon tea had produced a loss of only
£375,000. The reduction of the Stamp duties from threepence up
to ten shillings to one uniform duty of onepence had increased
their income, instead of the anticipated loss taking place, to the
amount of £36,000.

Mr. Gladstone proceeded, then showing the result of the
measures of last Session for the *augmentation of the taxes.* The
collection of the Income tax in Ireland had been delayed by
various circumstances, but it would yield £20,000 more than
calculated upon. The extension of the tax upon incomes, from
£150 to £100, in Great Britain would produce £100,000 beyond
this estimate, viz., £250,000. The revenue from the additional
duty of one shilling a gallon on spirits in Scotland had produced
an increase of only £209,000, he having estimated it at £278,000.

On the other hand, the Spirit duty in Ireland had realized an
increase of £213,000, while he had calculated upon an increase of
£198,000 only. The operation of the Succession duty on the
financial year would produce only half a million. So far the
statement of Mr. Gladstone on the finances of Great Britain
during the last twelve months, expiring on the 5th April.

The probable estimate of the revenue for the year 1854-55
will be:

Customs	£20,175,000	Post-tax	1,200,000
Excise	14,595,000	Crown lands	259,000
Stamps	7,090,000	Old stores	420,000
Taxes	3,015,000	Miscellaneous	320,000
Income-tax	6,275,000	Total income	£53,349,000

The probable estimate of expenditure on the other hand is given as

Funded debt	£27,000,000	Commissariat	645,000
Unfunded debt	546,000	Miscellaneous estim's	4,775,000
Consolidated fund	2,460,000	Militia	530,000
Army	6,857,000	Picket service	792,000
Navy	7,488,000	Eastern service	1,250,000
Ordnance	3,846,000		

Total expenditure £56,189,000
Causing a deficit of 2,840,000

Before adverting to the means by which this deficiency was to be made up, Mr. Gladstone enumerated the measures which Government would not recommend the House to adopt. He should not return to the reimposition of any of those reductions of duties he had proposed last year, which had already acquired the force of law. He would not assent to the reimposition of these taxes unnecessarily which former Governments had released. If, however, the struggle they were now entering upon should be prolonged for a year, it would hardly be in their power to maintain a permanent continuance of those reductions. In general, he would not propose any addition to indirect taxation. He should not resort to state-loans, there being no country whose means were already so heavily mortgaged as those of England. At length, after all these preambles, Mr. Gladstone came to the announcement what the Government intended to propose. This was to double the Income tax for six months, and to abolish altogether the existing distinction between home-drawn and foreign-drawn bills. The average rate of duty on present bills of exchange, although unequally distributed, was 1/6 per cent.; he proposed to equalize it to 1/ per cent. This change, he calculated, would produce an increase of revenue of £60,000. With regard to the Income tax, the increase would be from /7 to /10$^1/_2$ in the pound on incomes of £150 and upward, and from /5 to /7$^1/_2$ on incomes between £100 and £150. Simultaneously he proposed that the House should make a proposition to enable him, before the tax was levied, to issue £1,750,000 Exchequer bills to be paid out of the accruing produce of the Income tax. In conclusion, Mr. Gladstone endeavored, not very successfully, to vindicate his late measures for the reduction of the public debt, measures which resulted, as you know, in a lamentable failure.

In the discussion following upon this statement several members partook, but the only speech worth mentioning was that of Mr.

Disraeli.[a] He declared that he should make no opposition to any vote which Government, on their own responsibility, thought necessary to submit to the House for the purpose of conducting the impending war with vigor, and he hoped with success. But he protested, in case of the war being prolonged, against direct taxation being exclusively had recourse to for carrying on the war. As to the second part of Mr. Gladstone's statement, that which related to the actual state of the finances of the country, and as to the money in hand, it seemed to him involved in an obscurity which did not become a financial statement, and certainly not one delivered under such circumstances as the present one. The present state of the balance in the Exchequer was not sufficient or satisfactory. When the present Government took office, there had been, on the 3d January, 1853, balances in the Exchequer amounting to £9,000,000, but a year after, in January, 1854, they were reduced by one-half. He estimated that the balances in the Exchequer on April 5th next would be £3,000,000, while the expenditure, consisting of the dividends for the payment of the public creditors and the execution of his conversion scheme would altogether require from £9,000,000 to £10,000,000. The right honorable gentlemen said there was no use of meeting this with balances in the Exchequer, but that he would make up the sum wanted by deficiency bills. He maintained that it was of great importance they should have had at this moment an ample balance but instead of its being a question whether they were to have a balance, or an excess of balances, it was now a question whether they were to have a balance at all, or a large deficiency, and in fact, instead of having any balance, they had an enormous deficiency, which had been caused in two ways by the Chancellor of the Exchequer. First, by having reduced the interest on Exchequer bills to $1^1/_2$ per cent. when the value of money was rising, and secondly by his ill-devised conversion of the South Sea stocks,[58] a measure which had not only eaten up his balances but left him in a present deficiency of £2,000,000.

Some further remarks of an indifferent character having been made by other members, the Report on Supply was brought up and the resolution agreed to.

Written on March 7, 1854

First published in the *New-York Daily Tribune*, No. 4035, March 24; reprinted in the *New-York Semi-Weekly Tribune*, No. 921, March 24 and the *New-York Weekly Tribune*, No. 655, April 1, 1854

Reproduced from the *New-York Daily Tribune*

[a] Mr. Disraeli's speech in the House of Commons on March 6, 1854. *The Times*, No. 21682, March 7, 1854.— *Ed.*

The People's Paper

THE CHAMPION OF
POLITICAL JUSTICE AND UNIVERSAL RIGHT.

98   LONDON, SATURDAY, MARCH 18, 1854.   [Price Fourpence

Karl Marx

[LETTER TO THE LABOUR PARLIAMENT] [59]

28, Dean Street, Soho, London
9th March, 1854

I regret deeply to be unable, for the moment at least, to leave London, and thus to be prevented from expressing verbally my feelings of pride and gratitude on receiving the invitation to sit as Honorary Delegate at the Labour Parliament. [60] The mere assembling of such a Parliament marks a new epoch in the history of the world. The news of this great fact will arouse the hopes of the working classes throughout Europe and America.

Great Britain, of all other countries, has seen developed on the greatest scale the despotism of Capital and the slavery of Labour. In no other country have the intermediate stations between the millionaire commanding whole industrial armies and the wages-slave living only from hand to mouth so gradually been swept away from the soil. There exist here no longer, as in continental countries, large classes of peasants and artisans almost equally dependent on their own property and their own labour. A complete divorce of property from labour has been effected in Great Britain. In no other country, therefore, the war between the two classes that constitute modern society has assumed so colossal dimensions and features so distinct and palpable.

But it is precisely from these facts that the working classes of Great Britain, before all others, are competent and called for to act as leaders in the great movement that must finally result in the absolute emancipation of Labour. Such they are from the conscious clearness of their position, the vast superiority of their numbers, the disastrous struggles of their past, and the moral strength of their present.

It is the working millions of Great Britain who first have laid down the real basis of a new society—modern industry, which transformed the destructive agencies of nature into the productive power of man. The English working classes, with invincible energies, by the sweat of their brows and brains, have called to life the material means of ennobling labour itself, and of multiplying its fruits to such a degree as to make general abundance possible.

By creating the inexhaustible productive powers of modern industry they have fulfilled the first condition of the emancipation of Labour. They have now to realise its other condition. They have to free those wealth-producing powers from the infamous shackles of monopoly, and subject them to the joint control of the producers, who, till now, allowed the very products of their hands to turn against them and be transformed into as many instruments of their own subjugation.

The labouring classes have conquered nature; they have now to conquer man. To succeed in this attempt they do not want strength, but the organisation of their common strength, organisation of the labouring classes on a national scale—such, I suppose, is the great and glorious end aimed at by the Labour Parliament.

If the Labour Parliament proves true to the idea that called it to life, some future historian will have to record that there existed in the year 1854 two Parliaments in England, a Parliament at London, and a Parliament at Manchester—a Parliament of the rich, and a Parliament of the poor—but that men sat only in the Parliament of the men and not in the Parliament of the masters.

Yours truly,

Karl Marx

Written on March 9, 1854   Reproduced from the newspaper

First published in *The People's Paper*,
No. 98, March 18, 1854

The house re-assembled at nine o'clock.

Mr. Clark Cropper in the chair.

The minutes having been read and confirmed, it was ordered that instead of 300 copies, 1,500 copies of the balance sheet should be printed.

Mr. E. Jones then read the following letter from Dr. Marx, of London :—

"28, Dean Street, Soho, London.
"9th March, 1854,

"I regret deeply to be unable, for the moment at least, to leave London, and thus to be prevented from expressing verbally my feelings of pride and gratitude on receiving the invitation to sit as Honorary Delegate at the Labour Parliament. The mere assembling of such a Parliament marks a new epoch in the history of the world. The news of this great fact will arouse the hopes of the working classes throughout Europe and America.

"Great Britain, of all other countries, has seen developed on the greatest scale, the despotism of Capital and the slavery of Labour. In no other country have the intermediate stations between the millionaire commanding whole industrial armies and the wages-slave living only from hand to mouth so gradually been swept away from the soil. There exist here no longer, as in continental countries, large classes of peasants and artisans almost equally dependent on their own property and their own labour. A complete divorce of property from labour has been effected in Great Britain. In no other country, therefore, the war between the two classes that constitute modern society has assumed so colossal dimensions and features so distinct and palpable.

But it is precisely from these facts that the working classes of Great Britain, before all others, are competent and called for to act as leaders in the great movement that must finally result in the absolute emancipation of Labour. Such they are from the conscious clearness of their position, the vast superiority of their numbers, the disastrous struggles of their past, and the moral strength of their present.

It is the working millions of Great Britain who first have laid down the real basis of a new society— modern industry, which transformed the destructive agencies of nature into the productive power of man. The English working classes, with invincible energies, by the sweat of their brows and brains, have called into life the material means of ennobling labour itself, and of multiplying its fruits to such a degree as to make general abundance possible.

By creating the inexhaustible productive powers of modern industry they have fulfilled the first condition of the 'emancipation of labour. They have now to realise its other condition. They have to free those wealth-producing powers from the infamous shackles of monopoly, and subject them to the joint control of the producers, who, till now, allowed the very products of their hands to turn against them and be transformed into as many instruments of their own subjugation.

The labouring classes have conquered nature; they have now to conquer men. To succeed in this attempt they do not want strength, but the organisation of their common strength, organisation of the labouring classes on a national scale—such, I suppose, is the great and glorious end aimed at by the Labour Parliament.

If the Labour Parliament proves true to the idea that called it into life, some future historian will have to record that there existed in the year 1854 two Parliaments in England, a Parliament at London, and a Parliament at Manchester—a Parliament of the rich, and a Parliament of the poor—but that men sat only in the Parliament of the men and not in the Parliament of the masters.

Yours truly,
KARL MARX.

Part of the page from *The People's Paper* of March 18, 1854 with Marx's letter to the Labour Parliament

Karl Marx

THE LABOR PARLIAMENT[61]

London, Friday, March 10, 1854

Of all countries Great Britain has seen developed on the grandest scale the despotism of capital and the slavery of labor. In no other country have the intermediate degrees between the millionaire, commanding whole industrial armies, and the wages-slave living only from hand to mouth, so radically been swept away from the soil. There exist no longer, as in continental countries, large classes of peasants and artizans almost equally dependent on their own property and their own labor. A complete divorce of property from labor has been effected in Great Britain. In no other country, therefore, has the war between the two classes that constitute modern society assumed so colossal dimensions and features so distinct and palpable.

But it is precisely from these facts that the working classes of Britain, before all others, are competent and called upon to act as leaders in the great movement that must finally result in the absolute emancipation of labor. Such they are from the conscious clearness of their position, the vast superiority of their numbers, the disastrous struggles of their past and the moral strength of their present.

The London daily papers observe the "policy of abstention" with respect to the proceedings of the Labor Parliament. They hope to kill it by a vast "*conspiration de silence*". Having for whole months fatigued the public with interminable articles on the probable chances of realization for the scheme of such a Parliament, now they purposely avoid ever mentioning that it has actually sprung into life and already begun to work. This wisdom of the ostrich, that imagines it avoids dangers by feigning not to

see them, will not do now-a-days. They will be forced to notice the
Labor Parliament, and, notwithstanding their simulated indifference, some future historian will record that there existed in the
year 1854 two Parliaments in England, a Parliament in London
and a Parliament in Manchester, a Parliament of the rich and a
Parliament of the poor, but that men sat only in the Parliament of
the men, and not in the Parliament of the masters.

The following is the report of the Committee appointed to draw
up a plan of action for the Labor Parliament[62]:

Your Committee believe the duty of this Parliament to be the rendering of the
existing turn outs and lock outs victorious for the operatives, and the adoption of
means whereby both should be prevented for the future; the securing for the
working classes fair treatment during work; the rescuing of women and children
from the factory; the means of education, and the abolition of stoppages and
underhand abatements of wages. Believing further that it is their duty to endeavor
to secure to those who labor a fair participation in the profits of their work; and
above all this, to obtain for them the means of independent self-employment, with
a view to their *emancipation from wages-slavery altogether*; and, being convinced that
the final step thereto is the obtaining the pecuniary leverage for action,
recommend for your consideration.

1. The organization of a system for the collection of a national revenue for
labor.

2. A plan for the security of the funds thus raised.

3. The application of the same and the securing of the rights of the working
classes.

4. The constitution of the Mass Movement.

I. The Raising of a National Labor Revenue.

a. A weekly levy on the wages, graduated according to the price of labor, as
follows:

Up to 4/ per week ... $\frac{1}{2}$d.   Up to 20/ per week ... 2d.
Up to 8/ per week ... $\frac{3}{4}$d.   Up to 30/ per week ... 3d.
Up to 12/ per week ... 1d.   Up to 40/ per week ... 4d.
Up to 15/ per week ..1$\frac{1}{2}$d.

b. That the officers of the several bodies of working men, who act in
conjunction with the Mass Movement, forward the moneys thus raised to its
directing head.

II. Security of the Funds.

a. That the local officers forward weekly all moneys they receive on behalf of
the Mass Movement to the directing head of the same as shall be further specified
below. The duly appointed officers for the reception thereof to return receipts
immediately for the moneys thus received.

b. That the directing heads shall invest all moneys they receive on behalf of the
Mass Movement (having powers to retain in hand a sum not exceeding £50) in a
bank, in their collective names; no such sum or sums, nor any part of the same, to
be drawn out of the bank except on presentation of the minute-books of the said

directing body, containing an order for the same to be drawn, signed by such a majority of the members of that body as shall hereafter be determined.

c. That the money thus drawn shall be paper money, (unless under £5); that the numbers of such notes shall be entered in a book, open to inspection and published in the papers; that the notes thus received shall be cut into parts, and each part intrusted to a separate member of the directing body; and where large sums are drawn, that they be held in equal portions by each member.

d. That each member, thus intrusted with a portion of the said money, shall give a promissory note amounting to his proportionate share of the money drawn, supposing the same divided into equal parts according to the number of the directing body; and that, should he refuse to apply for the purposes for which the money was drawn, such part of note held by him, the document thus held against him shall at once be put in force, but be cancelled on his paying over said part of note; that the promissory notes thus given shall be deposited in a chest or safe, which shall be placed in the custody of an independent and responsible party (not a member of the directing body), who shall not allow any document to be taken therefrom except in presence of all the directing body.

e. That the money thus drawn for any payment or purchase be paid by the directors only in the mutual presence of each member of their body.

III.—*Application of the Funds.*

a. The funds collected shall be applied as follows: To support all towns and places now on strike, and for liquidating all debts contracted during the late and present strikes and lockouts. That equal support shall be afforded to towns in proportion to the number out of employ. That on the same principle as when provisions run short on board of ship, each receives alike; thus the same relief shall be given without distinction of high or low paid trader. That, although all existing strikes and lockouts shall be supported, no future assistance will be given to any body of men who do not recognize and support the Mass Movement.

b. That the department be opened to regulate the price of labor. That for this purpose a monthly statement be issued for the price of the raw material employed in all the trades in connection with the Mass Movement; the price of labor in the same, and the selling price of the articles produced, and the other working charges. That on the evidence thus furnished, the directing body shall issue a statement of the profits of the employer; being open to receive from the latter a statement of any peculiar and additional charges which the employers may have to meet. That on the basis thus laid the price of labor shall be regulated, and the tariff of wages be fixed in accordance with the same. That a similar plan be applied to the agricultural interests of the country.

c. That, while workingman has an undoubted right to participate in the profits of the employer, he has a right higher still—that of employing himself; and that, for the purpose of the self-employment, as also for the purpose of more effectually regulating wages, by removing the power of surplus labor from the employer's hands, the funds of the Mass Movement be further employed in the purchase of land. That the estates be purchased in the names of individuals not being members of the directing body. That the estates be divided into farms, varying in size according to the nature of the soil and the purposes to which they are to be applied, viz: whether as individual tenancies or large cooperative undertakings. That the said lands be retained by and never alienated from the Mass Movement. That the land be let to tenants on short leases and at a fair and moderate rental. That the clause be inserted in the lease whereby any tenant making the fault in payment of rent shall immediately lose his right of tenancy. That a fourth clause be inserted whereby the tenant binds himself to pay the rental to the parties appointed by the deed of assignment hereafter named. That the parties in whose names the estates are bought execute a deed of assignment, whereby the tenant shall pay the rent, not to them, but to the individuals then being directors of the Mass Movement. That the directors of the time being shall execute a deed, binding themselves in a penalty of £5,000 each, to two individuals, not being purchasers of any estate; such penalty to be enforced should they, on leaving office, not execute a deed of assignment of the said rental to their successors in office; those successors to be bound in the same way.

d. That independence of self-employment and relief of the labor market from its surplus be still more secure, your Committee recommend a further application of the available funds for the establishment of cooperative factories, workshops and stores, such to be the property of the Mass Movement. Those employed therein to receive that amount of wages regulated by the tariff for the price of labor previously named, and one-half of the net profits realized on the articles produced and sold, the other half of the profits to go to the revenue of the Mass Movement. That the chief manager of each cooperative undertaking be elected by the operatives engaged therein, subject to the approbation of the directing body. That the said manager of each respective undertaking regulate the purchases and sales connected therewith, and return monthly to the directing body a statement of the purchases, sales, payments, and loss or profit connected with the same. That, in case grounds of complaint at difference arise between the operatives and manager, the operatives shall have the power of dismissing the manager and electing another by the majority of not less than three-fourths of their number. That one-half of the net profits of each cooperative undertaking be sent by each respective manager to the directing body. That the property for cooperation purposes purchased by the Mass Movement be placed under a system of security similar to that applied to the landed estates.

After a long discussion, the report of the Committee up to end of the portion marked "II" was adopted on Wednesday's sitting of the Labor Parliament. [a] The Committee appointed for drawing up this programme of action for the Mass Movement consisted of Messrs. Ernest Jones, James Finlen, James Williams, Abraham Robinson and James Bligh.

Written on March 10, 1854

First published in the *New-York Daily Tribune*, No. 4039, March 29; reprinted in the *New-York Semi-Weekly Tribune*, No. 924, April 4, 1854

Signed: *Karl Marx*

Reproduced from the *New-York Daily Tribune*

---

[a] March 8, 1854.— *Ed.*

Frederick Engels

RETREAT OF THE RUSSIANS FROM KALAFAT [63]

The Russians have retreated from Kalafat, and have, it is stated, entirely remodelled their plan of campaign. This is the glorious end of the efforts and risks of a three months' campaign, during which the last resources of Wallachia have been completely exhausted. This is the fruit of that inconceivable march into Little Wallachia, which appeared to have been undertaken in utter contempt of the first rules of strategy. In order to take Kalafat, that only bridgehead held by the Turks on the left bank of the Danube, the mass of the army [a] was concentrated on the extreme right, in a position where the weakened centre and left appeared completely abandoned to any attack that the enemy might chance to undertake, and where an indifference was shown to the lines of communications and retreat which is without parallel in the history of warfare. That Omer Pasha has not profited by this blunder is only to be explained by the interference of our Ambassador at Constantinople. [b] How it is that, after all, the Russians have to retreat disgracefully without having effected their purpose, we shall have to show presently.

We say they have to retreat disgracefully, because an advance preceded by blustering, crowned by taking up a merely threatening position, and ending in a quiet and modest retreat, without even an attempt at serious fighting—because a move composed of an uninterrupted series of mistakes and errors, resulting in

---

[a] The *New-York Daily Tribune* has: "the Russian army".— *Ed.*

[b] The *New-York Daily Tribune* has: "How it happened that Omer Pasha has not profited by this blunder, we have already had occasion to show." (See this volume, pp. 6-7).— *Ed.*

nothing but the General's[a] conviction that he has made a complete fool of himself—is the very height of disgrace.

Now to the state of the case.

The Russians had, by the end of 1853, the following troops in Wallachia, Moldavia, and Bessarabia:—

1. 4th corps of the army (Dannenberg) three divisions infantry, one division cavalry, four brigades artillery—total, after deducting losses, say 45,000 men.

2. Of the 5th corps (Lüders) one division infantry, one division cavalry, two brigades artillery—say 15,000 men.

3. 3rd corps (Osten-Sacken) three divisions infantry, one division cavalry, four brigades artillery—say 55,000 men.

Total about 115,000 men, besides non-combatants and one division of Lüders' corps in the neighbourhood of Odessa, which, being wanted for garrison duty, cannot be taken into account.

The troops under Dannenberg and Lüders were the only ones that had been in the Principalities up to the beginning of December. The approach of Osten-Sacken's corps was to be the signal for the grand concentration for the attack on Kalafat.[b] His place, on the Bug and the Pruth, was to be filled up by the 6th corps (Cheodayeff), then on the road from Moscow. After the junction of this latter corps, the Danubian army would have consisted of about 170,000 men, but might have turned out to be stronger, if the new levies of recruits from the South Western provinces were at once directed to the theatre of war.

However, 115,000 to 120,000 men appeared to the Russian Commander a sufficient force to defend the whole line of the Danube from Brailow to Nicopolis, and spare a sufficient number to be concentrated, from the extreme right, for an attack on Kalafat.

When this movement was commenced, towards the end of December, Kalafat could hardly harbour more than 10,000 to 12,000 defenders, with 8,000 more at Vidin, whose support might be considered dubious, as they had to cross an unruly river in a bad season. The slowness of the Russian movements, however, the indecision of Prince Gorchakoff, and above all the activity and boldness of Ismail Pasha, the commander at Kalafat, permitted the Turks to concentrate some 40,000 men on the menaced point, and to change Kalafat from a simple bridgehead stormable by a force double that of its defenders into a

---

[a] M. D. Gorchakov.— *Ed.*

[b] The *New-York Daily Tribune* has: "for the grand concentration and the attack on Kalafat."— *Ed.*

fortification which could shelter at least 30,000 men, and withstand any but a regular siege attack. It has been justly said that the highest triumph for the constructor of a field fortification is the necessity for the enemy to open his trenches against it; if the Russians did not actually open the trenches, it is merely because, even with that extreme means, they did see no way of taking Kalafat in the time they might set apart for the operation. Kalafat will henceforth rank with Frederick II's camp at Bunzelwitz, with the lines of Torres-Vedras, with the Archduke Charles' entrenchments behind Verona, as one of those efforts of field fortification that are named as classical applications of the art in warlike history.[64]

Now let us look to the Russian means of attack. That they meant in good earnest to take Kalafat, is shown by their parks of siege artillery having been brought forward as far as Crajova. That Omer Pasha, we may state by the way, allowed these guns to go and return freely, is one of the many military inconceivabilities of this war, to be explained merely through diplomatic influences. The only thing,[a] then, for the Russians, was a sufficient mass of troops to drive in the Turks, and to protect the trenches and batteries, and to storm the breaches as soon as they should have been opened. Here, again, Ismail Pasha acted like an energetic and clever commander. His sally towards Chetatea on the 6th of January—his vigorous attack ending in the defeat of a superior Russian force, and the continued attacks of a similar nature he executed, while the Russian concentration was still going on, and, until he was fairly blockaded on his small Danubian Peninsula by a superior force—in short, his system of defending himself by concentrated offensive blows against single points of the Russian line, and thereby destroying his enemy, as far as he could, *in detail*, was exactly what a commander under his circumstances should have done, and forms a cheering contrast with Omer Pasha's passive[b] defence at Oltenitza, or his lazy passivity, all this while, on the lower Danube. For the petty attacks carried on by him here and there, which appear never to have been broken off at the proper moment, but carried on for days and days on the same point with blind obstinacy, even when no result could be expected from them, these petty attacks do not count, when a movement across the Danube with 40,000 to 60,000 men was wanted.

After all, the Russians completed, by the end of January, their concentration around Kalafat. They were evidently superior in the

---

[a] The *New-York Daily Tribune* has: "The only thing necessary, then, for the Russians...".— *Ed.*

[b] The *New-York Daily Tribune* has: "previous".— *Ed.*

open field; they must therefore have had some 30,000 or 40,000 men. Now deduct these from 115,000, deduct then, say 20,000 or 25,000 men[a] more for the defence of the line from Brailow to the sea, and there remained for the whole of Greater Wallachia, inclusive of garrisons, from 50,000 to 65,000 men—an army far from sufficient to defend such a long line of attack, and a line of communication *running parallel with the line of attack*, at a short distance behind it. A vigorous attack on any point, even with a force inferior to the whole of these 65,000 men, could not but have ended in the utter defeat, in detail, of all these dispersed Russian troops, and with the capture of all the Russian magazines. Omer Pasha will have to explain, some time or other, his motives for neglecting such an opportunity.

With all their efforts, then, the Russians could merely concentrate before Kalafat a force barely sufficient to drive in the outposts, but not to attack the stronghold itself. They took nearly five weeks to effect even this momentary and illusory success. General Schilder, of the Engineers, was sent with positive orders to take Kalafat. He came, he saw, and he resolved to do nothing[b] until the arrival of Cheodayeff should allow fresh troops to come up from the centre and left.

Five weeks the Russians stood in this dangerous position, rear and flank exposed, as if provoking that attack which they could not have resisted a moment; and five weeks Omer Pasha stood menacing their flank and rear, in a position where he could see their weakness without spectacles or telescopes—and he did nothing. Verily, this system of modern warfare, under the patronage of the Allied Courts,[c] is above comprehension!

All at once the news reaches London—"The Russians are in full retreat from Kalafat." "Oh," says *The Times*, "that is the effect of our *allies*, the Austrians, having concentrated an army in Transylvania, in the rear of the Russians[d]; that is the effect of the glorious Austrian alliance, which is again the effect of our glorious Aberdeen policy." Three cheers for Aberdeen! But next day Austrian authentic manifestoes show that no Austrian alliance exists,[e] and that the Austrians as yet have not said, and do not appear to know themselves, for what purpose they have sent that army

---

[a] The *New-York Daily Tribune* has: "20,000 or 30,000 men".— *Ed.*

[b] An ironical allusion to Julius Caesar's famous words: "Veni, vidi, vici."— *Ed.*

[c] The *New-York Daily Tribune* has: "Allied Powers".— *Ed.*

[d] *The Times*, No. 21686, March 11, 1854, leader.— *Ed.*

[e] Report from the Vienna correspondent of March 8. *The Times*, No. 21688, March 14, 1854.— *Ed.*

where it is,—and, consequently, great uncertainty reigns as to the cause of the Russian retreat.

We are now told that the Russians will try to cross the Danube at the opposite point, between Brailow and Galatz, and thus proceed on the direct road to Adrianople, as in 1828-29. If there does not exist a perfect understanding between the Russians on the one side, and the Anglo-French squadron on the other, this march is strategically impossible. We have another cause to account for this retreat. Cheodayeff is said to have been stopped in this march, in order to form a camp of 30,000 or 40,000 men above Odessa. If this be true, he cannot relieve any troops on the Pruth and Sereth, nor reinforce Gorchakoff before Kalafat. Consequently, Prince Gorchakoff has to retreat in as good order as he came, and thus would end the grand tragi-comedy of the Russian march against Kalafat.[a]

Written on March 13, 1854

First published in *The People's Paper*, No. 98, March 18, 1854 and in the *New-York Daily Tribune*, No. 4040, March 30; reprinted in the *New-York Weekly Tribune*, No. 655, April 1, 1854 as a leader

Reproduced from *The People's Paper* checked with the *New-York Daily Tribune*

---

[a] The two concluding paragraphs in the *New-York Daily Tribune* are as follows: "All at once the news reaches us that the Russians are in full retreat from Kalafat. The English journals hereupon exclaim that it is the effect of their allies, the Austrians, having concentrated an army in Transylvania, in the rear of the Russians! That it is the effect of the glorious Austrian alliance which is again the effect of the glorious policy of Lord Aberdeen. But presently an authentic Austrian manifesto shows that no Austrian alliance exists and that the Austrians have not said and as yet do not appear to know themselves for what purpose they have sent that army where it is. And consequently our British contemporaries are in great uncertainty as to the cause of the Russian retreat. But what is the cause of it? Why, simply this: French and British troops are to go to Constantinople. Nothing more easy or more plain than to send them thence to Odessa or Bessarabia and cut off the communications of the Russians.

"However harmless the real intentions of the Coalition may be, pressure from without may force them to act seriously. Gorchakoff evidently does not trust in the merely diplomatic mission of the Western armies. If he were quite sure of England, he could not be so of France. If he were sure of all the Cabinets, he could not be so of the Generals. He might risk flank marches in the presence of the Turks, but he supposes the matter must become serious so soon as French and British troops arrive and threaten to fall on his flanks. Consequently, Cheodayeff is stopped in his march to form a camp of 30,000 or 40,000 men above Odessa. Consequently he cannot furnish any troops for the Pruth or Sereth. Consequently no troops can come to reenforce Gorchakoff before Kalafat. Consequently the attack upon that place becomes an impossibility. Consequently prince Gorchakoff has to retreat in as good order as he came. And thus ends the great tragic-comedy of the Russian march against Kalafat."—*Ed.*

Karl Marx

THE GREEK INSURRECTION [65]

The insurrection among the Greek subjects of the Sultan, which caused such alarm at Paris and London, has now been suppressed, but its revival is thought not impossible. With regard to this possibility we are able to say that after a careful investigation of the documents relating to the whole affair so far, we are convinced that the insurgents were found exclusively among the mountaineers inhabiting the southern slope of the Pindus, and that they met with no sympathy on the part of the other Christian races of Turkey, save the pious freebooters of Montenegro; and that the occupants of the plains of Thessaly, who form the only compact Greek community still living under Turkish supremacy, are more afraid of their compatriots than of the Turks themselves. It is not to be forgotten that this spiritless and cowardly body of population did not dare to rise even at the time of the Greek war of independence. [66] As to the remainder of the Greek race, numbering perhaps 300,000 souls, distributed throughout the cities of the Empire, they are so thoroughly detested by the other Christian tribes that, whenever a popular movement has been successful, as in Servia and Wallachia, it has resulted in driving away all the priests of Greek origin, and in supplying their places by native pastors.

But although the present Greek insurrection, considered with reference to its own merits, is altogether insignificant, it still derives importance from the occasion it affords to the western Powers for interfering between the Porte and the great majority of its subjects in Europe, among whom the Greeks count only one million against ten millions of the other races professing the Greek religion. The Greek inhabitants of the so-called kingdom as well as those living in the Ionian Isles under British rule consider it, of course, to be their national mission to expel the Turks from wherever the Greek language is spoken, and to annex Thessaly and Epirus to a State of their own. They may even dream of a Byzantine restoration, although, on the whole, they are too astute a people to believe in such a fancy. But these plans of national aggrandizement and independence on the part of the Greeks, proclaimed at this moment in consequence of Russian intrigues, as is proved by the lately detected conspiracy of the priest Athanasius,[67] and proclaimed too by the robbers of the mountains without being reechoed by the agricultural population of the plain—all have nothing to do with the religious rights of the subjects of Turkey with which an attempt is made to mix them up.

As we learn from the English journals and from notice given in the House of Lords by Lord Shaftesbury, and in the Commons by Mr. Monckton Milnes,[a] the British Government is to be called upon in connection, partly at least, with these Greek movements to take measures to meliorate the condition of the Christian subjects of the Porte. Indeed, we are told explicitly that the great end aimed at by the western Powers is to put the Christian religion on a footing of equal rights with the Mahometan in Turkey. Now, either this means nothing at all, or it means the granting political and civil rights, both to Mussulmans and Christians, without any reference to either religion, and without considering religion at all. In other words, it means the complete separation of State and Church, of Religion and Politics. But the Turkish State, like all Oriental States, is founded upon the most intimate connection, we might almost say, the identity of State and Church, of Politics and Religion. The Koran is the double source of faith and law, for that Empire and its rulers. But how is it possible to equalize the faithful and the Giaour, the Mussulman and the Rajah before the Koran? To do that it is necessary, in fact, to supplant the Koran by a new civil code, in other words to break down the framework of Turkish society and create a new order of things out of its ruins.

On the other hand, the main feature that distinguishes the Greek confession from all other branches of the Christian faith, is the same identification of State and Church, of civil and ecclesiastical life. So intimately interwoven were State and Church

---

[a] The Earl of Shaftesbury's speech in the House of Lords on March 10, 1854. *The Times*, No. 21686, March 11, 1854; M. Milnes' speech in the House of Commons on March 13, 1854. *The Times*, No. 21688, March 14, 1854.— *Ed.*

in the Byzantine Empire, that it is impossible to write the history of the one without writing the history of the other. In Russia the same identity prevails, although there, in contradistinction to the Byzantine Empire, the Church has been transformed into the mere tool of the State, the instrument of subjugation at home and of aggression abroad. In the Ottoman Empire in conformity with the Oriental notions of the Turks, the Byzantine theocracy has been allowed to develop itself to such a degree, that the parson of a parish is at the same time the judge, the mayor, the teacher, the executor of testaments, the assessor of taxes, the ubiquitous factotum of civil life, not the servant, but the master of all work. The main reproach to be cast upon the Turks in this regard is not that they have crippled the privileges of the Christian priesthood, but, on the contrary, that under their rule this all-embracing oppressive tutelage, control, and interference of the Church has been permitted to absorb the whole sphere of social existence. Mr. Fallmerayer very amusingly tells us, in his *Orientalische Briefe*,[a] how a Greek priest was quite astonished when he informed him that the Latin clergy enjoyed no civil authority at all, and had to perform no profane business. "How," exclaimed the priest, "do our Latin brethren contrive to kill time?"

It is plain then that to introduce a new civil code in Turkey, a code altogether abstracted from religion, and based on a complete separation of State and Church, would be not only to abolish Mahometanism, but also to break down the Greek Church as now established in that Empire. Can any one be credulous enough to believe in good earnest that the timid and reactionary valetudinarians of the present British Government have ever conceived the idea of undertaking such a gigantic task, involving a perfect social revolution, in a country like Turkey? The notion is absurd. They can only entertain it for the purpose of throwing dust in the eyes of the English people and of Europe.

Written on March 14, 1854   Reproduced from the newspaper

First published in the *New-York Daily Tribune*, No. 4039, March 29, 1854 as a leader

---

[a] Fallmerayer, *Fragmente aus dem Orient.— Ed.*

Karl Marx

THE DOCUMENTS ON THE PARTITION OF TURKEY [68]

London, Tuesday, March 21, 1854

A most important event is the compulsory publication by Ministers of their secret correspondence with the Emperor of Russia during the first three months of their administration, as also of the memorandum of the interview between the Czar and Lord Aberdeen in 1844, which the *Journal de St. Pétersbourg* challenged the latter to produce.[69]

I begin with an analysis of the "memorandum" by Count Nesselrode, delivered to Her Majesty's Government, and founded on communications from the Emperor of Russia, subsequent to his visit to England in June, 1844. The present *status quo* of the Ottoman Empire is "the most compatible with the general interest of the maintenance of peace." England and Russia agree on this principle, and therefore unite their efforts to keep up that *Status quo*.

"With this object, the essential point is to suffer the Porte to live in repose, without needlessly disturbing it by diplomatic bickerings, and without interfering, without absolute necessity, in its internal affairs."

Now, how is this "system of forbearance" to be successfully carried out? Firstly, by Great Britain not interfering with the interpretation Russia may think fit to put upon her treaties with the Porte, but forcing it, on the contrary, to act in conformity with those treaties as interpreted by Russia; and, in the second place, by allowing Russia "constantly" to meddle between the Sultan and his Christian subjects. In a word, "the system of forbearance" toward the Porte means a system of complicity with Russia. This strange proposition is, however, far from being expressed in rude terms.

The memorandum affects to speak of "all the great Powers," but at the same time plainly intimates that there exist no great Powers at all besides Russia and England. France, it is said, will

"find herself *obliged* to act in conformity with the course agreed upon between St. Petersburg and London."

Austria is represented as a mere appendage to Russia, enjoying no life of her own, following no distinct policy, but one "closely united by the principle of *perfect identity*" with that of Russia. Prussia is treated as a nonentity, not worth mentioning, and consequently is not so much as mentioned. "All the great Powers," then, is only a rhetorical figure for the two Cabinets of St. Petersburg and London; and the line of conduct to be agreed upon by all the great Powers means the line of conduct drawn up at St. Petersburg and to be acted upon at London. The memorandum says:

"The Porte has a constant tendency to extricate itself from the engagements imposed upon it by the treaties which it has concluded with other powers. It hopes to do so with impunity, because it reckons on the mutual jealousy of the Cabinets. It thinks that if it fails in its engagements toward one of them, the rest will espouse its quarrel, and will screen it from all responsibility.

"It is essential not to confirm the Porte in this delusion. Every time that it fails in its obligations toward one of the great Powers, it is the interest of all the rest to make it sensible of its error, and seriously to exhort it to act rightly toward the Cabinet which demands just reparation.

"*As soon as the Porte shall perceive that it is not supported by the other Cabinets, it will give way*, and the differences which have arisen will be arranged in a conciliatory manner, without any conflict resulting from them."

This is the formula by which England is called upon to assist Russia in her policy of extorting new concessions from Turkey, on the ground of her ancient treaties.

"In the present state of feeling in Europe, the Cabinets cannot see with indifference the Christian populations in Turkey exposed to flagrant acts of oppression or religious intolerance. It is necessary constantly to make the Ottoman Ministers sensible of this truth, and to persuade them that they can only reckon on the friendship and on the support of the great Powers on the condition that they treat the Christian subjects of the Porte with toleration and with mildness....

"It will be the duty of the foreign representatives, guided by these principles, to act among themselves in a perfect spirit of agreement. If they address remonstrances to the Porte, those remonstrances must bear a real character of unanimity, though divested of one of exclusive dictation."

In this mild way England is taught how to back Russia's pretensions to a *religious Protectorate* over the Christians of Turkey. Having thus laid down the premises of her "policy of forbearance," Russia cannot conceal from her confidante that this very forbearance may prove more fatal than any policy of aggression, and fearfully contribute to develop all the "elements of dissolution" the Ottoman Empire contains: so that some fine morning

"*unforeseen circumstances* may hasten its *fall*, without its being in the power of the friendly Cabinets to prevent it."

The question is then raised: what would have to be done in the event of such unforeseen circumstances producing a final catastrophe in Turkey.

The only thing wanted, it is said, in the event of Turkey's fall becoming imminent, is *England and Russia's "coming to a previous understanding before having recourse to action."* "This notion," we are assured by the memorandum, "was in principle agreed upon during the Emperor's last residence in London" (in the long conferences held between the Autocrat on the one hand, and the Duke of Wellington, Sir Robert Peel, and the Earl of Aberdeen on the other hand). The result was

"the *eventual engagement* that, if *anything unforeseen* occurred in Turkey, *Russia and England should previously concert together as to the course which they should pursue in common.*"

Now, what means this *eventual engagement*? Firstly, that Russia and England should previously come to a common understanding as to the *partition of Turkey*; and secondly, that in such a case, England was to bind herself to form a Holy Alliance with Russia and Austria, described as Russia's *alter ego*, against France, who would be "*obliged*," i.e., forced to act in conformity with their views. The natural result of such a common understanding would be to involve England in a deadly war with France, and thus to give Russia full sway to carry out her own policy on Turkey.

Great stress is again and again laid upon the "unforeseen circumstances" that may accelerate the downfall of Turkey. At the conclusion of the memorandum the mysterious phrase, however, disappears, to be replaced by the more distinct formulation: "If we foresee that the Ottoman Empire must crumble to pieces, England and Russia have to enter into a previous concert, etc...." The only unforeseen circumstance, then, was the unforeseen declaration on the part of Russia that the Ottoman Empire must now crumble to pieces. The main point gained by the eventual engagement is the liberty granted to Russia to foresee, at a given moment, the sudden downfall of Turkey, and to oblige England to enter into negotiations, on the common understanding of such a catastrophe being at hand.

Accordingly, about ten years after the memorandum had been drawn up, due notice is given to England that the vitality of the Ottoman Empire is gone, and that they had now to enter upon their previously arranged concert to the exclusion of France, i.e. to conspire behind the backs of Turkey and France. This overture opens the series of secret and confidential papers exchanged between St. Petersburg and the Coalition Cabinet.

Sir G. H. Seymour, the British Embassador at St. Petersburg, sends his first secret and confidential dispatch to Lord J. Russell, the then Foreign Minister, on January 11, 1853. On the evening of the 9th January he had the "honor" to see the Emperor at the Palace of the Grand Duchess Helen,[a] who had condescended to invite Lady Seymour and himself to meet the Imperial family. The Emperor came up to him in his most gracious manner, expressing his great pleasure at the news of the formation of the Coalition Cabinet, to which he wished long life, desiring the Embassador to convey to old Aberdeen his congratulation on his part, and to beat into Lord John Russell's brains

"that it was very essential that the two Governments—the English Government and I, and I and the English Government—should be on the best terms; and that the necessity was never greater than at present."

Mark that these words were spoken in January, 1853, at the very time when Austria, "between whom and Russia"—according to the memorandum—"there exists an entire conformity of principles in regard to the affairs of Turkey," was openly engaged in troubling the waters at Montenegro.

"When we are agreed," said the Czar, "it is immaterial what the others may think or do. Turkey," he continued, in a hypocritical manner of condolence, "is in a very critical state, and may give us all a great deal of trouble."

Having said so much, the Czar proceeded to shake hands with Sir H. Seymour, very graciously, as if about to take leave of him; but Sir Hamilton, to whom it "instantly occurred that the conversation was incomplete," took "the great liberty" humbly to pray the Autocrat to "speak a little more explicitly with regard to the affairs of Turkey."

"The Emperor's words and manner," remarks this observer, "although still very kind, showed that His Majesty had no intention of speaking to me of the *demonstration which he is about to make in the South.*"

---

[a] Yelena Pavlovna.— *Ed.*

Be it remarked that already in his dispatch of Jan. 7, 1853, Sir Hamilton had informed the British Government that

"orders had been dispatched to the 5th *corps d'armée* to advance to the frontiers of the Danubian provinces..., and that the 4th corps ... would be ordered to hold itself in readiness to march if necessary;"

and in a dispatch dated Jan. 8, 1853, that Nesselrode had expressed to him his opinion of the "necessity that the diplomacy of Russia should be supported by a demonstration of force."

"The Emperor," Sir Hamilton continues his dispatch,[a] "said, at first with a little hesitation, but, as he proceeded, in an open and unhesitating manner:

"'The affairs of Turkey are in a very disorganized condition; the country itself seems to be falling to pieces (*menace ruine*); the fall will be a great misfortune, and it is very important that England and Russia should come to a perfectly good understanding upon these affairs, and that neither should take any decisive step of which the other is not apprized.'

"'Stay,' he exclaimed, 'we have on our hands a sick man, a very sick man: it will be, I tell you frankly, a great misfortune if, one of these days, he should slip away from us, especially before all necessary arrangements were made. But, however, this is not the time to speak to you on that matter.'"

The patient, in this bear's eyes, is so weak that he *must* eat him. Sir Hamilton, somewhat frightened at this "unforeseen" diagnostic of the Muscovite physician, answers in the true spirit of courtesy:

"Your Majesty is so gracious that you will allow me one further observation. Your Majesty says the man is sick; it is very true; but Your Majesty will deign to excuse me if I remark, that it is the part of the generous and strong to treat with gentleness the sick and feeble man."

The British Embassador comforts himself by the consideration, that this concurrence on his part in the Czar's view of Turkey and sickness and his appeal to forbearance with the sick man did "at least not give offense." Thus ends Sir H. Seymour's report on his first confidential conversation with the Czar; but, although appearing a perfect courtier in this *vis-à-vis*, he has sufficient good sense to warn his Cabinet and to tell them what follows:

"Any overture of this kind only tends to establish a dilemma. The dilemma seems to be this: If Her Majesty's Government do not come to an understanding with Russia as to what is to happen in the event of the sudden downfall of Turkey, they will have the less reason for complaining if results displeasing to England should be prepared. If, on the contrary, Her Majesty's Government should enter into the consideration of such eventualities, they make themselves in some degree consenting parties to a catastrophe which they have so much interest in warding off as long as possible."

----

[a] The reference is to the dispatch of Sir G. H. Seymour to Lord Russell dated January 11, 1853.— *Ed.*

Sir Hamilton winds up his dispatch with the following epigrammatic sentence:

"The sum is probably this, that England has to desire a close concert with Russia, with a view to preventing the downfall of Turkey—while Russia would be well pleased that the concert should apply to the events by which this downfall is to be followed."

On the 14th of January, as Sir G. H. Seymour informs Lord J. Russell, in his dispatch dated 22d January, 1853, he had another confidential interview with the Czar, whom "he found alone." The Autocrat condescended to give the English Embassador a lesson in Eastern affairs. The dreams and plans of the Empress Catherine II were known, but he did not indulge in them. On the contrary, in his opinion there existed, perhaps, only one danger for Russia, that of a further extension of his already too vast dominions. (Your readers will recollect that I alluded to this in extracting a passage from the dispatches of Count Pozzo di Borgo.[70]) The *status quo* of Turkey was the most consonant with Russian interests. On the one hand, the Turks had lost their spirit of military enterprise, and on the other,

"this country was strong enough, *or had hitherto been* strong enough, to preserve its independence and to ensure respectful treatment from other countries."

But in that empire there happened to be several millions of Christians he must take care of, hard and "inconvenient" as the task might be. To do this he was bound at once by his right, his duty and his religion. Then, all of a sudden, the Czar returned to his parable of the sick man, the very sick man, whom they must by no means allow "to suddenly die on their hands" (de leur échapper).[71]

"Chaos, confusion, and the certainty of a European war, must attend the catastrophe if it should occur unexpectedly, and *before some ulterior scheme had been sketched.*"

Having, thus, again given notice of the impending death of the Ottoman Empire, the summons to England followed in conformity with the "eventual engagement" to discount the heritage in common with Russia. "Still, he avoids sketching his own ulterior system," contenting himself by establishing, in a parliamentary way, the main point to be kept in view in the event of a partition.

"I desire to speak to you as a friend and a *gentleman*. If England and I arrive at an understanding of this matter, as regards the rest, it matters little to me; it is indifferent to me what others do or think. Frankly, then, I tell you plainly, that if England thinks of establishing herself one of these days at Constantinople, I will not allow it. I do not attribute this intention to you, but it is better on these occasions to speak plainly; for my part, I am equally disposed to take the engagement not to establish myself there, as proprietor that is to say, for as occupier I do not say; it might happen that circumstances, if no previous provision were made, if everything should be left to chance, might place me in the position of occupying Constantinople."

England, therefore, will be forbidden to establish herself at Constantinople. The Czar will do so, if not as proprietor, at least in the quality of a temporary occupier. The British Embassador thanked His Majesty for the frankness of this declaration. Nicholas then alluded to his past conversation with the Duke of Wellington, of which the memorandum of 1844 is the record, and, as it were, the *résumé*. Passing to the question of the day—to his claims to the Holy Places—the British Embassador expressed his fears:

"Two consequences that might be anticipated from the appearance of a Russian army—the one being the counter-demonstration which might be provoked on the part of France; the other, and the more serious, the rising, on the part of the Christian population, against the Sultan's authority, already so much weakened by revolts, and by a severe financial crisis. The Emperor assured me that no movement of his forces had yet taken place (n'ont pas bougé), and expressed his hope that no advance would be required. *With regard to a French Expedition to the Sultan's dominions,* His Majesty intimated that such a step would bring affairs to an immediate crisis; that a sense of honor would compel him to send his forces into Turkey without delay or hesitation: that if the result of such an advance should prove to be the overthrow of the *Great Turk* (*le Grand Turc*), he should regret the event, but should feel that he had acted as he was compelled to do."

The Czar has now given England the theme she has to work out, viz: to sketch an "ulterior system" for superseding the Ottoman Empire, and "to enter into a previous concert as to everything relating to the establishment of a new order of things, intended to replace that which now exists." He encouraged his pupil by holding forth the prize he might gain from a successful solution of this problem, dismissing him with the paternal advice:

"A noble triumph would be obtained by the civilization of the Nineteenth century, if the void left by the extinction of Mohammedan rule in Europe could be filled up without an interruption of the general peace, in consequence of the precautions adopted by the two principal Governments the most interested in the destinies of Turkey."

England being thus summoned, Lord J. Russell appears and sends in his answer in a secret and confidential dispatch dated Feb. 9, 1853. If Lord John had been fully aware of the Czar's perfidious plan to press England into a false position by the mere fact of her entering into secret communications with him, as to the future partition of an allied State, he would have acted like the Czar, and have contented himself with making a verbal reply to Baron Brunnow, instead of dispatching an official State paper to St. Petersburg. Before the secret papers were laid before the House, *The Times* had described Lord John's dispatch as a most powerful and "indignant refusal" of the Czar's proposals.[a] In its yesterday's number it withdraws its own eulogy of Lord John, declaring that "the document does not deserve the praise it had been led, on imperfect information, to apply to it."[b] Lord John incurred the wrath of *The Times* in consequence of his declaration, in Friday's sitting of the Commons,[c] that he certainly was not in the habit of making communications to *that* paper, and that he had not even read the article alluding to his answer to Sir G. H. Seymour until three days after its publication.

Any one acquainted with the humble and abject tone assumed by every English Minister since 1814, Canning not even excepted, in their communications with Russia, will be forced to own that Lord John's dispatch is to be regarded as a heroic performance on the part of that little earthman.

The document having the character of an important contribution to history, and being proper to illustrate the development of negotiations, your readers will be glad to be acquainted with it *in extenso*.

"LORD JOHN RUSSELL TO SIR G. H. SEYMOUR

("Secret and Confidential)

"Foreign Office, February 9, 1853

"Sir: I have received, and laid before the Queen, your secret and confidential dispatch of the 22d of January.

"Her Majesty, upon this as upon former occasions, is happy to acknowledge the moderation, the frankness, and the friendly disposition of His Imperial Majesty.

"Her Majesty has directed me to reply in the same spirit of temperate and amicable discussion.

"The question raised by His Imperial Majesty is a very serious one. It is, supposing the contingency of the dissolution of the Turkish Empire to be probable, or even imminent, whether it is not better to be provided beforehand for a contingency than to incur the chaos, confusion, and the certainty of a European war, all of which must attend the catastrophe if it should occur unexpectedly, and before some ulterior system has been sketched; this is the point, said His Imperial Majesty, to which I am desirous that you should call the attention of your Government.

---

[a] *The Times*, No. 21686, March 11, 1854, leader.— *Ed.*
[b] *The Times*, No. 21693, March 20, 1854, leader.— *Ed.*
[c] March 17, 1854.— *Ed.*

"In considering this grave question, the first reflection that occurs to Her Majesty's Government is that no actual crisis has occurred which renders necessary a solution of this vast European problem. Disputes have arisen respecting the Holy Places, but these are without the sphere of the internal government of Turkey, and concern Russia, and France rather than the Sublime Porte. Some disturbance of the relations between Austria and the Porte has been caused by the Turkish attack on Montenegro; but this again relates rather to dangers affecting the frontier of Austria, than the authority and safety of the Sultan; so that there is no sufficient cause for intimating to the Sultan that he cannot keep peace at home, or preserve friendly relations with his neighbors.

"It occurs further to Her Majesty's Government to remark, that the event which is contemplated is not definitely fixed in point of time. When William III and Louis XIV disposed, by treaty, of the succession of Charles II, of Spain,[72] they were providing for an event which could not be far off. The infirmities of the sovereign of Spain, and the certain end of any human life, made the contingency in prospect both sure and near. The death of the Spanish king was in no way hastened by the treaty of partition. The same thing may be said of the provision made in the last century for the disposal of Tuscany[73] upon the decease of the last prince of the house of Medici.[a] But the contingency of the dissolution of the Ottoman Empire is of another kind. It may happen twenty, fifty, or a hundred years hence.

"*In these circumstances it would hardly be consistent with the friendly feelings toward the Sultan which animate the Emperor of Russia, no less than the Queen of Great Britain, to dispose beforehand of the provinces under his dominion.* Besides this consideration, however, it must be observed, that an agreement made in such a case tends very surely to hasten the contingency for which it is intended to provide. Austria and France could not, in fairness, be kept in ignorance of the transaction, nor would such concealment be consistent with the end of preventing a European war. Indeed, such concealment cannot be intended by His Imperial Majesty. It is to be inferred that, as soon as Great Britain and Russia should have agreed on the course to be pursued, and have determined to enforce it, they should communicate their intentions to the Great Powers of Europe. An agreement thus made and thus communicated would not be very long a secret; and while it would alarm and alienate the Sultan, the knowledge of its existence would stimulate all his enemies to increased violence and more obstinate conflict. They would fight with the conviction that they must ultimately triumph; while the Sultan's generals and troops would feel that no immediate success could save their cause from final overthrow. Thus would be produced and strengthened that very anarchy which is now feared, and the foresight of the friends of the patient would prove the cause of his death.

"Her Majesty's Government need scarcely enlarge on the dangers attendant on the execution of any similar convention. The example of the Succession War[b] is enough to show how little such agreements are respected when a pressing temptation urges their violation. The position of the Emperor of Russia as depositary, but not proprietor, of Constantinople, would be exposed to numberless hazards, both from the long-cherished ambition of his own nation and the jealousies of Europe. The ultimate proprietor, whoever he might be, would hardly be satisfied with the inert, supine attitude of the heirs of Mohammed II. A great

---

[a] Gian Gastone.— *Ed.*
[b] The reference is to the war of the Spanish succession.— *Ed.*

influence on the affairs of Europe seems naturally to belong to the Sovereign of Constantinople, holding the gates of the Mediterranean and the Black Sea.

"That influence might be used in favor of Russia; it might be used to control and curb her power.

"His Imperial Majesty has justly and wisely said: My country is so vast, so happily circumstanced in every way, that it would be unreasonable in me to desire more territory or more power than I possess. On the contrary, he observed, our great, perhaps our only danger, is that which would arise from an extension given to an Empire already too large. A vigorous and ambitious State, replacing the Sublime Porte, might, however, render war on the part of Russia a necessity for the Emperor or his successors.

"Thus European conflict would arise from the very means taken to prevent it; for neither England nor France, nor probably Austria, would be content to see Constantinople permanently in the hands of Russia.

"On the part of Great Britain, Her Majesty's Government at once declare that they renounce all intention or wish to hold Constantinople. His Imperial Majesty may be quite secure upon this head. They are likewise ready to give an assurance that they will enter into no agreement to provide for the contingency of the fall of Turkey without previous communication with the Emperor of Russia.

"Upon the whole, then, Her Majesty's Government are persuaded that no course of policy can be adopted more wise, more disinterested, more beneficial to Europe than that which His Imperial Majesty has so long followed, and which will render his name more illustrious than that of the most famous sovereigns who have sought immortality by unprovoked conquest and ephemeral glory.

"With a view to the success of this policy, it is desirable that the utmost forbearance should be manifested toward Turkey; that any demands which the Great Powers of Europe may have to make should be made matter of friendly negotiation rather than of peremptory demand; that military and naval demonstrations to coerce the Sultan should as much as possible be avoided; that differences with respect to matters affecting Turkey, within the competence of the Sublime Porte, should be decided after mutual concert between the Great Powers, and not be forced upon the weakness of the Turkish Government.

"To these cautions Her Majesty's Government wish to add that, in their view, it is essential that the Sultan should be advised to treat his Christian subjects in conformity with the principles of equity and religious freedom which prevail generally among the enlightened nations of Europe. The more the Turkish Government adopts the rules of impartial law and equal administration, the less will the Emperor of Russia find it necessary to apply that exceptional protection which His Imperial Majesty has found so burdensome and inconvenient, though no doubt prescribed by duty and sanctioned by treaty.

"You may read this dispatch to Count Nesselrode, and, if it is desired, you may yourself place a copy of it in the hands of the Emperor. In that case you will accompany its presentation with those assurances of friendship and confidence on the part of Her Majesty the Queen, which the conduct of His Imperial Majesty was so sure to inspire.

"I am &c.

"J. Russell"

I am obliged to postpone the conclusion of this analysis to my next letter.[a] Before concluding, however, I will give you, in

---

[a] See this volume, pp. 84-99.— *Ed.*

addition to previous communications, the most recent news I have obtained, from a source not otherwise accessible to the public,[74] regarding the attitude and plans of Prussia.[a]

When the conflict between Russia on the one hand, and the Anglo-French Alliance on the other, already reached a certain climax, the Emperor Nicholas dispatched an autograph letter to his brother-in-law[b] at Berlin, in which he stated that though England and France might do him some damage at sea he feared nothing from them on land, having 600,000 soldiers ready to take the field at the end of April. Of these he would place 200,000 at the disposition of Frederick William, if the latter engaged himself to march on Paris and dethrone Louis Napoleon. The imbecile king was so much taken in by this proposition that *Manteuffel* required three days' discussion to dissuade him from taking the pledge. So much for the king.

As to *Herr von Manteuffel* himself, the "great character"[c] of whom the Prussian middle classes are so proud, the whole man lies open, as in a nutshell, in his secret instructions sent to Mr. Bunsen, his Embassador at London, at the same period as the above Russian letter was received, and which came into my possession through certainly a different manner than that by which Mr. Bunsen possessed himself of my private letters.[75] The contents of these instructions, betraying in the arrogant ambiguity of their style at once the schoolmaster and the drill-sergeant, are nearly as follows: "Look sharp whence the wind blows. If you observe that England is in earnest alliance with France, and determined to push on the war, take your stand on the 'integrity and independence' of Turkey. If you observe her wavering in policy and disinclined to war, out with your lance and break it cheerfully for the honor and character of the king, my master and yours."

Is the Autocrat wrong then in treating Prussia as a non-entity?

Written on March 21, 1854

First published in the *New-York Daily Tribune*, No. 4045, April 5; reprinted in the *New-York Semi-Weekly Tribune*, No. 925, April 7 and the *New-York Weekly Tribune*, No. 656, April 8, 1854

Signed: *Karl Marx*

Reproduced from the *New-York Daily Tribune*

---

[a] See this volume, p. 8.— *Ed.*
[b] Frederick William IV.— *Ed.*
[c] Presumably an allusion to Heine's "Kein Talent doch ein Charakter" from *Atta Troll,* Kap. 24.— *Ed.*

Karl Marx

THE SECRET DIPLOMATIC CORRESPONDENCE[76]

London, Friday, March 24, 1854

Although Lord J. Russell's dispatch[a] may, upon the whole, be described as a polite refusal of the Czar's proposition to enter into a previous concert on the eventual partition of Turkey, there occur some very strange passages, to which I call the attention of your readers. Lord John says:

"*There is no sufficient cause for intimating to the Sultan* that he cannot keep peace at home, or preserve friendly relations with his neighbors."[b]

Now, nowhere in the confidential communications of Sir H. Seymour do we meet an allusion to the Czar having proposed to intimate to the Sultan anything of the sort. We must, therefore, conclude either that Lord Russell, while simulating opposition to such a step, meant to insinuate it himself, or that some of Sir Hamilton's confidential communications are suppressed in the papers laid before the House. The matter looks the more suspicious as, only 16 days later, on Feb. 25, 1853, Lord Clarendon, on his accession to the Foreign Office, gave the following instructions to Lord Stratford de Redcliffe:

"Your Excellency will, with all the frankness and unreserve that may be consistent with prudence and the dignity of the Sultan, explain the reasons which lead Her Majesty's Government to fear that the Ottoman Empire is now in a position of peculiar danger. The *accumulated grievances of foreign nations* which the Porte is unable or unwilling to redress, the *mal-administration of its own affairs* and the *increasing weakness of executive power in Turkey,* have caused the allies of the

---

[a] See this volume, pp. 80-82.— *Ed.*
[b] Ibid., p. 81.— *Ed.*

Porte latterly to assume a tone alike novel and alarming and which, if persevered in, may lead to a general revolt of the Christian subjects of the Porte, and prove fatal to the independence and integrity of the Empire, a catastrophe that would be deeply deplored by Her Majesty's Government, but which it is their duty to represent to the Porte as considered probable and impending by *some* of the Great European Powers." (See the Blue Books on the Rights and Privileges of the Latin and Greek Churches, Vol. 1, pages 81 and 82.)

Was this not "*intimating*" to the Sultan, on the part of England, in plain words: "that he cannot keep peace at home or preserve friendly relations with his neighbors?" The Czar had told Sir Hamilton in a very off-hand way that he would not *allow* England to establish herself at Constantinople, but that he, on his part, intended to establish himself there, if not as *proprietor*, at least as depositary.[a] How does Lord John reply to this impertinent announcement? In the name of Great Britain he renounces "all intention or wish to hold Constantinople." He exacts no similar pledge from the Czar.

"The position of the Emperor of Russia," he says, "as *depositary*, but not proprietor, of Constantinople, would be exposed to numberless hazards, both from the long-cherished ambition of his own nation and the jealousies of Europe."[b]

The jealousies of Europe, but not the opposition of England! As to England, she would not allow—no—Lord John Russell dares not speak to Russia in the same tone in which Russia speaks to England—she would "*not be content* to see Constantinople *permanently* in the hands of Russia." She will, then, be content to see it *temporarily* so. In other words she fully concurs in the Czar's own proposal. She will not allow what he himself renounces, but is prepared to suffer what he intends doing.

Not "content" with installing the Czar as the eventual depositary of Constantinople, Lord John Russell declares in the name of the English Government that "they will enter into no agreement to provide for the contingency of the fall of Turkey without *previous* communication to Russia."[c] That is to say, although the Czar told Sir H. Seymour that he *had* entered into an agreement with Austria before making any previous communication to England, she on her part pledges herself to communicate with Russia previously to entering into an agreement with France.

---

[a] See this volume, pp. 78-79.— *Ed.*
[b] Ibid., p. 81.— *Ed.*
[c] Ibid., p. 82.— *Ed.*

"Upon the whole," says Lord John, "no course of policy can be adopted more wise, more disinterested, more beneficial to Europe than that which His Imperial Majesty has so long followed."

His Cossack Majesty happens to have followed, without ever swerving from it, the policy inaugurated at his accession to the throne, and which the liberal Lord John declares to have been so disinterested and so beneficial to Europe.

The ostensible and main point of dispute in the present Eastern complication is Russia's claim to a religious protectorate over the Greek Christians in the Ottoman Empire. The Czar, far from disguising his pretensions, told Sir Hamilton plainly that "by treaty he has a right to watch over those several millions," that he "made a moderate and sparing use of his right," and that it was "attended with obligations occasionally very inconvenient." Does Lord John Russell give him to understand that there exists no such treaty, and that the Czar had no such right? That he had no more right to meddle with the Greek subjects of Turkey than England with the Protestant subjects of Russia, or France with the Irishmen of Great Britain? Let him answer for himself.

"Her Majesty's Government wish to add, that in their view it is essential that the Sultan should be advised to treat his Christian subjects in conformity with the principles of equity and religious freedom: ...The more the Turkish Government adopts the rules of impartial law and equal administration, the less will the Emperor of Russia find it necessary to apply that *exceptional protection* which His Imperial Majesty has found so burdensome and inconvenient, though *no doubt prescribed by duty* and *sanctioned by treaty.*"

Russia's *exceptional protectorate* over the subjects of the Porte *sanctioned by treaty*! *No doubt* about that, says Lord John, and Lord John is an honest man,[a] and Lord John speaks in the name of Her Majesty's Government, and Lord John addresses the Autocrat himself. What, then, is England quarrelling about with Russia, and why doubling the Income tax, and troubling the world with war-like preparation? What was Lord John's business when, some weeks ago, he arose in Parliament, with the aspects, and in the tone of a Cassandra, screaming and bouncing and gesticulating bombastic imprecations against the faithlessness and perfidy of the Czar?[b] Had [he] not himself declared to Caesar that Caesar's

----

[a] Apparently an allusion to Antony's words
   "But Brutus says, he was ambitious;
   And Brutus is an honourable man"
from Shakespeare, *Julius Caesar*, Act III, Scene 2.— *Ed.*
   [b] Lord John Russell's speech in the House of Commons on February 17, 1854. *The Times*, No. 21668, February 18, 1854.— *Ed.*

claims to the *exclusive protectorate* were "prescribed by duty and sanctioned by treaty?"

What the coalition had to complain of, was certainly no dissimulation or reserve of the Czar's but, on the contrary, the impudent familiarity with which he dared to unbosom himself before them and make them the vessels of his most secret designs, thus transforming the cabinet of Downing-st. into a private cabinet in the Alexander Newski.[a] A man confides to you his intention to murder your friend. He entreats you to enter with him upon a previous concert about the booty. If the man be Emperor of Russia and you an English Minister, you will not call him to the bar, but thank him in humble terms for the great confidence placed in you, and feel happy "to acknowledge his moderation, frankness and friendly disposition," as Lord John Russell did.

Let us return to St. Petersburg.

On the night of the 20th Feb.—only eight days before Prince Menchikoff's arrival at Constantinople—the Autocrat came up to Sir Hamilton Seymour at the *soirée* of the Grand Duchess Hereditary's,[b] when the following conversation took place between these two "gentlemen."

The Czar:
"Well, so you have got your answer, and you are to bring it to me to-morrow."
Sir Hamilton:
"I am to have that honor, Sire, but Your Majesty is aware that the nature of the reply is very exactly what I had led you to expect."
The Czar:
"So I was sorry to hear; but I think your Government does not well understand my object. I am not so eager *about what shall be done when the sick man dies,* as I am to determine with England *what shall not be done* upon that event taking place."
Sir Hamilton:
"But, Sire, allow me to observe that we have no reason to think that the sick man is dying; countries do not die in such a hurry. Turkey will remain for many a year, unless some unforeseen crisis should occur. It is precisely, Sire, for the avoidance of all circumstances likely to produce such a crisis that Her Majesty's Government reckons upon your generous assistance."
The Czar:
"I will tell you that if your Government has been led to believe *that Turkey retains any elements of existence,* your Government must have received incorrect information. *I repeat to you that the sick man is dying,* and we can never allow such an event to take us by surprise. We must come to some understanding.... And remember, I do not ask for a treaty or a protocol; *a general understanding* is all I

---

[a] Nevsky Prospekt.— *Ed.*
[b] Maria Alexandrovna.— *Ed.*

require—that *between gentlemen* is sufficient.... So no more for the present; you will come to me to-morrow."[a]

Sir Hamilton "thanked His Majesty very cordially," but having hardly left the Imperial saloon and returned home, suspicion overcomes him, he sits down at his desk, reports to Lord John on the conversation, and sums up his letter with these striking marginal notes:

"It can hardly be otherwise but that the Sovereign who *insists with such pertinacity upon the impending fall of a neighboring State*, must have *settled* in his own mind that the hour, if not *of* its dissolution, at all events, *for* its dissolution, must be at hand.... This assumption would hardly be ventured upon unless some, *perhaps general, but at all events intimate understanding, existed between Russia and Austria.*

"Supposing my suspicion to be well founded, *the Emperor's object is to engage Her Majesty's Government, in conjunction with his own Cabinet, and that of Vienna, in some scheme for the ultimate partition of Turkey, and for the exclusion of France from the arrangement.*"

This dispatch arrived at London on the 6th of March, when Lord Russell was already supplanted in the Foreign office by Lord Clarendon.[b] The impression produced on the mind of this whining lover of Turkey by the Embassador's anxious warnings is quite surprising. Being fully aware of the Czar's treacherous design to partition Turkey to the exclusion of France, he tells Count Walewski, the French Embassador at London, that "they," in contradistinction to France, "were disposed to place reliance in the Emperor of Russia"—that "a policy of suspicion was neither wise nor safe"—and that "although he hoped the Governments of England and France would always act together, *when* their policy and their interests were identical, yet he must frankly say that *the recent proceedings of the French Government were not the best calculated to secure that desirable result.*" (See Blue Books, Vol. 1, pp. 93 and 98.)[c]

Be it also remarked, *en passant*, that at the same time when the Czar indoctrinated the British Embassador at St. Petersburg, *The Times* was repeating at London, day after day, that the state of Turkey was desperate, that the Ottoman Empire was crumbling to pieces and that there remained nothing of it except the phantom of "a Turk's head dressed up in a turban."[d]

The morning after the interview at the Imperial *soirée* Sir G. H. Seymour, according to the invitation received, waits upon the

[a] Sir G. H. Seymour to Lord John Russell. February 21, 1853.— *Ed.*
[b] See this volume, p. 84.— *Ed.*
[c] The Earl of Clarendon to Lord Cowley. March 22 and 29, 1853.— *Ed.*
[d] *The Times*, No. 21383, March 23, 1853, leader.— *Ed.*

Czar and a "*dialogue* lasting one hour and twelve minutes" takes place between them, on which he reports again in his dispatch to Lord J. Russell, dated Feb. 22, 1853.

The Emperor began by desiring Sir Hamilton to read to him aloud Lord John's secret and confidential dispatch of the 9th of February. The declarations contained in this dispatch he declared, of course, to be very satisfactory; he "could only desire that they should be a little amplified." He repeated that a Turkish catastrophe was constantly impending, and

"that it might be brought about at any moment, either by an external war, or by a feud between the old Turkish party and that of the 'new superficial French reforms,' or again, by a rising of the Christians, already known to be very impatient of shaking off the Mussulman yoke."

He does not allow the opportunity to slip without bringing forth his worn-out bravado, that "if he had not stopped the victorious progress of Gen. Diebich, in 1829, the Sultan's authority would have been at an end"—while it is a notorious fact, that of the 200,000 men he had then marched into Turkey 50,000 only returned to their homes, and the rest of Diebich's army would have been annihilated on the plains of Adrianople but for the combined treason of Turkish Pashas and foreign Embassadors.

He insists on his not requiring a system altogether arranged between England and Russia, as to the previous disposal of the provinces ruled by the Sultan, and still less a formal agreement to be concluded between the two Cabinets, but only some general understanding or exchange of opinions, each party confidentially stating what it did not wish,

"what would be contrary to English interests, what would be contrary to Russian interests, in order that, the case occurring, they might avoid acting in opposition to each other."[a]

By such a *negative* understanding the Czar would obtain all he cares for: 1st, the breaking up of the Ottoman Empire settled between England and Russia as a *fait accompli*, although in a negative and conditional form, while it would rest with him so to embroil matters as to be able to declare to England, with some show of reason, that the contingency foreseen *had* arrived. Secondly, a secret plan of action between England and Russia,

---

[a] Quotation from the confidential memorandum of the Russian Cabinet to the British Government dated February 21 (March 4), 1853 which was communicated by Count Nesselrode to Sir Seymour on March 7, and sent by the latter to London on March 9, 1853 (see this volume, pp. 92-93).— *Ed.*

however vague and negative, brought about behind the back and to the exclusion of France, and thus necessarily setting England and France by the ears. Thirdly, England being restrained by her negative pledges as to what she would *not* do, he would have liberty to elaborate very tranquilly his own plan of positive action. Besides, it is evident that two parties agreeing as to what they will *not* allow each other to do, in a given case, are only settling in an evasive way what they *will.* This negative sort of understanding gives only the greater facilities to the more cunning of the two parties.

"Perhaps your Majesty," perplexed Sir Hamilton muttered, "would be good enough to explain your own ideas upon this *negative policy.*" The Czar, after some show of coy resistance, feigns to yield under the gentle pressure and made the following highly remarkable declaration:

> "I will not tolerate the *permanent* occupation of Constantinople by the Russians; having said this, I will say that it never shall be held by the English, or French, or any other great nation. Again, I never will permit an attempt at the reconstruction of a Byzantine Empire, or such an extension of Greece as would render her a powerful State; still less will I permit the breaking up of Turkey into little republics, asylums for the Kossuths and Mazzinis and other revolutionists of Europe; rather than submit to any of these arrangements I would go to war, and as long as I have a man and a musket left would carry it on."

No Byzantine Empire, no powerful extension of Greece, no confederation of little republics—nothing of the sort. What, then, does he want? There was no need for the British Embassador to guess. The Emperor himself, in the course of the dialogue, bursts upon his interlocutor with the following proposition:

> "The Principalities are in fact an independent state under my protection: this might so continue. Servia might receive the same form of government. So again with Bulgaria: there seems to be no reason why this province should not form an independent state. As to Egypt, I quite understand the importance to England of that territory. I can then only say, that if, in the event of a distribution of the Ottoman succession upon the fall of the Empire, you should take possession of Egypt, I shall have no objections to offer. I would say the same thing of Candia: that island might suit you, and I do not know why it should not become an English possession."

Thus he proves that "in the event of the dissolution of the Ottoman Empire, it might be less difficult to arrive at a satisfactory territorial arrangement than was commonly believed." He declares frankly what he wants—*the partition of Turkey*—and he gives the clearest possible outlines of that partition; clear as well from what he reveals as from what his silence conceals. Egypt and

Candia for England. The Principalities, Servia and Bulgaria to exist as vassal states of Russia. Turkish Croatia, Bosnia and Herzegovina he intentionally abstains from mentioning, to be incorporated with Austria. Greece to be extended in a "not powerful way"—say lower Thessaly and part of Albania. Constantinople to be temporarily occupied by the Czar, and then to become the capital of a state comprising Macedonia, Thracia, and what remains of Turkey in Europe. But who is to be the definitive possessor of that little empire, perhaps to be aggrandized by some portions of Anatolia? He keeps close upon that point, but it is no secret that he has some one in reserve for that post, viz: his younger son,[a] who longs for an empire of his own. And France—is she to receive nothing at all? Perhaps so. But no: she is to be put off with—who will believe it?—with *Tunis*. "One of her objects," he tells Sir Hamilton, "is the possession of Tunis," and perhaps, in the event of a partition of the Ottoman Empire, he might be so magnanimous as to indulge her appetite for Tunis.

The Czar speaks throughout in an affected tone of the most haughty disdain of France. "It looks very much," he says, "as if the French Government were endeavoring to embroil us all in the East." As for himself, he cares not a straw about it:

"For his own part, he cared very little what line the French might think proper to take in Eastern affairs, and that little more than a month ago he had apprised the Sultan that if his assistance was required for resisting the menaces of the French, it was entirely at the service of the Sultan!

"In a word, the Emperor went on to observe, 'As I before told you, all I want is a good understanding with England, and this not as to what shall, but as to what shall not be done; this point arrived at, the English Government and I, I and the English Government, having entire confidence in one another's views, I care nothing about the rest.'"

"But Your Majesty has forgotten Austria!" exclaims Sir Hamilton.

"Oh!" replied the Emperor, greatly to his surprise, "but you must understand that *when I speak of Russia, I speak of Austria as well; what suits the one suits the other*, our interests as regards Turkey are perfectly identical."

When he says Russia, he says Austria. As to Montenegro, he states explicitly "that he approved the attitude taken by the Austrian Cabinet."

Having treated in a former conversation the Sultan as the

---

[a] Mikhail Nikolayevich.— *Ed.*

"Grand Turk"[a] of the *Vaudeville,* he designs him now, after the fashion of *Paul de Kock,* as "*Ce monsieur.*" And how forbearing did he not behave toward *ce monsieur?* He has only dispatched a Menchikoff to Constantinople. "If he chose, he certainly could send an army there—there is nothing to stop them," as he proved afterward at Oltenitza and Chetatea, and by his own army's glorious retirement from Kalafat.

His Cossack Majesty dismissed Sir Hamilton with the words: "Well, induce your Government to write again on these subjects— to write more fully, and to do so without hesitation."

On the 7th of March, shortly after this curious dialogue, or, rather, monologue, the British Embassador is summoned to appear before Count Nesselrode, who places in his hands "a very confidential memorandum[b] which His Imperial Majesty had caused to be drawn up, and which was intended as an answer to, or a comment upon, the communication" of Lord John Russell.[c] Count Nesselrode invites him to read the paper, which, in fact, "was intended for his use." Sir Hamilton, accordingly, peruses the document, and he who had not found a single word of protest against the Muscovite's[d] elaborate insults against France, all of a sudden trembles at discovering that "the impression under which it has been framed is an incorrect one; that impression being evidently that, in the disputes carried on between Russia and France, Her Majesty's Government had leant partially to the latter power."[e] The very next morning he hastily sends a *billet doux* to Count Nesselrode, asserting that,

"*far from having inclined,* as has been stated, to France in the course of the late critical transactions, it has been the desire of the Queen's advisers, *to the full extent permitted (!)* to a Government *compelled (!!)* to observe a *neutral* attitude, that ample satisfaction shall be given to the demands which His Imperial Majesty's Government were *justified* in making."[f]

In consequence of this begging letter, Sir Hamilton has, of course, another "very amicable and satisfactory conversation with the Chancellor," who comforts the British Embassador with the assurance that he had misunderstood one passage of the Emperor's memorandum which did not intend reproaching England with any partiality for France. "All," said Count

---

[a] See this volume, p. 79.— *Ed.*
[b] Of February 21 (March 4), 1853.— *Ed.*
[c] See this volume, pp. 80-82.— *Ed.*
[d] Nicholas I.— *Ed.*
[e] Sir G. H. Seymour to the Earl of Clarendon. March 9, 1853.— *Ed.*
[f] Sir G. H. Seymour to Count Nesselrode. February 24 (March 8), 1853.— *Ed.*

Nesselrode, "what was desired here was that, *while appealing to the Emperor's magnanimity and feelings of justice,* the British Government should employ some efforts toward opening the eyes of the French Minister." There is nothing wanted "*here*" but England's creeping and cringing before the Kalmuk, and assuming a tone of dictatory severity against the Frenchman. To convince the Chancellor of the conscientious manner in which the British Government had executed the latter part of their service, Sir Hamilton reads him an extract from one of Lord John Russell's dispatches,[a] "as a specimen of the *language* held by an English Minister against the French Government." Count Nesselrode finds his boldest expectations surpassed. He only "regretted that he had not long ago been put in possession of *evidence so conclusive.*"[b]

The Russian memorandum in answer to Lord John's dispatch is described by Sir Hamilton, as "one of the most remarkable papers which have been issued, not from the Russian, 'Chancellery', but from the Emperor's secret Cabinet."[c] So it is. But it is superfluous to dwell on it, as it merely resumes the views of the Czar as developed in his "dialogue." It impresses upon the British Government that "the result, whatever it might be, of these communications, should remain a *secret* between the two Sovereigns." The Czar's system, it observes, has, "as *admitted* by the English Cabinet itself, been *always* one of forbearance" against the Porte. France had adopted another line of conduct, thus compelling Russia and Austria to act in their turn by intimidation. In the whole memorandum Russia and Austria are identified. One of the causes which might lead to the immediate downfall of Turkey is *expressly* stated to be the *Question of the Holy Shrines,* and "the religious sentiments of the orthodox Greeks offended by the concessions made to the Latins." At the close of the memorandum "no less precious" than the assurances contained in Russell's dispatch are declared to be "the *proofs of friendship and personal confidence on the part of Her Majesty the Queen,* which Sir Hamilton Seymour had been directed on this occasion to impart to the Emperor." These "*proofs*" of Queen Victoria's allegiance to the Czar have been wisely withheld from the British public, but may perhaps, one of these days, appear in the *Journal de St.-Pétersbourg.*

In commenting upon his dialogue with the Emperor and on the

---

[a] Lord John Russell to Lord Cowley. January 28, 1853.— *Ed.*
[b] Sir G. H. Seymour to the Earl of Clarendon. March 10, 1853.— *Ed.*
[c] Sir G. H. Seymour to the Earl of Clarendon. March 9, 1853.— *Ed.*

Muscovite memorandum, Sir Hamilton again draws the attention of his Cabinet to the position of Austria:

"Assuming, as a certain and now acknowledged fact, the existence of an understanding or compact between the two Emperors as to Turkish affairs, it becomes of the deepest importance to know the extent of the engagements entered into between them. As to the manner in which it has been concluded, I conjecture that little doubt is to be entertained.

"Its basis was, no doubt, laid at some of the meetings between the Sovereigns which took place in the autumn; and the scheme has probably been worked out since under the management of Baron Meyendorf, the Russian Envoy at the Austrian Court, who has been passing the winter at St. Petersburg, and is still here."[a]

Does the British Government on receiving these revelations, call Austria to account? No, it finds fault with France only. After the Russian invasion of the Principalities, it appoints Austria as mediator, chooses Vienna, of all other towns, for the seat of the conference, hands over to Count Buol the direction of the negotiations, and to this very moment continues to stultify France into the belief that Austria is likely to be a sincere ally in a war against the Muscovite for the integrity and independence of the Ottoman Empire, although it knew for longer than a twelvemonth that Austria had agreed to the dismemberment of that Empire.

On March 19, Sir Hamilton's report on his dialogue with the Czar arrived at London. Lord Clarendon now fills the place of Lord John, and continues to improve upon his predecessor. Four days after the receipt of that startling communication, in which the Czar no longer deigns to dissimulate, but frankly reveals his conspiracy against Turkey and France, the noble Earl sends to Sir Hamilton the following dispatch:

"Her Majesty's Government regret that the alarm and irritation which prevail at Paris should have induced the French Government to order their fleet to sail for the waters of Greece; but the position in which the French Government stands, in many respects is different from that of Her Majesty's Government. They have not, to the knowledge of Her Majesty's Government, [received] assurances from the Emperor as to the policy he was determined to follow toward Turkey." (See Blue Books, Vol. 1, page 95.)[b]

If the Czar had communicated to France also that "the sick man was dying," and a complete plan for sharing his succession, France, of course, would have felt neither alarm nor hesitation as to the fate of Turkey, the real objects of Prince Menchikoff's mission, and the Emperor of Russia's immovable determination to maintain

---

[a] Sir G. H. Seymour to the Earl of Clarendon. March 9, 1853.— *Ed.*
[b] The Earl of Clarendon to Sir G. H. Seymour. March 23, 1853.— *Ed.*

the integrity and independence of the Empire, which he averred contained "no elements of existence."

On the same 23d of March, the Earl of Clarendon sends another dispatch to Sir Hamilton Seymour, one not "cooked" for the Blue Books, but the secret answer to the secret communication from St. Petersburg.[a] Sir Hamilton had closed his report of the dialogue with the very judicious suggestion:

"I might venture to suggest that *some expression might be used in the dispatch to be addressed to me, which might have the effect of putting an end to the further consideration*, or, at all events, discussion of points which it is highly desirable should not be regarded as offering *subject for debate.*"[b]

The Earl of Clarendon, who feels himself the true man to handle hot coals, acts in strict compliance with the Czar's invitation, and in direct contravention to his own Embassador's warning. He commences his dispatch by declaring that "Her Majesty's Government gladly comply with the Emperor's wish that the subject should be further and frankly discussed." The Emperor is "*entitled*" to "the most cordial declaration of opinion" on their part, because of the "generous confidence" placed in them that they will help him dismembering Turkey, betraying France, and, in the contingency of the overthrow of the Ottoman rule, suppressing all possible efforts on the part of the Christian populations to form free and independent States.

"Her Majesty's Government," continues the freeborn Briton, "are fully aware that, in the event of any understanding with reference to future contingencies being expedient, or indeed possible, the *word of His Imperial Majesty* would be *preferable* to any Convention that could be framed."

At all events, his word must be as good as any Convention that could be framed with him, *the law advisers of the British Crown having long ago declared all treaties with Russia at an end, through violations on her part.*

"Her Majesty's Government persevere in the belief, that Turkey still preserves the elements of existence."

To prove the sincerity of that belief, the Earl gently adds:

"If the opinion of the Emperor, that the days of the Turkish Empire were numbered, became notorious its downfall must occur even sooner than His Imperial Majesty now appears to expect."

---

[a] The Earl of Clarendon to Sir G. H. Seymour. March 23, 1853.— *Ed.*
[b] Sir G. H. Seymour to Lord John Russell. February 22, 1853.— *Ed.*

The Kalmuk, then, has only to divulge his opinion that the sick man is dying, and the man is dead. An enviable sort of vitality this! There is wanted no blast of the trumpets of Jericho. One breath from the Emperor's august mouth, and the Ottoman Empire falls to pieces.

"Her Majesty's Government *entirely* share the opinion of the Emperor, that the occupation of Constantinople by either of the great Powers would be incompatible with the present balance of power and the maintenance of peace in Europe, and must at once be regarded as impossible; that there are no elements for the reconstruction of a Byzantine Empire; that the systematic misgovernment of Greece offers no encouragement to extend its territorial dominion; and that, as *there are no materials for provincial or communal government,* anarchy would be the result of leaving the provinces of Turkey to themselves, or permitting them to form separate republics."

Observe that the British Minister, prostrate at the feet of his Tartar master and servilely reechoing his words, is not ashamed even to repeat the monstrous lie that in Turkey there are "no elements for provincial or communal government," while it is precisely the great development of communal and provincial life that has enabled Turkey to withstand till now the heaviest shocks both from without and from within. By indorsing all the Czar's premises the British Ministry justifies all the conclusions he intends to draw therefrom.

In the contingency of a dissolution of the Turkish Empire, says the gallant Earl, "the only mode by which a pacific solution could be attempted would be that of a European Congress." But he is afraid of the consequences of such a Congress—not because of Russian trickery, which cheated England at the Congress of Vienna to such a degree that Napoleon at St. Helena exclaimed: "Had he been victorious at Waterloo, he could not have imposed more humiliating conditions upon England"[a]—but from fear of France.

"The treaties of 1815 must then be open to revision, when France might be prepared to risk the chances of a European War to get rid of the obligations which she considers injurious to her national honor, and which, having been imposed by victorious enemies, are a constant source of irritation to her."

Her Majesty's Government "desire to uphold the Turkish Empire" not as a bulwark against Russia, and because its downfall would force England to fight out with Russia her *diametrically*

---

[a] The quotation from the book: Las Cases, *Mémorial de Sainte-Hélène,* T. VI, p. 186, is freely rendered.— *Ed.*

opposed interests in the East. Oh, no, says the Earl: *"The interests of Russia and England in the East are completely identical."*

They desire to uphold the Turkish Empire not from any Eastern consideration at all, but "from their conviction that no great question can be agitated in the East *without becoming a source of discord in the West.*" An Eastern question, therefore, will not bring about *a war of the Western Powers against Russia,* but a war of the Western Powers among themselves—*a war of England against France.* And the same Minister who wrote, and his colleagues who sanctioned these lines, would stultify us into the belief that they are about to carry on a serious war with France against Russia, and this "on a question agitated in the East," and although "the interests of England and Russia in the East are completely identical!"

The brave Earl goes further. Why does he fear *a war with France* which he declares must be the "necessary result" of the dissolution and dismemberment of the Turkish Empire? A war with France considered in itself would be a very pleasant thing. But there is this delicate circumstance connected with it,

— "that every great question in the West will assume a revolutionary character, and embrace a revision of the entire social system, for which the Continental Governments are certainly in no state of preparation.

"The Emperor is fully cognisant of the materials that are in constant fermentation beneath the surface of society, and their readiness to burst forth even in times of peace; and His Imperial Majesty will probably therefore not dissent from the opinion that the first cannon shot may be the signal for a state of things more disastrous even than those calamities which war inevitably brings in its train."

Hence, exclaims the sincere peacemonger, "hence the anxiety of Her Majesty's Government to *avert the catastrophe.*" If there lurked no war with France behind the partition of Turkey, and no revolution behind the war with France, Her Majesty's Government would be as ready to swallow the *Grand Turk* as his Cossack Majesty.

According to the instructions received from the Russian Chancellery, through the means of Sir H. Seymour, the gallant Clarendon winds up his dispatch with "appealing to the Emperor's magnanimity and feelings of justice."

In a second dispatch of our Earl, dated April 5, 1853, Sir Hamilton is directed to instruct the Russian Chancellor that

— "Viscount Stratford de Redcliffe was directed to return to his post, and a *special character* was given to his mission *by an autograph letter* from Her Majesty, under the impression that the Porte would be better disposed to listen to *moderate* councils, when offered by one of Viscount Stratford de Redcliffe's high position and great knowledge and experience of Turkish affairs..., to advise the Porte to treat the Christian subjects with the utmost leniency."

The same Clarendon who gave his *particular* instructions had written in his secret dispatch dated 23d March, 1853:

"The treatment of Christians is not harsh, and the toleration exhibited by the Porte toward this portion of its subjects might serve as an example to some Governments who look with contempt upon Turkey as a barbarous Power."

In this secret dispatch it is avowed that Lord Stratford was sent to Constantinople as the most able and willing tool for intimidating the Sultan. In the Ministerial papers, at the time, his errand was represented as a strong demonstration against the Czar, that nobleman having long since played the part of Russia's personal antagonist.

The series of secret documents laid before the House concludes with the Russian memorandum wherein Nicholas congratulates himself on perceiving that his views and those of the English Cabinet entirely coincide on the subject of the political combinations which it would be chiefly necessary to avoid in the extreme case of the contingency occurring in the East.

The memorandum is dated the 15th April, 1853. It asserts "that the best means of upholding the duration of the Turkish Government is *not to harass it by overwhelming demands supported in a manner humiliating to its independence and its dignity.*" This was exactly the time of action of the Menchikoff comedy, who, on the 19th of April, sent in his impudent "verbal note," and used "language fortunately very rare in diplomacy"—as declared by the Earl of Clarendon in the House of Lords.[a] The more firmly was his lordship convinced of the Czar's determination to gently manage the sick man. His conviction grows yet stronger when the Principalities are invaded by the Cossack.

The Coalition Cabinet have discovered but one hole to slip through from these branding documents. The ostensible object of Prince Menchikoff's mission, they say, was the question of the Holy Shrines, while the communications about the partition of Turkey only related to an uncertain and distant epoch. But the Czar had plainly told them in his first memorandum[b] that the question of Turkey's downfall was "by no means an idle and imaginary question, a contingency too remote;" that the English

---

[a] The Earl of Clarendon's speech in the House of Lords on August 12, 1853. *The Times*, No. 21506, August 13, 1853.— *Ed.*
[b] See this volume, p. 92.— *Ed.*

Ministry were wrong "in perceiving in the two questions of Montenegro and the Holy Shrines mere disputes which would not differ in their bearing from difficulties which form the ordinary business of diplomacy," and that the question of the Holy Shrines might "take a most serious turn," and lead to the "catastrophe." They had admitted themselves, not only that he was wronged in the affair of the Holy Shrines, but that he had "a right, sanctioned by treaty, to the exceptional protection" of eleven millions of the Sultan's subjects. When therefore, they failed in pressing the Porte into the acceptance of the Menchikoff demands, the Czar acted according to the spirit of the memorandum of 1844,[a] to their own agreement with him, and to his verbal declaration to Sir G. Hamilton Seymour, that "he would not be trifled with," when he prepared to put *ce monsieur* to death. There is no question as to whether he is in the right against them; the only question is, whether they be not, even at this moment, "all right" with him. So much must be clear to whoever closely peruses those documents, that, if this scandalous Ministry remain in office, the English people may be driven, by the mere influence of external complications, into a terrible revolution, sweeping away, at once, Throne, Parliament and the governing classes, who have lost the faculty and the will to maintain England's position in the world.

In challenging, by the *St.-Petersburg Gazette*,[b] the Coalition to produce the secret proofs of their own infamy Nicholas proved true to his known dictum:

"Je hais ceux qui me résistent; je méprise ceux qui me servent."[c]

Written on March 24, 1854

First published in the *New-York Daily Tribune*, No. 4050, April 11; reprinted in the *New-York Semi-Weekly Tribune*, No. 927, April 14 and the *New-York Weekly Tribune*, No. 657, April 15, 1854

Signed: *Karl Marx*

Reproduced from the *New-York Daily Tribune*

---

[a] See this volume, p. 73.— *Ed.*

[b] *Journal de St.-Pétersbourg.— Ed.*

[c] "I hate those who resist me, I despise those who serve me."— *Ed.*

Karl Marx

DECLARATION OF WAR.—ON THE HISTORY OF THE EASTERN QUESTION [77]

London, Tuesday, March 28, 1854

War has at length been declared. The Royal Message was read yesterday in both Houses of Parliament; by Lord Aberdeen in the Lords, and by Lord J. Russell in the Commons.[a] It describes the measures about to be taken as "active steps to oppose the encroachments of Russia upon Turkey." To-morrow *The London Gazette* will publish the official notification of war, and on Friday the address in reply to the message will become the subject of the Parliamentary debates.

Simultaneously with the English declaration, Louis Napoleon has communicated a similar message to his Senate and *Corps Législatif.*[b]

The declaration of war against Russia could no longer be delayed, after Captain Blackwood, the bearer of the Anglo-French *ultimatissimum* to the Czar, had returned, on Saturday last, with the answer that Russia would give to that paper no answer at all.[c] The mission of Capt. Blackwood, however, has not been altogether a gratuitous one. It has afforded to Russia the month of March, that most dangerous epoch of the year, to Russian arms.

The publication of the secret correspondence between the Czar and the English Government, instead of provoking a burst of public indignation against the latter, has — *incredibile dictu*[d] — been the signal for the press, both weekly and daily, for congratulating England on the possession of so truly national a Ministry. I

---

[a] Victoria R., "The Royal Message". *The Times,* No. 21700, March 28, 1854.— *Ed.*

[b] *Le Moniteur universel,* No. 87, March 28, 1854.— *Ed.*

[c] *The Times,* No. 21699, March 27, 1854, leader.— *Ed.*

[d] Incredible thing.— *Ed.*

understand, however, that a meeting will be called together for the purpose of opening the eyes of a blinded British public on the real conduct of the Government. It is to be held on Thursday next in the Music Hall, Store-st.; and Lord Ponsonby, Mr. Layard, Mr. Urquhart, etc., are expected to take part in the proceedings.

The *Hamburger Correspondent* has the following:

"According to advices from St. Petersburg, which arrived here on the 16th inst., the Russian Government proposes to publish various other documents on the Eastern question. Among the documents destined for publication are some letters written by Prince Albert."

It is a curious fact that the same evening on which the Royal Message was delivered in the Commons, the Government suffered their first *defeat* in the present session; the second reading of the Poor-Settlement and Removal bill[78] having, notwithstanding the efforts of the Government, been adjourned to the 28th of April, by a division of 209 to 183. The person to whom the Government is indebted for this defeat, is no other than my Lord Palmerston.

"His lordship," says *The Times* of this day, "has *managed* to put himself and his colleagues between two fires (the Tories and the Irish party) without much prospect of leaving them to settle it between themselves."[a]

We are informed that on the 12th inst. a treaty of triple alliance was signed between France, England and Turkey,[79] but that, notwithstanding the personal application of the Sultan to the Grand Mufti,[b] the latter supported by the *corps* of the Ulemas, refused to issue his *fetva*[80] sanctioning the stipulation about the changes in the situation of the Christians in Turkey,[81] as being in contradiction with the precepts of the Koran. This intelligence must be looked upon as being the more important, as it caused Lord Derby to make the following observation:

"I will only express my earnest anxiety that the Government will state whether there is any truth in the report that has been circulated during the last few days that in this convention entered into between England, France and Turkey, there are articles which will be of a nature to establish a protectorate on our part as objectionable at least, as that which, on the part of Russia, we have protested against."[c]

The Times of to-day, while declaring that the policy of the Government is directly opposed to that of Lord Derby adds:

---

[a] *The Times*, No. 21700, March 28, 1854, leader.— *Ed.*
[b] Arif Hikmet Bey.— *Ed.*
[c] The Earl of Derby's speech in the House of Lords on March 27, 1854. *The Times*, No. 21700, March 28, 1854.— *Ed.*

5*

"We should deeply regret if the bigotry of the Mufti or the Ulemas succeeded in opposing any serious resistance to this policy."[a]

In order to understand both the nature of the relations between the Turkish Government and the spiritual authorities of Turkey, and the difficulties in which the former is at present involved, with respect to the question of a protectorate over the Christian subjects of the Porte, that question which ostensibly lies at the bottom of all the actual complications in the East, it is necessary to cast a retrospective glance at its past history and development.

The Koran and the Mussulman legislation emanating from it reduce the geography and ethnography of the various people to the simple and convenient distinction of two nations and of two countries; those of the Faithful and of the Infidels. The Infidel is "*harby*," i.e. the enemy. Islamism proscribes the nation of the Infidels, constituting a state of permanent hostility between the Mussulman and the unbeliever. In that sense the corsair-ships of the Berber States[82] were the holy fleet of Islam. How, then, is the existence of Christian subjects of the Porte to be reconciled with the Koran?

"If a town," says the Mussulman legislation, "surrenders by capitulation, and its habitants consent to become *rayahs*, that is, subjects of a Mussulman prince without abandoning their creed, they have to pay the *kharatch* (capitation tax), when they obtain a truce with the faithful, and it is not permitted any more to confiscate their estates than to take away their houses.... In this case their old churches form part of their property, with permission to worship therein. But they are not allowed to erect new ones. They have only authority for repairing them, and to reconstruct their decayed portions. At certain epochs commissaries delegated by the provincial governors are to visit the churches and sanctuaries of the Christians, in order to ascertain that no new buildings have been added under pretext of repairs. If a town is conquered by force, the inhabitants retain their churches, but only as places of abode or refuge, without permission to worship."[b]

Constantinople having surrendered by capitulation, as in like manner has the greater portion of European Turkey, the Christians there enjoy the privilege of living as *rayahs*, under the Turkish Government. This privilege they have exclusively by virtue of their agreeing to accept the Mussulman protection. It is, therefore, owing to this circumstance alone, that the Christians submit to be governed by the Mussulmans according to Mussul-

[a] *The Times*, No. 21700, March 28, 1854, leader.— *Ed.*

[b] Here and below Marx quotes documents on the situation of Christian subjects in the Ottoman Empire from César Famin, *Histoire de la rivalité et du protectorat des églises chrétiennes en Orient*, pp. 12, 13.— *Ed.*

man law, that the patriarch of Constantinople,[a] their spiritual chief, is at the same time their political representative and their Chief Justice. Wherever, in the Ottoman Empire, we find an agglomeration of Greek *rayahs,* the Archbishops and Bishops are by law members of the Municipal Councils, and, under the direction of the patriarch, [watch] over the repartition of the taxes imposed upon the Greeks. The patriarch is responsible to the Porte as to the conduct of his co-religionists. Invested with the right of judging the rayahs of his Church, he delegates this right to the metropolitans and bishops, in the limits of their dioceses, their sentences being obligatory for the executive officers, kadis, etc., of the Porte to carry out. The punishments which they have the right to pronounce are fines, imprisonment, the bastinade, and exile. Besides, their own church gives them the power of excommunication. Independent of the produce of the fines, they receive variable taxes on the civil and commercial law-suits. Every hierarchic scale among the clergy has its moneyed price. The patriarch pays to the Divan a heavy tribute in order to obtain his investiture, but he sells, in his turn, the archbishoprics and bishoprics to the clergy of his worship. The latter indemnify themselves by the sale of subaltern dignities and the tribute exacted from the popes. These, again, sell by retail the power they have bought from their superiors, and traffic in all acts of their ministry, such as baptisms, marriages, divorces, and testaments.

It is evident from this *exposé* that this fabric of theocracy over the Greek Christians of Turkey, and the whole structure of their society, has its keystone in the subjection of the rayah under the Koran, which, in its turn, by treating them as infidels—i.e., as a nation only in a religious sense—sanctioned the combined spiritual and temporal power of their priests. Then, if you abolish their subjection under the Koran by a civil emancipation, you cancel at the same time their subjection to the clergy, and provoke a revolution in their social, political and religious relations, which, in the first instance, must inevitably hand them over to Russia. If you supplant the Koran by a *code civil,* you must occidentalize the entire structure of Byzantine society.

Having described the relations between the Mussulman and his Christian subject, the question arises, what are the relations between the Mussulman and the unbelieving foreigner?

As the Koran treats all foreigners as foes, nobody will dare to present himself in a Mussulman country without having taken his

---

[a] Anthinos.— *Ed.*

precautions. The first European merchants, therefore, who risked the chances of commerce with such a people, contrived to secure themselves an exceptional treatment and privileges originally personal, but afterward extended to their whole nation. Hence the origin of capitulations. Capitulations are imperial diplomas, letters of privilege, octroyed by the Porte to different European nations, and authorizing their subjects to freely enter Mohammedan countries, and there to pursue in tranquillity their affairs, and to practice their worship. They differ from treaties in this essential point that they are not reciprocal acts contradictorily debated between the contracting parties, and accepted by them on the condition of mutual advantages and concessions. On the contrary, the capitulations are one-sided concessions on the part of the Government granting them, in consequence of which they may be revoked at its pleasure. The Porte has, indeed, at several times nullified the privileges granted to one nation, by extending them to others; or repealed them altogether by refusing to continue their application. This precarious character of the capitulations made them an eternal source of disputes, of complaints on the part of Embassadors, and of a prodigious exchange of contradictory notes and firmans revived at the commencement of every new reign.

It was from these capitulations that arose the right of a *protectorate* of foreign powers, not over the Christian subjects of the Porte—the rayahs—but over their co-religionists visiting Turkey or residing there as foreigners. The first power that obtained such a protectorate was France. The capitulations between France and the Ottoman Porte made in 1535, under Soliman the Great[a] and Francis I; in 1604 under Ahmed I and Henry IV; and in 1673 under Mohammed IV and Louis XIV, were renewed, confirmed, recapitulated, and augmented in the compilation of 1740, called "ancient and recent capitulations and treaties between the Court of France and the Ottoman Porte, renewed and augmented in the year 1740, A.D., and 1153 of the Hegira, translated (the first official translation sanctioned by the Porte) at Constantinople by M. Deval, Secretary Interpreter of the King, and his first Dragoman at the Ottoman Porte." Art. 32 of this agreement constitutes the right of France to a protectorate over all monasteries professing the Frank religion to whatever nation they may belong, and of the Frank visitors of the Holy Places.

---

[a] Soliman I the Magnificent.— *Ed.*

Russia was the first power that, in 1774, inserted the capitulation, imitated after the example of France, into a *treaty*—the treaty of Kainardji.[83] Thus, in 1802, Napoleon thought fit to make the existence and maintenance of the capitulation the subject of an article of treaty, and to give it the character of synallagmatic contract.

In what relation then does the question of the Holy Places stand with the protectorate?

The question of the Holy Shrines is the question of a protectorate over the religious Greek Christian communities settled at Jerusalem, and over the buildings possessed by them on the holy ground, and especially over the Church of the Holy Sepulcher. It is to be understood that possession here does not mean proprietorship, which is denied to the Christians by the Koran, but only the right of *usufruct*. This right of *usufruct* excludes by no means the other communities from worshipping in the same place; the possessors having no other privilege besides that of keeping the *keys*, of repairing and entering the edifices, of kindling the holy lamp, of cleaning the rooms with the broom, and of spreading the carpets, which is an Oriental symbol of possession. In the same manner now, in which Christianity culminates at the Holy Place, the question of the protectorate is there found to have its highest ascension.

Parts of the Holy Places and of the Church of the Holy Sepulcher are possessed by the Latins, the Greeks, the Armenians, the Abyssinians, the Syrians, and the Copts. Between all these diverse pretendents there originated a conflict. The sovereigns of Europe who saw, in this religious quarrel, a question of their respective influences in the Orient, addressed themselves in the first instance to the masters of the soil, to fanatic and greedy Pashas, who abused their position. The Ottoman Porte and its agents adopting a most troublesome *système de bascule*[a] gave judgment in turns favorable to the Latins, Greeks, and Armenians, asking and receiving gold from all hands, and laughing at each of them. Hardly had the Turks granted a firman, acknowledging the right of the Latins to the possession of a contested place, when the Armenians presented themselves with a heavier purse, and instantly obtained a contradictory firman. Same tactics with respect to the Greeks, who knew, besides, as officially recorded in different firmans of the Porte and "*hudjets*" (judgments) of its agents, how to procure false and apocryph titles. On other

---

[a] System of weights.— *Ed.*

occasions the decisions of the Sultan's Government were frustrated
by the cupidity and ill-will of the Pashas and subaltern agents in
Syria. Then it became necessary to resume negotiations, to appoint
fresh commissaries, and to make new sacrifices of money. What
the Porte formerly did from pecuniary considerations, in our days
it has done from fear, with a view to obtain protection and favor.
Having done justice to the reclamations of France and the Latins,
it hastened to make the same conditions to Russia and the Greeks,
thus attempting to escape from a storm which it felt powerless to
encounter. There is no sanctuary, no chapel, no stone of the
Church of the Holy Sepulcher, that had been left unturned for
the purpose of constituting a quarrel between the different
Christian communities.

Around the Holy Sepulcher we find an assemblage of all the
various sects of Christianity, behind the religious pretensions of
whom are concealed as many political and national rivalries.

Jerusalem and the Holy Places are inhabited by nations
professing religions: the Latins, the Greeks, Armenians, Copts,
Abyssinians, and Syrians. There are 2,000 Greeks, 1,000 Latins,
350 Armenians, 100 Copts, 20 Syrians, and 20 Abyssinians—
3,490. In the Ottoman Empire we find 13,730,000 Greeks,
2,400,000 Armenians, and 900,000 Latins. Each of these is again
subdivided. The Greek Church, of which I treated above, the one
acknowledging the Patriarch of Constantinople, essentially differs
from the Greco-Russian, whose chief spiritual authority is the
Czar; and from the Hellens, of whom the King and the Synod of
Athens are the chief authorities. Similarly, the Latins are
subdivided into the Roman Catholics, United Greeks, and Maro-
nites; and the Armenians into Gregorian and Latin Armenians—
the same distinctions holding good with the Copts and Abyssinians. The three prevailing religious nationalities at the Holy
Places are the Greeks, the Latins, and the Armenians. The Latin
Church may be said to represent principally Latin races, the Greek
Church, Slav, Turko-Slav, and Hellenic races; and the other
churches, Asiatic and African races.

Imagine all these conflicting peoples beleaguering the Holy
Sepulcher, the battle conducted by the monks, and the ostensible
object of their rivalry being a star from the grotto of Bethlehem, a
tapestry, a key of a sanctuary, an altar, a shrine, a chair, a
cushion—any ridiculous precedence!

In order to understand such a monastical crusade it is
indispensable to consider firstly the manner of their living, and
secondly, the mode of their habitation.

"All the religious rubbish of the different nations," says a recent traveler,[a] "live at Jerusalem separated from each other, hostile and jealous, a nomade population, incessantly recruited by pilgrimage or decimated by the plague and oppressions. The European dies or returns to Europe after some years; the pashas and their guards go to Damascus or Constantinople; and the Arabs fly to the desert. Jerusalem is but a place where every one arrives to pitch his tent and where nobody remains. Everybody in the holy city gets his livelihood from his religion—the Greeks or Armenians from the 12,000 or 13,000 pilgrims who yearly visit Jerusalem, and the Latins from the subsidies and alms of their co-religionists of France, Italy, etc."[b]

Besides their monasteries and sanctuaries, the Christian nations possess at Jerusalem small habitations or cells, annexed to the Church of the Holy Sepulcher, and occupied by the monks, who have to watch day and night that holy abode. At certain periods these monks are relieved in their duty by their brethren. These cells have but one door, opening into the interior of the Temple, while the monk guardians receive their food from without, through some wicket. The doors of the Church are closed, and guarded by Turks, who don't open them except for money, and close it according to their caprice or cupidity.

The quarrels between churchmen are the most venomous, said Mazarin. Now fancy these churchmen, who not only have to live upon, but live in, these sanctuaries together!

To finish the picture, be it remembered that the fathers of the Latin Church, almost exclusively composed of Romans, Sardinians, Neapolitans, Spaniards and Austrians, are all of them jealous of the French protectorate, and would like to substitute that of Austria, Sardinia or Naples, the Kings of the two latter countries both assuming the title of King of Jerusalem; and that the sedentary population of Jerusalem numbers about 15,500 souls, of whom 4,000 are Mussulmans and 8,000 Jews. The Mussulmans, forming about a fourth part of the whole, and consisting of Turks, Arabs and Moors, are, of course, the masters in every respect, as they are in no way affected with the weakness of their Government at Constantinople. Nothing equals the misery and the sufferings of the Jews at Jerusalem, inhabiting the most filthy quarter of the town, called *hareth-el-yahoud*, the quarter of dirt, between the Zion and the Moriah, where their synagogues are situated—the constant objects of Mussulman oppression and

---

[a] J. Mislin.— *Ed.*

[b] C. Famin, *Histoire de la rivalité...*, pp. 49, 50; Famin cites the phrase "Everybody in the holy city ... Italy, etc." from J. Mislin, *Les Saints Lieux...*, T. II, p. 291.— *Ed.*

intolerance, insulted by the Greeks, persecuted by the Latins, and living only upon the scanty alms transmitted by their European brethren. The Jews, however, are not natives, but from different and distant countries, and are only attracted to Jerusalem by the desire of inhabiting the Valley of Jehosaphat, and to die in the very places where the redemptor is to be expected.

"Attending their death," says a French author, "they suffer and pray. Their regards turned to that mountain of Moriah, where once rose the temple of Solomon, and which they dare not approach, they shed tears on the misfortunes of Zion, and their dispersion over the world."[a]

To make these Jews more miserable, England and Prussia appointed, in 1840, an Anglican bishop at Jerusalem, whose avowed object is their conversion. He was dreadfully thrashed in 1845, and sneered at alike by Jews, Christians and Turks. He may, in fact, be stated to have been the first and only cause of a union between all the religions at Jerusalem.

It will now be understood why the common worship of the Christians at the Holy Places resolves itself into a continuance of desperate Irish rows between the diverse sections of the faithful; but that, on the other hand, these sacred rows merely conceal a profane battle, not only of nations but of races; and that the Protectorate of the Holy Places which appears ridiculous to the Occident but all important to the Orientals is one of the phases of the Oriental question incessantly reproduced, constantly stifled, but never solved.

Written on March 28, 1854

First published in the *New-York Daily Tribune*, No. 4054, April 15; reprinted in the *New-York Semi-Weekly Tribune*, No. 928, April 18, 1854

Signed: *Karl Marx*

Reproduced from the *New-York Daily Tribune*

---

[a] C. Famin, op. cit., pp. 54-55.— *Ed.*

Frederick Engels

THE FORTRESS OF KRONSTADT[84]

Ever since Sir Charles Napier set sail for the Baltic, with the First Lord of the Admiralty's "full permission to declare war", the more sanguine portion of the British public expect shortly to hear of Kronstadt bombarded, the approaches to St. Petersburg forced, and who knows? perhaps even the Union Jack hoisted on the glittering spire of the Russian Admiralty Palace.

There is a very correct idea at the bottom of these anticipations; it is this, that Kronstadt *is* the decisive point for any naval attack against Russia in the Baltic. Take Kronstadt, and St. Petersburg is at your feet, the Russian Navy exists no longer, and Russia is reduced to what she was before Peter the Great. If England *has* the forces in the Baltic required for such a feat, and if these forces should fritter away their strength in attacks against minor points, more than might be absolutely necessary, they would commit a blunder of the first magnitude, decisive in its effects perhaps for two or three campaigns to come. But if *we* know the vital importance of Kronstadt, the Russians know it also, and have acted up to their knowledge. That key of Russia has been surrounded by double and triple armour, bristling with something like a thousand guns.

It is well known that Kronstadt takes up the south-eastern angle of a small island,[a] about five miles in length, which closes up the narrowing portion of the Gulf of Finland, about 16 miles from the mouth of the Neva. The water on both sides of the island is generally very shallow, having only two channels navigable for

---

[a] Kotlin.— *Ed.*

sea-going vessels. The one passing to the north of the island has a depth of not less than four fathoms[a] about two or three miles distant from its northern shore, bends round at four miles from its eastern extremity, approaching this latter to within 1,400 yards, but losing about a fathom in its depth of water. Thus the whole of the north-eastern coast of the island is out of cannon range for any men-of-war coming round by this channel, except the western and eastern extremities only. These alone are therefore fortified, the first by the forts *Katharine, Alexander* and *Michael,* the second by the walls of the town itself and by two batteries erected on the sands, about 1,000 yards in advance; the larger one of these batteries, however, is reported to be in ruins. Abreast of the north shore of the island, between its eastern and western defences, and fully a mile from the shore, another battery is constructed on the sands, which however is still out of gun-shot range from the four-fathom channel.

This northern passage, then, from its general distance from the defences, from the very intricate navigation it offers, and from the considerable shallowing of its south-eastern extremity, may be considered useless for a serious attack upon Kronstadt. Under circumstances where a dispersion of forces is to a certain extent not likely to bring on disastrous results, it may serve for sending a number of the lighter ships round the island, where, after silencing the not very formidable fire of the East Battery, they might take up a very convenient station for bombarding the town. Kronstadt, containing not only the chief naval magazines and dock-yards of Russia in the Baltic, but also plenty of timber in private hands, is full of combustible materials, and a few lucky hits with shell-guns might create a conflagration destroying in one night the naval stores amassed during years. Whether the taking up of such a position by a sufficient number of light men-of-war is actually possible, a close survey of the state of matters on the spot, combined with renewed soundings, must show; whether it is advisable, will depend upon the balance of forces; here we can only state what may, even at a distance, appear feasible from a comparison of the best evidence that can be collected.

The main line of attack, then, remains the South Channel, leading to the Great and Little Roads, otherwise called the Narrows. Here the four-fathom channel, several miles wide off the north-western point of the island, suddenly contracts to about a mile in width at two miles distance from the inner harbour, and

---

[a] 1 fathom=6 feet=1.82 metres.— *Ed.*

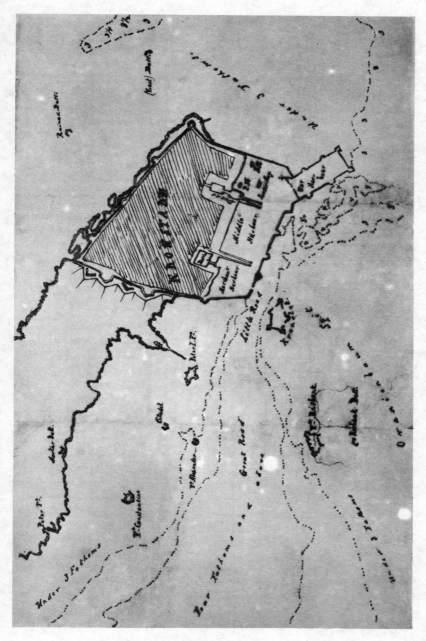

Plan of Kronstadt drawn by Engels while writing the article
"The Fortress of Kronstadt"

thence forms an extremely acute angle, the apex of which is situated in front of the man-of-war harbour. Here a narrow bar, passing from the great sand-bank of Oranienbaum to the island, cuts the channel off and reduces its extreme depth to $3^1/_2$ fathoms. The Russians have taken good care to preserve this natural fortification for their man-of-war harbour, although a little dredging would remove it. This four-fathom channel, then, the central passage of which is nowhere less than $4^1/_2$ fathoms deep, and admits the largest men-of-war, is the line of approach to Kronstadt, and the decisive struggle must take place in its apex, which, for a mile and a half, is nowhere more than 400 yards wide.

The fortifications which defend this channel are of all sorts, from the antediluvian buildings of Peter the Great, to the most modern and formidable constructions with two or three tiers of guns one above the other. It is remarkable that the most important points are defended by fortifications of old and faulty construction: *this is the weak side of Kronstadt.* The old fortifications are small bastioned works, with guns firing from behind an open parapet, and with few or no casemated guns at all; with exceedingly small and narrow bastions, and therefore carrying a number of guns exceedingly small in proportion to their extent of frontage. It must, besides, be stated that one half of their guns is generally directed towards shallow water from which at the very utmost a gun-boat attack could be expected. But to such fortifications even gun-boats were formidable.

The modern constructions, on the contrary, are planned upon the system which *Montalembert* first introduced and which since, with more or less modification, has been generally adopted, especially for coast and harbour defences. Besides Kronstadt, Cherbourg and Sevastopol may be quoted as examples of its extensive application for this latter purpose. These constructions are distinguished by their two or three tiers of guns ranging one above the other, the lower tiers of guns standing in casemates, small vaulted rooms, as it were, where both guns and men are as much protected from the enemy's fire as it can be done. The upper tier of guns alone stands behind a parapet not covered in, but from their elevated station which commands the upper decks of the largest three-deckers, are well protected against the effects of shot. The trial of an attack will show, whether these forts have actually been constructed solidly enough to bear the concussion of their own and the effect of the enemy's fire; but if they are, they will prove the hardest nuts to crack.

We may distinguish three lines of fortifications around the Kronstadt channel.

The first, or outer, line embraces in a semi-circle the mouth of the Great Road, or that part of the four-fathom channel which is from one mile to half a mile in width. The right, or northern, wing of the position is formed by the *Peter Fort*, an insignificant lunette on the island, about 1,400 yards from the deep water channel; a *mortar battery*, also on the island, half a mile to the east, which may be considered as almost useless, and the *Fort Constantine*, a strong lunette closed to the rear, built on the sands, within 1,000 yards from the edge of deep water, exactly in front of the mortar battery. This fort is of modern construction and carries 50 guns in two tiers. It serves to defend the outer approaches, and may become troublesome to a fleet while forming; but if once passed, one half of its guns become useless. The centre of the first line is made up by *Fort Alexander* (not the one on the north end of the island, mentioned before); a semi-circular building erected in three fathoms water within four hundred yards of the deep channel where it narrows to half a mile. This fort therefore sweeps the channel from side to side, and small as it looks on plans and charts, it carries no less than seventy two guns in three tiers. If it be of sufficiently solid construction, and with well-ventilated casemates so as to draw off the smoke, this tower-like fort will give enough to do to a couple of three-deckers. Behind it lies the old *Citadel*, a lunette the insignificance of which is proved by the very existence of the new fort, which intercepts the fire of one half of its guns.

The left or southern wing, finally, is formed by the *Risbank Fort* and *Battery*, situated south of the entrance to the Great Road. This fort, constructed in the last century, has undergone a modernizing process, in consequence of which part of its guns are disposed in two tiers and their total number is increased to fifty. But for all that it occupies a far larger area than the modern forts, offering a frontage towards the roads of some 300 yards, which frontage, besides, is enfiladed, partially from the deep water channel, and entirely by a position which vessels of lighter draft may take up in $3\frac{1}{2}$ to 3 fathoms water within half a mile westwards. To obviate this, the *Risbank Battery* has been built 600 yards to the rear, but in a position little adapted for that purpose. The Risbank Fort lies exactly a mile south from *Fort Alexander*, and both sweep the entrance to the Great Road with cross fire.

This first line of defences would not in itself prove very formidable, if it were not materially supported by the more distant fire of the second line. The second line protects the whole of the Great Road along with the entrance to the Little Road. It consists of the two flanking works of *Fort Peter the First* (old, badly constructed, a sort of crown-work situated half a mile east of Fort Alexander, and carrying on a frontage of 250 yards only 24 guns), *Kronslot* (bastioned old-fashioned work of five fronts, two of which look towards the shallow water and are therefore useless, carrying, although 400 yards in its longest diagonal, no more than 36 guns) and lastly, the fortified western wall of the *Merchant Harbour* in the centre. This wall, projecting from the island of Kronstadt itself, comes down to the very edge of the deep channel with which it forms a right angle, and which is here but 300 yards wide. It carries 70 guns and 12 mortars, part of which however appear so placed as to have little effect upon the shipping, and offers, in conjunction with both the main fronts of Peter I Fort and two fronts of Kronslot, a most effective cross fire over the inner half of the Great Road, where because of the obstacles created by the fire of the first line, and the narrowness of the channel, it must be extremely difficult for any ships but screw-steamers to take up a good position in sufficient force.

The third line, the direct defence of the Little or Inner Road, is formed, on the south side of the channel, by a third (the North East) front of Kronslot, and on the north and east side by the fortified walls of the Merchant, Middle, and Man-of-war harbours. The latter, projecting at an obtuse angle at the eastern end of the Middle Harbour, rakes the whole of the Little Road, while the south wall of the Merchant and Middle harbours protects it by a front fire. Both walls are flanked by several bastions, fortified gates and other projections. The width of the deep water channel, here, being nowhere greater than 250 yards, the fighting would be very murderous, but it is hardly to be doubted that before ships could penetrate so far, Kronstadt would have to capitulate. The central work of this third line, and the only one which may ever have any practical utility, is *Fort Menchikoff*, the first bastion, from the west, on the Merchant Harbour south wall. This bastion has been reconstructed into a tower of imposing proportions, carrying 44 guns in *four tiers* above one another one half of which enfilade the greater part of the Little and Great roads, the other half appearing, from the direction of their embrasures, almost useless. Whether the four tiers of guns will not prove too heavy for the narrow foundation of the building, remains to be seen.

We may add that on the land-side Kronstadt is fortified by regularly bastioned fronts, requiring a siege in due form to be forced; and such a siege in the swampy ground of the little island, with only a fleet for base of operations, offers very great difficulties. If Kronstadt is to be taken, it must be done from the sea.

It is understood that we could only describe the permanent fortifications such as they existed according to the latest surveys and military reports. There may have been some alterations during the last few years, but it is not probable that they have been very important.

To recapitulate. The fate of any attack against Kronstadt must be decided in the Great Road, and here the only fortifications that can effectually play against the attacking fleet, are Forts Alexander, Peter I, Risbank, two fronts of Kronslot, the western Harbour Wall, and Fort Menchikoff. Altogether they may bring 350 guns at once to bear upon the attack, most of them well protected by walls and vaults, and firing through narrow embrasures. The other batteries are either directed towards other points of attack, or they are insignificant, or they are not within effective range. The question is: Can a sufficient naval force be brought up this narrow and intricate channel, to face both the northern and southern fronts of defence and to silence their fire, while that force is itself exposed to a raking fire from the Harbour Wall, Fort Menchikoff and Kronslot? Naval men may answer that question, unless they prefer to wait till the actual trial has been made. From what little we have had occasion to learn of naval tactics, we should say that here, if anywhere, is the point where the superiority of screw-ships of the line can produce results which to sailing-ships and paddle-steamers would appear equally unattainable.

The great weakness of Kronstadt, we repeat it, are the forts of old construction. They occupy the best positions and the largest portion of available space with the least possible effect of fire. If Risbank has been improved, Peter I and Kronslot remain inefficient. They might be silenced with comparative ease, perhaps even occupied, and in that case might be used to bombard the town. But from the moment ships have penetrated as far as between Alexander and Risbank, they have the town within shell-range, and can do immense mischief, unless sufficiently occupied by the forts.

Written at the end of March (not later than 30), 1854

First published in: Marx and Engels, *Works*, Second Russian Edition, Vol. 44, Moscow, 1977

Printed from the manuscript

Published in English for the first time

Karl Marx

BRITISH FINANCES.—
THE TROUBLES AT PRESTON[85]

London, Friday, March 31, 1854

The Income Tax bill has been passed.[86] Sir G. Pakington spoke against it plainly and justly, although in a dull manner, observing that the recent publications of the Blue Books and of the secret and confidential correspondence had thrown quite a new light on the past financial policy of the Chancellor of the Exchequer. Mr. Gladstone brought in a peace budget on the 18th April, 1853, when he [must] have been quite sure of war being imminent.[87] Three days before he made his statement the Coalition had received from Colonel Rose the information that

"Prince Menchikoff had tried to exact a promise from the Grand Vizier, before he made known to him the nature of his mission and of his demands, that he should make a formal promise that he would not reveal them to the British and French representatives."[a]

They were also aware, by the secret correspondence, of the Emperor's[b] intention to kill the dying man lest he should slip through his fingers.[c] With this information in his hands the unctuous Puseyite[88] comes forward and addresses the House:

"If you will adopt the income tax for seven years, I will only ask you for 7d. in the pound for the first two years; I will ask 6d. in the pound for the next two years; and for the last three years I will only ask 5d. in the pound, and then the income tax will expire."

---

[a] G. Pakington's speech in the House of Commons on March 30, 1854. *The Times*, No. 21703, March 31, 1854.— *Ed.*

[b] Nicholas I.— *Ed.*

[c] See this volume, p. 77.— *Ed.*

The income tax, as your readers will remember,[a] Mr. Gladstone described as a mighty engine of war that must be got rid of in these times of peace. This he said with the knowledge that war was almost inevitable, and that it would be necessary to double the tax of 7d. in the pound before twelve months had elapsed. It is now 1s. 2d. in the pound. If anybody should tell me that the overscrupulous Chancellor of the Exchequer deluded himself as to the position of affairs, I reply that only last Monday week[b] a fall in the funds occurred, because the stock jobbers said that the publication of the secret papers proved to demonstration that the Czar had determined to pursue his schemes, and that no trust could be placed in his most positive assertions. The members of the "Cabinet of all the Talents" must be supposed to possess at least equal perspicacity with the members of the Stock Exchange.

At the same time that the *Duns Scotus* of the Coalition, the Doctor Subtilissimus,[89] proposed his financial schemes for the conversion of the funds, and thus prepared, notwithstanding the warnings he received, an emptiness of the Treasury at the very moment of the "catastrophe". The balances in the Exchequer were as follows, in the years named:

1844	£6,254,113	1847	£8,457,691	1850	£9,[245,676][c]
1845	8,452,090	1848	8,105,561	1851	8,[381,637]
1846	9,131,282	1849	9,748,539	1852	8,[841,822]

By the commencement of 1853 Mr. Gladstone had contrived to reduce it to £4,485,230, and soon there will be no balance at all, as this ingenious *financier* has to take back the remainder of the South Sea stock[90] at £100, when it can hardly be sold on 'change at £85.

This financial policy of the Coalition perfectly t[akes up] with their diplomatic policy, which "thanks" the Czar for confiding to them his plans of partition; with their parliamentary policy, which always told the House the contrary of their information in hand; and with their military policy, which forced Omer Pasha to inaction till the Czar had completed his preparations for invasion, which dispatches the troops by steamers and the horses by sail

---

[a] Marx, "Feargus O'Connor.—Ministerial Defeats.—The Budget" (present edition, Vol. 12).— *Ed.*

[b] March 20, 1854.— *Ed.*

[c] The figures are taken from Pakington's speech published in *The Times*, No. 21703, March 31, 1854.— *Ed.*

vessels, retains the officers at London, and disembarks soldiers at Constantinople, and thinks fit to occupy neither Odessa nor the Crimea, nor Finland, nor the mouths of the Danube, nor any point threatening the Russians, but Constantinople, of all other places, in order not to crush the Cossack,[a] but to teach at this momentous crisis both the Mussulman and the Byzantine priest the occidental law and civil equality.

Notwithstanding the strong opposition of the Irish members, the House seems resolved to, proceed with Mr. Chambers's motion, and to appoint a Committee of Inquiry for the practices and household arrangements of the nunneries. The principal plea on which Mr. Chambers's motion intends to be based is the seclusion of girls forcibly held from their natural and legitimate protectors. The middle classes of England shudder at the probability of girls being kidnapped for nunneries, but their justice, shown in a recent case, becomes impotent when girls are kidnapped for satisfying the lust of aristocrats or caprice of cotton lords. Last week a girl of sixteen had been lured away from her parents, enticed into a Lancashire factory, and kept there night and day, made to sleep there, and take her meals there, locked up as in a prison. When her father discovered what had become of his child, he was not allowed to see her, but was driven away from the factory by the police. In this case the Factory law was violated, the law of personal liberty, the law that gives the father the custody of his child under age, the very right of *habeas corpus* was set at nought. A gross and flagrant case of abduction had been committed. But how did the magistrates act in this case, when the disconsolate father appealed to them for redress? Their answer was: "They could do nothing in the matter."

Mr. Thom. Duncombe presented a petition, signed within 24 hours by above 7,600 inhabitants of the borough of Preston, complaining of the manner in which the laws for the maintenance of peace and order were administered by the local authorities in that borough. He gave notice that he should move for a committee of inquiry into the subject immediately after the Easter recess.

"The agitators of Preston, the great fomentors of the strike—the men who pretended to form a new estate of the realm, and to be the nursing fathers of the Labor Parliament, have at length received a check. Some dozen of them have been arrested and examined before the local magistrates on a charge of conspiracy, released on bail and sent before the Liverpool assizes".[b]

---

[a] Nicholas I.— *Ed.*
[b] "The Week", *The Morning Post*, No. 25033, March 27, 1854.— *Ed.*

Such are the words in which *The Morning Post* announces an event[91] which I was prevented from writing about earlier by the pressure of other matter. The charge against the leaders rests upon the fact that the masters had sent to Manchester and induced men to come down to Preston. They were mostly Irishmen. The people met them at the railway station, where they presented a scene of misery and wretchedness. About fifty-four of them were persuaded to go to the Farmer's Arms[a] where they were regaled all day, and, having consented to return, were escorted in the evening to the railway station amidst the exclamations of 15,000 persons. The employers got hold of seven of these people and brought them back to Preston to convict Mr. Cowell and his colleagues of conspiracy. Now, if we consider the [real facts] of the case, there remains no doubt on the question who are the real conspirators.[b]

In 1847 the Preston cotton lords reduced wages on a solemn promise to restore them as soon as trade should have become brisk. In 1853, the year of prosperity, they refused to keep their word. The working men of four mills struck, and were supported by the contributions of the remaining at work. The masters now conspired together that they would lock their mills, and entered each into a £5,000 bond to enforce their conspiracy.[92] The operatives then appealed for support to the other towns of Lancashire, and that support was given. The employers had sent emissaries to persuade and incite the cotton lords of other towns to lock out their hands, and succeeded in their endeavor. Not content with this, a vast subs[cription was] opened among them to counterbalance the [subscription] of the operatives. When they found that all these efforts were of no avail, they sent their agents far and near to induce laborers and their families, needlewomen, and paupers from the workhouses of England and Ir[eland to come] to Preston. Finding the surplus did not flow in fast enough for their wishes, they tried to provoke the people to a breach of the peace. They aggravated them by their insolence. They forbade meetings in the Marsh, but the people held meetings in Blackstone Edge and other interdicted localities. They introduced one hundred new police, they swore in special constables,[93] they turned out the fire-brigade, they kept troops under arms, and

---

[a] The premises of the workers' committee during the Preston weavers' strike.— *Ed.*

[b] Below Marx uses data from E. Jones' article "The Cotton Law of Preston. Who Are the Real Conspirators?", *The People's Paper*, No. 99, March 25, 1854.— *Ed.*

went so far as to read the riot act[94] in order to provoke a riot. Such was the conspiracy of the masters [but] they were defeated in each of their attempts. Notwithstanding these facts, an indictment of conspiracy is charged, not against the masters, but against the men. Besides, there is a special case bringing the masters under the law of conspiracy. The men of a certain factory resumed the work. The masters' committee and the men's committee alike called for explanations. The men published a placard to the effect that they had gone to work on condition of payment at a certain rate. The masters' committee threatened proceedings against the master[a] of that mill to recover £5,000 as penalty on a bond given to support the masters' strike. The mill-owner thereupon said something which, being a flat contradiction of men's statement, occasioned them all to withdraw. If [making] of this bond of £5,000 was a conspiracy in the terms of the law, the menace to enforce it was still more so. But this is not all. The very indictment of the men's leaders was brought about by a conspiracy committed by the magisterial benches at Preston. According to *The Times*[b] itself, the magistrates got up evidence, sought for it, brought up their surplus slaves[c] in cabs to their council chamber, dreading the publicity of the town hall, there to arrange their evidence, and there, in the dead of night to pounce on their intended victims.

The expectations of these little Napoleons of Lancashire [were,] however, set at naught by the good sense of the working people, who neither allowed themselves to be provoked into a breach of peace, nor to be frightened into [submission] to the dictates of the Preston *parvenus.*

A public meeting was held in London on Wednesday night in St. Martin's Hall, Long Acre, for the purpose of affording the working classes of the metropolis an opportunity of expressing their opinion on the conduct of the Preston masters. The following two resolutions were unanimously accepted:

"That the present Lord Chancellor of England, when Baron Rolfe[d], [and] in his capacity of judge, laid down the law thus:

"That if there were no other object than to persuade people that it was their interest not to work except for certain wages, and not to work under certain regulations, complied with in a peaceful manner, it was not illegal.

"That the operatives of Preston have for a period of thirty weeks been engaged

---

[a] John Swainson.— *Ed.*
[b] "The Wages' Movement", *The Times*, No. 21694, March 21, 1854.— *Ed.*
[c] Recruited workers.— *Ed.*
[d] Rolfe, Robert Monsey, Baron Cranworth.— *Ed.*

in a contest with their employers, and during the whole of that time have conducted themselves in the most peaceable and orderly manner.

"That, notwithstanding these facts, four[a] members of the Operatives' Committee have been committed to take their trial at the present Liverpool Assizes on a charge of conspiracy, although neither violence nor intimidation has been proved or even charged against them.

"This meeting is therefore of opinion that the conduct of the manufacturers and magistrates of Preston is reprehensible; that they have been guilty of an unwarrantable assumption of power; that they have destroyed at once the equality of the law and personal freedom; and that such proceedings ought to be condemned by the unanimous voice of the people.

"That the sympathy and help of the entire of the working classes of the United Kingdom should be devoted to the vindication of justice and the maintenance of right. This meeting, therefore, pledges itself to an extraordinary and continuous support of the Preston operatives in their present trying position, and earnestly exhorts all who have an interest in the elevation of labor to join with them in supporting its best interests."[b]

[The] London press generally condemn the proceedings [of the] Preston masters, not from any sense of justice but [from fear] of the probable results. They apprehend that [the] working classes will now understand that the indivi[dual] capitalist who oppresses them is backed by the whole machinery [of state], and that in order to hit the former they [must] deal with the latter.

Written on March 31, 1854   Reproduced from the newspaper

First published in the *New-York Semi-Weekly Tribune*, No. 929, April 21, 1854

Signed: *Karl Marx*

---

[a] *The People's Paper* has "eleven".— *Ed.*

[b] The resolution is given according to the article "Prosecution of the Lancashire Leaders" (*The People's Paper*, No. 100, April 1, 1854). *The People's Paper* for April 1, 1854 came out in the evening of March 31 as was then the custom and was used by Marx for this article.— *Ed.*

Frederick Engels

THE RUSSIAN ARMY

TO THE EDITOR OF *THE DAILY NEWS*[95]

Sir,—It is getting high time that we should look our enemy straight in the face, to see what sort of an opponent he may turn out to be. The most contradictory opinions are afloat as to the real military strength and capabilities of Russia. Overrated by some, underrated by others, the reality appears still to be hidden by a veil, removable, not by any "Revelations of Russia,"[a] but by the actual events of war only.

Yet there exists a good deal of valuable matter in our western literatures which requires nothing but sifting and combining. Russia herself has contributed plenty of such matter. For Russian military literature makes as much, if not more, use of the French and German languages than of its own. Witness Major Smitt's valuable work on the Polish campaign of 1831, and Col. Tolstoi's account of the invasion of Hungary. The military works written in Russian are decidedly inferior to those written in foreign languages by officers of the Russian army. Mikhailovsky-Danilevsky's and Buturlin's Campaigns of 1812, Lukianovich's Campaign of 1828-29, and similar works, too much resemble the accounts of campaigns which we generally meet with in second-rate French historical works. The sobriety of facts is drowned in floods of inflated bombast, events are distorted according to the exigencies of national vanity, the victories achieved on the field of battle are put into the shade by greater victories achieved on paper by the authors, and detraction from the character of the enemy, whoever he be, predominates from beginning to end.

---

[a] Ch. F. Hennigsen, *Revelations of Russia*, Vols. I-II, London, 1844.— *Ed.*

There is little of that soldierly feeling which knows that there is more merit in defeating a brave than a cowardly enemy, and which makes, for instance, Sir W. Napier's *Peninsular War* so pre-eminently the production, not only of an "officer," but of a "gentleman" also. The necessity of keeping up warlike ardour amongst the Russian population may explain the existence of such a style of writing history. But as soon as a western language is chosen, the thing is different. Europe, then, is to judge, and the publicity of the west would soon scatter to the winds assertions which, in Russia, pass off for gospel truth, because there the opponent has not the right of reply. The tendency to glorify Holy Russia and her Czar remains the same, but the choice of means becomes more limited. Accuracy of fact must be more strictly adhered to; a more sedate and businesslike diction is adopted; and in spite of attempts at distortion which generally betray themselves soon enough, there remains at least enough of positive information to make such a book in many cases an important historical document. If, besides, it should happen to have been written by a man in a relatively independent position, it may even be excellent as a military history, and this is actually the case with Smitt's *History of the Polish War.*

The composition and organisation of the Russian army is known well enough to military men all over Europe. The extreme simplicity of this organisation, as far at least as the "army of operation" is concerned, makes it easy to understand it. The actual difficulty is merely to know how far this organisation has been really carried out, how much of this army exists not merely on paper but can be brought forward against a foreign foe. It is on this point that these Russian military writings in western languages are principally important. National pride prevents their authors, wherever the enemy has been partially successful and offered a lively resistance, from overrating the numbers of combatants on the Russian side. In order to guard the honour of the Russian arms, they must unveil the differences between the real and nominal strength of Russian armies. Smitt's work, which gives the official muster-rolls, is particularly useful for this purpose. Tolstoi's *Hungarian Campaign,* on the contrary, quite in harmony with the proceedings of the Russians in that country, appears to be intended to show off not so much the valour as the formidable and overwhelming numbers of the Russian armies, ready to be launched upon the revolutionary west.

But if we can arrive at something like certainty regarding that part at least of the Russian army which more directly menaces the rest of Europe, it is far more difficult to ascertain the real state of the fleet. We shall, later on, collect whatever information we have met with, but must wait for something more definite until "Charley"[a] gives a better account of it, or sends a few specimens over for home inspection.

The fortificatory system, the preliminary preparation of the theatre of war for defence and attack, is of course very difficult of access in a country like Russia. The coast defences are to a certain degree delineated in charts and plans, and cannot, from their very nature, be kept entirely hidden. Kronstadt and Sevastopol, although many details of military importance are not well known, are yet not half as mysterious places as they appear to some parties. But of the fortifications of Poland, of that very group of fortresses the very existence of which proclaims intentions of offensive war and of conquest, very little is known besides the spots upon which they have been built.[b] Some European war offices may have obtained, by dint of gold, plans of these fortresses from Russian *employés*; if so, they have kept the information for themselves. If the Polish Emigration could procure such plans, which to them should not be impossible, they might, by publishing them, do to Russia a great deal more harm than ever they did.

The Russian army is made up of four great divisions: the great army of operation, the reserves for it, the special and local corps, the Cossacks (amongst which are here comprised all irregular troops, whatever be their origin).[c]

The peculiar circumstances in which Russia is placed require a military organisation totally different from that of all other European countries. While on the south-east, from the Pacific to the Caspian Sea, her frontiers, guarded by deserts and steppes, are exposed to no other irruptions but those of nomadic robber tribes, who on such ground are best met by troops somewhat similar to themselves; while on the Caucasus she has to struggle against a hardy race of mountaineers, best combated by a judicious mixture of regular and irregular forces; her south-western and western frontiers require the immediate presence of a large army organised upon the most regular European footing and equipped with arms equal to those of the western armies it may have to fight. But as it is impossible to maintain permanently

---

[a] Charles Napier.— *Ed.*
[b] For details see this volume, p. 502.— *Ed.*
[c] For details see this volume, pp. 498-501.— *Ed.*

upon the war footing such an army in a country the resources of which are only very partially developed, part of the soldiers have to be dismissed on furlough, to form a reserve for the war. Thus arise the four great divisions of the Russian army.

This organisation of the Russian army, the origin of which may be traced back as far as the first partition of Poland,[96] has been successively developed by the succeeding partitions of that country, the conquests on the Black Sea, the great wars with France; it has been brought to its present state of perfection after the Polish revolution of 1830.

The Great Army of Operation, which is almost exclusively stationed on the European frontier of Russia, is more especially a production of the partition of Poland, the wars with France, and the Polish revolution. Its object is twofold—to maintain in subjection the western, more civilised, and non-Russian portions of the empire, and to hang like a threatening cloud over the west of Europe, ready to come down upon it with thunder and lightning at a moment's notice. How far this object has been, or rather has not been, obtained during the past, is a matter of notoriety. How far it may in the present war be carried out, we shall have to consider by and by.

The grand army of operations or active army (deistvuyushtsheye voisko) consists of eleven corps d'armée, the corps of guards, the corps of grenadiers, six corps of infantry, and three corps of cavalry of reserve.

This whole organisation is imitated from the system introduced by Napoleon. The eight first named corps correspond exactly to the army corps of the French during the great war. The guards and grenadiers appear specially destined to form the general reserves of the army, while the cavalry corps are expected to produce those special decisive effects for which Napoleon always kept in reserve large masses of that arm and of artillery. Thus all the first named eight corps, although called infantry corps, are provided by their very organisation with cavalry and a numerous artillery. They have each a complete staff, engineers, pontoon and ammunition trains, parks of artillery, and every other requisite of an army destined to act independently. The guards and grenadiers are rather weaker in infantry than the other corps, their regiments having each three battalions only instead of four. The guards are, on the other hand, considerably stronger in cavalry and artillery; but it may be expected that in order of battle the greater part of this will be joined to the general cavalry and artillery reserve. The first and second cavalry corps consist of heavy cavalry and horse artillery exclusively (the light regular cavalry is attached to the infantry corps); the third cavalry or dragoon corps has an especial organisation, as these dragoons are intended, same as was the fashion formerly, to fight both as infantry and cavalry, and thus to form a corps of reserve of all arms, having at the same time the mobility and rapidity of locomotion exclusively possessed by cavalry. Whether this will have been attained remains to be seen; the experience of all other armies, resulting in the almost complete and general conversion of dragoons into simple cavalry, is of no very favourable augury. This idea has even been carried to the extent of attaching both to the dragoon corps and to the guards battalions of mounted sappers, miners, and pontonniers—an institution highly lauded by the admirers of the Russian system, but equally wanting, as yet, the test of actual experience.

It may be added that this organisation in eleven corps, with their divisions, brigades, regiments composing each, does not merely exist on paper or for mere administrative purposes. On the contrary, the last Turkish war,[97] the Polish campaign, the Hungarian invasion, and the present Turkish war have shown the dispositions prevailing during peace to be so entirely calculated for war that no division, brigade, or regiment has to be separated from its corps, and to be attached to another whenever the movement towards the frontier begins. This is a great military advantage, resulting from the almost constant state of impending war in which Russia is accustomed to find herself. Other more peaceable states find, on a war approaching, every wheel and pulley of their war-machinery covered with rust, and the whole gearing out of trim; the organisation of army corps, divisions, brigades, complete as it may appear, has to be revolutionised in order to bring troops quick enough to the menaced frontiers; commanders, generals, and staffs are appointed afresh, regiments are shifted from brigade to brigade, from corps to corps, until, when the army is assembled for active operations, you have a motley reunion of commanders more or less unknown to each other, to their superiors, and to their troops; most of them, perhaps, big with a good deal of wounded vanity; and yet you must rely upon this brand-new machinery working well together. The disadvantage is undeniable, although in an army like those of the West it has far less importance than in a Russian one. It is a disadvantage not to be avoided except in an army on a permanent war footing (such as the Austrian army has been since 1848, in consequence of which its corps are also pretty firmly organised);

but for all that the higher degree of industrial perfection existing in western countries makes up, even in a merely military point of view, for this and any other disadvantage which the exigencies of their civilisation may impose upon them.

Written between April 3 and 12, 1854

First published in: Marx and Engels, *Works*, Second Russian Edition, Vol. 44, Moscow, 1977

Printed from the original proofs

Published in English for the first time

Karl Marx and Frederick Engels

THE EUROPEAN WAR [98]

The most important feature of the news from Europe, brought by the *Arctic* which arrived yesterday morning, is the certainty that the Russians have crossed the Lower Danube, some 50,000 strong, in three corps under the immediate command of Prince Gorchakoff, Gen. Lüders and Gen. Oushakoff, and have occupied a part of the Turkish district of Dobrodja. This district belongs to the province of Bulgaria, and is a narrow plain inclosed on the west and north by the Danube,—which bends northwardly at Chernavoda, and makes a large detour before reaching its mouth,—and on the east by the Euxine. A large part of the district is marshy and liable to be overflowed; it contains several fortresses, such as those of Babadagh, Isaktsha, Matchin and Tultcha, which it is stated have been captured by the Russians, but this report our well-informed London correspondent pronounces a mere stock-jobbing invention. Between the plain of the Dobrodja and the interior of Turkey the Balkan stretches its protecting chain. The Russians are no nearer Constantinople than they were previous to this movement, and have gained by it no new advantage over the Turks. In fact, it seems perfectly clear that it is merely a defensive movement, indicating simply their intention to withdraw from the most western portions of Wallachia. Their entire force in Wallachia mustered seven divisions of infantry, one reserve division at Ismail, and further back the corps of Cheodayeff, numbering three divisions, which is now supposed to have reached Jassy. The eight divisions, together with the cavalry, are hardly above 110,000 strong. Considering the possibility of the landing of an Anglo-French corps on the north-western shores of the Black Sea, menacing the Russian rear, it is plain that the object [of the] occupation of the Dobrodja is to secure the Russian flank with the smallest possible sacrifice of ground. There were but two means of securing a position which would guard them against the danger of being cut off,—either a direct retreat upon the Sereth, making the Lower Danube their line of defense, with Fokshani, Galatch and Ismail as supporting points; or to dash at the Dobrodja, with their front leaning upon Kustendje, Hirsova, Oltenitza and Bucharest; the wall of Trajan, the Danube and the Argish to be the first, Buseo the second and the Sereth the third line of defense. The latter plan was decidedly the best, as for the *terrain* abandoned on the one side a new one is gained on the opposite flank, which gives to the retreat the character of an advance, and saves the military *point d'honneur* of the Russians. The possession of the Dobrodja shortens the Russian front, allowing them, in the worst case, to retire upon Chotin on the Dniester, even if a landing should take place at Akerman or Odessa. For the details of the maneuvers by which this change in the Russian position has been effected, we have yet to wait.

Next in interest is the moral certainty that the Greek insurrection will be supported by what influence belongs to the monarchy of Greece, the King and Queen[a] both having gone to the frontier to encourage the insurgents. In this emergency, war between Greece and Turkey, backed by the allies, is nearly inevitable, adding to the complications if not seriously increasing the dangers of the general conflict. On the other hand we have the news of another proposal of peace from the Czar himself, communicated by way of Prussia.[99] Nicholas offers to settle the quarrel if the allies will obtain from Turkey an act of complete emancipation for all her Christian subjects. In that case he will evacuate the Principalities when the allied fleet passes the Dardanelles. Had these terms been openly proffered sooner they might have greatly diminished the chances of the war, as there is no doubt that the allies mean to procure just such an emancipation, and refusal to admit at least a part of it has already led to the dismissal by the Sultan[100] of two important members of his government.[b] But the offer cannot probably now prevent the war; for to the allied fleet a French and English army is now added, while Sir Charles Napier will have probably attacked and taken Aland before new orders could be sent out and reach him. Still this proposal may have a greater importance than we are inclined to attribute to it; on

---

[a] Otto I and Amalie.— *Ed.*
[b] Rifaat Pasha and Arif Hikmet Bey.— *Ed.*

that head we shall doubtless have full information by the next steamer.

Amid all this confusion and uncertainty, one thing alone seems clear, and that is the extinction of the Moslem power as a distinct polity in Europe. The emancipation of the Christians of Turkey, whether effected by peaceful concession or by violence, degrades Islamism from a political authority to a religious sect, and utterly uproots the old foundations of the Ottoman Empire. It not only perfectly recognizes the truth of the Czar's statement that the Ottoman Porte is laboring under a dangerous malady, but cuts the patients' throat by way of medication. After that operation the Sultan may possibly be retained as a political fiction upon the throne of his fathers, but the real rulers of the country must be looked for elsewhere. It is clear why in such a case the Russian autocrat should be willing to settle quietly with his western antagonists. They will have effected in Turkey the most complete revolution conceivable, and effected it wholly in his interest. After such a dissolution of the present ruling authority, his relations to the Greek Church in the country, and to the Slavonians, will really endow him with the supreme power over it; he will then have the oyster while the western governments are obliged to content themselves with the shells. Such a consummation, though now improbable, is not impossible. But we may be sure there are plenty of elements, not yet developed, which will presently rush in to exercise a powerful influence on the progress of this great struggle. Among these how far the long-slumbering European Revolution is to play a leading part is a question which the statesmen of that hemisphere affect to ignore, but of which they may soon be unpleasantly reminded.

Written on April 3 and 4, 1854

First published in the *New-York Daily Tribune*, No. 4055, April 17; reprinted in the *New-York Weekly Tribune*, No. 658, April 22, 1854 as a leader

Reproduced from the *New-York Daily Tribune*

Karl Marx

THE WAR DEBATE IN PARLIAMENT[101]

London, Tuesday, April 4, 1854

A singularity of English tragedy, so repulsive to French feelings that Voltaire used to call Shakespeare a drunken savage,[a] is its peculiar mixture of the sublime and the base, the terrible and the ridiculous, the heroic and the burlesque. But nowhere does Shakespeare devolve upon the Clown the task of speaking the prologue of a heroic drama. This invention was reserved for the Coalition Ministry. Mylord Aberdeen has performed, if not the English Clown, at least the Italian Pantaloon. All great historical movements appear, to the superficial observer, finally to subside into the farce, or at least the common-place. But to commence with this is a feature peculiar alone to the tragedy entitled, *War with Russia*, the prologue of which was recited on Friday evening[b] in both Houses of Parliament, where the Ministry's address in answer to Her Majesty's message[c] was simultaneously discussed and unanimously adopted, to be handed over to the Queen yesterday afternoon, sitting upon her throne in Buckingham Palace. The proceedings in the House of Lords may be very briefly delineated. Lord Clarendon made the Ministerial, and Lord Derby the Opposition statement of the case. The one spoke as the man in office, and the other like the man out of it.[d]

Lord Aberdeen, the noble Earl at the head of the Government, the "acrimonious" confidant of the Czar, the "dear, good, and

---

[a] Voltaire. *Dissertation sur la tragédie ancienne et moderne* (Preface to the tragedy *Sémiramis*).— *Ed.*

[b] March 31, 1854.— *Ed.*

[c] See this volume, p. 100.— *Ed.*

[d] Marx analyses the debate in Parliament according to the report published in *The Times*, No. 21704, April 1, 1854.— *Ed.*

excellent" Aberdeen of Louis Philippe, the "estimable gentleman" of Pius IX although concluding his sermon with his usual whinings for peace, caused, during the principal part of his performance, their lordships to be convulsed with laughter, by declaring war not on Russia, but on *The Press*,[a] a London weekly periodical. Lord Malmesbury retorted on the noble Earl; Lord Brougham, that "old, foolish woman," as he was styled by William Cobbett, discovered that the contest on which they were engaged was no "easy" one; Earl Grey, who, in his Christian spirit, had contrived to make the British Colonies the most miserable abodes of the world, reminded the British people that the tone and temper in which the war was referred to, the feeling of animosity evinced against the Czar and his Cossacks, was not the spirit in which a Christian nation ought to enter upon war. The Earl of Hardwicke was of opinion that England was weak in the means she possessed for dealing with the Russian navy; that they ought not to have a less force in the Baltic than 20 sail of the line, well armed and well manned, with disciplined crews, and not begin, as they had done, with a mob of newly raised men, a mob in a line of battle-ship during an action being the worst of all mobs. The Marquis of Lansdowne vindicated the Government, and expressed a hope as to the shortness and ultimate success of the war, because (and this is a characteristic mark of the noble lord's powers of conception) "it was no dynastic war, such a war involving the largest consequences, and which it was the most difficult to put an end to."

After this agreeable *conversazione* in which everybody had given his sentiment, the address was agreed to *nemine contradicente*.[b]

All the new information to be gathered from this *conversazione* is limited to some official declarations on the part of Lord Clarendon, and the history of the secret memorandum of 1844.

Lord Clarendon stated that "at present the *agreement with France* consists simply of an *exchange of notes* containing arrangements with respect to military operations."

Consequently there exists, at this moment, *no treaty* between England and France. In reference to Austria and Prussia he stated that the former would maintain an armed neutrality, and the other a neutral neutrality; but that "with such a war as is now about to be waged upon the frontiers of both countries, it would

---

[a] The reference is to Lord Russell's polemic with the London *Press* on the history of the 1844 memorandum.— *Ed.*

[b] Without opposition.— *Ed.*

be impossible for either power to preserve a neutrality." Finally he declared that the peace to be brought about by the impending war, would only be a glorious peace "if they did secure equal rights and immunities for the Christian subjects of Turkey."

Now we know that the Sheik-ul-Islam[a] has already been deposed for having refused to sanction by a fetva the treaty granting this equalization of rights; that the greatest excitement exists on the part of the old Turkish population at Constantinople; and by a telegraphic dispatch received to-day we learn that the Czar has declared to Prussia that he is willing to withdraw his troops from the Principalities if the Western Powers should succeed in imposing such a treaty upon the Porte.[b] All he wants is to break the Osman rule. If the Western Powers propose to do it in his stead, he, of course, is not the madman to wage war with them.

Now to the history of the secret memorandum, which I collect from the speeches of Derby, Aberdeen, Malmesbury and Granville. The memorandum was

"intended to be a provisional, conditional and secret arrangement between Russia, Austria and England, to make certain arrangements with respect to Turkey, which France, without any consent on her part, was to be obliged to concur in."

This memorandum, thus described in the words of Lord Malmesbury, was the result of private conferences between the Czar, the Earl of Aberdeen, the Duke of Wellington and Sir Robert Peel. It was by the advice of Aberdeen that the Czar addressed himself to the Duke and to Sir Robert Peel. It remains a matter of controversy between Lord Aberdeen and his opponents, whether the memorandum was drawn up by Count Nesselrode, on the return of the Czar to St. Petersburg subsequently to his visit to England in 1844, or whether it was drawn up by the English Ministers themselves as a record of the communications made by the Emperor.

The connection of the Earl of Aberdeen with this document was distinguished from that of a mere Minister with an official document as proved, according to the statement of Malmesbury, *by another paper not laid before the House.* The document was considered of the greatest importance, and such as might not be communicated to the other powers, notwithstanding Aberdeen's

---

[a] Arif Hikmet Bey.— *Ed.*
[b] Telegraphic dispatch from Berlin of April 3. *The Times*, No. 21706, April 4, 1854.— *Ed.*

assurance that he had communicated the "substance" to France.
The Czar, at all events, was not aware of such a communication
having been made. The document was sanctioned and approved
by the Duke of Wellington and Sir Robert Peel. It was not brought
under the cognizance and consideration of the Peel Cabinet, of
which Lord Derby was at that time a member. It remained not
with the ordinary papers of the Foreign Office, but in the private
custody of each successive Secretary of State, with no copy of it
whatever in the Foreign Office. When Lord Derby acceded to
office, he knew nothing of it, although himself a member of the
Peel Cabinet in 1844. When the Earl of Aberdeen left office, he
handed it over in a box to Lord Palmerston, who handed the box
of Pandora over to his successor, Earl Granville, who, as he states
himself, at the request of Baron Brunnow, the Russian Embassador, handed it over to the Earl of Malmesbury on his accession
to the Foreign Office. But, in the meantime, there appears to have
been an alteration, or rather a falsification in the original
indorsement of the document, since the Earl of Granville sent it to
the Earl of Malmesbury with a note stating that it was a
memorandum drawn up by *Baron Brunnow*, as the result of the
conferences between the Emperor of Russia, Sir Robert Peel and
Lord Aberdeen, the name of the Duke of Wellington not being
mentioned at all. No other motive can be supposed for this false
allegation but the anxiety to conceal the importance of the
memorandum by describing it as a mere annotation of the
Embassador, instead of an official document issued from the
Chancellory at St. Petersburg.

Such was the importance Russia attached to this document that
48 hours after Lord Malmesbury had been in office, Baron
Brunnow came and asked him whether he had read it; but
Malmesbury had not then done so, it being not forwarded to him
till a few days after. Baron Brunnow urged on him the necessity
of reading this document, which he stated *constituted the key of all
conferences with Russia.* From that moment, however, he never
mentioned the document again to the Derbyites, apparently
judging the Tory Administration too powerless or too transitory
for carrying out the Russian policy. In December, 1852, the Derby
Government went out, and shortly after the intelligence of the
formation of the Coalition [102] reaching St. Petersburg, on Jan. 11,
the Czar again opened this question—a sufficient evidence this
that he thought the cabinet of all the talents ready to act on the
basis of this memorandum.

Here, then, we have the most compromising revelations made in the House of Lords by the most irreversible witnesses, all of them having been Prime or Foreign Ministers of Great Britain. An "eventual engagement"—the expression used in the memorandum—is secretly entered into with Russia by an English Foreign Minister, not only without the sanction of Parliament, but behind the backs of his own colleagues, two of them only having been initiated into the mystery. The paper is for ten years withheld from the Foreign Office and kept in clandestine custody by each successive Foreign Minister. Whenever a ministry disappears from the scene, the Russian Embassador appears in Downing-st. and intimates to the new-comer that he had to look closely at the bond, the secret bond, entered into not between the nation as legally represented, but between some Cabinet-Minister and the Czar, and to act according to the line of conduct prescribed in a Russian memorandum drawn up in the Chancellory of St. Petersburg.

If this be not an open infraction of the Constitution, if not a conspiracy and high treason, if not collusion with Russia, we are at a loss to understand the meaning of these terms.

At the same time we understand from these revelations why the criminals, perfectly secure, are allowed to remain at the helm of the State, at the very epoch of an ostensible war with Russia, with whom they are convicted to have permanently conspired, and why the Parliamentary opposition is a mere sham, intended to annoy but not to impeach them. All Foreign Ministers, and consequently all the successive Administrations since 1844 are accomplices, each of them becoming so from the moment he neglected to accuse his predecessor and quietly accepted the mysterious box. By the mere affectation of secrecy each of them became guilty. Each of them became a party to the conspiracy by concealing it from Parliament. By law the concealer of stolen goods is as criminal as the thief. Any legal proceeding, therefore, would ruin not only the Coalition, but their rivals also, and not only these Ministers, but the Parliamentary parties they represent, and not only those parties, but the governing classes of England.

I may remark, *en passant*, that the only speech delivered in the House of Lords worth mentioning is that of the Earl of Derby; but his criticism of the memorandum and the secret correspondence— and I may say the same with respect to the debate in the Commons—contains nothing that I have not stated before in the full analysis I gave you of that fatal memorandum and that extraordinary correspondence.[a]

---

[a] See this volume, pp. 73-83 and 84-99.— *Ed.*

"The power of declaring war is a prerogative of the Crown, a real prerogative; and if Her Majesty summons her Parliament, and informs them that she has found it necessary to engage herself in war, it is not an occasion when the Commons enter on the policy or impolicy of the war. It is their duty, under such circumstances, to rally round the throne, and to take a proper, subsequent and constitutional occasion of commenting on the policy which may have led to the war."

So said Mr. Disraeli in the sitting of the Commons, and so said all the Commoners, and yet *The Times* fills seventeen columns with their comments on that policy. Why was this? Even because it was not the "occasion," because their talk would remain resultless. But we must except Mr. Layard, who stated plainly:

"If it should be the feeling of the House, after what he should state to them, that the conduct of the Ministers should force the subject of a Parliamentary inquiry, he should not shrink from the duty thus imposed upon him, and would be ready to ask the Ministers to fix an early day on which the matter might be brought forward."

You will comprehend now the reason why *The Times* begins to doubt the justice of the Assyrian discoveries of Mr. Layard.[a]

Lord J. Russell, who introduced the address in the House of Commons, distinguished himself from Lord Clarendon only by his intonation of the words integrity, liberty, independence, civilization, whereby he secured the cheers of his more common audience.

Mr. Layard, who rose to reply to him, committed two great blunders, which disfigured his otherwise remarkable speech. In the first place, he sought to establish the existence of opposite elements in the Coalition, the Russian element and the English element, the Aberdeen fraction and the Palmerston fraction, these two fractions possessing no other distinction than their language and their modes of subserviency to Russia. The one is a partisan of Russia, because he does not understand her, and the other although he understands her. The former is, therefore, an open partisan, and the other a secret agent. The former, therefore, serves gratuitously, and the latter is paid. The former is less dangerous because placed in open antagonism to the feelings of the English people; the latter is fatal, because he makes himself pass for the incarnation of the national animosity against Russia. With Mr. Layard we must presume that it is ignorance of the man whom he places in opposition to Aberdeen. For Mr. Disraeli, who employed the same contrast, there is no such excuse. No man knows Lord Palmerston better than that chief of the Opposition,

---

[a] *The Times*, No. 21705, April 3, 1854, leader.—*Ed.*

who declared already in 1844, that no foreign policy of any
Minister had ever been so fatal to British interests as that of the
noble Lord. The second blunder committed by Mr. Layard was his
argument that *The Times* was the direct organ of the Aberdeen
party because the secret and confidential correspondence, two or
three days after arrival, furnished materials for its leading articles,
which endeavored to bring the country to consent to the nefarious
transaction intended at St. Petersburg, especially its articles during
February and March of last year. Layard would have done better
to conclude with Lord Palmerston that those materials were
furnished by the Russian Embassy at London, when he would
have been able to charge both *The Times* and the Foreign Office
with being the organs of the St. Petersburg Cabinet.

Holding the opinion that *The Times* is, in fact, a greater power
than the Coalition not as to its opinions but as to the data which
constitute the treasonable character of this secret correspondence,
I subjoin the whole statement of Mr. Layard against that paper:

"The first of these secret dispatches was received in this country on the 23d of
January, 1853, and on the 26th of the same month appeared in *The Times* the first
of those articles to which he had referred. The next dispatch was received on the
6th of February, 1853, and on the 11th of the same month, four days afterward,
there appeared an extraordinary article in *The Times*, from which he would now
quote. In one part of the article it was stated:

"'We do not suppose that it is the intention or the policy of Russia to accelerate
a catastrophe in the East, and the good offices of this country will again be
employed to lessen the perils of a situation which is becoming critical. We cannot,
however, forget that the attempt to prolong the brutal and decrepit authority of
the Turks in Europe is purchased by the surrender of fine provinces and a large
Christian population to barbarous misgovernment; and we shall rejoice when
civilization and Christianity are able to repair the injuries of the Ottoman
conquest.'

"Again, it was stated in *The Times* on the 23d of February, 1853, after various
comments on the exhausted state of Turkey:

"'With the utmost political caducity, with a total want of ability and integrity in
the men who are still its rulers, with a declining Mussulman population, and an
exhausted treasury, the Porte unites as if by way of derisory contrast a dominion
over some of the most fertile regions, the finest ports and the most enterprising
and ingenious people of Southern Europe.... It is hard to comprehend how so
great a positive evil can have been so long defended by politicians as a relative
good; and, though we are not insensible to the difficulties attending any change in
the territories of so huge an empire, we are disposed to view with satisfaction
rather than with alarm the approach of a period'"

How did *The Times* know the period was approaching?

"'when it will be impossible to prolong the dominion of such a Government as
that of the Porte over such a country as that which is now subject to its authority.
Perhaps that period is less distant than is commonly supposed; and it may be the

part of wise statesmen to provide against such a conjuncture, which it is beyond their power indefinitely to postpone. We do not believe, and we do not mean to imply, that any combination of Austria and Russia, hostile to the territorial claims of the Ottoman Empire, is now in existence, or is likely to be formed without the knowledge of the other European powers. We have strong grounds to believe'"—

When *The Times* says that we know what it means—

"'that Prince Menchikoff is sent from St. Petersburg to Constantinople upon a special embassy, for the express purpose of declaring, in the name of the Emperor Nicholas, that as head of the Greek Church he cannot submit, or allow the Eastern Church to submit, to the conditions of the firman recently obtained by the French Embassador with reference to the Holy Shrines in the Holy Land.'

"Now, the first intimation of Prince Menchikoff's mission was contained in Sir H. Seymour's dispatches, received February 14 and February 21. It was important to observe that on the 6th of March, 1853, arrived the dispatch giving the whole of the Emperor of Russia's plan for the partition of Turkey. The answer to it, as he had before said, was not returned before the 23d of March, and no Cabinet Council was held until the 13th of March, though certain members of the Government had seven days previously received the Emperor's proposal. That proposal was not submitted to their colleagues till the 13th of March, but it had been previously submitted to *The Times,* for on the 7th of March, the morning following the receipt of the dispatch, which then could not have been known to more than two or three members of the Cabinet, and which could not then have been seen by any clerk in the Foreign Office, there appeared a particular article in *The Times.* (Hear, hear.) The article said, among other things, that

"'The state of the Turkish Empire and the relations of the European Powers to the East are subjects on which it may be useful for reflecting politicians and the independent press to form and express opinions, though the consummation to which these opinions point be still unwelcome and remote. Statesmen, bound to transact the business of the day, and to recognize at every turn the obligations of what is called State necessity, are restrained within narrower limits, and would probably be unable to give effect to any novel or original conception if it had not previously been entertained by the mind and reason of the public.'

"He entreated the noble Lord to mark the words which followed, for they referred to the objection which he had offered.

"'We are therefore by no means surprised that, in adverting to the differences which have recently taken place in Turkey, and especially on its European frontiers, Lord John Russell should have expressed his dissent from the opinions which have been recently put forward on this subject, and should have repeated in his place in Parliament, speaking under the weight of official responsibility, the old story of the integrity and independence of the Ottoman Empire. We ourselves, however, are not affected by similar considerations.'

"How did the writer know that the noble Lord dissented? (Hear.) The article proceeded:

"'We do not, therefore, concur in the opinion of Lord J. Russell that no greater calamity could occur to Europe at the present time than the necessity of considering what ought to be done in such a case as the dismemberment of that empire.'

"Let the House mark the following words, for they were almost identical with those of the Emperor of Russia:

"'It would, we think, be a far greater calamity that the dismemberment commenced before any such consideration had taken place.'

"(Hear, hear.) They were the very words. The writer went on thus:

"'And here we must be allowed to express our surprise that any statesman should, for an instant, confound the policy which it might be proper to pursue in the event of a dissolution of the Turkish Empire with that which led to the partition of Poland. No doubt the argument of State necessity still remains to support the integrity and independence of the Turkish Empire; but that argument stands alone against a host of evils, and it means, in reality, no more than the fear of dealing with a momentous and uncertain question. Yet, so strange are the prepossessions on this subject which have been fostered, especially of late years, that an attempt to discuss this question on its own merits is viewed in some quarters as an act of political depravity, and a violation of all the laws which bind nations together.'

"The next article appeared on the 10th of March. The House might, perhaps, have been of opinion that hitherto he had not shown that the writer in *The Times* employed the exact words used in the dispatches; but the article he was about to read would remove all doubt upon that point. On the 10th of March an article appeared in *The Times* commencing with these words:

"'Prince Menchikoff arrives in a more strictly diplomatic capacity, and we have reason to believe that his instructions are more conciliatory than those of Count Leiningen.'

"A similarity of expression would be found in Sir H. Seymour's dispatch of the 21st of February:

"'His Excellency (Count Nesselrode) wished to assure me that the instructions with which Prince Menchikoff would be provided were of a conciliatory nature.'

"The article continued:

"'We must venture to say that it implies some penury of resources in modern statesmen that, when they have to deal with a question which involves the civilization of great provinces, the restoration of Christianity itself to that supremacy which it once enjoyed in all parts of Europe, and the progressive welfare of millions of human beings, the only expedient on which they can agree is to dress up a Turk's head in a turban, and agree to treat it as if it was still a symbol of force and empire.'

"A Cabinet Council was held on the 19th of March, at which the dispatch received on the 6th of that month was discussed, and an answer to it was returned on the 23d of March, containing this passage:

"'Although Her Majesty's Government feel compelled to adhere to the principles and the policy laid down in Lord John Russell's dispatch of the 9th of February, yet they gladly comply with the Emperor's wish, that the subject should be further and frankly discussed.'

"On the same day an article appeared in *The Times*, in which some of the phrases used in Lord Clarendon's dispatch might be found. The article commenced thus:

"'The opinions we have expressed on the present condition and future prospects of the Ottoman Empire do not coincide with the views entertained by Lord J. Russell, and communicated by him to the House of Commons; they differ from the course of policy which this country has pursued in former times and on several occasions; and they are entirely at variance with the system which a large numerical proportion of the London press is attempting, not very brilliantly or successfully, to defend.'

"Honor to the British press that, though wanting the brilliant epigrammatic pen which had shaken a Colonial Minister and almost upset a Cabinet, it did not support the views of *The Times*. *The Times* added near the end of its article:

"'He (the Emperor) has said that it is an object of his ambition to stand well with this country, and to deserve its confidence. His proceedings on this occasion will bring that assurance to the test, and he can give us no greater proof of moderation and good. faith toward Turkey and the rest of Europe than a willingness to cooperate on these subjects, as he has before done, with the British Government.'"

"On the same day on which *The Times* announced that its endeavors to reconcile the British public to the partition of Turkey had failed, the answer to the dispatch which had been delayed for 16 days was sent to St. Petersburg. (Hear, hear.) He need not trouble the House with further extracts from *The Times*."

Mr. Bright supported the character of Mr. Cobden, in order to afford another opportunity to Lord Palmerston to gather popularity by abuse of Russia and sham-energetic defense of the war-policy. Among other things Palmerston stated:

"Now, it is known, I think, to those who have given their attention to the affairs of Europe for a considerable time past, that the views of Russia upon Turkey are not of yesterday, or indeed of any recent date. (Hear.) It is known that for a great length of time it has been the standing and established policy of Russia to endeavor to obtain possession of at least the European part of Turkey, and subsequently of Asiatic Turkey. This policy has been pursued with undeviating and systematic perseverance. It has been ever kept in view. When opportunities have offered, steps in advance have been made, and when checks have been experienced, those steps have been withdrawn; but only for the purpose of taking advantage of the next opportunity which offers. (Hear, hear.) Delay has been no element in mitigating or in inducing Russia to abandon its schemes. Its policy has been to keep one object in view—not to hurry, not to lose its object by prematurely grasping at its possession, but to watch the course of the other Governments of Europe, and to take advantage of every opportunity which might present itself, by which it could get even the slightest advance toward the ultimate object of its ambition."

Now compare this declaration of Lord Palmerston with those he made in 1829, '30, '31, '33, '36, '40, '41, '42, '43, '46, '48, '49, and you will find that the above is less a reply to Mr. Bright than to his own former policy.[103] But while this cunning foe, by such onslaughts upon Russia, conciliates the sympathies of the public, he on the other hand secures favor with the Czar, by the following observation:

"Now, Sir, do I blame the Russian Government for entertaining such a policy? A policy of aggrandizement pursued by legitimate means is a policy which you may condemn as dangerous to yourselves, which you may oppose as destructive of the independence and the liberties of other States, but which is not a reproach to the Government which pursues it, provided it be pursued by open, undisguised, and avowed means, without concealment, without subterfuge, and without fraud. Now, the course which, I am sorry to say, the Russian Government has pursued in all these recent transactions has not been that open and straightforward course which would justify it in avowing and in boldly declaring its policy."

But the only reproach to be made against the Russian Government was just, as Mr. Disraeli termed it, her *fatal frankness.* Palmerston, accordingly, by disapproving only of what Russia did not do, justifies entirely that which she really has done.

Mr. Disraeli's criticism of the secret papers was clever, as usual, but missed its effect by his declaration that it was out of place, and that his only intention in addressing the House was to support the address. It is painful to see a man of his genius cajoling a Palmerston, not only in the House, but also in his reputed organ, *The Press,* from so sordid a motive as the politics of place and party.

In yesterday's sitting of the House, Sir J. Graham stated that he had received intelligence that the fleet had entered the Black Sea, and was in the neighborhood of Varna.[a]

In the House of Lords, Lord Aberdeen gave notice that on Tuesday, the 11th, he should move the adjournment of the House till Thursday, 27th inst.

Written on April 4, 1854

First published in the *New-York Daily Tribune*, No. 4055, April 17; reprinted in the *New-York Weekly Tribune*, No. 658, April 22, 1854

Reproduced from the *New-York Daily Tribune*

---

[a] Sir J. Graham's speech in the House of Commons on April 3, 1854. *The Times*, No. 21706, April 4, 1854.— *Ed.*

Karl Marx

[RUSSIA AND THE GERMAN POWERS.—CORN PRICES] [104]

London, Friday, April 7, 1854

Lord Clarendon declared last night in the House of Lords that "he had reason to believe" that the news of the landing of 4,000 Russians in the Dobrodja by means of transports from Odessa was untrue. He was not aware that the Russian fleet had left Sevastopol which point had been watched, now and then, by English and French steamers. With regard to the alleged inactivity of the fleets, he begged to say that a blockade of Sevastopol and Odessa could only be undertaken by the whole of the combined squadron, which would have been a dangerous undertaking during the bad season. He believed, therefore, that it had been politic to retain them at Beikos. The Vienna correspondent of *The Times* concurs in this view of Lord Clarendon, and moreover, states the true motives of his policy.[a] The apprehension of riots at Constantinople has never been more justified than since the negotiations for "Christian emancipation" have become known, and it would have been highly "impolitic" to move the fleets from the Bosphorus before the arrival of a sufficient land force, i.e., sufficient to put down the Turks.

In the House of Commons Lord John Russell said the responsibility for the Greek insurrections rested with the Court of Athens, which had favored them at first secretly, and now openly.[b]

The debates of the week offer nothing of interest, except that on Mr. Moore's motion for a Select Committee to take into

---

[a] Report from the Vienna correspondent of April 2. *The Times*, No. 21709, April 7, 1854.— *Ed.*

[b] Lord John Russell's speech in the House of Commons on April 6, 1854. *The Times*, No. 21709, April 7, 1854.— *Ed.*

consideration the case of the appointment of H. Stonor to the office of a Judge in the colony of Victoria,[a] the said Stonor having been reported by a Committee of the House to have been guilty of bribery at the elections in the borough of Sligo in 1853, the appointment of the Committee was granted. The prosecution of Mr. Stonor is, however, a mere pretext for renewing, on fresh ground, the battle between the two fractions of the broken Irish Brigade.[105] To what degree the sanctimonious *clique* of Mr. Gladstone and his co-Peelites are involved and comprised in these Irish scandals, may be judged from the following remark of *The Morning Post*:

"In the letters that have been produced, the gossip that has been retailed and the evidence which has been given before Parliamentary Committees within the last few weeks, there is much calculated to give strength to the suspicion that the Peelite section of the coalition have, for some time past, systematically employed agents to influence many of the Irish elections, and that they have supplied them largely with money for the purpose. The Duke of Newcastle is especially compromised.... There certainly appears to have been a conference of preferment upon individuals conducting election business, seemingly under his instruction."[b]

The Daily News of to-day publishes the treaty between France, England and Turkey, which, however, merely contains the arrangements for military action. The western powers are careful not to bring the real conditions of their "assistance to the Sultan" into the form of a treaty. These are imposed by Lord Stratford de Redcliffe and his minatory apparatus *in loco*,[c] and made to appear as the voluntary act of the Turkish Government.

The peace mission of the Prince of Mecklenburg to Berlin had no other object in view but to furnish the King of Prussia[d] with a new pretext for keeping aloof from the Western Alliance. I am informed from Berlin that Russia would only acknowledge the Swedish declaration of neutrality after the King[e] had bound himself to re-issue to the commandants of the Swedish harbors the old regulations, according to which no more than four foreign men-of-war are allowed to anchor within the range of the guns of any port. As this order considerably departs from the stipulations of neutrality agreed upon between Sweden and Denmark, new

[a] The debates in the House of Commons on Mr. Moore's motion are given according to *The Times*, No. 21709, April 7, 1854.— *Ed.*
[b] *The Morning Post*, No. 25043, April 7, 1854, leader.— *Ed.*
[c] On the spot.— *Ed.*
[d] Frederick William IV.— *Ed.*
[e] Oskar I.— *Ed.*

negotiations between the Scandinavian powers on the one hand, and the western powers on the other hand, are to be anticipated. It is generally believed at Stockholm that the Russians will abandon their occupation of Aland, and raze their fortifications on that island, carrying away the guns and other material of war. A telegraphic dispatch received to-day states that this step had already been carried out.[a]

The Austrian *corps d'observation* in the south-eastern portions of Hungary is now on a complete war footing, and drawn up in the different positions allotted to it. The concentration required from ten to twelve days. The German papers generally assume that this army would be destined to take the Turkish army in the flank, in case of Austria joining actively with Russia, and there would be no difficulty in doing so. But the Austrians can only enter Turkey either by Mehadia, when they would have the Turkish army in their front, or by Belgrade, when they would find themselves in a line with the extended left flank of the Turks. It is much more probable, therefore, that if the Austrians enter Turkey with hostile intentions, they will march from Belgrade upon Sofia by Kruschevatz and Nissa; but even in that case the Turks would have a shorter way to Sofia, by marching from Vidin in a direct line southward.

The report of the Prussian Loan-Committee in the Second Chamber contains an account of the policy pursued by Prussia in the Eastern Question, and publishes several diplomatic documents which have not yet found their way into the English press. I propose, therefore, to give you some important extracts from that report.[b]

At the end of January the Russian Embassador at Berlin[c] handed a proposition to the Prussian Government, simultaneously with the propositions made by Count Orloff to the Austrian Court, according to which the three Courts of Prussia, Austria and Russia were to sign a joint protocol. In the preamble to the draft of this protocol it is stated that the motive of this common engagement was the desire to draw closer the alliance of the three powers, in view of the dangers threatening the peace of Europe, and to regulate the relations both between them and with

---

[a] This erroneous telegraphic dispatch from Berlin of April 5 was published in *The Times*, No. 21709, April 7, 1854.— *Ed.*

[b] The reference is to "Erster Bericht der Kommission zur Vorprüfung der Gesetz-Entwürfe, betreffend die Kredit-Bewilligung...."— *Ed.*

[c] A. F. Budberg.— *Ed.*

the western powers under the impending juncture. This draft contained the following three points:

1. The two German powers bind themselves formally, in the case of an active participation by England and France in the Russo-Turkish war, to observe the strictest neutrality; and declare if they should be again pressed or menaced by the western powers, that they are resolved to defend their neutrality, in case of need, with arms.

2. The three powers will consider any attack by France or England on the respective territories of Austria, Prussia, or any other German State, as a violation of their own territory, and will defend each other, as circumstances may require, and in accordance with a common military understanding (now arranged between General Hess and the Prussian Minister of War[a] at Berlin).

3. The Emperor of Russia repeats his assurance that he intends to bring the war to a close *as soon as compatible with his dignity and the well-understood interests of his empire.* Considering, however, that the ulterior development of events is likely to alter the existing state in Turkey, His Majesty obliges himself, if he should come to any understanding on that point with the naval powers, to take no definitive resolution without previous concert with *his German allies.*

This draft was accompanied by a dispatch from Count Nesselrode, in which the Chancellor reminds Prussia and Austria of the importance of that triple alliance which had so long been the shield of Europe. In sight of the impending war his imperial master considered himself obliged to earnestly appeal to his friends and allies. Their common interest made it necessary to define the position which they had now to occupy under these grave eventualities. Pointing out the one-sided advance of the western powers, he called attention to their want of consideration for the interests of the German powers. Russia acted differently. She was prepared to submit alone to the burdens of war, and would ask neither sacrifices nor aid from her friends and allies. The welfare of both powers and of Germany depended on their union. In this way they would succeed in preventing the crisis from extending, and perhaps shorten it. The Russian dispatch next proceeds to examine the three alternative positions open to the German powers: Common action with Russia against the naval

---

[a] Ed. Bonin.— *Ed.*

powers; alliance with the latter against Russia, or lastly, a strict neutrality. As to an alliance with Russia, the Czar did not require it; and as to an action against him, it was impossible if the German powers would not submit to the menace of the western powers. This would be the acknowledgment of a disgraceful necessity to the end of bringing about a deplorable future. Russia, inattackable in her own territory, apprehended neither military invasions nor the more pernicious invasions of the revolutionary spirit. If her allies deserted her, she knew how to restrict herself to her own resources, and would arrange herself so as to dispense with them in future. (M. de Nesselrode writes his dispatches in German taking care that translation into another language becomes a matter of downright despair. As a specimen of his German exercises I give you the last sentence in the original words: *Wenn seine Alliierten es verließen, so würde es sich gesagt sein lassen, sich auf sich selbst zurückziehen und sich so einrichten, ihrer in Zukunft entbehren zu können.*) But the Czar had full confidence in the known sentiments of his friends and allies, and in their gallant armies, which had been connected long since with those of Russia by the baptism of blood (*Bluttaufe*), and by an identity of principles not to be denied. The third alternative only the Russian Cabinet thinks worthy of the German Courts, as corresponding with their interests, and appropriate; by continuing their parts as mediators, to realize the particular desires of Russia. It must, however, be understood that this neutrality could not be an indefinite one, or merely provisional, or an expectant one, because such an attitude would be construed as hostile by either belligerent, especially by Russia. That neutrality should rather be founded on the principles (of the Holy Alliance) which, during many trials, had secured the general tranquillity and the peace of the world. It was the duty of the German powers to give effect to this basis of their policy, if need be, by arms. If the one (France) of the two maritime powers should meditate or venture upon an attack of Germany, the other one (England) would instantly change her position. At all instances, if such an event should occur, Russia was ready to come forth and support them with all the forces at her command.

This proposition was declined at Berlin, and some days later at Vienna too. Manteuffel then still played the independent states-man, and declared in a dispatch to St. Petersburg that, by the desire of a renewed triple alliance, Russia, which pretended not to require the aid of Prussia, yet asked for it, though in an indirect form. "With regard to the revolutionary spirit, which Russia did not fear, he would observe that Prussia, too, had subjected it without foreign aid." The independent minister, who "saved" Prussia by putting himself at the head of the counter-revolution, cannot suppress his irritation at seeing Prussia, which had no Hungary, placed in a line with Austria.

While Prussia thus boasts of her security, the other documents alluded to in the report prove that in the last days of February Austria submitted to Prussia the draft of a convention to be concluded between the four powers.[106] Prussia declined it in a dispatch dated the 5th of March. But it is characteristic of this power that it declares at the same time that the Government of Frederick William IV still considered the concert of the four powers as the best means to arrive at a satisfactory solution of the complication. Austria, consequently, was forced also to drop the convention which would have put an end to the equivocal position of both German powers.

A Prussian dispatch of March 16 contains the following important passage:

> "The Prussian Cabinet had noticed the measures taken by Austria with a view to maintain her interests on the south-eastern frontiers. It was true that Prussia, like all other German States, had to protect its own particular interests; but this should not exclude an understanding with Austria. On the contrary, Prussia was ready to enter into a concert, as far as the maintenance of German interests required. From this motive she looked forward to communications on the following points:
>
> "1. Whether Austria was prepared, in order to secure the tranquillity of her own frontier provinces, to occupy the contiguous Turkish provinces?
>
> "2. Whether she would take possession of the latter, and hold them as a pledge, till the restoration of peace?
>
> "3. Whether she intended to participate actively in the war?"

It would wholly depend on the answer to these several questions for Prussia to come to a conclusion as to what the maintenance of German interests would require, and whether she could do anything to mitigate the pressure applied to Austria by the *western powers* (not by Russia!).

On March 14, the Prussian Government addressed a circular Note to the German Courts in the one sense, and the Austrian Government in the opposite sense. The Prussian *circulaire* says the impending war will be of a purely local character. Austria, on the contrary, maintains that the struggle is likely to take a turn which would intimately affect her own relations. As long as circumstances should permit, she would not participate in the war; but she had to consider also the eventuality of a participation in it. The interests involved in this question were likewise those of the German States. The Imperial Cabinet, therefore, trusted that in such a contingency Prussia and the other German Courts would join their forces with those of Austria. The German Confederation would then be called upon to show that, beyond its present defensive attitude, it knew also how to fill an active part in this question. Austria would make a further declaration as soon as the war between the western powers and Russia should have been actually declared. If there were yet any means to prevent the increase of those dangers which now threatened Europe, it would be found in the common action of Austria and Prussia, joined by their German confederates.

The last, but not least remarkable information contained in the report, is the melancholy answer given by M. de Manteuffel to a question of the Committee members, viz: That Russia had made no communication whatever of her partition schemes to the Prussian Government.

In conclusion, we learn from this document that the juggle of the Vienna Conferences has not at all come to an end. On the contrary, it states, on the authority of the Prussian *Premier*, that a new protocol was about to be drawn up, which would establish the *continued understanding between the four powers.*

The corn market is again rising. The cause of the late fall in France and England was the pressure acting upon speculators who, for want of sufficient capital and in a tight money market, were driven to forced sales which overstocked the markets. Another cause was the fact that the dealers, millers and bakers allowed their supplies to run out, in the belief that enormous cargoes were on the way to the European ports. I am, therefore, still of opinion that prices are yet far from having reached their maximum. It is certain that in no previous year were such erroneous and illusory speculations about the probable and possible supply of the corn market entertained as in the present year, illusions which are to a great extent encouraged by the cant of the free-trade papers.

Written on April 7, 1854

First published in the *New-York Daily Tribune*, No. 4059, April 21 and in the *New-York Semi-Weekly Tribune*, No. 929, April 21, 1854

Signed: *Karl Marx*

Reproduced from the *New-York Daily Tribune*

Frederick Engels

POSITION OF THE ARMIES IN TURKEY [107]

When the intelligence of the Russian occupation of the Dobrodja was first received, and long before the real intentions of the Russians in passing the Danube could be developed by their acts, we stated our opinion that the leading idea of the movement could not be any other than the improvement of their defensive position.[a] That this was actually the case is shown by all their steps since, and by those of their opponents also. The Russians sent from 40,000 to 50,000 men into the Dobrodja, who have not, as far as reliable information goes, passed the line from Chernavoda to Kustendje. They appear to have sent an equal if not a superior number to Kalarash, opposite Silistria, with the intention of menacing, or under favorable circumstances, of attacking that fortress. They have withdrawn all their troops west of Bucharest with the exception of a rear guard, which, incapable of holding out any longer in front of Kalafat, has, it appears, made an excursion upon the opposite Servian shore of the Danube, for the purpose apparently of showing the contempt of the Russians for Servian neutrality, and trying what effect the presence of a few Russian uniforms would produce among the Servian peasantry—or even perhaps to furnish occasion for the occupation of the country by Austria.

There is no doubt that we shall very shortly hear of the whole of Lesser Wallachia being abandoned by the Russians, and what, then, will be their position? Their line will extend from Tirgovest by Oltenitza and Kalarash to Chernavoda and thence, crossing the Danube, to the Black Sea near Kustendje. It is, in fact, a position

---

[a] See this volume, pp. 129-30.— Ed.

which sacrifices more ground than it gains. This is the case notwithstanding [that] this shortening of the Russian front is in itself an advantage. At the same time it is a movement toward their left, by which their line of retreat, formerly in the direction of the prolongation of that front, is now placed perpendicularly behind it. Two months ago Omer Pasha could have cut off their retreat by merely passing the Danube at any point between Silistria and Hirsova; but now that cannot be done, except, perhaps, by landing troops near the mouth of the Dniester. And it is in this that the great advantage of the movement lies—an advantage not even balanced by the risk encountered by placing the corps in the Dobrodja in an oblong rectangle, one side of which is closed by the strong position of the enemy, another by the sea, and the other two by the two bends of the Danube with no more than three bridges for communication, reenforcements or retreat.

But here ends the advantage gained by the Russians. They have obtained a position from which they can retreat, but not one from which they can advance. Before them, from Oltenitza to Chernavoda, is the Danube, passable at a few points only, and those points defended either by strong batteries on a commanding shore, or, as at Silistria by a regular fortress. Further on, from Chernavoda to the sea are the lakes and morasses of Karasu, the Wall of Trajan, (refitted for defense on the points of passage) the fortress of Kustendje, and the allied fleets on their flank in the Black Sea. Beyond the Danube, as well as beyond Trajan's Wall, stretches a comparatively barren country, generally of high ground, intersected in every direction by precipitous ravines formed by numerous rivers, none of which are bridged over. This country is certainly not impassable for an army, but can only be traversed by a force which may safely expect to find a good position, a weak enemy, and plenty of provisions and forage on the other side. But here just the reverse is the case. If the Russians advance from Trajan's Wall and from Oltenitza or Turtukai toward Bazardjik and Rasgrad, they must leave troops behind them to blockade Silistria and to observe Rustchuk. Thus weakened, they pass the difficult country to Rasgrad and Bazardjik, and where do they arrive? Why, before the first advanced range of the Balkans, which runs right across their line of operations, and which must be passed in detached corps on different and diverging roads. Supposing this to be attempted, their divided corps risk being beaten in detail by a concentrated force emerging from Shumla, the retreat of which they cannot in any case cut off. But supposing even that they should overcome all these difficulties, and should appear, say 100,000 men strong, in the neighborhood of

Shumla and Varna—what then? Shumla is a position which not only can be held by 40,000 men against 100,000, but in which the smaller force cannot be kept in check by the larger. At the same time, it covers Varna, which on the other flank is covered by the allied fleets. And Varna and Shumla form, combined, a line far stronger than Verona and Legnago formed, in 1848, upon the Adige for Field-Marshal Radetzky, when he was pressed on all sides by the Piedmontese and insurgent Italian troops.[a] Moreover, Shumla and Varna have as their complements Rustchuk and Silistria, both of which are situated in the direction of the enemy's flank, and which, weak as they may appear in themselves, cannot successfully be attacked as long as the main force of the Turkish army is capable of a sally from Shumla in either direction. Both fortresses are situated on the Danube, Silistria in front of the right center of the present Russian position, Rustchuk on its right flank. They must be blockaded on the right bank of the river; that is to say, the blockading force must take its station directly between the fortresses and Shumla, where, according to all appearances, Omer Pasha is concentrating the bulk of his troops. Any force, blockading Rustchuk and Silistria, must, therefore, be of sufficient strength to resist at least two-thirds of the Turkish army concentrated at Shumla, with the garrisons of these fortresses besides. On the other hand, if the Russian force advances by way of Bazardjik, it must also be strong enough to resist two-thirds of the army of Shumla in open battle. Besides, troops must be detached to blockade Varna at least on the north side, and if possible on the south side also; for unless Varna is blockaded it cannot be taken, and unless it is taken, the Russians cannot pass the Balkans. If, beside all these requirements, we take into consideration the detachments necessary to keep up the communication between the different corps on the long line from Rustchuk to Varna, and to secure the arrival of supplies, there is no doubt that in order to make a successful advance upon Shumla and Varna, the two decisive points of the defense of the eastern Balkans, the Russians must have more than double the force which the Turks can concentrate at Shumla.

From these facts we see that the Turks have acted very wisely. The abandonment of the Dobrodja is the first positive and undeniable proof of good generalship on the part of Omer Pasha. The country and its fortresses are not worth holding. Instead of incurring defeats and losses of men and material, the Turkish General at once ordered his troops to abandon all points as soon as it could be done with

---

[a] The reference is to the revolution of 1848.— *Ed.*

safety for the retreat of all, and to fall back on Trajan's Wall. Thus the Russians obtained an easy apparent triumph, while the Turks did them serious damage in the process, and gained their true position of defense before the enemy could retaliate. The Turks have no garrisons except in important places, and where the main army or the fleets in the Black Sea can support them. Thus they will be able to bring together at least 80,000 or 90,000 men in case of need, between Shumla and Varna, a force which might be increased by the speedy recall of some of the troops that a political panic, without any real reason, sent to Kalafat. And that the Russians should bring twice as many, or even more men, across the Danube is impossible, at least during this campaign. In saying this, we are supposing that they actually intend to carry forward a vigorous offensive, and we leave out of the account the arrival of the Anglo-French auxiliary troops, whose presence would make any passage of the Balkans an act of folly. We have considered the subject in this light, because it is quite as well to know the real state of the present combatants. The truth is, that if the Russians and the Turks alone had to fight the matter out, even after the superiority required for offensive action has been lost to the Turks by diplomatic delays, Constantinople is, for the present year at least, safe enough from a Russian invasion.

Written on April 13, 1854

First published in the *New-York Daily Tribune*, No. 4065, April 28; reprinted in the *New-York Weekly Tribune*, No. 660, May 6, 1854 as a leader

Reproduced from the *New-York Daily Tribune*

Karl Marx

[RESHID PASHA'S NOTE.—AN ITALIAN NEWSPAPER ON THE EASTERN QUESTION][108]

London, Tuesday, April 18, 1854

The Governments of England and France are said to have at last exchanged copies of an offensive and defensive treaty, comprising Five Articles. The contents are not yet known.

The treaty between Austria and Prussia is not yet concluded, the point of dissension being the occupation of the frontiers touching on Russian Poland, which the Prussian Court partly declines.

On the 6th April a *Te Deum* was celebrated at Athens in honor of the anniversary of Greek Independence. It was not attended by the Embassadors of the Western Powers. On the same day the *Observer* of Athens[a] registered sixteen royal *ordonnances* accepting the resignation of twenty-one generals, colonels, and other officers, all of whom were about to join the insurgents. On the day following the news reached Athens that the insurgents had been fearfully beaten near Arta. The very place where the battle was fought denotes that the insurrection had made not the slightest progress, and that its only victims until now have been the Greek peasants themselves who inhabit the frontier districts of the kingdom of Greece.

You will remember that in 1827 the Embassadors of Russia, England and France demanded that the Sublime Porte should recall every Turk from Greece, whether settled there or not. The Turks refusing to acquiesce, obedience was enforced by the battle of Navarino.[109] A similar order has now been issued against the Greeks, on the part of the Sublime Porte; and as neither the letter

---

[a] *L'Observateur d'Athènes.* The report is given as reprinted in *L'Indépendance belge*, No. 108, April 18, 1854.— *Ed.*

of Reshid Pasha to Mr. Metaxas, the Greek Embassador, nor the circular of Lord Stratford de Redcliffe to the British Consuls, has yet been published in the London papers, I give you a translation of each from the *Journal de Constantinople* of April 5[a]:

"Answer of Reshid Pasha, Minister of Foreign Affairs,
to the note of M. Metaxas

"Constantinople, 3d Redjeb, 1270 (lst April, 1854)

"I have taken cognizance of the note which you addressed to me on March 26, with respect to your resolution to quit this capital. The Government of the Sublime Porte not having obtained from that of Greece due satisfaction in return for its just reclamations, with respect to the actual events, and the Chargé d'Affaires[b] of the Sublime Porte being obliged to quit Athens in conformity to his instructions, it is proper, Sir, that you also quit this city. I remit you, accordingly, in compliance with your demand, your passports. As from this day the diplomatic relations as well as the commercial ones are broken off between the two countries, we have come to the decision that the Hellenic Chancelleries established in the different provinces of our empire, as well as all the Greek Consuls, are to return immediately to their country. The merchants and other Hellenic subjects residing in Turkey must likewise withdraw from Constantinople; but in order to protect the interests of Greek commerce, we will grant them a delay of fifteen days. As to those who are established in the provinces, this delay will only be counted from the day of reception of the order for their departure. It is proved by positive statements that it is not in consequence of any neglect, but rather of the tolerance of the Greek Government, that our frontier provinces have been invaded. Although the Imperial Government has unquestionably the right to stop and confiscate all vessels found in our harbors, as pledges of the very considerable expenses incurred by us, my august master thinks it corresponds better with his sense of moderation not to inflict any losses on Greek subjects in a question only regarding the Greek Government. When that government shall have returned to more equitable sentiments, taking into its consideration international rights and the rules of the *jus gentium*,[c] then the occasion will have arrived for examining the question of the expenses caused by this insurrection. All Hellenic ships are, therefore, allowed to return without any hindrance, during the term fixed for them, to their own country. It has been enjoined on the proper authorities to facilitate the departure of those Greek subjects who are poor and destitute, and to use as much indulgence as possible toward the sick and infirm."

(The most Christian and civilized Government of Austria manages these things in a different style—witness the expulsion of the Ticinese.)[110]

"I think it expedient to repeat once more that the Hellenic Government alone has enforced upon us this decision, and that all the responsibility consequent upon it must entirely rest with Greece.

"Reshid Pasha"

---

[a] These documents are given according to *L'Indépendance belge*, No. 108, April 18, 1854.—*Ed.*

[b] Nesset Bey.—*Ed.*

[c] International law.—*Ed.*

According to this order 3,000 Greeks embarked at Constantinople on the 5th of April, and we hear that the Pasha of Smyrna has already published the order for the Greeks inhabiting that city.[a]

The circular addressed by Lord Stratford de Redcliffe to the British Consuls in Turkey and Greece, runs as follows:

"Constantinople, Saturday, April 1, 1854

"Sir: It has come to my knowledge that the Hellenes who have invaded the frontier provinces of Turkey are exciting the Greek subjects of the Sultan to revolt, by declaring that the Governments of France and England are ready to support them in overthrowing the authority of the Sultan. I am also informed that similar maneuvers are employed with a view to persuading people that the French and English Embassadors will give protection to all the Hellenic subjects in Turkey, as soon as the Porte—in consequence of its diplomatic and commercial rupture with Greece—shall notify its intention to expel them from the States of the Sultan. Whereas such suppositions have a tendency to encourage false hopes, to mislead well-disposed men and to aggravate, criminally, the evils inseparable from a state of war, I hasten to give you the assurance that these assertions have no foundation at all. Those who for one moment rely on falsehoods so transparent and so incompatible with common sense and facts, must be very ignorant and credulous indeed. But such is unfortunately the case everywhere, in countries where the means of publicity are only imperfectly developed. You know as well as I do, that England and France are entirely with the Sultan in the noble resistance he opposes to a violent and unjust aggression. It necessarily follows that the two allied Governments cannot view, but with painful feelings of indignation and reprobation, a movement calculated only to benefit Russia, without even having the merit of being spontaneous, and which must ultimately embarrass the Porte and its allies, while it offers no other prospect but the ruin of those who thus expose their lives for so chimerical an illusion. We must pity the innocent families unfortunately implicated in the consequences of a brutal and unprincipled policy; but on our part there can exist no relations with the leaders, nor any dissimulation of the sentiments which the conduct of a senseless party cannot fail to inspire. I have to recommend to you not to neglect any opportunity of making known the contents of this circular to all those who may be disposed to allow themselves to be misled by the false assertions which it denounces.

"Stratford de Redcliffe"

The populations most immediately interested in the issue of the eastern complications are, besides the Germans, the Hungarians and Italians. It is of some consequence, therefore, to know the intentions of the diverse parties of these nations with regard to their relations toward one another. The following article from the Turin *Unione*, which I translate for this purpose, will show you the views of the constitutional party in Italy,[111] which seems to be quite prepared to sacrifice Hungary in order to recover Italian independence. The

---

[a] Report from the Constantinople correspondent of April 3. *The Times*, No. 21718, April 18, 1854.— *Ed.*

secret of the duration of the Austrian Empire is no other than this provincial egotism which blinds each people with the illusion that they can conquer their liberty at the sacrifice of their fellow-people's independence.

"The English journals take great pains to give the impending war with Russia a character of liberty and European independence, while, in fact, they have nothing in view but their own commercial interests; in proof of which Lord John Russell recommends us Italians to remain quiet, and gives us to understand that Austria may one day or other become more humane. Thus he recognizes, at least, that at present she has nothing humane at all about her. Nevertheless, philanthropic England is trying to secure her alliance for the 'triumph of the *liberty and independence of Europe.*' As to the French press, it is not free, and under the dread of receiving warnings for the first time and being suspended for the second one, it cannot but make itself the echo of what is desired by the Government. Besides, the French papers are not accustomed to consider the questions of the day on a grand scale, and undergo too much the impulse of fashion. The German liberal papers write under the pressure of the immense fear which Russia causes them and justly so, if we consider the influence she has already acquired over the two principal powers of Germany. But what do we want? The independence of Italy. As long, however, as there is talk about the territorial integrity of Turkey and European *equilibrium* as based on the treaty of Vienna,[112] it is quite natural that we should continue to enjoy that identical *status quo* so contradictory to our wishes. What does Russia pretend to? To get rid of the Ottoman Empire and consequently of the equilibrium of the *status quo* and to revise the map of Europe. This is the very thing which we want. But it will be said that Russia wants to revise it in her own fashion. It is exactly this which may turn to our benefit, because neither France, nor England, nor Germany can tolerate this new aggrandizement of the territory or influence of an Empire that possesses already too much of both, and thus they will be forced to look out for a bulwark against her. This bulwark can be no other State but Austria, toward whom the occidental States are obliged to show generosity and to give her the whole Valley of the Danube, from Orsova to the Black Sea and below the Danube, the Dobrodja and the keys of the Balkans. Austria would then possess:

"1. A vast territory, with a population kindred to her own.

"2. The whole course of a great river, so necessary to the commerce of Germany.

"In such a case Austria would no longer want Italy, as far at least as her defense is concerned, and she would concentrate about six millions of South Slavonians and four millions of Daco-Romanians, in order to associate them with three other millions of the former and about as many of the latter, who are already subject to her dominion.

"Integrity and Independence of Turkey! Two solemn paradoxes. If you understand by independence the liberty enjoyed by a nation to govern itself according to its own principles, and without the right of any foreigner to intermeddle, that independence was already much compromised by the treaty of Kainardji,[113] and received its death-blow (colpo di grazia) from the recent treaty with the Occidental Powers.[114] Consequently it is no longer the Sultan who governs Turkey, but the European Powers; and from the moment that Mussulmans and Christians, conquerors and conquered, are subjected to an equality before law; from the moment that the rayahs—forming four-fifths of the population—are to have arms in their hands, Turkey no longer exists, but a transformation is set on foot that cannot realize itself without violence and the most serious disorders, and without the two sects who, during four centuries, have been accustomed to detest each other, coming to blows. Then let us hear no more of the independence of Turkey, except as a fable.

"And the territorial integrity! Was it then not France and England which, in agreement with Russia, wrested from Turkey the Greek Kingdom, viz: the Peloponnesus, Attica, Boeotia, Phocis, Acarnania, Aetolia, the Island of Negropont, etc., with a million of inhabitants? Was it not they? Is it not the French who took Algiers? Was it not France, England and Russia who gave to Egypt a half-independence? Was it not the Englishman who, fifteen years ago, seized upon Aden, on the Red Sea? Is it not also the Englishmen who covet Egypt?[115] And Austria that covets Bosnia and Servia? Why then speak of preserving a state of things against which all conspire, and which is unable to continue by its own force?

"We conclude, therefore, that Russia, while intending the overthrow of Turkey, is intending a good thing; that also the western Powers are justly inspired, if they intend to oppose the encroachments of Russia, but if the latter powers want to gain their object, they must dispense with the diplomatic hypocrisy in which they have enveloped themselves, and must be resolved to undo Turkey and revise the map of Europe. That is the point they must come to."[a]

Written on April 18, 1854

First published in the *New-York Daily Tribune*, No. 4068, May 2 and in the *New-York Semi-Weekly Tribune*, No. 932, May 2, 1854

Signed: *Karl Marx*

Reproduced from the *New-York Daily Tribune*

---

[a] *L'Unione*, No. 138, April 12, 1854.— *Ed.*

Karl Marx

[GREECE AND TURKEY.—
TURKEY AND THE WESTERN POWERS.—
FALLING OFF IN WHEAT SALES
IN ENGLAND] [116]

London, Friday, April 21, 1854

We are informed by the *Prussian Correspondence*[a] that the famous Chevalier Bunsen is not recalled, but has only obtained, on his own demand, a lengthened leave of absence. Count Bernstorff is designed as his temporary *locum tenens.*

The Commission of Constitution of the Swedish Diet has decided, by a majority of 12 to 11, that the ministers should be impeached before the High Court of the Kingdom, for their conduct in the affair of the simplification of the taxes which has lately been under consideration.

According to a report from Mr. Meroni, Consul at Belgrade, the Austrians must be prepared to meet the armed resistance of the Servians, in case they should march their armies into Servia.

On the 3d inst., Mr. Metaxas left Constantinople, to be followed, within a delay of less than fourteen days, by 40 to 50,000 of his compatriots. No embassy was willing to act as his temporary substitute for carrying on the current business. The Austrian Embassador declined, because, England and France being the protecting powers of Greece, it was the duty of their Chancelleries to represent Greece in the interim. Prussia would not accept, because Austria had declined. The Embassadors of England and France declared the time rather unseasonable for constituting themselves the representatives of Mr. Metaxas. The Charges d'Affaires of the smaller powers thought fit anxiously to avoid making any manifestation either of sympathy or antipathy. Thus Mr. Metaxas was obliged to leave behind an Attache of his own. But

---

[a] *Preussische Lithographische Correspondenz.—Ed.*

it was soon discovered that his substitute, abusing the power
granted to him by the Porte, busily engaged himself in distributing
passports among the Greek Rayahs, in order to enable them to
join the insurgents in Albania. Consequently, the functions of the
Greek Chancellery have been altogether suspended, the issuing of
passports being now devolved on a commission consisting of two
Turks and two Rayahs.

Simultaneously, a notice was posted up that any subject of the
Kingdom of Greece, who wished to become a subject of the Sultan,
might be allowed to do so on finding two respectable persons to
guarantee his good conduct. As the Hellenic inhabitants of
Constantinople had uttered loud threats of setting Constantinople
on fire and pillaging it before their marching off, extraordinary
measures have been taken by the Government. The Turks patrol
by day and night, and on the promenade of Pera [117] fifty cannons
are mounted. From sunset to midnight every one walking or
riding through the streets or the field must be provided with
a lantern; after midnight all circulation is forbidden. Another
edict prohibits the export of grain. Greeks confessing the Latin
religion have been allowed to remain on the responsibility of the
Latin Bishops of Pera. For the greater part, these natives from
Tinos, Andros, and Syros, belong to the servant class. The inhabitants of the Isle of Hydra have addressed a petition to the
Porte, sharply censuring the Greek insurrection, and entreating
the Government to except them from the general measure.
There has also arrived a deputation of the Greek subjects of
the Porte from Trikala in Thessaly, requesting it to protect them
energetically against the Hellenian robbers, as whole villages had
been laid in ashes by them, and their inhabitants, without distinction of sex or age, dragged to the frontiers, there to be tormented
in the most cruel manner.

A feeling of doubt, mistrust and hostility against their western
allies is gaining possession of the Turks. They begin to look on
France and England as more dangerous enemies than the Czar
himself, and the general cry is—"they are going to dethrone the
Sultan, and divide the land—they are going to make us slaves to
the Christian population." Landing south of Constantinople
instead of north of Varna, the allies are fortifying Gallipoli against
the Turks themselves. The tract of land on which the village is
situated is/a long peninsula joined by a narrow isthmus to the
continent and admirably adapted for a stronghold for invaders. It
was there the Genoese of old defied the Greek Emperors of
Constantinople. [118] Besides, the appointment of the new Sheik-ul-

Islam[a] fills the orthodox Moslems with indignation, since they regard him as little better than a tool of the Greek priesthood, and a strong feeling begins to pervade the Turks that it was better to yield the one demand of Nicholas than be made the plaything of a knot of greedy powers.

The opposition to the Coalition Ministry and the popular indignation at their manner of carrying on the war has grown so strong that even *The Times* is obliged to choose between damaging its own circulation and its subserviency to the Cabinet of all the Talents, and has thought fit to make a furious onslaught on them in its Wednesday's number.[b]

The Quebec correspondent of *The Morning Post* writes:

"Our fleet in the Pacific is quite strong enough to capture the whole of the Russian forts and posts along the coasts of Russian America (and they have none in the interior) and those which they possess here and there among the Fox, Aleutian and Kurile Islands, the whole forming a chain from the American coast to Japan. With the capture of these islands, which are also very valuable in furs, copper, in the mildness of their climate and in some of them containing excellent harbors near the Asiatic main shore, where no good harbors exist, and of Russian America, our influence in the Pacific would be materially increased, at a period when the countries of that ocean are likely to become of that importance which has long been their due. The greatest resistance which would be offered to our fleet would be at New-Archangel, in the Island of Sitka, which, besides being strong by nature, has been completely fortified, and has now some 60 or 70 guns mounted. There are about 1,500 persons there, the garrison being about 500, and there is a dockyard where many vessels of war have been built. At most of the other posts there are but from 50 to 300 persons and few of them have works of any importance. Should France desire to acquire territory as a set off to this conquest, should we make it, she might be allowed to possess herself of Kamchatka and the neighboring coast."[c]

The Gazette's returns of wheat sold in the market towns of England and Wales exhibit a remarkable falling off as compared with those of the corresponding period of 1853, and this may be taken as a criterion of the quantity grown in each of the preceding harvests. The sales were, in

	January	February	March
1853	qrs. 532,282	345,329	358,886
1854	qrs. 266,477	256,061	227,556

The last weekly return is 36,628 quarters against 88,343 quarters in the corresponding week of 1853. These returns, then,

---

[a] Arif Bey.— *Ed.*
[b] *The Times*, No. 21719, April 19, 1854, leader.— *Ed.*
[c] *The Morning Post*, No. 25055, April 21, 1854.— *Ed.*

show for the three months a falling off of about half a million of quarters, when compared with the corresponding months of 1853, afford the most striking proof of the deficiency in the last crop.

The Mark Lane Express says:

"The liberal character of the foreign supply has thus far prevented the shortness of the home deliveries being severely felt, and there are still considerable quantities of wheat and flour on passage from different quarters to this country; but can we expect that the importations during the time which must necessarily elapse before the next crop can be rendered available will be on an equally liberal scale? America has drained her ports on the seaboard to furnish what we have received from thence; and, though we do not doubt that she has still considerable stores in the far west, it will need high prices to cover the expenses of transporting the same to the east coast, and from thence to England. The northern ports of Europe have been nearly cleared of previous accumulations, and the war with Russia cuts off further supplies from the Black Sea and Azoff."[a]

We offer the foregoing for the consideration of our readers, without further comment.

Written on April 21, 1854

First published in the *New-York Daily Tribune,* No. 4072, May 6; reprinted in the *New-York Semi-Weekly Tribune,* No. 934, May 9, 1854

Signed: *Karl Marx*

Reproduced from the *New-York Daily Tribune*

---

[a] This quotation is given as reprinted in *The Morning Post,* No. 25052, April 18, 1854.— *Ed.*

Frederick Engels

THE TURKISH WAR[119]

On the Danube there is nothing new except the complete evacuation of Lesser Wallachia by the Russians, and their preparations to storm the fortress of Silistria. With a view to this they had concentrated a large force of artillery on the opposite bank, and were, as it is reported, about to fling across some 30,000 men for the assault. It remains to be seen how far this report is true, but at any rate such a plan is not improbable. Its success is another question. It is certain that Silistria is the weakest of all the great Turkish fortresses, commanded within comfortable dis-mounting and breaching range by hights which have not, that we are aware, been fortified since the last war.[120] But this same Silistria, which fell in 1810 after four days' attack, sustained in 1828-29 two blockades of ten months' duration, and held out thirty-five days after the opening of a regular siege, and *nine days* after the completion of a practicable breach in the main wall. A fortress which has undergone such varying fates may well be said to be beyond any reasoning as to its strength and defensibility.[a]

But supposing Silistria to be carried by storm by an overwhelm-ing superiority of force, it by no means follows that the road to Constantinople is clear for them. In order to advance on Shum-la and Varna, they must leave at least 6,000 men behind at Silistria, which would then have to serve them as bridge-head for another and more conveniently situated bridge. Shumla they could hardly attack; for even if they took this famous intrenched camp, they would simply deprive the enemy of a good position

---

[a] For details see this volume, pp. 239-40.— *Ed.*

without gaining one for themselves. Shumla shuts against the Russians the passage of the Balkans, but if taken it does not open that passage to them.

The importance of Shumla consists in the fact that Varna is the key to the Lower Balkan, and Shumla is the key to Varna. Whatever may be the defects of the fortifications of Varna—and they are many—if fully garrisoned it requires a siege-corps of 20,000 to 30,000 men; and unless there remain troops enough, after deducting these, to cover the siege against any sallies from the intrenched camp of Shumla, where the Turks can concentrate all their forces, the siege cannot be carried on successfully. Varna held out, in 1828, *three weeks* after two practicable breaches had been made in its ramparts, and that at a time when the Russian fleet commanded the Black Sea, and the Turks had hardly the shadow of an army to attempt an attack upon the besiegers. Now, supposing Silistria taken, the various and very difficult river-lines before Varna and Shumla forced, and Varna blockaded, is there a chance that enough Russian troops would remain to neutralize Shumla? For the Turks at Shumla could act not only against the besiegers of Varna, but in the direction of the Danube, and at least one of the lines of communication of the Russians, so as to force them to detach more and more troops from their main body, which ultimately might be weakened to a dangerous extent.

And if Varna should fall what would Paskievich do if Omer Pasha sullenly remained in his stronghold of Shumla, ready to profit by the very first mistake the Russians made? Would he dare to push on toward Constantinople with but a single line of communication, which at the same time would be hemmed in and menaced by the Shumla army on one side, and by the allied fleets in the Black Sea on the other? Not he, indeed, if we are to judge from his exploits in Asia and Poland. He is an almost overcautious general, a sort of military slow-coach, with nothing of the Radetzky in him. And if he had he would find that maneuver extremely hazardous, for he knows very well what a plight his predecessor Diebich was in when he arrived, in 1829, at Adrianople. Thus, even without taking into account the Anglo-French troops landing in Thrace, and making no more of the allied fleets than what they have justified us in, namely, supposing they will do next to nothing, we find that it is not such an easy thing for the Russians to march straight ahead to Constantinople with banners displayed and bands playing. That against Turkey unaided they were sure ultimately to get there no one ever denied except those new-fangled military writers who form their judgment not from facts but from a conviction that "right against might" is necessarily victorious, and that in a "good cause" no blunders can possibly be committed.[a]

We may add that the British forces in the Baltic have done even less so far than those in the Black Sea.

Written on April 24, 1854

First published in the *New-York Daily Tribune*, No. 4080, May 16; reprinted in the *New-York Weekly Tribune*, No. 662, May 20, 1854 as a leader

Reproduced from the *New-York Daily Tribune*

---

[a] Arnold, "The Coming War", *The Leader*, Vol. V, No. 200, January 21, 1854, pp. 59-60.— *Ed.*

Karl Marx

[THE GREEK INSURRECTION.—
THE POLISH EMIGRATION.—THE AUSTRO-
PRUSSIAN TREATY.—RUSSIAN DOCUMENTS][121]

London, Friday, April 28, 1854

The last authentic news from Turkey fully confirms the views of *The Tribune*, with respect to the retreat of the Russians from Kalafat, the occupation by the Russians of the Dobrodja, and the character of the Greek insurrection.[a]

The *Lloyd* confirms the report that the Russians have raised the investment of Kalafat, and that the evacuation of Lesser Wallachia is now complete. The latest news received at Constantinople states that the Russians do not advance, but, on the contrary, are fortifying the Dobrodja.[b]

With regard to the Greek insurrection, the following letter from Vienna, of the 21st April, appeared in yesterday's *Moniteur*:

"The Greek insurrection does not make any progress in Epirus, but begins to show itself in its true character. If anybody could have thought that the interests of Christianity and nationality were anything else than a vain pretext, the acts of the chiefs of the Hellenic bands from the kingdom of Greece must dissolve all such doubts. The altercations which, since the commencement of the struggle, have taken place between Grivas and Tsavellas, with respect to the chief command of the insurgents, are known. These two chiefs continue to act separately, and make no scruple of taking advantage of any opportunity to injure each other. Grivas, especially, has only carried pillage and incendiarism to the Christian Rayahs, of whom he pretends to be the liberator. The Suliotes,[c] who have come to the resolution to interdict the access to their territory to several Hellenic chiefs, particularly denounce Grivas. At the beginning of last month, this chief went to demand hospitality of the Greek Primate, Deventzista, and left the day after, but not until he had pillaged his house, and carried off his wife by force. The Primate has gone to Abdi Pasha and asked permission to serve under his orders with a view

---

[a] See this volume, pp. 65-69, 70-72 and 129-31.— *Ed.*

[b] *Der Lloyd*'s report is given as reprinted in *The Morning Post*, No. 25061, April 28, 1854: "Withdrawal of the Russians from Kalafat. Vienna, April 26", and in *Le Moniteur universel*, No. 116, April 26, 1854.— *Ed.*

[c] Population of Southern Ioannina (Yannina) (Ancient Epirus).— *Ed.*

to revenge himself for this savage act. It is, however, at Mezzovo where Grivas distinguished himself by his skill in plundering. That town, misled by the Russian propaganda, spontaneously opened its gates to 'generallissimus' Grivas. His first act was to impose upon the Christian population a 'patriotic' contribution of 200,000 piasters. The sum not being extravagant, it was paid. But Grivas did not stop there. He called by turns, individually, on all the principal inhabitants, and all those in comfortable circumstances residing in the town, asking them to deposit, likewise as an offering, all articles of luxury in gold or silver which might be at their disposal. This mode of extortion excited murmurs, and it appeared neither expeditious nor very productive. It was then that Grivas took it into his mind an idea which seems to us a masterpiece of brigandage. Taking as a pretext the approach of the Ottoman troops which were marching on Mezzovo, he announced that the defense of the place necessitated the almost general burning of the town, and, in consequence, he invited the inhabitants to assemble with their families in the principal church of Mezzovo, where nearly 4,000 persons soon after collected. Grivas had anticipated that they would bring their money with them, as also their jewels and their most valuable articles, and thus he would get into his power all the wealth of Mezzovo. He then let them out in small numbers, and handed them over to his followers, who robbed them without ceremonies. Such are the exploits of the Greek chief, who has, up to this moment, played the most prominent part in the insurrection of Epirus. Grivas then only opposed a feeble resistance to the Turks. After setting the town on fire, he retired toward Archelous, in the direction of Rodovizzi. Mezzovo, previously the most flourishing city of Epirus, next to Yannina and Buat, is now a mere heap of ruins, and the inhabitants are reduced to misery. Only about 100 houses remain standing."[a]

Reshid Pasha has declared, on the unfounded rumor that Kossuth and Mazzini proposed to come to Constantinople, that he would not permit them to enter the Turkish territory.

The formation of a Polish Legion is said to have found no opposition from the Embassadors of France and England, but to have met with obstacles of a different nature. General Wysocki submitted to the Porte and to Lord Redcliffe a document covered with several thousands of signatures, authorizing him to act in the name of a large portion of the Polish Emigration. On the other hand, Colonel Count Zamoiski, nephew of Prince Czartoryski, presented a similar document, also covered with many signatures, by which another fraction of the same Emigration authorize him to act on its behalf. In consideration of their divisions, in order to conciliate the alternative pretensions and rivalries, and in order to combine the services of both Wysocki and Zamoiski, the Ambassador of England advised the formation of two Polish Legions instead of one.[122]

Marshal Paskievich arrived on the 17th April at Jassy, and proceeded on the same day on his journey to Bucharest.

---

[a] Report from Vienna of April 21, 1854. *Le Moniteur universel*, No. 116, April 26, 1854.— *Ed.*

According to the *Hannoversche Zeitung* the following are the main stipulations of the treaty of offensive and defensive alliance concluded between Austria and Prussia.[a]

"1. Austria and Prussia guarantee to each other their German dominions and others (in und ausserdeutschen Besitzungen) in such manner that an attack directed against either of the two powers shall be considered as an attack directed against itself.

"2. Austria and Prussia mutually oblige themselves to support each other, and if need be, to proceed to a common aggression, as soon as one or the other of the contracting parties shall consider the interests of Germany as compromised, in which view they will agree with each other. The particular cases in which support is to be given, are provided in a separate stipulation, forming an integral portion of the convention. In order to secure its efficacy, the adequate military resources shall be placed on the necessary footing at certain provided epochs. The time, the extent and the employment of the troops, are reserved for special arrangement.

"3. All the members of the German *Bund*[b] are invited to accede to this offensive and defensive alliance, and to support it in conformity with the obligations imposed upon them by the federal act."

On comparison, you will find that these stipulations closely resemble the terms in which Count Nesselrode made his propositions of neutrality to the Prussian Court.[c] It is to be observed also that, practically, the convention is only adapted to the exigencies of a defensive policy, while with regard to the eventuality of an offensive policy, everything is reserved to the several Courts.

The First Chamber of Prussia passed, on the 25th inst., a vote of credit for thirty millions of dollars, in conformity with the recommendations of its Committee. The ministerial explanations given on this occasion by Herr von Manteuffel are so characteristic of that Prussian diplomacy which affects to conceal its intrinsic impotency under patriotic flourishes and nonsensical sublimity, that I will give you the document *in extenso.* Herr von Manteuffel says:

"The complications which have occurred between Russia and Turkey, and then extended to the Occidental powers, are generally known. The Prussian Government thought it expedient, in view of its position and interest, to unravel these complications and to arrange this difference. All its efforts and labors have proved abortive. Some fatality seems to have controlled this affair. Many attempts, which were likely to contribute to the reestablishment of peace, have resulted in nothing—perhaps because they were not made at the opportune moment and in a suitable manner. Thus the difficulties have been pushed to the extremity of war. The efforts of Prussia and of Austria to insure the maintenance of peace afford, as it were, a leading-string to which to tie again negotiations. Such was the great end

---

[a] Signed on April 20, 1854. *Hannoversche Zeitung*, No. 187, April 22, 1854.— *Ed.*
[b] Confederation.— *Ed.*
[c] See this volume, pp. 145-47.— *Ed.*

aimed at by the Vienna Conference. In this Conference the Government has not ceased to make the utmost efforts for the maintenance of peace. It has acted in a spirit of conciliation"

as the "Angel of Peace" of the Emperor Nicholas

"but always in a firm and decided manner, and with the consciousness of its position as a great power"

in the same manner in which the Emperor of Russia expressed it in his secret correspondence.

"It is precisely because it is uninterested"

about its becoming a Russian province and changing decorations

"and because its disinterested (uninteressiert) position has been acknowledged by the other powers, that it was able to speak frankly and energetically. Its offers and its efforts have been received by the two parties alternately with gratitude and with regret. But the Government did not allow itself to be drawn from its career. The first condition for the existence of a great power is independence. This independence the Prussian Government has known to uphold, by taking steps in the interest of peace, without troubling itself by a doubt whether they would be agreeable to this or that power,"

altogether a fine definition of what is to be understood by the independence of a great power.

"When circumstances became more threatening, the Government thought that, besides its generous efforts for the preservation of peace, it was its duty to consider, above all, the Prussian and German interests. With this view, a Convention has been entered into with Austria. The other States of the German Confederation will adhere to this alliance. Consequently, we may be sure of cooperation with Austria and the whole of Germany. According to the Government, the most certain and efficient guarantee of the German powers, consists in this cooperation. Besides this intimate union, the anterior concert of Prussia and Austria with the Occidental powers on the basis of the Vienna Conference,[123] will continue. Prussia has not estranged itself from the Occidental powers, notwithstanding the assertions of the contrary in the English press. This concert with the Occidental powers still exists. The protocol manifesting this concert, has already been signed by the Embassador of Prussia; but this protocol cannot be laid before the Chamber. The respective positions of the four powers up to this day, and their efforts for the restoration of peace, will continue, although two of these powers have commenced operations of war—"

a proof that the war is a sham, and peace-negotiations the real business of the western Cabinets.

"As far as Russia is concerned, the Cabinet of St. Petersburg has recently made more favorable and more conciliatory overtures, and though they hold out only weak hopes of peace at present, they give, nevertheless, the point of issue for new negotiations of peace. The Prussian Government has shown its readiness to hope in peace until the last moment. As long as there will remain only a spark of hope for peace, Prussia will continue its efforts and pains (Mühen). When the decisive moment shall arrive for Prussia",

Trema, Byzantium! [a]

"*the Government will act* without delay, without hesitation, and with energy. Prussia must prepare for that moment. Its words will have the greater weight, because it will be ready to draw the sword. When the conflict between Russia and Turkey broke out, the Occidental powers exhibited firmness and strengthened the Ottoman Porte. Prussia had not then the mission to play the part of an umpire. It considered, besides the violated right of a third power, above all the welfare of its own subjects. Its own interest in the Oriental question is more remote than that of Austria, which has a more direct interest in it, and Austria has urgently begged of Prussia not to refuse her cooperation. Prussia and Austria have pursued the object of moderating, on both sides, the pretensions pushed too far, and rendering difficult the work of pacification. It was their efforts that led to the Vienna Conference, justly considered as a fortunate event. Our Government cannot abandon a situation which still permits it to exercise a salutary influence"

for Russia

"on the Occidental powers. It is the mediating link for those powers, and may serve as a support for the hopes of peace. As to the project of note communicated by the four powers to the Russian Government, you must not forget that Russia never acknowledged the conference, and also that this project, in consequence of new circumstances, ceased to be acceptable to Turkey. The new Vienna protocol"

and this is a very important revelation on the part of *Herr von* Manteuffel,

"affords new means toward a general peace, and at all events to keep the war aloof from Prussia and Germany. With regard to the anterior demand on the part of Austria to propose to the German Diet a strict neutrality, binding for Prussia, too, the government acting spontaneously was unable to consent to it. It was unable to compromise its position as a great independent power, and the liberty of its resolutions. Besides, by such a neutrality we should have afforded to the other powers a pretext for assuming a hostile attitude, if these powers should consider such an attitude consonant with their interests. To-day the situation of the Occidental powers is essentially altered by their engagement,"

Vienna Protocol.

"In the most unfavorable case peace will not be obtained, but in the most favorable case all the great calamities which are the consequences of war will be diverted from our fatherland; and this is an immense and inappreciable advantage."

If anybody can make anything out of this alternative, I congratulate him on his acuteness.

"The military events which may take place in the Baltic and Black Seas between Russia and the Occidental powers have forced Prussia, in consequence of her geographical position as a great power"

---

[a] "Tremble, Byzantium!" G. Donizetti's opera *Belisario*, libretto by S. Cammarano, Act II, Scene 3.— *Ed.*

rather longer than great

"to prepare the means required for the defense, if need be, of its interests with arms in hand. At all events, the government has not shrunk before the past,"

meaning, perhaps, if anything, that it is not ashamed of its past,

"and is glad to have found an occasion for publicly explaining its views."[a]

The Committee, it is needless to say, found these explanations exceedingly gratifying.

The following new documents have been published by the *Journal de St.-Pétersbourg*:

"*Ordre du Jour of the Commissioner of Police*

April 15, 1854

"His Majesty, the Emperor, has been pleased to order the extension to the men retired from the Marine, and the train of the Guards who feel yet able-bodied and zealous to enter a second period of service the advantages granted to the pensioners of the Guards and of the army, etc.

"Aide-de-camp—General *Galakhoff*."

"*Ukase addressed to the Directing Senate*

"In order to increase the means of defense of the coasts of the Gulf of Finland, we have thought fit to form a reserve-fleet of oar-boats, and order:

"1. The organization of four new legions of rowers.

"2. These troops will be formed by an appeal for voluntary service, made in the Governments of Petersburg, Novgorod, Olonez and Tver.

"3. The measures to be taken for the organization of this corps are intrusted to a Committee composed of His Imperial Highness, the Grand Duke Constantine, Director of the Ministry of the Marine, and of the Ministers of the Imperial domains and apanages of the interior, etc.[b]

"April 14, 1854   "*Nicholas*"

"*A Regulation concerning the Maritime Armament*

"I. Object of the institution and composition of the maritime armament:

"1. The maritime armament is made with a view to complete the reserve flotilla of oar-boats destined to defend the coasts of the Gulf of Finland.

"2. This armament is composed of four legions, the formation and organization of which are left to the Minister of the Marine.

"3. Individuals of all conditions are allowed to enter the corps of this armament.

---

[a] Manteuffel's speech at a sitting of the First Chamber of the Prussian Diet on April 22, 1854.—*Ed.*

[b] P. D. Kiselyev, L. A. Perovsky, D. G. Bibikov.—*Ed.*

"II. Enlistment:

"4. Persons desirous of entering the maritime corps must be provided with legal passports, and serfs must have a special authorization from their proprietors.

"5. At St. Petersburg the volunteers have to present themselves to the department of inspection of the Ministry of the Marine, in government towns to the Governors, and in district towns to the police authorities.

"6. The passports will be deposited in exchange for a ticket of an appointed form. The passports will be transmitted to the department of inspection, where the bearers have to present themselves. At the same time they will receive, if they demand it, one month's pay, to be marked on the ticket.

"7. The police are to watch the departure of the volunteers for St. Petersburg, and to give them all aid and protection for facilitating their journey. In case of sickness of a volunteer, he is to be taken care of.

8 and 9 are without interest.

"III. Conditions of service:

"10. Those who wish to enter the oar-marine shall receive on the day of their inspection:

"A. Eight rubles silver per month.

"B. Ammunition and provisions like the regular soldiers of the marine.

"C. A peasant's suit of clothes. The volunteers may wear their beards and hair *à la paysanne*.[a]

"11. The term of expiration of the service is to be the 1st November, 1854.

"12. After this day no volunteer will be retained for service.

"13. Those who shall distinguish themselves will be rewarded like the regular troops.

"14. In case of 'prizes' being made with the assistance of the gun-boats the oar-volunteers are to have their shares according to the laws of distribution.

"15. In case of their being wounded the volunteers acquire the rights enjoyed by the soldiers.

"16. Their families are to be provided for by the local authorities and corporations.

"Constantine
"Count Kisseleff
"Count Perowski
"Dmitry Bibikoff"[b]

It would have been impossible to give a better bird's-eye view of Russia than is offered by the preceding documents: the Emperor, the bureaucracy, the serfs, the beards *à la paysanne*, the police, the oar-marine, the corporations, the lands and the seas—"all the Russias."

Written on April 27 and 28, 1854

First published in the *New-York Daily Tribune*, No. 4079, May 15, 1854

Signed: *Karl Marx*

Reproduced from the newspaper

---

[a] In peasant style.— *Ed.*

[b] Marx cites these documents according to *Le Moniteur universel*, No. 117, April 27, 1854.— *Ed.*

Karl Marx

[THE BOMBARDMENT OF ODESSA.—GREECE.— PROCLAMATION OF PRINCE DANIEL OF MONTENEGRO.—MANTEUFFEL'S SPEECH] [124]

London, Tuesday, May 2, 1854

The bombardment of Odessa, so many times performed by a boastful imagination, has at length been realized. But the telegraphic dispatches hitherto received are too meager and deficient in detail to deserve a commentary. According to the most trustworthy news, the bombardment began on the 22d, was suspended on the 23d (a summons to surrender being sent to the Governor of the place [125]), and recommenced on the 24th April. On one side, it is affirmed that a great portion of the town was laid in ruins; on the other, that only the forts were destroyed by rockets and shells. In some quarters it is even asserted that the bombardment had remained without any effect whatever. Several dispatches announce the destruction of eight Russian vessels— merchant vessels, of course, as there were no Russian men-of-war at Odessa. The latest dispatch—dated Odessa, 26th April—states that the whole of the combined fleet had taken its departure on that morning.[a]

In order to prepare the public mind for this event, the French Government had just published in the *Moniteur* an extract from Admiral Hamelin's latest report to the Minister of the Marine,[b] in which he states:

"The English steam-frigate *Furious* had gone on the 6th of April to Odessa, in order to claim and take on board the Consuls and such French and English subjects as might wish to quit that town on the approach of hostilities ... that, in spite of the flag of truce which she had hoisted, and which her landing-boat also

---

[a] Telegraphic dispatch from Odessa of April 26. *The Times*, No. 21731, May 3, 1854.— *Ed.*

[b] Théodore Ducos.— *Ed.*

bore, the Russian batteries treacherously fired seven shots upon this boat a few moments after it had left the pier. ...Admiral Dundas and himself were deliberating on the measures of retribution required by such a barbarous proceeding." [a]

The Russians give a different version of the affair. They allege that the sending of a flag of truce was only a pretext for examining their works of defense. The fact of the ship *Retribution,* having entered the port of Sevastopol, some time ago, under pretext of remitting dispatches, but with the real object of making drawings of the interior batteries, had highly irritated the Czar—the more so, as the noise made about this achievement by the English press had confirmed this supposition. Orders had consequently been given to the effect that in future all vessels presenting themselves before a Russian port should be received with cannon-shots. The *Indépendance belge* publishes a letter illustrating these circumstances, apparently by a Russian officer at Odessa, but probably having no other author than M. de Kisseleff himself.

"On the 27th of March (8th of April) at 6 o'clock a.m., the *Furious,* a steamer of the English royal fleet, approached the pier of the quarantine-port of Odessa without hoisting the flag of truce. Although the captain of the port had orders to fire a rocket over any English man-of-war, he resolved nevertheless to abstain from executing his orders at once, admitting that the steamer might not yet be aware of the English declaration of war. The *Furious* cast anchor, lowered her boat, and sent it on shore with a flag of truce. The captain of the port immediately dispatched his aide-de-camp to meet the officer of the boat. This officer declared that he came with the mission to fetch the Consuls of France and England. He was answered that these gentlemen had quitted Odessa a long time since, and was consequently invited to remove instantly; whereupon the boat was taken on board the pyroscaphe, the flag of truce being removed. But instead of weighing anchor, the officers of the steamer set about taking drawings of the batteries. It was then that, in order to prevent the *Furious* from doing this, blind shots were fired over her. The *Furious* taking no notice of them, a ball was sent into one of her wheels. The *Furious* immediately withdrew." [b]

It is certainly ridiculous that the English and French fleets had to wait to be furnished with "reasons" by the Russians before entering upon the hostilities now directed against a Russian port, and not then even to take it but merely to launch a few broadsides into it.

About the same time when the *Furious* was dispatched on her mission, the letters received from Odessa at Constantinople

---

[a] Hamelin's report to the Minister of the Marine of April 10, 1854. *Le Moniteur universel,* No. 120, April 30, 1854.— *Ed.*

[b] *L'Indépendance belge,* No. 121, May 1, 1854.— *Ed.*

affirmed that the Russian Government had seized all grain in bond, without any respect for the private property of foreign merchants. The quantity confiscated amounted to 800,000 chetverts.[a][126] Besides, the Russian Government had enjoined the foreign merchants to supply 150,000 sacks and 15,000 waggons for transporting to the interior the confiscated grain. All reclamations were met by the Governor[b] with the declaration that the policy of the western powers reduced the Russian Government to such extremities, and that in seizing their property they only saved it from the plunder of an exasperated population. On the reclamations of the neutral consuls remaining at Odessa, the Governor at last consented—not to pay for the seized goods—but to issue simple receipts to the owners.

The following is an extract from a Stockholm paper:

"The whole town swarms with fugitives from Finland; many, too, come from Aland," (which seems to be still occupied by the Russians,) "in order to escape the Russian press-gangs. The Russian fleet is in great want of seamen, and the authorities lay violent hands on young and old. In the dead of the night fathers of families are hurried off without a moment's grace, and the result is that whole households fly to Sweden, with bag and baggage, in order to escape from such tyranny."[c]

The *Journal de St.-Pétersbourg* of the 23d ult. contains a proclamation from the Czar to his subjects, representing the war against the Occidental powers as a war of the orthodox church against the heretics, and aiming at the liberation of its suppressed brethren in the Ottoman Empire.[d]

The Paris *Presse* of to-day has the following article:

"One of our correspondents at Constantinople has sent us important details on the Russian complot which was discovered some time ago, and the inquiry into which has just terminated. This inquiry clearly proves that Russia has long been preparing the crisis which was to carry off the sick man under the very hands of his physicians. The inquiry proves that Baron Oelsner had feigned to place himself at the service of the Turkish Police in order the better to deceive his *surveillants.* He was in the receipt of 1,000 piasters per month. Notwithstanding his astuteness, his double game was detected in the following manner: He had entered into relations

---

[a] An old Russian measure of liquid and dry substances. It equals 2.099 hectolitres.— *Ed.*

[b] N. N. Annenkov.— *Ed.*

[c] The name of the newspaper has not been established. Marx quotes from the item "Sweden" in *The Times,* No. 21723, April 24, 1854.— *Ed.*

[d] Marx took the report about the manifesto of April 23 (11), 1854 from the telegraphic dispatch "Turkey and Russia" in *The Times,* No. 21731, May 3, 1854.— *Ed.*

with Mr. Aska, a physician in the Turkish service, and believing that he could trust him, he avowed to him that, although paid by the Turkish Police, he had never ceased to serve Russia. According to Mr. Oelsner, Russia proposed to recruit among the Greeks and the Slavs in Turkey an army of 60,000 conspirators ready to rise at a given signal. The decisive blow was to be struck at Constantinople. The chief of the complot in that city was an Englishman, a certain Plantagenet Harrison. Mr. Aska feigned to enter into the views of Oelsner, and gave a hint to the Turkish Police. The police, having suspected Oelsner for a considerable time, caused him to be watched with increased care, and discovered that he was in the habit of sending regular reports to Prince Gorchakoff. Finally they succeeded in intercepting one of these reports. Oelsner, though very cautious on the whole, had the unlucky idea of showing the above report to Mr. Aska, who immediately informed Mr. Palamari, the secret agent of the Turkish Police, and contrived to give it in his presence to Radschiskz, an Austrian Slavonian who was in communication with Oelsner and his accomplices. The letter was seized upon this individual and forms one of the *pieces* of conviction. It was also averred that Oelsner had established a concert with Constantinos, captain of a Greek merchant ship, and that they had arranged for the affiliation of forty other captains of Greek ships who, at a given day, were to arrive at Constantinople, provided with ammunition and furnishing the materials for raising in rebellion the Greek population of the metropolis. Constantinos was in permanent relation not only with Oelsner, but also with Mr. Metaxas, the Greek Embassador at the Porte. Bodinaroff, a Russian Colonel, afforded the means of communication between Oelsner and Prince Gorchakoff." [127]

There has appeared in the *Augsburger Zeitung* a series of articles extremely hostile toward Russia, which have created a great sensation in Germany, as that journal was, until now, the most ardent partisan of Russian interests, and is known, at the same time, to receive its inspirations from the Austrian Cabinet. Austria is represented in these articles as released from her obligations toward Russia, in consequence of the revelations contained in the confidential correspondence of Sir H. Seymour. In one of these articles it is said:

"When the proceedings of Russia rendered it necessary to make representations at St. Petersburg, they were received in so peremptory a manner, and the Vienna Cabinet was treated so unceremoniously, that every new dispatch from Constantinople evoked painful presentiments. This want of respect, of consideration, engaged Count Mensdorff to ask for the command of a brigade, in order to be relieved from his post at St. Petersburg, although personally he had no cause for complaints."

Consequently he was replaced by Count Esterházy. In another article there occurs this passage:

"When the Emperor of Russia came to Olmütz, [128] his conduct toward Count Buol-Schauenstein was so improper, not to say offending, that it was remarked by everybody, and that Nesselrode and Meyendorf were embarrassed by it."

Let me remind your readers that it is a habit of Nesselrode to provoke such arrogant behavior of his august master in order to deplore it afterward.

"The young Emperor,[a] witnessing these proceedings against his minister, has not forgot[ten] them. The letters of Sir H. Seymour could only accelerate the fixed resolution of His Majesty"

to oppose the encroachments of Russia upon Austria herself.

"During his stay at Vienna, Count Orloff refused to engage himself, in the name of his sovereign, to respect under all circumstances the integrity of the Ottoman Empire."[b]

The Constantinople correspondent of *The Times* lays a special accent upon the statement that the Greek insurrection would infallibly lead to a revolution in Greece, that is, a struggle between the national party and the partisans of Russia. On the other hand, it appears that the cruelties of the Pasha's bayonets in Bulgaria are disposing the population in favor of Russia. Let me illustrate by a few facts the position of Greece toward the Occidental powers. We read in the *Nouvelliste de Marseille*, dated Constantinople, April 17:

"The European residents at Athens have to undergo all sorts of insults. They are even assailed with sticks, no obstacle being opposed by the Greek *gendarmerie*. On the 15th ult. Mr. Gaspari, a member of the French Embassy, and the son of an old French Consul at Athens, received blows and was knocked down in the presence of three *gendarmes*, who remained indifferent witnesses of this scene. On the same day other Frenchmen received warnings that a list of ninety-six *Franchi* destined for 'chastisement' had been drawn up. In consequence of these excesses a collective note of the French and English Representatives[c] was addressed to the Government of King Otto, informing him that any violence committed against the persons of French and English residents would immediately give occasion for an indemnity of 25,000 drachmas. On the 12th of April a new ultimatum was transmitted to the Greek Government, in which a delay of only five days was given, expiring on the 17th. This ultimatum calls upon King Otto to redress the wrongs suffered by the French, to pronounce in a categorical manner against the insurrection, and to retrieve the evils done and permitted. No satisfactory answer was expected on the part of the King. In case of a negative answer, the Embassadors had resolved to break off completely all relations with the Government, and at the same time to constitute themselves, in the collective name of France and England, as the *Administrators of Greece*, according to the provisions of the protocol establishing that kingdom.[129]"

---

[a] Francis Joseph I.— *Ed.*
[b] Marx gives the material published in the *Augsburger Zeitung* according to *The Times*, No. 21731, May 3, 1854, except for the last sentence which is taken from *Le Moniteur universel*, No. 122, May 2, 1854.— *Ed.*
[c] Rouen and Wyse.— *Ed.*

The Greek Government has addressed circulars to its foreign agents, in apology of its conduct during its recent quarrel with the Porte, the latest measures of which, against Greek subjects, says Mr. Paikos, arise from the resentment of Turkey at having no longer the privilege of considering Greece as a Turkish province, and which form merely the keystone of twenty years' intrigues against Greece, with the insurrections in Thessaly and Epirus as pretexts.

The *Wiener Presse*[a] of 28th April publishes the following proclamation of Prince Daniel[b] to the Montenegrin chiefs:

"I wish that you, too, Czernogoras (Montenegrins), now as before prove yourselves as heroic as the Greeks and other nations, after the example of our victorious ancestors who bequeathed us the liberty of which we are so proud in the eyes of the world. It is, therefore, that I desire to address the soldiers who have already entered their service, in order that I may know whether I can depend upon them, and I order the chiefs to assemble each his tribe. Each soldier is to declare spontaneously whether he is ready to march with me against the Turk, the common enemy of our faith and of our land. You, Captain, are to receive every volunteer, and report to me at Cettinie. But I conjure all those who are not ready to brave death, to stay at home. Whoever wishes to march with me must forget his wife and his children, and all he loves in this world. I tell you, my brave people, and you, my brethren, that whoever desires not to die with me, need not stir; because I know that whoever marches with me into war is worth more than fifty cowards. Thus I invite all gallant men whose hearts are not cold, and who do not hesitate to spill their blood for their country, the orthodox church and the holy cross, to share with me in the glory and the honor. We are, indeed, the sons of the old Montenegrins who vanquished three Turkish viziers, defeated French troops, and stormed the fortresses of the Sultan. Let us not betray our fatherland, nor disown the glory of our ancient friends, and let us meet to fight, in the holy name of God.

          "Cettinie, March 16, 1854

                                                        "*Daniel*"

We read in the *Agramer Zeitung* that in consequence of this appeal to the pious freebooters of Montenegro, the chiefs called together, in each of the Montenegrin clans, the young warriors and communicated this proclamation, when 4,000 men swore, at the altar, to conquer or die under the flag "For Faith and Fatherland." It is impossible not to recognize the interesting affinity of this movement with the phrases and hopes of the Prussian war of independence, whose memory is so faithfully kept up by Gen. Dohna at Königsberg, and the Prussian *Treubund*[130] generally. The attack of the Montenegrins against Herzegovina,

---

[a] *Die Presse.—Ed.*
[b] Danilo I Petrović Njegoš.— *Ed.*

by way of Nixitshy, will be commanded by Prince Daniel himself. The attack in the south (toward Albania), by way of Zabliak, will be led by the Woywode George Petrović.

"The mountaineers," says the *Agramer Zeitung*, "are well provided with ammunition, and each of the two corps will have twelve three-and-a-half-pounders at their disposal."[a]

The signal for opening the hostilities will be given by Col. Kovalevsky, who receives his instructions direct from St. Petersburg.

Herr von Manteuffel, having got his $30,000,000,[b] has sent the Chambers home with a speech from which I extract the following eminently characteristic passage:

"Gentlemen: By granting the credit you have given the Government the means to proceed on the way it has hitherto pursued, in entire union (*in voller Einigkeit*) with Austria and the whole of Germany, and in concert with the other great powers, and to preserve to Prussia the position due to her in the solution of the great European question of the day."[c]

Let me observe, that [in] the telegraphic report of this speech, given by the English papers, the "concert with all the other great powers" was falsely translated into a "concert with the Occidental powers." Prussia has chosen a higher aim. She wants, in concert with both parties apparently at war, to arrange measures of peace—with whom?

Herr von Manteuffel, on the same day on which he dismissed the Chambers, had the good fortune to deliver a second speech, in a *réunion* of his party, a speech far more precise and eloquent than the above official slang. That speech is the most eminently Prussian production of modern times. It is, as it were, Prussian statesmanship *in nuce*[d]:

"Gentlemen," said he, "there is a word which has been much abused—this word bears the name of liberty. I do not disown the word, but my motto is another one; my motto is the word *service*. (Dienst.) Gentlemen, all of us who meet here have the duty to serve God and the King, and it is my pride that I am able to serve that King. That word *service* holds together the Prussian State, scattered as it lies throughout German lands (*in deutschen Gauen*). This word must unite us all in the

---

[a] Marx quotes the *Agramer Zeitung* according to *The Times*, No. 21731, May 3, 1854.— *Ed.*

[b] See this volume, p. 168.— *Ed.*

[c] Manteuffel's speech at a sitting of the two Chambers of the Prussian Diet on April 29, 1854.— *Ed.*

[d] In a nutshell.— *Ed.*

different situations we hold. The word *service to the King* is my standard, it is the banner of all those who have met here, and in this lies the salvation of these times. Gentlemen, the service of the King shall live."

Manteuffel is right: there is no other Prussia than that which lives upon service of the King.

Written on May 2 and 3, 1854

First published in the *New-York Daily Tribune*, No. 4080, May 16; reprinted in the *New-York Semi-Weekly Tribune*, No. 937, May 19 and the *New-York Weekly Tribune*, No. 662, May 20, 1854

Signed: *Karl Marx*

Reproduced from the *New-York Daily Tribune*

Frederick Engels

NEWS FROM THE EUROPEAN CONTEST[131]

Our journals and letters by the *Europa* contain a positive confirmation of the reported bombardment of Odessa. The present advices on that subject are official and leave no possibility of doubt as to the event. The works of the harbor have been destroyed, two powder magazines blown up, twelve small Russian vessels-of-war sunk and thirteen transports captured, all with the loss of eight men killed and eighteen wounded in the allied fleet. This trifling loss of men proves that it was [by] no means a formidable achievement. After it was done the fleet sailed away for Sevastopol, the destruction of which we fancy they will find to be a different sort of work.

From the Danube there is a new report of a decisive victory gained by Omer Pasha over Gen. Lüders, but of this affair we have nothing beyond a telegraphic dispatch by way of Vienna,[a] the great manufactory of stock-jobbing hoaxes. The story runs that the Turks, 70,000 strong, overhauled Lüders somewhere between Silistria and Rassova, the latter being a place on the Danube some ten miles above Chernavoda, and that while Omer Pasha was pressing the Russians in front, another corps, sent around for the purpose, fell upon their flank, and so between the two fires they were used up. This is not an impossible thing, but we do not see how Omer Pasha could concentrate so large a force at any point below Silistria with such rapidity as to take Lüders unprepared.[132] According to the last previous advices, the gross of his army,— which altogether cannot be more than 120,000 strong, including

---

[a] "Defeat of the Russians", *The Times*, No. 21732, May 4, 1854.— *Ed.*

the garrisons that must be provided for along his extended line,—was being collected at Shumla, some hundred miles from the scene of the reported battle, and it is not an easy thing to surprise an enemy at such a distance where 70,000 men have to be brought upon the field to do it. Still we repeat, it is possible; the next steamer will probably inform us whether it is true.[133]

The Greek insurrection has suffered another defeat, but that it is extinguished by the disaster it would be impossible to believe. Men and leaders will no doubt appear to renew the contest and carry on a harassing guerrilla war at least against the Turkish forces on the frontiers. Whether it will become anything more serious must depend upon circumstances; as our readers will see in another column[134] an extensive conspiracy of Greeks and Russians came near exploding in the midst of Turkey; accident put the whole into the hands of the Porte,[135] but other such conspiracies may occur without any interposing event to hinder their course. Meanwhile the allied powers ply the Greek Court with menaces, and land troops in Turkey as if to take final possession of the country for themselves. Most of these forces still remain near Constantinople, though at the instance of the French Embassador,[a] a detachment has gone north to Varna, where there is likely to be fighting any day. It is doubtful, however, whether the body of the allied forces will so soon engage in the active work of the campaign. This point cannot be determined till the commanding generals arrive at Constantinople.[b]

In the Baltic Sir Charles Napier still remains in the vicinity of Stockholm, attacking none of the Russian strongholds on the coast. It appears that he is anxious with respect to the gun-boat flotilla with which the Russians propose to operate against him in the shallow waters and among the islands of the Gulf of Finland, and has sent to England for small steamers of light draught, which can pursue these boats to their places of refuge. On the other hand, it is reported by the St. Petersburg correspondent of a journal of Berlin[c] that the Russian Court is fearful that Kronstadt cannot stand the onslaught which is expected from the British Rough and Ready,[d] that the men-of-war in the harbor do not succeed well in

---

[a] Baraguay d'Hilliers.— *Ed.*

[b] Raglan and Saint-Arnaud.— *Ed.*

[c] The reference is to a report of the *National Zeitung* reprinted in *The Times*, No. 21732, May 4, 1854.— *Ed.*

[d] A nickname for British soldiers in the nineteenth century, which became common after the battle of Waterloo when Colonel Rough distinguished himself. The Duke of Wellington used to say to him "Rough and ready, Colonel".— *Ed.*

maneuvering and firing even for the purposes of a review; and that preparations are even [in] making to resist the debarkation of a hostile land force at that place.

It is not likely, however, that any attack will take place in the Baltic until the French fleet has also arrived, and then Kronstadt will very probably receive the honor of the first bombardment. Its capture or destruction is another question; but before such means of destruction as the allies will bring against it, its fall would not be surprising.

The western powers flatter themselves that Austria is coming over to their side, and derive encouragement from agreeable things said to the Duke of Cambridge at the festivities of the Emperor's[a] wedding. But from Prussia there is no such pleasing intelligence. Altogether, Germany stands just where she did before, and the allies have no prospect of drawing her into any engagement in their favor. There is no doubt that Austria will be ready to occupy Serbia and Montenegro,—where a positive rebellion has broken out against the Sultan,[b]—but such an occupation, as we have previously shown,[136] would only be another step toward the partition of Turkey, and would be, in fact, more favorable to Russia than to her antagonists.

Written on May 4, 1854   Reproduced from the newspaper

First published in the *New-York Daily Tribune*, No. 4084, May 20, 1854 as a leader

---

[a] Francis Joseph I.— *Ed.*
[b] On the rebellion in Montenegro see this volume, pp. 178-79.— *Ed.*

Karl Marx

BRITISH FINANCES [137]

London, Tuesday, May 9, 1854

Although the bombardment of Odessa, which appears, after all, to have been a very indifferent affair, highly excites the public mind, there is another bombardment which, at this very moment, works upon it still more powerfully—namely, the bombardment of the public purse. Before entering into an analysis of the financial statement made by Mr. Gladstone in yesterday's sitting of the Commons, we must cast a retrospective glance at his official transactions hitherto.

Mr. Disraeli, when in office, had reduced the interest of Exchequer Bills to $1^1/_4$d. a day, which was lower than it had ever been before; but Mr. Gladstone, anxious to improve upon his predecessor, went on further, reducing it to 1d., neglecting to notice the circumstance that when Mr. Disraeli reduced the interest of Exchequer Bills money was abundant and cheap, while it was scarce and dear when Mr. Gladstone undertook to surpass his rival. Consequently, the great man was called upon to pay three millions of money for Exchequer Bills, which, if left alone, would have floated at the rate of interest at which he found them. This was not all. Having hardly paid off the Exchequer Bills at great public inconvenience, they had to be reissued again at a higher rate of interest. This was the first proof of the transcendent genius of the Oxford casuist, who was supposed to unite, as it were, all the talents in his single person, the coalition of all the talents having ejected the Tory Government upon their financial scheme, and thus proclaimed finances the strong point of their policy.

Mr. Gladstone, not content with dealing with the floating debt, made a still more curious experiment upon the funded debt. In April, 1853, he went down to the House of Commons with a very complicated scheme for the conversion of the South Sea stock and other funds, with an arrangement which might compel him to pay off nine and a half millions at the end of six months and twelve months. It has been very justly remarked that when he did so he had before him the secret dispatches of Sir Hamilton Seymour, and the warnings of Col. Rose and Consul Cunningham, communications which could leave no doubt of the hostile intention of the Russian Government and the proximity of a European war. But your readers will recollect that at the very period when Mr. Gladstone proposed his scheme I foretold its failure,[a] and the necessity in which it would place the Government of borrowing, at the end of the financial year, to the amount of five or six millions. I made this statement without any respect to the Eastern complication. Besides, the scholastic air of Mr. Gladstone's scheme not being likely to seduce the stock-jobbing mob of the Exchange, there was wanted no great sagacity to foretell that the harvest must prove a failure, because the extent sowed was far below the average on account of the very wet season; that a bad harvest would cause a drain of bullion; that a drain of bullion could certainly not counteract the already existing tendency to a rise of interest in the money market, and that, with the general money market rising, it was absurd to suppose that the public creditor would allow the interest of his stock to be reduced or not eagerly grasp at the opportunity afforded him by Mr. Gladstone's experiment to insist on the repayment of his stock at par in order to invest it the following day at a net profit. Indeed, at the close of the financial year, Mr. Gladstone was obliged to pay off at par six millions of South Sea annuities which, without his intermeddling, would at this moment only command £85 for every £100 of stock at the Exchange. Thus he not only made needlessly away with six millions of the public funds, but the public incurred by this brilliant operation an actual loss of at least one million,

---

[a] Marx, "The New Financial Juggle; or Gladstone and the Pennies", "Achievements of the Ministry", "Feargus O'Connor.—Ministerial Defeats.—The Budget", "Riot at Constantinople.—German Table Moving.—The Budget", "Soap for the People, a Sop for *The Times.*—The Coalition Budget" (see present edition, Vol. 12).—*Ed.*

while the balance in the Exchequer, which was in April, 1853, £7,800,000, has been reduced in April, 1854, at a time of war, to only £2,778,000, being a loss of more than £5,000,000. The abortive conversion scheme of Mr. Gladstone is at the foundation of all the monetary difficulties against which the Government has now to contend. On the 6th of March, only 24 days before the declaration of war, Mr. Gladstone laid down[a] as the very basis of all his operations that the supplies should be provided within the year to pay the current expenses, and declared he had taken measures to cast the burdens of war only upon the present, and that a resort to the money market for a loan was out of question. He repeated his statement again on the 22d of March, and even on the 12th of April.[b] Yet on the 21st of April, when Parliament was not sitting, an official notice appeared that a loan would be required, and that Exchequer Bonds to the amount of six millions would consequently be issued.[c] The Exchequer Bonds, you will remember, are an invention of Mr. Gladstone, cotemporaneously introduced with his conversion scheme.

The ordinary Exchequer Bill is a security for 12 months, and is generally exchanged or paid off at the end of that time, and its rate of interest fluctuates with the market rate of interest. The Exchequer Bonds, on the contrary, bear a fixed rate of interest for years, and are a terminable annuity, transferable from hand to hand by a simple indorsement, without any cost whatever to either buyer or seller. Upon the whole, they may be described as imitations of railway debentures. When Mr. Gladstone first invented them in 1853, he took power to issue 30,000,000, and so proud he was of his invention that he thought the 30,000,000 would not be sufficient to answer the public demand, and that they would be at a high premium. However, "the public were glutted by very little more than £400,000, or about one-seventh of the amount he expected would be required." In order to raise his loan of 6,000,000, Mr. Gladstone brought out three sorts of Exchequer Bonds, such as have four years to run, such as have five years to run, and such as have six years to run. To make them

---

[a] Mr. Gladstone's speech in the House of Commons on March 6, 1854. *The Times*, No. 21682, March 7, 1854.— *Ed.*

[b] This refers to Gladstone's speeches in the House of Commons on March 21 and April 11, 1854 published in *The Times*, No. 21695, March 22 and No. 21713, April 12, 1854.— *Ed.*

[c] Notice of the Exchequer dated April 21, 1854. *The Times*, No. 21722, April 22, 1854.— *Ed.*

more acceptable to the Exchange, he decided that the interest would be allowed on installments not yet paid. He pretended to issue them at par, with an interest of three and one-half per cent., considering the extraordinary advantages belonging to the new form of securities as being equivalent to from 10 to 16 per cent., on the amount of the dividend. When the tenders were opened, it was found that the amount bid for was but £800,000 of bonds of the first series, to be paid off in 1858; while with respect to the other series of bonds of 1859 and 1860 no offers were made at all. This is not all. He was forced to issue his commodities at a discount, selling them at the minimum of ninety-eight and three-fourths, and throwing in a few months interest, so that he is simply borrowing at four per cent. in exchange for the South Sea Stocks, which were at three per cent. annuity, thus losing on the capital fifteen per cent., and on the interest twenty-five per cent. Notwithstanding all these concessions, his failure was complete, he being obliged to extend the period for receiving tenders to the 8th inst., and to come down from his demand of 6,000,000 to the "ridiculously small sum" of 2,000,000. The failure was necessary, because his commodity was neither well adapted for permanent investment nor for temporary use, because the repayment in 1858 and 1860 appears, under the present circumstances, to be very problematical, and, finally, because, with a rising market, bonds with a fixed rate of interest for years cannot be as acceptable as Exchequer Bills, of which the interest is sure to be raised if the value of money increases.

Mr. Gladstone, not content to throw upon the market three different sorts of Exchequer commodities, felt himself obliged to bring to the House of Commons not one but two, and perhaps three or four budgets. For contradistinction to the former Chancellors of [the] Exchequer he made his financial statement on March 6, before the termination of the financial year with the view, as he said, to make the country clearly understand its position. The House were then told that there was a surplus of £3,000,000, but that in consequence of the perilous position in which they were placed, they had to incur an increased expenditure of £6,000,000, so that they were to be prepared for a deficiency of three millions this year. Before eight weeks have passed, he comes down to the House and asks for about seven millions more, although certainly in March he ought to have formed more correct estimates of the demands to be made upon the public resources.

The new supplementary estimates he asks for are:

The Navy	£4,550,000
Army	300,000
Ordnance	650,000
Supplementary militia vote	500,000
Unknown charges	2,100,000
Total	£8,100,000

The navy, army and ordnance estimates have already been voted without division on Friday evening,[a] and I shall give a short resumé of the different items on account of which they were asked for, viz: £300,000 were voted for addition of the army by 14,799 men of all ranks, which would raise the number of land forces to 40,493 above that voted last year, or 142,000 men. The supplementary ordnance estimates amount in the whole to £742,132. The supplementary navy estimates, amounting to £4,553,731 and including a part of the supplementary ordnance estimates, may be classed under the following heads:

I.

1. On account of wages to seamen and marines, 11,000 of whom were added to the navy, 2,500 from the Coast Guard and 8,500 by voluntary enlistment	£461,760
(a.) To defray the charges of wages which will come in course of payment in the year ending the 31st of March, 1854, for 5,000 seamen to be employed for 6 months additional	110,000
(b.) To meet the extra pay, beyond seamen's pay, of the 2,500 coast guard men and seamen riggers now employed afloat	51,700
(c.) For raising 5,000 reserve seamen	220,000
(d.) For provisions of 5,000 men, for an additional period of 6 months to the 31st of March, 1855	80,000
(e.) For additional victualing, stores required for freight of provisions, and for increase in the prices of several species of stores and provisions	50,000
(f.) For provisions, victualing, stores, etc., for an additional sum of 5,000 men to be employed in the fleet for one year	100,000
(g.) To provide for an additional number of clerks necessary in consequence of the war at the establishments at Whitehall and Somerset House [138]	5,000
(h.) For the additional expense to be incurred for salaries in the several naval, victualing and medical establishments at home	2,000
(i.) For additional wages to artificers and others in the naval establishments abroad	1,000

---

[a] May 5, 1854.— Ed.

2. £697,331 for naval stores:

(a.)	For the purchase of coal and other fuel for steam vessels	160,000
(b.)	For the purchase of stores required to replace those issued to the fleet	40,000
(c.)	For the purchase and repair of steam machinery, it having been decided that the reserve fleet should have the advantage of steam	252,674
(d.)	For the purchase of steam vessels, gun boats, etc.	244,657
3.	For new works, improvements and repairs in the yards	7,000
4.	For medicines and medical stores	30,000
5.	For miscellaneous services	6,000

Sum total £1,457,031

II.

Items which, although included in the navy estimate, refer rather to the army than the navy. Under this head demanded:

1. For freight of transports on monthly pay including steam vessels, and for the purchase of the same, covering the hire of eight new steam vessels and 86 sailing transports, of which 75 were frigates with cavalry £2,610,200

2. For the freight of ships hired for the conveyance of troops including rations, the Government having taken up 18 steam vessels and 86 sailing transports for the entire year   108,000

Sum total £3,096,700

Grand total £4,553,731

Mr. Gladstone proposes to raise new taxes by continuing the double income tax to the end of the war, by increasing the malt duty from 2/9 to 4/-, by augmenting the duty on spirits 1/- per gallon in Scotland and 8d. per gallon in Ireland, and by putting off the fall upon the duty on sugar, which was to occur on the 5th of next July. The resolutions respecting spirits, malt and sugar were passed immediately.

The duty on spirits will cancel itself, because it will greatly reduce the consumption of spirits. The duty on malt is a punishment inflicted on the licensed victualers and their customers, because their official organ, *The Morning Advertiser*, signalised itself by sounding the trumpet of war. The duty on sugar is calculated to embitter the pickles and preserves of the current year. As to the income tax, it is well-known that on the 18th of April, Mr. Gladstone proclaimed its death at the end of seven years,[a] only three days after having received the communications from Col. Rose and Consul Cunningham describing the Russian preparations for war. It is no less known that on the 6th of March he declared it sufficient to double the income tax for half a year only.[b] Mr. Gladstone is either the most improvident and short-sighted Chancellor of Exchequer that ever existed, or it was his deliberate plan to grope in the dark, to mislead, to bewilder and to mystify the public.

The British public has not only to pay for the war against Russia, and also for the quackery and the hair splitting ingenuity of Mr. Gladstone, but besides it has to furnish the Czar with the means of carrying on the war against itself, as Lord John Russell declared on Friday evening,[c] that the British Government would continue to pay the principal and the interest of the debt called the Russo-Dutch loan,[139] inserted in the treaty of Vienna, one of whose principal arrangements is that Poland should remain an Independent Constitutional Kingdom, that Cracow should be protected as a free town, and that the navigation of all European rivers, consequently of the Danube, should be free.

The distrust in Irish loyalty must be very great, as Lord Palmerston declared that during the present year Her Majesty's Government did not intend to enrol the Irish militia; the same Palmerston having broken up the Russell Cabinet on the pretext that Lord John exasperated Ireland by excluding it from his Militia bill.

Ministers have sustained a virtual defeat on their Railway bill, which contained only some enactments recommended by a Parliamentary Committee sitting on that subject.[d] As the railway interest is powerfully organized, the gallant Mr. Cardwell preferred, in the name of the Ministry, to withdraw his original bill and to substitute for it one framed by the railway directors themselves, which enforces nothing nor adds anything to the stringency of

---

[a] See this volume, p. 117.— *Ed.*

[b] Mr. Gladstone's speech in the House of Commons on March 6, 1854. *The Times*, No. 21682, March 7, 1854.— *Ed.*

[c] Lord John Russell's speech in the House of Commons on May 5, 1854. *The Times*, No. 21734, May 6, 1854.— *Ed.*

[d] The debates on the Railway Bill are given according to parliamentary reports in *The Times*, No. 21733, May 5, 1854.— *Ed.*

already existing enactments. When the bill was discussed there was nobody present in the House except those railway directors who are M.P.s.

"It appears," says a weekly paper, "that Ministers and Parliament are not strong enough to protect the property of shareholders and the pockets of travellers, or the life and limb of the public, against the right which the railway companies claim to dispose of those valuables at pleasure."

Written on May 9, 1854

First published in the *New-York Daily Tribune*, No. 4086, May 23; reprinted in the *New-York Weekly Tribune*, No. 663, May 27, 1854

Signed: *Karl Marx*

Reproduced from the *New-York Daily Tribune*

Frederick Engels

A FAMOUS VICTORY[140]

The English journals indulge in liberal bursts of derision at the fact that the Czar has rewarded Gen. Osten-Sacken for his share in the late fight between the allied fleets and the fortifications that defend the port of Odessa. This fight they claim as altogether a victory of their own, pronouncing the opposite exultations of their enemy as but a new specimen of Muscovite braggadocio and imperial lying. Now, while we have no special sympathy with the Czar or with Osten-Sacken, though the latter is no doubt a clever and resolute man (he is the brother of the General of the same name[141] commanding an army corps in the Principalities), it may perhaps be worth while to look a little more carefully into the merits of this victory at Odessa, and ascertain, if possible, on which side the braggadocio and humbug really figure, especially as this is the first and only battle between the allies and the Russians of which we have yet received any report.

As appears by the official documents on both sides, the object of the allied fleet in appearing before Odessa was to summon the Governor[142] to deliver up, as reparation for the round shot fired at a British flag of truce, all British, French and Russian vessels in the harbor. Now they must have known that he would not make any reply to such a summons, and must therefore have been prepared to take by force what they had asked for in vain, and if they failed in this object they suffered a genuine defeat, whatever damage they may have done to the enemy.

What, then, were the odds? The very decree of the Russian Government, which appointed Osten-Sacken to the command of the vast territory he governs, situated immediately in the rear of the army of the Danube, and the fact of his selecting for his residence the town of Odessa, shows the importance naturally and justly attributed by the Russians to this point. Odessa is the place, of all others, where a hostile landing might do them the most harm. There the enemy would find not only all the resources of a large town, but those, too, of the granary of all Europe; and there they would be nearest to the line of communication and retreat of the Russian army in Turkey. Under these circumstances, the two Admirals[a] must have known that they would find the place defended by a numerous garrison, and that any attempt at landing, with what sailors and marines they might have to spare for that purpose, would at once be repelled. But without landing and taking possession of the harbor, if not the town, at least for a moment, they could not expect to liberate the British and French ships now confined there. Their only remaining chance for accomplishing their object would have been to bombard the town itself most furiously, so as to make it unsafe for any body of troops to remain in it, and then to attempt a rescue of the ships. But it is doubtful whether that purpose could have been effected by a bombardment upon a large town with very wide streets and extensive squares, where comparatively little room is occupied by combustible buildings. The Admirals, then, must have known that if their demand on Osten-Sacken was refused, they had no means of enforcing it. They thought, however, that after the firing on a flag of truce, something must be undertaken against Odessa, and so they went on their errand.

The approaches to Odessa, on the seaside, were defended by six batteries, which must have been armed with some forty or fifty guns of 24 and 48 pounds caliber. Of these batteries only two or three were engaged, the attacking force keeping out of range of the remainder. Against these batteries eight steam frigates carrying about 100 guns were brought to act; but as from the nature of the maneuver, the guns of only one side of the ships could be used, the superiority in the number of the guns on the part of the allies was considerably diminished. In respect of the caliber, they must have been about equal, for if a 24-pound gun is inferior to a long 32-pounder, a 48-pounder of heavy metal must certainly be equal to 56- or 68-pound shell guns, which cannot stand full charges of powder. Finally, the vulnerable nature of ships, as compared with breastworks, and the insecurity of aim produced by the ship's motion, are such that even a still greater

----

[a] Dundas and Hamelin.— *Ed.*

numerical superiority in the artillery of a fleet over that of strand-batteries will leave some odds in favor of the latter. Witness the affair at Eckernförde [143] in Schleswig (1849), where two batteries with 20 guns between them destroyed an 84-gun ship, disabled and captured a 44-gun frigate, and beat off two heavily armed steamers.

The fight, as long as it was confined to artillery and to the eight steamers, may therefore be considered a pretty equal one, even allowing for the superiority of range and accuracy which, during the struggle, the Anglo-French guns were found to possess. The consequence was that the work of destruction went on very slowly. Two Russian guns dismounted were the only result of several hours firing. At length the allies came up closer and changed their tactics. They abandoned the system of firing against the stone walls of the batteries in order to send shells and rockets into the Russian shipping and the military establishments in and around the harbor. This told. The object aimed at was large enough to make every shell hit some vulnerable part, and the whole was soon on fire. The powder-magazine behind that battery on the mole-head, which had offered the most effective resistance and had been principally attacked, blew up; this and the spreading of the fire all around forced its garrison at length to retire. The Russian artillerymen had shown on this point, as usual, very little skill but very great bravery. Their guns and shot must have been very defective and their powder extremely weak.

This was the only result of the whole action. Four Russian guns had been silenced in the battery on the mole-head; all the other batteries hardly received any damage at all. The explosion of the powder-magazine cannot have been very severe; from its situation close behind the battery, it is evident that it was the special magazine of this battery containing merely the ammunition for a single day, say 60 or 100 rounds for each of the four guns; now, if we deduct the probable number of rounds already used in the course of the day, there can hardly have remained more than 300 weight of powder. What the damage done to other establishments may amount to, we have no means of judging; the allies, of course, could not ascertain it, while the Russians put it down at the very lowest figure. [144] From the Russian report, however, it would appear that the vessels burnt were *not* men-of-war, as the Anglo-French reports state them to have been; probably they were, besides some merchantmen, transports and government passenger steamers. We have, besides, never received any previous information that any Russian men-of-war were at Odessa.

Two French and one or two English merchantmen succeeded during the action in escaping from the harbor; *seven British merchantmen* remain confined there to the present day. Thus the "gallant" Admirals have not succeeded in enforcing their demand, and as they had to retreat without obtaining any positive result, without even silencing more than one out of six batteries, they may consider themselves fairly beaten off. They lost very few men; but several ships' hulls were damaged and the French steamer *Vauban* was once set on fire by a red-hot ball, and had to retire for a while from the action.

This is the sum of what the British press calls "Glorious news from Odessa," and which in British eyes has wiped out all the former shortcomings of Admiral Dundas. Nay, this action has so much raised the public expectations in England that we are seriously told, the Admirals, having now ascertained the excessive superiority of the range of their guns over the Russian ones, have positively resolved to try a bombardment of Sevastopol; indeed, they did go there and fire a few shots. But this is the purest humbug, for whoever has once looked upon a plan of Sevastopol, knows that an attack, bombardment or not, upon that town and harbor, unless it be a mere sham-fight outside the bay, must take place in narrow waters and within range even of field guns.

We may properly add to this simple exposé, that the gasconade of our English friends about this action,—in which they suffered a complete repulse and totally failed of their object— does not vary much from the general tone of their previous discussions and statements concerning the war. Whatever be the result of the struggle, impartial history must, we think, place upon her record that its early stages were marked by quite as much humbug, prevarication, deception, diplomatic bad faith, military bragging and lying on the side of England as on that of Russia.

Written on May 15, 1854   Reproduced from the newspaper

First published in the *New-York Daily Tribune*, No. 4098, June 6, 1854 as a leader

8-2970

Karl Marx

[ATTACK UPON SEVASTOPOL.— CLEARING OF ESTATES IN SCOTLAND] [145]

London, Friday, May 19, 1854

The "first attack upon Sevastopol," of which we have a telegraphic announcement in to-day's papers, seems to be about the same glorious exploit as the bombardment of Odessa, where both parties claimed the victory. The attack is described as having been made by means of shells projected from "long-ranging" guns, and directed against the outward fortifications. That you cannot attack the harbor of Sevastopol or the town itself by guns of any range without going up the bay and coming to close quarters with the protecting batteries, and that you cannot take it at all without the assistance of a considerable landing army, is evident from a glance at the map, and is, moreover, conceded by every military authority. The operation, if it has really taken place, is therefore to be considered as a sham exploit, for the edification of the same *gobe-mouches*[a] whose patriotism is elated by the laurels of Odessa.

The French Government has sent M. Bourrée on an extraordinary mission to Greece. He goes accompanied by a brigade under command of General Forey, and has orders to claim from King Otto immediate payment of the whole interest on the one hundred millions of francs advanced by France to the Greek Government in 1828. In case of refusal, the French are to occupy Athens and divers other points of the kingdom.

Your readers will remember my description of the process of clearing estates in Ireland and Scotland,[b] which within the first

---

[a] Simpletons.— *Ed.*

[b] Marx, "Elections.—Financial Clouds.—The Duchess of Sutherland and Slavery", "The Indian Question.—Irish Tenant Right" (see present edition, Vols. 11 and 12).— *Ed.*

half of this century swept away so many thousands of human beings from the soil of their fathers. The process still continues, and with a vigor quite worthy of that virtuous, refined, religious, philanthropic aristocracy of this model country. Houses are either fired or knocked to pieces over the heads of the helpless inmates. At Neagaat in Knoydart, the house of Donald Macdonald, a respectable, honest, hard-working man, was attacked last autumn by the landlord's order. His wife was confined to bed unfit to be removed, yet the factor and his ruffians turned out Macdonald's family of six children, all under 15 years of age, and demolished the house with the exception of one small bit of the roof over his wife's bed.

The man was so affected that his brain gave way. He has been declared insane by medical men, and he is now wandering about looking for his children among the ruins of the burnt and broken cottages. His starving children are crying around him, but he knows them not, and he is left roaming at large unaided and uncared for, because his insanity is harmless.

Two married females in an advanced stage of pregnancy had their houses pulled down about their ears. They had to sleep in the open air for many nights, and the consequence was that, amid excruciating sufferings, they had premature births, their reason became affected, and they are wandering about with large families, helpless and hopeless imbeciles, dreadful witnesses against that class of persons called the British aristocracy.

Even children are driven mad by terror and persecution. At Doune, in Knoydart, the cottagers were evicted and took refuge in an old storehouse. The agents of the landlord surrounded that storehouse in the dead of night and set fire to it as the poor outcasts were cowering beneath its shelter. Frantic, they rushed from the flames, and some were driven mad by terror. *The Northern Ensign* newspaper says:

"That one boy is deranged; that he will require to be placed in confinement; he jumps out of bed crying, 'Fire! fire!' and assures those near him that there are men and children in the burning storehouse. Whenever night approaches, he is terrified at the sight of fire. The awful sight at Doune, when the storehouse was in flames, illuminating the district—when men, women, and children ran about half frantic with fear, gave such a shock to his reason."

Such is the conduct of the aristocracy to the able-bodied poor who make them rich. Listen now to their parochial mercies. I extract the following cases from the work of Mr. Donald Ross, of Glasgow, and from *The Northern Ensign*:

1. Widow Matherson, aged 96, has only 2s. 6d. per month from the parish of Strath, Skye.

2. Murdo Mackintosh, aged 36 years, is totally disabled, by reason of a cart falling on him fourteen months ago. He has a wife and seven children; the oldest 11 years, the youngest 1 year, and all that the parish of Strath allows him is 5s. per month.

3. Widow Samuel Campbell, aged 77, residing at Broadford, Skye, in a wretched house, had 1s. 6d. a month from the parish of Strath. She complained that it was inadequate, and the parochial authorities, after much grudging, increased it to 2s. per month.

4. Widow M'Kinnon, aged 72, parish of Strath, Skye, has 2s. 6d. per month.

5. Donald M'Dugald, aged 102 years, resides at Knoydart. His wife is aged 77 years, and both are very frail. They only receive 3s. 4d. each in the month from the parish of Glenelg.

6. Mary McDonald, a widow, aged 93 years, and confined to bed. Her husband was in the army, and there he lost an arm. He died 20 years ago. She has 4s. 4d. in the month from the parish of Glenelg.

7. Alexander M'Isaak, aged 53 years, totally disabled, has a wife aged 40 years; has a blind son aged 18 years; and four children under 14 years of age. The parish of Glenelg allows this wretched family only 6s. 6d. per month between them, just about 1s. each per month.

8. Angus M'Kinnon, aged 72, has a rupture; wife aged 66 years. They have 2s. 1d. each per month.

9. Mary M'Isaak, aged 80 years, frail and stone-blind, has 3s. 3d. a month from the parish of Glenelg. When she asked more, the Inspector said: "You should be ashamed to ask more when others have less;" and refused to listen to her.

10. Janet M'Donald, or M'Gillivray, aged 77 years, and totally disabled, has only 3s. 3d. per month.

11. Catherine Gillies, aged 78 years, and totally disabled, has only 3s. 3d. from the parish of Glenelg.

12. Mary Gillies, or Grant, aged 82 years, and for the last eight years confined to bed, gets twenty-eight pounds of meal and 8d. in the month from the parish of Ardnamurchan. The Inspector of poor did not visit her for the last two years; and she gets no medical aid, no clothing, no nutrition.

13. John M'Eachan, aged 86 years, and bed-ridden, resides at Auchachraig, parish of Ardnamurchan, has just one pound of meal a day, and 8d. of money in the month from said parish. He has no clothing nor anything else.

14. Ewen M'Callum, aged 93 years, and has sore eyes, I found begging on the banks of the Crinan Canal, parish [of] Knapdale, Argyllshire. He has just 4s. 8d. in the month; nothing whatever in the way of clothing, medical aid, fuel or lodgings. He is now a moving collection of rags, and a most wretched-looking pauper.

15. Kate Macarthur, aged 74, and bed-ridden, lives alone at Dunardy, parish of Knapdale. She has 4s. 8d. per month from the parish, but nothing else. No doctor visits her.

16. Janet Kerr, or M'Callum; a widow, aged 78 years, in bad health; has 6s. a month from the parish of Glassary. She has no house, and has no aid but the money allowance.

17. Archibald M'Laurin, aged 73, parish of Appin, totally disabled; wife also disabled; have 3s. 4d. each per month in the name of parish relief—no fuel, clothing or lodging. They live in a wretched hovel, unfit for human beings.

18. Widow Margaret M'Leod, aged 81 years; lives at Coigach, parish of Lochbroom; has 3s. a month.

19. Widow John Makenzie, 81 years, resides at Ullapool, parish of Lochbroom. She is stone-blind and in very bad health, and has just 2s. a month.

20. Widow Catherine M'Donald, aged 87 years, Island of Luing, parish of Kilbrandon; stone-blind and confined to bed, is allowed 7s. a month in name of aliment; out of which she has to pay a nurse! Her house fell to the ground, and yet the parish refused to provide a lodging for her, and she is lying in an open out-house on the earthen floor. The Inspector declines doing anything for her.

But the ruffianism ends not here. A slaughter has been perpetrated at Strathcarron. Excited to frenzy by the cruelty of the evictions and the further ones that were expected, a number of women gathered in the streets on hearing that a number of sheriff's officers were coming to clear out the tenantry. The latter, however, were Excisemen, and not sheriff's officers; but on hearing that their real character was mistaken, these men instead of correcting the mistake, enjoyed it—gave themselves out for sheriff's officers, and said they came to turn the people out and were determined to do so. On the group of women becoming excited, the officers presented a loaded pistol at them. What followed we extract from the letter of Mr. Donald Ross, who went over from Glasgow to Strathcarron, and spent two days in the district, collecting information and examining the wounded. His letter is dated Royal Hotel, Tain, April 15, 1854, and states as follows:

"My information goes to show a shameful course of conduct on the part of the sheriff. He did not warn the people of the intention on his part to let the police loose on them. He read no Riot Act.[146] He did not give them time to disperse; but, on the contrary, the moment he approached with his force, stick in hand, cried out: 'Clear the way,' and in the next breath said: 'Knock them down,' and immediately a scene ensued which baffles description. The policemen laid their heavy batons on the heads of the unfortunate females and leveled them to the ground, jumped and trampled upon them after they were down, and kicked them in every part of their bodies with savage brutality. The field was soon covered with blood. The cries of the women and of the boys and girls, lying weltering in their blood, was rending the very heavens. Some of the females, pursued by the policemen, jumped into the deep and rapid-rolling Carron, trusting to its mercies more than to that of the policeman or the sheriff. There were females who had parcels of their hair torn out by the batons of the policemen, and one girl had a piece of the flesh, about seven inches long by one and a quarter broad, and more than a quarter of an inch thick, torn off her shoulder by a violent blow with a baton. A young girl, who was only a mere spectator, was run after by three policemen. They struck her on the forehead, cut open her skull, and after she fell down they kicked her. The doctor abstracted from the wound a portion of the cap sunk into it by the baton of the savage police. The marks of their hobnails are still visible in her back shoulders. There are still in Strathcarron thirteen females in a state of great distress, owing to the brutal beating they received at the hands of the police. Three of these are so ill that their medical attendant has no hopes whatever of their recovery. It is my own firm conviction, from the appearance of these females and the dangerous nature of their wounds, coupled with medical reports which I have procured, that not one-half of these injured persons will recover; and all of them, should they linger on for a time, will bear about on their persons sad proofs of the horrid brutality to which they had been subjected. Among the number seriously wounded is a woman advanced in pregnancy. She was not among the crowd who met the sheriff, but at a considerable distance, just looking on; but she was violently struck and kicked by the policemen, and she is in a very dangerous condition."

We may further add that the women who were assailed numbered only eighteen. The name of the sheriff is Taylor.

Such is a picture of the British aristocracy in the year 1854.

The authorities and Government have come to an arrangement that the prosecution against Cowell, Grimshaw and the other Preston leaders shall be withdrawn, if the investigation against the magistrates and cotton lords of Preston is withdrawn also. The latter was accordingly done, pursuant to this arrangement.

Mr. Duncombe's postponement for a fortnight of his motion for a Committee of Inquiry into the conduct of the Preston magistrates is said to be in pursuance of the above arrangement.[147]

Written on May 19, 1854

First published in the *New-York Daily Tribune*, No. 4095, June 2; reprinted in the *New-York Semi-Weekly Tribune*, No. 941, June 2, 1854

Signed: *Karl Marx*

Reproduced from the *New-York Daily Tribune*

Frederick Engels

THE WAR [148]

At last, then, we have to report an exploit of the "British Tar." The fleet of Admiral Napier has destroyed, after eight hours' bombardment, the fort of Gustavsvaern (which translated from the Swedish means "Gustav's defence, or stronghold," "Gustav's Wehr") and taken the garrison prisoners of war, to the number of 1,500. This is the first serious attack upon Imperial Russian property, and compared with the drowsy and torpid affair at Odessa, shows at least that Charles Napier is not going to sacrifice his own renown and that of his family if he can help it. The fort of Gustavsvaern is situated on the extremity of a peninsula, forming the south-west corner of Finland, close to the lighthouse of Hango-Udd, well known as a landmark to all skippers going up the Finnish Gulf. Its military importance is not very great; it defends a very small area either of land or water, and might have been left in the rear by the attacking fleet without any risk whatever. The fort itself cannot have been large, as is evident from the numbers of its garrison. But in the present blessed ignorance existing even in the British Admiralty and War Office as to the real strength and importance of the Baltic Coast defences of Russia, we may be excused if we delay any comments upon the tactical merits of the affair until fuller particulars have arrived. We can, for the present, only say this much: the eight hours' duration of the cannonade proves a brave, if not over-skilful defence on the part of the Russians, and forebodes a greater obstinacy than may have been expected, in the defence of the first class fortresses in that same gulf. On the other hand, the fifteen hundred prisoners of war are no appreciable loss at all to Russia (they make up about two average days' loss by sickness on the Danube), while they must prove a serious embarrassment to Napier. What in the world will he do with them? He cannot release them on parole; or without parole; and there is no place nearer to bring them to than England. For a safe transport of these 1,500 men he would require at least three ships of the line or twice that number of steam frigates. The very effects of his victory cripple him for a fortnight or three weeks. Lastly, as he has no landing troops, can he hold the ground he has conquered? I do not see how he could, without again crippling his thinly-manned fleets by a further weakening of each ship's contingent of sailors and marines. This circumstance brings us to a subject which is discussed with great vehemence in the British press, although far too late as usual.

The British press has, all at once, found out that a fleet, however powerful, is of very little avail unless it has troops on board, strong enough to go on shore and complete the victory which ships' guns, in the best case, can obtain only very incompletely against land defences. It appears there was not a man in the British official world directing the war, nor in the official world directing British public opinion—who was ever struck by this idea up to the end of last month. Now, all available troops and means of transport are engaged for the Black Sea, and the whole land force under orders for the Baltic, of which not a man has been sent off, the very staff of which has not yet been organised, consists of one brigade of 2,500 men!

As to the French, they are woefully limping[a] behind. Their Baltic fleet—you recollect the pompous report of secretary Ducos: "Your Majesty ordered the equipment of a third fleet; the orders of your Majesty are executed"[b]—this splendid armament which was to be ready for the sea by the middle of March to the tune of ten ships of the line, has never consisted of more than five ships of the line, which with frigates and small vessels, are at present creeping slowly along the mouth of the Great Belt, to reach which from Brest, it has taken them fully three weeks, westerly winds prevailing all the time. The grand Camp of Saint Omer,[c] to

---

[a] The *New-York Daily Tribune* has: "lingering".— *Ed.*

[b] Ducos, Report of the Minister of the Marine of February 25, 1854. *Le Moniteur universel,* No. 57, February 26, 1854.— *Ed.*

[c] Department of Pas-de-Calais.— *Ed.*

contain 150,000, in case of need, 200,000 troops pretended for a Baltic expedition, has been formed, on paper, three or four weeks ago, and not a brigade is, as yet, concentrated. The French, however, might easily spare some 10,000 to 15,000 infantry and field artillery from their coast garrisons, without the fuss and pomp of a large theatrical camp demonstration, but where are the means of transport? British merchantmen would have to be chartered; they would, according to the rate of sailing of the French fleet, require from four to six weeks to arrive, one by one, on the scene of action; and where should the troops be landed, the brigade and division concentrated, the staff and commissariats organised? That is the vicious circle in which the allies move; in order to have a land-army in the Baltic, they must first conquer an island or peninsula where to concentrate and organise it for attack; and in order to conquer this desideratum, they must first have a landing force on the spot. There is no difficulty in getting out of this scrape, as soon as you have a good admiral who knows as much of land-warfare as is necessary to enable him to command a land-force; and there is no doubt Charles Napier is quite up to that, as he has fought a great deal on shore. But with an Aberdeen[a] reigning supreme, with four different ministries meddling with the fighting force, with the eternal antagonism of army and navy, and with French and English forces combined, and jealous of each other's glory and comforts, how can you expect anything like unity of action?

Then there cannot now be brought up any effective land-force to the Baltic before the end of June; and unless the war is decided and peace concluded in four months, the whole of the conquests made will have to be given up, troops, guns, ships, provisions, all will have to be withdrawn, or abandoned, and for seven winter months the Russians will be again in possession of all their Baltic territory. This shows clear enough that all serious and decisive attacks upon Baltic Russia are out of the question for the present year; it is too late. Only when Sweden joins the Western Powers, have they a base of operations in the Baltic which will admit of their carrying on a winter campaign in Finland. But here again we have a vicious circle, though vicious only, as the former one, to the pusillanimous. How can you expect the Swedes to join you, unless you show them by sending a land-force, and taking part of Finland, that you are in earnest? And, on the other side, how can

---

[a] The *New-York Daily Tribune* has: "with an Aberdeen and Palmerston".— *Ed.*

you send that force thither without having made sure of Sweden as a base of operations?

Verily, Napoleon the Great, the "butcher" of so many millions of men, was a model of humanity in his bold, decisive, home-striking way of warfare, compared to the hesitating "statesman-like" directors of this Russian war, who cannot but eventually sacrifice human life and hard cash to a far greater amount if they go on as they do.

Turning to the Black Sea, we find the combined fleets before Sevastopol amusing themselves with a little harmless long-range exercise against some paltry outworks of that fortress. This innocent game, we are informed, has been carried on for four days by the majority of the ships, and during all this time the Russians, having only twelve ships of the line ready for sea, did not show their faces outside the harbour, to the great astonishment of Admiral Hamelin (vide his report, May 1-5).[a] That heroic sailor is, however, old enough to recollect the time when French squadrons were not only blocked up, but even attacked in harbour by English squadrons of far inferior strength [149]; and certainly it is expecting a little too much, that the inferior Russian squadron should come out of Sevastopol to be shattered and sunk by twice their number of ships, and thus offer themselves up in expiation for the "hideous crime" of Sinope!

In the meantime, two ships of the line (screws) and seven steam-frigates are on their road to Circassia. They were to explore the coasts of the Crimea, and then to destroy the forts on the Circassian coast. But in this latter attack only three steam-frigates were to participate, the remaining four being instructed to return to the fleet as soon as the Crimea was duly reconnoitred. Now the three forts the Russians still occupy on the Circassian coast, viz: Anapa, Sukhum-Kaleh and Redut-Kaleh, are, as far as we know, of considerable strength, built upon heights which entirely command the offing (except Redut-Kaleh), and it may be doubted whether the force sent will be sufficient to effect their purposes, especially as it is not accompanied by landing troops. The squadron, which is commanded by Rear Admiral Lyons, is at the same time to communicate with the Circassians, and especially with their chief, Shamyl. What Rear Admiral Lyons is to communicate to him the report telleth not, but there is this certain that he

---

[a] Review of current events, May 20. *Le Moniteur universel*, No. 141, May 21, 1854.— *Ed.*

cannot bring him what he wants most, viz: arms and ammunitions, for men-of-war on active service have no room to spare for goods shipped to order. Two paltry merchant brigs or schooners freighted with these valuable articles would be far more acceptable than all the moral but perfectly useless support of five men-of-war. At the same time we learn that the Turkish fleet has sailed for the same destination, this time carrying along with it the articles required for arming the Circassians. Thus two allied fleets are going on the same errand, the one not knowing of the other. This is unity of plan and of action with a vengeance. May be, each may take the other for Russians, and a famous sight it will be for the Circassians, these two squadrons firing one into the other!

The allied land-forces, in the meantime, fraternise at Gallipoli and Scutari in their own way, annihilating enormous quantities of the strong and sweet wine of the country. Those who happen to be sober are employed upon the construction of field-works, so situated and so constructed, that they will be either never attacked, or never defended. If a proof was wanted that neither the British nor the French Government have any intention of doing Friend Nicholas any serious harm, it is given to the very blindest in their way of spending the time of the troops. In order to have a pretext to keep their troops away from the field of action, the allied commanders set them to dig a continuous line of field-works across the neck of the Thracian Chersonesus. Everybody, and particularly every French engineer, knows that continuous lines of defence are under almost all circumstances to be rejected in field fortifications, but it was reserved to the Anglo-French army of Gallipoli to employ continuous lines upon a ground, two-thirds of which are commanded by heights, situated on the side where the enemy is expected from. However, as the slow-coach system cannot be carried on without making at least a snail-like sort of progress, we are informed that 15,000 French are to go to Varna, there to form what? The garrison of the place. And to do what? To die of fever and ague.

Now, if there is any sense in this warfare, the chiefs must know that what the Turks are deficient in, is the art of manoeuvring in the open field, in which again the Anglo-French troops are masters, and that, on the other hand, the Turks are fit for the defence of walls, ramparts, and even breaches, against stormers, in a degree which neither the British nor the French can lay any claim to. Therefore, and because Varna, with a Turkish garrison, did that which no fortress before it had ever done, that is, held

out for twenty-nine days after three practicable breaches had been
laid in the rampart—therefore[a] the half-disciplined Turks are
taken out of Varna and sent to meet the Russians in the open
field, while the well-drilled French, brilliant in attack, but unsteady
in lengthy defence, are sent to guard the ramparts of Varna.

Other reports inform us that all these movements are mere
gammon. They say that great things are in preparation. The
combined troops are not intended to act on the Balkans, but they
are to execute, with the help of the fleets, tremendous exploits in
the rear of the Russians. They are to land at Odessa, to cut off the
retreat of the enemy, and to combine in his rear with the
Austrians in Transylvania. They are, besides, to send detachments
to Circassia; they are, finally, to furnish 15,000 to 20,000 men for
the attack of Sevastopol on the land-side, while the fleets are to
force the harbour. If you cast a glance at the whole past history of
the war and the diplomatic transactions preceding it, you will no
doubt very soon dispose of these rumours. They came from
Constantinople, shortly after the arrival of Marshal Leroy,
commonly called Saint-Arnaud. Whoever knows the past history of
this worthy,[b] recognises in these bravadoes the man who blustered
himself up to the rank he occupies, although three times cashiered
as an officer of the army.

The long and the short of this war is this: England, and
particularly France, are being dragged "unavoidably, though
reluctantly," into engaging the greater part of their forces in the
East and the Baltic, that is, upon two advanced wings of a military
position which has no centre nearer than France. Russia sacrifices
her coasts, her fleets, and part of her troops, to induce the
Western Powers to engage themselves completely into this
anti-strategical move. As soon as this is done, as soon as the
necessary number of French troops are sent off to countries far
from their own, Austria and Prussia will declare in favour of
Russia, and at once march with superior numbers upon Paris. If
this plan succeeds, there is no force at the disposal of Louis
Napoleon to resist that shock. But there is a force which can
"mobilise" itself upon any emergency, and which can also
"mobilise" Louis Bonaparte and his minions as it has mobilised
many a ruler before this. That force is able to resist all these

---

[a] The words "Therefore and because", "three practicable breaches had been
laid in the rampart—therefore" are italicised in the *New-York Daily Tribune.—Ed.*
[b] Here the *New-York Daily Tribune* has: "I shall send it you some of these
days."[150]*—Ed.*

invasions, and it has shown it once before to combined Europe, and that force, the Revolution, be assured, will not be wanting the day its action is required.

Written on May 22, 1854

First published in *The People's Paper*, No. 108, May 27, signed: *K. M.* and in the *New-York Daily Tribune*, No. 4101, June 9; reprinted in the *New-York Semi-Weekly Tribune*, No. 941, June 13, 1854, signed: *Karl Marx*

Reproduced from *The People's Paper* checked with the *New-York Daily Tribune*

Frederick Engels

THE PRESENT CONDITION OF THE ENGLISH ARMY
—TACTICS, UNIFORM, COMMISSARIAT, &c.[151]

London, Friday, May 26, 1854

If the war in the East is good for nothing else it will at least demolish a portion of the military renown of the late Duke of Wellington. Whoever knew England during the lifetime of this much over-estimated General, will recollect that it was considered an insult to the British nation to speak even of Napoleon as of a soldier approaching in any way the invincible Iron Duke. This glorious Duke is now dead and buried, after having had the command of the British army, at least virtually, for the last forty years. Never was a man more independent or irresponsible in the exercise of command. The "Duke" was an authority above all authorities, neither king nor queen[a] daring to contradict him in professional matters. Well, after enjoying many a year of those honors and comforts which usually fall to the lot of happy mediocrity, and which so strongly contrast with the tragic revulsions generally belonging to the career of genius—Napoleon for instance—the Iron Duke died, and the command of the British army fell into other hands. About eighteen months after his death, the British army is called upon to enter on a campaign against the Russians, and before the first regiment is ready to embark, it is found that the Iron Duke has left the army in a state entirely unfit for active service.

The "Duke," in spite of his generally sound English sense, had but a small and narrow mind in many respects. The unfairness with which he habitually alluded to the part his German allies bore in the decision of the struggle at Waterloo, taking to himself all the credit of a victory which would have been a defeat but for the timely appearance of Blücher, is well known. The pettishness with

---

[a] William IV and Victoria.— Ed.

which he stuck to all abuses and absurdities in the English army, replying to all criticism: "Those abuses and absurdities made us victorious in Spain and Portugal"—perfectly agrees with his conservative notion that a certain degree of traditional absurdity and corruption was essential to a proper working of the "demonstrably best" of Constitutions. But while in politics he knew how to give way upon important points in critical moments, in military matters he clung all the more stubbornly to antiquated notions and traditional Tory fooleries. There was not one single important improvement introduced into the British army during his lifetime, unless it was in the purely technical department of the artillery. Here it was simply impossible that the rapid progress of manufacturing industry and mechanical science should have been left entirely unnoticed. The consequence is, that though the British army has the best artillery material in existence, the organization of that artillery is as clumsy as that of the other arms; and that in the dress, general armament, and organization of the British forces there is not a single item in which it is not inferior to any civilized army in Europe.

I must again call the attention of your readers to the fact that the direction of military affairs is not confided, as in other countries, to a single branch of the administration.[a] There are four departments, each clashing with and independent of the other. There is the Secretary of War, a mere paymaster and accountant. There is the Commander-in-Chief at the Horse Guards,[152] who has the infantry and cavalry under him. There is the Master-General of the Ordnance, who commands the Artillery Engineers, and is supposed to have the general direction of the *materiel* of the army. Then there is the Colonial Secretary, who apportions the troops to the various foreign possessions, and regulates the distribution of war-material to each. Beside these, there is the Commissariat Department; and lastly, for the troops in India, the Commander-in-Chief of the Army in that empire. It is only since the death of Wellington that the absurdity of such an arrangement has been publicly alluded to, the report of the Parliamentary Committee of 1837 having been superseded by the Duke's authority. Now that war has begun, its inefficiency is felt everywhere; but change is deprecated as being liable to upset all possibility of order and regularity in the transaction of the business.

As an instance of the confusion created by this system, I mentioned, on a former occasion, that there are hardly two articles

---

[a] See this volume, p. 203.— *Ed.*

for which a regiment is not obliged to apply to different and independent administrations. The clothing is supplied by the Colonel, but the great-coats by the Ordnance; the belts and knapsacks by the Horse Guards; but the fire-arms again by the Ordnance. On any foreign station, military officers, ordnance officers, storekeepers and commissariat employers are all more or less independent of each other, and responsible to distinct and independent boards at home. Then there is the nuisance of the "clothing colonels." Every regiment has a titular colonel, a general officer, whose duty it is to pocket a certain government allowance for clothing his regiment, and to spend a portion only for the purpose. The balance is considered as his wages for the trouble.

There is the sale of commissions, which puts all the higher posts in the army at the almost exclusive disposal of the aristocracy. After a few years' service in the capacity of lieutenant, captain, and major, an officer is entitled, on the first vacancy occurring, to buy up the next rank which becomes vacant, unless there should be an officer of the same rank, and of older standing, inclined to anticipate him. The consequence is, that a man with ready money can advance very rapidly, as many of his seniors have not the means to buy the vacancy as soon as it occurs. It is clear that such a system greatly narrows the class of useful men from which the corps of officers is recruited, and the advancement or active employment of general officers being subject almost exclusively to seniority or aristocratic connection, the circle from which these are drawn must necessarily exclude a large mass of talent and knowledge from the higher commands. It is, no doubt, attributable to this system chiefly that the mass of British officers are so lamentably deficient in the general and more theoretical branches of military science.

The number of officers is disproportionately large for that of the men. Gold lace and epaulettes abound in a British regiment to an extent unknown anywhere else. Consequently, the officers have nothing to do, and their *esprit de corps* hardly admitting of any degree of study, they pass their time in all sorts of extravagant amusements, trusting that if it comes to fight, native bravery and "Her Majesty's regulations" will be quite sufficient to carry them through all difficulties. Yet when the Chobham camp[153] was formed, the helplessness of very many of the officers was conspicuous enough to anybody who could judge a little better of the maneuvers than the poor enthusiastic penny-a-liners who, with true cockney spirit, admired everything in the strange spectacle which they saw for the first time of their lives.

The drill regulations and system of exercise are of the most old-fashioned character. The maneuvering is exceedingly clumsy, all the movements being complicated, slow, and pedantic. The old system of movements in line, which has been maintained in the British longer than in the Austrian army, as the grand form of all tactical maneuvers, has a few well-known advantages where the ground allows of its application; but there is more than one way to counterbalance this, and above all it is applicable under very exceptional circumstances only. The system of evolutions in column, especially in small columns of companies, as introduced into the best regulated continental armies, insures a far greater mobility and an equally rapid formation of lines when required.

The armament of the British soldier is of good material and capital workmanship, but disfigured in many cases by old-fashioned regulations. The old muskets of smooth bore are well made, of large caliber, but rather more heavy than is necessary. The old Brunswick rifle was good of its kind, but has been superseded by better arms. The recently introduced Pritchett rifle, considered an improvement upon the French Minié rifles, appears to be a capital weapon, but it has only been after a hard struggle that this arm has been forced upon the authorities. As it is, it is very irregularly and unsystematically introduced; one-half of a regiment carries muskets, and the other half rifles, thereby deranging the whole armament. The swords of the cavalry are good, of a better shape for thrust and sharp edge blows than those of Continental armies. The horses are also first-rate, but the men and equipments are too heavy. The *materiel* of the field artillery is the best in the world, admirably simplified in some respects, but indulging in too great a variety of calibers and guns of different weight, by which different charges of powder are necessitated.

The dress, on the contrary, and the general accoutrement of the British soldier is the greatest nuisance in existence. A high, tight, stiff stock round the neck; a shabby-looking, close-fitting coatee with swallow-tails, badly cut and uncomfortable; tight trousers; disgraceful looking great-coats; an ugly cap, or shako; a system of strapping and belting, of carrying ammunition and knapsack, the like of which even the Prussians cannot show—all this has been of late the theme of so many newspaper comments that a mere allusion to it is sufficient. Besides the almost intentional discomfort of the dress, it must not be forgotten that the British soldier carries a far heavier weight than any other in the world; and, as if to make mobility the ruling principle of the army, it has a far more considerable train of *impediments* dragging along with it than any other. The clumsiness of the commissariat arrangements contributes a great deal to this, but even the regimental train, and particularly the great amount of officers' luggage, surpasses anything known out of Turkey and India.

Now see how this army managed when the troops reached Turkey. The French soldiers, having permanently incorporated into their army system all the arrangements found to be of practical utility in their Algerian campaigns, had no sooner landed than they made themselves comfortable. They carried everything with them which they wanted, little as it was, and whatever was deficient was soon supplied by the inborn ingenuity of the French soldier. Even under the joint-stock swindling Administration of Louis Bonaparte and Saint-Arnaud, the system was found to work smoothly enough. But the English! They came to Gallipoli before their commissariat stores had arrived; they came in numbers four times greater than could encamp; there were no preparations for disembarking, no portable ovens for baking, no properly responsible administration. Orders and counter-orders succeeded each other, clashing most fearfully, or rather ludicrously. There was many an old sergeant or corporal who had made himself comfortable in the Kaffir Bush, or in the burning plains of the Indus; but here he was helpless. The improved arrangements, which each foreign commander on a campaign might have introduced, were made for the duration of the campaign only; the different regiments once separated Her Majesty's old-fashioned regulations were again the only rule, and the administrative experience of the campaign was totally lost.

Such is the glorious system to which the Iron Duke stuck with iron tenacity, and which was necessarily the best, because with it he had beaten Napoleon's generals in the Peninsula. The British soldier, when strapped in his leather cuirasse, with 60 or 70 pounds weight to carry over the steppes of Bulgaria, creeping along under occasional attacks of ague, badly supplied by neglectful and unbusinesslike commissariat officers, may well be proud of his glorious Iron Duke, who has prepared all these benefits for him.

The mischievous results naturally flowing from the Duke's traditional routine are still aggravated by the oligarchic character of the English Administration, which intrusts the most important offices to men who, although their parliamentary support may be needed by the set of place-hunters just in power, are altogether destitute even of elementary professional knowledge and fitness.

Take for instance Mr. Bernal Osborne, the Coalition Clerk of Ordnance.[154] Mr. Bernal Osborne's nomination was a concession made to the Mayfair Radicals,[155] represented in the ministry by Sir W. Molesworth, the "humble" editor of Hobbes. Mr. Bernal Osborne

> "Pecks up wit, as pigeons peas,
> And utters it again when Jove doth please:
> He is wit's pedlar; and retails his wares
> At wakes, and wassails, meetings, markets, fairs."[a]

But although a small trader in stale jokes, Mr. Bernal Osborne is hardly competent to distinguish a common musket from a Minié rifle, and, nevertheless, he is Her Majesty's Parliamentary Clerk of Ordnance.

Your readers will remember that some time ago he applied to Parliament for a grant of money to enable the Board of Ordnance to manufacture all the small arms required for the army and navy. He asserted that in the United States of America, Government manufactories supplied the arms at a cheaper rate than could be done by private industry, and that on several occasions serious difficulties had arisen from the contractors failing to deliver the arms at the time agreed upon.

The vote of the House was, however, postponed on the motion of M. Muntz, to appoint a Select Committee "to inquire as to the cheapest, the most expeditious, and the most sufficient mode of obtaining fire-arms for Her Majesty's service." The report of this Committee is now before the public,[b] and what are the conclusions it has come to? That the private manufacturers had failed to supply the arms at the time contracted for,

"because of the vexatious manner of the *view* of their work, as required by the Board of Ordnance, and its habit of employing different contractors for each individual part of the numerous pieces which compose a musket."

The report states further that

"the Board of Ordnance had scarcely any knowledge of either the price at which muskets were made in America, or the extent to which machinery was used in their manufacture, and had never seen any fire-arms which had been made at any of the Government manufactories of that country."

Finally, we learn from the report that

---

[a] Shakespeare, *Love's Labour's Lost*, Act V, Scene 2.— *Ed.*
[b] Report from the Select Committee on Small Arms; together with the proceedings of the Committee, Minutes of Evidence, and Appendix, [London,] 1854.— *Ed.*

"from the manufactory the Government intended to build, not a musket could be issued for eighteen months."

These extracts from the Parliamentary Report may suffice to characterize the professional abilities of Mr. Osborne, the Coalition's own Clerk of Ordnance. *Ex ungue leonem.*[a]

Written on May 25, 1854

First published in the *New-York Daily Tribune*, No. 4102, June 10; reprinted in the *New-York Semi-Weekly Tribune*, No. 944, June 13, 1854

Signed: *Karl Marx*

Reproduced from the *New-York Daily Tribune*

---

[a] By his claw one may recognise the lion.— *Ed.*

Karl Marx

[THE TREATY BETWEEN AUSTRIA AND PRUSSIA.— PARLIAMENTARY DEBATES OF MAY 29][156]

London, Tuesday, May 30, 1854

The Times is highly indignant that the British general has issued an order prohibiting its "own correspondents" to accompany the British army.[a] If the war were a *bona fide*[b] war, it would be absurd to object to this measure, since the dispatches of the Duke of Wellington repeatedly complain of the information about his intended movements and dispositions which Napoleon was able to transmit to his peninsular generals through the columns of the English newspapers.[c] As it is, the object of the order can only be to keep the English public in the dark about the treacherous designs of their expeditionary troops, and receives a suitable complement in the order just enforced upon the Sultan by the heroes of the 2d of December[157] to forbid, by a decree read in all mosques, any political conversation to the Turks. But why should the Turks be better off in this respect than the English public itself?

In yesterday's sitting of the House of Commons[d] Mr. Blackett asked Lord J. Russell whether, by the last Vienna protocol,[158] Great Britain had given any recognition or sanction to the first article of the treaty of 20th April, 1854, between Austria and Prussia, whereby the contracting powers

"reciprocally guarantee to each other the possession of their German and non-German territories, so that any attack made upon the territory of the one, no matter whence it may come, shall be regarded as a hostile attack on the territory of the other."[159]

---

[a] *The Times*, No. 21753, May 29, 1854, leader.— *Ed.*

[b] In good faith.— *Ed.*

[c] The Duke of Wellington to the Earl of Liverpool, November 21, 1809 in: Wellington, the Duke of, *Selections from the Dispatches and General Orders of Field Marshal the Duke of Wellington.—Ed.*

[d] Parliamentary debates of May 29 are reported according to *The Times*, No. 21754, May 30, 1854.— *Ed.*

Lord John Russell answered that

"the protocol does not contain any *special* recognition or sanction of that first article of the treaty between Austria and Prussia."

Special, or not special, we read in the French *Moniteur* of yesterday that

"the last protocol of Vienna connects the Anglo-French Convention for the present war with the Austro-Prussian treaty for the eventual war,"[a]

i.e. connects the actual Anglo-French war against Russia with the eventual Austro-Prussian war for Russia, and is at all instances a guarantee given by the western powers to Prussia and Austria for their undisturbed possession of Posen, of Galicia, of Hungary, and of Italy. Lord John Russell further avows that this protocol

"has a tendency to confirm and maintain the principles which are constituted by the Vienna protocols—namely, the integrity of the Turkish Empire, and the evacuation of the Principalities by the Russian forces."

In fact, it is a fresh engagement to maintain the *status quo ante bellum*. The western powers cannot pretend to have gained any advantage over Russia by this protocol; for, the Austro-Prussian treaty expressly stipulates:

"An offensive and defensive action on the part of the two contracting powers would be occasioned, firstly, by the incorporation of the Principalities; and in the second place, by an attack on, or a passage of, the Balkans by the Russians."

These two conditions have manifestly been dictated by Russia herself. From the very first, she declared that it was not her intention to incorporate, but to keep the Principalities as a "material guaranty" for the satisfaction of her demands. To cross the Balkans in the face of some 89,000 French troops,[b] is an idea which never entered into the Russian plan of campaign, the only object of which is to secure some of the fortresses on the right bank of the Danube as têtes-de-pont[c] for her army, and as constant facilities for an inroad into Bulgaria. Be it remarked, *en passant*, that *The Times*, in noticing this new protocol, is content at the best to hope that Austria may have been gained over to the western powers, Prussia being "notoriously" now governed by "Russian agents;"[d] while *The Morning Chronicle* even despairs of any sincere adhesion of Austria. The great Napoleon would have

---

[a] Report from Vienna, *Le Moniteur universel*, No. 149, May 29, 1854.— *Ed.*
[b] Presumably a mistake—should be 29,000 (see this volume, p. 223).— *Ed.*
[c] Bridgeheads.— *Ed.*
[d] *The Times*, No. 21753, May 29, 1854, leader.— *Ed.*

forced Austria and Prussia into open alliance with Russia; the little one permits Russia to impose upon him an alliance with the German Powers which removes his army to the greatest possible distance from its basis of operations.

On the interpellation of Mr. Milnes, Lord John Russell declared that

"a force, consisting of about 6,000 men, had been sent from France with instructions to occupy the Piraeus. An English regiment of infantry which had left this country about a week ago should likewise be posted in occupation of the Piraeus."

The cause of this measure was the conspiracy of the Greek Government with Russia. The troops were to occupy Athens only in certain contingencies. We read in the French papers of to-day that

"King Otto has accepted the ultimatum, and promised the return of the Maurocordatos Ministry, in case the occupation were suspended. If not, he was decided to transfer his Government to the interior, and there to concentrate his troops."

That this alternative will not remain altogether a gratuitous offer, follows from a further declaration by Lord J. Russell:

"If the King of Greece disapproves of the attempts of his people to violate the duties of a neutral Power, he will find protection in the forces which have been sent, and the means of compelling his people to observe those duties. If, on the other hand, the protestations which we have received from the Greek Government should turn out not to be sincere, those forces might prove useful in another way."

Consequently, the Greek Government may do as it pleases, Greece will be occupied.

The Times mentions with a certain moroseness that

"French troops form at this moment the larger portion of the garrisons of Rome, Athens and Constantinople—the three great capitals of the ancient world."[a]

Old Napoleon was in the habit of occupying the capitals of the new world. Napoleon the Little, content with the theatrical show of greatness, disperses his armies over insignificant countries, and locks up the better portion of his troops in so many *culs de sac*.[b]

The withdrawal of the Bribery Prevention bill in last night's House gave occasion to a highly amusing tournament between Little Johnny, Disraeli, and Bright. Mr. Disraeli remarked that

"The Government had introduced, during the session, seven important bills. Out of the seven, they had been defeated on three; three had been withdrawn, and

---

[a] *The Times*, No. 21754, May 30, 1854, leader.—*Ed.*
[b] Blind alleys.—*Ed.*

on the seventh, they had suffered considerable, though partial, defeats. They had been defeated on a bill for the entire change of the law of settlement[160]—on a bill for public education for Scotland—and on a bill for the total reconstruction of parliamentary oaths. They had withdrawn the present Bribery Prevention bill; they had withdrawn a most important measure for the complete change of the civil service, and they had withdrawn a measure for Parliamentary reform. The Oxford University Reform bill would come out of the House in a very mutilated state."

If they had not had a fair prospect of carrying these measures they ought not to have been introduced.... They were told that the Government had no principles, but "all the talents," and one might have expected that, as every minister had made a sacrifice of his private opinions, some public advantage should at least have accrued from such heroism.

Lord John's answer was not rendered less weak by his great indignation. He exalts the merits of the bills defeated as well as of the bills withdrawn. At all events, he adds, the House was not for Mr. Disraeli and his friends. The latter had accused the Government of credulity or connivance in the conduct of their foreign policy, but he had never dared to take the opinion of the House on that point. He had pretended an unwillingness to disturb the Government in their arrangements for the war; nevertheless, he had brought forward a motion to deprive them of the means of carrying on the war. That motion had been defeated by a majority of more than 100 votes. With regard to the Jews,[161] whose emancipation he pretended to advocate, he gave or withheld his support to that measure according to the conveniences of the hour.

This answer drew upon the poor leader of the Commons a fresh onslaught of his antagonist, much fiercer than the first.

"The noble Lord," said Mr. Disraeli, "seems to think that I am surprised that he has not quitted office; on the contrary, I should have been immensely surprised if he had. [Loud laughter.] Many more defeats, if possible more humiliating, and, if possible, more complete, must occur before the noble Lord will feel the necessity of taking such a step as that. [Cheers.] I know the noble Lord too well; I have sat opposite to him too long; I have seen him too often in the same position. Many a time have I seen him experience the most signal defeats, and I have seen him adhere to office with a patriotism and a pertinacity which cannot be too much admired. [Cheers and laughter.] With regard to the war, they had announced to Parliament that they would lay on the table all the papers on the subject, while in fact they kept back the most important part, and the country would have remained in total ignorance of what was going on, except for the revelations in the *St. Petersburg Gazette*.[a] After these revelations he had to modify his opinion only so far as to dispense with any hypothesis, and to positively declare that the Government

---

[a] *Journal de Saint-Pétersbourg.—Ed.*

can only have been guilty of connivance or credulity. He was quite convinced that before long that would be the general opinion of the country."

Mr. Disraeli then proceeded to defend the Government of Lord Derby, and to show that Lord John's opposition to it had been "factious." Lord John had made great sacrifices:

"He parted from the colleagues of his life, who had been faithful to him, to take into his bosom the ancient foes who had passed their lives in depreciating his abilities and decrying his career. He gave up the confidence—I may say he almost broke up the being of that historic party, the confidence of which to a man like the noble Lord ought not to have been less precious than the favor of his Sovereign. [Cheers.] And for what did he do it? Because he was devoted to great principles and was resolved to carry great measures. But now that every one of his measures had foundered, he still remained in office. As to his conduct upon the Jewish question, Mr. Disraeli gave to the statement of the noble Lord a most unequivocal and most unqualified denial."

In fact, he left no other resource to Lord John Russell but to plead his "misfortune," and to represent the continuance of the coalition as an indispensable evil.

Mr. Bright thought that

"The noble Lord came out of the discussion with some scars. The elements of the Government were such, that, from the day of its formation, it was not very likely that it could act for the benefit of the country. He recollected an ingenious gentleman in the House, and a great friend of the noble Lord and of the Government, saying that the Cabinet would get on admirably if they could only avoid politics. That appeared to be about the course that the Government had pursued. Upon every other matter except free trade the Government appeared altogether unable to advise, to lead, or to control the House. It was quite clear that the noble Lord who was by courtesy called the Leader of the House did not lead the House, and that the House did not follow the noble Lord, and that their measures were kicked overboard in a very unceremonious manner. You have got us into a war, and you must get us out of it. We will not undertake the responsibility. This was the condition that they were now driven to by the Government. While they were undermining and destroying the constitution of Turkey, they were also doing something to undermine and destroy the Parliamentary system of this country."

It may be asked of what use this system is? Domestic questions must not be agitated because the country is at war. Because the country is at war, war must not be discussed. Then why remains Parliament? Old Cobbett has revealed the secret. As a safety-valve for the effervescing passions of the country.

Written on May 30, 1854

First published in the *New-York Daily Tribune*, No. 4103, June 12; reprinted in the *New-York Semi-Weekly Tribune*, No. 944, June 13, 1854

Signed: *Karl Marx*

Reproduced from the *New-York Daily Tribune*

Karl Marx

[THE FORMATION OF A SPECIAL MINISTRY OF WAR IN BRITAIN.—THE WAR ON THE DANUBE.— THE ECONOMIC SITUATION] [162]

London, Friday, June 2, 1854

The formation of a special Ministry of War having now been determined upon, the great question of the moment is to know who may be selected to fill that office. The Duke of Newcastle, who has hitherto combined both the functions of Colonial and War Secretary, has long shown a great disinclination to relinquish either of his two posts, and seems disposed, if we may judge from the tone of *The Morning Chronicle*,[a] to stick at all events to the Administration of the War Department. *The Times* of to-day recommends for the third time the appointment of Lord Palmerston.

"Lord Palmerston would certainly seem more in his place as Minister of War, directing the forces of this country *against what we may call his old enemy, Russia*, than engaged in a series of squabbles with parochial vestries and sewers commissions."[b]

The Daily News likewise recommends Lord Palmerston. Yesterday's *Morning Herald* brought a denunciation of this intrigue from the pen of Mr. Urquhart. At all instances, these movements in Downing-st. are of greater importance for the "war" than all the military demonstrations at Gallipoli or Scutari.

Perhaps you will remember that great expectations were held out to the public of immediate and energetic measures as soon as the commanders of the expeditionary forces should have arrived at Constantinople. On the 18th May, Marshal St. Arnaud, Lord

---

[a] *The Morning Chronicle*, No. 27282, June 2, 1854, leader.— *Ed.*
[b] *The Times*, No. 21757, June 2, 1854, leader.— *Ed.*

Raglan and the Turkish Sereskier[a] proceeded to Varna where a council of war was to take place with Omer Pasha and the Admirals[b] on the 20th. Yesterday a telegraphic dispatch arrived in London stating that

"at the military council, held at Varna, it was decided that the allied troops should proceed from Gallipoli to Adrianople."[c]

Simultaneously *The Times* published a leading article in which the whole plan of the campaign as settled on at the Varna conference was revealed.

"This conference," says *The Times*, "must have taken place at the very time when the Russians, under Prince Paskievich, were directing their fiercest attacks against the fortress of Silistria, and consequently the principal officers of the allied army were in the best position to decide on the measures which might be taken for the relief of that place."[d]

And *consequently* they ordered their forces to come up from Gallipoli to Adrianople—for the relief of Silistria; and *consequently* they arrived at the following heroic determination:

"That it is not expedient to expose the Turkish army to the risk of a general action for the sake of repelling the attack of the Russians on the fortresses which cover the right bank of the Danube: ... nor to throw any considerable portion of the allied armies on the coast, so as to come into immediate collision with the present advanced posts of the Russians."

In other words, the allied generals have resolved not to oppose anything to the exertions of the Russians to carry the fortresses on the right bank of the Danube. *The Times* confesses that this plan of operations

"may disappoint the natural impatience of the public;"

but, on the other hand, it discovers that

"these fortified places are in reality the outworks of the Turkish position, and do not constitute its principal strength."

Formerly we were told that Moldavia and Wallachia were the *outworks* of Turkey, and that the latter could not be a great loser by surrendering them to Russian occupation. Now we learn that Turkey may, with the same tranquility, abandon Bulgaria to the Russians.

---

[a] Riza Pasha.— *Ed.*
[b] Dundas and Hamelin.— *Ed.*
[c] Telegraphic dispatch from Paris. *The Times*, No. 21756, June 1, 1854.— *Ed.*
[d] *The Times*, No. 21756, June 1, 1854, leader.— *Ed.*

"The Balkans is the real bulwark of the Ottoman Empire, and it can profit the Russians nothing to carry the outer line of circumvallation with heavy loss, if fresh obstacles of incalculably greater magnitude rise up before them as they proceed. The further they advance within this region north of the Balkans, the worse their position becomes.... The invading army exhausts its strength against the fortified places on the river and the scattered detachments of the enemy; but in the meantime the forces in defense of the main position remain comparatively fresh and unbroken."

There is no doubt that if the beef-eating allies[a] can only avoid encountering an enemy their forces will remain very fresh. But how will it be if the Russians do not further advance within the region north of the Balkans, contenting themselves with the possession of the fortresses, the keys of Bulgaria, and with the Principalities? How will their evacuation be effected?

"Behind the lines of the Balkans a European army is preparing to *advance*, at the proper time, with irresistible force, and the concluding months of the campaign *ought* to effect the annihilation of the enemy."

This irresistible advance will, of course, be greatly facilitated by the Russian possession of the Danube fortresses, and what may not be achieved by the allied armies, the *season* will have no difficulty to finish.

The *Moniteur*, it is true, announces that Omer Pasha was preparing to come to the relief of Silistria[b]; and *The Morning Chronicle* finds fault with the above article of *The Times*, observing:

"The author of this project probably hopes that Austrian diplomacy may induce, in the meanwhile, the Czar to withdraw his troops, with the satisfaction of having obtained uninterrupted and unresisted success; and on the other hand, it is, perhaps, imagined that, in the alternative of an advance on the Balkans, the remote contingency contemplated in the Austro-Prussian treaty would at once come into operation."[c]

The news of the *Moniteur*, however, is notoriously so arranged as to keep the Parisians in good humor; and the manner in which *The Chronicle* comments on the plan of *The Times* only increases the probability that it is the plan of the coalition. Other sources of information further confirm this assumption. The Constantinople correspondent of *The Chronicle*, under date of 18th May, observes:

"A campaign will scarcely be undertaken on the Danube in midsummer, as more men would be lost by fever and disease than otherwise."[d]

---

[a] An allusion to the nickname of the Yeomen of the Tower of London (Beefeaters).— *Ed.*

[b] Report from Belgrade of May 29, 1854. *Le Moniteur universel*, No. 151, May 31, 1854.— *Ed.*

[c] *The Morning Chronicle*, No. 27282, June 2, 1854, leader.— *Ed.*

[d] Ibid., No. 27281, June 1, 1854.— *Ed.*

Besides, the ministerial *Globe* of last evening publishes an article conceived entirely in the same spirit as that of *The Times*. It tells us, firstly, that there are at this moment "*only*" 45,000 allied troops in Turkey—29,000 French and 16,000 English, the same *Globe* stating, in another column, that the Russians have only 90,000 men before and around Silistria, and that the regular Turkish army in the field amounts to 104,000 men. But this aggregate of nearly 150,000 Turkish, French and English troops is not deemed sufficient by *The Globe* to prevent 90,000 Russians from taking the Bulgarian fortresses, not to mention the cooperation which might be given by three powerful fleets. *The Globe* thinks it sheer superfluity that either Turks or allies should fight against the Russians, as "time is fighting against them." In revealing the plan of campaign concocted by the allied commanders, *The Globe* even goes a step further than *The Times*, for it says:

"Whatever becomes of the fortresses on the Danube, adequate force must be brought up to render hopeless the invader's *further* progress, and punish his audacious advance."

Here we have the clear proof that the Austro-Prussian treaty has been acceded to in the last Vienna Protocol, by England and France. The fortresses on the Danube and Bulgaria are to be given up to Russia, and a case of war will only be constituted by her *further* advance.

When the 15,000 Russians who first invaded Moldavia crossed the Pruth, Turkey was advised not to stir, as she would be unable to prevent such a formidable force of 15,000 men from occupying Wallachia also. The Russians then occupied Wallachia. When war had been declared by the Porte no operations could be undertaken against the Russians because it was winter. On the arrival of spring, Omer Pasha received orders to abstain from any offensive movement, because the allied forces had not arrived. When they arrived nothing could be done because it was now summer, and summer [is] an unwholesome season. Let autumn arrive, and it will be "too late to open a campaign". This proceeding *The Times* calls a combination in strategies with tactics, the essence of tactics, in its opinion, being the sacrifice of the army in order to keep "fresh" the reserves. Observe also that all the time since this juggle has been going on under the very noses and eyes of the opposition journals and the British public at large, *The Morning Advertiser* rivals with *The Times* in expressions of angry denunciation against Prussia, against Denmark and Sweden, for not "joining" the western powers! That the motives which determine the tendencies of all the smaller Courts to side with Russia are not without a very good foundation, is seen from the tone, for instance, of the Danish Government journals. Thus the Copenhagen correspondent of *The Morning Chronicle* writes:

"The threat, by holding out which the Ministerial party manage to keep the National party quiet and discouraged, is that England has ever been perfidious toward Denmark, and that if the latter now joined with the western powers, 100,000 Prussians, perhaps with a corps of Austrians, would ravage Jutland down to the Eider, and occupy the whole Danish continent."[a]

It might be expected, and certainly was expected, by the coalition, that the delicate services—diplomatic, military and otherwise—rendered by them to the "good cause" of Russia would at least meet with a certain delicate gratitude from the Autocrat. So far from this, they receive a great deal of abuse from him beyond the understanding, and in excess of the exigencies of the case. In illustration of the manner of expressing this sovereign contempt of the Russian Court for their sham-adversaries, I will give you a translation of a fable lately published by the *Nordische Biene*,[b] by some anonymous Tyrtaeus of Russia. Its child-like simplicity of language and structure must be accounted for as an exigency of the semi-barbarian understanding to which the poet addresses himself, exactly as the ironical urbanity of criticism to which the late Odessa report of Admiral Hamelin has been subjected by the *St. Petersburg Gazette*, is to be explained by the circumstance of its being addressed to the diplomatists of Europe.[c] The fable is headed: The Eagle, the Bull-Dog, the Cock, and the Hare.

"A royal eagle, great and strong, sat on the summit of a rock, and from his lofty seat surveyed the whole world, far behind the Baltic, (*Weit hinter Belt die ganze Welt*); there he sat quietly and contently, satisfied by his modest meal, scorning to store up provisions from the valley beneath him, since he commands everything at every hour. A bull-dog viewed him with envious mien, and thus he spoke to the cock: Be my ally, we will combine, from vengeance thou, myself from envy, and put down yonder eagle. So said, so done. They marched on, and taking council on the road how they would best subdue the eagle, the cock said: Stop! look at his talons, his wings—may God assist him who would try them! More than once heard I the curses of my ancestors, lamenting their sad fate when beaten by his wings. "Tis true,' said the bull-dog; but we will devise a plan to catch the eagle. Let's send

---

[a] Report from Copenhagen of May 23. *The Morning Chronicle*, No. 27278, May 29, 1854.— *Ed.*

[b] *Северная пчела.— Ed.*

[c] *Journal de Saint-Pétersbourg*, No. 402, May 11 (23), 1854.— *Ed.*

a hare near him; he will clutch the hare. Meanwhile do thou turn his attention by crowing and jumping, as thou always know'st how to do, affecting to begin a fight with him. When thus we shall have diverted his attention and his talons, I will attack him in the back, so that he cannot defend himself, and soon he will be torn to pieces by my sharp teeth. The scheme pleased the cock, and he took his stand at a near post. The bull-dog enters a wood and barks, driving a hare toward the eagle, who watches quietly. The hare, stupid and blind, falls quickly into the eagle's clutch. The cock, faithful to his agreement, leaves his post and jumps after the hare; but lo! what disgrace! The eagle without stirring from his seat, lifts but his wings and, disdaining to take hold of the hare, drives him away with one and with the other, just touches the cock, who neither stirs nor crows any more. One knows the tendency of hares to fly; behold him run, senseless and unconscious into the sea, and there expires. The eagle saw the fat bull-dog at a distance conducting the intrigue—for, what escapes the eagle's eyes? He has discovered the hero concealed behind a bush. The eagle spreads his large and sturdy wings, and rises up in majesty. The bull-dog barks and flies with hasty leaps. In vain, it is too late. The eagle rushes down upon him and plunges his talons into the traitor's back, and there he lies, torn in pieces."

In consequence of the favorable harvest prospects, and through the absence of speculative buyers, the prices of grain have experienced a small decline during the week. A reaction, however, is inevitable, because

"all the evidence which can be brought to bear on the subject tends to lead to the belief that the stocks in farmers' hands, are reduced to a much smaller compass than is usual at the corresponding period of the season."—(*Mark Lane Express*.)

The advices from Danzig, Stettin, Rostock, etc., concur in the statement that the stocks on hand are very small, that the surrounding farmers had little or nothing more to deliver, and that assistance from those quarters could not be expected but at very high prices. The deliveries from the grower in France appear, also, not to have increased, and the wheat brought forward at the markets of the interior is described as scarcely sufficient to meet the demand for consumption.

I have also learned from a private source of information [163] that *The Times* reports of the state of trade in the manufacturing districts around Manchester[a] are generally misrepresentations, and that trade is everywhere in a declining condition except at Birmingham. *The Manchester Guardian* confirms this, and adds that the resumption of work by so large a number of operatives on strike could not be expected to act otherwise than to depreciate prices.

For the measure announced by Sir J. Graham in last Monday's

---

[a] *The Times*, No. 21753, May 29, 1854.—*Ed.*

House of Commons,[164] viz: The non-blockade of the port of Archangel, *The Morning Herald* accounts in the following laconic paragraph: "There is a house at Archangel which bears the name of the Chancellor of the Exchequer.[a]"

Written on June 2, 1854

First published in the *New-York Daily Tribune*, No. 4105, June 14; reprinted in the *New-York Semi-Weekly Tribune*, No. 945, June 16, 1854

Signed: *Karl Marx*

Reproduced from the *New-York Daily Tribune*

---

[a] Gladstone.— *Ed.*

Karl Marx

[REORGANISATION OF THE BRITISH WAR ADMINISTRATION.— THE AUSTRIAN SUMMONS.— BRITAIN'S ECONOMIC SITUATION.—ST. ARNAUD][165]

London, Friday, June 9, 1854

The speech delivered by Kossuth, at Sheffield,[a] is the most substantial ever heard from him during his stay in England. Nevertheless one cannot help finding fault with it. Its historical expositions are partly incorrect. To date tne decline of Turkey from the support given by Sobieski to the Austrian capital,[166] is a proposition for which no grounds whatever exist. The researches of Hammer[b] prove beyond dispute that the organization of the Turkish Empire was at that period already in a state of dissolution, and that the epoch of Ottoman grandeur and strength had been rapidly disappearing for some time before. Similarly incorrect was the proposition that Napoleon discarded the idea of attacking Russia by sea for other reasons than those suggested by his having no fleet, and his being excluded from the command of the ocean by the British. The menace that if England entered into alliance with Austria, Hungary might ally herself with Russia, was an act of imprudence. In the first place it furnished a weapon to the ministerial journals, of which *The Times* has not failed to make ample use by "convicting" all revolutionists as agents of Russia.[c] Secondly, it came with a singular propriety from the lips of the man whose mir try already in 1849 had offered the Hungarian crown to a Cesarewitch. Lastly, how could he deny that if ever his threat should be carried into execution, either at his own or others' instigation, the national existence of the Magyar race would

---

[a] L. Kossuth's speech at a meeting in Sheffield on June 5, 1854. *The Times*, No. 21761, June 7, 1854.— *Ed.*

[b] J. Hammer, *Geschichte des Osmanischen Reiches.*— *Ed.*

[c] *The Times*, No. 21762, June 8, 1854, leader.— *Ed.*

be doomed to annihilation, the major part of the population of Hungary being Slavonians? It was equally a mistake to describe the war against Russia as a war between liberty and despotism. Apart from the fact that if such be the case, liberty would be for the nonce represented by a Bonaparte, the whole avowed object of the war is the maintenance of the balance of power, and of the Vienna treaties—those very treaties which annul the liberty and independence of nations.

A more than usually vigorous speech has also been delivered by Mr. Urquhart at Birmingham, where he developed again his charge of treachery against the Coalition. However, as Mr. Urquhart is strictly opposed to the only party prepared to overthrow the rotten Parliamentary basis on which the Coalition Government of the Oligarchy rests, all his speeches are as much to the purpose as if they were addressed to the clouds.

In the House of Commons, last night, Lord John Russell announced the formation of a special Ministry of War, which ministry, however, is not to absorb the various departments at present constituting the administration of war, but only to have a nominal superintendence over all.[a] The only merit of the change is the erection of a new ministerial place. With regard to the appointment, *The Morning Post* of yesterday stated that the Peelite [167] section of the Cabinet had been victorious, and that the Duke of Newcastle would become the new Secretary for War, while the Colonies would be offered to Lord John Russell.[b] *The Globe* of last evening confirmed this statement, adding that, as Lord John was not likely to accept, Sir George Grey would be nominated Colonial Secretary. Although the Peelite journals affect still to be ignorant of a final decision, the Palmerstonian journal[c] of to-day announces in positive terms that the Duke of Newcastle and Sir George Grey have been appointed.

The Morning Post has the following in reference to the Austrian "peremptory summons:" [168]

"We have reason to believe that Russia will not treat the Austrian communication with silence, nor meet it by a refusal, and we shall not be surprised if we shortly learn that Russia is disposed to accept the Austrian proposal for the complete evacuation of the Turkish territory, on condition that Austria shall arrange an armistice with a view to negotiation."[d]

----

[a] *The Times*, No. 21763, June 9, 1854.— *Ed.*

[b] "The New Ministry of War", *The Morning Post*, No. 25095, June 8, 1854.— *Ed.*

[c] *The Morning Post.— Ed.*

[d] *The Morning Post*, No. 25095, June 8, 1854, leader.— *Ed.*

The Morning Chronicle of to-day likewise grants that "the communication may be of the greatest importance". It adds, nevertheless, that it must not be considered as an ultimatum, that it is couched in the usual courteous language, and that a rupture was only held out in case Russia should ignore the communication altogether. If Russia gave an evasive answer, or made a partial concession, new suggestions and negotiations might follow.

Let us suppose, for a moment, that the assumption of *The Post* was just, and about to be realized; it will be seen that the service rendered by Austria would be only to procure another armistice in favor of Russia. It is highly probable that something like this may have been contemplated, founded on the supposition that Silistria, in the meantime, would fall, and the "character and honor of the Czar" be guaranteed. The whole scheme, however, must fall to the ground, if Silistria holds out, and the valor of the Turks should at last force the allied troops to enter into the campaign, much as it may be against the inclination of their commanders and Governments.

If there be anything fit to render the frequent gaps and omissions in this great war less unendurable, it is the amusing uncertainty of the English press and public about the value and the reality of the alliance between the western and the German powers. Scarcely is the "peremptory summons" of Austria started to the satisfaction of all the world, when all the world is distressed by the news of a meeting between the Austrian and Prussian monarchs, a meeting which, in the words of *The Times*, "forbodes no good to the western powers."

The Board of Trade tables for the last month have been published.[a] The results are less favorable than those of the preceding months. The declared value of exports has fallen off £747,527, as compared with the corresponding month of 1853.[b] The articles chiefly affected have been those connected with the Manchester markets; but linen, woolen and silk manufactures likewise exhibit a decline.

In the usual monthly circular of Messrs. Sturge of Birmingham, we read that the wheat-plant has not tillered nor stooled well, and this is accounted for in the following way:

"The high price of seed caused a smaller quantity to be used per acre than in ordinary years, and the inferiority of the wheat of last year's growth committed to

---

[a] "Accounts relating to Trade and Navigation. III. Exports of British and Irish Produce and Manufactures from the United Kingdom", *The Economist*, No. 562, June 3, 1854.— *Ed.*

[b] "Our Trade", *The Economist*, No. 562, June 3, 1854.— *Ed.*

the soil may not have done so well as would have been the case if it had been better harvested."

In regard to this statement, *The Mark Lane Express* observes:

"This inference appears to us exceedingly probable and deserving of attention, as unsound seed can scarcely be expected to produce so healthy a plant as that gathered under more auspicious circumstances. The progress of the growing crop will be watched with more than ordinary interest, it being an admitted fact that stocks, not only in this country but almost in all parts of the world, have, owing to the extreme deficiency of the harvest of 1853, been reduced into a very narrow compass. The future range of prices will depend mainly on the character of the weather; the present value of wheat is too high to encourage speculation, and though it is more than probable that the supplies from abroad will, during the next three months, be on a much less liberal scale than they have hitherto been, still, if nothing should occur to give rise to uneasiness in respect to the probable result of the next harvest, those having anything to dispose of will naturally be anxious to clear out old stocks, while millers and others are likely to act on the hand-to-mouth system.... At the same time, it must be borne in mind that the country generally is bare of wheat."

You cannot at present pass through the streets of London without being stopped by crowds assembled before patriotic pictures exhibiting the interesting group of the Sultan, Bonaparte and Victoria—"the three saviors of civilization." To help you to a full appreciation of the characters of the personages who are now charged with saving civilization, after having "saved society," I resume my sketch of their generalissimo, Marshal St. Arnaud.[169]

The famous days of July[170] rescued Jacques Leroy, (old style), or Jacques Achille Leroy de St. Arnaud, (new style), from the grasp of his creditors. The grave question then arose how to improve the circumstance of French society being thrown into a general confusion by the sudden fall of the old regime. Achille had not participated in the battle of the three days, nor could he pretend to have done so, the fact being too notorious that at the memorable epoch he found himself carefully locked up in a cell at St. Pélagie. He was therefore unable to claim, like many other adventurers of the day, any remuneration under the false pretense of having been a *combattant* of July. On the other hand, the success of the *bourgeois regime* appeared by no means favorable for this notorious outcast of the Parisian Bohemia, who had always professed an implicit faith in Legitimacy, and never belonged to the Society of the "Aide-Toi,"[a] (a want of foresight which he has mended by becoming one of the first members of the Society of the "Dix-mille,")[171] nor played any part whatever in the great "comedy of fifteen years." Achille, however, had learned some-

---

[a] Help yourself.—*Ed.*

thing from his ancient master, M. E. de P.,[a] in the art of extemporization. He boldly presented himself at the War Office, pretending to be a non-commissioned officer who, from political motives, had tendered his resignation at the time of the Restoration. His banishment from the *Gardes du Corps*,[b] his expulsion from the Corsican Legion, his absence from the ranks of the 51st Regiment setting out for the colonies, were easily turned into as many proofs of his eccentric patriotism, and of the persecution he had suffered at the hands of the Bourbons. The conduct-list gave his assertions the lie, but the War Office feigned to believe in their truth. The withdrawal of numerous officers refusing to take the oath under Louis Philippe had caused a great void which must be filled up, and every public apostasy from Legitimacy, whatever might have been the motives of the conversion, was accepted as a valuable support to the usurper's government. Achille, consequently, was commissioned in the 64th Regiment of the Line, but not without undergoing the humiliation of being simply rehabilitated in his post of non-commissioned officer, instead of being promoted to a higher grade, like the others who had resigned under the Restoration.

Time and his brevet, advanced him at last to the rank of lieutenant. At the same time he was given an opportunity to make valid his special talents of servile apostasy. In 1832 his regiment was quartered at Parthenay, in the midst of the Legitimist insurrection of the Vendée. His former connection with some former *Gardes du Corps*, rallied around the Duchess of Berry, enabled him to combine the offices of soldier and of police-spy—a combination singularly agreeing with the genius matured in the gaming houses of London and the *cafés borgnes*[c] of Paris. The Duchess of Berry having been sold by the Jew Deutz to Mons. Thiers was arrested at Nantes, and Achille became intrusted with the mission of accompanying her to Blaye, where he was to act as one of her jailers under the orders of General Bugeaud.[173] Anxious not to let slip the occasion of exhibiting a conspicuous zeal for the dynastic interest, he over-shot the mark, and contrived to scandalize even Bugeaud himself by the abject services he allowed the police to impose upon him, and the brutal treatment to which he subjected the Duchess. Bugeaud, however, had not the power to dismiss an aide-de-camp whom the police had

---

[a] Eugène Courtray de Pradel.[172] — *Ed.*

[b] Royal Guard.— *Ed.*

[c] Low pubs.— *Ed.*

selected for the special duty of guarding the Duchess, who was under the particular superintendence of M. Joly, the Commissary of Police, and who, after all, depended more on the Ministry of the Interior than on that of War. The future generalissimo of the Anglo-French troops played the part of the mid-wife, it being his special mission to state and prove by witnesses the pregnancy of the Duchess, the discovery of which dealt the death-blow to the partisans of the old régime. It was in this same quality that the name of M. de St. Arnaud figured for the first time in the *Moniteur*, in whose columns of May 1833, we read that

"M. Achille de St. Arnaud, thirty-four years old, habitually residing at Paris, aide-de-camp to General Bugeaud, was summoned to sign, in his official capacity, the act of birth of the child of which the Duchess was delivered at her prison on May 10, 1833".[a]

The gallant St. Arnaud continuing to play his part of a jailer, accompanied the Duchess on board the corvette which disembarked her at Palermo.

Having returned to France, Achille became the laughing stock and the scapegoat of his regiment. Disliked by the other officers, excluded from their *réunions*, harassed by undisguised proofs of their utter contempt, put as it were in quarantine by the whole regiment, he was forced to take refuge in the Foreign Legion at Algiers, which was then organizing at Paris under the care of Colonel Bedeau. This Foreign Legion may be fairly characterized as the Society of the Tenth December of the European armies. Notorious desperadoes, adventurers of broken fortune, deserters from all countries, the general offal of the European armies, constituted the nucleus of this *corps d'élite*, which was properly called the *refugium peccatorum*.[b] There was no situation that could have better suited the genius of Achille than the fellowship of such a corps, the official mission of which preserved it from the fangs of the police, while the character of its constituting members removed all the checks weighing on the officers of the regular army. Notwithstanding Achille's habitual prodigality, he gave such slender proofs of military courage and capacity that he continued to vegetate during four years in the subaltern place of lieutenant in the 1st battalion of the Foreign Legion, until on the 15th August, 1837 when a new brevet conferred upon him the rank of captain. It is an unhappy circumstance that the company's chest is

---

[a] Report of May 13, 1833. *Le Moniteur universel*, No. 134, May 14, 1833.— *Ed.*
[b] The sinners' refuge.— *Ed.*

placed under the control of the captains in the French army, who are accountable for the pay of the men and their provisions. Chests were exactly the spot in which the modern Achille was most vulnerable; and thus it happened that some months after his promotion a terrible deficit was discovered in his. The Inspector-General, M. de Rullière, having detected this embezzlement, insisted on the punishment of the captain. The report to the Ministry was ready, it was on the point of being committed to the post, and M. de St. Arnaud would have been lost forever, if M. Bedeau, his lieutenant-colonel, affected by the despair of his inferior, had not interfered and appeased the wrath of General Rullière.[a]

St. Arnaud has quite a manner of his own of showing his gratitude for past obligations. Appointed to the ministry of war, on the eve of the *coup d'état*,[b] he caused General Bedeau to be arrested, and struck the name of General Rullière from the lists. Rullière addressed to him the following letter, which he circulated among his friends at Paris, and published in the Belgian journals:

"In 1837, the General Rullière refused to break the sword of the Captain Leroy de St. Arnaud, unwilling to dishonor him; in 1851, the Minister of War, Leroy de St. Arnaud, unable to dishonor the General Rullière, has broken his sword."[c]

Written on June 9, 1854

First published in the *New-York Daily Tribune*, No. 4114, June 24; reprinted in the *New-York Semi-Weekly Tribune*, No. 948, June 27, 1854

Signed: *Karl Marx*

Reproduced from the *New-York Daily Tribune*

[a] *Le trois maréchaux*, p. 9.— *Ed.*
[b] The reference is to the coup d'état of Louis Bonaparte on December 2, 1851.— *Ed.*
[c] Cited from the anonymous article: "Les Spoliateurs", *Le Bulletin français*, No. 5, January 29, 1852, p. 96.— *Ed.*

Frederick Engels

THE SIEGE OF SILISTRIA [174]

After an interval of time filled up by military movements below criticism, because they were made, not upon strategical and tactical, but upon diplomatic and parliamentary grounds, the investment and attack of Silistria affords at last an event of military interest.

This attack shows that the Russians still keep the initiative, and that, up to the present moment, the Turks, allied armies and allied fleets, are directed by an impulse received from the enemy. The allied fleets are instinctively, irresistibly attracted by the Russian fleet in its safe retreat at Sevastopol; being unable to attack that stronghold without a land force, they are thus held in check and paralyzed by a fleet far inferior in quality and number of ships. Even the evacuation of the forts on the Caucasian coast, carried out in proper time and under the nose of the British and French steamers, shows the determination of the Russians to hold the lead as long as possible. And in war this is a great thing. It is a proof of superiority—whether in numbers, in quality of troops, or in generalship. It keeps up the *morale* of the soldier under all checks and retreats short of the loss of a decisive battle. It was this initiative which held together Wellington's little army in the midst of hundreds of thousands of French troops in Spain, and which made it the center around which all the events of that five years' war grouped themselves. You may be forced to retreat, you may suffer a repulse, but as long as you are able to give the impulse to the enemy instead of receiving it from him, you are still to a degree his superior; and what is more, your soldiers will feel themselves, individually and collectively, superior to his men. The attack upon Silistria is, besides, the first real forward movement of the Russians since they completed the occupation of the Danube.

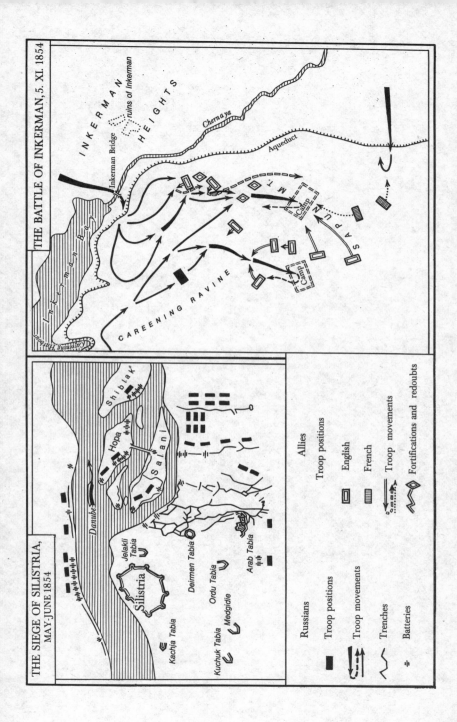

THE BATTLE OF INKERMAN, 5. XI. 1854

INKERMAN HEIGHTS

ruins of Inkerman

Chernaya

Aqueduct

Inkerman Bridge

Camp

S A P U N (M T)

Camp

CAREENING RAVINE

Careening Harbour

Inkerman Bay

THE SIEGE OF SILISTRIA, MAY-JUNE 1854

Shiblak

Hopa

Salani

Danube

Jelakli Tabia

Silistria

Kachia Tabia

Kuchuk Tabia

Medgidie

Ordu Tabia

Deirmen Tabia

Arab Tabia

Russians

Troop positions

Troop movements

Trenches

Batteries

Allies

Troop positions

English

French

Troop movements

Fortifications and redoubts

The entrance into the Dobrodja was eminently defensive; a shortening of their front line, and a step to secure the mouths of the Danube. But the attack upon Silistria is not only a bold, but an extremely well calculated movement.

In 1828-29 the Russians, then masters of the Black Sea, very properly neglected Silistria in order to secure Varna first, because Varna opened a new line of sea-communication with their own country. Yet Silistria was important enough to induce them to take it before they crossed the Balkans. At present, when the allied fleets command the Black Sea, Varna loses most of its importance to the Russians, and Silistria and Shumla are the main points of attack. To them Varna can now have but a negative value; if they take it, they gain no improved base of operations, but merely deprive the enemy of what may be called a maritime bridge-head, under cover of which he can suddenly concentrate, by his ships, a number of troops for a special operation. Thus the Danes in 1849, after enticing the Prussian army into Jutland, suddenly trans-shipped a strong body of troops to their maritime bridge-head of Fredericia, and, in a sally, destroyed the fine, but far weaker Schleswig-Holstein corps left before it to conduct the siege.[175] If therefore the Russians, driven from the Black Sea, cannot under any circumstances pass the Balkans before they have secured Varna, they cannot advance against Varna before they are masters at least of Silistria.

But these are considerations of secondary importance for the present; Russia, unaided by Austria, cannot think of passing the Balkans in the face of her present enemies. The defensive importance of Silistria to the Russians is at this moment paramount; it is such that unless they take it, they may consider their campaign of the year as lost. Silistria is situated exactly in front of the center of the Russian position, extending from Giurgevo by Kalarash and Chernavoda to Kustendje. With a strong system of fortresses before this position, with Omer Pasha in Shumla, like a spider in the center of its web, watching every movement of its intended prey, with allied forces expected on the Kamtchik and Devna, there is very little chance that the force Russia can spare for the Danubian war, single-handed, will ever get a glimpse of those Thracian valleys whose verdure charmed the fatigued soldiers of Diebich from the hights of the Balkans. Russia must calculate, for this year at least, upon a simple defense of her present conquests, until either Austria joins her, or some circumstance disables or draws away her most formidable oppo-nent, the Anglo-French army. A defensive war presupposes a system of field, or, if possible, of permanent, fortifications. Now, Silistria being in the hands of the enemy, the Russians have no permanent fortifications at hand but the small forts of the Dobrodja, which will be entirely useless as soon as Wallachia is lost. They may have reconstructed some of the fortifications of Ibraila and Rustchuk and formed an entrenched camp at Bucharest, but as long as Silistria is not theirs, their first line of serious defense lies as far back as the Sereth, Fokshani, Galatch and Ismail.

But suppose Silistria in the hands of the Russians, the aspect of the war changes at once. Silistria is a splendid point for a Russian bridge-head on the Danube. It is situated in a reentering angle formed by a bend in the Danube, just the situation best fitted for the purpose. There is a large island to the north and west, which is crossed by the dyke to Kalarash, and which commands the plains west of the fortress, at a distance of 1,000 yards—quite near enough to enfilade trenches or to shell columns. There are two little islands to the east that sweep the eastern approach, and temporary batteries erected there at low water would annoy a besieger very materially. Thus part of the ground which the Turks, attacked from the north, cannot use in the defense and must therefore abandon to the enemy, would give the Russians excellent positions for batteries flanking an attack coming from the south. The front open to an attack would thus be confined to the base of the triangle, at the apex of which Silistria is situated, or in other words to its southern or land front; and a Turkish or allied army could not think of seriously attacking Silistria before Wallachia, at least, was taken from the Russians.

The main advantages, however, would be not so much of a tactical as of a strategical nature. With the Dobrodja and Silistria, Russia commands the Danube, and can, according to circumstances, debouch for momentary offensive action either from Trajan's Wall, or from Silistria. The enemy would not be able, unless he were twice as strong as the Russians, to cross at any point higher up without exposing Shumla. As to his crossing lower down than Silistria, it is out of the question; there is no crossing point nearer than Hirsova to reach which he must first take the position of Karasu and then Hirsova itself, which is as strong against an attack from the land side as it is weak against one from the river side. Thus by the possession of Silistria, the forts of the Dobrodja become of great importance to the Russians. Their army obtains a double pivot around which it can freely maneuver without exposing its communications, and even if a superiority of two to one should enable the enemy to cross at Oltenitza or

Giurgevo to take Bucharest and to repel the Russians behind the Jalomitza, the siege of Silistria would be an indispensable operation before any decisive advance into Bessarabia could be considered safe. Until Silistria had actually fallen, the Russians, therefore, might consider themselves as possessors of Wallachia even if they had not a soldier in that province. Silistria, in a word, would be equivalent, to Russia, to six months tenure of Wallachia and six months, bringing us to the winter when no sieges can be carried on at all in that country, would be equivalent to four months more. Silistria would be the winning, and a repulse from Silistria would almost be the loss, of the campaign.

For once, then, in spite of diplomacy, bribery, cowardice and irresolution, we are come, through the inherent necessities of the war, to a decisive turning point. Either Silistria is abandoned to its fate, and then its fall is a matter of more than mathematical certainty; or the allies advance to its relief, and then there will be a decisive battle; for without demoralizing their army and losing all their prestige, the Russians cannot retreat from before Silistria without fighting, nor do they appear willing to do so.

Silistria has undergone more varied fates than any other fortress. In 1810 the Russians took it after nine days' investment and five of serious attack. In 1828, the fortress being exactly in the same state as before, they invested it on the 21st of June with their land forces, and on the 10th of August with thirty-six gun-boats also. But their siege-artillery did not arrive till September, and then there was no ammunition with it, so that a regular attack could not be made. On the 10th of November they had to raise the siege, the winter having set in, and the Danube having begun to drift ice. The retreat of the disorganized and disheartened Russians was followed up most vigorously by the garrison; part of the Russian siege-artillery had been left in the batteries and the remainder was taken by the Turks in the pursuit toward Rassova. In the next year Diebich renewed the attack, invested the fortress on the 7th May by driving the Turks out of the lines and redoubts constructed by the Russians the year before, and opened fire from thirty-one heavy guns placed, it would seem without any preparation, on an elevation about 900 yards from the town. On the 26th dismounting batteries were opened at about 600 yards from the wall. At the same time the second parallel was opened; the third was opened on the 4th of June, and on the 12th the advance toward the crowning of the glacis was begun. The glacis was crowned at one point on the 17th, but this operation was completed on the 26th, only when five batteries were opened at the very edge of the ditch, thirty yards from the main wall. At the same time General Schilder, the same who now directs the engineering part of the siege, had carried on his favorite extensive mining operations. Large mines laid under the counterscarp and the main wall had been sprung on the 21st (effecting at once a practicable breach), on the 25th, 27th, 28th and 29th, when at last the fortress surrendered. Even then there appears not to have been any urgent necessity for a surrender, save the terror produced by the subterranean explosions among a superstitious and irregular soldiery. Behind the whole attacked front and second rampart a *coupure* or new intrenchment had been made, which would of course have required fresh mining or artillery operations before it could have been taken. Thus this singular fortress, in no way improved upon its state in 1810, had yet held out thirty-five days after the opening of the trenches, and nine days after a practicable breach had been effected in the main wall; it had forced the Russians to expend 30,000 shot and shell in the artillery attack, and 336 hundredweight of powder in the mining attack.

Financial difficulties and the Egyptian wars compelled the Turks to neglect this important point after the peace of Adrianople [176] to such a degree that even in 1836 the breaches of 1829 were not only not completely repaired and the ditches cleared, but the traces of the attack of 1810 even were still visible. The Sultan[a] intended to construct detached forts then, but for some time this intention was not carried out. At the present day, Silistria is in a far different state, owing mostly to the exertions of a Prussian officer in the Turkish service, Col. Grach. The original faulty construction of the place perhaps hardly admits of much improvement, but the detached forts constructed on the hights have already proved their utility. The fortress forms a semi-circle, the diameter of which, about 1,800 yards long, runs along the shore of the Danube. It has ten bastioned fronts of an average length of 500 yards. The construction, as with all Turkish fortresses of the sixteenth and seventeenth centuries, teems with all the imperfections of the old Italian fortifications; long curtains, small and narrow bastions, short flanks offering hardly any defense of the ditch, the ditch itself shallow (not above eight feet deep), no covered way, but a mere glacis, the crete or highest part of which was hardly four feet above the top of the counterscarp. The rampart itself was eight feet high by twenty feet in thickness,

_____
[a] Mahmud II.— *Ed.*

and constructed of earth; scarp and counterscarp were rivetted to the hight of the ditch, viz., eight feet. The ditch itself is from the hight of its level necessarily dry. There were not even lunettes in front of the curtains. Such was Silistria up to 1836; and these weaknesses of its defenses were crowned by the fact that, within 600 yards from the wall, the fortress is commanded by a range of hights extending to the south of it. These hights are the abutment of the Bulgarian Plateau, which, perfectly flat at the top, extends within 1,500 yards of the town, and then slopes down toward the river, offering a splendid emplacement for terraced batteries for front or enfilading fire, with the narrow arm of the river on one side and the hights on the other. Major Moltke, who surveyed the place in 1836, and to whose work on the campaign of 1829 we are indebted for the above particulars, gives it as his opinion

"that Silistria cannot be made capable of a serious defense without four detached forts on the hights, and a bridge-head on the large island opposite." [a]

The bridge-head was an impossibility, the island belonging to Wallachia, from which the Turks were excluded by treaty; but the forts are there, and if we are well informed, almost on the identical spots pointed out by Major Moltke.

What Col. Grach may have been able to do with the faulty main wall, we cannot tell. There is, however, hardly a doubt that he must have constructed at least a covered way and introduced loop-holes for enfilading the ditch at the middle of the curtain in each of the most menaced and least defended fronts. As to the four detached forts, we know nothing as yet respecting their mode of construction, but from Col. Grach's being a Prussian, and cheapness being a great object with the Porte, we should say they must most likely be constructed upon the system which is now almost generally adopted on the continent, and especially in Prussia, viz: plain square or octagonal redoubts with loop-holes on every alternate corner. Their situation is pointed out by the four promontories which form the final projections of the plateau toward the town, and which are separated by three ravines. Their distance from the main wall must be, on an average, 1,500 yards so that they cannot be very effectually protected by the fire from the fortress. But there is no absolute necessity for this; and there appear to be no spots nearer the town, on the slope, where a fort could be well defiladed against the commanding edge of the plateau.

---

[a] Moltke, *Der russisch-turkische Feldzug in der europäischen Türkei 1828 und 1829,* S. 206.— *Ed.*

Beside these permanent works, Col. Grach has constructed on the plateau itself an earthwork, not of a permanent nature, called Arab Tabiassi, (Fort Arabia,) situated in front of the two central forts, at about 1,000 yards distance. Some reports would lead to the conclusion that other field-redoubts have been erected so as to form an outer line of forts, thus giving three lines of successive defense. Arab Tabiassi, however, remains the key of this position, and must be taken before the inner line of forts can be approached. This disposition of the works endows Silistria with great defensive and offensive strength. As the regular attack can lead to decisive results on its southern front only, a garrison from 15,000 to 18,000 strong can spare a great number of men for sallies. The sally troops find a splendidly covered position on the slope behind the detached forts, from which they can advance unseen up the ravines, until near the enemy. In a storm upon Arab Tabiassi, therefore, it would not be so much the garrison of that fort as the sallying troops from Silistria who would decide the battle. Now to the siege itself.

From the end of April the Russians had occasionally fired across the Danube into Silistria. In May they began to construct a regular approach on the large island opposite the town, close to the dyke leading to Kalarash, and by the 10th they had their batteries completed along the shore of the river. A violent bombardment against the town as well as horizontal firing against the northern front took place on the 11th. It was repeated on the 12th, when Lieut. Nasmyth, Bengal Artillery, who had just arrived, witnessed it, and gives his report in *The London Times.*[a] The main point of aim was the northeastern or Tshengel Bastion, from which the Turks replied most vigorously, and with great steadiness of aim. The practice of the Russians, on the contrary, is described as very indifferent. Numbers of shells were found in the town which had been fired without taking off the caps of the fuses, so that they could not take fire and explode. Such an oversight, though common in rapid field-practice in the beginning of a campaign, is unheard of in siege-firing, where the fire is always comparatively slow. It proves what a hurry the Russians must have been in to get rid of their ammunition. The Russians had, besides, erected batteries during the night on the island of Shiblak, to the east of Silistria. (They had two batteries on the same spot in 1829.) The four guns of this battery must have been intended to enfilade the whole of the northern front.

---

[a] [Nasmyth,] "The Siege of Silistria". *The Times*, No. 21762, June 8, 1854.— *Ed.*

From the 13th to the 16th nothing much appears to have been done; the reports at least are entirely silent. It is not improbable that the Russian generals, finding, as they might well have expected, a bombardment of no avail against a Turkish fortress, prepared for an attack on the right bank of the river. Accordingly on the 16th a bridge was completed below Silistria; 20,000 men crossed on it, and were shortly afterward joined, it is said, by 20,000 more from the Dobrodja. A general movement of concentration toward Silistria and Turtukai took place among the Russians; for as soon as the attack was to be carried on upon the right bank, a force was necessary to cover it against Omer Pasha at Shumla, and any Anglo-French troops which might be landed at Varna.

On the 19th the first reconnoitering took place against Arab Tabiassi; large masses of troops were concentrated just out of gun-range, while a line of skirmishers advanced. After a short cannonade, Mussa Pasha sent some Bashi Buzouks [177] upon the plateau, who drove the skirmishers in. On the 20th, another Russian advance took place, which looks too serious for a mere reconnoitering—not serious enough for a real attack. On the 21st the first assault upon Arab Tabiassi was carried out; the details are wanting, but the Russians were repulsed with great loss. Two Russian officers passed over to the Turks, and reported the enemy to be 90,000 strong, combined from three army-corps (this is correct, the 3rd, 4th and 5th), and to be commanded by the Grand Duke Constantine. This latter statement is evidently a mistake, as Constantine is notoriously commanding the fleet, troops and coast defenses in Finland. The report of an intended renewal of the attack on the following day was not confirmed by the event. The Russians were under arms, but did not approach the fort. We are, then, again without news of what happened up to the 26th; but at daybreak on the 27th the Russians assaulted the Arab Tabiassi again with very considerable forces. Three times was the assault renewed, and three times the assailants were repulsed with immense loss. The Turkish reports speak of 1,500 killed, and 3,000 wounded Russians, which may be a little exaggerated, but is not much beyond probability. Determined to take the fort, *à la* Suvoroff, the next morning Paskievich had his columns again ready for the attack. The massacre appears to have been fearful; Gen. Selvan was killed. Col. Count Orloff, Jr., was shot in the eye and died afterward.[178] Another colonel was severely wounded. The Russians themselves admit a loss of 186 dead and 379 wounded; but this is evidently not one-third of what they must have lost;

with the masses they brought to the attack, a loss of 2,000 is the least they can have suffered.

In the night following the Turks made a sortie in mass, fell suddenly on the Russian lines and drove the Russians back with great loss (1,500 to 1,800, as the reports go). This successful sally, and the circumstance that on the last assault the troops could not be brought up too close, although the cavalry was employed in driving them up and cutting off their retreat, made Prince Paskievich resign the attempt to carry the place with the bayonet. There is no doubt that the defense of this redoubt is one of the most glorious feats of arms, not only in this, but even in all the Russo-Turkish campaigns. The ground admitted of an attack by very large numbers, and the Russians are not the men to omit sending as many thousands to a storm as they possibly can. The superiority of numbers on their part must, therefore, have been very great, and required not only brilliant gallantry, but also well planned and harmoniously executed sally operations on the part of the Turks to repulse it. There is hardly a doubt that against the Turks of 1829 the Russians would have carried the place. Their present repeated defeat shows that the Turks, at least part of them, have improved in tactical proficiency and military science, without losing any of their bravery. In this respect the defense of Arab Tabiassi and the engagement of Chetatea are the most remarkable affairs of the campaign.

As to the Russian attack, we cannot say much good of it. Paskievich appears to be in such a hurry to take Silistria that he has not even time for measures the most indispensable to effect his object. His irresolution is plainly betrayed. First he tried a bombardment, though he might have known how useless that is against a Turkish town. A bombardment can lead to nothing but a great loss of ammunition to the Russians, with perhaps a breach in the wall on the river front, where the vicinity of the Danube, a natural ditch of 1,000 yards wide, prevents all idea of a storm. Then the land front is attacked, but the fire of Arab Tabiassi appears never to have been silenced nor any serious attempt made to ruin its defenses. All that is too circumstantial for a successor of Suvoroff. As said that arch-Russian general, "The bullet is a foolish girl, the bayonet is a brave fellow," and if this is true with regard to the Russian bayonet, which, according to the same gallant authority, pierces through the Alps, it is certainly still more true with regard to Russian bullets, which have an invariable and irresistible tendency to deviation. So the storm is ordered, executed, repeated, and again repeated, in vain. It appears that the earthen parapets of a small but strongly built Turkish fort are harder than the Alpine granite, against which Suvoroff fought, and that the balls and bullets of the Turks are not so foolish as those of the Russians. After all, Paskievich will have to return to the old maxim: Never storm a work before silencing its fire and ruining its defenses. Thus, about the 30th or 31st of May the regular siege begins, and Paskievich at last has recourse to the "foolish bullet."

But, no! this even is a mere show. Here is Gen. Schilder of 1829 notoriety, who promises to bring down the place with his eternal mines; and in a few days too. Mines against a field-work are the last expression of military despair, of ignorant rage brought to bay. If mines are to be employed, then, in order to be able to work them with effect, the primary condition is that the *glacis* be crowned. Before the glacis can be crowned, the enemy's fire must be silenced; that is, one, two, three parallels laid, with all their respective batteries. In fact, mines are the concluding operation of a siege, not its beginning. Unless Schilder proposes to undermine some twenty square miles of ground, or lay a tunnel under the Danube, he cannot escape the necessity of a regular siege. In spite of Suvoroff, the bullets are indispensable.

Now, a regular siege against Arab Tabiassi might be certainly concluded in a very few days, as the work has almost completely fulfilled its purpose and a prolonged defense would weaken the garrison too much. But this would be a regular siege against at least two forts, and then another against the town. Five weeks is certainly the *very shortest* time in which the Russians can complete this, slovenly as they are in siege operations. If, then, the Turks should have plenty of provisions and ammunition, and no unforeseen accidents should occur, the fortress may be considered as safe up to the beginning of July. We suppose, of course, that the forts are of an average strength and that the walls are not too much out of repair. But if Silistria stood 35 days of opened trenches in 1829, surely with the new additions, with a brave and intelligent commander, an experienced director of artillery, and a first-rate garrison, it will be able to stand at least as long in 1854. If it were possible to rely on the allies, we might safely say, therefore, that the campaign must prove a total failure for the Russians, if not a great deal worse.

Written on June 10, 1854

First published in the *New-York Daily Tribune*, No. 4115, June 26; reprinted in the *New-York Weekly Tribune*, No. 668, July 1, 1854 as a leader

Reproduced from the *New-York Daily Tribune*

Karl Marx and Frederick Engels

STATE OF THE RUSSIAN WAR [179]

Our European correspondence and files of journals received last evening by the arrival of the *America*'s mail, fully confirm the reported expulsion of the Russians from their trenches before Silistria and their subsequent withdrawal from Wallachia back to the line of the Sereth. We learn also that there is no doubt of the immediate entrance of the Austrians into the evacuated province of Wallachia, under the treaty concluded at Constantinople on the 14th ult.[180]—an event under the circumstances of no small value to the Czar, brought about too, as we learn, under the immediate direction of Prince Metternich, who, in fact, again controls the foreign policy of the Hapsburgs.

Besides the curious coincidence of the Russians evacuating and of the Austrians occupying Wallachia, the very manner in which the siege of Silistria was undertaken, carried on, and finally abandoned, indicates that agencies were at work altogether distinct from mere military considerations. From the official Russian report, which comes down to the night of May 28,[181] and which differs from the Turkish bulletins only with regard to the respective numbers of killed and wounded, it appears that the operations were of a strangely precipitate character; that the rudest efforts to dismount the outworks were not made until the impossibility of taking the place by storm was practically ascertained, and that the attack was more wild and unscientific than any known even in the annals of Russian sieges. As to the operations between the 28th of May and the 15th of June, the reports which we have received are yet too fragmentary to allow of a detailed description; the fact, however, that during the repeated desperate assaults, nearly all the commanding officers were wounded and disabled — Paskievich, Schilder, whose leg has since been amputated, Gorchakoff, Lüders and Orloff who was shot through the eye, clearly proves that the Russians were under orders, not merely to take the place at any cost, but to take it within a certain fixed time. Indeed the whole was conducted on their part in a manner which reminds us more of the barbarian method of carrying the cities of Koordistan by Timur Tamerlane, than of the proceedings of regular modern warfare. On the other hand, it is evident that the heroic and able defense of Silistria created equal surprise with the allied powers and the Ottoman Divan. Our readers may remember that about six weeks ago the allied commanders met at Varna, that they discovered that the Balkan line formed the natural defense of Turkey,[a] and that now many of the British journals not only confess, but glory in the avowal, that Silistria was not relieved by a single French or English soldier. Lastly, it cannot be denied that Silistria was a point of great military importance, that the fate of this fortress decides the fate of the campaign, and that with the abandonment of its siege and the sudden retreat of the Russians upon the Sereth, the whole of the Russian conquests of territory made this year as well as the last are lost.

Still it must be said that our English cotemporaries, many of them, greatly exaggerate the extent of the present Muscovite reverses. It certainly requires a high degree of credulity to believe that the sortie made by the garrison of Silistria on June 13, and the succor of 2,000 men they are said to have received from Omer Pasha, resulted in the total defeat of the Russians, and forced 90,000 to 100,000 men to fly before 15,000. The sudden retreat of the Russians is, so far as we can judge, quite as mysterious as their sudden attack. It is only to be explained by a previous understanding with Austria, involving the occupation of Wallachia by Austrian troops. Under these circumstances, the following passage which we find in a letter of *The Morning Chronicle*'s Constantinople correspondent, revealing this plot on June 10, as early as four days before the conclusion of the Austro-Turkish treaty, is of a peculiarly interesting character:

"The Turks think that diplomacy is playing with them, and that it is their intention to allow Silistria to fall into the hands of Russia. These suspicions receive confirmation from the news that has been received here of the *preparation of a new protocol at Vienna*, in which the fall of Silistria is, I learn, spoken of *as if it were*

---

[a] See this volume, p. 222.— *Ed.*

accomplished; and, *the military honor of Russia being satisfied,* Austria would consider the time to have arrived for her armed intervention to bring about an arrangement by the means of her co-operation— *occupying the Danubian Principalities, which would be evacuated by the armies of Russia.*"

According to this, if the Russians had taken Silistria in due time, all would have been right. But though they did not succeed in satisfying the military honor of the Czar, they must, according to the compromise with Austria, beat back in a somewhat inglorious manner. The Russians receding behind the Sereth, the Austrians advance to the Sereth and Danube, and thus place themselves between the Muscovites and the Turks and their allies. In this position they are arbiters of the quarrel, preventing both parties from moving forward. The Russians remain in Moldavia, while the Vienna Conference will be more than ever busy itself with protocols, and thus the winter will be gained. If the Conferences end in nothing—a result which is sure since the Emperor of Russia has got the money on his new loan of $37,000,000 from Hope & Co. of Amsterdam[a]—the position of the Russian army behind the Danube and the Sereth will be twice as strong as was its line between Bucharest and Kustendje. Besides, if we look at the relative strength of the Russians before Silistria and in Bulgaria, now on their retreat behind the Sereth, and of the allied armies as far as they can, thanks to their ingenious arrangements, be thrown at all into the balance, it is plainly seen that, with even the best intentions, the latter would not be capable of baffling this combination of Austria with Russia.

The Russian forces employed against Turkey and the allies on the European shores of the Black Sea amount to thirteen divisions of infantry, three of the third, three of the fourth, one of the fifth, three of the sixth army corps, and three reserve divisions. Besides these, the third, fourth, fifth and sixth divisions of light cavalry, and the third, fourth and fifth divisions of artillery. These troops, making up nearly one-half of the grand army of operations, should amount, according to the official statements, to 16,000 men per division of infantry, 5,000 per division of cavalry, and 160 guns per division of artillery; altogether something like 250,000 to 260,000 men, inclusive of train and camp followers. But, if we measure the strength of a Russian army by what it actually was in the Hungarian war,[182] we cannot estimate a division of Russian infantry at more than 13,000 to 14,000 men, and the cavalry and artillery must be reduced in proportion. The actual

---

[a] See this volume, pp. 267-68.— *Ed.*

forces, then, which the Russians have successively marched into the Principalities would be reduced to about 210,000 men, and even from this number must be deducted, on account of loss in battle and by sickness, at least 20,000 to 25,000 more. Recollecting the ravages made by the marsh-fever in the ranks of the Russian army during 1828-29, and comparing the letters of a Russian surgeon [183] in the Vienna *Medical Journal,*[a] we cannot consider a loss of from eight to ten per cent. upon the total of the army as exaggerated. Thus about 180,000 Russians are left as the disposable number of their army.

It is interesting to learn what portion of this force can have been employed in the operations against Silistria. A large body of troops was required to guard the communications and magazines established in the rear of the line of battle. Bucharest and the line of the Dobrodja had to be occupied. Detachments were indispensable to cover the flanks, and partly the front of the army; and if we deduct 60,000 men for these various duties we obtain a net result of 130,000 men available for the siege of Silistria and the covering of that operation. This is rather above than below the mark. Now the position of Silistria on a large river made it unavoidable that the besieging army should divide itself, with a view to inclose the fortress from all sides. It further necessitated the establishment of strong reserves on the northern bank, in order to receive the troops pushed forward from the southern bank in case of a defeat. Finally these troops occupying the southern or right bank had to divide themselves again into a double army, the one to carry on the siege and to repel any sallies of the besieged, the other to cover the siege and defeat any army marching to the relief of the fortress. About 35,000 to 40,000 men were required to occupy the left bank and carry on the siege on the right. Thus an army of 80,000 Russians would have remained available for active field-operations against a relieving army, and this was the utmost the Russians could bring to battle on Bulgarian ground within from ten to twenty miles of Silistria.

Now let us see what force the allies have to oppose to the 180,000 Russian total at this moment. The Turkish army at Shumla was stated, some time ago, to be about 80,000 strong, but short of everything required for action in the open field, and is, according to the latest report of Lord Raglan and French staff officers, badly officered, altogether in a condition which peremptorily forbids offensive operations. It is neither our purpose nor

---

[a] *Wiener medizinische Wochenschrift.—Ed.*

within our present means to determine the accuracy of this report. Suffice it to say that such is the character of the Turkish main army in the official opinion of its allies. Since then the troops from Kalafat have been drawn to Rustchuk, where a camp of 40,000 men is said to be establishing. It would be difficult to conceive the policy of thus rendering idle a corps of such strength, which, if it had marched upon Bucharest instead of Rustchuk, might have compelled the Russians to raise immediately the investment of Silistria, but for the conduct of the war being entirely in the hands of diplomacy. Setting apart the present garrison at Rustchuk and the garrison and reserve at Shumla, it may well be doubted whether the Turks can muster 50,000 men in the open field in a condition fit for the work before them. An Anglo-French soldier being equal, in the estimation of western military authorities, to at least two Russians, there would still be required a force of 65,000 allies to balance the strength of the Russian army of occupation. Unless, therefore, they can muster that force at Varna they would hardly go to battle, the case of extreme necessity excepted.

They have however been most careful not to drop at once into the field in such force as would leave no further pretext for abstaining from active operations. The whole Anglo-French force now in Turkey does not amount to more than 80,000 men, besides from 15,000 to 20,000 more now on their way thither, including almost the entire cavalry and artillery. The amount of transports at hand in the Bosphorus is, whether intentionally or not, very limited, so that it would take many a journey there and back, if they were to be transported to Varna by sea alone. But,

"according to the latest and most accurate accounts,"—says the correspondent we have already quoted—"there are at present but 12,000 British and French troops who have been transported by sea, while the bulk of the French army is slowly advancing from Gallipoli toward Constantinople and Adrianople."

The roads being notoriously bad and the difficulty of victualling extreme, an arrangement which allows their famous General—St. Arnaud—to be permanently under steam between Varna and Constantinople, where we may be sure he does not lose an opportunity for turning every intrigue in the Divan to a solid advantage for his unfathomable purse. As to the two British divisions still at Scutari, we are informed by the same correspondent that

"they do not seem ready to start yet, though there is a whole fleet of transports and steamers at anchor, waiting to embark them."

From all these facts it is sufficiently clear to everybody that the allied powers have taken full care not to be in a state to frustrate directly the present arrangement between Russia and Austria. For, if it were intended to pursue that object, a very simple alternative for doing so offers itself either by an Anglo-Swedish alliance in the Baltic, which would give a basis of operations for auxiliary troops by facilitating an invasion of Finland and a turning on the land-side of the fortresses of Sweaborg and Kronstadt; or by a combined attack by sea and land on the Crimea and Sevastopol. With regard to the first supposition, it is amusing to see how *The London Times* which, not three weeks before, preached the necessity of sending the Black Sea squadron to the Baltic, now recommends a simple blockade of the harbors of the Baltic and an immediate return of the greater portion of the Baltic fleet to the Black Sea, where it suddenly advocates the occupation of the Crimea.[a] This is the same journal which affected to regret that nothing could be undertaken by Napier before the French fleet should have joined him.[b] Now that it has done so, it is supposed that nothing *will* be done, after all, and that both the French and English fleet had better take another excursion through the Kattegat, the Channel, and the straits of Gibraltar sound to the Euxine. Reflecting on the time which the juncture of these fleets has required, and again on the time which their junction with the forces under Admiral Dundas would require, it becomes plain that to do nothing either in the Baltic or in the Black Sea is the great object of these propositions.

The only point on which the Russians—apart from their unforeseen and unexpected defeat at Silistria—have undergone substantial losses and are surrounded with dangers, is the Caucasus—though this is not altogether certain. They had abandoned nearly all their fortresses on the eastern shore of the Black Sea, not from any fear of the allied fleets, but in order to strengthen their Georgian army. On their retreat across the Dariel Pass they are stated to have been suddenly attacked by a large force of mountaineers, in the van and rear, to have had their advanced guard cut to pieces, while their center and rear were compelled to retire with severe loss. At the same time the army of Selim Pasha advanced from St. Nicholas upon Ussurgheti, whence the Russians had frequently molested and menaced the Turks, and now forced

---

[a] *The Times,* No. 21774, June 22, 1854, leader.— *Ed.*
[b] *The Times,* No. 21747, May 22, 1854, leader; report from Gothland, May 16, 1854, *The Times,* No. 21751, May 26, 1854.— *Ed.*

the Russians to evacuate that fortress, a result by which the communications between Selim Pasha and the main Turkish army at Kars have been secured. When it is recollected that even this army was throughout the winter and spring in the most deplorable state of inefficiency, the maneuver of the Russians indicates at least that they felt their position in Georgia to be no less precarious, and that they were sadly in want of reenforcements from the coast. If, now, this reported defeat at Dariel be true or even partially so, the consequence is that the army of Woronzoff is cut off, and must try either to procure a tenable basis at Tiflis with a view to hold out until next winter—a matter of no slight difficulty—or it must attempt to make its way at any loss through the pass. This operation would at all events be preferable to a retreat upon the Caspian Sea, the pass leading thither being of infinitely greater danger than that of Dariel. On this point, however, we shall be better able to speak positively on the receipt of more complete and authentic information from that quarter. So far we may set down Russia as having certainly gained two victories by the recent operations,—one in the loan from Hope & Co., and one in the Austrian treaty with the Porte; and as having suffered one defeat—that of Silistria. Whether the former will have permanent advantages enough to compensate for the disgrace of the latter, the future only can decide.

Written on June 16 and 23, 1854

First published in the *New-York Daily Tribune*, No. 4125, July 8; reprinted in the *New-York Semi-Weekly Tribune*, No. 952, July 11 and the *New-York Weekly Tribune*, No. 670, July 15, 1854 as a leader

Reproduced from the *New-York Daily Tribune*

Karl Marx and Frederick Engels

THE RUSSIAN RETREAT

The retrograde movement of the Russians in Turkey is much more complete than we had supposed it could be, and more than, even in the worst case, now seems necessary from a military point of view. It appears that the pledge of the Czar to the Emperor of Austria and his orders to his generals include the total evacuation of Moldavia as well as Wallachia, leaving not a Russian soldier on Turkish ground, while a powerful Austrian force will instantly come forward to take their place and enforce a separation between the recent combatants. But it would be an error to suppose that the Russians withdraw because of their defeat at Silistria or to accept for truth the blustering assertions of the English journals, which give to that defeat the character of a rout, and would fain make the world believe that 15,000 or at the utmost 17,000 men, sallying from the fortress, could drive away 100,000 or at the least 90,000. The Russians were repulsed beyond a doubt, bloodily and utterly repulsed again and again, as their precipitate, ill considered, unscientific, confused attacks deserved to be, bravely as they were executed; the Turks fought with heroic courage that never was surpassed, and with a degree of military skill that must make this siege memorable in all history; but we have yet to see any reason for believing that they compelled the enemy to raise the siege. Indeed, our best information is to the effect that the Russian batteries on the left bank were still held and employed against the fortress after that last murderous sortie, in which some exaggerated dispatches affirm that these batteries were captured by the garrison. The truth evidently is that the Russians finally withdrew from before Silistria simply because the Czar had agreed with Austria that on a certain day his troops should all be out of the Principalities. He had ordered them to take Silistria beforehand, in order to leave Turkey with the prestige of at least one victory; in that they failed and had to march away under the disgrace of the failure; but their march was not a flight with a pursuing enemy in their rear. They might not, and probably would not, have been able to take Silistria even by a regular siege; they probably could not have gained anything from the campaign, and in that event might have retired upon the Sereth; but they were still stronger than the allies, Turks and all, and, for defensive purposes at least, far stronger. Besides, the allies had not yet been brought against them, and no decisive battle had been fought. It is, therefore, certain that this retreat to the Pruth is dictated by diplomatic considerations, and not by any military necessity growing out of the superior power or better strategy of Omer Pasha and the allies in Turkey.

But while it would be a mistake to suppose the Russians were actually driven from before Silistria, it would be equally a mistake not to see that the war generally is going against them, and that the Austrian intervention offers the best means of mending their fortunes. We do not here allude to their successive reverses at Oltenitza, Chetatea, Caracal, or Silistria, comparatively small affairs, in which the Turks beat them, and which they have nowhere matched with successes of equal brilliancy. All of these conflicts together had no decisive or desperate results; but in Asia their game has steadily been a losing one, and the loss now threatens to become final. Of their numerous forts on the Black Sea only two remain; while inland Shamyl and his mountaineers have not only freed their immediate hills and valleys from the hated Muscovite,[a] but have cut off the communications of Count Woronzoff with Russia, and, acting with the Turks on the south are marching upon Tiflis with a strength which may possibly compel the surrender of the Count with all the hard-got and painfully-held Transcaucasian possessions of Russia. To lose these provinces, which have cost such vast amounts of blood and treasure, would be, if possible, a greater mortification to the Czar than defeat in a pitched battle in Turkey; and there is no doubt that, so soon as his armies are back across the Pruth, he will at once devote all the forces he can spare from the defense of the

---

[a] Nicholas I.— *Ed.*

Crimea and of Sevastopol, to the work of regaining the passes of the Caucasus and relieving Woronzoff. The success of Shamyl has in all probability contributed much toward the Russian compliance with the Austrian summons to evacuate the Principalities.

In this important transaction, which so changes and complicates the aspect of the war, Austria holds the post of honor and of advantage. It is a great triumph for her diplomacy, and testifies to the respect in which her military resources are held by all the contending parties. She intervenes as the friend of both sides; the Russians go quietly out to make room for her; and the Porte only follows the advice of France and England in signing the treaty which gives the Principalities to her occupation. She is there, then, as an armed arbitrator intervening between the combatants by their joint consent, because each believes the intervention to be for his benefit. The western powers openly proclaim that it is an act in their favor—and the concert with regard to it, which the facts prove to have existed between St. Petersburg and Vienna, before it was known to the world that such an event would take place, and before the army under Paskievich had met with the repulse at Silistria, renders it impossible to doubt that Russia also regards it as an act in her favor. Which, then, is the dupe? and to which party will Austria prove treacherous?

Of course, like every other power, Austria pursues her own interest alone. That interest requires on the one hand that Russia should not hold the Principalities and control the mouths of the Danube and the Black Sea, because a large and increasing part of Austrian commerce goes in that direction. Besides, for Russia to annex Turkey or any part of it might breed disturbance in the Slavonic tribes of the Austrian empire, among whose members Panslavism, or a union with Russia, already has numerous partisans. It is therefore plain that Austria never can consent to the absorption of Turkey by Russia, unless she receives at the same time an equivalent addition of territory and power elsewhere, which is impossible. But on the other hand, the sympathies of Austrian policy are all with the Czar and opposed to France and England, and her real leanings will always be against the western powers. That Russia should be humiliated as a punishment for making a needless war, cannot be regarded as a cause of mourning at Vienna; but that she should be seriously crippled Austria will never suffer, because in that case the Hapsburgs would be left without a friend to help them out of the next revolutionary slough. This brief statement appears to us to comprise the motives that must govern the Viennese Cabinet throughout the further developments of the war. It will be treacherous to either of the belligerents or to both, just so far as the interest of Austria and the imperial dynasty shall seem to require, and no farther.

Now by the fact that Russia withdraws and ceases from her encroachments, and that the evacuated provinces are handed over to Austria, the latter is at once enlisted to prevent any further injury being done to the former. Austria may remain in nominal friendship with the allies, but it is for her interest that they should fail in any ulterior attacks on the Czar, and we may be sure that she will do everything to make them fail, short of an actual declaration of war, which in any case she dare not resort to. She must then be treacherous to the western powers; they are the dupes in the treaty which allows an Austrian army to occupy the Turkish provinces; and that they will in due time discover as the war goes on.

It was apparently the plan of Lord Aberdeen, the English Prime Minister, that it should not go on, but that the quarrel should now be settled according to the wish of Austria, on the basis of the *status quo*, with possibly a transfer of the protectorate of the Principalities from Russia to the house of Hapsburg. This plan we may, however, now set down as defeated through the self-exposures of Lord Aberdeen's notorious speech, and the subsequent debate in Parliament, of which we give a full report in this paper.[184] The British people, excited by these revelations, will not consent, at least not at present, to make peace without having, for the enormous sums the war costs them, some result more substantial than the mere restoration of things as they were. They hold the crippling of Russia to be indispensable, so that she cannot soon again thus upset the world; and they expect impatiently some brilliant feat of arms, such as the capture of Kronstadt or Sevastopol. Without such a tangible achievement to pay for going to war, they will not now agree to make peace. This disposition of theirs will probably lead at once to a change in the ministry and to a prolongation of the war. But it by no means follows that, because the war is prolonged, any harder blow will be struck at Russia than she has already suffered,—except it be the conquest of her Transcaucasian provinces by the Turks and Circassians without any Western help. And, judging the men who will probably remain in power at London after Lord Aberdeen has retired to private life, by their acts hitherto since the beginning of the war, it would be no occasion for surprise if at some future day we should see them signing a treaty of peace on the very basis for favoring which Lord Aberdeen is now driven from office. So far Austrian diplomacy has carried the day, and it is very likely to win at last.

Written on June 19 and 23, 1854

First published in the *New-York Daily Tribune*, No. 4126, July 10; reprinted in the *New-York Semi-Weekly Tribune*, No. 952, July 11 and the *New-York Weekly Tribune*, No. 670, July 15, 1854 as a leader

Reproduced from the *New-York Daily Tribune*

Karl Marx

THE WAR.—DEBATE IN PARLIAMENT [185]

London, Tuesday, June 27, 1854

The Russian *Moniteur* of Bucharest [186] officially declares that, in obedience to orders sent from St. Petersburg, the siege of Silistria is raised, Giurgevo evacuated, and the whole Russian army about to recross the Pruth. *The Times*, in a third edition of yesterday, published a telegraphic dispatch from its Vienna correspondent to a similar effect, viz: that

"the Emperor of Russia accepts the Austrian summons out of high consideration for his ancient ally, and has ordered his troops to recross the Pruth." [187]

Lord John Russell in last night's House of Commons confirmed the statement with regard to the abandonment of the siege of Silistria, but had received no official information about the answer given by Russia to the Austrian summons.[a]

The result of the Austrian intervention will be to interpose a barrier between the Turks and the Russians, to secure the retreat of the latter from all molestation, to enable them to reenforce the garrison of Sevastopol and the Crimea, and perhaps to reestablish their communications with the army of Woronzoff. Besides the reconstruction of the Holy Alliance between Russia, Austria and Prussia must be looked upon as certain the moment the allied powers refuse to acquiesce in the simple restoration of the *status quo ante bellum*, with perhaps some slight concessions made by the Czar in favor of Austria.

---

[a] Lord John Russell's speech in the House of Commons on June 26, 1854. *The Times*, No. 21778, June 27, 1854.— *Ed.*

The whole fabric of this fine "solution," devised, it is said, by Metternich, is now, however, shattered to pieces by the indiscretion of old Aberdeen and the intrigues of Palmerston.

It will be remembered that in the late ministerial reconstruction[a] the endeavor to place Lord Palmerston in the War Office, the cry for the establishment of which was mainly raised by the Palmerstonian press, had failed, and the Peelite Duke of Newcastle supplanted the noble Lord in his contemplated new office. This failure seems to have reminded Lord Palmerston that it was high time to break up the whole Cabinet, and accordingly he has raised a perfect storm against its chief, the occasion for which was afforded by Lord Aberdeen's inconsiderate speech in reply to Lord Lyndhurst.[b] The whole English press immediately laid hold of that speech. It is, however, important to add, that *The Morning Herald* denounced the existence of a conspiracy against Lord Aberdeen before the speech was delivered. Mr. Layard rose in the House of Commons on Friday last, and gave notice that on Thursday next he should move a resolution that

> "the language held by the first Minister of the Crown was calculated to raise grave doubts in the public mind as to the objects and ends of the war, and to lessen the prospects of an honorable and durable peace."[c]

There are two weak points in this resolution: firstly, its being unconstitutional and apt to be set aside for being in contradiction to the parliamentary rule which forbids the criticism of a speech delivered in the Lords by a member of the Commons; and, secondly, because it pretends to distinguish between the occasional language of the Premier and the whole acts of the coalition Cabinet. Nevertheless, its result was to give such serious apprehensions to Lord Aberdeen that, two hours after the announcement of the above resolution, he rose in his place and gave notice, in an unusually excited tone, that

> "on Monday next (thus anticipating Mr. Layard by three days), he should move for a copy of the dispatch he had addressed to Russia, after the treaty of Adrianople, and that he would take the opportunity of alluding to the misconstructions which had been placed on the remarks he had recently addressed to their Lordships on the subject of the war."[d]

---

[a] See this volume, p. 220.— *Ed.*
[b] Lord Aberdeen's speech in the House of Lords on June 19, 1854. *The Times*, No. 21772, June 20, 1854.— *Ed.*
[c] Mr. Layard's speech in the House of Commons on June 23, 1854. *The Times*, No. 21776, June 24, 1854.— *Ed.*
[d] Lord Aberdeen's speech in the House of Lords on June 23, 1854. *The Times*, No. 21776, June 24, 1854.— *Ed.*

So strong was the belief that Mr. Layard's motion would result in the expulsion of Lord Aberdeen from the Cabinet, that *The Morning Advertiser*, for instance, has published already the list of the Ministry which is to succeed him; a list including the names of Lord John Russell as Premier, and of Lord Palmerston as Minister of War. It may be imagined, then, that the sitting of the Lords of last night attracted an unusual number of the curious and excited *intrigants* of the aristocracy, anxious to witness in what manner Lord Aberdeen would clear himself from his somewhat difficult and intricate position.

Before giving a *resumé* of the speech of Lord Aberdeen, and of the attack made upon him by the Marquis of Clanricarde, I must recur to the epoch and the circumstances, to which both speakers particularly referred, in the year 1829, when Lord Aberdeen found himself at the head of the British Foreign Office. At that time a Russian fleet under the command of Admiral Heiden was blockading the Dardanelles, the Gulfs of Saros and Enos, as well as those of Adramyti and Smyrna, notwithstanding an agreement concluded between the Cabinets of St. Petersburg and London in 1815, that Russia should not exercise any belligerent rights in the Mediterranean. These blockades, threatening to injure the British commerce in the Levant, aroused the otherwise dull opinion of the English of that time into vehement declamations against Russia and against the Ministry. Interviews, accordingly, took place between the Russian Embassadors Prince Lieven and Count Matusczewicz on the one side, and Wellington and Aberdeen on the other side. In a dispatch under date of London 1st (13th) June 1829, Prince Lieven reports as follows on the character of these interviews:

"The conversation with Lord Aberdeen which took place some hour later,"

than that with the Duke of Wellington, which had not been altogether very satisfactory to the Russian diplomatist

"was not less remarkable. As he was acquainted only imperfectly with our conversation with the first Minister, he labored, when he learned the details of it, to *soften* the disagreeable impressions that might have been left upon us by his language at the commencement of it, by the reiterated assurance *that at no period had it entered into the intentions of England to seek a quarrel with Russia*; that if the ministry had sought to induce us not to insist on the blockade of Enos, it was in the full desire to prevent importunate reclamations, and to cement the good intelligence between the two cabinets, *that we should have to congratulate ourselves more than perhaps we were aware on the benefits we received from that happy and constant concurrence*. He was flattered that he could place the maintenance of that harmony higher than the momentary advantages that the blockade of the Gulf of Enos would have offered us; but he feared that the position of the English Ministry was not well understood at St. Petersburg. They attributed to malevolent intentions, and to hostile views, the difficulties that he sometimes raised, as in the matter that had just been terminated, while these intentions and these *arrières pensées*[a] were very far from his spirit and from his policy. But, on the other hand, he found himself in a delicate situation. Public opinion was always ready to burst forth against Russia. *The British Government could not constantly brave it,* and it would be dangerous to excite it on questions (of maritime law) that touched so nearly the *national prejudices.* On the other side we could reckon upon the well-disposed and friendly dispositions of the English Ministry *which struggled against them* (the national prejudices).

"I know, I replied, the weight of public opinion in England, and I have seen it change in a few days. It is against us in our war because it thinks us aggressors, while we have been attacked; because it imputes to us the idea of overthrowing the Ottoman Empire, while we *declare* that such is not our object; because, finally, it believes that we pursue an ambitious policy against which *we ourselves protest. To enlighten it on this point* would be the surest way to correct it.

"Lord Aberdeen replied to me, that the matter was not exactly as I represented; public opinion was pronounced against us, because generally in England it took with ardor the side of the Whigs—but *au reste,*[b] the British Cabinet was far from not *wishing us success;* on the contrary, *it wished us success, prompt and decisive,* because it knew that it was the only means of terminating the war, which could not be regarded except as a great misfortune, since it was impossible to foresee its results! In conclusion, the English Minister entered into long deductions to demonstrate that we lent to him intentions that he could not have, and ended by saying that the Cabinet of London desired that the war should be terminated *to the honor and advantage of Russia.*"[188]

It is strange that none of the opponents of Lord Aberdeen have thought proper to recur to this dispatch, so conclusive against his conduct at the time before the treaty of Adrianople, that it would have been impossible to attach any importance to anything contained in a secret dispatch of his Lordship, written *after* the conclusion of that treaty. The production of the above dispatch would have demolished at one stroke the only argument of defense which Lord Aberdeen could bring forward in his speech of yesterday. His true defense would have been an open recrimination against Lord Palmerston, since the whole "row" was exclusively between these two old rival servants of Russia.

Lord Aberdeen began by saying that he had nothing either to retract or to contradict, but only to "explain."[c] He had been falsely accused of having claimed the honor of having framed the treaty of Adrianople. Instead of having framed it, he had protested

---

[a] Ulterior motives.— *Ed.*

[b] Nevertheless.— *Ed.*

[c] Lord Aberdeen's speech in the House of Lords on June 26, 1854. *The Times,* No. 21778, June 27, 1854.— *Ed.*

against it, as their lordships would see from the dispatch for the production of which he now made a motion. Such had been the alarm produced on his mind, and on his colleagues' mind, by that treaty, that the whole policy of the Government had been changed in a most material point in consequence of its existence. Which was this change of policy? Before the treaty of Adrianople was signed, he, Lord Aberdeen and the Duke of Wellington, therein following the policy of Canning, had never contemplated constituting Greece an independent kingdom, but only as a vassal state under the *suzeraineté* of the Porte, somewhat similar to Wallachia and Moldavia. After the treaty of Adrianople had been signed, the condition of the Turkish Empire appeared to them so perilous, and its existence so precarious, that they proposed to convert Greece from a vassal state into an independent kingdom. In other words, it was resolved, since the treaty of Adrianople did so much to weaken Turkey, to counteract its perilous consequences by *dismembering* whole provinces from it. This was the "change."

Although their alarm for the consequences of that treaty had been exaggerated, Lord Aberdeen was far from not considering it as in the highest degree disastrous and prejudicial. He had said that "Russia had not acquired great territorial acquisitions by that treaty," and even now he contended that the Russian empire had not greatly increased in Europe within the last fifty years, as Lord Lyndhurst had asserted.(Bessarabia, Finland, and the Kingdom of Poland, appear not to be any significant acquisitions in the view of the noble Lord.) But, as he had stated in his dispatch of December, 1829, if the territorial acquisitions of Russia had been small, they had been important in their character—the one giving Russia "exclusive authority over the navigation of the Danube, and the other ports in Asia which, though small in extent, yet had the character of high political importance." (The vast territory acquired in the Caucasus is again not present to Lord Aberdeen's mind.) Starting from this point of view, he asserts that the treaty of Adrianople was the commencement of a change of policy on the part of Russia, which, since the time of that treaty, had looked to an extension of political influence rather than to the acquisition of territory. This change of policy had not been a change of intention. "Satan had only grown wiser than in days of yore." The fact that Russia concerted a plan with Charles X for the acquisition of Turkey—not through alarming conquests, but through a series of treaties—is passed over in silence. Nor did Lord Aberdeen think fit to mention that even before the treaty of Adrianople and the treaty of Unkiar–Skelessi,[189] which he quotes in proof of the change in Russian policy, Russia had bound herself to France and England already, in 1827, not to seek to derive any further territory from the war against Turkey, and that, but for the permission of England, she would never have been able to advance an army upon Constantinople in 1833.

Lord Aberdeen next stated that his expression that "if we could obtain a peace which should last twenty-five years, as had been the case by the treaty of Adrianople, we should not have done amiss," had been falsely construed into the meaning that he would return to a treaty similar to that of Adrianople. He had only meant to say that

"if by any treaty which the fortune of war might enable them to make, they could secure a peace for twenty-five years, considering the instability of human affairs they would not have done amiss. *He had never recommended a return to the status quo, nor did he not object to the status quo.* Before the declaration of war the *status quo* had been all they hoped for or desired, and all that they attempted to attain, and it was that which the Turkish Government consented to give, and it was much more than they had a right to expect. But, from the instant war had been declared, the whole question was changed entirely, and everything depended upon the war itself.... How far they might ultimately deviate from the *status quo* no man could say, as it depended on events not in their power absolutely to control. This he would say, that the independence and integrity of the Ottoman Empire must be secured, effectually secured."

How it is to be secured Lord Aberdeen could not say, as this, again, depended on the events of the war.

He had been understood to express some doubt or disbelief as to the danger of Russian aggression, but, in fact, he had the greatest alarm at Russian aggression on Turkey, although he did not feel great alarm with respect to the danger of Russian aggression on Europe, and "he was inclined to feel less so every day." He considered France more powerful than Russia and Austria put together. The noble Lord then complained of the "extraordinary absurdity and malignity of the personal imputations to which he had been exposed." It was true that there was no greater peacemonger in the country than himself, but his very love of peace peculiarly fitted him to carry on the war in the most vigorous manner.

"His colleagues would admit that he personally had been more urgent than perhaps any other man in exhorting a speedy advance and concentration of the allied forces beyond the Balkans, in order to support the gallant army of Omer Pasha, and to extend a hand to Austria, in order to enable her to take a more active part in the operations of the war."

This was the course he invariably urged. On the interpellation of Lord Beaumont[a] he declared that

"intimate as he formerly was with Prince Metternich, since he had been in office, for the last eighteen months, he had not communicated with him, directly or indirectly, until a few days ago, when a friend told him she was about to write to Metternich, and asked him whether he had anything to say to the Prince; whereupon he said: 'Pray, make my best remembrances to him.'"

Aberdeen's speech was on the whole favorably received by the House; but it is a curious fact that the acrimonious answer that he met with from the Marquis of Clanricarde—a disappointed place-hunter, and Lord Palmerston's old Embassador at St. Petersburg—was not replied to by any member of the Cabinet, and that none of them came forward to certify to his having been the foremost in urging a vigorous war.

The Marquis of Clanricarde[b] principally dwelt upon Aberdeen's participation in the treaty of Adrianople; the general character of his political past, and on the shortcomings of his present administration. He said that Lord Aberdeen had produced now, for his own personal convenience and from a merely personal motive, a dispatch which he had some months ago refused to other members of either House. It was, however, quite different from what the noble lord had written to St. Petersburg in December, 1829, when the treaty of Adrianople had been signed in September. The real question was what instructions he had given to their Embassador[c] at that time, and what steps he had taken to *prevent* the signing of the treaty. The Russian general commanding at Adrianople[d] had not had above 15,000 men, and that amount had to be diminished by some 5,000 or 6,000 who, either from disease or wounds, were literally *hors de combat*[e]. The Turkish general,[f] on the other hand, was within a short distance with 25,000 Albanians. The Russian general gave a very short respite to Turkey to sign or not to sign, for he knew that his real position might be discovered if he gave a long one. Consequently he did not give beyond five or eight days. At Constantinople the

---

[a] Lord Beaumont's interpellation to the House of Commons on June 26, 1854. *The Times*, No. 21778, June 27, 1854.— *Ed.*
[b] The Marquis of Clanricarde's speech in the House of Lords on June 26, 1854. *The Times*, No. 21778, June 27, 1854.— *Ed.*
[c] Gordon.— *Ed.*
[d] General Diebich.— *Ed.*
[e] Out of action.— *Ed.*
[f] Apparently Mustapha Pasha.— *Ed.*

Minister of Turkey summoned to his council the French and English Embassadors and the Prussian Minister, and asked for their advice.[190] The English Embassador, under instructions from Lord Aberdeen, tendered the advice to sign as soon as possible that treaty which the noble lord now told them was so disastrous.

The noble Marquis did not like to allude to the circumstance, that it was exactly the vehement denunciation which his friend Palmerston, then in opposition, directed against Lord Aberdeen, when he charged him with being yet too anti-Russian, which induced the latter to give the order for the signing of the treaty.

The Marquis proceeded to reproach the Premier with having been always the most zealous, the most constant, and the most powerful supporter of the arbitrary governments of Europe, in proof of which he reviewed the history of Portugal, Belgium, and Spain, alluding to Aberdeen's opposition to the famous Quadruple Alliance of 1834.[191] It certainly wanted all the cool impudence of an old Whig Lord to exult, at this moment, in the glory of Belgium, the constitutionalism in Portugal and Spain, and the general blessings Europe derives from the Quadruple Alliance which Palmerston, in his defense, falsely stated to have been devised not by himself but by Talleyrand.

As to the operations of the present war, Clanricarde said that the plan of the campaign had been drawn up by the highest military authorities in Russia, in December last, and that the British Government had been informed of that plan, aiming not at the mere occupation of the Principalities, but at crossing the Danube, seizing Silistria, masking Shumla, and marching on the Balkans. The noble Lord, with such information in his possession, had come down to this House talking of peace, and neglecting to give those orders which were at the time given by the Cabinet to the Ministry of War until the end of February or the beginning of March.

If Lord Clanricarde had chosen to remember the answers given by Lord Palmerston[a] to Mr. Disraeli in the Commons and by Lord Clarendon[b] to himself in the Lords, he would have abstained from the ridicule of charging with those neglects of duty only Lord Aberdeen, and exempting his Whig friends from a blame equally attaching to the whole Cabinet.

---

[a] Lord Palmerston's speech in the House of Commons on February 20, 1854. *The Times*, No. 21670, February 21, 1854.— *Ed.*
[b] Lord Clarendon's speech in the House of Lords on February 6, 1854. *The Times*, No. 21658, February 7, 1854.— *Ed.*

"If," exclaimed the Marquis—"if a proper, he would almost say an honest, course had been taken by the Government fifteen months ago, there never would have been a war."

Now, these are the very same words which Mr. Disraeli addressed to Lord John Russell.

Finally, the Marquis has the absurdity to charge also Lord Aberdeen, individually and exclusively, with all the failures of the coalition, and their continuous defeat in Parliament on all important questions. It does not occur to his memory that at the very formation of the Cabinet it was declared by every judicious man, that it could not hold together for six weeks except it left all legislation an open question, and abstained from politics.

After a silly speech from Lord Brougham,[a] who expressed himself very much contented with Lord Aberdeen's first speech, but still more so with his second one, the subject dropped.

The serious result of this whole incident is the baffling of the secret protocol drawn up at Vienna, and consequently the continuance of hostilities, and of a war, the speedy cessation of which was so confidently anticipated that consols rose 3 per cent. notwithstanding heavy loans in the market, and that any bets were taken at the military clubs against the prolongation of war beyond four weeks.

Written on June 27, 1854

First published in the *New-York Daily Tribune*, No, 4126, July 10; reprinted in the *New-York Semi-Weekly Tribune*, No. 952, July 11 and the *New-York Weekly Tribune*, No. 670, July 15, 1854

Signed: *Karl Marx*

Reproduced from the *New-York Daily Tribune*

---

[a] Lord Brougham and Vaux's speech in the House of Lords on June 26, 1854. *The Times*, No. 21778, June 27, 1854.— *Ed.*

Karl Marx

[THE INSURRECTION AT MADRID.— THE AUSTRO-TURKISH TREATY.— MOLDAVIA AND WALLACHIA] [192]

London, Tuesday, July 4, 1854

The long-expected military insurrection at Madrid has at length been accomplished under the leadership of Generals O'Donnell and Dulce.[193] The French Government journals hasten to inform us that, according to their dispatches, the Spanish Government has already overcome the danger and that the insurrection is suppressed.[a] But the Madrid correspondent of *The Morning Chronicle*, who gives a detailed account of the rising and communicates the proclamation of the insurgents, says that they have only withdrawn from the capital in order to join the garrison of Alcala, and that in case of Madrid remaining passive they would have no difficulty in reaching Saragossa.[b] Should the movement be more successful than the last rebellion in that town,[194] the consequences would be to cause a diversion in the military action of France, to afford a subject for dissent between France and England, and probably also to affect the pending complication between Spain and the United States Government.

It appears now that the new Russian loan has not been positively contracted for by the Messrs. Hope of Amsterdam, as I was led to believe[c] from announcements made at ·the London and Manchester Exchanges; and that these bankers have not advanced any portion of the money to the Russian treasury. They merely

---

[a] Report from Bayonne of July 3, 1854. *Le Moniteur universel*, No. 185, July 4, 1854.— *Ed.*

[b] Report from Madrid of June 28. *The Morning Chronicle*, No. 27309, July 4, 1854.— *Ed.*

[c] See this volume, p. 248.— *Ed.*

undertook to bring it out at the different European Exchanges, but at no risk of their own. The success of the loan is reported to be very doubtful, and we have news that at Berlin and Frankfort it has met with very little favor. The Hamburg Senate has prohibited its official quotation, and the English diplomatic agents and Consuls, according to *The Morning Chronicle*, have issued warnings to British subjects not to become subscribers to a loan "intended for carrying on war against the Queen."

The intelligence of the movements of the Russian troops since the abandonment of the siege of Silistria is contradictory. The *Moniteur* having announced the retreat of the Russians behind the Pruth, the Vienna *Presse* states that there was not the slightest reason to believe in the fact of such a move.[a] It appears, on the contrary, that not even Wallachia is intended to be evacuated, General Liprandi having taken up a position at Plojesti and Kimpina, with his outposts stationed at the entrance of the *Rothenthurm Pass*, while the main army, retiring by Slobodzic and along the left bank of the Danube, is stated to have halted at Brailow. On the other hand, the corps of Lüders occupying the Dobrodja, has not yet abandoned the line of Trajan's Wall, and it is not likely that, even in case of further retreat, they will surrender Matchin and Isaktsha. Fresh troops are said to be pouring into Moldavia, where it seems to be the plan of the Russians to concentrate a large force. The corps of General Panyutin has entered from Podolia, and additional resources are being drawn in from Bessarabia. The entire force of the Russians in Upper Moldavia, between Jassy, Roman and Botushani, is said to amount to 60,000; and a division of 20,000 is encamped near Kamenicz. "Paskievich," says the *Ost-Deutsche Post*, "has declared that in no case will he abandon the mouths of the Danube."[b] The retreat is explained by the Russians to be only a consequence of the plague having broken out on the Higher Danube.

The movements of the Austrians are still quite undefined. The corps of Coronini is stated to have orders to embark on steamers at Orsova, and to go down the river to Giurgevo, thence to march upon Bucharest. The *Corriere Italiano*, an Austrian Government organ, announces that the object of this move is only to take up a

---

[a] The report of *Die Presse* is given according to *Le Moniteur universel*, No. 184, July 3, 1854.— *Ed.*

[b] The *Ost-Deutsche Post* is quoted according to the *Journal des Débats*, June 29, 1854.— *Ed.*

neutral position in Wallachia,[a] and yet at the same time we hear that the Austrian "ultimatum" has been declined by Russia.

"The Russian Emperor," says the dispatch published in *The Morning Chronicle*, "in his answer to the Austrian summons, expresses his readiness to negotiate with the four powers on all points, except on the privileges of the Christian subjects of the Sultan. On this subject he will only treat directly with the Porte, and he refuses to admit the interference of the four powers. He also refuses to give any guarantees for the evacuation of the Principalities."[b]

Now, it is quite possible that in consequence of this refusal, a sham war between Austria and Russia may occur, to end in some such famous *rencontre*[c] as the remarkable affair at Bronzell,[195] which ended the sham war between Austria and Prussia in 1850, while the newspapers were yet lost in conjectures on the terrible eventualities of that "middle European crisis." In lieu of similar speculations on the possible meaning of Austria's present policy, we shall betake ourselves to the fact of the Austro-Turkish treaty of June 14, which is now fully and officially made known.[d]

There are two points to be considered—the relations between Austria and Turkey and the relations of the Moldo-Wallachian people to Turkey and Austria or other foreign powers, the latter point being, strange to say, entirely neglected by the diplomacy-ridden opinion of Europe.

By the first article of the treaty,

"the Emperor of Austria undertakes to exhaust every means of negotiation and others, to obtain the evacuation of the Danubian Principalities by the foreign army now occupying them, and even to employ, in case of need, the number of troops necessary to attain that end."

The Emperor of Austria is thereby entitled to march any number of troops into Wallachia, without a previous declaration of war on his part against Russia. Thus a Turkish dependency is subjected to an operation converting it into a neutral possession under Austria against Turkey. By the second article it is agreed that

"it shall belong exclusively to the Imperial commander-in-chief to direct the operations of his army. He shall, however, be careful to inform in proper time the commander-in-chief of the Ottoman armies of his operations."

---

[a] The *Corriere Italiano* statement is given as reprinted in *Le Moniteur universel*, No. 184, July 3, 1854.— *Ed.*

[b] Telegraphic dispatch from Berlin. *The Morning Chronicle*, No. 27309, July 4, 1854.— *Ed.*

[c] Duel.— *Ed.*

[d] The text of the treaty is given according to the report of *The Times* correspondent in Paris of June 30, 1854. *The Times*, No. 21783, July 3, 1854.— *Ed.*

By this agreement the Austrians escape not only from all control, on the part of Turkey, over any movement they may think fit, but obtain a perfect control of all the operations possibly intended on Wallachian ground by the Turkish commander, whom they have only to inform that they want to occupy such and such a point, when the Turks will be prevented from marching there. Considering, now, that the Principalities, besides the narrow territory of the Dobrodja, are the only possible battle-field between the Turks and the Russians, the Austrian intervention simply forbids Turkey to follow up her victories and punish the invader.

By virtue of Article 3,

"the Emperor of Austria engages to reestablish, in common accord with the Ottoman Government, in the Principalities, *as soon as possible*, the legal state of things such as results from the privileges secured by the Sublime Porte relative to the government of these countries. *The local authorities thus reconstituted* shall not, however, extend their action so far as to exercise any control over the Imperial army...."

Thus the Emperor of Austria reserves to himself full liberty of restoring the legal state when he shall think it *possible*; and even then, he may reconstitute the local authorities only in order to place them under Austrian martial law, quite after the fashion of the Russian General Budberg.

According to Article 4,

"the Imperial Court of Austria engages not to enter into any plan of accommodation with the Imperial Court of Russia which shall not have for its starting point the sovereign rights of the Sultan and the integrity of his empire."

Article 5 adds,

"that as soon as the object of the present convention shall have been attained by the conclusion of a treaty of peace between the Sublime Porte and the Court of Russia, the Emperor of Austria will make arrangements to withdraw his forces *as soon as possible*. The details connected with the withdrawal of the Austrian troops will form the object of a special arrangement with the Sublime Porte."

By the former of these articles Austria reserves to herself the right to an arrangement with Russia based simply on the *status quo*, as embodied in the Vienna note.[196] By the latter Austria promises not to withdraw her troops after an arrangement between herself and Russia, but only after the conclusion of a treaty between Russia and Turkey. The "material guaranty," no longer safe in the direct keeping of Russia, is transferred to Austria, and Austria empowered to hold it for her—with the consent of the Porte—until Turkey shall have adhered to the "accommodation between the two Imperial Courts."

Article 6 entitles the Austrians to feed, without even a semblance of payment, upon the remainder left by the Russians in the Principalities. The advantages of this arrangement can only be appreciated in Germany, where the people are wont to receive Austrian garrisons for the punishment of their revolutionary sins, and where they grazed off whole districts in 1849-50.

The treaty is a virtual surrender of the Principalities to Austria, and an abandonment of the Turkish suzerainty over them. The Turks have committed thereby as flagrant a violation of the rights of the Moldo-Wallachian people as any previously committed by the Russians. The Turks have as little right to surrender the Principalities to Austrian occupation as they have to declare them Russian provinces.

The claims of the Porte to the suzerainty of Moldo-Wallachia are founded on the treaties of 1393, 1460 and 1511. The treaty concluded in 1393 between Wallachia and Turkey [197] contains the following articles:

"Art. I. We, Bayazet, etc. determine, by our extreme condescendence toward Wallachia, which has made its submission to our invincible Empire, with its reigning Prince,[a] that this country is to continue to govern itself by its own laws, and that the Prince of Wallachia shall have the entire liberty of declaring war or making peace with his neighbors, how and when it may please him.

"Art. III. The Princes (Christians) will be elected by the Metropolitans and Boyards.

"Art. IV. The Prince of Wallachia will have to pay annually to our Imperial Treasury 500 piasters of our money."

The treaty concluded in 1460 between Vlad V, Prince of Wallachia, and Mohammed II stipulates:

"Art. I. The Sultan consents and engages, for himself and successors, to protect Wallachia and to defend it against every enemy, without exacting anything but the suzerainty over this sovereign Principality, of which the Voyvodes will be expected to pay to the Sublime Porte a tribute of 10,000 ducats.

"Art. II. The Sublime Porte will in no way interfere in the local administration of the said Principality, and no Turk will be allowed to come into Wallachia without an ostensible motive.

"Art. III. The Voyvodes will continue to be elected by the Metropolitan Archbishop, the Bishops and Boyards, and the election will be recognized by the Porte.

"Art. IV. The Wallachian nation will continue to enjoy the free exercise of its own laws, and the Voyvodes will have the right of life and death over their subjects, as also that of making peace or war, without being subjected for any of their acts to any kind of responsibility toward the Sublime Porte." [198]

The third treaty is that of 1511 in which Moldavia acknowl-

---

[a] Mircea the Old.— *Ed.*

edged the suzerainty of the Porte, obtaining even better conditions in exchange than Wallachia had obtained.

The treaties which intervened between Russia and Turkey could not of course invalidate the treaties concluded by the Moldo-Wallachians themselves with the Porte, since this people never treated with the Russians nor gave the Porte power to treat for them. It may be stated, besides, that Russia herself recognized the above-mentioned capitulations in the treaty of Adrianople, Art. V of which says:

> "The Principalities of Wallachia and Moldavia, having placed themselves by capitulation under the suzerainty of the Sublime Porte, and Russia having warranted their prosperity(!), it is understood that they continue to enjoy all those privileges and immunities which have been granted to them in virtue of their capitulation." [199]

It follows, then, from the above-cited capitulations, which, not having been superseded by any subsequent treaty, still remain in vigor, that the Principalities form two sovereign States under the suzerainty of the Porte, to which they pay a tribute on the condition that the Porte shall defend them against every and any external enemy, and not interfere at all in their internal administration. So far from being entitled to surrender Wallachia to foreign occupation, the Turks themselves are forbidden from entering Wallachia without an ostensible motive. Nay, more: Since the Turks have thus violated their capitulations with the Wallachians and forfeited the claims of suzerainty, the Russians might even, when appealed to by the Wallachians, found their right of driving the Austrians out of the Principalities on the show of broken treaties. And this would be by no means surprising, as it has been the constant policy of Russia to encourage, and even oblige the Turks to violate the rights of the Wallachians, so as to produce hostilities between them, and create for herself a pretext for intervention. What happened, for instance in 1848? [200] Some Boyards in the spring of that year had presented a petition to the Hospodar of Moldavia,[a] demanding certain reforms, which request was, by the influence of the Russian Consul,[b] not only refused but caused its authors to be thrown into prison. The commotion produced by this act furnished the Russians with a pretext to cross the frontier, on June 25, and to march upon Jassy. Simultaneously the Hospodar of Wallachia,[c] like the other continental govern-

---

[a] Sturdza.— *Ed.*
[b] Kotzebue.— *Ed.*
[c] George Bibesco.— *Ed.*

ments, granted a number of reforms demanded by the Liberal party of the Wallachian Boyards. This was on June 23. It is scarcely necessary to remark that these reforms infringed in no way upon the suzerainty of the Porte. But they happened to destroy entirely all the influence Russia had obtained through the fundamental law decreed during their occupation of 1829,[201] which the reforms abolished. The constitution replacing it suppressed serfdom, and a portion of the land occupied by the peasant was ceded to him as property, while the landlord was to be indemnified by the State for the land given up and for the loss of his peasant's labor.[202] The reigning hospodar was then induced by the Russians to remove, and a Provisional Government took up the management of the public affairs. The Porte which, as we have shown, had no right to interfere in the internal affairs of the Principalities, and had omitted to protest against the Russian entrance into Moldavia, dispatched Soliman Pasha with a Turkish army into Wallachia, and published a very threatening address of the Sultan to the inhabitants,[a] the measures of the Divan being taken of course under the influence of Russia. The Wallachians went out to meet the Pasha and the Turks, and fraternised with them. An agreement was made that the Provisional Government should be replaced by a *Lieutenance Princière*, composed at first of six, and afterward of three members. This Government was then recognized by the Pasha, and at the Pasha's desire, by the foreign Consuls. A modification was introduced into the new constitution after which that also was confirmed by the Sultan.

Meanwhile the Russian Government fulminated against the Wallachian people in manifestoes addressed to Europe, wherein they were charged to have established a republic, and proclaimed communism.[203] On the 1st August, 1848, a large Russian force crossed the Pruth on its march to Bucharest. Suddenly Soliman Pasha was recalled by the Porte; the Sultan refused to receive the Wallachian deputies who had gone to Constantinople in answer to his own invitation; and on September 25, Fuad Effendi, at the head of a Turkish army, presented himself before Bucharest, declaring that he had only come to deprive Russia of all pretext for entering the Principality. Confiding in the word of the Turks, more than 100,000 inhabitants went out from Bucharest and the surrounding country, unarmed, in festive garments, and with the clergy at their head to welcome them. Fuad Effendi then invited

---

[a] This refers to Soliman Pasha's letter of July 31, 1848.— *Ed.*

them to send a deputation to his camp, so that he might communicate to them his instructions.

"No sooner," says M. Bratiano in his account of these events, "no sooner did the deputation present themselves before Fuad Effendi, than they were made prisoners, and at the same time the Turkish army precipitated itself in a forced march upon Bucharest, trampling down under the hoofs of his cavalry the peaceful inhabitants who had gone out to meet the Turks as friends, tearing down their banners, destroying their crosses, bombarding a military barrack which it found on its passage, as well as a whole quarter of the town, firing grape-shot at the Wallachian soldiers who occupied those barracks, inducing them to capitulate and lay down their arms, putting to death the sick, and after having reached the town giving themselves up to pillage, massacre and other horrible deeds!"[a]

It was here that Gen. Duhamel, the Russian Commissioner, accompanied, and in fact commanded the Turkish army. He was followed by the Russian army, and the result was the treaty of Balta Liman,[204] i.e. among other things the restoration of the Russian fundamental law, or *statato* which is nothing else than the *status quo* as to which Austria engages [to] reduce Wallachia.

It is clear that if Omer Pasha should now enter Wallachia with his victorious army, the Turks with all their late experience and at war with Russia would [have] reestablished the Constitution of 1848, with the "republic, communism," and the revival of all the creations of 1848 following in its wake. Nobody will believe that Austria would have been less displeased with that contingency than Russia. On the other hand, it is equally clear, that the Porte must have been subject to extraordinary pressure to allow itself to be dragged into another violation of its treaties with the Wallachians, the consequences of which it knows by experience. That pressure can have proceeded from no quarter but the English Embassador. It is, therefore, interesting to record how the same Lord Redcliffe and his superiors in Downing-st. behaved in 1848 and '49 with regard to the violations of the rights of Moldo-Wallachia by both Russians and Turks.

When the Russian Army first crossed the Moldavian frontier, in June 1848, Lord Palmerston declared in the House of Commons, in answer to the inevitable Dudley Stuart:

"that the Russian troops entered Moldavia without any orders from the Cabinet of St. Petersburg, that they only aimed at the maintenance or establishment of order, that they would be withdrawn when the occasion had ceased, that the entry

---

[a] D. Bratiano, *Documents Concerning the Question of the Danubian Principalities*, pp. 10-11.— *Ed.*

was on the authority of the Hospodar, and there was no disposition for the acquisition of territory."[a]

In August 1848, when the Russian army again crossed the Pruth, on their march to Bucharest, and when the Moldo-Wallachians had sent a deputation to Constantinople, the Divan applied to the Embassadors of England and France for advice, and was recommended by Lord Redcliffe to adopt the line of policy enjoined by Russia.

In October, when the Turks and Russians in common occupied Wallachia, a Wallachian officer was pursued by the Russians into the dwelling of the commander of the Turkish troops at Bucharest, Omer Pasha, who in common with Fuad Effendi protested. The Porte, informed of this insult, declared it would have no more to do with the Russians and order its troops to recross the Danube, in order to cease to be the accomplice of the Russians in the Principalities, and threatened to address to the great powers a solemn protestation, accompanied by a detailed memorandum of all that had occurred in the Principalities. The same Embassador interfered again and baffled these intentions of the Porte.

Lastly, at the time when the combined Russo-Turkish occupation in 1848 had assumed the character of a reign of terror, and when Magheru, the commander of the Wallachian irregulars alone resisted, he was induced to withdraw beyond the Carpathian mountains "by the persuasion of the British Consul-General,[b] who represented to him that the presence of his army would paralyze the action of diplomacy, but that his country would soon be righted." [205]

Written on July 4, 1854

First published in the *New-York Daily Tribune*, No. 4134, July 19; reprinted in the *New-York Semi-Weekly Tribune*, No. 955, July 21 and the *New-York Weekly Tribune*, No. 671, July 22, 1854

Signed: *Karl Marx*

Reproduced from the *New-York Daily Tribune*

---

[a] Lord Palmerston's speech in the House of Commons on September 1, 1848, is cited from the book: *The Russians in Moldavia and Wallachia*, p. 17.— *Ed.*
[b] Colquhoun.— *Ed.*

Frederick Engels

THE WAR ON THE DANUBE[206]

About eighty years ago, when the victorious armies of Catherine II were severing from Turkey province after province, prior to their transformation into what is now called South Russia, the poet Derzhavin, in one of the bursts of lyrical enthusiasm in which he was wont to celebrate the glories, if not the virtues of that Empress, and the destined grandeur of her empire, uttered a memorable couplet in which we may still find condensed the scornful boldness and self-reliance of the Czarian policy:

> "And what to thee O Russ, is any ally?
> Advance and the whole Universe is thine!"[a]

This may be true enough, even now, if the Russ only could advance, but on that process a pretty decided check has been put. Consequently he is constrained for the present moment at least, to postpone the possession of the Universe. But what is very bitter to his pride is that in retracing his steps he not only fails to carry with him the pledge of universal dominion, but is even obliged to leave behind the keys of the simple fortress of Silistria, on the Danube, which he had sworn to have. And still more painful, he leaves behind him also the remains of some fifty thousand of his brethren, who have perished by disease and battle in this single campaign.

There is no doubt that from a military point of view the siege of Silistria is the most important among all the military events since the beginning of the war. It is the failure to take that fortress which renders the campaign a failure for the Russians and adds

---

[a] G. Derzhavin, "On the Capture of Warsaw".— Ed.

disgrace and the Czar's disfavor to the retreat behind the Sereth, in which they are now engaged. Of the earlier stages of the siege we have already laid before our readers a careful, and, we hope, a clear analysis[a]; and now, at last, having received by the *Pacific*[207] the official Russian reports, we are able to follow the whole affair to its conclusion without doing any injustice to either party. Besides the Russian reports, which are distinct, clear and business-like in what they state, but abound in faults of omission, we now have Lieutenant Nasmyth's (Bengal Artillery,) report to *The London Times*,[b] a complete journal of the siege, giving some interesting particulars, but made up in rather a slovenly way, and sometimes incorrect in the dates. It is only proper to say that the views and conclusions we have previously expressed concerning the siege, are altogether confirmed by these later and more detailed narratives, except in the particular that the Turks did not abandon the defense of the fort Arab Tabiassi, as in the latter part of the siege we supposed they would be constrained to do.[c] It appears too, that the Russians were still more extravagant in their operations than we suspected. First they made a regular attack on the fortress on its eastern side, on the low lands of the Danube, hoping to be able to turn the detached forts altogether and to make a breach in the main wall of Silistria at once. If this attempt had the merit of originality, it certainly had no other. It affords, perhaps the first instance of trenches, and approaches being thrown up against a fortress, on ground which was not only flanked, but actually commanded in the rear by hights fortified by the enemy. But then a second, an irregular attack was directed against these very hights, and so cleverly combined that after the loss of a fortnight on reconnoitering and storming, in which thousands of Russians were killed or disabled, a regular siege against them had also to be employed. So much for the skill displayed by the Russians. Let us now pass to the details of the period of the siege.

On the 1st of June the Russians got a fresh train of siege-artillery, brought over from the left bank of the Danube, which they arranged in battery against Arab Tabiassi. The Turks sunk shafts and pushed mines under the counterscarps and glacis of this fort. On June 2, Mussa Pasha, commander of Silistria was

---

[a] See this volume, pp. 234-45.— *Ed.*

[b] [Nasmyth,] "The Siege of Silistria". *The Times*, No. 21783, July 3, 1854.— *Ed.*

[c] See this volume, p. 245.— *Ed.*

killed by a shell. Toward evening the Russians exploded a mine under one of the bastions of Arab Tabiassi. As at that time they could not yet have arrived at the crest of the glacis, this mine could not have been very accurately laid. The distances, as well as the line of shortest resistance must have been wrongly calculated, and, accordingly, when the mine sprung, so far from injuring the Turkish defenses, it exploded backward and overwhelmed the Russian trenches with a hail of stones and earth. But here the storming columns were assembled ready for an assault, and the effect of this hail of stones among them may be readily imagined. How far the Russians succeeded in effectually blockading the fortress is shown by the fact that on this day 5,000 Turkish irregulars from Rasgrad west of Silistria made their way into the besieged town.

From the 4th to the 8th of June the trenches against the Arab Tabiassi were continued. The Russians arrived at the glacis, pushed a sap boldly forward toward its crest, which was very poorly supported however by the fire of their artillery. They commenced sinking a mine below the ditch and pushed it under the scarp of the bastion. While this was going on Marshal Paskievich on the 9th again made one of his inexplicable displays of armed force in a grand reconnaissance against the fortress, consisting of 31 battalions, 40 squadrons, and 144 field pieces. What he expected to gain by this exhibition nobody can tell. It looks like one of those displays volunteered only in the hope of some chance offering itself for doing something serious, or at least to impress your enemy with the notion that you are irresistible. But no such effect was produced upon the Turks. On the contrary, they sent forth 4,000 cavalry, who, according to the Russian *bulletin* were dreadfully beaten; Nasmyth, however, asserts that they brought in sixty Russian horses taken in the affray. At the same time, Paskievich instead of reconnoitering something to his advantage, was, according to the report, himself reconnoitered by a Turkish cannon-ball, which put him *hors de combat*[a] and necessitated his being transported to Jassy.

On the 10th the siege was at its crisis. The grand mine, Schilder's last hope, was sprung. It produced indeed a practicable breach in the front bastion of Arab Tabiassi. The Russian columns advanced to the assault; but, as they might have expected, the Turks had long since made a *coupure* or second parapet with a ditch, a little to the rear of the main wall, and the Russians on

---

[a] Out of action.— *Ed.*

coming up found themselves arrested and exposed to murderous fire. Now, when the advance of an assaulting column is once brought to a stand, that column is beaten; for the fire of the enemy covered behind ramparts and supported by artillery, at a distance where every shot tells, forces it to retreat in a very few minutes. The Russians, therefore, had to make the best of the way back across the breach, and were followed by the Turks, who pursued them as far as the Russian trenches and destroyed part of the siege works. This assault was the last serious enterprise of the Russians against Silistria. If the siege was apparently and nominally continued until orders for the raising of it arrived, it was merely to save appearances. On the 12th the blockade was so little sustained that European officers from Shumla had no difficulty in entering the fortress.

The Russians had opened their trenches in the low ground on the 19th of May. Their batteries against Arab Tabiassi, seven in number, commenced work on the 22d. Fifteen more guns were brought up against that fort on the following day. Still the regular attack against Arab Tabiassi did not take place, according to the Russian account, until the 31st of May. This appears to indicate that the batteries erected on the 21st and 22d merely did the office of a first parallel, and were armed with heavy field pieces, for the purpose of enfilading the fort. From May 31 to June 10 the Russian batteries advanced within one hundred yards of the fort, that is from the first to the third parallel, at the foot of the glacis. Neither was the glacis crowned, nor were trenching batteries erected; but, as before stated, a sap was pushed up the slope of the glacis, in order to sink the shaft of the mine at its top. As we learn from all reports that Arab Tabiassi was hardly more than a field fortification, of large proportions but little permanent strength, the conduct of its defenders, composed of four battalions and 500 irregulars under Hussein Pasha, certainly deserves the highest praise. Nine days of distant cannonading, eleven days of open trenches, two mines and four or five assaults, all ending in the discomfiture of the enemy, we remember no other instance in the history of war where a mere outwork, of such construction as Arab Tabiassi, has stood so much. The instances coming nearest to it are the defense of Colberg by the Prussians in 1807, and of Danzig by the French in 1813.

It has seemed very surprising that during the whole siege nothing was done by Omer Pasha to support or relieve so important a place. From his letter addressed to Sami Pasha, the Governor of Vidin, we learn, however, that he was actually preparing to succor Silistria when the Russians withdrew to the left side of the Danube.

"You know," says this letter, "that I had collected all our forces in front of Shumla, and that I was preparing to march to the relief of the place. Six regiments of cavalry and three batteries had already left Shumla for this destination. The Russians, having gained information of this movement, have withdrawn precipitately over to the left bank, with the whole of their artillery. During the forty days they invested the place, the Russians lost 25,000 men killed." [a]

What the Russians are now about to do it is impossible to decide. According to some Vienna papers, they purpose to take up a position behind the Buseo, but the same papers pretend that it is the fear of Austria which drives them back, and the Buseo is equally outflanked by Austria. If the Russians try to hold Moldavia, they would be outflanked by Austria from Galicia and the Bukovina. But a timely junction of the Russian troops in Poland with the late Danubian army in Podolia and Volhynia would again outflank Austria and expose the north-eastern part of Galicia as far as the San and the Dniester.

Abstaining, for a moment, from political considerations, and supposing Austria to be ready to join with the allied forces in an attack upon Russia, matters would stand thus: Austria could bring into the field from 200,000 to 250,000 men to join the allies, who themselves dispose of about 100,000 to 120,000 Turks, and 60,000 Anglo-French troops. To these forces Russia could oppose the four corps of the Danubian army, with their reserves, amounting, after due deduction on account of losses, to about 200,000 men. The second corps, commanded by Panyutin, and the three cavalry reserve corps, with some further infantry reserves, and reenforcements by fresh levies, might together amount to 180,000 men: so that the entire military strength of Russia would be composed of 350,000 men, from which the garrisons necessary for guarding the Crimea and parts of Southern Russia would have to be deducted. This would still leave the guards, the grenadiers, and the first army corps disposable for the defense of Poland and the Baltic provinces—not to speak of the Finnish corps of about 15,000 men. Everything considered, the discrepancy between the relative belligerent forces would not be so great as to forbid Russia from calculating on moderate success, if she would restrict herself to a proper defense.

If Austria, as the latest diplomatic news and her total inactivity

---

[a] *Le Moniteur universel*, No. 190, July 9, 1854.—*Ed.*

on the Moldavian frontier appear to indicate, has no other intention but to interfere between the belligerents, then we may safely assume that there is no chance of anything occurring in the course of the year in either Moldavia or Bessarabia.

Written on July 6, 1854

First published in the *New-York Daily Tribune*, No. 4139, July 25; reprinted in the *New-York Semi-Weekly Tribune*, No. 957, July 28 and the *New-York Weekly Tribune*, No. 672, July 29, 1854 as a leader

Reproduced from the *New-York Daily Tribune*

Karl Marx

[THE DETAILS OF THE INSURRECTION AT MADRID.— THE AUSTRO-PRUSSIAN SUMMONS.— THE NEW AUSTRIAN LOAN.—WALLACHIA] [208]

London, Friday, July 7, 1854

The news we receive of the military insurrection at Madrid continues to be of a very contradictory and fragmentary character. All the Madrid telegraphic dispatches are, of course, government statements, and of the same questionable faith as the bulletins published in the *Gaceta.* A review of the scanty materials at hand is consequently all I can give you.

It will be recollected that O'Donnell was one of the generals banished by the Queen [a] in February; that he refused to obey, secreted himself in Madrid, and from his hiding place kept up secret correspondence with the garrison of Madrid, and particularly with General Dulce, the Inspector-General of the Cavalry. The Government were aware of his sojourn at Madrid, and on the 27th June, at night, General Blaser, the Minister of War, and General Lara, the Captain-General of New Castile, received warnings of an intended outbreak under the leadership of General Dulce. Nothing, however, was done to prevent or stifle the insurrection in its germ. On the 28th, therefore, General Dulce found no difficulty in assembling about 2,000 cavalry under pretext of a review, and marching with them out of the town, accompanied by O'Donnell, with the intention of kidnapping the Queen, then staying at the Escurial. The design failed, however, and the Queen arrived at Madrid on the 29th, attended by Count San Luis, the President of the Council, and held a review, while the insurgents took up quarters in the environs of the capital.

---

[a] Isabella II.— *Ed.*

They were joined by Colonel Echague and 400 men of the Regiment "Prince," who brought along the regimental cashbag containing 1,000,000 francs. A column composed of seven battalions of infantry, one regiment of cavalry, one detachment of mounted *gendarmerie*, and two batteries of artillery left Madrid on the evening of the 29th inst., under command of General Lara, in order to meet the rebels quartered at the *Venta del Espiritu Santo* and the village of Vicálvaro. A battle took place on the 30th between the two armies, of which we have received three accounts—the official one addressed by General Lara to the Minister of War, published in the *Gaceta*; the second published by the *Messager de Bayonne*, and the third a report from the Madrid correspondent of the *Indépendance belge*, an eye-witness of the affair. The first named report, which may be found in all the London papers,[a] is easily disposed of, General Lara stating at one time that he attacked the insurgents, and at another that they charged him, making prisoners in one place and losing them in another, claiming the victory and returning to Madrid—*enfin*, leaving the insurgents masters of the field, but covering it with the dead of the "enemy," while pretending himself to have only thirty wounded.

The following is the version of the *Messager de Bayonne*:

"On the 30th June, at 4 A.M., General Quesada left Madrid at the head of two brigades, in order to attack the rebel troops. The affair lasted but a short time, General Quesada being vigorously repulsed. General Blaser, the Minister of War, having assembled the whole garrison of Madrid"

which, by the way, consists of about 7,000 or 8,000 men

"made a *sortie*, in his turn at 7 o'clock in the evening. A combat immediately commenced, and lasted almost without interruption until evening. The infantry, threatened by the numerous cavalry of the insurgents, formed in squares. Colonel Garrigó, at the head of some *escadrons*, charged one of these squares so vigorously as to break through it, but was received by the fire of a masked battery of five guns, the grape-shot of which dispersed his *escadrons*. Colonel Garrigó fell into the hands of the Queen's troops, but General O'Donnell lost not a moment in rallying his squadrons, and threw himself so vehemently on the infantry that he shook their ranks, delivered Colonel Garrigó, and seized the five pieces of artillery. The Queen's troops having suffered this check, retired to Madrid, where they arrived at 8 o'clock in the evening. One of their generals, Messina, was slightly wounded. There was a great number of dead and wounded on both sides in their murderous engagements."

---

[a] Marx used General Lara's account according to *The Times*, No. 21787, July 7, 1854.— *Ed.*

We come now to the report of the *Indépendance*, dated Madrid, lst July, which seems to be the most trustworthy:

"The Venta del Espiritu Santo and Vicálvaro were the theater of a murderous combat, in which the troops of the Queen were repulsed this side the *Fonda de la Alegría*. Three squares successively formed on different points, were spontaneously dissolved by order of the Minister of War. A fourth was formed beyond the *Retiro*.[209] Ten squadrons of insurgents commanded by Generals O'Donnell and Dulce in person, attacked it in the center (?) while guerrillas took it in the flank (?)."

It is difficult to conceive what this correspondent understands by *center*! and *flank*! attacks on a square.

"Twice the insurgents came to close fighting with the artillery but were repulsed by the grape-shot poured upon them. The insurrectionists evidently intended seizing some pieces of artillery placed in each of the corners of the square. Night having approached in the meantime, the governmental forces retired in echelons on the gate of Alcala, where a squadron of the cavalry that had remained faithful was suddenly surprised by a detachment of insurrectionist lancers who had concealed themselves behind the *Plaza de Toros*. In the midst of the confusion produced by this unexpected attack, the insurrectionists seized four pieces of artillery that had remained behind. The loss was nearly equal on both sides. The insurgent cavalry suffered much from the grape-shot, but their lances have almost exterminated the regiment de la Reina Gobernadora, and the mounted *gendarmerie*. Latest accounts inform us that the insurrectionists received reenforcements from Toledo and Valladolid. There is even a rumor afloat that General Narvaez is expected today at Vallecas where he is to be received by Generals Dulce, O'Donnell, Ros de Olano and Armero. Trenches have been opened at the gate of Atocha. Crowds of curious are thronging the railway station whence the advance posts of General O'Donnell may be perceived. All the gates of Madrid are, however, rigorously watched....

"*Three O'Clock P. M. same Day*.—The insurgents occupy the place of Vallecas, three English miles from Madrid, in considerable force. The Government expected today the troops from the provinces, especially the battalion *del Rey*. If we are to believe the most recent information, this force had joined the insurgents.

"*Four P. M.*—At this moment almost the whole garrison leaves Madrid, in the direction of Vallecas, in order to meet the insurgents who show the greatest confidence. The shops are closed. The Guard of the *Retiro* and generally of all Government offices have been armed in haste. I hear at this moment that some companies of the garrison yesterday joined the insurgents. The Madrid garrison is commanded by General Campuzano, who was falsely stated to have gone over to the insurgents, General Vista Hermosa, and Blaser, the Minister of War. Till now no reenforcements have come to the support of the Government; but the 4th Regiment of the line and the lst Cavalry are said to have left Valladolid and to be marching in all haste upon Madrid. The same is assured with respect to the garrison of Burgos, commanded by General Turon. Lastly, General Rivero has left Saragossa with imposing forces. More bloody encounters are, therefore, to be expected."[a]

Up to the 6th inst. no papers or letters had arrived from

---

[a] *L'Indépendance belge*, No. 187, July 6, 1854.— *Ed.*

Madrid. The *Moniteur* alone has the following laconic dispatch, dated Madrid, the 4th of July:

"Tranquillity continues to reign at Madrid and in the provinces."[a]

A private dispatch states that the insurgents are at Aranjuez. If the battle anticipated for the lst inst. by the correspondent of the *Indépendance* had resulted in a victory of the Government, there would be wanting neither letters, nor papers, nor bulletins. Notwithstanding that the state of siege had been proclaimed at Madrid, the *Clamor Público*, the *Nación*, the *Diario*, the *España*, and the *Época* had reappeared without previous notice to the Government, whose *fiscal* informed them of this dismal fact. Among the persons arrested at Madrid are named Messrs. Antonio Guillermo Moreno and José Manuel Collado, bankers. A warrant was issued against Sijora Sevillano, Marquis de Fuentes de Duero, a particular friend of Marshal Narvaez. Messrs. Pidal and Mon are placed under *surveillance*.

It would be premature to form an opinion on the general character of this insurrection. I may say, however, that it does not seem to proceed from the Progresista party,[210] as General San Miguel, their soldier, remains quiet at Madrid. From all the reports it seems, on the contrary, that Narvaez is at the bottom of it, and that Queen Cristina,[b] whose influence had of late much decreased through the Queen's favorite Count San Luis, is not entirely a stranger to it.

There is perhaps no country, except Turkey, so little known to, and so falsely judged by Europe as Spain. The numberless local pronunciamentos and military rebellions have accustomed Europe to view it on a level with Imperial Rome at the era of the pretorians. This is quite as superficial an error as was committed in the case of Turkey, by those who fancied the life of the nation extinct because its official history for the last century consisted only of palace-revolutions and Janissary *émeutes*.[c] The secret of this fallacy lies in the simple fact that historians, instead of viewing the resources and strength of these peoples in their provincial and local organization, have drawn at the source of their Court almanacs. The movements of what we are used to call the State, have so little affected the Spanish people that they were quite content to leave that restricted domain to the alternative passions

---

[a] *Le Moniteur universel*, No. 187, July 6, 1854.— *Ed.*
[b] Maria Cristina.— *Ed.*
[c] Mutinies.— *Ed.*

and petty intrigues of Court minions, soldiers, adventurers, and a few so-called statesmen, and they have had little cause to repent themselves of their indifference. The character of modern Spanish history deserving to receive a very different appreciation than it has until now experienced, I will take an opportunity to treat this subject in one of my next letters.[a] This much I may yet remark in this place, that little surprise ought to be felt if a general movement should now arise in the Peninsula from a mere military rebellion, since the late financial decrees of the Government[211] have converted the tax-gatherer into a most efficient revolutionary propagandist.

Austria holds at this moment the balance of war. If she has not yet marched her troops into Wallachia, it is only because she awaited the reply of the Emperor of Russia. The electric telegraph reports that Gorchakoff has now arrived at Vienna, the bearer of a disagreeable answer.[b] For the first time the Austro-Prussian summons, dispatched on June 3d, has been published in the *Kölnische Zeitung*. The principal passages in the Austrian summons are the following:

"The Emperor of Russia weighing in his wisdom all these considerations, will appreciate the value which the Emperor of Austria must attach to a discontinuance of the advance of the Russian army in the Transdanubian countries, and to the obtaining from him positive indications as to the epoch, it is to be hoped not very distant, when the occupation of the Principalities shall come to an end. The Emperor Nicholas, we are far from doubting it, desires peace; he will therefore consider the means of bringing to an end a state of things tending every day more to become a source of internal trouble to Austria and Germany. We are sure that he will not drive the Emperor Francis Joseph to the necessity of considering for himself the means of saving his interests, so much compromised by the present situation, by prolonging indefinitely this occupation, or by attaching such conditions to the evacuation which it would be impossible for us to obtain."

The Prussian note[c] destined to support the Austrian "summons" terminates as follows:

"The King hopes that the Emperor will consent to place the question at dispute on a ground offering a practical issue, in order to facilitate a satisfactory solution, by abridging and circumscribing the general action of both parties. Our august master hopes, therefore, that the present step will meet, on the part of the Emperor of Russia, with a reception similar in spirit to that which inspired it, and

---

[a] See this volume, pp. 389-446.— *Ed.*

[b] Telegraphic report from Vienna of July 6, 1854. *The Times,* No. 21787, July 7, 1854. The text of the Austro-Prussian summons is cited from *L'Indépendance belge,* No. 188, July 7, 1854.— *Ed.*

[c] This refers to the Dispatch of Baron von Manteuffel to Baron von Werther, June 12, 1854.— *Ed.*

that the answer which we and the Cabinet of Vienna expect, with an interest corresponding to its importance, will be of a character to allow the King to withdraw from the painful necessities which would be imposed upon him by his duty and by his engagements."

Hess, the generalissimo of the Oriental army, will establish his headquarters at Czeraswitz. The *Soldatenfreund*[a] of Vienna gives the following biography of Gen. Hess:

"*Feldzeugmeister*[b] *von Hess* was born at Vienna in 1788; in 1805 he entered the regiment Gyulay as ensign, was lieutenant of the staff at the end of 1815, and appointed lieutenant-colonel and military commissary at Turin in 1822. Colonel since 1829, he became in 1831 quartermaster of the mobile corps of Upper Italy. In 1842 he obtained the rank of lieutenant-marshal, and was chief of the staff of Radetzky's army in 1848. To him must be ascribed the plan of the march upon Mantua, Curtatone and Vicenza in 1848, and that of the short campaign of 1849, terminating with the battle of Novara."[c]

With regard to the avowed intentions of Austria in the occupation of Wallachia, I will quote from Austrian journals.

The *Oberpostamts-Zeitung*[d] of Frankfort, organ of the Austrian embassy at the Bundestag remarks:

"By its geographical position, Austria is obliged to work in the most effective manner at the reestablishment of peace, by actually separating, through the occupation of the Principalities, the belligerent parties, and interposing between them at the most important place. If the Russians retire behind the Pruth, the Turks and their allies cannot then cross the Danube. If we take further into account that both parties have gained one experience and lost one illusion—the Russians having lost the delusion of their military predominance and the maritime powers that of the omnipotence of their fleets—it is clear that the actual situation renders the resumption of peace negotiations almost inevitable."

The *Lloyd*,[e] in its turn, observes:

"The disputed Territory, viz. the Principalities, would be left to the protection of a neutral power. A Turkish army could not take up a position on the banks of the Pruth. An armed mediator would stand between the forces of the western powers and those of Russia, and would prevent a collision in the Danubian Principalities. Thus there would be, in point of fact, an armistice on the most important theater of war. If, indeed, the possibility of peace still exists, this measure might promote it. There can be no doubt entertained either at St. Petersburg or elsewhere, but that the determination of Austria to occupy the

---

[a] *Oesterreichischer Soldatenfreund.*—*Ed.*
[b] Master of Ordnance.—*Ed.*
[c] Marx cites Hess' biography from *Oesterreichischer Soldatenfreund* as it was reprinted in the *Journal des Débats*, July 6, 1854.—*Ed.*
[d] *Frankfurter Postzeitung.*—*Ed.*
[e] *Der Lloyd* is quoted according to *L'Indépendance belge*, No. 187, July 6, 1854.—*Ed.*

Principalities has been adopted with a view to peace, and that at the same time it is the last step which can be taken for the prevention of a general war."

The last and most curious article in this line occurs in the *Spenersche Zeitung*[a] published at Berlin:

"It is confirmed that the embassadors of the four great powers will hold a new conference at Vienna, firstly with a view to take cognizance of the convention of Austria with the Porte, and to declare it to be in conformance with the anterior protocols of the conference; and secondly to come to a mutual understanding as to the manner in which the principles established by the Vienna Protocol of 9th April may be so modified as to serve for the positive basis of the future preliminaries, not of war, but of peace."[b]

In the meantime Austria has profited by these contingencies to project a new loan, of which the following are the terms of its official announcement:

"1. The amount of the loan is provisionally fixed at from 350 to 500 millions of florins. If the subscriptions reach this sum, the payments are to be effected during three, four, or five years, according to the amount of the subscription.

"2. The rate of emission is fixed at 95 in bank paper.

"3. The interest to be at 5 per cent., paid in real coin.

"4. The subscription is no forced one, the Imperial Government being about to appeal, through the constituted authorities of all provinces, to the *patriotism* of the subjects of the State.

"5. The loan will be employed to pay the State debt to the Bank, to the amount of 80 millions, with a view of thus restoring the value of the Bank paper. The surplus"

it is very ingenious to call four-fifths of the whole a surplus

"will be employed as resource for the budgets of coming years."[c]

The *Lloyd*, of course, assures that this grand financial operation now contemplated (and almost for the first time!) must and will do away with the existing depreciation of the Austrian currency. Your readers will not have forgotten that it was this pretext which introduced almost every Austrian loan in this century.[d] There are some points, however, in this grand operation which they might not hit upon, as they are carefully omitted from the above announcement. On this score *The Globe* of last evening remarks:

"This loan will be national, i.e. every tax-payer will be called upon to subscribe in proportion of the amount of taxes he pays. For the present some moral

---

[a] *Berlinische Nachrichten von Staats- und gelehrten Sachen.—Ed.*

[b] The quotation from the *Berlinische Nachrichten von Staats- und gelehrten Sachen* is given according to the *Journal des Débats*, July 7, 1854.—*Ed.*

[c] "Die österreichische Nationalanleihe." *Allgemeine Zeitung*, No. 183, July 2, 1854. Supplement.—*Ed.*

[d] See this volume, pp. 43-49.—*Ed.*

compulsion will be employed to precede positive compulsion. In point of fact, therefore, the measure amounts to the raising of an additional sum of taxes at once, with the promise that this particular sum shall be repaid."

It is curious what resemblance this grand operation bears in point of its pretexts as well as in point of execution, with the late Spanish decrees that now prelude to a revolution.

In my last letter I called your attention to the rights and position of the Wallachian people,[a] in opposition to the diplomatic quarrels pretending to originate in their violation. A report has just appeared in the Paris *Siècle*, of M. Barbu Bibesco, prefect of Mehedintzi, in Little Wallachia, addressed to the Foreign Minister of the Porte,[b] in which at length we hear a voice raised for the people of the Principalities treated with such shameful indifference by the "defenders of civilization." It commences with stating that

"the Russians, to avenge themselves of the passive resistance of a completely disarmed people, abandoned themselves to the most abominable acts of cruelty and dilapidation on their retreat from Little Wallachia. They have carried away the cash in the public chests, the seals and the archives of the Administration, and the sacred vessels of the churches. When retiring they slaughtered the cattle which the numberless requisitions had spared; and these cattle they took not away, but left to rot, merely to make the people feel their cruelty and hatred."

M. Bibesco remarks with respect to the then rumored entrance of the Austrians into Wallachia, that

"even a benevolent foreign army is always burdensome for the country it occupies."

He says that Wallachia does not want the Austrians; that it is able to furnish a contingent of 50,000 men, drilled in arms and disciplined. In each of the seventeen departments of Wallachia there are at this moment 3,000 *gendarmerie*, wood-keepers, game-keepers and ancient soldiers, who require only arms and to hear the drums beat, when they would burst upon the Russians. He concludes in the following words:

"It is arms we want; if there be not enough in your arsenals, the many factories in France, England and Belgium do not want them, and we are ready to pay for them. Arms! and again arms, Excellency, and before three months there will not remain one single Russian in the Principalities, and the Sublime Porte will find a force of 100,000 Roumans as eager as the Osmanlis to pursue and punish their common and implacable enemy."

---

[a] See this volume, pp. 269-75.— *Ed.*
[b] Reshid Pasha.— *Ed.*

The poor Prefect of Mehedintzi does not understand that it is precisely for preventing them to have arms, and along with the Osmanlis to pursue and punish the Russians that Austria subjects the Wallachians to her occupation.

Sir Charles Napier, say the cockney papers, is trying to make the Czar's admirals come out from Kronstadt, and leave the protection of the granite-walls behind which they "tremble" before the Anglo-French fleet. But why don't the English sailors come out from their wooden walls and fight the Russians on their element, the land? Be it observed, that in spite of the English bravadoes, the Russians came out from Sevastopol, and "damaged" the *Fury*.

Baraguay d'Hilliers has been appointed commander of a division of troops to be embarked for the Baltic, the departure of which is fixed for the 14th inst.; England is to furnish the transports for 6,000 men. An equal number of troops with one field battery will be embarked on board the French ships. If we add to these numbers that of the marine-soldiers commanded by Col. Fieron, the effective of the whole Baltic division will amount to from 13,000 to 14,000 men, while at the same time the embarkation of troops for the Black Sea from Marseilles has not yet ceased; the process of disarming France having apparently not yet reached the desired point of "safety."

Written on July 7, 1854

First published in the *New-York Daily Tribune*, No. 4136, July 21 and the *New-York Semi-Weekly Tribune*, No. 955, July 21, 1854

Signed: *Karl Marx*

Reproduced from the *New-York Daily Tribune*

Karl Marx

[EXCITEMENT IN ITALY.—THE EVENTS IN SPAIN.—
THE POSITION OF THE GERMAN STATES.—
BRITISH MAGISTRATES][212]

London, Friday, July 14, 1854

Sir Charley[a] has quietly returned from Kronstadt, with no other killed or wounded than some of his gallant tars carried off by the cholera. To keep the public in good humor, the same farce is now to be repeated before Sevastopol, fifty sail of the combined fleets having been seen at Odessa, "making direct" for that place.

The embarkation of the French troops from Calais, fixed for this day,[b] has been adjourned until the 20th inst., in order, it is said, to await the development of events in Spain.

General Budberg has forced upon the inhabitants of the Principalities an address expressing their thanks to the Emperor Nicholas, for the occupation of their country, and for its defense against the "cruel and barbarous Turk."[c] The *Euphrates*, which left Constantinople on the 5th and arrived at Marseilles on the 13th inst., brings the important news that the Dobrodja has not at all been evacuated by the Russians, and that the "illustrious" Reshid (wretched) Pasha has resumed the office of Foreign Minister.

It is stated from Cracow, July 8, that Prince Paskievich has arrived at Castle Homel, on his estates in Lithuania, and that he is not to take any more part in the present campaign. It is added that not only himself, but also his plan of campaign, has been given up, and this is the more probable as the Russian troops already in retreat to Moldavia have been ordered forward again by

---

[a] Admiral Sir Charles Napier.— *Ed.*

[b] July 13.— *Ed.*

[c] Report from Bucharest of June 30, 1854. *Le Moniteur universel*, No. 195, July 14, 1854.— *Ed.*

Prince Gorchakoff, who is said to be collecting a strong force in
front of Bucharest.[a] The present position of the Russian troops is,
therefore, as follows: their right wing on the Upper Jalomnitza,
leaning with its extreme on the Transylvanian Alps, where they
occupy the Temesher Pass with twenty-four pieces of heavy
artillery; their center extending from Fokshani to Bucharest; their
left, under Lüders, at Brailow; and their extreme left, under
Oushakoff, in the Dobrodja.

The latest news from the theater of war states that the Turks
have crossed the Danube in force (40,000, including 12,000 allies),
and that they have occupied Giurgevo. French journals report that
the Russian establishment at the Sulina mouth has been bombarded and destroyed by the steamers detached from the
combined fleet[b]; but this news is probably to be classed with the
hoax about the second bombardment and destruction of Bomarsund in the Baltic. The operations of Marshal St. Arnaud in the
East seem to have inspired the Tuileries with some dread, lest they
might be on too grand a scale. At least, it is said that the French
Government has dispatched a special superintendent—of course, a
financial one—to control his excess of zeal (*son excès de zèle*).

In Italy, a strange excitement has taken hold both of the Governments and the people. Gen. La Marmora, the Piedmontese
Minister of War, has ordered the formation of military camps in
Savoy, at St. Maurice, at Alessandria, and even in the Island of
Sardinia. A great number of soldiers on unlimited leave have been
recalled under arms. Simultaneously the fortresses of Alessandria
and Casale are being provisioned. Marshal Radetzky, on the other
hand, has likewise ordered the formation of a camp between
Verona and Volta, where more than 20,000 troops are daily
exercised in the operations of war on a small scale (*petite guerre*).
Troubles occasioned by the dearness of provisions have taken
place at Codogno, Casalpusterlengo, and in some Lombardian
towns. About two hundred persons have been arrested and
conveyed to Mantua. According to letters from Naples, numerous
arrests had been made there as well as in Sicily, where the son of
Count Caraffa has been imprisoned. King Bomba[c] is taking
extraordinary measures for armaments by land and sea. He has
ordered the fortress of Gaeta to be put in readiness for all

---

[a] Telegrams from Vienna of July 10 and 11. *The Times*, No. 21790, July 11
and No. 21791, July 12, 1854.— *Ed.*

[b] *Le Moniteur universel*, No. 194, July 13, 1854.— *Ed.*

[c] Ferdinand II.— *Ed.*

eventualities. All Europe has been declared pestiferous by him, and a strict quarantine is established for all vessels arriving. All shipping from Portugal, Glasgow and the Sardinian States are subjected to a quarantine of ten days; that of Tuscany and the Roman States, seven days. Almost every other country being already subject to similar restrictions, the free arrival of any ship at all is a rare exception. Foreign correspondence by land is subjected to all the measures of precaution observed with regard to arrivals from pestiferous countries. Communication with the Papal States is still carried on by Monte Casino and Sora, and by the Abruzzi, but a sanitary cordon is about to be established along the whole frontier.

The last mail due from Madrid, via Bordeaux, had not arrived at Paris up to yesterday evening. The royal troops are stated to be still in pursuit of the rebels, to have reached them, and to be on the point of cutting them to pieces. We were told in the first instance that the rebels were on their flight to Estremadura, in order to gain the Portuguese frontier. Now we hear they are on the way to Andalusia, a circumstance which shows no very great determination on their part to expatriate themselves so soon. According to private letters Gen. Serrano has joined them with 300 cavalry, while the *Gaceta* pretends that he joined them single-handed.[a] At Madrid it was rumored that the King's regiment (*del Rey*) had gone over to the insurgents. The correspondent of *The Morning Chronicle* adds that they were joined besides by 200 officers of all arms, several companies of the regiments stationed at Toledo, and two battalions of volunteers from Madrid. The *Gaceta* announces that the division ordered to pursue the rebels left Madrid on the evening of the 5th, being composed of three brigades of infantry, one of cavalry, two batteries of artillery, one company of engineers, and one detachment of the workmen of the military administration.[b] It set out under command of Gen. Vista Hermosa, who was replaced, however, on the following day by Gen. Blaser, the Minister of War. A royal decree of 7th July intrusts the ministry of War to Gen. San Roman during the absence of Blaser. The *Gaceta* states that the division above mentioned was at Tembleque, and proceeding in the direction of Cuidad Real by the valley of the

Guadiana. On the same day, Blaser published a proclamation to the soldiers and non-commissioned officers in the rebel army, inviting them to return to their standards, and promising them full pardon in the name of the Queen. We read the following in the *Messager de Bayonne*:

"According to the latest news we have received, Gen. O'Donnell made a movement in the direction of Valdepeñes. The vanguard of the royal army was assembled at Tembleque. Gen. O'Donnell is employing his leisure in exercising his little army, composed of 2,000 horse, six pieces of artillery, and 800 infantry."[a]

The proclamations of O'Donnell and Dulce are of a different character, the one appealing to the Constitution of 1837, the other to the ancient Castilian right of insurrection against monarchs guilty of having broken the coronation-oath.[213] A new feature is the formation of republican guerrillas in Valencia. Under date of 6th inst., a communication has been received to the effect that some towns and villages have risen against the Government, among others Alcira, Xativa and Carlet. Orozko, a retired colonel, has entered the last-named town at the head of an armed band, confiscated all fire-arms, and invited the inhabitants by proclamation to join the movement. The Government sent off detachments of cavalry, infantry and civil guard, to suppress the insurrections in Valencia.

The *Indépendance belge* gives quite a new version of the Russian note addressed to Austria and Prussia.[214] According to this paper, which may be regarded as the private *Moniteur* of the retired Russian diplomatists at Brussels, the Russian note was not addressed directly to the Austrian Cabinet, but to Prince Gorchakoff, who left a copy with M. de Buol, expressing the belief that Austria, while demanding the evacuation of the Principalities by the Russians, only meant to propose an armistice, since it could not be her wish to expose the retreating Russian armies to an attack of the allied forces. The Austrian meaning, accordingly, must have been a suspension of arms. Turks, English and French would then have to abstain from all forward movements and from every act of fresh hostility to Russia. As to the evacuation of the Principalities by the Russian troops, the note dwells on the absolute necessity for Russia of maintaining certain strategical points in those provinces while attending the conclusion of peace, as she would otherwise be placed in too disadvantageous

---

[a] This quotation is given according to a reprint in *L'Indépendance belge*, No. 194, July 13, 1854.— *Ed.*

a position with regard to the armies of the allies. On the other hand, the note protests against any supposed intention of threatening Austria by the said strategical occupation. Proceeding from these promises, the note expresses the disposition of Russia to enter upon new negotiations of peace, to be on the following basis: The integrity of the Ottoman empire, which the Russian Government has never intended to injure; the equality between the Christian and Mussulman subjects of the Porte, such as it is understood in the protocol of April 9 [215]; finally, the revision of the conventions referring to the Straits. The note admits a common protectorate of the powers over the Christians of Turkey; but with regard to the Russian protectorate of the Greek Christians, the article in the *Indépendance* confesses that some vague phrases are attached to it which would give sufficient latitude for diverging interpretations. Prince Gorchakoff, it is said, speaks even in a more subdued tone than the note itself. His dispatch does not contain the *last word* of Russia; he may be authorized to go further, with a view of enabling Austria to enter into fresh negotiations. On the 9th inst., however, the Vienna Cabinet had not yet come to a decision.

"Now," says the *Indépendance*, or rather Baron Brunnow, "we must not conceal from ourselves that whatever the dispositions at St. Petersburg might be, a single incident, an actual act of war, an attack against Kronstadt, or what is more probable, against Sevastopol, and even the occupation of the Aland Isles by the Anglo-French, must necessarily modify those dispositions, and give more force to the party opposed to any concession." [a]

At all events, this Russian note has satisfied Prussia, which considers it as a sort of escape into new negotiations, and as a means of preventing the Austrians from entering Wallachia. The *Moniteur* itself admits that the objections raised by Prussia against this Austrian entrance have produced the fresh hesitation evinced by the Court of Vienna. On the other hand, we are told in the sanctimonious *Morning Chronicle* that

"it was urged from Berlin, that the contingent duty with which the Court of Berlin charged itself, of protecting the Austrian territory from invasion, entitled it to protest against any fresh provocation of Russia." [b]

It is known, besides, that the treaty between Austria and Prussia [c] was arranged in precisely such a manner as to allow

---

[a] Review of current events. *L'Indépendance belge*, No. 193, July 12, 1854.— *Ed.*
[b] *The Morning Chronicle*, No. 27318, July 14, 1854, leader.— *Ed.*
[c] See this volume, p. 168.— *Ed.*

either of the powers to stop its military operations as long as it
should not be convinced of the necessity of the warlike steps
contemplated by the other. Thus Austria may appear anxious to
act with the western powers, while it finds itself stopped by the
remonstrances of Prussia. I, for my part, am sure that all these
eventualities were arranged for long ago by the three northern
powers in common, and that even the new difficulties raised
against Austria are only intended to give her occupation of
Wallachia the appearance of a heroic opposition to Russia. A little
sham war, after the fashion of the Austro-Prussian war of 1850,[216]
may not be excluded from that arrangement, as it would only
contribute to give Austria a more decisive vote at the conclusion of
peace. Be it observed that the *Austrian Correspondence*[a] expressly
announces that Austria consents in every point to the policy of the
western powers, *except* as to any eventual infringement on the
present territories of Russia.[b]

In judging the position of Austria, it is important to notice the
"Protest of the Servian Government against Austrian occupation,"
dated June 22,[c] which has now been laid before the House of
Commons. This protest is addressed by the Servian Government
to the Sublime Porte. It begins with stating that

"according as Austria believed the Servian Government to be more or less well
disposed toward Russia or toward Turkey, she held to it a language corresponding
to these sentiments, and constantly promised it her support for the defense of the
frontiers of the Principality against all hostile aggression."

Then took place a very considerable concentration of troops on
the frontiers of Servia. The Government of Servia asked for
information "directly from the Cabinet of Vienna, and indirectly
from the Sublime Porte, as to the object and meaning of this
military movement of Austria." Austria gave evasive declarations,
while the Porte and the representatives of the western powers at
Constantinople professed to know nothing about the object of the
Austrian demonstrations, and appeared even to participate in the
anxieties and doubts of the Servian Government.

---

[a] *Oesterreichische Correspondenz.—Ed.*
[b] Marx draws on an article from the *Oesterreichische Correspondenz* according to
the Vienna correspondent's report of July 9, 1854, published in *The Times*,
No. 21793, July 14, 1854.— *Ed.*
[c] A misprint in the newspaper. The reference is to the "Memorandum of the
Serbian Government to the Sublime Porte concerning the occupation of this
Principality by the Austrian troops" of April 17 (5), 1854. The Memorandum was
debated in the House of Commons on June 20 and 22, 1854.— *Ed.*

"The Pasha of Belgrade[a] remained without instructions, or, to speak more correctly, he remained provided with the old instructions that had formerly been given to him, and in virtue of which he was to consider any military intervention of Austria in Servia as a hostile attempt directed against the Ottoman Empire itself, and as such to repel it with all his power."

Austria appearing to lean more and more toward the western powers, their agents at Belgrade began to give satisfactory assurances as to the disposition of Austria. Simultaneously, the Cabinet of Vienna informed the Servian Government that the military measures in question had nothing in them hostile to Servia; that Austria only intended to protect her own frontiers; and would not interpose in Servia, unless the Russian troops entered it, or revolts against legitimate authority should break out there; that, consequently, even in that case, she would interpose as a friend, and with a view to lending assistance to the Government and legitimate authority. The Servian Government was not tranquillized with these assurances of Austria. It saw, on the one side, Austria pretending to an arbitral intervention, and on the other her isolated action under pretense of co-operating with the western powers in support of the Ottoman Empire. In conclusion, it suspected her intention to provoke those very disorders which she professed to be so anxious to prevent. As the military preparations of Austria assumed, day by day, a more threatening aspect, the Servian Government, in concert with Izzet Pasha, took active steps at Vienna and Constantinople for the prevention of any combination which should make Austria the arbiter of the present destinies of Servia. It is for this object that Azzis Pasha was first sent to Vienna, and is now at Constantinople. At the same time, every measure for the defense of the country was taken in concert with the Turkish representative. Austria holds out two reasons which might occasion her intervention in Servia: 1. The entrance of the Russians; 2. The breaking out of an insurrection in Servia. The first is absurd, as the theater of war is too distant from Servia, and should the Russians attempt to enter it, the Servian and Turkish troops would perfectly suffice to repel them. If auxiliary troops were required, others would be preferable to Austrian.

"The Servian nation has so decided a mistrust, if not a hatred of Austria, that the entrance of the Austrians into Servia would be immediately considered by every Servian as so imminent a danger, so great a misfortune, that all the proceedings of the Servians would be directed against the Austrian troops, all the energy of the

---

[a] Izzet Pasha.— *Ed.*

nation would be employed in resisting those enemies in whom is always supposed to be personified that cupidity which urges Austria to seek to exercise in Servia, no matter under what patronage, a selfish influence."

As to internal insurrections, they are only to be apprehended in consequence of Austrian intervention. Servia will always be loyal to the Porte.

"All that the Servian Government requires, is to be honored henceforth with the same confidence the Sublime Porte has hitherto shown it, and not to see its country given over to Austrian occupation, which would be the signal for, and the commencement of, incalculable misfortunes. On this condition, the Servian Government fully answers for the maintenance of public tranquillity, of order in Servia."

This protest of the Servians is at the same time a fair indication with what enthusiasm the Austrian entrance into Wallachia is looked forward to by the Wallachian people.

The neutral or rather hostile attitude of the minor powers toward England can surprise no one who has followed her present acts of war against Russia, who considers the marauding expeditions of the English fleet in the Baltic, and the measures that have been taken to disable the troops at Varna from doing anything in the field, so that even the medical ambulances of the British troops in Turkey have but just now been sent out by the *Himalaya* from Southampton.[a] Sweden, accordingly, has definitely declared her resolution to remain neutral, and to abstain from any steps in common with the western powers, while Denmark and Holland, as members of the German Confederation,[217] have only assented to the Austrian communication of May 24, on the express understanding that nothing but absolute neutrality and endeavors to restore peace are meant by it.

A police case has occurred before the magistrate of Bow-st., Mr. Jardine, which has caused infinitely greater excitement in London than either Bonaparte's harangue at Boulogne[b] or Charley's glorious retreat from Kronstadt. A German, named Dr. Peitman, having been locked up during four days, was brought up by warrant and charged with being a person of unsound mind and unfit to be at large. Mr. Reynolds, the Solicitor to the Treasury, desired the exclusion of the public and the press, and the proceedings were conducted accordingly; with the strictest secrecy, in the magistrate's private room. Mr. Otway, M.P., a friend of

---

[a] "Naval and Military Intelligence". *The Times*, No. 21792, July 13, 1854.— *Ed.*

[b] Napoleon III's address to the soldiers in Boulogne on July 12, 1854. *Le Moniteur universel*, No. 194, July 13, 1854.— *Ed.*

defendant, indignantly protested against the attempt to exclude him from the inquiry, and was subsequently admitted, and Mr. Lewis, a lawyer, also demanded and obtained admission as the solicitor of the defendant. Mr. Lewis asked why Dr. Peitman had been confined in a felon's cell four whole days without having been taken before any magistrate. Mr. Jardine replied that two medical gentlemen had signed certificates as to the insanity of the defendant, upon which he must order him to a lunatic asylum. Mr. Lewis offered to produce contrary certificates, but Mr. Jardine refused to hear any proposal for adjourning the case, as he must act upon the certificates before him. Mr. Lewis then said he would appeal to a higher tribunal, where the case would not be prejudged and both parties would be heard. He should now advise his client to make no answer to the charge, although invited to do so by the magistrate. Mr. Otway protested against the *ex parte*[a] character of the entire proceedings and declared he would bring the whole matter before the House of Commons, by moving for the particulars of Dr. Peitman's former apprehension and committal to a lunatic asylum. The defendant was removed to Colney Hatch.

I now subjoin the statement of Mr. Percival, the physician who lately released Dr. Peitman from Bedlam, which is given in to-day's *Morning Advertiser*:

"Dr. Peitman, a German Professor, who has studied at Bonn, Berlin, and Halle, is the son of a Hanoverian officer, who fought for George III, and died in his service, and step-son of Baron Ripperta, a Prussian *Landrath*. He came to England about thirty years ago, and, having soon become acquainted with the disgracefully defective system of education pursued in our public schools and colleges, he went to Oxford and Cambridge to give lectures on the subject. In 1835 he was recommended to the Marquis of Normanby, and he went to Ireland under his protection. Lady Normanby having already a tutor for Lord Mulgrave, recommended Dr. P. to an Irish nobleman, to whose two sons he became tutor. After seven months, it was discovered that the eldest son was deeply attached to a Saxon maid, servant in the family, and in fact that she was *enceinte* by him. His mother applied to Dr. Peitman to assist her in getting the girl back to Germany, but the Doctor refused to interfere. He left the family and commenced a course of public lectures at Dublin, when about March 1836, the Saxon girl, delivered of a child on the nobleman's estate, came there in a state of great destitution, and soon after informed him that she would employ an attorney to commence an action for seduction against the nobleman's son, and that he would be subpoenaed as witness. Dr. Peitman then resolved to call on Col. Phipps, Chamberlain of the Marquis of Normanby, and very intimate with that nobleman's family. Having repeatedly called upon this Phipps, brother of Normanby, and present Secretary of Prince Albert, he got neither answer nor admittance, and was at length taken before Mr.

---

[a] One-sided.— *Ed.*

Studdert, a magistrate in Dublin, who on the evidence of the same Phipps, sent him to a lunatic asylum without any certificate for a breach of the peace, in May, 1836. Under Lord Normanby's Vice-Royalty, he was removed to Dean Swift's Hospital, on the certificate of a Dr. Lytton, which contained, in his opinion no ground of Peitman's insanity. He was released nine months after, through the interference of Dr. Dawson, Dean of St. Patrick's, by whose introduction he gave a course of lectures before the Royal Society of Dublin, and was engaged in Lord Fortescue's family. On the arrival of Prince Albert in England, he applied to the Prince for the office of a librarian, and permission to carry out his school reforms. The Duke of Sussex, after a long interview, ordered his librarian to give him free access to his library. Subsequently he sent in his application to Prince Albert, accompanied by his testimonials and by eleven volumes published by him. The Prince returned no answer to his application, and Dr. Peitman ultimately called to request an interview or to have his testimonials restored to him. About this time young Oxford fired at the Queen, *and a female came over from Germany with whom the Prince had been intimate at Bonn,* where he had studied under the same tutor with Peitman. The Court were nervous, and Dr. Peitman's pertinacity excited suspicion. Report was made to the Home Secretary, the Marquis of Normanby, against whom Peitman complained for having had him detained unjustly in a lunatic asylum in Dublin; and a policeman in plain clothes was sent one morning in June, 1840, to fetch the Doctor from his lodgings at Whitehall. Lord Normanby sent for his brother, Col. Phipps, on whose testimony the magistrate in attendance ordered the Doctor to be removed to Bedlam, where he remained confined fourteen years. His conduct there was always exemplary; he was never subject to restraint nor medicine, and he employed himself in attaining an improvement of the treatment of the patients, forming classes of such of them as were capable of receiving his instruction. When released he petitioned on the advice of his friends to the Queen, and on Saturday last, conceiving that he might now go anywhere without exciting apprehension, he went to the royal chapel in Buckingham Palace, where he attended divine service in order to come under the notice of the Queen. It was here that he was again arrested."

Your readers may see from this sample how dangerous it is in this free country to excite the nervousness of the Court, and to become initiated into the family scandals of the moral English aristocracy.

Written on July 13 and 14, 1854

First published in the *New-York Daily Tribune*, No. 4142, July 28; reprinted in the *New-York Semi-Weekly Tribune*, No. 957, July 28 and the *New-York Weekly Tribune*, No. 673, August 5, 1854

Signed: *Karl Marx*

Reproduced from the *New-York Daily Tribune*

Karl Marx

[A CONGRESS AT VIENNA.—THE AUSTRIAN LOAN.— PROCLAMATIONS OF DULCE AND O'DONNELL.— THE MINISTERIAL CRISIS IN BRITAIN][218]

London, Tuesday, July 18, 1854

There was a Congress at Vienna on July 13, composed of rather different elements than the late famous Conferences.[219] Count Buol, the Austrian Premier, gave a dinner on that day, in honor of Prince Gorchakoff, the Russian Envoy, whose task it is to cover the position of Prince Gorchakoff, the General commanding in the Principalities. Besides the *personnel* of the Russian Legation, there were present Count Flemming, the representative of Prussia during the absence of Count Arnim; Gen. Mansbach, Embassador of Sweden; Count Bille-Brahe, Embassador of Denmark; M. de Heeckeren, Embassador of Holland; M. de Wendtland, the expelled Secretary of the King of Greece; lastly, Count O'Sullivan de Grass, Minister of Belgium and the senior of the *corps diplomatique.* Here you have the complete list of the persons openly sailing under the Russian flag. Bamberg,[220] of course, was strongly represented, but the names of its great men have not been given.

The official English press cannot suppress the uneasiness felt at the Austrian order for the suspension of Count Coronini's advance into Wallachia, and about the dispatches forwarded to Paris and London, according to which Russia proposes to accede to the terms of the Protocol of 9th April, as a basis for negotiations of peace,[221] but subject to conditions. The semi-official *Austrian Correspondence*[a] thinks that, although the Russian propositions are not quite satisfactory, there is really something in them which deserves to be taken into consideration by the western

---

[a] *Oesterreichische Correspondenz.—Ed.*

powers.[a] *The Times, Morning Chronicle,* and *Observer* suggest as a
sort of consolation, that it is all the fault of Prussia.[b] If anything
were still wanting to reinforce the impression produced by the
dinner, the altered position of the Russian troops would be
sufficient to prove how much Russia relies on the intentions of
Austria. We read in the *Neue Preussische Zeitung,* the Russian
Moniteur at Berlin, with respect to the latest movements of the
Russian troops in the Principalities:

> "In consequence of an order of Prince Gorchakoff, all that had been ordered
> some days ago has been countermanded. The retreat of the garrison (of
> Bucharest), the evacuation of Bucharest had been ordered; General Dannenberg
> was to leave that town in a few days with the *gendarmerie,* and to establish the
> headquarters of the rear guard at Fokshani. Now, in conformity with the new
> orders, the line of Oltenitza, Bucharest, Buseo and Fokshani is to be maintained."[c]

From other sources we learn that the Russian cavalry are again
pushing forward on Statira, to the left of the Aluta. How serious
was the intention of evacuating Bucharest is evident from the
severe measures taken for carrying off the archives in that town,
which are said to contain some documents extremely compromising for the court of Peterhoff.[222]

All these apparently whimsical and contradictory movements of
the Russians receive their explanation from the inopportune
interference of the Turkish army with the diplomatic arrangements. As the successive settlements of the diplomatists at Vienna
were blown up by the Turkish exploits at Oltenitza, Chetatea and
Silistria, so also have their last shams been dispersed by the
general advance of Omer Pasha's army.

> "The policy of these crafty swearing rascals, that stale old mouse-eaten dry
> cheese, Nestor—and that same old dog-fox, Ulysses—is not proved worth a
> blackberry; ... whereupon the Grecians begin to proclaim barbarism, and policy
> grows into an ill opinion."[d]

If you had passed through the streets of London on Saturday,[e]
you would have heard all the newsvenders shouting their

> "great Anglo-Turko-Gallo victory over the Russians at Giurgevo, and capture of
> Bucharest by the allied troops."

---

[a] Report from Vienna of July 17. *The Times,* No. 21799, July 21, 1854.— *Ed.*

[b] *The Times,* No. 21796, July 18, 1854, leader; *The Morning Chronicle,* No.
27321, July 18, 1854, leader.— *Ed.*

[c] Quoted according to a reprint in *L'Indépendance belge,* Nos. 197 and 198, July
16 and 17, 1854.— *Ed.*

[d] Shakespeare, *Troilus and Cressida,* Act V, Scene 4.— *Ed.*

[e] July 15, 1854.— *Ed.*

The reason of these pompous announcements you will learn by-and-by, when I come to speak of the new ministerial crisis. As to the cooperation of the Anglo-French forces in the battle of Giurgevo, we know by the regular post from Varna, with dates down to the 4th inst., that "no move" had taken place in the camps. According to the latest Vienna advices, on July 13,[a] the auxiliary troops were in full march upon Rustchuk by way of Shumla, and on the 8th a division of French troops had arrived at Rustchuk, and on the 9th only a division of English troops arrived there. Now the battle of Giurgevo ended at 4 a.m. on the 8th, having commenced at an early hour on the 7th, and after an interruption of some hours at noon, being resumed and continued until the morning of the 8th. Thus it is impossible that any French or English troops can have participated in it. The Turks found eight Russian guns spiked, and immediately threw up intrenchments around Giurgevo. The town did not suffer, notwithstanding the shells thrown by the Turks from Rustchuk and the islands. After the retreat of the Russians, Omer Pasha issued a proclamation calling upon the inhabitants to remain tranquil, as no further danger menaced their towns.[b] Giurgevo was only occupied by a feeble detachment of regulars, the principal force of the Turks being encamped around the town and on the three islands of the Danube. Omer Pasha remains at Giurgevo, Said Pasha at Rustchuk. The Turks are masters of the road communicating between Giurgevo and Oltenitza on the left bank of the Danube.

With regard to a second battle, which is asserted to have been followed by the capture of Bucharest, the French *Moniteur* itself limits it to a small defeat inflicted by the Turks on the Russian rear at Frateshti, on the road from Giurgevo to Bucharest. The *Moniteur* adds that an Anglo-French corps of 25,000 men has joined the Turks, that the allied forces concentrated amount to about 60,000 men, that Prince Gorchakoff is at the head of a force nearly equal in numbers, and that a great battle might be expected, decisive of the fate of Bucharest. Frateshti is a small fortified place, about twelve miles from Giurgevo and thirty miles from Bucharest. According to the *Moniteur*, the battle at this place was fought on the 11th,[c] but according to the *Journal des Débats*, on

---

[a] Reprint from *Der Lloyd* of July 13, 1854 in the *Journal des Débats*, July 18, 1854.— *Ed.*

[b] Ibid.— *Ed.*

[c] *Le Moniteur universel*, No. 197, July 16, 1854.— *Ed.*

the 14th inst.[a] The Russians are said to have had 700 wounded in this affair, including two generals.[b]

The last Marseilles steamer from Constantinople reports the capture of the Sulina mouth of the Danube by the English steamer *Terrible*. It is said to have entered the Roads, to have destroyed the Russian fortifications, dispersed the garrison and captured its commander.[c] The news appears to me to require more positive confirmation.

A rumor circulated by English journals, which is, however, not repeated by any French paper, pretends that Admiral Lyons is cruising before Anapa with a view to support an expedition of Admiral Bruat, who is said to have on board 7,000 men for landing.

Letters from Constantinople state that the Porte shows a disposition, on the representations of the English and French Ministers,[d] to resume immediately commercial relations with Greece on the following conditions: 1. That Greece engage herself to pay at convenient terms the expenses of the war and an indemnity for the pillage organized by the late insurrectionists; and 2. That she sign, within two months, the commercial treaty hitherto declined. This treaty acknowledges the actual limits of the Turkish and Greek territories.

No news from the Baltic. The *Hamburger Correspondent* describes the result of the English marauding expedition on the Finnish coast, in its effects on the mind of the Finlanders, as follows:

"It is confirmed that the Russian Government, assured since the burning of Brahestad and Uleaborg, upon the sentiments of the Finnish population along the two gulfs, has ordered arms to be distributed among the able-bodied men, with a view of enabling them to resist all fresh attempts of disembarkment of the English squadrons. The immediate creation of two battalions of Finnish riflemen, of 1,000 men each, has been sanctioned, and the recruitment is to take place in the districts of Abo, Vasa, and Uleaborg. A greater number of these battalions is successively to be formed in the other provinces."

The Austrian loan turns out to be a forced contribution, as I predicted.[e] The whole is now to be distributed on the different crown lands of the empire; for instance, Upper Austria has to take 115,000,000 florins, Lower Austria 15,000,000, Vienna 2,500,000,

[a] *Journal des Débats*, July 17, 1854.— *Ed.*
[b] Stepan Khrulev and David Bebutov. These data are given according to the report of the Vienna correspondent. *The Times*, No. 21798, July 20, 1854.— *Ed.*
[c] Report of the Vienna correspondent. *The Times*, No. 21795, July 17, 1854.— *Ed.*
[d] Wyse and Rouen.— *Ed.*
[e] See this volume, pp. 288-89.— *Ed.*

Hungary 70,000,000, etc., in proportion. If the Emperor of Russia has not obtained anything for himself, he has at least contrived to plunge all the other governments into a serious quarrel with their subjects about the question of cash. The Prussians will have to pay an increased income tax on the lst of August. Bonaparte, too, is said to be projecting another loan of 500,000,000, the effect of which on France will not be diminished by the present prospects of the wine and corn harvest, and the stagnation of trade, especially at Lyons since the outbreak in Spain. An appeal to the English pockets is also contemplated by the Coalition Ministry, and expected for next week.

The Spanish insurrection appears to assume a new aspect, as is evident from the proclamations of Dulce and O'Donnell,[a] the former of whom is a partisan of Espartero, and the latter was a stout adherent of Narvaez and perhaps secretly of Queen Cristina. O'Donnell having convinced himself that the Spanish towns are not to be set in motion this time by a mere palace-revolution, suddenly exhibits liberal principles. His proclamation is dated from Manzanares, a borough of the Mancha, not far from Ciudad Real. It says that his aim is to preserve the throne, but to remove the camarilla; the rigorous observation of the fundamental laws; the amelioration of the election and press laws; the diminution of taxes; advancement in the civil service according to merit; decentralization, and establishment of a national militia on a broad basis. It proposes provincial juntas and a general assembly of Cortes at Madrid, to be charged with the revision of the laws. The proclamation of General Dulce is even more energetic. He says:

"There are no longer Progresistas and Moderados; all of us are Spaniards, and imitators of the men of July 7th 1822. Return to the Constitution of 1837; maintenance of Isabella II; perpetual exile of the Queen Mother; destitution of the present Ministry; re-establishment of peace in our country; such is the end we pursue at every cost, as we shall show on the field of honor to the traitors whom we shall punish for their culpable folly."

According to the *Journal des Débats*, papers and correspondence have been seized at Madrid which are said to prove beyond doubt that it is the secret aim of the insurgents to declare the throne vacant, to reunite the Iberian Peninsula into one State, and to offer the crown to Don Pedro V, Prince of Saxe-Coburg-Gotha.[b]

---

[a] The proclamations of Dulce and O'Donnell were published in the *Journal des Débats* on July 17, 1854.— *Ed.*

[b] S. de Sacy, Account of current events. *Journal des Débats*, July 16, 1854.— *Ed.*

The tender interest taken by *The Times* in the Spanish insurrection, and the simultaneous presence of the said Don Pedro in England, appears indeed to indicate that some new Coburg dodge is afloat. The Court is evidently very uneasy, as all possible Ministerial combinations have been tried, Isturiz and Martinez de la Rosa having been applied to in vain. The *Messager de Bayonne* asserts that the Count de Montemolin left Naples as soon as he received news of the insurrection.

O'Donnell has entered Andalusia, having crossed the Sierra Morena in three columns, one marching by Carolina, the other by Pozo Blanco, and the third by Despeñaperros. The *Gaceta* confesses that Colonel Buceta succeeded in surprising Cuenca, by the possession of which place the insurgents have secured their communications with Valencia. In the latter province the rising now comprises about four or five towns, besides Alcira where the Government troops received a severe check.

It is stated also that a movement had broken out at Reus in Catalonia, and the *Messager de Bayonne* adds that disturbances had taken place in Aragon.

> "Aimes-tu le front, sevère,
> Du sa(i)ge Napoléon?
> Aimes-tu que l'Angleterre,
> T'oppose Lord Palmerston?"[a]

With this apostrophic song, the embarkation of the French troops at Calais has been celebrated.

In order to really oppose Lord Palmerston to the Czar, immense movements have shaken the town from Saturday to Monday, with a view to put him in the place of the Duke of Newcastle. Great agitation has prevailed once more in the ministerial, as well as in the opposition camp. It was known that the estimates for the new ministry of war were to be laid before the House on Monday night,[b] and this occasion was to be seized to make a murderous onslaught on the Coalition, and to place the invincible Palmerston in the War Ministry.

"On Saturday a Cabinet Council was summoned before two o'clock. Ministers did not assemble until three. They then met with the exception of the Foreign Secretary, who was detained by an audience with the Queen. Lord Clarendon joined his colleagues at four. Their deliberations then lasted until half past six, and

---

[a] Are you fond of wise Napoleon's stern looks?
Are you glad that England opposed Lord Palmerston to you?— *Ed.*
[b] July 17, 1854.— *Ed.*

immediately upon the breaking up of the Council Lord Aberdeen proceeded to the palace of Her Majesty." [a]

You may see from this excited narrative of *The Morning Herald* how greatly the hopes of the Tories were raised by these "important" moves. Lord John Russell summoned his adherents to Whitehall for Monday, and Mr. Disraeli, in his turn, assembled the Opposition members. One hundred and seventy-nine gentlemen presented themselves at Whitehall, almost in hysterics with the anticipation of the great revelations intended for them by Russell. They were most deplorably deceived by the Parliamentary Squeers, [b] who drily told them that the vote of the war-estimate being a matter of course, he expected them to be quiet and behave:

"The Cabinet would shortly want more money for carrying on the war, and so the question of confidence or no confidence in the Coalition would be taken next week, when such money vote would be presented to the House." [c]

Not being initiated in the secrets of Lord Clarendon, he could not give them any information on the state of foreign affairs. Well, the result was that Russell saved the whole Coalition for the present session; for, if the vote of confidence had been taken on the estimates of the War Ministry, a defeat would have been a victory of Palmerston over Newcastle, while on the general war estimates a vote of non-confidence would be a victory of the Tories over the combined Whig Peelites—an eventuality, of course, out of the question.

Accordingly, the votes for the War Ministry were taken last night in a very quiet House, nothing occurring but a delivery by Russell and Pakington of all the stale common-places on the present military administration.

It is to be regretted that the obstinate resistance of the Queen keeps Lord Palmerston out of the War Office, as by his installation in that office the last false pretense under which the Radicals yet defend the foreign policy of England would fall to the ground.

On the announcement of Mr. Otway in last Friday's sitting of the Commons, that he would bring the case of Dr. Peitman before them, [d] Lord Palmerston rose and declared that he was ready to

---

[a] *The Morning Herald*, No. 22174, July 17, 1854.— *Ed.*

[b] Ch. Dickens, *The Life and Adventures of Nicholas Nickleby.*— *Ed.*

[c] Lord John Russell's speech on July 17, 1854 is cited from a report in *The Leader*, No. 226, July 22, 1854.— *Ed.*

[d] *The Times*, No. 21794, July 15, 1854. See also this volume, pp. 299-300.— *Ed.*

give every explanation, and that everything would be found to be "all right." Meanwhile, Dr. Peitman has published a letter in *The Morning Advertiser*, which proves that if he never was insane in other respects, he continues to believe in the generosity of Queen Victoria and Prince Albert, whom he petitions to let him go back to Germany—the very thing which they want.

The mean servility of the so-called Radical press is exemplified by its absolute silence on this unexampled case, where a *lettre de cachet*[a] buried a man for eighteen years, just because he had the misfortune to know something of the royal and aristocratic relations with German maid-servants.

Written on July 18, 1854

First published in the *New-York Daily Tribune*, No. 4147, August 3; reprinted in the *New-York Semi-Weekly Tribune*, No. 959, August 4, 1854

Signed: *Karl Marx*

Reproduced from the *New-York Daily Tribune*

---

[a] Royal warrant for arrest and imprisonment.— *Ed.*

Karl Marx

[THE SPANISH REVOLUTION.— GREECE AND TURKEY] [223]

London, Friday, July 21, 1854

"*Ne touchez pas à la Reine*" (Touch not the Queen) is an old Castilian maxim, but the adventurous Madame Muñoz[a] and her daughter Isabella have too long overstepped the rights of even Castilian Queens not to have outworn the loyal prejudices of the Spanish people.

The pronunciamentos of 1843 [224] lasted three months; those of 1854 have scarcely lasted as many weeks. The Ministry is dissolved, Count San Luis has fled, Queen Cristina is trying to reach the French frontier, and at Madrid both troops and citizens have declared against the Government.

The revolutionary movements of Spain since the commencement of the century offer a remarkably uniform aspect, with the exception of the movements in favor of provincial and local privileges which periodically agitate the northern provinces, every palace-plot being attended by military insurrections, and these invariably dragging municipal pronunciamentos in their train. There are two causes for this phenomenon. In the first place, we find that what we call the State in a modern sense has, from the exclusively provincial life of the people, no national embodiment in opposition to the Court, except in the army. In the second place, the peculiar position of Spain and the Peninsular war [225] created conditions under which it was only in the army that everything vital in the Spanish nationality was permitted to concentrate. Thus it happens that the only national demonstrations (those of 1812 and of 1822 [226]) proceeded from the army;

---

[a] María Cristina.— *Ed.*

and thus the movable part of the nation has been accustomed to regard the army as the natural instrument of every national rising. During the troublesome epoch from 1830 to 1854, however, the cities of Spain came to know that the army, instead of continuing to uphold the cause of the nation, was changed into an instrument for the rivalries of the ambitious pretenders to the military guardianship of the Court. Consequently, we find the movement of 1854 very different even from that of 1843. The *émeute* of General O'Donnell was looked upon by the peoples as anything but a conspiracy against the leading influence at the Court, especially as it was supported by the ex-favorite Serrano. The towns and country accordingly demurred to giving any response to the appeal made by the cavalry of Madrid. It was thus that General O'Donnell was forced to alter entirely the character of his operations, in order not to remain isolated and exposed to failure. He was forced to insert in his proclamation three points[a] equally opposed to the supremacy of the army: the convocation of the Cortes, an economical Government, and the formation of a national militia—the last demand originating in the desire of the towns to recover their independence of the army. It is a fact, then, that the military insurrection has obtained the support of a popular insurrection only by submitting to the conditions of the latter. It remains to be seen whether it will be constrained to adhere to them and to execute these promises.

With the exception of the Carlists,[227] all parties have raised their cry—Progresistas, partisans of the Constitution of 1837,[228] partisans of the Constitution of 1812, Unionists (demanding the annexation of Portugal), and Republicans. The news concerning the latter party is to be received with caution, since it has to pass the censure of the Paris police. Beside these party struggles, the rival pretensions of the military leaders are in full development. Espartero had no sooner heard of the success of O'Donnell than he left his retreat at Leganes and declared himself the chief of the movement. But as soon as Caesar Narvaez learned of the appearance of his old Pompey in the field, he forthwith offered his services to the Queen, which were accepted, and he is to form a new Ministry. From the details I am about to give you, it will be seen that the military has by no means taken the initiative in all places, but that in some they have had to yield to the overpowering pressure of the population.

---

[a] See this volume, p. 305.— *Ed.*

Besides the pronunciamentos in Valencia, reported in my last,[a] there has been one at Alicante. In Andalusia, pronunciamentos have taken place at Granada, Seville and Jaen. In Old Castile, there has been a pronunciamento at Burgos; in Leon, at Valladolid; in Biscay, at San Sebastian and Vitoria; in Navarre, at Tolosa, Pamplona and Guipuzcoa; in Aragon, at Saragossa; in Catalonia, at Barcelona, Tarragona, Lerida and Gerona; there is said, also, to have been a pronunciamento in the Islas Baleares. In Murcia, pronunciamentos were expected to take place, according to a letter from Cartagena, dated July 12, which says:

"In consequence of a *bando*[b] published by the Military Governor of the place, all the inhabitants of Cartagena possessed of muskets and other arms, have been ordered to depose them with the civil authorities within twenty-four hours. On the demand of the Consul of France,[c] the Government has allowed the French residents to depose their arms, as in 1848, at the Consulate."[d]

Of all these pronunciamentos, four only deserve particular mention, viz.: those of San Sebastian in Biscay, Barcelona the capital of Catalonia, Saragossa the capital of Aragon, and Madrid.

In Biscay the pronunciamentos originated with the Municipalities, in Aragon with the military. The Municipality of San Sebastian was pronouncing in favor of the insurrection, when the demand for the armament of the people was raised. The city was immediately covered with arms. Not till the 17th could the two battalions garrisoning the town be induced to join. The fusion between the citizens and the military having been completed, 1,000 armed citizens accompanied by some troops set out for Pamplona, and organized the insurrection in Navarre. It was only the appearance of the armed citizens from San Sebastian which facilitated the rising of the Navarrese capital. General Zabala joined the movement afterward and went to Bayonne, inviting the soldiers and officers of the Cordova regiment, who had fled there upon their late defeat at Saragossa, immediately to return to their country and to meet him at San Sebastian. According to some reports he subsequently marched upon Madrid to place himself under the orders of Espartero, while other reports state that he was on the march to Saragossa to join the Aragonese insurgents.[e]

[a] See this volume, p. 306.—*Ed.*
[b] Order.—*Ed.*
[c] Ligier.—*Ed.*
[d] *Le Moniteur universel*, No. 201, July 20, 1854.—*Ed.*
[e] Telegraphic dispatch from Paris of July 21, 1854. *The Times*, No. 21799, July 21, 1854.—*Ed.*

General Mazarredo, the commander of the Basque provinces, refusing to take part in the pronunciamento of Vitoria, was obliged to retire to France. The troops under orders of General Zabala are two battalions of the regiment of Bourbon, a battalion of carabiniers, and a detachment of cavalry. Before dismissing the subject of the Basque provinces I may state as something characteristic, that the Brigadier Barrastegui, who has been named Governor of Guipuzcoa, is one of Espartero's former aides-de-camp.

At Barcelona the initiative was apparently taken by the military, but the spontaneity of their act becomes very doubtful from the additional information we have received. On the 13th of July, at 7 o'clock P.M., the soldiers occupying the barracks of San Pablo, and of the Buen Suceso, yielded to the demonstrations of the populace and declared their pronunciamento, under the cry of *Vive la Reine; Vive la Constitution*; death to the Ministers; away with Cristina! After having fraternized with the mass, and marched along with them over the Rambla, they halted at the Plaza of the Constitution. The cavalry, kept indoors at the Barceloneta[a] for the previous six days, because of the distrust it inspired to the Captain-General, made a pronunciamento in its turn. From this moment the whole garrison passed over to the people, and all resistance on the part of the authorities became impossible. At 10 o'clock General Marchesi, the Military Governor, yielded to the general pressure, and at midnight the Captain-General of Catalonia[b] announced his resolution to side with the movement. He went to the place of the *Ayuntamiento* where he harangued the people, filling the place. On the 18th, a junta was formed composed of the Captain-General and other eminent persons, with the cry of the Constitution, the Queen and Morality. Further news from Barcelona states that some workmen had been shot on the order of the new authorities, because they had destroyed machinery and violated property; also, that a Republican Committee convened in a neighboring town, had been arrested[c]; but it should be recollected that this news passes through the hands of the Second of December[229] whose special vocation it is to calumniate republicans and workmen.

---

[a] A suburb of Barcelona situated on the peninsula (partly artificial) which separates the port of Barcelona from the open sea.— *Ed.*

[b] La Rocha.— *Ed.*

[c] This information is given according to the official French Bonapartist newspapers *Le Moniteur universel*, Nos. 200 and 201, July 19 and 20 and the *Journal des Débats*, July 21, 1854.— *Ed.*

At Saragossa it is said that the initiative proceeded from the military—a statement which becomes invalidated, however, by the additional remark that the formation of a militia corps was immediately resolved upon. So much is certain, and is confirmed by the Madrid *Gaceta* itself,[a] that before the pronunciamento of Saragossa 150 soldiers of the Montesa regiment (cavalry) on the march to Madrid and quartered at Torrejon (five leagues[b] from Madrid) revolted and abandoned their chiefs, who arrived at Madrid on the evening of the 13th with the regimental chest. The soldiers, under command of Captain Baraiban, mounted horse and took the road to Huete, being supposed to intend joining the force under Colonel Buceta at Cuenca. As for Madrid, against which Espartero is said to be marching with the "army of the center," and General Zabala, with the army of the north, it was natural that a town which subsists upon the Court should be the last to join in the insurrectionary movement. The *Gaceta* of the 15th inst. still published a bulletin from the Minister of War[c] asserting the factions to be in flight, and the enthusiastic loyalty of the troops increasing. Count San Luis, who seems to have very correctly judged of the situation at Madrid, announced to the workmen that General O'Donnell and the anarchists would deprive them of all employment, while if the Government succeeded, it would employ all workingmen on the public works for six reals (75 cents) a day. By this stratagem San Luis hoped to enroll the most excitable portion of the Madrileños under his banner. His success, however, was like that of the party of the *National* at Paris in 1848.[230] The allies he had thus gained soon became his most dangerous enemies—the funds for their support being exhausted on the sixth day. How much the Government dreaded a pronunciamento in the capital is evident from General Lara's (the Governor's) proclamation forbidding the circulation of any news respecting the progress of the insurrection.[d] It appears, further, that the tactics of General Blaser were restricted to the care of avoiding any contact with the insurgents, lest his troops should catch the infection. It is said that the first plan of General O'Donnell was to meet the Ministerial troops on the plains of La

---

[a] The data from the Madrid *Gaceta* given here and below have been taken from the reprint in *Le Moniteur universel*, Nos. 200 and 201, July 19 and 20, 1854.— *Ed.*

[b] A league is equal to 4.83 kilometres.— *Ed.*

[c] Blaser y San Martin. Bulletin of July 15, 1854, *Le Moniteur universel*, No. 201, July 20, 1854.— *Ed.*

[d] General Lara's proclamation of June 28, 1854. *Le Moniteur universel*, No. 185, July 4, 1854.— *Ed.*

Mancha, so favorable to cavalry operations. This plan, however, was abandoned in consequence of the arrival of ex-favorite Serrano, who was in connection with several of the principal towns of Andalusia. The Constitutional army thereupon determined, instead of remaining in La Mancha, to march upon Jaen and Seville.

It may be observed, *en passant*, that the *boletines*[a] of General Blaser bear a wonderful resemblance to the orders of the day of the Spanish generals of the sixteenth century, which gave such occasion for hilarity to Francis I, and of the eighteenth century, which Frederick the Great turned into ridicule.

It is plain that this Spanish insurrection must become a source of dissension between the Governments of France and England, and the report given by a French paper that General O'Donnell was concealed previous to the outbreak, in the palace of the British Embassador,[b] is not likely to lessen the misgivings of Bonaparte on its account. There exists already some commencement of irritation between Bonaparte and Victoria; Bonaparte expected to meet the Queen at the embarkation of his troops from Calais, but Her Majesty answered his desire by a visit to the ex-Queen Amélie on the same day. Again, the English Ministers when interpellated about the non-blockade of the White Sea, the Black Sea, and the sea of Azov, alleged as their excuse the alliance with France. Bonaparte retorted by an announcement of those very blockades in the *Moniteur*, without waiting for the formal consent of England.[c] Lastly, a bad effect having been produced in France by the embarkation of French troops in British vessels only, Bonaparte published a list of French vessels destined for the same use and applied to it.

The Porte has communicated to the representatives of the four allied powers a note[d] concerning the authority given to the Greek merchant ships again to enter Turkish ports. This authorization is to be valid for two months, on condition that the Greek Government does not render itself guilty of any act justifying its suspension. If, at the expiration of this term, the Greek Government shall have failed to give satisfactory reparation to the

---

[a] Bulletins.— *Ed.*

[b] Sir John Caradoc.— *Ed.*

[c] This information is taken from *Le Moniteur universel*, No. 196, July 15, 1854.— *Ed.*

[d] Marx, apparently, got this information through the Polish or Hungarian refugees in London. The text of the note was published later in the *Journal des Débats* on July 28, 1854.— *Ed.*

Porte, the latter reserves to itself the right of reestablishing the actual *status quo.* Greek ships in the Turkish ports will be subject to the local authorities, and deprived of any appeal to other protection. Within the two months the basis of an arrangement and of a commercial treaty will be negotiated. The indemnity claimed by the Porte for the immense damage done by the Greek insurrection is to be regulated by arbitration, on the report of a committee of inquiry, to be sent to the proper places, and composed of Frenchmen, Englishmen, Turks and Greeks.

Shamyl has been officially invested by the Porte with the title of Generalissimo of the army of Circassia and Georgia.

Three dragomans in the service of the French army have been shot at Varna, all of them having been found to correspond with the Russians. Two of them were Greeks and one Armenian. At the moment of his execution, one of them swallowed a paper of a compromising character.

We are informed from Hermannstadt, on the 16th inst., that no engagement has yet taken place in the vicinity of Frateshti.[a]

The arrival of the allied forces at Rustchuk was, of course, a lie,[b] and their whole aim, in the present instance, will be to keep under restraint—as *The Times* calls it—the barbarous fury of the victorious Turks.[c]

Written on July 21, 1854

First published in the *New-York Daily Tribune*, No. 4148, August 4; reprinted in the *New-York Semi-Weekly Tribune*, No. 960, August 8 and the *New-York Weekly Tribune*, No. 674, August 12, 1854

Signed: *Karl Marx*

Reproduced from the *New-York Daily Tribune*

---

[a] *Le Moniteur universel,* No. 202, July 21, 1854.—*Ed.*
[b] See this volume, p. 303.—*Ed.*
[c] *The Times,* No. 21799, July 21, 1854, leader.—*Ed.*

Karl Marx

THE WAR DEBATES IN PARLIAMENT[231]

London, Tuesday, July 25, 1854

At last Thursday's evening sitting of the House of Commons, in reply to an inquiry of Mr. Disraeli, Lord J. Russell stated that her Majesty had been pleased to order that a message should be sent to the House, in pursuance of which he proposed to move on Monday a vote of credit for £3,000,000. There would be no necessity for a Committee of Ways and Means.[a] To Mr. Disraeli's question whether there would be an autumnal session this year, Lord John gave no reply. Accordingly the vote of credit was accomplished without a division, in the sitting of both Houses which took place yesterday.[b]

In the House of Lords, Lord Aberdeen, in moving the vote, delivered the shortest, dryest, and most common-place speech that ever he has favored us with since his accession to the Premiership. He had to ask for three millions, and he was sure their lordships would have no objection. They might entertain different opinions, but all of them must be unanimous as "to the necessity of adopting all such measures as were best calculated to lead to an early and successful termination of the war." This result was mainly to be produced "by the activity and energy of the efforts of England and France, with the concurrence of the other powers." He did not say whether he meant the efforts to be made by war, or negotiation; nor even exclude Russia from "the other powers" with whom England and France are to concur. Parliament being about to be prorogued, there was so much more reason to provide

---

[a] See Debates in Parliament in *The Times*, No. 21799, July 21, 1854.— *Ed.*

[b] The debate on the budget in Parliament on July 24, 1854 is given according to *The Times*, No. 21802, July 25, 1854.— *Ed.*

the Government with money. Possibly some noble lords might prefer to see the money intrusted to other hands than his, but such fanciful wishes ought not to interfere with business. Which business, the business on hand, was to vote three millions of pounds.

The Earl of Ellenborough, who has the particular gift of never speaking to the question, thought this the fittest occasion for recommending the Government "to carry the most searching economy into all those civil departments which have no connection with the war."

The Earl of Hardwicke saw a very great force in the Baltic ready for any emergency, a similar force in the Black Sea, and the greatest army sent out that ever left this country. He did not know what the Government intended to do with them, and, therefore, he appealed to every noble Lord to grant the credit demanded from them.

Earl Fitzwilliam, an out-of-place Whig, protested against "this country being described as being the highest taxed in Europe; it ought to be described as that in which the taxes fall more lightly on the people than in any other section of the European commonwealth." If the noble Lord had spoken of the lords instead of the people, he would have been right. "As to the speech of his noble friend at the head of the Government," there had never been made one on such an occasion "of which it might be more truly said that it conveyed scarcely a single idea to the House addressed," and the noble Lord ought to know better what the wants of the House are in respect to ideas. Earl Fitz-William desired to learn from Lord Aberdeen who were "the other powers," whose concurrence he was anxious to have? Perhaps Austria? He feared they might be induced by that power to consider certain minor objects, as the evacuation of the Principalities, and the free navigation of the Danube, as justifying them in concluding peace. (Ridiculous fear, since Lord Aberdeen will certainly not be induced by any one to demand so much.) He wanted also to know what was to be understood by the integrity of Turkey—whether it was that circumscribed by the treaty of Adrianople,[232] or something else? Finally, he considered that they found themselves in a very singular position, Parliament having no information whatever of the intentions of the Government. Accordingly he would vote for the credit.

The Marquis of Clanricarde, whose temper is getting sourer each day which separates him further from office, claimed at least some explanation as his due for the unexampled liberality with

which he had hitherto treated the ministry—an explanation
respecting the progress which had been made and the course
pursued since the former supplies were asked for; he wanted to
know something of the conditions and prospects of the war, and
of the state of the country with respect to its allies. There had
been successes on the side of the Turks, but not on the side of the
British government or the British arms, which should not prevent
him, however, from passing a eulogium on the bravery of the
sailors in the Baltic and Black Sea. As to the relations with their
allies he would fix a day when he would move the production of
the recent treaty entered into between Turkey and Austria,[a] as
well as of other documents likely to throw a light on their present
position.

"From general rumor it appeared that through the pressure and persuasion of
the British government, the Divan, which was much averse to it, and the Turkish
minister[b] recently concluded a convention with Austria, by which the Austrian
troops were to enter the Danubian provinces, and occupy a portion of the Turkish
empire."

How was it that, at the hour of danger, Austria, instead of
hurrying into the field, held back and commenced fresh negotiations? He wanted also to know whether the Vienna Conferences
went on,[233] and what they were consulting about? On the whole
they depended too much on the German Powers.

In order to prove that Austria "ought" to be the best possible
ally, Lord Clarendon showed how she was circumscribed and
threatened by Russia in all parts of her dominions. The
Austro-Turkish treaty could not have been laid before the House,
no ratified copy of it having been received as yet. He thought he
might assure them that the time was not far distant when they
should have Austria cooperating with them; he "answered,
however, for nothing." Still, from the general character of Austria,
and from his own administration of the Foreign Office, their
lordships were satisfied to draw the most cheering conclusions.
Having twice been convicted of the most unblushing falsehoods,
Lord Clarendon naturally expects implicit belief in his assurance

"that there is no intention of returning to the *status quo*, and that there is no
intention of listening to a patched-up peace, which could only be a hollow truce,
and which would render a return to war inevitable."

After this brilliant display of their own highly educated minds,

---

[a] See this volume, pp. 269-71.— *Ed.*
[b] Reshid Pasha.— *Ed.*

the Lords naturally turned to the subject of national education, and we will leave them there.

During the discussion in the Lords the Commons were occupied upon several indifferent subjects, until the speech of Lord Aberdeen was communicated to them, which produced "a disagreeable sensation." Lord John Russell perceived at once that it was necessary to produce a counter sensation.

When the first extraordinary grant was about to be asked, the Government dispatched the "magnificent" Baltic fleet; on the occasion of the second one, the famous bombardment of Odessa had to serve as a catcher; now the watchword selected was Sevastopol.

Lord John began by certifying to the "patriotic" spirit of the House in having given its aid so liberally when asked for the first grants, and thanked the House for having hitherto so judiciously abstained from putting any embarrassing questions to the Government. Great, very great things had been achieved thereby, namely, a very great number of ships and men had been procured. Of first, second and third-rate steamers they had now 17, against only one on the 1st of January, 1853; of sailing line-of-battle ships 17 against 11; and a marine force of 57,200 against 33,910. They had also placed on the Turkish shores a force of above 30,000 soldiers, "a great part of which was lately at Varna." So much for the material of war. As to the operations of war, they had

"but just commenced, and all he could say was, that the Turkish army had performed deeds of valor. Nobody would now say that it required only a fillip from the Emperor of Russia to overthrow the whole Ottoman Power. Beside the chivalrous deeds of the Turks, the glories of this war consisted in the perfect union and harmony between the French and English armies."

Now, with respect to the vote he asked for, he could not tell them what the money was exactly required for. Some two millions might be absorbed by the Commissariat, ordnance, and transports; besides, a large body of Turkish troops might be joined with the British army and receive pay from the British Government. On the whole, he asked the money not on the ground of detailed estimates, but for the use of the Government, "as it might have occasion for it."

Austria, said the noble Lord, had a greater interest in protecting Turkey than even France or England. The Czar would have the complete command of the Government of Austria as soon as he domineered over the Principalities, with a predominant influence in Turkey. However, to judge Austria justly, it should be borne in

mind with what difficulties she was beset. On more than one side
Russian armies could approach to within no great distance of the
Austrian capital, and on the other hand, some of the kingdoms
submitted to her were so disturbed as to make it a perilous thing
for her to enter into hostilities. It had, therefore, been her policy
to attempt, as long as possible, to obtain the settlement of these
questions by negotiation. But recently she had dispatched a
message to the Emperor of Russia, whose answer could not be
termed evasive.

"Firstly, Russia does not profess herself ready to fix any time for the evacuation
of the Principalities. She states, now that war has been declared, and now that
England and France are engaged in that war, and are superior to her in the Black
Sea and the Baltic, while her fleets do not leave her ports, that there remains only
the seat of war in the Principalities, and the navigation of the Danube, where she
can hope to restore the balance, and by the successes of her arms to obtain a
victory for herself. She therefore declines on those terms the evacuation of the
Principalities."

Russia was ready to adopt the principles contained in the
protocol of the 9th of April,[234] except the admission of Turkey
into the European concert. With regard to the future conduct of
Austria, Lord John considers on the one side that she is mistaken
in her present policy, but on the other he cannot believe that she
will forfeit the engagements into which she has entered. By those
engagements with the western powers and with Turkey, she was
bound to take part in the attempt to drive back Russia. It was
possible that she might attempt again to obtain from St.
Petersburg some better assurance. They, of course, had no control
over the councils of Austria, and Austria had no control over the
King of Prussia. All the powers were, accordingly, in the most
favorable position for jointly counteracting Russia.

Lord John then came to a great and enthusiastic exposition of
what they—England and France—proposed to do. The integrity
of Turkey was not compatible with a return to the *status quo* in
the Principalities. He said:

"But, Sir, there is another mode in which the position of Russia is menacing to
the independence and integrity of Turkey. I mean the establishment of a great
fortress, prepared with all the combinations of art, made as impregnable as it is
possible for art to make it, and containing within its port a very large fleet of
line-of-battle ships, ready at any time to come down with a favorable wind to the
Bosphorus. I say that that is a position so menacing to Turkey, that no treaty of
peace could be considered wise which left the Emperor of Russia in that same
position of menace. (Enormous cheering.) We shall be ready, as we have been
ready, to communicate with the Government of France upon that subject, and I
have every reason to believe, that the views of the Government of the Emperor of
the French coincide with our own in that respect." (Cheers.)

With respect to Mr. Disraeli's proposition of an autumnal session, Lord John "declined to accept at the hand of members of this House restrictions on freedom of ministers."

It would be as tedious as it is superfluous to report the saying of the Humes, Bankes, Knights, Alcoxes, and *tutti quanti,* on this occasion.

Mr. Cobden, believing in the words of Lord John, and thinking that he had turned the House into a council of war, very anxiously labored to show why Sevastopol and the Crimea should on no account be taken. A point of more interest was raised by him through means of the question whether this country was in alliance with the sovereignties against the nationalities. A great delusion prevailed with the people who fancied that the war had been undertaken in favor of any oppressed nationalities. It had, on the contrary, been conducted with a view of riveting still closer the chains by which Hungary and Italy were bound in the grasp of Austria. There were honorable and deluded gentlemen in the House who

"had been crying out that the Government were not carrying on the war as they ought to do, that they ought to have some other man at the head of the War Department; nay, sometimes they had even said, at the head of the Government. They had called out for Lord Palmerston. And this was all done for the interest of Hungary and the Italians. He had heard it from the lips of two of the greatest chiefs of Hungary and of Italy[a] declared, that so far from their hopes and aspirations resting upon that noble Lord, they knew that when the noble Lord had an opportunity of giving them a moral support, he would not so much as lift up his finger in their favor. If there was any member in the present Government at this moment, upon whom these leaders would be less disposed to rely than upon another, it was that noble Lord. He did not believe that the noble Lord was aware of the great imposture practiced in his name, but the delusion had happily exploded."

Mr. Layard and Lord Dudley Stuart did nothing but repeat their old speeches, with this variation, that Lord Dudley's opinion of the magic force of the name "Palmerston" was "more exalted than ever."

It was reserved for Mr. Disraeli to blow up by one single breath the whole bubble speech of Lord John. Having briefly justified his proposition of an autumnal session by an allusion to Sinope[235] and other exploits that occurred during the last autumnal vacation, he confessed himself to be surprised, bewildered, alarmed at the announcement of the impending destruction of Sevastopol and the conquest of the Crimea. Lord John here expressed dissent, but did

---

[a] Kossuth and Mazzini.— *Ed.*

Karl Marx

not rise; Mr. Disraeli, however, sitting down on his part, forced Lord John to an explanation. In a voice of humility and confusion he came forward, at last:

"I may as well state that what I said was, that I thought Russia could not be allowed to maintain the menacing attitude she has done by keeping so large a fleet at Sevastopol."

Having elicited this confession from Lord John, Mr. Disraeli delivered one of his most savage and sarcastic speeches on record, which would well repay a perusal in extenso, (it is copied at length below among the news from Great Britain,[236]) and which ended with the following words:

"Really, after what we have heard there seems great unfairness in the painful distinction which is made at times between the policy of Lord Aberdeen and the policy of some of his colleagues. I am no admirer or supporter of Lord Aberdeen, but I am no admirer either of the parliamentary policy which would exonerate members of a Cabinet at the expense of their colleagues. It does not at all appear to me, after the statement which the noble Lord opposite has made of what it was he says he said, that his policy as to Russia, substantially differs from that of Lord Aberdeen, and this, after all, is some satisfaction to the people of England. We have not, then, a divided Cabinet; the session at last closes upon Ministers in unison upon this subject; and, so far as conducting the war with small purposes goes, so far as having from great objects of policy mean and insignificant results, the Coalition Government appear to be unanimous."

Lord Palmerston's jokes were of no use. After the speech of Mr. Disraeli, and a number of other members having risen to protest that they had been entirely deluded by Lord John's first speech, the motion for the supply was indeed voted, but only on the condition that the debates should be resumed to-night, Lord Dudley Stuart announcing at the same time his intention to move an address to the Queen,

"praying that she would be graciously pleased not to prorogue Parliament until she might be enabled to afford the House more full information with respect to the relations existing with foreign powers, and of her views and prospects in the contest in which her Majesty was engaged."

Written on July 25, 1854

First published in the *New-York Daily Tribune*, No. 4150, August 7; reprinted in the *New-York Semi-Weekly Tribune*, No. 960, August 8 and the *New-York Weekly Tribune*, No. 674, August 12, 1854

Signed: *Karl Marx*

Reproduced from the *New-York Daily Tribune*

Karl Marx

[THE POLICY OF AUSTRIA.—
THE WAR DEBATES IN THE HOUSE OF COMMONS] [237]

London, Friday, July 28, 1854

In one of my former letters I gave you an analysis of the Austro-Turkish Treaty of the 14th of June,[a] and stated as the purposes aimed at by that curious diplomatic transaction: 1st. To give the allied armies a pretext for not crossing the Danube, and for not confronting the Russians; 2d. To prevent the Turks from reoccupying the whole of Wallachia, and forcing them out of that part which they had already conquered: 3d. To restore in the Principalities the old Reactionary Government, forced upon the Roumans by Russia in 1848. We are now actually informed from Constantinople, that Austria has protested against Omer Pasha's presumption in crossing the Danube; that she claims an exclusive occupation of the Principalities for herself, and the right of shutting them not only against the Anglo-French troops, but equally against the Turks. Upon this remonstrance, the Porte is said to have forwarded orders to Omer Pasha not to cross the Danube for the present, while refusing to admit, in principle, the exclusive occupation of the Principalities by Austria. Wretched Pasha[b] who has learned something from his master and contriver, Lord Palmerston, has of course little objection to admitting in fact what he refuses in principle. You may perhaps think that Austria has already violated as well as practically canceled the treaty of the 14th June, by not entering Wallachia at the moment when the Russian army was disorderly retreating in three different directions, and was exposed in the flank and the rear to an Austrian

---

[a] See this volume, pp. 269-71.— *Ed.*
[b] Reshid Pasha. See this volume, p. 291.— *Ed.*

attack, if it had failed to retire at once behind the Sereth. Only remember that by the very words of this famous treaty Austria is bound neither to enter the Principalities at once, nor to leave them at any exact epoch, nor even to force the Russians to evacuate them within any definite term. It is now stated that the Austrians are really entering Little Wallachia, and that the Russians are recalling their troops from the Carpathian passes and concentrating them at Fokshani. This, however, means nothing but that the Austrians, instead of expelling the Russians from Great Wallachia, have resolved to eject the Turks from Little Wallachia, thus preventing their operations on the banks of the Aluta. It is evident that no better contrivance could have been imagined to work up a military insurrection in Turkey than their exclusion from the territory conquered by the Turkish army, and by an occupation of Bulgaria through Anglo-French troops, who are fully avoiding the Russians, keep the Turks under a sort of state of siege—as you may see from the common proclamation of the Anglo-French commanders to the inhabitants of Bulgaria—a proclamation almost literally copied from a Budberg, a Gorchakoff and *tutti quanti*. I have told you long before this that the western powers would render one service to progress—the service of revolutionizing Turkey, that keystone of the antiquated European system.[a]

Besides the protest against the Turkish presumption of occupying Turkish territories, Austria demands the reinstallation of the two hospodars now residing at Vienna, whose return to Wallachia and Moldavia, along with the first Austrian troops, Herr von Bruck has announced to the Porte. Reshid Pasha replies that the Porte will take the propriety of their restoration into consideration—Herr von Bruck, on his part, insisting, however, on the fulfillment of Article III of the Convention, which stipulates the reestablishment of the late Government. It will be remembered that I called attention to the ambiguous construction liable to be put on this article.[b] Reshid Pasha retorts that this reestablishment could not take place before the Porte had made sure that the hospodars had not failed in their duty as loyal subjects. The Porte had no serious complaints against Prince Ghica of Moldavia, but the conduct of Stirbey, the hospodar of Wallachia, had been very compromising, having proved himself a partisan of Russia in the most scandalous manner, so that his expulsion had been imposed upon the Porte. Herr von Bruck then appealed to the Sultan, who

---

[a] See this volume, pp. 70-72 and 129-31.—*Ed.*
[b] Ibid., p. 270.—*Ed.*

assembled an extraordinary Council, in which the compromise was made that both hospodars should be recalled to their posts *provisionally*, while the Porte would appoint a High Commissioner to inquire into their conduct, and then come to a definitive resolution. Now it will be at once understood that Prince Ghica, against whom Reshid pretends to have no serious objections, is only nominally recalled, Moldavia remaining in the hands of the Russians. The recall of Prince Stirbey, expelled by the Porte itself, and stigmatized as a Russian agent, is, on the contrary, a real restoration, as a portion of Wallachia is already evacuated by the Russians, and the other likely to become so at no distant time.

But the action of Austrian diplomacy does not stop there. We read in yesterday's *Morning Post*, dated Belgrade, July 19[a]:

"An order arrived yesterday, from Constantinople, immediately to suspend all armaments and military exercises. It is confidently stated that there is another order for disarmament. The intelligence was forwarded at once to Prince Alexander." [b]

This, then, is the answer of the Porte to the Servian protest against an Austrian occupation. Thus that miserable Turkish Government is simultaneously prevented from thwarting its avowed enemy, and driven into hostile and usurpatory acts against its own loyal dependencies. By the treaty of the 14th June it broke its Conventions with the Principalities, and by the order for disarmament it breaks the fundamental laws of Servia.[238] By the same stroke of policy, the Turkish army is worked into a state of insurrection, and Servia and the Principalities are thrown into the arms of Russia. The Austrian summons for the evacuation of the Principalities turns out to be a prohibition to the Turks to enter them, and the boasted armaments of Austria to be the disarmament of Servia.

With all that stupid Austria, a mere tool in the hands of the Czar and his English confederates, is only preparing the elements of a general revolution, the first victim of which she herself will be, and of which nobody can complain except utopian reactionaries like David Urquhart.

You are already informed of the first movements in Italy. The public papers speak of riots at Genoa, Modena, Parma, &c.[c]; but,

---

[a] Telegraphic dispatch from Belgrade of July 19. *The Morning Post*, No. 25137, July 27, 1854.— *Ed.*

[b] Alexander Karageorgević.— *Ed.*

[c] Telegraphic dispatch from Vienna of July 25. *The Times*, No. 21803, July 26, 1854.— *Ed.*

in my opinion, the scenes which have occurred at Ferrara remind us more of the general insurrection of 1848 than all the rest.

That I have justly characterized, from the first, the patriotic voluntary loan of the arrogant and bankrupt Austrian Government,[a] you will see from the notification Chevalier le Burger has lately addressed to the loyal subjects of Lombardy. He informs them that the quota the Lombardian territory has to pay to the voluntary loan will amount to 40,000,000 florins, equivalent to 104,400,000 francs, which, divided among the population, makes 40 francs per head.

"This voluntary loan," says the *Unione*, "resolves itself into a gigantic confiscation—every province, every commune and every individual being assigned a quota which it *must* pay *voluntarily*."

In order to leave no doubt as to the true meaning of this voluntary loan, the notification of Chevalier Burger ends in the following terms:

"It must be more than evident, that in case the voluntary loan should not succeed, an extraordinary and forced contribution must be levied upon the various elements of the produce of land, capital, commerce and industry in the most convenient proportions."

At Monday's sitting of the Commons,[b] for the first time in the annals of Parliament, the Lord President of the Ministry[c] and Leader of the House rose on the pretext of giving a deliberate exposition of the intentions of the Cabinet, which he completely recanted six hours later in the same place. At 7 P.M. Sevastopol was bombarded, dismantled, destroyed and dismembered from Russia. At 1.15 A.M. the Russian fleet at Sevastopol was to be reduced by one or two sail of the line, and "Russia by no means to be disturbed in her present rank and position." During six hours little Johnny brawled, swaggered, bullied, hectored, rodomontized,[d] cheered, congratulated, amplified to his Commoners[239]; during six hours he caused Parliament to revel in "a fool's paradise," when, by no more than one sting of Mr. Disraeli's tongue, this bubble speech suddenly shrunk together, and the false lion was forced to hang his usual calf-skin round his shoulders. This was a "day of humiliation" for the Ministry, but they carried their three millions of pounds.

---

[a] See this volume, pp. 288-89.— *Ed.*
[b] July 24.— *Ed.*
[c] Lord John Russell.— *Ed.*
[d] Derived from the name of Rodomonte, a character from Ariosto's *L'Orlando furioso.— Ed.*

At Tuesday's sitting the debate on Lord Stuart's motion for the non-adjournment of Parliament took place.[a] They had voted away the money of the country; they could not but vote their confidence in the Ministry. This being generally understood by the honorable members, the House was but thinly attended, the debate dull, the Ministry more provoking than ever, and the motion of Dudley negatived without a division. The Ministry contrived to turn their very disgrace into a victory over the Commoners. This was the "day of humiliation" for Parliament. Nevertheless, the sitting became important from the defense of the warfare furnished by Mr. Herbert, the British Secretary at War, and Woronzoff's brother-in-law; from Berkeley, the Lord of the Admiralty's indiscretions; and from little Johnny's magisterial declarations on the internal state of the English Ministry.

In answer to the complaints about the deficient organization of the commissariat, Mr. Herbert, a thin-headed ex-young Tory, entered into an elaborate eulogy of Commissary-General Filder, who was certainly the fittest man for the place, because, some fifty years ago, he had enjoyed the confidence of the Iron Duke,[b] and held high offices under him. To the disagreeable letters of the newspaper correspondents, he opposed the high-colored reports of "the very best paymasters in the service", and the obligatory compliments of some French officers. He uttered not a word about the army being destitute of any means of transport, being supplied neither with mules nor horses to carry the baggage and the water necessary for an army marching from Varna and Devna toward the Danube, and the other necessaries required on a march. He uttered not a word about the deficient means of the army to supply itself with food. He did not refute the fact that no commissariat was appointed until several divisions of troops had been sent out, and the fleets were at Constantinople. He dared not contradict the assertion that Lord Raglan himself had stated that his troops had been stationed at one place nearly two months, but could not advance from the deficiency of the commissariat, although they were almost within cannonshots hearing of the half-starved enemy.

In a similar way the ingenious brother-in-law of Prince Woronzoff got rid of the complaints on the ordnance. He spent much breath upon an answer to a reproach made by nobody but

---

[a] The parliamentary debates on July 25, 1854 are given according to *The Times*, No. 21803, July 26, 1854.— *Ed.*
[b] Wellington.— *Ed.*

himself, viz: that there were only six-pounders out with the army
in Turkey, while he passed under obstinate silence the facts that
there was no battering train with the army, that the infantry was
almost unsupported by cavalry, the most essential arm for
operations in the plains of Wallachia, and that the 40,000 men at
Varna had not 40 pieces of artillery to oppose to the Russians
where every corps of 40,000 men deploys 120 pieces.

To the attacks on the negligence of the Government in
supplying the army with the necessary implements, the brother-in-
law of Woronzoff answered by an indignant defense of the
military commanders who were ·not at all to blame.

As to the fatal accidents and the British monopoly of fatal
accidents, none of which happened to the French expedition, the
Hon. Mr. Herbert replied, first, that it was true that a ship which
carried out a portion of the 6th Dragoons was lost by fire, but that
the commander,

"a noble old man, faced the most terrible death which man can be subject to,
and refused, at the solicitation of his own men, to leave the ship until, alas! it was
too late, and he perished at his post."

The imbecile Commoners cheered this nonsensical answer. As to
the loss of the *Tiger*,[240] he declared it to belong to the chapter of
accidents. As to the "grievous casualty in the Baltic—why, it
proved the foolhardiness of our seamen." [241]

The small-headed man then proceeded to answer the question
whether "no practical results had been brought about by our fleets
and armies?" and he glories in the "complete, effective, and
irresistible blockade of the Russian ports." This blockade was so
effective that, for instance, eight Russian war-steamers have
reached Odessa from Sevastopol, notwithstanding bombardments,
fights and obstruction. It was so effective that the Baltic trade is
carried on through Russia to such an extent that Russian produce
is selling at London at a price very little higher than that at which
it sold before the war; that at Odessa commerce is carried on
exactly as last year, and that even the nominal blockades of the
Black and White Seas were only some days ago forced upon the
English by Bonaparte.

But the English Government did more, exclaims the noble
young man called Herbert. Had they not wrested from Russia the
ability of communicating supplies by the Black Sea, and cut them
off from all access by sea? He forgot that for four months they left
the Russians in the command of the Danube, that they allowed
them to appropriate with only 15,000 men the European

corn-houses of Moldavia and Wallachia, that they abandoned to them the rich flocks of the Dobrodja almost under their eyes, and that they prevented the Turkish fleet from annihilating the Russian squadron at Sinope.

They had an ample share in the military success of the Turks, because by forming their reserve they enabled them to use every man and every gun against the invading army. Need I repeat to your readers[a] that, as long as the Russians were unable to concentrate a superior force in the Principalities, the British Government interdicted Omer Pasha the use of his own numerical superiority and the fruits of his first victories?

Had their forces done anything else?

"How many pounds sterling had been expended by Russia in erecting a line of forts along the coast of Circassia? In one short campaign, all these strong places, which formed the chains with which Circassia was bound, had, with one exception, fallen into their hands or into those of their allies."

Woronzoff! Woronzoff! Do you not remember that, when advised, at the beginning of the session, to take those forts, you refused to do so, thus allowing the Russians to withdraw their garrisons to Sevastopol? You have only taken the forts which the Russians chose to abandon, and that single "exception," which you neither destroyed nor captured, nor attacked, is the only one worth taking, the only one thought worth holding by the Russians, and the only one by which you could communicate with the Circassians—Anapa.

Mr. Herbert reached the climax of his insipid diatribe when he pretended that in the glorious defense of Silistria, which they neither relieved, nor allowed Omer Pasha to relieve, England had a share, because of one dead young man, called Captain Butler. Lieutenant Nasmyth, as a living man, is of course not mentioned. Captain Butler, let me tell you, went to Silistria, only after the Government had refused to send him there, and the more ground for Marshal Herbert to claim credit for his conduct. As to Lieutenant Nasmyth, he belongs to the class who were shortly to be expelled from the British camp, and went to Silistria in the capacity of a newspaper correspondent.

Lord Dudley Stuart having assailed the Government for not procuring steamers drawing only three feet of water and carrying one or two heavy guns, Admiral Berkeley—who spoke after Gen. Herbert—begged the noble Lord "to teach the Surveyor of the

---

[a] See this volume, p. 223.— Ed.

Navy[a] how to build such steamboats." This was the answer given
by the gallant Whig admiral to the question how the Admiralty
could fit out a fleet for the Baltic without providing a large
number of gun-boats. Brave Berkeley and his scientific Surveyor
of the Navy would do well to apply for instruction at the Swedish
and Russian Admiralties than to poor and deluded Dudley Stuart.

We have now done with the defense of British warfare as put
forward by elegant Herbert and gallant Berkeley, and we come
now to the indiscreet revelations of that same Berkeley. On the
previous evening the Sevastopol bubble was blown up by little
Johnny; on this evening the Kronstadt bubble exploded through
the means of Berkeley. As the Austrians alone will fight out the
case in the Principalities, there remains no field of action "for the
most formidable armies and navies, with screw-propellers,
paixhans, and other monster powers of destruction ever fitted and
sent out by any country." From a letter written by the gallant
commander of the Baltic fleet[b] the following quotation was made
by gallant Berkeley:

"It has not been in my power to do anything with this powerful fleet; for
attacking either Kronstadt or Sweaborg would have been certain destruction."

This was not all. Brave Berkeley exulting at what the most
powerful fleet could not do, went on babbling:

"Admiral Chads, than whom no man possesses a greater amount of scientific
knowledge, wrote also in these terms: 'After two days inspection from the
lighthouse, and full views of the forts and ships, the former are too substantial for
the fire of ships. They are large masses of granite. With respect to an attack on the
ships where they are, it is not to be entertained.'"

As to Napier, brave Berkeley concludes with the words:

"There never was a British officer who had more completely *carte blanche* to
undertake what he pleased. So far from his hands being tied up by the
Government it has afforded him every encouragement to proceed"

from Bomarsund to Kronstadt, and from Kronstadt to Bomarsund.

On the remark of Mr. Hildyard, a Tory, that "in the whole
course of his life he never heard such indiscretion," that Berkeley
had spoken as a plain agent of Russia, and that all the
rodomontades about Kronstadt had notwithstanding experienced
his silent approval, brave Berkeley recanted his indiscretions so far

---

[a] Sir Baldwin Wake Walker.— *Ed.*
[b] Sir Charles Napier.— *Ed.*

as to say that Napier had only spoken of his present position with ships alone, and without being backed by any land forces. That nothing could be done in the Baltic without land troops and without an alliance with Sweden, I have repeated to you all the time, since Napier left the English shores,[a] and my opinion was participated in by every scientific military man.

I come now to the last point of this memorable debate, the magisterial declarations of Lord John Russell. After having got his note for 3,000,000 he was as barefaced as he was shamefaced, 20 hours before, when quailing under the sarcasms of Disraeli.

"He certainly did not think it necessary to give any further explanation of the statements which he made last night."

As to the "painful distinctions" which certain parties had attempted to draw between Aberdeen and his colleagues, he would tell them that

"with regard to the general measures of the war, those measures had been considered, step by step, by those advisers of Her Majesty who are usually called the Cabinet, and for the decisions which had been adopted, all the colleagues of Lord Aberdeen are alike responsible to Parliament and the country with that noble Lord."

In fact, he dared—but at no risk—to tell the House:

"If we are fit to be ministers of the Crown, we are fit to have the discretion to call or not to call Parliament together; if we are not fit to have that discretion, on the other hand, we are no longer fit to remain the ministers of the Crown."

Being present at the sittings of the English Parliament on Monday and Tuesday, I confess to my error in having stigmatized, in 1848, in the *New-Rhenish Gazette*,[b] the Berlin and Frankfort assemblies as the lowest possible expressions of Parliamentary life.[c]

It will be amusing for your readers to see opposed to the declarations of Woronzoff's British brother-in-law,[d] the *fades*[e] bravadoes of a Russell, and the roaring leaders of *The Times*, the following extracts from the latest letter of *The Times* correspondent at the British camp near Varna, dated July 13.

"The night before this there was a general belief that peace would soon be proclaimed, inasmuch as an Austrian Envoy was reported to be dining with Gen.

---

[a] See this volume, pp. 202-04 and 251.— *Ed.*
[b] *Neue Rheinische Zeitung.— Ed.*
[c] See articles on the Frankfort National Assembly published in Vols. 8 and 9 of the present edition.— *Ed.*
[d] S. Herbert.— *Ed.*
[e] Insipid.— *Ed.*

Brown, and this Austrian Envoy was on his way from Shumla, where he had held long interviews with Omer Pasha, to Varna, where he was to consult with Lord Raglan and Marshal St. Arnaud. It was reported that the Duke of Cambridge had said that the cavalry would be home by November, and the infantry by May. Surely it cannot be affirmed we are at war, or that the allied armies have taken a belligerent part, or exhibited warlike actions since they landed in Turkey. Our parades, reviews, drills, and inspections are as harmless, as innocent, as if they took place at Satory or at Chobham, and our whole operations of offence by land have been confined to, first, a reconnoitering excursion by Lord Cardigan; secondly, the dispatch of some engineer officers and sappers to Silistria and Rustchuk; thirdly, the march of a few French pontoniers in the same direction; and, fourthly, the further dispatch of a company of sappers and of 150 sailors to Rustchuk, to construct a bridge across from the bank to the islands and thence across to the other side."[a]

There exists no Bastille in England, but there exist lunatic asylums to which every individual obnoxious to the Court, or standing in the way of certain family arrangements, may simply be confined by a *lettre de cachet*. In Wednesday's debate on the case of Dr. Peitman,[b] this was fully proved by Mr. Otway, backed by Mr. Henley. There were wanted only some words of Lord Palmerston, the *civis Romanus*,[242] and the notorious advocate of "the rights and privileges of the British subject"—and the subject [was] dropped. Palmerston did not so much as pretend that Peitman was a real madman, but only that "he appeared to imagine to have some claim upon Government," and imagining to pursue that claim in a very troublesome way to the Queen, or rather that anonymous personage called Prince Albert. The Coburgs are everywhere; they pretend at this very moment to appropriate the Spanish nation.[c]

"It is," says the Ministerial *Globe*, "a question of the rights of the doctor and of the rights of the Queen, and we believe that there is no man in or out of Parliament who can hesitate in balancing these rights."

No wonder, then, that Thomas Paine's "Rights of Man" were publicly burned in this free and blessed country.[243]

Another little Parliamentary comedy was performed on the same Wednesday evening. At the sitting of last Friday,[d] Mr. Butt had moved the resolution that British subjects should be forbidden, under certain penalties, to trade in Russian Government securities; this bill relating only to loans contracted by the Russian

---

[a] Report from Varna of July 13, 1854. *The Times*, No. 21805, July 28, 1854.— *Ed.*

[b] The debate on Dr. Peitman's case on July 26 is given according to the parliamentary report published in *The Times*, No. 21804, July 27, 1854.— *Ed.*

[c] See this volume, pp. 305-06.— *Ed.*

[d] July 21.— *Ed.*

Government during the present war. The British Government had not proposed the bill, but it could hardly dare to oppose it, as Bonaparte had already falsely announced in the *Moniteur* that the British Government concurred with him in considering subscriptions to the Russian loan as illegal.[a] Palmerston, therefore, supported Mr. Butt's motion, but found himself opposed in no very courteous manner by Mr. Wilson, the sage editor of *The Economist*, and Secretary of the Treasury. Now, on Wednesday the same Palmerston, having defended the Coalition Cabinet on Monday, having abstained from speaking on Tuesday and thus secured the real success of the Coalition, could not but seize upon this opportunity to resume his position as the "unprotected female" of the Cabinet. He spoke with the aspect and in the tone of a male Sibyl, as if overpowered by the spontaneous explosion of his patriotic feelings, which he, poor man, was forced to suppress on the two preceding evenings, fettered as he was by the cold necessity of an official position. He elicited the inevitable cheers of the honorable and deluded gentlemen when he declared

"the bill simply affirmed the principle that British subjects should not supply the Russians with funds to carry on the war. The arguments adduced by the Secretary of the Treasury went to show that we should abolish our laws of high treason. Such arguments were sheer nonsense."[b]

Note that this is the same man who, during twenty-four years, imposed the Russo-Dutch loan [244] upon England, and is at this very moment the most influential member of a Cabinet which continues to pay the capital and interest of that loan, thus supplying him with "funds to carry on the war."

Written on July 28, 1854

First published in the *New-York Daily Tribune*, No. 4152, August 9; reprinted in the *New-York Semi-Weekly Tribune*, No. 961, August 11, 1854

Signed: *Karl Marx*

Reproduced from the *New-York Daily Tribune*

---

[a] *Le Moniteur universel*, No. 189, July 8, 1854.— *Ed.*
[b] The debates on the Russian government securities bill are given according to *The Times*, Nos. 21800 and 21804, July 22 and 27, 1854.— *Ed.*

Karl Marx and Frederick Engels

THAT BORE OF A WAR [245]

It is now very near a twelvemonth since a small Turkish corps, two battalions, succeeded in crossing the Danube near Turtukai, opposite Oltenitza, threw up intrenchments there, and being attacked by the Russians, repulsed them in a very spirited little affair, which, being the first engagement in the war, took the style and title of the Battle of Oltenitza. There the Turks alone were opposed to the Russians; they had no British or French troops behind them as a reserve, and could not even expect any support from the allied fleets. And yet they held their ground on the Wallachian side of the river for a fortnight at Oltenitza, and for the whole winter at Kalafat.

Since then, England and France have declared war against Russia; sundry exploits, of a doubtful nature it is true, have been achieved. Black Sea fleets, Baltic fleets, and an army of now nearly a hundred thousand English and French soldiers are there to assist the Turks or to make diversions in their favor. And the upshot of all this is nothing but a repetition of the Oltenitza business on a larger scale, but rather less successfully than last year.

The Russians laid siege to Silistria. They went about it stupidly but bravely. They were defeated day after day, night after night; not by superior science, not by Captain Butler or Lieutenant Nasmyth, the two British officers present who, according to *The Times*, saved Silistria.[a] They were defeated by the ignorance of the Turks, an ignorance extending so far as not to know when a fort

---

[a] See this volume, p. 329.— *Ed.*

or rampart ceases to be tenable, and sticking doggedly to every inch of ground, every molehill which the enemy appears to covet. They were defeated, besides, by the stolidity of their own Generals, by fever and cholera; finally by the moral effect of an allied army menacing their left, and an Austrian army menacing their right wing. When the war began, we stated that the Russian army had never been able to lay a regular siege, and the ill-managed operations before Silistria show that they have not improved since. Well, they were defeated; they had to decamp in the most discreditable way imaginable; they had to raise the siege of an incomplete fortress in the midst of a fine season, and without any troops coming to relieve the garrison. Such an event occurs not more than once in a century; and whatever the Russians may try to do in the autumn, the campaign is lost, disgracefully lost for them.

But now for the reverse of the medal. Silistria is free. The Russians retreat to the left bank of the Danube. They even prepare for, and gradually execute the evacuation of the Dobrodja. Hirsova and Matchin are dismantled. The Sereth seems to be the line to which the Russians trust for the defense, not of their conquests, but of their own territory. Omer Pasha, the wily old Croat, who can hold his tongue or tell a lie as well as anybody, "in the execution of his duty," at once sends a corps to the Dobrodja and another to Rustchuk, thus engaging the two wings of the Russians at once. There were far better maneuvers possible at the time, but poor old Omer appears to know the Turks and the allies better than we do. The correct military move to be made would have been to march through the Dobrodja or by Kalarash upon the communications of the enemy; but after what we have seen, we cannot even accuse Omer of having missed a good opportunity. We know that his army is very badly cared for —provided with almost nothing—and cannot, therefore, execute rapid movements which would remove it to a distance from its base, or open up fresh lines of operation. These movements, decisive as they are in their effect, when undertaken by a sufficient force, are not within the reach of an army which lives from hand to mouth, and has to pass through a barren country. We know that Omer Pasha went to Varna, imploring the aid of the allied generals, who at that time had 75,000 capital soldiers there, within four days' march of the Danube; but neither St. Arnaud nor Raglan thought proper to come up to where they could meet the enemy. Thus Omer could do no more than he has done. He sent 25,000 men toward the Dobrodja, and marched with the rest of his army to Rustchuk. Here his troops passed from island to island until the Danube was crossed, and then, by a sudden march to the left, took Giurgevo in the rear, and forced the Russians to quit it. On the next day the Russians were drawn up on some hights to the north of Giurgevo, where the Turks attacked them. A sanguinary battle ensued, remarkable for the number of English officers who, with rare success, competed for the honor of being shot first. They all got their bullets, but with no benefit to anybody, for it would be preposterous to think that the sight of a British officer being shot could inflame a Turkish soldier to invincibility. However, the Russians having a mere advanced guard on the spot—a brigade, the two regiments of Kolyvan and Tomsk—got beaten, and the Turks made good their footing on the Wallachian bank of the Danube. They at once set about fortifying the place, and as they had British sappers, and as at Kalafat they did very well for themselves, there is no doubt that they were making a formidable position of it. But thus far they were allowed to go, and no further. That Emperor of Austria who now for eight months has been trying hard to act the part of an independent man, steps in at once. The Principalities have been promised to his troops as a feeding ground, and he intends to have them. What business have the Turks there? Let them go back to Bulgaria. So down comes the order from Constantinople to withdraw the Turkish troops from the left bank, and to leave "all that plot of land" to the tender mercies of the Austrian soldiers. Diplomacy is above strategy. Whatever may come of it, the Austrians will save their own frontiers by occupying a few yards of ground beyond; and to this important end even the necessities of the war must give way. Besides, is not Omer Pasha an Austrian deserter? And Austria never forgets. In Montenegro she interrupted his victorious career; and she repeats the process again, to make the renegade feel that he is not yet out of the allegiance of his lawful sovereign.

It is entirely useless to enter into the military details of this present stage of the campaign. The actions possess little tactical interest, being plain, straightforward front attacks; the movements of troops on either side are ruled more by diplomatical than strategical motives. Most likely we shall see the campaign closing without any great enterprise, for on the Danube there is nothing prepared for a grand offensive, and as to the taking of Sevastopol, of which we hear so much, the beginning will probably be delayed until the season is so far advanced that it must be postponed till next year.

It would seem that whoever may have had any conservative leanings in Europe must lose them when he looks at this everlasting Eastern Question. There is all Europe, incapable, convicted for the last sixty years of incapability to settle this puny little strife. There they are, France, England, Russia, going actually to war. They carry on their war for six months; and unless by mistake, or on a very shabby scale, they have not even come to blows. There they are, eighty or ninety thousand English and French soldiers at Varna, commanded by old Wellington's late military secretary,[a] and by a Marshal of France[b] (whose greatest exploits, it is true, were performed in London pawnshops)—there they are, the French doing nothing and the British helping them as fast as they can; and as they may think this sort of business not exactly honorable, the fleets are come up to Baltshik Roads to have a look at them and to see which of the two armies can enjoy the *dolce far niente*[c] with the greatest decorum. And yet, although the allies have hitherto only been eating up the provisions upon which the Turkish army had calculated, idling away day after day at Varna for the last two months, they are not yet fit for duty. They would have relieved Silistria if required by about the middle of May next year. The troops that have conquered Algeria and learned the theory and practice of war on one of the most difficult theaters in existence,[246] the soldiers who fought the Sikhs on the sands of the Indus, and the Kaffirs in the thorny bush of South Africa,[247] in countries far more savage than Bulgaria—there they are, helpless and useless, fit for nothing in a country which even exports corn!

But if the allies are miserable in their performances, so are the Russians. They have had plenty of time to prepare. They have done whatever they could, for they knew from the beginning what resistance they would find. And yet, what have they been able to do? Nothing. They could not take a yard of contested ground from the Turks; they could not take Kalafat; they could not beat the Turks in one single engagement. And yet they are the same Russians who, under Münnich and Suvoroff conquered the Black Sea coast from the Don to the Dniester. But Schilder is not Münnich, Paskievich is not Suvoroff, and though the Russian soldier can bear flogging with the cane beyond all others, yet when

---

[a] Raglan.— *Ed.*
[b] On Saint-Arnaud see this volume, pp. 230-33.— *Ed.*
[c] Sweet doing-nothing.— *Ed.*

it comes to habitual retreating, he loses his steadiness as well as anybody else.

The fact is, that conservative Europe—the Europe of "order, property, family, religion"—the Europe of monarchs, feudal lords, moneyed men, however they may be differently assorted in different countries—is once more exhibiting its extreme impotency. Europe may be rotten, but a war should have roused the sound elements; a war should have brought forth some latent energies, and assuredly there should be that much pluck among two hundred and fifty millions of men that at least one decent struggle might be got up, wherein both parties could reap some honor, such as force and spirit can carry off even from the field of battle. But no. Not only is the England of the middle classes, the France of the Bonapartes, incapable of a decent, hearty, hard-fought war; but even Russia, the country of Europe least infected by infidel and unnerving civilization, cannot bring about anything of the kind. The Turks are fit for sudden starts of offensive action, and stubborn resistance on the defensive, but seem not to be made for large combined maneuvers with great armies. Thus everything is reduced to a degree of impuissance and a reciprocal confession of weakness, which appears to be as reciprocally expected by all . parties. With governments such as they are at present, this Eastern war may be carried on for thirty years, and yet come to no conclusion.

But while official incompetency is thus displaying itself all over Europe, in the south-western corner of that continent a movement breaks out which at once shows that there are still other forces more active than the official ones. Whatever may be the real character and the end of the Spanish rising, so much at least may be affirmed, that it bears to a future revolution the same relation as the Swiss and Italian movements of 1847 to the revolution of 1848.[248] There are two grand facts in it: first, the military, the actual rulers of the continent since 1849, have got divided among themselves, and have given up their calling of preserving order, for the purpose of asserting their own opinion in opposition to the Government. Their discipline taught them their power, and this power has loosened their discipline. Secondly, we have had the spectacle of a successful barricade fight. Wherever barricades had been raised since June, 1848,[249] they had hitherto proved of no avail. Barricades, the resistance of the population of a large town against the military, seemed of no effect whatever. That prejudice has fallen. We have again seen victorious, unassailable barricades. The spell is broken. A new revolutionary era is rendered possible, and it is significant that while the troops of official Europe are showing themselves useless in actual war, they are at the same time defeated by the insurgent inhabitants of a town.

Written on July 29 and August 1, 1854

First published in the *New-York Daily Tribune*, No. 4159, August 17; reprinted in the *New-York Semi-Weekly Tribune*, No. 963, August 18 and the *New-York Weekly Tribune*, No. 675, August 19, 1854 as a leader

Reproduced from the *New-York Daily Tribune*

Karl Marx

ESPARTERO [250]

It is one of the peculiarities of revolutions that just as the people seem about to take a great start and to open a new era, they suffer themselves to be ruled by the delusions of the past and surrender all the power and influence they have so dearly won into the hands of men who represent, or are supposed to represent, the popular movement of a by-gone epoch. Espartero is one of those traditional men whom the people are wont to take upon their backs at moments of social crises, and whom, like the ill-natured old fellow that obstinately clasped his legs about the neck of Sindbad the sailor, they afterward find it difficult to get rid of. Ask a Spaniard of the so-called Progressist School [251] what is the political value of Espartero, and he will promptly reply that "Espartero represents the unity of the great liberal party; Espartero is popular because he came from the people; his popularity works exclusively for the cause of the Progresistas." It is true that he is the son of an artisan, who has climbed up to be the Regent of Spain; and that, having entered the army as a common soldier, he left it as a Field-Marshal. But if he be the symbol of the unity of the great liberal party, it can only be that indifferent point of unity in which all extremes are neutralized. And as to the popularity of the Progresistas, we do not exaggerate in saying that it was lost from the moment it became transferred from the bulk of that party to this single individual.

We need no other proof of the ambiguous and exceptional character of Espartero's greatness, beyond the simple fact that, so far, nobody has been able to account for it. While his friends take refuge in allegoric generalities, his enemies, alluding to a strange feature of his private life, declare him but a lucky gambler. Both, then, friends and enemies, are at an equal loss to discover any logical connection between the man himself, and the fame and the name of the man.

Espartero's military merits are as much contested as his political shortcomings are incontestable. In a voluminous biography, published by Señor de Florez,[a] much fuss is made about his military prowess and generalship as shown in the provinces of Charcas, Paz, Arequipa, Potosi and Cochabamba, where he fought under the orders of General Morillo, then charged with the reduction of the South American States under the authority of the Spanish Crown. But the general impression produced by his South American feats of arms upon the excitable mind of his native country is sufficiently characterized by his being designated as the chief of the *Ayacuchismo*, and his partisans as *Ayacuchos*, in allusion to the unfortunate battle at Ayacucho, in which Peru and South America were definitively lost for Spain.[252] He is, at all events, a very extraordinary hero whose historical baptism dates from a defeat, instead of a success. In the seven years' war against the Carlists, he never signalized himself by one of those daring strokes by which Narvaez, his rival, became early known as an iron-nerved soldier. He had certainly the gift of making the best of small successes, while it was mere luck that Maroto betrayed to him the last forces of the Pretender,[b] Cabrera's rising in 1840 being only a posthumous attempt to galvanize the dry bones of Carlism.[253] Señor de Marliani, himself one of Espartero's admirers, and the historian of modern Spain, cannot but own that the seven years' war is to be compared with nothing but the feuds waged in the tenth century between the petty lords of Gaul, when success was not the result of victory.[254] It appears, by another mischance, that of all the Peninsular deeds of Espartero, that which made the liveliest impression upon the public memory was, if not exactly a defeat, at least a singularly strange performance in a hero of liberty. He became renowned as the bombarder of cities—of Barcelona and Seville. If the Spaniards, says a writer, should ever paint him as Mars, we should see the god figuring as a "wall-batterer."[c]

When Cristina was forced, in 1840, to resign her Regency and to fly from Spain, Espartero assumed, against the wishes of a very

---

[a] José Segundo Florez. *Espartero. Historia de su vida militar y política y de los grandes sucesos contemporáneos.*—*Ed.*

[b] Don Carlos (Charles V).—*Ed.*

[c] [Hughes,] *Revelations of Spain in 1845. By an English Resident*, p. 14.—*Ed.*

large section of the Progresistas, the supreme authority within the limits of parliamentary government. He surrounded himself with a sort of camarilla, and affected the airs of a military dictator, without really elevating himself above the mediocrity of a Constitutional King. His favor extended to Moderados [255] rather than to old Progresistas, who,with a few exceptions, were excluded from office. Without conciliating his enemies, he gradually estranged his friends. Without the courage to break through the shackles of the parliamentary regime, he did not know how to accept it, how to manage it, or how to transform it into an instrument of action. During his three years' dictatorship, the revolutionary spirit was broken step by step, through endless compromises, and the dissensions within the Progresista party were allowed to reach such a pitch as to enable the Moderados to regain exclusive power by a *coup de main*. Thus Espartero became so divested of authority that his own Embassador at Paris[a] conspired against him with Cristina and Narvaez; and so poor in resources, that he found no means to ward off their miserable intrigues, or the petty tricks of Louis Philippe. So little did he understand his own position that he made an inconsiderate stand against public opinion when it simply wanted a pretext to break him to pieces.

In May, 1843, his popularity having long since faded away, he retained Linage, Zurbano and the other members of his military camarilla, whose dismissal was loudly called for; he dismissed the Lopez Ministry, who commanded a large majority in the Chamber of Deputies, and he stubbornly refused an amnesty for the exiled Moderados, then claimed on all hands, by Parliament, by the people and by the army itself. This demand simply expressed the public disgust with his administration. Then, at once, a hurricane of pronunciamentos against the "tyrant Espartero" shook the Peninsula from one end to the other; a movement to be compared only, for the rapidity of its spreading, to the present one. Moderados and Progresistas combined for the one object of getting rid of the Regent. The crisis took him quite unawares— the fatal hour found him unprepared.

Narvaez, accompanied by O'Donnell, Concha and Pezuela, landed with a handful of men at Valencia. On their side all was rapidity and action, considerate audacity, energetic decision. On the side of Espartero all was helpless hesitation, deadly delay,

---

[a] Olozaga.— *Ed.*

apathetic irresolution, indolent weakness. While Narvaez raised the siege of Teruel, and marched into Aragon, Espartero retired from Madrid, and consumed whole weeks in unaccountable inactivity at Albacete. When Narvaez had won over the corps of Seoane and Zurbano at Torrejon, and was marching on Madrid, Espartero at length effected a junction with Van Halen, for the useless and odious bombardment of Seville. He then fled from station to station, at every step of his retreat deserted by his troops, till at last he reached the coast. When he embarked at Cadiz, that town, the last where he retained a party, bade its hero farewell by also pronouncing against him. An Englishman who resided in Spain during the catastrophe, gives a graphic description of the sliding-scale of Espartero's greatness:

"It was not the tremendous crash of an instant, after a well-fought field, but a little and bit by bit descent, after no fighting at all, from Madrid to Ciudad Real, from Ciudad Real to Albacete, from Albacete to Cordova, from Cordova to Seville, from Seville to Port St. Mary,[a] and thence to the wide ocean. He fell from idolatry to enthusiasm, from enthusiasm to attachment, from attachment to respect, from respect to indifference, from indifference to contempt, from contempt to hatred, and from hatred he fell into the sea."[b]

How could Espartero have now again become the savior of the country, and "Sword of the Revolution," as he is called? This event would be quite incomprehensible were it not for the ten years of reaction Spain has suffered under the brutal dictatorship of Narvaez, and the brooding yoke of the Queen's minions, who supplanted him. Extensive and violent epochs of reaction are wonderfully fitted for reestablishing the fallen men of revolutionary miscarriages. The greater the imaginative powers of a people—and where is imagination greater than in the south of Europe?—the more irresistible their impulse to oppose to individual incarnations of despotism individual incarnations of the revolution. As they cannot improvise them at once, they excavate the dead men of their previous movements. Was not Narvaez himself on the point of growing popular at the expense of Sartorius? The Espartero who, on the 29th of July, held his triumphant entrance into Madrid, was no real man; he was a ghost, a name, a reminiscence.

It is but due to justice to record that Espartero never professed to be anything but a constitutional monarchist; and if there had ever existed any doubt upon that point, it must have disappeared

---

[a] Puerta de Santa María.— *Ed.*
[b] [Hughes,] op. cit., pp. 15-16.— *Ed.*

before the enthusiastic reception he met with during his exile, at
Windsor Castle and from the governing classes of England. When
he arrived in London the whole aristocracy flocked to his abode,
the Duke of Wellington and Palmerston at their head. Aberdeen,
in his quality of Foreign Minister, sent him an invitation to be
presented to the Queen; the Lord Mayor and the Aldermen of the
city entertained him with gastronomic homages 'at the Mansion
House; and when it became known that the Spanish Cincinnatus
passed his leisure hours in gardening, there was no Botanical, or
Horticultural, or Agricultural Society which was not eager to
present him with membership. He was quite the lion of that
metropolis. At the end of 1847 an amnesty recalled the Spanish
exiles, and the decree of Queen Isabella appointed him a Senator.
He was, however, not allowed to leave England before Queen
Victoria had invited him and his Duchess to her table, adding the
extraordinary honor of offering them a night's lodging at Windsor
Castle. It is true, we believe, that this halo thrown round his
person was somewhat connected with the supposition that
Espartero had been and still was the representative of British
interests in Spain. It is no less true that the Espartero demonstration looked something like a demonstration against Louis Philippe.

On his return to Spain he received deputation upon deputation,
gratulations upon gratulations, and the city of Barcelona dispatched an express messenger to apologize for its bad behavior in
1843. But has anybody ever heard his name mentioned during the
fatal period from January, 1846, till the late events? Has he ever
raised his voice during that dead silence of degraded Spain? Is
there recorded one single act of patriotic resistance on his part?
He quietly retires to his estate at Logroño, cultivating his cabbages
and flowers, waiting his time. He did not go even to the revolution
till the revolution came for him. He did more than Mahomet.[a] He
expected the mountain to come to him, and the mountain came.
Still there is one exception to be mentioned. When the revolution
of February[b] burst out, followed by the general European
earthquake, he caused to be published by Señor de Principe, and
some other friends, a little pamphlet entitled *Espartero, his Past, his
Present, his Future*,[256] to remind Spain that it still harbored the man
of the past, the present, and the future. The revolutionary
movement soon subsiding in France, the man of the past, of the
present, and of the future once more sank into oblivion.

---

[a] Mohammed.— *Ed.*
[b] 1848.— *Ed.*

Espartero was born at Granátula, in La Mancha, and like his famous fellow countryman,[a] he also has his fixed idea—the Constitution; and his Dulcinea del Toboso—Queen Isabella. On January 8, 1848, when he returned from his English exile to Madrid, he was received by the Queen and took leave of her with the following words:

"I pray your Majesty to call me whenever you want an arm to defend, or a heart to love you."[b]

Her Majesty has now called and her knight-errant appears, smoothing the revolutionary waves, enervating the masses by a delusive calm, allowing Cristina, San Luis and the rest to hide themselves in the palace, and loudly professing his unbroken faith in the words of the innocent Isabella.

It is known that this very trustworthy Queen, whose features are said to assume year after year a more striking resemblance to those of Ferdinand VII, of infamous memory, had her majority proclaimed on November 15, 1843. She was then only thirteen years old on November 21 of the same year. Olozaga, whom Lopez had constituted her tutor for three months, formed a Ministry obnoxious to the Camarilla and the Cortes newly elected under the impression of the first success of Narvaez. He wanted to dissolve the Cortes, and obtained a royal decree signed by the Queen giving him power to do so, but leaving the date of its promulgation blank. On the evening of the 28th, Olozaga had the decree delivered to him from the hands of the Queen. On the evening of the 29th he had another interview with her; but he had hardly left her when an Under-Secretary of State came to his house, and informed him that he was dismissed, and demanded back the decree which he had forced the Queen to sign. Olozaga, a lawyer by profession, was too sharp a man to be ensnared in this way. He did not return the document till the following day, after having shown it to at least one hundred deputies, in proof that the signature of the Queen was in her usual, regular handwriting. On December 13, Gonzalez Bravo, appointed as Premier, summoned the Presidents of the Chambers, the principal Madrid notables, Narvaez, the Marquis de la Santa Cruz, and others, to the Queen that she might make a declaration to them concerning what had passed between her and Olozaga on the evening of

---

[a] Don Quixote of La Mancha.— *Ed.*

[b] [Principe, Giron, Satorres, Ribot,] *Espartero: su pasado, su presente, su porvenir*, p. 58.— *Ed.*

November 28. The innocent little Queen led them into the room where she had received Olozaga, and enacted in a very lively, but rather overdone manner, a little drama for their instruction. Thus had Olozaga bolted the door, thus seized her dress, thus obliged her to sit down, thus conducted her hand, thus forced her signature to the decree, in one word, thus had he violated her royal dignity. During this scene Gonzalez Bravo took note of these declarations, while the persons present saw the alleged decree which appeared to be signed in a blotted and tremulous hand. Thus, on the solemn declaration of the Queen, Olozaga was to be condemned for the crime of *laesa majestas*,[a] to be torn in pieces by four horses, or at the best, to be banished for life to the Philippines. But, as we have seen, he had taken his measures of precaution. Then followed seventeen days' debate in the Cortes, creating a sensation greater even than that produced by the famous trial of Queen Caroline in England.[257] Olozaga's defense in the Cortes contained among other things this passage:

"If they tell us that the word of the Queen is to be believed without question, I answer, No! There is either a charge, or there is none. If there be, that word is a testimony like any other, and to that testimony I oppose mine."[b]

In the balance of the Cortes the word of Olozaga was found to be heavier than that of the Queen. Afterward he fled to Portugal to escape the assassins sent against him. This was Isabella's first *entrechat* on the political stage of Spain, and the first proof of her honesty. And this is the same little Queen whose words Espartero now exhorts the people to trust in, and to whom is offered, after eleven years' *school for scandal*,[c] the "defending arm," and the "loving heart" of the "Sword of the Revolution."

Written on August 4, 1854

First published in the *New-York Daily Tribune*, No. 4161, August 19; reprinted in the *New-York Semi-Weekly Tribune*, No. 964, August 22 and the *New-York Weekly Tribune*, No. 676, August 26, 1854 as a leader

Reproduced from the *New-York Daily Tribune*

---

[a] Lese-majesty, high treason.— *Ed.*
[b] [Hughes,] op. cit., p. 80.— *Ed.*
[c] An allusion to Sheridan's famous comedy.— *Ed.*

Frederick Engels

THE ATTACK ON THE RUSSIAN FORTS[258]

At last it seems that the allied French and English are to make a genuine attack on Russia. The outmost fortifications of the Empire, on the Aland Isles and at Sevastopol in the Black Sea, are successively, if not simultaneously, to be assailed. Indeed, it is rumored in Western Europe that the former point has already been taken after a brief bombardment, but the report wants confirmation, and is probably premature. As for the attempt upon Sevastopol, we have no official information that it is to be made, but it is positively asserted by *The London Times*[a] and generally believed in that city. So far only a couple of divisions of French and English troops have been embarked at Varna, and though it is supposed they form part of the expedition to the Crimea, it is possible, on the other hand, that they are destined to besiege the Russian fortress of Anapa in Asia. On this point all doubt will probably be removed by the arrival of the next steamer.[259]

The attack upon Bomarsund will be an event of great military interest. It will be the first time that Montalembert's casemated town-fortifications are put to the proof. To judge from views and plans of the place, the forts there, although on a far smaller scale than those of Helsingfors, Kronstadt, or Sevastopol, are defended against a land attack as much as against a bombardment by ships, and are exclusively constructed upon Montalembert's principles. A long bomb-proof fort, with about one hundred guns flanked by temporary earth works, forms the main defense against ships, while it is commanded and protected in the rear by large towers,

---

[a] *The Times*, No. 21814, August 8, 1854, leader.— *Ed.*

mounting one thirty, and one ten guns. While the main fort would chiefly engage the ships, the attack on the towers would occupy the land forces. According to our last accounts the garrison is very much weaker than we had supposed; it consists of but little more than three thousand men. It is not quite clear, from the information attainable, how far the sea-attack and the land-attack can, not merely coincide, but actually cooperate and support each other; for a sea-attack is necessarily an attack *de vive force*,[a] which must be decided in a very short time, while any land-attack against masonry presupposes preparatory operations, with at least one parallel and batteries, and therefore is a matter of some duration. This kind of questions, however, can only be decided on the spot. At all events the taking of Bomarsund will have, in a military point of view, a far higher interest than even the capture of Sevastopol, inasmuch as it contributes to the solution of a much-discussed question, while the latter feat would merely be the successful carrying out of old-established military rules.

The proposed attack upon Sevastopol is to be mainly executed by land forces; while the action of the fleets must be almost entirely confined to the close blockade of the harbor. It thus amounts to a land and sea blockade of a sea-port incompletely fortified on the land side. We have no means of knowing what fortifications may have been raised by the Russians on the south of the town and bay; but that they have established redoubts and lines which may necessitate a regular siege, unless great sacrifices are submitted to, there can hardly be a question. At all events, we know that a permanent and to all appearance well-constructed fort—a large square with ample ditch-defenses on each of its sides, and mortar-batteries in each of its salient angles—crowns the hill on the north of the bay, just opposite the town.[b] That hill is the only position near the town which appears not to be commanded within gun-range by other hights, and which itself commands the bay and its opposite slope. Here, then, at all events, will be the chief resistance; but it may be doubted if the possession of the town and harbor can be maintained, even if all the coast-forts on the southern shore are taken, unless this fort is reduced. There will be some regular siege work, there, at least. Now, the extent of the bay from Cape Constantine to its head is about eight miles; and allowing a moderate range to the town and

---

[a] By sheer strength.— *Ed.*

[b] The reference is to the fortification on the northern shore of the Big Bay.— *Ed.*

forts, the allied forces would have to extend on a semi-circle of twenty-two or twenty-four miles around them, in order to insure the blockade on land. They must be strong enough on all points to resist the sallies of the garrison, and the attacks of any troops which might be collected in their rear. Although we have no means of knowing the forces which Russia can bring directly or indirectly to the defense of her Black Sea stronghold, yet these details show that no inconsiderable body of troops is required for its capture. There is, besides, a dangerous enemy to be encountered in the deadly climate of the Lower Crimea. As in this attack the strand-batteries can be hardly of any utility to the Russians, the attempt must lose a great deal of its military interest, reducing itself to a siege of very large, but by no means unprecedented, proportions. The force destined for the movement is nowhere stated at above 100,000 men, including a detachment of Turks. Taking all the circumstances into account, this army does not seem sufficient for the purpose

Written on August 7, 1854

First published in the *New-York Daily Tribune*, No. 4162, August 21; reprinted in the *New-York Semi-Weekly Tribune*, No. 964, August 22 and the *New-York Weekly Tribune*, No. 676, August 26, 1854 as a leader

Reproduced from the *New-York Daily Tribune*

Karl Marx

[EVACUATION OF THE DANUBIAN PRINCIPALITIES.—
THE EVENTS IN SPAIN.—
A NEW DANISH CONSTITUTION.—THE CHARTISTS][260]

London, Tuesday, Aug. 8, 1854

On the 28th ult. Prince Gorchakoff passed with the center of his army through Shlawa, a village about six miles from Kalugereni; leaving it again on the 29th *en route* for Fokshani. The vanguard, commanded by Gen. Soimonoff, consists of eight battalions of the 10th division of infantry, of the regiments of *chasseurs* of Tomsk and Koliwan, and of the regiment of hussars of the Grand Duke, Heir of the Empire.[a] This vanguard was to pass the Jalomitza on the 1st inst. at Ureshti and Merescyani, where bridges had been constructed. It would be expected to arrive at Fokshani about the middle of the month.

The Turkish army advances in three columns. The center was, on July 29, at Kalugereni, on the 30th skirmishers of its vanguard were seen at Glina, two miles from Bucharest, where Omer Pasha's headquarters were expected to be established on the 1st. The right wing marched along the Argish, in the direction from Oltenitza on Bucharest. The left which, on the 28th, was at Mogina, is to take the road from Slatina to Bucharest.

"The retrograde movement of the Russian army," says the *Moniteur de l'Armée*, "seems to partake more of a strategic than of a political character. The Muscovite General finds in it the advantage of concentrating his troops in a good position where they can draw breath from the sufferings undergone in the Dobrodja, and inflicted upon them, on the left bank of the Danube by the Turks. He will be nearer to his basis of *approvisionnement*,[b] while continuing to occupy an important portion of the territory invaded last year. Finally he gets a position that is formidable, even in the presence of superior forces."

---

[a] Alexander Nikolayevich (Alexander II).—*Ed.*
[b] Supply.— *Ed.*

On the 26th of July Baron Budberg addressed the following proclamation to the Wallachians:

"His Majesty the Emperor of all the Russias, King of Poland, and Protector of the Principalities of Moldavia and Wallachia, and Protector of all those who profess the orthodox Greek faith, has determined to withdraw the imperial troops for a very short period from the insalubrious countries of the Danube, in order to quarter them on the more healthy hills. The enemy, in the short-sightedness of his views, imagined that we retired from fear of him, and consequently he attempted to attack our troops during their retreat. But Prince Gorchakoff, the Commander-in-Chief, had hardly ordered his troops to repulse them when they fled ignominiously, abandoning their arms and ammunition, which our gallant soldiers carry away. When the season shall be more favorable we shall return to you in arms, to deliver you forever from the barbarous Turk. Our retreat will be effected with caution, and without hurry, so that the enemy may not imagine that we are flying before him."[a]

It is curious that in 1853, in the very same month of July, the Russians found the season not at all unfavorable to the occupation of Wallachia.

"The emigration of the Bulgarian families from the Dobrodja," says a letter from Galatch published in a German paper, "is constantly going on. About 1,000 families, with 150,000 head of cattle, have crossed near Reni."

This "voluntary emigration," to which the inhabitants were invited by the Russians, on the plea of the dangers from Turkish vengeance, is very similar in character to the "voluntary" Austrian loan.[b] The Vienna correspondent of *The Morning Chronicle* relates that the same families,

"on learning that they were to be employed on the fortifications in Moldavia, wished to return to their homes; but they were forced by the Cossacks to proceed to Fokshani, where they are now at work at the trenches."

The barricades were scarcely removed at Madrid, at the request of Espartero, before the counter-revolution was busy at work. The first counter-revolutionary step was the impunity allowed to Queen Cristina, Sartorius, and their associates. Then followed the formation of the Ministry, with the Moderado O'Donnell as Minister of War, and the whole army placed at the disposal of this old friend of Narvaez. There are in the list the names of Pacheco, Lujan, Don Francisco Santa Cruz, all of them notorious partisans of Narvaez, and the first a member of the infamous Ministry of 1847.[261] Another, Salazar, has been appointed on the sole merit of

---

[a] Baron Budberg's address is given according to *Le Moniteur universel*, No. 219, August 7, 1854.— *Ed.*

[b] See this volume, pp. 288-89 and 304.— *Ed.*

being a playfellow of Espartero. In remuneration for the bloody sacrifices of the people, on the barricades and in the public place, numberless decorations have been showered upon the Espartero generals on the one hand, and on the Moderado friends of O'Donnell on the other hand. In order to pave the way for an ultimate silencing of the press, the press law of 1837 has been reestablished. Instead of convoking a general Constituent Cortes, Espartero is said to intend convoking only the Chambers after the Constitution of 1837, and, as some say, even as modified by Narvaez. To secure as far as possible the success of all these measures and others that are to follow, large masses of troops are being concentrated near Madrid. If any consideration press itself especially on our attention in this affair, it is the suddenness with which the reaction has set in.

On the first instant the chiefs of the barricades called upon Espartero, in order to make to him some observations on the choice of his Ministry. He entered into a long explanation on the difficulties with which he was beset, and endeavored to defend his nominations. But the Deputies of the people seem to have been little satisfied with his explanation. "Very alarming" news arrives at the same time, about the movements of the republicans in Valencia, Catalonia, and Andalusia. The embarrassment of Espartero is visible from his decree sanctioning the continued activity of the provincial juntas.[a] Nor has he yet dared to dissolve the junta of Madrid, though his Ministry is complete and installed in office.

On the demand of Napoleon the Little, Col. Charras has been expelled from Belgium. The Paris correspondent of the *Indépendance belge* speaks of a pamphlet, written and published by Prince Murat, which claims the crown of King Bomba[b] as the legitimate inheritance of the Murats.[c] The pamphlet had been translated into Italian.

The Danish Ministry obstinately persists in refusing to accord to the western powers the harbors and landing-places which would enable them to keep their forces in the Baltic during the winter. This is, however, not the only manner in which that Government manifests its contempt for the powers arrayed against its patron, the Emperor of Russia. It has not hesitated to make its long

------

[a] Isabella II. The decree sanctioning the existence of the provincial juntas of August 1, 1854, countersigned by Espartero. *Le Moniteur universel*, No. 220, August 8, 1854.— *Ed.*

[b] Ferdinand II.— *Ed.*

[c] *L'Indépendance belge*, No. 219, August 7, 1854.— *Ed.*

meditated *coup d'état*, one entirely in the interest of Russia, in the very face of the fleets and armies of the occidental powers. On July 26 a state paper was published at Copenhagen, headed: "Constitution of the Danish Monarchy for its common affairs." Strange to say, the English press has scarcely taken any notice at all of this measure. I give you, therefore, the more important points of this new Danish Constitution:

Section 1. The succession of the Danish monarchy is settled by the law of 31st July, 1853.

Sec. 5. Common affairs of the monarchy are all those which are not expressly stated to refer to any particular part of it.

Sec. 6. The common expenses of the monarchy in excess of its receipts are to be borne in the following proportion, viz: Denmark 60 per cent.; Schleswig 17 per cent.; Holstein 23 per cent.

Sec. 7. The common affairs of the monarchy are to be in charge of a *Rigsrad.*

Sec. 8. The present Rigsrad will be composed only of members nominated by the King. Future Rigsrads are to be *partly* elected.

Sec. 10. The Rigsrad will then be composed of fifty members, the King nominating twenty, and the other thirty members will be elected in the following proportion, viz: The Diet of Denmark will elect 18, the Provincial States of Schleswig 5, those of Holstein 6, and the Ritterschaft of Lauenburg 1.

Sec. 11. The fundamental law of the Kingdom of Denmark of 5th June, 1849, is to be restricted to the affairs of that kingdom.

Sec. 15. The members of the Rigsrad receive an annual pay of 500 thalers.

Sec. 16. The Rigsrad is to be convoked at least once within every two years, for a term as shall be decreed by the King.

Sec. 17. Its sittings are to be at Copenhagen; but the King may remove them to any other place.

Sec. 18. Its deliberations will be guided by a President, nominated by the King. The debates may be either in the German or the Danish languages, but the resolutions must be put in the latter.

Sec. 19. The deliberations of the Rigsrad are secret.

Sec. 21. No tax common to the whole Monarchy can be levied, altered, or suppressed, nor any loan contracted for the whole Monarchy without the consent of the Rigsrad.

Sec. 22. The Rigsrad has only a consultative voice in all other except the money affairs of the common Monarchy.

A decree of the same date convokes the Rigsrad for Sept. 1st, 1854, and another decree publishes the nominations of the King, the nominees being all courtiers, high functionaries, and knights of the Danebrog.[a]

The principal points gained by this new *coup d'état* are the suppression of the fundamental law, of the representative institutions of Denmark, and the creation of an easy machine for

---

[a] All the decrees mentioned above are cited from the report of the Copenhagen correspondent of July 31. *Le Moniteur universel*, No. 216, August 4, 1854.— *Ed.*

the supply of as much money as the Court and the Government may want.

Ernest Jones has started on another tour through the manufacturing districts, in order to agitate them in favor of the Charter. At Halifax, Bacup, and the other localities he had already visited, the following petition to the Parliament was adopted:

"To the Honorable, the Commons of Great Britain and Ireland in Parliament assembled.— The humble Petition of the Inhabitants of Bacup, in public meeting assembled, on Sunday, the 30th of July, 1854,
Sheweth,—

"That your Petitioners have long and closely observed the conduct of the present Ministers of the Crown, in their home and foreign policy, and are convinced from calm observation that in both they are utterly undeserving the confidence of the country.

"That your Petitioners feel convinced no domestic amelioration will take place, and no external vigor be displayed so long as such men remain at the helm of national affairs.

"Your Petitioners therefore pray your honorable House to present an address to the throne, to the effect that Her Majesty may be pleased to discard her present advisers, and call to her assistance men more in harmony with the progressive spirit of the age, and better suited to the requirements of the times.

"And your Petitioners will ever pray."[a]

On Sunday[b] a large meeting assembled at Dirpley Moor, Bacup; where the agitator[c] delivered one of the most powerful speeches ever made by him, some extracts from which deserve a place in your journal[262]:

"The time for action has at last arrived, and we are commencing now such a revival of Chartism in England as never yet succeeded on a pause of apathy. At last the hour is drawing nigh when we shall have the Charter....

"Against the fall of wages you have struggled—and struggled vainly; hunger led you to the breach; ...but poverty was your teacher, even as hunger was your drill-sergeant; and after every fresh fall you rose in intelligence and knowledge. At first combinations and strikes were your remedy. You sought to conquer by them—forgetting that, not having the means of working for yourselves, you had not the means of resisting the capitalist—whose purse sat very comfortably watching your belly—seeing which could stand out longest.... You thought short time would do it, and were told that if each man worked two hours less, there would be two hours' work for those who had not worked at all. But you forgot that while you shortened the hours of labor one per cent, monopoly increased machinery one hundred....

"You then flew to co-operation. You compassed a great truth—the salvation of labor must depend on co-operation—but you overlooked the means of insuring that salvation. If you manufacture, you require a market—if you have something

---

[a] *The People's Paper*, No. 118, August 5, 1854.— *Ed.*
[b] July 30, 1854.— *Ed.*
[c] Ernest Jones.— *Ed.*

to sell, you require somebody who wants to buy it—and you forgot that that somebody was not at hand. Co-operative manufacture starts—but where's the market.... Where then are you to get the market? How can you make the poor rich, which alone can enable them to become purchasers of what co-operation manufactures? By those British Californians, whose gold is on the surface of the soil, and tints the waving wheatfield of the harvest. Look at your feet!—there, on the grassy banks whereon you sit—there, on the broad field whereon you stand—there lies liberty—there lies co-operation—there lies high wages—there lies prosperity and peace! In the fifteen millions of our public lands—the twenty-seven millions of our uncultivated British prairies[a] here at home. A Greek fable says Hercules wrestled with the giant Antæus, whose mother was the Earth, and threw him often—but every time he fell upon his mother's breast he gained fresh force, and bounded up more strong. Hercules discovering this, lifted him up, and held him in the air, till he had conquered him. Thus does the Hercules monopoly tear giant labor from its parent soil, and hold it by the grasp of competition, weak, powerless, and suspended, like Mahomet's tomb, 'twixt heaven and hell—only much nearer to the latter place!

"But how get to the land? There are some men who tell you that political power is not needed for the purpose. Who are they who tell you so? Is it the leaders of ten per cent. movements, and ten hours' movements, and short time movements, and restriction on machinery movements, and burial club movements, and partnership movements, and benefit society movements, and church separation movements, and education movements, and municipal movements, and all the other movements besides? What a lot of 'movements', and yet we have not *moved*. Not want political power? Why, these are the very men who go dancing around a political Tidd Pratt,[b]—or send whining deputations to a political Palmerston,—or petition a political parliament, or wheedle around a political throne! Why, then it is political power we must go to after all, by their own showing. Only those men tell you to go to the political power of your *enemies*, and I tell you to go to a political power of your *own*.... I lay down this sovereign truth:—

"The charter is the universal remedy.

"What have we opposed to us? First, a coalition ministry. What does it mean? The leaders of factions, not one of which can stand alone. Some dozen men, too weak to stand on their own legs, and so they lean against each other, and the whole lot of them can't make one proper man at last. That is a coalition. What have we besides? A Tory opposition that would kick them out, but dare not; for it knows that it would be kicked out in turn; and then comes the Deluge, in which Noah himself could not save Class Government. What have we else? A landed aristocracy, three-fourths of whose estates are mortgaged for above two-thirds of their value—a glorious power that to crush a people! 38,000 bankrupt landlords, with 300,000 farmers, who groan beneath high rents, game laws and landlord tyranny. What have we more? A minocracy becoming bankrupt beneath the working of their own vile race of competition—who soon will not be able to keep their mills over their own heads. A precious power that to strike the pedestal of freedom from your feet! What remains? The working man and the shopkeeper. Often has it been endeavored to unite the two on the basis of a compromise. I for one have always

---

[a] *Sic* in the original.— *Ed.*

[b] Apparently a misprint. The reference to a book by the well-known English lawyer W. Tidd, *Practice of the Court of King's Bench.*—*Ed.*

opposed it, because a compromise of the franchise would only have strengthened the moneyed interest, and perfected class legislation. But the time for that union has now come at last—and come without the need of compromise or treason. The retail shopkeepers are fast becoming democratic. It is said the way to a working man's brain is through his belly. Aye! and the way to a shopkeeper's heart is through his pocket? For every shilling less he takes he gets a new idea. Insolvency is teaching him the truth.... Thus the moral force of our enemies is annihilated— and new allies are joining us. Their physical force is gone as well. The Czar's done that! In Ireland there are scarce 1,000 men! In England there is now no standing army. But there's the militia! Ah, the militia! of which the desertions are so immensely numerous, says *The London Times*, that the 'Hue and cry' is no longer enough, but special circulars are sent to every parish, to every place where the deserter ever lived, if but a week, to see if force and terror can drag him back. I wish the Government joy of their new force. Thus the field is clear—the people's opportunity has come. Do not suppose from this I mean violence. No! Far from it! *We mean a great peaceable moral movement.* But because *we* mean moral force, it does not follow our *enemies* should mean it *too*....

"England has begun to think, and listening. As yet she is listening for the drums of Poland and the tramp of Hungary. As yet she is listening for the cries of Milan and the shouts of Paris! But amid the passing pause she is beginning to hear the beating of her own proud heart—and cries 'I also have a work to do—a foe to vanquish, and a field to conquer.'"[a]

The Chairman of the meeting[b] adverted to the presence of the Superintendent and other men of the police—trusting that no misrepresentations of what was said would be reported by those employed by Government.[c] Referring to this warning Ernest Jones said:

"For my part, I don't care what they say—they may say what they choose. I go into agitation like a soldier into battle—taking my chance amid the balls that fly—to fall and perish, or to live and conquer; for I'm a soldier of Democracy."[d]

Written on August 8, 1854

First published in the *New-York Daily Tribune*, No. 4162, August 21; reprinted in the *New-York Semi-Weekly Tribune*, No. 964, August 22 and partly in the *New-York Weekly Tribune*, No. 676, August 26, 1854

Signed: *Karl Marx*

Reproduced from the *New-York Daily Tribune*

---

[a] *The People's Paper*, No. 118, August 5, 1854.—*Ed.*

[b] Shoesmith.—*Ed.*

[c] This warning was not pronounced by the Chairman but by James Mooney who was the first to speak. *The People's Paper*, No. 118, August 5, 1854.—*Ed.*

[d] This is a quotation from Ernest Jones' speech extracts from which are given by Marx above.—*Ed.*

Karl Marx

[EVACUATION OF MOLDAVIA AND WALLACHIA.— POLAND.—DEMANDS OF THE SPANISH PEOPLE][263]

London, Friday, Aug. 11, 1854

Yesterday's *Moniteur* states that

"the Russian Envoy at Vienna[a] has announced to the Austrian Cabinet that the Emperor Nicholas has ordered the complete evacuation of Wallachia and Moldavia. Notwithstanding this declaration, Count Buol exchanged notes on the 8th inst. with Baron de Bourqueney and Lord Westmorland, from which it results that Austria, like France and England, is of opinion that *guarantees* must be exacted from Russia to prevent a return of complications which disturb the quiet of Europe, and engages itself until the reestablishment of general peace not to enter into any treaty with the Cabinet of St. Petersburg unless those *guarantees* are obtained."[b]

Of what sort these guarantees are to be, may be seen from *The Times* of this morning. Firstly, the evacuation of the Principalities; secondly, the substitution of a common European protectorate in *lieu* of the Russian protectorate; thirdly, the

"revision of the Convention of the Straits, and the adoption of such measures as are necessary to reduce the naval ascendancy of Russia within limits less formidable to the existence of Turkey and the independence of navigation both on the waters of the Euxine and at the mouths of the Danube."[c]

The statement of the *Moniteur* is on the whole confirmed by the declarations of Lord Clarendon in yesterday's sitting of the House of Lords.[d] We know also, from other sources, that the Russian headquarters are removed to Buseo; that four Russian regiments have crossed the Pruth, and that the Austrian Government, on its part, has countermanded the order given to several corps of

---

[a] A. M. Gorchakov.— *Ed.*
[b] *Le Moniteur universel*, No. 222, August 10, 1854.— *Ed.*
[c] *The Times*, No. 21817, August 11, 1854, leader.— *Ed.*
[d] *The Times*, No. 21817, August 11, 1854.— *Ed.*

troops to reenforce the armies drawn up *en échelon* on the
frontiers of Galicia and Transylvania.

There was scarcely ever a more curious operation in the history
of wars than this evacuation of the Principalities by the armies of
Russia. The fact is that it cannot be accounted for from any
strategical, but only from a diplomatic point of view. As has been
explained in *The Tribune*,[a] a plan had been arranged between
Austria and Russia, according to which the Austrians were to
occupy the Principalities as soon as the honor of the Czar should
be satisfied by the capture of Silistria; the chance of a Russian
defeat being provided for by a clause, according to which the
Austrian occupation was to take place in that case, too. Accordingly, one day before the Russians raised the siege of Silistria, a treaty
was concluded between Turkey and Austria, giving the latter
power the right to enter Wallachia.[264] The treaty aimed at three
purposes—to withhold the Principalities from Turkey; to "raise a
cordon against the plague of revolution around the Austrian
frontiers;" lastly, to secure the safe retreat of the Russian army.
This treaty, as we may safely infer from the confessions of Lord
Clarendon, was forced upon the Porte by Lord Stratford de
Redcliffe, the English Embassador at Constantinople—the Divan
simultaneously issuing an order for allowing the Russians to retire
without being molested by pursuit. The precipitate withdrawal of
the Russians from the Danube is therefore without an explanation,
unless it entered into Russia's agreements with Austria. The
Austrians had fixed the 3d of July for the entrance of their troops
into Wallachia. Whence their procrastination? They were securing
concession upon concession from the Porte: firstly, in respect of
the form of government to be established in Wallachia; secondly,
in respect to the exclusion of the Turks from their own province.
Subsequently they made known that their occupation of Wallachia
would not include a declaration of war.

"The Austrian Government," says Lord Clarendon, "at the end of June, when
the Russians were about to evacuate Wallachia, sent an officer from the staff of
General Hess to inform the allied Commanders that the Austrian Government
intended to occupy a portion of Wallachia, in the name of the Sultan, and for the
purpose of restoring his authority there; but that they would not enter as
belligerents, *because* they were not at war with Russia, and had not received an
answer to the demands which they had addressed to her."

This imbecile sincerity of Austria caused embarrassment, and a
new delay was necessitated. Then came the protest of Prussia,

---

[a] See this volume, pp. 246-52.—*Ed.*

jealous of the aggrandizement of Austrian power on the Danube. The fact of both these powers being the tools of Russia does not exclude their remaining jealous of each other, as was sufficiently exemplified by the "potato-war" of 1850.[265] If Mr. Urquhart had perused the Warsaw protocol of that year,[266] he would not have tumbled into the Quixotic idea of suddenly propping up Prussia as the European bulwark against Russia.

Seeing Austria losing her opportunity, the Russians already in retreat turned round and advanced once more to the Danube, for, if the evacuation of Wallachia was complete before Austria had moved, their subsequent entrance into that Principality would have been deprived of any pretext. Meanwhile, however, the Turkish General at Rustchuk[a]—to use the phraseology of The Times— "imagining"[b] the Russians in full retreat, went over to Giurgevo, and beat them so soundly as to render impossible any attempt at retaking possession of the line of the Danube. In consequence of this defeat the Russians were obliged to think seriously of retreat, a resolution to which they were prompted by the discovery that the ostensible allies of Turkey would no longer be able to remain inactive, and that the English Government would be forced, in deference to their army as well as to the public, to undertake something against them. By retiring from the Principalities they increased their defensive force in Bessarabia and the Crimea. Thus we learn by a telegraphic dispatch that the Russian regiments in Bessarabia and Kherson are to move in all possible haste to the Crimea, while those in Moldavia march to occupy their places.[c]

It was to be presumed that the Turks would not be slow in improving their opportunity. Their vanguard, under Iskander Bey, entered Bucharest on the 6th inst., and their General received a deputation from the Wallachian Capital on the anniversary of the day in which, in 1853, their enemies had entered it.

Thus the Austrians have again lost their opportunity and are deprived of their false pretenses for entering Wallachia. An occupation at this moment would bring them infallibly into collision with the Turks. While, therefore, the Austrian papers denounce the advance of the Turks upon Bucharest as a breach of contract, the Austrians themselves are denounced by the English

---

[a] Omer Pasha.—Ed.

[b] The Times, No. 21807, July 31, 1854, leader.—Ed.

[c] Telegraphic dispatch from Vienna of August 8. The Times, No. 21816, August 10, 1854.—Ed.

ministerial press for their slowness and stupidity, in having set at nought the fine spun plot. In *The Times* of Thursday we read for instance:

"The Austrians have lost by their procrastination the effect of the position they might have assumed in the Principalities. Omer Pasha has taken advantage of this opportunity and closed up on the heels of the retreating enemy. Wallachia is now in a great degree occupied by the troops of the Sultan. The Danube from Orsova to Galatch is in their possession and there is no reason to suppose that any claim can be urged by a foreign power to induce the Turkish commander to recede from a province which he holds by the right of the master and by the valor of his army." [a]

All that is left for the Austrians to do now is the occupation of Moldavia.

The dispatches from Constantinople dated July 30, almost exclusively allude to the projected expedition against the Crimea.[b] The division of twenty ships which started from Balchik on the 21st of July, accompanied by Generals Brown and Canrobert, and commanded by Admiral Bruat, in order to *reconnoitre* the coast from Anapa to Sevastopol, returned on the 27th. After their return Canrobert and Brown immediately proceeded to Varna to communicate the results of their mission to St. Arnaud and Lord Raglan.[c] The Anglo-French troops were drawn up from Varna to Kustendje, in order to facilitate their embarkation at the different ports. This embarkation must have taken place on the 29th or 30th of July. The Turkish fleet had entered the Black Sea, and all the Anglo-French naval forces must have been assembled in the latitude of Varna as on the 1st inst., numerous transports were accumulated there. On the destination of these forces the *Gazette du Midi* has the following:

"Some speak of Anapa, and the neighboring fortress which contain together about 20,000 men, and the capture of which would at once establish communications between Abkhazia, Circassia, and the Crimea, so that the Circassians could easily take part in any attack directed against the Crimea. According to others the attack is to be directed against Odessa, which, at this moment, musters a garrison of about 40,000 men, and which would be fortified by the allied troops, in order to stay there during the winter, and to threaten Bessarabia on one side and the Crimea on the other side. A third version points to Nikolayev as the point to be attacked, there being there the arsenals of the Russian army, and this place

[a] *The Times*, No. 21816, August 10, 1854, leader.— *Ed.*
[b] *Journal des Débats*, August 10, 1854.— *Ed.*
[c] *The Times*, No. 21816, August 10, 1854, leader.— *Ed.*

occupying the triangle formed by the Dnieper in the east, and the Bug in the west."[a]

The Dobrodja has been entirely abandoned by the Russians, and is now occupied by 36,000 Turks and French. The Turks are at Babadagh and are said to be under orders to attack Tultsha, while the French are to attack Galatch.

On the 16th of July, the little town established by the Russians at the Sulina mouth, which was already partly dismantled, is said to have been completely destroyed by the English steamers *Spitfire* and *Vesuvius*, no buildings having been spared except the lighthouse and the church.

In the White Sea the English have effected a landing on some point on the Coast of Onega and destroyed a village.

The *Vladimir* affair in the Black Sea[267] has called forth a violent attack from *The Times* against Admiral Dundas,[b] to which *The Herald* answers as follows:

"Sir Charles Napier in the Baltic could permit the Sweaborg fleet to pass unmolested to their anchorage—could allow Hango Udd to be well fortified, and then most ineffectively bombarded—could permit the buoys to be removed and the ships to run aground in consequence, and not one word of reflection would *The Times* cast upon him; but with Admiral Dundas the case is altogether different."[c]

By letters from Paris of the 9th inst. we learn that 50,000 French troops are to be added to the Oriental army.[d] If the war produce no other good, it has at least the merit of ridding France of her Decembrist army.

It may have occurred to your notice that the Emperor of Russia, since his discomfiture in Turkey, has recommenced using the title of King of Poland, which he had resigned as superfluous after his victory in Hungary, the absorption of that country being considered to have been effected. In a letter published by the *Vienna Presse*, dated Warsaw, 1st Aug., we read:

"The approaching arrival of the Czar at Warsaw will be marked, it is said, by certain concessions to the Poles in the point of view of their nationality. It is said that the assembly of notables mentioned in the organic statute for the Kingdom of Poland of 1832[268] is to be convoked. The establishments of public instruction are,

---

[a] This quotation is given according to a reprint in *L'Indépendance belge*, No. 223, August 11, 1854.— *Ed.*

[b] *The Times*, No. 21815, August 9, 1854, leader.— *Ed.*

[c] *The Morning Herald*, No. 22194, August 10, 1854.— *Ed.*

[d] Report by the Paris correspondent of August 9. *L'Indépendance belge*, No. 222, August 10, 1854.— *Ed.*

it is said, to be reopened, and the employment of the Polish language in official acts, the publication of the annual expenses and receipts, and the right to consent to direct taxes ordered. The Polish army is also, as the report goes, to be reestablished, but under command of Russian officers. The fourth recruitment is finished. Never had the population been subjected to contributions to such an extent."[a]

We read also in the *Düsseldorfer Zeitung* under date of 7th August:

"According to reports from Warsaw, Gen. Rüdiger, the stadtholder of the Kingdom of Poland, has summoned the marshals of the Polish nobility to petition the Crown for the restoration of an independent Polish Kingdom."

Many solutions of the Polish question have been offered by diverse parties, but never did any one imagine such a solution as that proposed and ordered by the Russian general.

I am informed from Copenhagen that the idiot king of Denmark,[b] accompanied by the Minister of the Interior, M. de Tillisch, has embarked to meet the king of Sweden[c] at Karlskrona. Tillisch is one of the most fanatical partisans of Russia, and it is generally supposed that the meeting of the two kings is destined to renew the bond of Russian partisanship called the Northern armed neutrality.[269] If Denmark and Sweden mean neutrality toward Russia, it does not follow that they mean the same toward England and France, as the following circumstance sets forth. Some days ago General Mesa, Commander-in-chief of the Danish Artillery, passed in review the Artillery of the National Guard and addressed to them an unusually ardent allocution, hinting that the day approached perhaps when the National Artillery, united to that of the army, would be appealed to by the king for the common defense of the Scandinavian fatherland.

Parliament will be prorogued to-morrow. The session is remarkable for its abandoned measures, as the campaign, for its postponement of warlike operations.

Some days ago the *Charivari* published a caricature exhibiting the Spanish people engaged in battle and the two sabers— Espartero and O'Donnell—embracing each other over their heads. The *Charivari* mistook for the end of the revolution, what is only its commencement. The struggle has already commenced

---

[a] This letter is quoted from a reprint in *The Morning Post*, No. 25150, August 11, 1854.— *Ed.*

[b] Frederick VII.— *Ed.*

[c] Oscar I; report by the Hamburg correspondent of August 8. *L'Indépendance belge*, No. 223, August 11, 1854.— *Ed.*

between O'Donnell and Espartero, and not only between them, but also between the military chiefs and the people. It has been of little avail to the Government to have appointed the toreador Pucheta as Superintendent of the slaughter-houses, to have nominated a committee for the reward of the barricade-combatants, and finally to have appointed two Frenchmen, Pujol and Delmas, as historiographers of the revolution. O'Donnell wants the Cortes to be elected according to the law of 1845, Espartero according to the Constitution of 1837,[270] and the people by universal suffrage. The people refuse to lay down their arms before the publication of a Government program, the program of Manzanares[a] no longer satisfying their views. The people demand the annulment of the Concordat of 1851,[271] confiscation of the estates of the counter-revolutionists, an *exposé* of the finances, cancelling of all contracts for railways and other swindling contracts for public works, and lastly the judgment of Cristina by a special Court. Two attempts at flight on the part of the latter have been foiled by the armed resistance of the people. *El Tribuno* makes the following account of restitutions to be made by Cristina to the National Exchequer: Twenty-four millions illegally received as Regent from 1834 to 1840; twelve millions received on her return from France after an absence of three years; and thirty-five millions received of the Treasury of Cuba.[b] This account even is a generous one. When Cristina left Spain in 1840, she carried off large sums and nearly all the jewels of the Spanish Crown.

Written on August 11, 1854

First published in the *New-York Daily Tribune*, No. 4166, August 25; reprinted in the *New-York Semi-Weekly Tribune*, No. 966, August 29 and partly in the *New-York Weekly Tribune*, No. 677, September 2, 1854

Signed: *Karl Marx*

Reproduced from the *New-York Daily Tribune*

[a] See this volume, p. 305.—*Ed.*
[b] The account from *El Tribuno* is given according to *L'Indépendance belge*, No. 221, August 9, 1854.—*Ed.*

Karl Marx

[THE EASTERN QUESTION.—THE REVOLUTION IN SPAIN.—THE MADRID PRESS][272]

London, Tuesday, Aug. 15, 1854

It is stated in the *Cologne Gazette*[a] that

"after many years negotiations the American Government has declared its refusal to renew the existing treaty with Denmark, unless article V. be replaced by a stipulation according free passage through the Sound to all American vessels. At the same time the United States Government has declined to offer any compensation. Denmark, menaced by these American measures, has appealed to the other powers, and the Prussian Government is said to be willing to send 20,000 men for the protection of the Sound."

Since the Sound duties weigh on no one more oppressively than on Prussia herself, the measure attributed to her would marvellously suit the genius of Prussian policy. Altogether — *se non è vero, è ben trovato*.[b]

The Frankfort Diet has published the new law on the press and association which has occupied its deliberations for a long time. The law affecting public associations simply prohibits every sort of political meetings or reunions, and the law on the press imposes heavy sums of *cautionnement*,[c] makes the issue of all publications dependent on Government permission, and withdraws offenses of the press from the jurisdiction of the jury trial.

The long-pending affair of the Berlin revolutionist conspiracy[273] has been abandoned by the Prussian Government, the chief witness against the accused parties, Mr. Hentze, being declared "suspect" by the public prosecutor. This Hentze is the same

---

[a] *Kölnische Zeitung.—Ed.*
[b] If it is not true, it's cleverly invented.—*Ed.*
[c] Caution money.—*Ed.*

person on whose evidence, at the Cologne trial, a number of my friends were condemned to imprisonment in 1852.[274] But we are no longer in 1852, and the Prussian Government perhaps did not like to run the risk of seeing all its police agents branded a second time, reviving the *souvenirs* of Cologne in the very Capital, and at a time when the *terreur* of counter-revolution no longer imposes on the people.

On the 1st of August the Servian Government sent a courier to Brestovac, where Prince Alexander is using the waters, with the answer proposed to be made to the injunctions of the Sublime Porte.[a] The answer was signed by the Prince and immediately forwarded to Constantinople. It alleges the impossibility of a disarmament, on account of the many dangers that would surround it, but states that in deference to the wishes of Austria and the orders of the Porte the military exercises had been suspended. Izzet Pasha, the Governor of Belgrade, has been recalled, at his own request. His successor is not yet known.

Ten thousand Turks are said to occupy Bucharest; but at the same time we read in today's *Moniteur* that Austria is only waiting for the reply of Omer Pasha to the last communication of Colonel Kalik, in order to command the entrance of an Austrian corps into the Principalities.[b] When Count Buol received the notification from Prince Gorchakoff, announcing the departure of the Russians from the Principalities, he answered that

"the Austrian troops would occupy the Principalities, but that such occupation had nothing hostile to Russia."[c]

By the prorogation of Parliament in 1854 the Eastern Question is brought back to the stage it occupied at the prorogation of Parliament in 1853. The Vienna Conference[275] is once more to set to work, to paralyze active operations, to bewilder public opinion, and to offer a new occasion to Sir James Graham, at the reopening of Parliament, to say that a noble mind is slow to suspect.[d] It is worthy of observation that the dodge originates this time not with Austria, but with England itself, as you will see from *The Times* Vienna correspondence:

---

[a] See this volume, p. 325.—*Ed.*
[b] Report from Vienna of August 10, 1854. *Le Moniteur universel*, No. 226, August 14, 1854.—*Ed.*
[c] Report from Vienna of August 10, 1854, reprinted from the *Journal français de Francfort* in *Le Moniteur universel*, No. 227, August 15, 1854.—*Ed.*
[d] See this volume, pp. 12-13 and 27.—*Ed.*

"The English and French Ministers have informed Count Buol that they have been instructed by their Governments to *propose* that the Vienna Conference should meet. The reply is said to have been that nothing could be more agreeable to the Imperial Court." [a]

The basis of the new deliberations of the Conference is a sort of revived Vienna note, furnished by the answer of M. Drouyn de Lhuys to the last communication of M. de Nesselrode, the cardinal points of which differ very little from what I expected they would be after the analysis I gave you in my last letter [b] of the terms named by *The Times.* There is not a word about an indemnity to the Turks, nor even to the allies. The usurped Russian protectorate over Moldavia, Wallachia and Servia, is to be transformed into European usurpation; the same is to be done with the "protectorate" over the Christians in Turkey; the fruits of the Turkish victories to be restricted to free navigation of the Danube for Austria, and a change of the treaty of 1841 [276] in favor, not of the Porte, but of the Powers.

The speech of Lord Clarendon on Thursday, the main points of which I have already reported, contained a most important revelation on the policy observed by the English Ministry in the Oriental question. He stated in plain words:

"I beg you to remember, that it was on the 29th of March that war was declared —a little more than four months ago—and it was then universally believed—and, when I say universally believed I do not speak of her Majesty's Government, but of the most able and experienced officers both of England and France—that at that time Russia meditated a war of further aggression. Nobody believed that, with the great forces she had concentrated on the north of the Danube, with all the efforts she had made, and with all the vast supplies she had accumulated, she did not intend—on the contrary that she did intend—a march southward. Although we did not doubt the known bravery of the Turks, we could not bring ourselves to believe that they would be able to resist the well-disciplined and numerically superior Russian troops, under the most experienced generals, while the only Turkish general whom we know even by name was Omer Pasha, who had not then had the opportunity, which he has since so nobly profited by, to establish for himself a lasting fame and renown. So much were the French Government and we convinced of this that Sir J. Burgoyne and an experienced French officer of engineers were sent to Constantinople in order to devise means of defending that capital and the strait of the Dardanelles, and so much importance was attached to their mission, and so entirely was the whole plan of the campaign supposed to be connected with it, that the departure of Lord Raglan and Marshal St. Arnaud was delayed, in order that they might have personal communications with the officers sent out on that service. The united armies of the Allies then went to Gallipoli

---

[a] Report from Vienna of August 10. *The Times*, No. 21820, August 15, 1854.—*Ed.*
[b] See this volume, p. 357.—*Ed.*

where great works were thrown up. They went to Constantinople, always having the necessity of defending the Dardanelles in view."[a]

The whole plan, then, of the Allied Powers, was that Russia should advance into and occupy the provinces, and the allied forces the capital of the Ottoman Empire and the Dardanelles. Hence the delays and all the misunderstood movements of the Anglo-French forces. The bravery of the Turkish troops which baffled this Russo-Anglo-French trick was, of course, "unexpected."

Some months before the outbreak of the present Spanish revolution, I told your readers that Russian influences were at work in bringing about a Peninsular commotion.[b] For that Russia wanted no direct agents. There was *The Times*, the advocate and friend of King Bomba,[c] of the "young hope" of Austria,[d] of Nicholas, of George IV, suddenly turned indignant at the gross immoralities of Queen Isabella and the Spanish Court. There were, besides, the diplomatic agents of the English Ministry, whom the Russian Minister Palmerston had no difficulty in bamboozling with visions of a Peninsular Coburg kingdom.[277] It is now ascertained that it was the British Embassador[e] who concealed O'Donnell at his palace, and induced the banker Collado, the present Minister of Finance, to advance the money required by O'Donnell and Dulce, to start their pronunciamento. Should anybody doubt that Russia really had a hand in Peninsular affairs, let me remind him of the affair of the *Isla de Leon*. Considerable bodies of troops were assembled at Cadiz, in 1820, destined for the South American colonies. All at once the army stationed on the Isle declared for the Constitution of 1812, and its example was followed by troops elsewhere. Now, we know from Chateaubriand, the French Embassador at the Congress of Verona,[278] that Russia stimulated Spain to undertake the expedition into South America, and forced France to undertake the expedition into Spain. We know, on the other hand, from the message of the United States President,[f] that Russia promised him to prevent the expedition against South America.[g] It requires, then, but little judgment to

---

[a] Lord Clarendon's speech in the House of Lords on August 10, 1854. *The Times*, No. 21817, August 11, 1854.—*Ed.*

[b] See this volume, pp. 40-41.—*Ed.*

[c] Ferdinand II.—*Ed.*

[d] Francis Joseph I.—*Ed.*

[e] John Caradoc, Baron Howden.—*Ed.*

[f] James Monroe.—*Ed.*

[g] All this information is taken from David Urquhart, *Progress of Russia in the West, North, and South*, pp. 31-35, 40-50.—*Ed.*

Karl Marx

infer as to the authorship of the insurrection of the Isla de León. But I will give you another instance of the tender interest taken by Russia in the commotions of the Spanish Peninsula. In his *Historia política de la España moderna*, Barcelona, 1849, Señor de Marliani, in order to prove that Russia had no reason to oppose the constitutional movement of Spain, makes the following statement:

"There were seen on the Neva Spanish soldiers swearing to the Constitution (of 1812) and receiving their banners from imperial hands. In his extraordinary expedition against Russia Napoleon formed from the Spanish prisoners in France a special legion, who, after the defeat of the French forces, deserted to the Russian camp. Alexander received them with marked condescension, and quartered them at Peterhoff, where the Empress[a] frequently went to visit them. On a given day Alexander ordered them to assemble on the frozen Neva, and made them take the oath for the Spanish Constitution, presenting them at the same time with banners embroidered by the Empress herself. This corps, thenceforth named 'Imperial Alexander,' embarked at Kronstadt, and was landed at Cadiz. It proved true to the oath taken on the Neva, by rising, in 1821, at Ocaña for the reestablishment of the Constitution."

While Russia is now intriguing in the Peninsula through the hands of England, it, at the same time, denounces England to France. Thus we read in the *New-Prussian Gazette*[b] that England has made the Spanish revolution behind the back of France.

What interest has Russia in fomenting commotions in Spain? To create a diversion in the West, to provoke dissensions between France and England, and lastly to seduce France into an intervention. Already we are told by the Anglo-Russian papers that French insurrectionists of June[279] constructed the barricades at Madrid. The same was said to Charles X at the Congress of Verona.

"The precedent set by the Spanish army had been followed by Portugal, spread to Naples, extended to Piedmont, and exhibited everywhere the dangerous example of armies meddling in measures of reform, and by force of arms dictating laws to their country. Immediately after the insurrection had taken place in Piedmont, movements had occurred in France, at Lyons and in other places, directed to the same end. There was Berton's conspiracy at Rochelle in which 25 soldiers of the 45th regiment had taken part. Revolutionary Spain retransfused its hideous elements of discord into France, and both leagued their democratic factions against the monarchical system."[c]

Do we say that the Spanish revolution has been made by the Anglo-Russians? By no means. Russia only supports factious

Yelizaveta Alexeyevna.—*Ed.*
Neue Preußische Zeitung.—*Ed.*
Marliani, *Historia política de la España moderna*, p. 293.—*Ed.*

movements at moments when it knows revolutionary crises to be at hand. The real popular movement, however, which then begins, is always found to be as much opposed to the intrigues of Russia as to the oppressive agency of the Government. Such was the fact in Wallachia in 1848—such is the fact in Spain in 1854.

The perfidious conduct of England is exhibited at full length by the conduct of its Embassador at Madrid, Lord Howden. Before setting out from England to return to his post, he assembled the Spanish bondholders, calling upon them to press the payment of their claims on the Government, and in case of refusal, to declare that they would refuse all credit to Spanish merchants. Thus he prepared difficulties for the new Government. As soon as he arrived at Madrid, he subscribed for the victims fallen at the barricades. Thus he provokes ovations from the Spanish people.

The Times charges Mr. Soulé with having produced the Madrid insurrection in the interest of the present American Administration.[a] At all events, Mr. Soulé has not written The Times's articles against Isabella II, nor has the party inclined to Cuban annexation gained any benefit from the revolution. With regard to this question, the nomination of General de la Concha as Captain-General of the Island of Cuba is characteristic, he having been one of the seconds of the Duke of Alba in his duel with the son of Mr. Soulé. It would be a mistake to suppose that the Spanish Liberals in any way partake in the views of the English Liberal, Mr. Cobden, in reference to the abandonment of the colonies.[280] One great object of the Constitution of 1812 was to retain the empire over the Spanish colonies by the introduction of a united system of representation into the new code.[281] In 1811 the Spaniards even equipped a large armament, consisting of several regiments from Galicia, the only province in Spain then not occupied by the French, in order to combine coercion with their South American policy. It was almost the chief principle of that Constitution not to abandon any of the colonies belonging to Spain, and the revolutionists of today share the same opinion.

No revolution has ever exhibited a more scandalous spectacle in the conduct of its public men than this undertaken in the interest of "morality." The coalition of the old parties forming the present Government of Spain (the partisans of Espartero and the partisans of Narvaez) has been occupied with nothing so much as the division of the spoils of office, of places, of salaries, of titles, and of decorations. Dulce and Echague have arrived at Madrid, and

---

[a] The Times, No. 21820, August 15, 1854, leader.— Ed.

Serrano has solicited permission to come, in order to secure their shares in the plunder. There is a great quarrel between Moderados and Progresistas, the former being charged with having named all the generals, the latter with having appointed all the political chiefs. To appease the jealousies of the "rabble," Pucheta the toreador has been promoted from a director of the slaughter-houses to a director of police. Even the *Clamor Público*, a very moderate paper, gives vent to feelings of disappointment.

"The conduct of the generals and chiefs would have been more dignified if they had resigned promotion, giving a noble example of disinterestedness, and conforming themselves to the principles of morality proclaimed by the revolution." [a]

The shamelessness of the distribution of the spoils is marked by the division of the Embassadors' places. I do not speak of the appointment of Señor Olozaga for Paris, although being the Embassador of Espartero at the same Court in 1843, he conspired with Louis Philippe, Cristina and Narvaez; nor of the appointment for Vienna of Alejandro Mon, the Finance Minister of Narvaez in 1844; nor of that of Rios y Rosas for Lisbon, and Pastor Diaz for Turin, both Moderados of very indifferent capacity. I speak of the nomination of Gonzalez Bravo for the Embassy of Constantinople. He is the incarnation of Spanish corruption. In 1839 he published *El Guirigay (The Slang)*, a sort of Madrid *Punch*, in which he made the most furious attacks against Cristina. Three years afterward his rage for office transformed him into a boisterous Moderado. Narvaez, who wanted a pliant tool, used him as Prime Minister of Spain, and then kicked him away as soon as he could dispense with him. Bravo, in the interval, appointed as his Minister of Finance one Carrasco, who plundered the Spanish treasury directly. He made his father Under-Secretary of the Treasury, a man who had been expelled from his place as a subaltern in the Exchequer because of his malversation; and he transformed his brother-in-law, a hanger-on at the Principe Theater, into a state-groom to the Queen. When reproached with his apostasy and corruption, he answered: "Is it not ridiculous to be always the same?" This man is the chosen Embassador of the revolution of morality.

It is somewhat refreshing to hear, in contrast with the official infamies branding the Spanish movement, that the people have forced these fellows at least to place Cristina at the disposal of the

---

[a] The quotation from *El Clamor Público* is given according to *L'Indépendance belge*, No. 221, August 9, 1854.— *Ed.*

Cortes, and to consent to the convocation of a National Constituent Assembly, without a Senate, and consequently neither on the election law of 1837 nor that of 1845.[282] The Government has not yet dared to prescribe an election law of their own, while the people are unanimously in favor of universal suffrage. At Madrid the elections for the National Guard have returned nothing but *Exaltados*.[283]

In the provinces a wholesome anarchy prevails, juntas being constituted, and in action everywhere, and every junta issuing decrees in the interest of its locality—one abolishing the monopoly of tobacco, another the duty on salt. Contrabandists are operating on an enormous scale, and with the more efficiency, as they are the only force never disorganized in Spain. At Barcelona the soldiers are in collision, now among each other, and now with the workmen. This anarchical state of the provinces is of great advantage to the cause of the revolution, as it prevents its being confiscated at the capital.

The Madrid press is at this moment composed of the following papers: *España, Novedades, Nación, Época, Clamor Público, Diario Español, Tribuno, Esperanza, Iberia, Catolico, Miliciano, Independencia, Guarda Nacional, Esparterista, Union, Europa, Espectador, Liberal, Eco de la Revolución.* The *Heraldo, Boletin del Pueblo,* and the *Mensajero,* have ceased to exist.

Written on August 14 and 15, 1854

First published in the *New-York Daily Tribune*, No. 4172, September 1; reprinted in the *New-York Semi-Weekly Tribune*, No. 968, September 5 and the *New-York Weekly Tribune*, No. 678, September 9, 1854 (abridged)

Signed: *Karl Marx*

Reproduced from the *New-York Daily Tribune*

Karl Marx

[REVOLUTION IN SPAIN.—BOMARSUND][284]

London, Friday, August 18, 1854

The "leaders" of the *Assemblée Nationale, Times,* and *Journal des Débats* prove that neither the pure Russian party, nor the Russo-Coburg party, nor the Constitutional party are satisfied with the course of the Spanish revolution.[a] From this it would appear that there is some chance for Spain, notwithstanding the contradiction of appearances.

On the 8th inst. a deputation from the Union Club[285] waited on Espartero to present an address calling for the adoption of universal suffrage. Numerous petitions to the same effect were pouring in. Consequently, a long and animated debate took place at the Council of Ministers. But the partisans of universal suffrage, as well as the partisans of the election law of 1845,[286] have been beaten. The Madrid *Gaceta* publishes a decree for the convocation of the Cortes on the 8th of November[b] preceded by an *exposé* addressed to the Queen. At the elections, the law of 1837 will be followed, with slight modifications. The Cortes are to be one Constituent Assembly, the legislative functions of the Senate being suppressed. Two paragraphs of the law of 1845 have been preserved, viz.: the mode of forming the electoral *mesas* (boards receiving the votes and publishing the returns), and the number of deputies; one deputy to be elected for every 5,000 souls. The

---

[a] This refers to the article by A. de St.-Albin, "La révolution espagnole" published in the newspaper *L'Assemblée Nationale,* No. 674, August 14; S. de Sacy's article published in the *Journal des Débats,* August 15 and the leader in *The Times,* No. 21819, August 14, 1854.—*Ed.*

[b] For his analysis of this decree Marx used the text of *La Gaceta* of August 12 as reprinted in *Le Moniteur universel,* No. 230, August 18, 1854.—*Ed.*

Assembly will thus be composed of from 420 to 430 members. According to a circular of Santa Cruz, the Minister of the Interior, the electors must be registered by the 6th of September. After the verification of the lists by the provincial deputations, the electoral lists will be closed on the 12th of September. The elections will take place on the 3d of October, at the chief localities of the Electoral Districts. The scrutiny will be proceeded to on the 16th of October, in the capital of each province. In case of conflicting elections, the new proceedings which will thereby be necessitated, must be terminated by the 30th of October. The *exposé* states expressly that

"the Cortes of 1854, like those of 1837, will save the monarchy; they will be a new bond between the throne and the nation, objects which cannot be questioned or disputed."

In other words, the Government forbids the discussion of the dynastic question; hence, *The Times* concludes the contrary,[a] supposing that the question will now be between the present dynasty or no dynasty at all—an eventuality which, it is scarcely necessary to remark, infinitely displeases and disappoints the calculations of *The Times*.

The Electoral law of 1837 limits the franchise by the conditions of having a household, the payment of the *mayores cuotas* (the ship taxes levied by the State), and the age of twenty-five years. There are further entitled to a vote: the members of the Spanish Academies of History and of the Artes Nobles, doctors, licentiates in the faculties of Divinity, law, of medicine, members of ecclesiastical chapters, parochial curates and their assistant clergy, magistrates and advocates of two years' standing; officers of the army of a certain standing, whether on service or the retired list; physicians, surgeons, apothecaries of two years' standing; architects, painters and sculptors, honored with the membership of an academy; professors and masters in any educational establishment, supported by the public funds. Disqualified for the vote by the same law are defaulters to the common pueblo-fund, or to local taxation, bankrupts, persons interdicted by the courts of law for moral or civil incapacity; lastly, all persons under sentence.

It is true that this decree does not proclaim universal suffrage, and that it removes the dynastic question from the forum of the Cortes. Still it is doubtful that even this Assembly will do. If the Spanish Cortes forbore from interfering with the Crown in 1812, it was because the Crown was only nominally represented—the King[a] having been absent for years from Spanish soil. If they forbore in 1837, it was because they had to settle with absolute monarchy before they could think of settling with the constitutional monarchy. With regard to the general situation, *The Times* has truly good reasons to deplore the absence of French centralization in Spain,[b] and that consequently even a victory over revolution in the capital decides nothing with respect to the provinces, so long as that state of "anarchy" survives there without which no revolution can succeed.

There are, of course, some incidents in the Spanish revolution peculiarly belonging to them. For instance, the combination of robbery with revolutionary transactions—a connection which sprung up in the guerrilla wars against the French invasions, and which was continued by the "royalists" in 1823, and the Carlists since 1835.[287] No surprise will therefore be felt at the information that great disorders have occurred at Tortosa, in Lower Catalonia. The *Junta Popular* of that city says, in its proclamation of 31st July:

"A band of miserable assassins, availing themselves for pretext of the abolition of the indirect taxes, have seized the town, and trampled upon all laws of society. Plunder, assassination, incendiarism have marked their steps."[c]

Order, however, was soon restored by the Junta—the citizens arming themselves and coming to the rescue of the feeble garrison of the place. A military commission is sitting, charged with the pursuit and punishment of the authors of the catastrophe of July 30. This circumstance has, of course, given an occasion to the reactionary journals for virtuous declamation. How little they are warranted in this proceeding may be inferred from the remark of the *Messager de Bayonne*, that the Carlists have raised their banner in the provinces of Catalonia, Aragon and Valencia, and precisely in the same contiguous mountains where they had their chief nest in the old Carlist wars. It was the Carlists who gave origin to the *ladrones facciosos,* that combination of robbery and pretended allegiance to an oppressed party in the State. The Spanish guerrillero of all times has had something of the robber since the time of Viriathus; but it is a novelty of Carlist invention that a pure robber should invest himself with the name of guerrillero. The men of the Tortosa affair certainly belong to this class.

---

[a] Ferdinand VII.— *Ed.*
[b] *The Times*, No. 21800, July 22, 1854, leader.— *Ed.*
[c] Quoted from *L'Indépendance belge*, No. 229, August 17, 1854.— *Ed.*

At Lerida, Saragossa and Barcelona matters are serious. The two former cities have refused to combine with Barcelona, because the military had the upper hand there. Still it appears that even there Concha is unable to master the storm, and General Dulce is to take his place, the recent popularity of that general being considered as offering more guarantees for a conciliation of the difficulties.

The secret societies have resumed their activity at Madrid, and govern the democratic party just as they did in 1823.[288] The first demand which they have urged the people to make is that all ministers since 1843 shall present their accounts.

The ministry are purchasing back the arms which the people seized on the day of the barricades. In this way they have got possession of 2,500 muskets, formerly in the hands of insurgents. Don Manuel Sagasti, the Ayacucho *Jefe Politico*[a] of Madrid of 1843, has been reinstated in his functions. He has addressed to the inhabitants and the national militia two proclamations, in which he announces his intention of energetically repressing all disorder.[b] The removal of the creatures of Sartorius from the different offices proceeds rapidly. It is, perhaps, the only thing rapidly done in Spain. All parties show themselves equally quick in that line.

Salamanca is not imprisoned, as was asserted. He had been arrested at Aranjuez, but was soon released, and is now at Malaga.

The control of the ministry by popular pressure is proved by the fact, that the Ministers of War, of the Interior, and of Public Works,[c] have effected large displacements and simplifications in their several departments, an event never known in Spanish history before.

The Unionist or Coburg-Braganza party is pitifully weak.[289] For what other reason would they make such a noise about one single address sent from Portugal to the National Guard of Madrid? If we look nearer at it, it is even discovered that the address (originating with the Lisbon *Journal de Progrès*) is not of a dynastic nature at all, but simply of the fraternal kind so well known in the movements of 1848.

The chief cause of the Spanish revolution was the state of the finances, and particularly the decree of Sartorius, ordering the

---

[a] Governor.— *Ed.*

[b] The contents of Sagasti's addresses are given according to *Le Moniteur universel*, No. 229, August 17, 1854, which reprinted the material from the Madrid *Gaceta.—Ed.*

[c] O'Donnell, Santa Cruz, Lujan.— *Ed.*

payment of six months' taxes in advance upon the year.[290] All the
public chests were empty when the revolution broke out,
notwithstanding the circumstance that no branch of the public
service had been paid; nor were the sums destined for any
particular service applied to it during the whole of several months.
Thus, for instance, the turnpike receipts were never appropriated
to the use of keeping up the roads. The moneys set aside for
public works shared the same destiny. When the chest of public
works was subjected to revision, instead of receipts for executed
works, receipts from court favorites were discovered. It is known
that financiering has long been the most profitable business in
Madrid. The Spanish budget for 1853 was as follows:

Civil List and Appanages	47,350,000 reals.
Legislation	1,331,685 reals.
Interest of Public Debt	213,271,423 reals.
President of Council	1,687,860 reals.
Foreign Office	3,919,083 reals.
Justice	39,001,233 reals.
War	278,646,284 reals.
Marine	85,165,000 reals.
Interior	43,957,940 reals.
Police	72,000,000 reals.
Finances	142,279,000 reals.
Pensions	143,400,586 reals.
Cultus	119,050,508 reals.
Extras	18,387,788 reals.
Total	1,209,448,390 reals.

Notwithstanding this budget, Spain is the least taxed country of
Europe, and the economical question is nowhere so simple as
there. The reduction and simplification of the bureaucratic
machinery in Spain are the less difficult, as the municipalities
traditionally administer their own affairs; so is reform of the tariff
and conscientious application of the *bienes nacionales*[a] not yet
alienated. The social question in the modern sense of the word has
no foundation in a country with its resources yet undeveloped,
and with such a scanty population as Spain—15,000,000 only.

---

[a] State lands.— *Ed.*

You will see from the English press the first exploits of the British army at Bomarsund. These poor journals, which had never anything brilliant to report, are in great enthusiasm about the successes of 10,000 French troops over 2,000 Russians. I shall pass over these glories, and occupy myself with the consideration of the result of this capture of an island—the *faubourg* of Stockholm, and not of St. Petersburg. The French *Siècle* had announced, and its announcement was echoed by many journals, that Sweden would presently join the western powers against Russia in active measures.[a] The probabilities of this announcement may be measured by the fact that Sweden concluded a treaty of armed neutrality [291] at the very time it might have operated with success against the swamps and woods of Finland. Will it alter its policy now that the time for operations is gone by? England and France have refused to King Oscar the required pecuniary and territorial guarantees for his adhesion. Moreover, how are we to explain the order of the Swedish Government for the disarmament of a whole squadron, on the supposition that Sweden is about to take the field? This disarmament extends to the ships of the line *Charles XII* and *Prince Oscar*, the frigate *Désiré*, and the corvettes *Gefle* and *Thor*.

The capture of Bomarsund, now that the waters in those latitudes will soon be covered with ice, can have no importance. At Hamburg an opinion prevails that it is to be followed by the capture of Riga, an opinion based upon a letter of Captain Heathcote, commander of the *Archer*, to the English Consul, Mr. Hartslet, at Memel, to the effect that all foreign vessels must have cleared from the harbor of Riga by the 10th inst.[b]

Prussia is said to be greatly encouraging smuggling articles contraband of war on its Russian frontier, and at the same time preparing for a rupture with the occidental powers. The commanders of the harbors of Königsberg, Danzig, Colberg, and Swinemunde, have received orders to arm these places.

The most influential papers of Norway and Sweden declare that "it would be worse than madness to join the allies and make enormous sacrifices, unless on the fixed and well-understood condition that Russia shall be broken up and Poland restored.

---

[a] This information is taken from *L'Indépendance belge*, No. 230, August 18, 1854.— *Ed.*

[b] The contents of Captain Heathcote's letter are given according to a report from Hamburg in *L'Indépendance belge*, No. 230, August 18, 1854.—*Ed.*

378 Karl Marx

Otherwise even the transfer of Finland to Sweden would be a delusion and a snare."

It ought to be remembered that all these northern Governments are in conflict with their own people. At Copenhagen for instance, matters stand thus: the Schleswig-Holsteiners have determined to abstain from all elections for the Rigsråd; while at the same time the electors of Copenhagen have sent an address to Dr. Madvig, Deputy of the Landsthing, calling upon him not to accept a place in the Rigsråd, since the decree of the King was an infraction of the Danish Constitution and the rights of the Danish people.

Written on August 18, 1854

First published in the *New-York Daily Tribune*, No. 4174, September 4; reprinted in the *New-York Semi-Weekly Tribune*, No. 968, September 5 and partly in the *New-York Weekly Tribune*, No. 678, September 9, 1854

Signed: *Karl Marx*

Reproduced from the *New-York Daily Tribune*

Frederick Engels

THE CAPTURE OF BOMARSUND[292]

(ARTICLE I)

The allied armies have at length begun to act. They have taken Bomarsund. On the 3d or 4th ult., the French troops and British marines were landed on the island of Aland; on the 10th, the place was invested; on three succeeding days the batteries were erected and armed; on the 14th fire was opened; on the 15th the two round towers were taken by storm, one by the French, the other by the English; on the 16th, after a short engagement in which the allies lost very few men, the large casemated fort surrendered. This short way of proceeding certainly looks rather spirited. From all the information we possessed, it was to be expected that a regular siege, with at least one parallel and about a fortnight of open trenches, would be necessary to reduce the place. Even *The London Times*, which for a long time had talked in a way as if the allied infantry had but to charge the stone walls with the bayonet in order to make them crumble, had to admit, that after all a siege was inevitable, and that this tedious operation would probably last a fortnight.

If, then, the attack has been brought to a successful issue in about a week from the investment, and on the sixth day after breaking ground, the natural inference is that the besiegers must have found far less difficulty than they expected. What it was that facilitated the attack, we of course can merely guess until the detailed accounts of the siege arrive; but there are many circumstances which may have operated in their favor. A considerable number of the garrison were Finlanders, and in part even Alanders. They certainly were not very much inspired with Russian patriotism, and if the reports from deserters may be

trusted, they were even resolved not to fight if they could help it.
The inhabitants of the island appear to have received the allies, as
soon as they saw they were about to attack Bomarsund seriously,
as deliverers from the Russian yoke, and must have given them all
kinds of information and assistance. But the main point, after all,
must have been something very defective in the construction of
the fortress itself. As no ground plans of it are to be had, and all
our knowledge of it is derived from views and sketches, and from
non-professional (at least as far as engineering is concerned)
descriptions, which are necessarily very vague, and as both views
and descriptions are of a somewhat conflicting nature in the
details, we cannot pretend to state where the defect lay.

To judge from the sketches, however, the two round towers
flank each other by their fire in a certain degree; but as in every
round fortification the guns must have a radiating position, and
their fire must be exceedingly eccentric, the smaller the fort, and
with it the number of guns, the greater becomes the eccentricity
and the less effectual is the fire. Montalembert, therefore, took
great care not to propose the employment of such towers unless
this eccentricity was counteracted by the strong support which
each tower would receive from its neighbors on the right and left
and from the main fortress in the rear. If five or six such towers
could concentrate their fire on one point, the fire would then
become as concentric and effectual as it would be eccentric and
weak before. Montalembert, besides, knew very well that in the last
stages of a siege, whenever it comes to storming, infantry fire is
the most effectual that can be brought to bear on the assailants.
Therefore, beside the contrivances in his towers for admitting
infantry defense, he generally connected the separate towers by a
sort of covered way or trench, not for safe communication only,
but also for infantry fire. What such a trench can do, we have just
seen at Arab Tabiassi, where the whole flanking defense was
confined to such a trench, and where the Russians were driven
back, time after time, by a mere handful of Arnauts.[a] Finally,
Montalembert tried to make his towers entirely safe against a *coup
de main.*[b] He surrounded them with a ditch, with a covered way,
and sometimes considered them merely as the *réduit,* or last
reserved position in a large, strong redoubt. This was his maturest
plan, and evidently the best. It has been adopted with more or less
alteration in almost all recent fortifications where the smaller

---

[a] See this volume, p. 279.—*Ed.*
[b] Sudden attack.—*Ed.*

towers of Montalembert were adopted. Beside these difficulties of access he has the whole of the lower storey or cellar of the tower arranged for infantry defense in a very ingenious way.

Now, in every one of these respects the Russians appear to have omitted important features. The time occupied by the breaching fire, twenty to thirty hours, is evidently too short to enable even thirty-two pounders to effect a practicable breach, unless, indeed, the masonry was of a nature not usually seen in fortifications. It may, therefore, be presumed that the towers were taken by scaling, the soldiers entering through the embrasures, and by bursting open the gates. This presupposes a very ineffectual flanking fire, and as it appears that the large fort has no batteries in the rear to assist the towers, each tower was flanked by the fire of the other only. This fault is the greater, as from the sketches it would appear that the ground was very uneven, allowing storming parties to creep up, covered by accidents of ground, to a pretty close proximity. Then, to judge from the sketches and from the event, preparations against a *coup de main* must have been altogether neglected. There is no trace of a redoubt thrown up around the towers, and the redoubts which the Russians had constructed in front of them were abandoned almost without resistance. There was, it is said, a ditch around each tower; but it must have been very shallow with no contrivances for infantry defense within it. The towers once taken, the larger fort, which they command, was necessarily at the mercy of the Allies. It consequently fell, very likely with no more than a show of resistance.

Judging these fortifications from what this short siege makes them appear to be, it would almost seem that their constructors never calculated upon a serious attack on the land side. They must have built the towers with a view merely to resisting the attacks of parties of marines, which at the most could not exceed a couple of thousands, and not muster in sufficient strength either to attempt an assault or to conduct to its close a regular siege. Consequently the water-front was the strongest, and the land-front, formed by the towers, more show than reality. And yet the result would almost show that a party of 1,000 marines might have stormed the towers many months ago, and thereby reduced the main fort!

As to the storming itself, it must have been done very well by both French and English. The English are well-known stormers; it is their favorite maneuver, and hardly ever fails them. The French prefer to charge a body of troops in the open field; and in sieges their mathematical turn of mind prefers the methodical march of that eminently French science which Vauban invented. But the ardor of a British veteran seems to have driven them on. There was at Bomarsund an old Colonel Jones—the man who improved upon Vauban, when, with hardly half-sufficient means, and against brave and determined garrisons, at Badajos, Ciudad Rodrigo and Saint Sebastian, he contrived to shorten a siege by about one-third of its prescribed duration. Colonel Jones is not a common engineer. He does not, like the rest of his profession, see in a siege a mere school-festival in which the chief engineer is under examination, and must prove before the eyes of the army how far all the rules and regulations of formal sieges and of Vauban's "*attaque des places fortes*" are retained and properly arranged in his memory. He does not think that the whole army is there for the sake of the engineers, to protect them while they exhibit their tricks. Instead of this, Colonel Jones is first a soldier, and then an engineer. He knows the British soldier well, and knows what he can trust him with. And the short, determined, and yet unpretending way in which Bomarsund was taken in half the prescribed time, is so much like the breaching and storming of the Spanish fortresses that nobody but old Jones can be at the bottom of it. As to the French, they could never have invented this way of taking a fortress. It goes against their grain; it is too blunt, too destitute of manners and politeness. But they could not contest the authority of the man who had tried his irregular way of taking fortresses upon themselves fifty years before, and found it to answer in every case. And when they came to the storming, they appear not to have been behind the English in resolution.

It is singular that the Russians, who have prided themselves so much upon their storming capacities, from Perekop and Ochakov down to Warsaw and Bistritz, these Russians have been repulsed in every assault upon field-works, and, indeed, were not able, before Silistria, to reduce a field-work by a regular siege, and had to decamp without the fortress being relieved; while on the other hand, the very first act of the war was the storming by the Turks of a permanent Russian fortification—St. Nikolai—while the celebrated fortress of Bomarsund has been taken by assault almost without the honor of an open trench. We must not forget to note that the fleets appear not to have in any way effectually contributed to this victory. They seem, after all, to shun the neighborhood of casemated batteries as much as ever.

This success of the allies, however, is of such a nature that it will very likely induce them to do nothing more in the ensuing autumn. At all events, the grand expedition to Sevastopol has not yet sailed, and a few weeks more delay is already promised. Then it will be too late, and thus that repose and relaxation during the winter, which is so necessary after the fatigues of the camp at Varna, will be secured to the heroes of the allied forces.

Written on August 19, 1854

First published in the *New-York Daily Tribune*, No. 4174, September 4; reprinted in the *New-York Semi-Weekly Tribune*, No. 968, September 5 and the *New-York Weekly Tribune*, No. 678, September 9, 1854 as a leader

Reproduced from the *New-York Daily Tribune*

Frederick Engels

THE CAPTURE OF BOMARSUND [293]

(ARTICLE II)

The particulars of the capture of Bomarsund, so far as published, are still couched in vague and unbusiness-like language. We do not, in fact, learn at what distance from the forts the breaching batteries were erected or the ships anchored during the naval attack. We hear no further details, such as might be expected, on the construction of the forts, now that the allied troops have possession of them. Indeed, almost every point of importance is passed over in order to amuse the public with the more picturesque and less professional part of the business. In so slovenly a manner are concocted even the official reports, that nobody can make out distinctly whether Fort Tzee (as they spell it), when taken by the French, had to be stormed or not, as it seems that hardly any one but the commanding officer[a] resisted.

The little we can make out is that, as we suspected from the sketches, the two towers were erected upon ground of so broken a nature that ravines, slopes and rocks formed natural approaches even up to their very ditches. In these ravines the allies could comfortably establish themselves, safe from the Russian shot, which passed over their heads; and being thus enabled to construct their batteries close to the place, at once began the siege with those which are generally the last used in such cases, namely, breaching batteries. That the Russians built their forts upon such ground, without at once leveling it up to at least six or eight

---

[a] Teshe.— *Ed.*

hundred yards in front of them, proves that a serious land attack was never calculated upon by them. The breaching batteries must have been erected at no greater distance than five or six hundred yards from the forts, as the French battered them with sixteen-pounders, generally considered not heavy enough for breaching a wall even at one hundred or one hundred and fifty yards distance. Thirty-six hours' firing, however, so injured the tower that twelve hours' more would have brought down a whole front. The British battered Fort Nottich with sixty thirty-two-pounders of forty-five cwt. each.

These guns, according to Sir Howard Douglas's *Naval Gunnery,* are used with a regulation charge of seven lbs. powder, and would, at the distance of four to five hundred yards, make the ball penetrate from two to two and a half feet into solid oak. The French sixteen-pound guns, with a charge of five lbs., would have, at four to five hundred yards, a penetration into oak of from one and a half to two feet. If the British, as may be expected, increased the regulation charge to at least eight lbs., there is no wonder that with twice the number of guns and double the caliber, they laid one side of the fort open in less than twelve hours.

As to the sea attack, it was a mere diversion. Only Captain Pelham profited by the occasion to make a scientific experiment. He used his long eight-inch pivot gun with all the steadiness and regularity of breaching fire, invariably hitting, as nearly as possible, the same place. These long eight-inch guns are the finest in the British navy. Their great weight of metal (ninety-five cwt.) permits a charge of sixteen pounds of powder to a solid shot of sixty-eight pounds. The effect of this shot, even at a distance of five or six hundred yards, is inconceivably greater than that of the eighteen or twenty-four-pound balls hitherto generally used in breaching batteries; and when properly used, could not fail to produce a tremendous result. Accordingly, Captain Pelham's steady firing very speedily unraveled the mystery of Russian granite fortresses. A few shots detached what hitherto appeared a large block of solid granite, but turned out to be a mere facing slab, the thickness of which was in no wise proportionate to its hight and width. Some more shots, and the next adjoining slabs fell in, and then followed an avalanche of rubbish, rattling down the walls, and laying bare the very heart of the fortress. It then was clear that the "granite" was nothing but show; that as soon as the comparatively thin slabs which faced the escarpe were knocked down, there was no solid masonry inside to resist the inroads of bullets. The walls, in fact, were mere casings, the interstices of which were filled up with all sorts of broken stones, sand, &c., having neither cohesion nor stability. If the main fortress was thus constructed, there is no doubt the masonry of the towers was equally bad, and the rapid breaching is fully explained. And these walls, of so little intrinsic strength, had by their imposing outside sufficed to keep the whole Anglo-French fleet at bay for nearly four months! The disappointment of Sir Charles Napier when he saw what they really were made of cannot, however, have been greater than that of the Czar, when he learned of what the "granite," for which he had so dearly paid, consisted. In the land attack, another feature is remarkable. We have already seen that broken ground surrounded the forts not only within gun-range, but even within musket-range. This was taken advantage of by the Chasseurs of Vincennes, who crept up very close, sheltering themselves behind stumps of trees, boulder stones, rocks, &c., and opened a murderous fire upon the embrasures of the casemates. As at a distance of four to five hundred yards their rifles have an unerring aim, and moreover, the sloping-side embrasures, like a tunnel, make every bullet which strikes them enter the central opening at the bottom, it may well be imagined how much the gunners in the fortress were annoyed while loading.

The Russians appear to have entirely neglected the commonest precautions against this rifle fire. They, too, had rifles. Why did they not post them behind the parapet of the roof of the tower, where they commanded the enemy's skirmishers? But the Finnish rifles at Bomarsund appear to have had no inclination to fight for the glory of Holy Russia. Finally, the French employed, besides the three breaching guns, some mortars and three howitzers. The mortars sent their shells at a high angle on the bomb-proof roof of the tower, trying to crush it by the combined force of the fall and the explosion. This, however, does not appear to have been of great effect. On the other hand, the French howitzers stuck to direct horizontal firing, and aimed at the embrasures. At the short distance of four or five hundred yards a long twenty-four-pound brass howitzer, throwing a shell of six inches diameter, might very well hit such an object as an embrasure once in three times; and every shell entering would disable the men at the gun, besides dismounting the gun itself. This fire, therefore, must have been very effective.

Thus we see that the granite walls of Bomarsund turned out mere Russian humbug—heaps of rubbish kept in shape by thin stone-facings, not fit to resist a good and steady fire for any time.

If Nicholas had been cheated by their constructors, he has succeeded for all that in cheating the allies out of a whole campaign by these sham fortresses. The defense on the part of the Russians was, upon the whole, indifferent; and this may be traced to the pretty plainly pronounced disaffection of the Finnish troops. The attack of the allies was characterized by a resolution unheard of hitherto in their proceedings, and due, evidently, to General Jones. The difficulties overcome in moving and placing the guns, though exaggerated by Sir Charles Napier, were certainly great. The French attacked with breaching guns of too weak caliber and with mortars that could be of little use under the circumstances, but their mode of horizontal shell-firing and rifle-firing at the embrasures deserves high eulogium. The English, as usual, came down with the heaviest caliber they could move, gave plain, straight-forward and effective fire, underwent difficulties and stood fire with their usual steadiness, and carried their point without fuss, but also without any special distinction.

Bomarsund being taken, the question next arises, what is to be done with it? According to the latest dispatches from Hamburg, at a council of war held by the Admirals,[a] the Generals-in-Chief of the expeditionary troops and the principal commanders resolved upon destroying all the fortifications and abandoning the island, if Sweden should not be inclined to occupy it and buy it at the price of a declaration of war against Russia. If this dispatch prove true, the expedition against the Aland Islands, so far from being a military move, as announced by the *Moniteur*,[b] would prove simply a diplomatic one, undertaken with a view to entangle Sweden in a dangerous alliance with the same powers whose friendship, to use the words of Mr. Bright, "has brought upon Turkey in a single year such calamities as Russia in her wildest dreams of ambition never imagined."[c] The Swedish Court hesitates, the Swedish press warns the people against the *Danaos et dona ferentes*,[d] but the Swedish peasants have already passed a motion that the Chamber should petition the King to take steps that Aland may never again

[a] Napier and Parseval.— *Ed.*

[b] Review of current events. *Le Moniteur universel*, No. 232, August 20, 1854.— *Ed.*

[c] Mr. Bright's speech in the House of Commons on March 31, 1854. *The Times*, No. 21704, April 1, 1854.— *Ed.*

[d] Greeks, even bearing gifts. Virgil, *Aeneid*, II, 49.— *Ed.*

become Russian. There is little probability that the petition of the peasants will be listened to, and we may expect soon to hear that the fortress has been blown up.

Written on August 26, 1854

First published in the *New-York Daily Tribune*, No. 4182, September 13; reprinted in the *New-York Semi-Weekly Tribune*, No. 941, September 15, 1854 as a leader

Reproduced from the *New-York Daily Tribune*

Karl Marx

REVOLUTIONARY SPAIN [294]

Written in August-November 1854

First published in the *New-York Daily Tribune*, Nos. 4179, 4192, 4214, 4220, 4222, 4244, 4250 and 4251, September 9 and 25, October 20, 27 and 30, November 24, December 1 and 2, 1854 as leaders

I

The revolution in Spain has now so far taken on the appearance of a permanent condition that, as our correspondent at London[a] has informed us, the wealthy and conservative classes have begun to emigrate and to seek security in France.[295] This is not surprising; Spain has never adopted the modern French fashion, so generally in vogue in 1848, of beginning and accomplishing a revolution in three days.[296] Her efforts in that line are complex and more prolonged. Three years seems to be the shortest limit to which she restricts herself, while her revolutionary cycle sometimes expands to nine. Thus her first revolution in the present century extended from 1808 to 1814; the second from 1820 to 1823; and the third from 1834 to 1843. How long the present one will continue, or in what it will result, it is impossible for the keenest politician to foretell; but it is not much to say that there is no other part of Europe, not even Turkey and the Russian war, which offers so profound an interest to the thoughtful observer, as does Spain at this instant.

Insurrectionary risings are as old in Spain as that sway of court favorites against which they are usually directed. Thus in the middle of the fifteenth century the aristocracy revolted against King Juan II[b] and his favorite, Don Alvaro de Luna. In the fifteenth century still more serious commotions took place against King Henry IV and the head of his camarilla, Don Juan de Pacheco, Marquis de Villena. In the seventeenth century the people at Lisbon tore to pieces Vasconcellos, the Sartorius of the

---

[a] F. A. Pulszky.— *Ed.*
[b] John II.—*Ed.*

Spanish Viceroy in Portugal,[297] as they did at Catalonia with Santa Coloma, the favorite of Philip IV. At the end of the same century, under the reign of Carlos II, the people of Madrid rose against the Queen's[a] camarilla, composed of the Countess de Berlepsch and the Counts Oropesa and Melgar, who had imposed on all provisions entering the capital an oppressive duty, which they shared among themselves. The people marched to the royal palace, forced the King to appear on the balcony, and himself to denounce the Queen's camarilla. They then marched to the palaces of the Counts Oropesa and Melgar, plundered them, destroyed them by fire, and tried to lay hold of their owners, who, however, had the good luck to escape, at the cost of perpetual exile. The event which occasioned the insurrectionary rising in the fifteenth century was the treacherous treaty which the favorite of Henry IV, the Marquis de Villena, had concluded with the King of France, according to which Catalonia was to be surrendered to Louis XI. Three centuries later, the treaty of Fontainebleau, concluded on October 27, 1807, by which the favorite of Carlos IV and the minion of his Queen,[b] Don Manuel Godoy, the Prince of Peace, contracted with Bonaparte for the partition of Portugal and the entrance of the French armies into Spain, caused a popular insurrection at Madrid against Godoy, the abdication of Carlos IV, the assumption of the throne by Ferdinand VII, his son, the entrance of the French army into Spain, and the following war of independence. Thus the Spanish war of independence commenced with a popular insurrection against the camarilla, then personified in Don Manuel Godoy, just as the civil war of the fifteenth century commenced with the rising against the camarilla, then personified in the Marquis de Villena. So, too, the revolution of 1854 commenced with the rising against the camarilla, personified in the Count San Luis.

Notwithstanding these ever-recurring insurrections, there has been in Spain, up to the present century, no serious revolution, except the war of the Holy League[298] in the times of Carlos I, or Charles V, as the Germans call him. The immediate pretext, as usual, was then furnished by the clique who, under the auspices of Cardinal Adrian, the Viceroy, himself a Fleming, exasperated the Castilians by their rapacious insolence, by selling the public offices to the highest bidder, and by open traffic in law-suits. The opposition against the Flemish camarilla was only at the surface of

---

[a] María Anna of Neuburg.— *Ed.*
[b] María Luisa of Parma.— *Ed.*

the movement. At its bottom was the defense of the liberties of medieval Spain against the encroachments of modern absolutism.

The material basis of the Spanish monarchy having been laid by the union of Aragon, Castile and Granada, under Ferdinand the Catholic, and Isabella I, Charles I attempted to transform that still feudal monarchy into an absolute one. Simultaneously he attacked the two pillars of Spanish liberty, the Cortes and the *Ayuntamientos*[299]—the former a modification of the ancient Gothic *concilia*, and the latter transmitted almost without interruption from the Roman times, the *Ayuntamientos* exhibiting the mixture of the hereditary and elective character proper to the Roman municipalities. As to municipal self-government, the towns of Italy, of Provence, Northern Gaul, Great Britain, and part of Germany, offer a fair similitude to the then state of the Spanish towns; but neither the French States General,[300] nor the British Parliaments of the Middle Ages, are to be compared with the Spanish Cortes. There were circumstances in the formation of the Spanish kingdom peculiarly favorable to the limitation of royal power. On the one side, small parts of the Peninsula were recovered at a time, and formed into separate kingdoms, during the long struggles with the Arabs. Popular laws and customs were engendered in these struggles. The successive conquests, being principally effected by the nobles, rendered their power excessive, while they diminished the royal power. On the other hand, the inland towns and cities rose to great consequence, from the necessity people found themselves under of residing together in places of strength, as a security against the continual irruptions of the Moors; while the peninsular formation of the country, and constant intercourse with Provence and Italy, created first-rate commercial and maritime cities on the coast. As early as the fourteenth century, the cities formed the most powerful part in the Cortes, which were composed of their representatives, with those of the clergy and the nobility. It is also worthy of remark, that the slow recovery from Moorish dominion through an obstinate struggle of almost eight hundred years, gave the Peninsula, when wholly emancipated, a character altogether different from that of cotemporaneous Europe, Spain finding itself, at the epoch of European resurrection, with the manners of the Goths and the Vandals in the North, and with those of the Arabs in the South.

Charles I having returned from Germany, where the imperial dignity had been bestowed upon him, the Cortes assembled at Valladolid, in order to receive his oath to the ancient laws and to invest him with the crown.[301] Charles, declining to appear, sent commissioners who, he pretended, were to receive the oath of allegiance on the part of the Cortes. The Cortes refused to admit these commissioners to their presence, notifying the monarch that, if he did not appear and swear to the laws of the country, he should never be acknowledged as King of Spain. Charles thereupon yielded; he appeared before the Cortes and took the oath—as historians say, with a very bad grace. The Cortes on this occasion told him: "You must know, Señor, that the King is but the paid servant of the nation." Such was the beginning of the hostilities between Charles I and the towns. In consequence of his intrigues, numerous insurrections broke out in Castile, the Holy League of Avila was formed, and the united towns convoked the assembly of the Cortes at Tordesillas, whence, on October 20, 1520, a "protest against the abuses" was addressed to the King, in return for which he deprived all the deputies assembled at Tordesillas of their personal rights. Thus civil war had become inevitable; the commoners appealed to arms; their soldiers under the command of Padilla seized the fortress of Torre Lobaton, but were ultimately defeated by superior forces at the battle of Villalar on April 23, 1521. The heads of the principal "conspirators" rolled on the scaffold, and the ancient liberties of Spain disappeared.

Several circumstances conspired in favor of the rising power of absolutism. The want of union between the different provinces deprived their efforts of the necessary strength; but it was, above all, the bitter antagonism between the classes of the nobles and the citizens of the towns which Charles employed for the degradation of both. We have already mentioned that since the fourteenth century the influence of the towns was prominent in the Cortes, and since Ferdinand the Catholic, the Holy Brotherhood (Santa Hermandad)[302] had proved a powerful instrument in the hands of the towns against the Castilian nobles, who accused them of encroachments on their ancient privileges and jurisdiction. The nobility, therefore, were eager to assist Carlos I in his project of suppressing the Holy League. Having crushed their armed resistance, Carlos occupied himself with the reduction of the municipal privileges of the towns, which, rapidly declining in population, wealth and importance, soon lost their influence in the Cortes. Carlos now turned round upon the nobles, who had assisted him in putting down the liberties of the towns, but who themselves retained a considerable political importance. Mutiny in his army for want of pay obliged him, in 1539, to assemble the

Cortes, in order to obtain a grant of money. Indignant at the misapplication of former subsidies to operations foreign to the interests of Spain, the Cortes refused all supplies. Carlos dismissed them in a rage; and, the nobles having insisted on a privilege of exemption from taxes, he declared that those who claimed such a right could have no claim to appear in the Cortes, and consequently excluded them from that assembly. This was the death-blow of the Cortes, and their meetings were henceforth reduced to the performance of a mere court ceremony. The third element in the ancient constitution of the Cortes, viz: the clergy, enlisted since Ferdinand the Catholic under the banner of the Inquisition, had long ceased to identify its interests with those of feudal Spain. On the contrary, by the Inquisition, the Church was transformed into the most formidable tool of absolutism.

If after the reign of Carlos I the decline of Spain, both in a political and social aspect, exhibited all those symptoms of inglorious and protracted putrefaction so repulsive in the worst times of the Turkish Empire, under the Emperor at least the ancient liberties were buried in a magnificent tomb. This was the time when Vasco Núñes de Balboa planted the banner of Castile upon the shores of Darien, Cortés in Mexico, and Pizarro in Peru; when Spanish influence reigned supreme in Europe, and the Southern imagination of the Iberians was bewildered with visions of Eldorados, chivalrous adventures, and universal monarchy. Then Spanish liberty disappeared under the clash of arms, showers of gold, and the terrible illuminations of the auto-da-fe.[303]

But how are we to account for the singular phenomenon that, after almost three centuries of a Habsburg dynasty, followed by a Bourbon dynasty—either of them quite sufficient to crush a people—the municipal liberties of Spain more or less survive? that in the very country where of all the feudal states absolute monarchy first arose in its most unmitigated form, centralization has never succeeded in taking root? The answer is not difficult. It was in the sixteenth century that were formed the great monarchies which established themselves everywhere on the downfall of the conflicting feudal classes—the aristocracy and the towns. But in the other great States of Europe absolute monarchy presents itself as a civilizing center, as the initiator of social unity. There it was the laboratory in which the various elements of society were so mixed and worked, as to allow the towns to change the local independence and sovereignty of the Middle Ages for the general rule of the middle classes, and the common sway of civil society.[304] In Spain, on the contrary, while the aristocracy sunk into degradation without losing their worst privilege, the towns lost their medieval power without gaining modern importance.

Since the establishment of absolute monarchy they have vegetated in a state of continuous decay. We have not here to state the circumstances, political or economical, which destroyed Spanish commerce, industry, navigation and agriculture. For the present purpose it is sufficient to simply recall the fact. As the commercial and industrial life of the towns declined, internal exchanges became rare, the mingling of the inhabitants of different provinces less frequent, the means of communication neglected, and the great roads gradually deserted. Thus the local life of Spain, the independence of its provinces and communes, the diversified state of society originally based on the physical configuration of the country, and historically developed by the detached manner in which the several provinces emancipated themselves from the Moorish rule, and formed little independent commonwealths—was now finally strengthened and confirmed by the economical revolution which dried up the sources of national activity. And while the absolute monarchy found in Spain material in its very nature repulsive to centralization, it did all in its power to prevent the growth of common interests arising out of a national division of labor and the multiplicity of internal exchanges—the very basis on which alone a uniform system of administration and the rule of general laws can be created. Thus the absolute monarchy in Spain, bearing but a superficial resemblance to the absolute monarchies of Europe in general, is rather to be ranged in a class with Asiatic forms of government. Spain, like Turkey, remained an agglomeration of mismanaged republics with a nominal sovereign at their head. Despotism changed character in the different provinces with the arbitrary interpretation of the general laws by viceroys and governors; but despotic as was the government it did not prevent the provinces from subsisting with different laws and customs, different coins, military banners of different colors, and with their respective systems of taxation. The oriental despotism attacks municipal self-government only when opposed to its direct interests, but is very glad to allow those institutions to continue so long as they take off its shoulders the duty of doing something and spare it the trouble of regular administration.

Thus it happened that Napoleon, who, like all his cotemporaries, considered Spain as an inanimate corpse, was fatally surprised at the discovery that when the Spanish State was dead, Spanish society was full of life, and every part of it overflowing

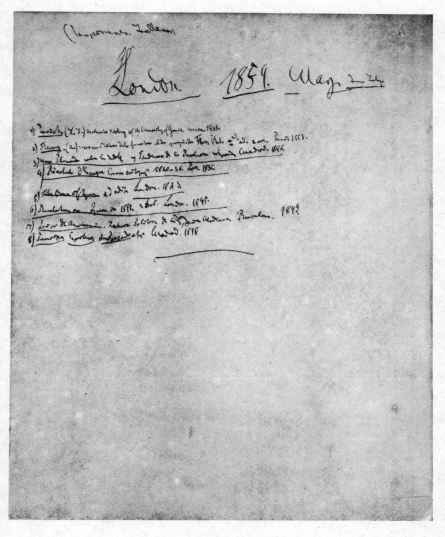

Title page of one of Marx's notebooks containing excerpts
on the history of Spain

with powers of resistance. By the treaty of Fontainebleau he had got his troops to Madrid; by alluring the royal family into an interview at Bayonne he had forced Carlos IV to retract his abdication, and then to make over to him his dominions; and he had intimidated Ferdinand VII into a similar declaration. Carlos IV, his Queen and the Prince of Peace conveyed to Compiègne, Ferdinand VII and his brothers imprisoned in the castle of Valençay, Bonaparte conferred the throne of Spain on his brother Joseph, assembled a Spanish Junta at Bayonne, and provided them with one of his ready-made constitutions.[305] Seeing nothing alive in the Spanish monarchy except the miserable dynasty which he had safely locked up, he felt quite sure of this confiscation of Spain. But, only a few days after his *coup de main,* he received the news of an insurrection at Madrid. Murat, it is true, quelled that tumult by killing about 1,000 people; but when this massacre became known, an insurrection broke out in Asturias, and soon afterward embraced the whole monarchy. It is to be remarked that this first spontaneous rising originated with the people, while the "better" classes had quietly submitted to the foreign yoke.

Thus it is that Spain was prepared for her more recent revolutionary career, and launched into the struggles which have marked her development in the present century. The facts and influences we have thus succinctly detailed still act in forming her destinies and directing the impulses of her people. We have presented them as necessary not only to an appreciation of the present crisis, but of all she has done and suffered since the Napoleonic usurpation—a period now of nearly fifty years—not without tragic episodes and heroic efforts,—indeed, one of the most touching and instructive chapters in all modern history.[306]

II

We have already laid before our readers a survey of the earlier revolutionary history of Spain, as a means of understanding and appreciating the developments which that nation is now offering to the observation of the world. Still more interesting, and perhaps equally valuable as a source of present instruction, is the great national movement that attended the expulsion of the Bonapartes, and restored the Spanish Crown to the family in whose possession it yet remains. But to rightly estimate that movement, with its heroic episodes and memorable exhibition of vitality in a people supposed to be moribund, we must go back to the beginning of the Napoleonic assault on the nation. The efficient cause of the whole was perhaps first stated in the treaty of Tilsit, which was concluded on July 7, 1807, and is said to have received its complement through a secret convention, signed by Prince Kurakin and Talleyrand. It was published in the Madrid *Gaceta* on August 25, 1812, containing, among other things, the following stipulations:

"*Art. I.* Russia is to take possession of European Turkey, and to extend her possessions in Asia as far as she may think it convenient.

"*Art. II.* The Bourbon dynasty in Spain and the house of Braganza in Portugal will cease to reign. Princes of the Bonaparte family will succeed to both of these crowns."

Supposing this treaty to be authentic, and its authenticity is scarcely disputed, even in the recently published memoirs of King Joseph Bonaparte,[307] it formed the true reason for the French invasion of Spain in 1808, while the Spanish commotions of that time would seem to be linked by secret threads with the destinies of Turkey.

When, consequent upon the Madrid massacre and the transactions at Bayonne, simultaneous insurrections broke out in Asturias, Galicia, Andalusia and Valencia, and a French army occupied Madrid, the four northern fortresses of Pamplona, San Sebastian, Figueras and Barcelona had been seized by Bonaparte under false pretenses; part of the Spanish army had been removed to the island of Fünen, destined for an attack upon Sweden; lastly, all the constituted authorities, military, ecclesiastic, judicial and administrative, as well as the aristocracy, exhorted the people to submit to the foreign intruder. But there was one circumstance to compensate for all the difficulties of the situation. Thanks to Napoleon, the country was rid of its King, its royal family, and its government. Thus the shackles were broken which might else have prevented the Spanish people from displaying their native energies. How little they were able to resist the French under the command of their Kings and under ordinary circumstances, had been proved by the disgraceful campaigns of 1794 and 1795.[308]

Napoleon had summoned the most distinguished persons in Spain to meet him at Bayonne, and to receive from his hands a King[a] and a Constitution. With very few exceptions, they appeared there. On June 7, 1808, King Joseph received at Bayonne a deputation of the grandees of Spain, in whose name the Duke of Infantado, Ferdinand VII's most intimate friend, addressed him as follows:

"Sire, the grandees of Spain have at all times been celebrated for their loyalty to their Sovereign, and in them your Majesty will now find the same fidelity and adhesion."[b]

The royal Council of Castile assured poor Joseph that "he was the principal branch of a family destined by Heaven to reign." Not less abject was the congratulation of the Duke del Parque, at the head of a deputation representing the army. On the following day the same persons published a proclamation,[c] enjoining general submission to the Bonaparte dynasty. On July 7, 1808, the new Constitution was signed by 91 Spaniards of the highest distinction; among them Dukes, Counts and Marquises, as well as several

---

[a] Joseph Bonaparte.— Ed.

[b] Quoted from [Bonaparte, Joseph,] Memoires et correspondance politique et militaire du roi Joseph, T. IV, p. 290.— Ed.

[c] R. Southey, History of the Peninsular War, Vol. I, pp. 318-21.— Ed.

heads of the religious orders. During the discussions on that Constitution, all they found cause to remonstrate against was the repeal of their old privileges and exemptions. The first Ministry and the first royal household of Joseph were the same persons who had formed the ministry and the royal household of Ferdinand VII. Some of the upper classes considered Napoleon as the providential regenerator of Spain; others as the only bulwark against revolution; none believing in the chances of national resistance.

Thus from the very beginning of the Spanish War of Independence the high nobility and the old Administration lost all hold upon the middle classes and upon the people, because of their having deserted them at the commencement of the struggle. On the one side stood the *Afrancesados* (the Frenchified), and on the other the nation. At Valladolid, Cartagena, Granada, Jaen, San Lucar, Carolina, Ciudad Rodrigo, Cadiz and Valencia, the most prominent members of the old Administration—governors, generals, and other marked personages presumed to be French agents and obstacles to the national movement—fell victims to the infuriated people. Everywhere the existing authorities were displaced. Some months previous to the rising, on March 19, 1808, the popular commotions that had taken place at Madrid, intended to remove from their posts *El Choricero* (the sausage-maker, a nickname of Godoy) and his obnoxious satellites. This object was now gained on a national scale, and with it the internal revolution was accomplished so far as contemplated by the masses, and as not connected with resistance to the foreign intruder. On the whole, the movement appeared to be directed rather *against* revolution than *for* it. National by proclaiming the independence of Spain from France, it was at the same time dynastic by opposing the "beloved" Ferdinand VII to Joseph Bonaparte; reactionary by opposing the old institutions, customs, and laws to the rational innovations of Napoleon; superstitious and fanatical by opposing "holy religion," against what was called French Atheism, or the destruction of the special privileges of the Roman Church. The priests, terrified by the fate that had fallen upon their brethren in France, fostered the popular passions in the interest of self-preservation.

"The patriotic fire," says Southey, "flamed higher for this holy oil of superstition."[a]

---

[a] R. Southey, op. cit., Vol. I, p. 301.—*Ed.*

All the wars of independence waged against France bear in common the stamp of regeneration, mixed up with reaction; but nowhere to such a degree as in Spain. The King appeared in the imagination of the people in the light of a romantic prince, forcibly abused and locked up by a giant robber. The most fascinating and popular epochs of their past were encircled with the holy and miraculous traditions of the war of the cross against the crescent; and a great portion of the lower classes were accustomed to wear the livery of mendicants and live upon the sanctified patrimony of the Church. A Spanish author, Don José Clemente Carnicero, published in the years 1814 and '16, the following series of works: *Napoleon, the True Don Quixote of Europe; Principal Events of the Glorious Revolution of Spain; The Inquisition Rightly Re-established*[a]; it is sufficient to note the titles of these books to understand this one aspect of the Spanish revolution which we meet with in the several manifestoes of the provincial juntas, all of them proclaiming the King, their holy religion, and the country, and some even telling the people that

"their hopes of a better world were at stake, and in very imminent danger."[b]

However, if the peasantry, the inhabitants of small inland cities, and the numerous army of the mendicants, frocked and un-frocked, all of them deeply imbued with religious and political prejudices, formed the great majority of the national party, it contained on the other hand an active and influential minority which considered the popular rising against the French invasion as the signal given for the political and social regeneration of Spain. This minority was composed of the inhabitants of the seaports, commercial towns, and part of the provincial capitals, where, under the reign of Charles V, the material conditions of modern society had developed themselves to a certain degree. They were strengthened by the more cultivated portion of the upper and middle classes, authors, physicians, lawyers, and even priests, for whom the Pyrenees had formed no sufficient barrier against the invasion of the philosophy of the XVIIIth century. As a true manifesto of this faction may be considered the famous memorandum of Jovellanos on the improvements of agriculture and the agrarian law, published in 1795, and drawn up by order of the

---

[a] J. C. Carnicero, *Napoleon o El verdadero D. Quixote de la Europa; Historia razonada de los principales sucesos de la gloriosa revolución de España; La Inquisición justamente restablecida.— Ed.*

[b] Quoted from the anonymous book: *The Crisis of Spain*, pp. 21-22.— *Ed.*

royal Council of Castile.ᵃ There was, finally, the youth of the middle classes, such as the students of the University, who had eagerly adopted the aspirations and principles of the French Revolution, and who, for a moment, even expected to see their country regenerated by the assistance of France.

So long as the common defense of the country alone was concerned, the two great elements composing the national party remained in perfect union. Their antagonism did not appear till they met together in the Cortes, on the battleground of a new Constitution there to be drawn up. The revolutionary minority, in order to foment the patriotic spirit of the people, had not hesitated themselves to appeal to the national prejudices of the old popular faith. Favorable to the immediate objects of national resistance, as these tactics might have appeared, they could not fail to prove fatal to this minority when the time had arrived for the conservative interests of the old society to intrench themselves behind these very prejudices and popular passions, with a view of defending themselves against the proper and ulterior plans of the revolutionists.

When Ferdinand left Madrid upon the summons of Bonaparte, he had established a Supreme Junta of government under the Presidency of the Infante Don Antonio. But in May this Junta had already disappeared. There existed then no central government, and the insurgent towns formed juntas of their own, presided over by those of the provincial capitals. These provincial juntas constituted, as it were, so many independent governments, each of which set on foot an army of its own. The Junta of Representatives at Oviedo declared that the entire sovereignty had devolved into their hands, proclaimed war against Bonaparte, and sent deputies to England to conclude an armistice. The same was done afterward by the Junta of Seville. It is a curious fact that by the mere force of circumstances these exalted Catholics were driven to an alliance with England, a power which the Spaniards were accustomed to look upon as the incarnation of the most damnable heresy, and little better than the Grand Turk himself. Attacked by French Atheism, they were thrown into the arms of British Protestantism. No wonder that Ferdinand VII, on his return to Spain, declared, in a decree re-establishing the Holy Inquisition, that one of the causes

---

ᵃ G. M. Jovellanos, *Informe de la Sociedad económica de esta corte al real y supremo consejo de Castilla, en el expediente de ley agraria.—Ed.*

"that had altered the purity of religion in Spain was the sojourn of foreign troops of different sects, all of them equally infected with hatred against the holy Roman Church."[a]

The provincial juntas which had so suddenly sprung into life, altogether independent of each other, conceded a certain, but very slight and undefined degree of ascendancy to the Supreme Junta of Seville, that city being regarded as the capital of Spain while Madrid was in the hands of the foreigner. Thus a very anarchical kind of federal government was established, which the shock of opposite interests, local jealousies, and rival influences made a rather bad instrument for bringing unity into the military command, and to combine the operations of a campaign.

The addresses to the people issued by these several juntas, while displaying all the heroic vigor of a people suddenly awakened from a long lethargy and roused by an electric shock into a feverish state of activity, are not free from that pompous exaggeration, that style of mingled buffoonery and bombast, and that redundant grandiloquence which caused Sismondi to put upon Spanish literature the epithet of Oriental.[b] They exhibit no less the childish vanity of the Spanish character, the members of the juntas for instance assuming the title of Highness and loading themselves with gaudy uniforms.

There are two circumstances connected with these juntas—the one showing the low standard of the people at the time of their rising, while the other was detrimental to the progress of the revolution. The juntas were named by general suffrage; but "the very zeal of the lower classes displayed itself in obedience." They generally elected only their natural superiors, the provincial nobility and gentry backed by clergymen and very few notabilities of the middle class. So conscious were the people of their own weakness that they limited their initiative to forcing the higher classes into resistance against the invader, without pretending to share in the direction of that resistance. At Seville, for instance, "the first thought of the people was that the parochial clergy and the heads of the Convents should assemble to choose the members of the junta." Thus the juntas were filled with persons chosen on account of their previous station, and very far from being revolutionary leaders. On the other hand, the people when

---

[a] Decree of King Ferdinand VII of Spain of July 21, 1814. *Le Moniteur universel*, No. 214, August 2, 1814.— *Ed.*

[b] Sismondi, *De la Littérature du Midi de l'Europe*, T. IV, pp. 259-60.— *Ed.*

appointing these authorities did not think either of limiting their power or of fixing a term to their duration. The juntas, of course, thought only of extending the one and of perpetuating the other. Thus these first creations of the popular impulse at the commencement of the revolution remained during its whole course as so many dykes against the revolutionary current when threatening to overflow.

On July 20, 1808, when Joseph Bonaparte entered Madrid, 14,000 French, under Generals Dupont and Vedel, were forced by Castaños to lay down their arms at Bailén, and Joseph a few days afterward had to retire from Madrid to Burgos. There were two events besides which greatly encouraged the Spaniards; the one being the expulsion of Lefebvre from Saragossa by General Palafox, and the other the arrival of the army of the Marquis de la Romana, at Coruña, with 7,000 men, who had embarked from the island of Fünen in spite of the French, in order to come to the assistance of their country.

It was after the battle of Bailén that the revolution came to a head, and that part of the high nobility who had accepted the Bonaparte dynasty or wisely kept back, came forward to join the popular cause—an advantage to that cause of a very doubtful character.

III

The division of power among the provincial juntas had saved Spain from the first shock of the French invasion under Napoleon, not only by multiplying the resources of the country, but also by putting the invader at a loss for a mark whereat to strike; the French being quite amazed at the discovery that the center of Spanish resistance was nowhere and everywhere. Nevertheless, shortly after the capitulation of Bailén and the evacuation of Madrid by Joseph, the necessity of establishing some kind of central government became generally felt. After the first successes, the dissensions between the provincial juntas had grown so violent that Seville, for instance, was barely prevented by General Castaños from marching against Granada. The French army which, with the exception of the forces under Marshal Bessières, had withdrawn to the line of the Ebro in the greatest confusion, so that, if vigorously harassed, it would then have easily been dispersed, or at least compelled to repass the frontier, was thus allowed to recover and to take up a strong position. But it was, above all, the bloody suppression of the Bilbao insurrection by General Merlin,[309] which evoked a national cry against the jealousies of the juntas and the easy *laissez-faire* of the commanders. The urgency of combining military movements; the certainty that Napoleon would soon reappear at the head of a victorious army, collected from the banks of the Niemen, the Oder, and the shores of the Baltic; the want of a general authority for concluding treaties of alliance with Great Britain or other foreign powers, and for keeping up the connection with, and receiving tribute from Spanish America; the existence at Burgos of a French central power, and the necessity of setting up altar against altar—all these circumstances conspired to force the Seville Junta to resign, however reluctantly, its ill-defined and rather nominal supremacy, and to propose to the several provincial juntas to select each from its own body two deputies, the assembling of whom was to constitute a *Central Junta*, while the provincial juntas were to remain invested with the internal management of their respective districts, "but under due subordination to the General Government."[a] Thus the *Central Junta*, composed of 35 deputies from provincial juntas (34 for the Spanish juntas, and one for the Canary Islands), met at Aranjuez on September 26, 1808, just one day before the potentates of Russia and Germany prostrated themselves before Napoleon at Erfurt.[310]

Under revolutionary, still more than under ordinary circumstances, the destinies of armies reflect the true nature of the civil government. The Central Junta, charged with the expulsion of the invaders from the Spanish soil, was driven by the success of the hostile arms from Madrid to Seville, and from Seville to Cadiz, there to expire ignominiously. Its reign was marked by a disgraceful succession of defeats, by the annihilation of the Spanish armies, and lastly by the dissolution of regular warfare into guerrilla exploits. As said Urquijo, a Spanish nobleman, to Cuesta, the Captain-General of Castile, on April 3, 1808:

"Our Spain is a Gothic edifice, composed of heterogeneous morsels, with as many forces, privileges, legislations, and customs, as there are provinces. There exists in her nothing of what they call public spirit in Europe. These reasons will prevent the establishment of any central power of so solid a structure as to be able to unite our national forces."[b]

If, then, the actual state of Spain at the epoch of the French invasion threw the greatest possible difficulties in the way of creating a revolutionary center, the very composition of the Central Junta incapacitated it from proving a match for the terrible crisis in which the country found itself placed. Being too numerous and too fortuitously mixed for an executive government, they were too few to pretend to the authority of National Convention.[311] The mere fact of their power having been delegated from the provincial juntas rendered them unfit for

---

[a] R. Southey, op. cit., Vol. I, pp. 301-05.—*Ed.*
[b] Urquijo's letter is apparently quoted from D. Pradt, *Mémoires historiques sur la révolution d'Espagne*, p. 360.—*Ed.*

overcoming the ambitious propensities, the ill will, and the capricious egotism of those bodies. These juntas—the members of which, as we have shown in a former article, were elected on the whole in consideration of the situation they occupied in the old society, rather than of their capacity to inaugurate a new one—sent in their turn to the "Central" Spanish grandees, prelates, titularies of Castile, ancient ministers, high civil and military officials, instead of revolutionary upstarts. At the outset the Spanish revolution failed by its endeavor to remain legitimate and respectable.

The two most marked members of the Central Junta, under whose banners its two great parties ranged themselves, were Floridablanca and Jovellanos, both of them martyrs of Godoy's persecution, former ministers, valetudinarians, and grown old in the regular and pedantic habits of the procrastinating Spanish regime, the solemn and circumstantial slowness of which had become proverbial even at the time of Bacon, who once exclaimed, "May death reach me from Spain: it will then arrive at a late hour!" [a]

Floridablanca and Jovellanos represented an antagonism, but an antagonism belonging to that part of the eighteenth century which preceded the era of the French Revolution; the former a plebeian bureaucrat, the latter an aristocratic philanthropist; Floridablanca, a partisan and a practicer of the enlightened despotism represented by Pombal, Frederick II and Joseph II; Jovellanos, a "friend of the people", hoping to raise them to liberty by an anxiously wise succession of economic laws, and by the literary propaganda of generous doctrines; both opposed to the traditions of feudalism, the one by trying to disentangle the monarchical power, the other by seeking to rid civil society of its shackles. The part acted by either in the history of their country corresponded with the diversity of their opinions. Floridablanca ruled supreme as the Prime Minister of Charles III, and his rule grew despotic according to the measure in which he met with resistance. Jovellanos, whose ministerial career under Charles IV was but short-lived, gained his influence over the Spanish people, not as a minister, but as a scholar; not by decrees, but by essays. Floridablanca, when the storm of the times carried him to the

---

[a] These words, ascribed to Bacon, are quoted from the book of the Spanish historian J. M. Toreno, *Historia del levantamiento, guerra y revolución de España*, T. I, p. 278.— *Ed.*

head of a revolutionary Government, was an octogenarian,
unshaken only in his belief in despotism, and his distrust of
popular spontaneity. When delegated to Madrid he left with the
Municipality of Murcia a secret protest, declaring that he had only
ceded to force and to the fear of popular assassinations, and that
he signed this protocol with the express view to prevent King
Joseph from ever finding fault with his acceptance of the people's
mandate. Not satisfied with returning to the traditions of his
manhood, he retraced such steps of his ministerial past as he now
judged to have been too rash. Thus, he who had expelled the
Jesuits from Spain[312] was hardly installed in the Central Junta,
when he caused it to grant leave for their return "in a private
capacity." If he acknowledged any change to have occurred since
his time, it was simply this: that Godoy, who had banished him,
and had dispossessed the great Count of Floridablanca of his
governmental omnipotence, was now again replaced by that same
Count of Floridablanca, and driven out in his turn. This was the
man whom the Central Junta chose as its President, and whom its
majority recognized as an infallible leader.

Jovellanos, who commanded the influential minority of the
Central Junta, had also grown old, and lost much of his energy in
a long and painful imprisonment inflicted upon him by Godoy.
But even in his best times he was not a man of revolutionary
action, but rather a well-intentioned reformer, who, from over-
niceness as to the means, would never have dared to accomplish
an end. In France, he would perhaps have gone the length of
Mounier or Lally-Tollendal, but not a step further. In England, he
would have figured as a popular member of the House of Lords.
In insurrectionized Spain, he was fit to supply the aspiring youth
with ideas, but practically no match even for the servile tenacity of
a Floridablanca. Not altogether free from aristocratic prejudices,
and therefore with a strong leaning toward the Anglomania of
Montesquieu, this fair character seemed to prove that if Spain had
exceptionally begot a generalizing mind, she was unable to do it
except at the cost of individual energy, which she could only
possess for local affairs.

It is true that the Central Junta included a few men—headed by
Don Lorenzo Calvo de Rosas, the delegate of Saragossa—who,
while adopting the reform views of Jovellanos, spurred on at the
same time to revolutionary action. But their numbers were too few
and their names too unknown to allow them to push the slow
State-coach of the Junta out of the beaten track of Spanish
ceremonial.

This power, so clumsily composed, so nervelessly constituted, with such outlived reminiscences at its head, was called upon to accomplish a revolution and to beat Napoleon. If its proclamations were as vigorous as its deeds were weak, it was due to Don Manuel Quintana, a Spanish poet, whom the Junta had the taste to appoint as their secretary and to intrust with the writing of their manifestoes.

Like Calderón's pompous heroes[a] who, confounding conventional distinction with genuine greatness, used to announce themselves by a tedious enumeration of all their titles, the Junta occupied itself in the first place with decreeing the honors and decorations due to its exalted position. Their President received the predicate of "Highness," the other members that of "Excellency," while to the Junta *in corpore* was reserved the title of "Majesty." They adopted a species of fancy uniform resembling that of a general, adorned their breasts with badges representing the two worlds, and voted themselves a yearly salary of 120,000 reals. It was a true idea of the old Spanish school, that, in order to make a great and dignified entrance upon the historical stage of Europe, the chiefs of insurgent Spain ought to wrap themselves in theatrical costumes.

We should transgress the limits of these sketches by entering into the internal history of the Junta and the details of its administration. For our end it will suffice to answer two questions. What was its influence on the development of the Spanish revolutionary movement? What on the defense of the country? These two questions answered, much that until now has appeared mysterious and unaccountable in the Spanish revolutions of the nineteenth century will have found its explanation.

At the outset the majority of the Central Junta thought it their main duty to suppress the first revolutionary transports. Accordingly they tightened anew the old trammels of the press and appointed a new Grand Inquisitor, who was happily prevented by the French from resuming his functions. Although the greater part of the real property of Spain was then locked up in mortmain—in the entailed estates of the nobility, and the unalienable estates of the Church—the Junta ordered the selling of the mortmains, which had already begun, to be suspended, threatening even to amend the private contracts affecting the

[a] An allusion to the monologue of Floripes from Calderón's *La puente de Mantible* in which she extols the valour of her father Almirante (Act I). Marx and Engels made use of this monologue earlier in *The German Ideology* (see present edition, Vol. 5, p. 450).— *Ed.*

ecclesiastical estates that had already been sold. They acknowledged the national debt, but took no financial measure to free the
civil list from a world of burdens, with which a secular succession
of corrupt governments had encumbered it, to reform their
proverbially unjust, absurd and vexatious fiscal system, or to open
to the nation new productive resources, by breaking through the
shackles of feudalism.

IV

Already at the time of Philip V, Francisco Benito la Soledad had said: "All the evils of Spain are derived from the *abogados*" (lawyers).[a] At the head of the mischievous magisterial hierarchy of Spain was placed the *Consejo Real*[b] of Castile. Sprung up in the turbulent times of the Don Juans and the Enriques,[313] strengthened by Philip II, who discovered in it a worthy complement of the *Santo Oficio*,[c] it had improved by the calamities of the times and the weakness of the later kings to usurp and accumulate in its hands the most heterogeneous attributes, and to add to its functions of Highest Tribunal those of a legislator and of an administrative superintendent of all the kingdoms of Spain. Thus it surpassed in power even the French Parliament which it resembled in many points, except that it was never to be found on the side of the people. Having been the most powerful authority in ancient Spain, the *Consejo Real* was, of course, the most implacable foe to a new Spain, and to all the recent popular authorities threatening to cripple its supreme influence. Being the great dignitary of the order of the lawyers and the incarnate guaranty of all its abuses and privileges, the *Consejo* naturally disposed of all the numerous and influential interests vested in Spanish jurisprudence. It was therefore a power with which the revolution could enter into no compromise, but which had to be swept away unless it should be allowed to sweep away the

---

[a] The quotation is presumably from Francisco Benito la Soledad, *Memorial historico y politico.—Ed.*
[b] Royal Council.— *Ed.*
[c] The Holy Office (of the Inquisition).— *Ed.*

revolution in its turn. As we have seen in a former article,[a] the *Consejo* had prostituted itself before Napoleon, and by that act of treason had lost all hold upon the people. But on the day of their assumption of office the Central Junta were foolish enough to communicate to the *Consejo* their constitution, and to ask for its oath of fidelity, after having received which they declared they would dispatch the formula of the same oath to all the other authorities of the kingdom. By this inconsiderate step, loudly disapproved by all the revolutionary party, the *Consejo* became convinced that the Central Junta wanted its support; it thus recovered from its despondency, and, after an affected hesitation of some days, tendered a malevolent submission to the Junta, backing its oath by an expression of its own reactionary scruples exhibited in its advice to the Junta to dissolve, by reducing its number to three or five members, according to Ley 3, Partida 2, Titulo 15[314]; and to order the forcible extinction of the provincial juntas. After the French had returned to Madrid and dispersed the *Consejo Real*, the Central Junta, not contented with their first blunder, had the fatuity to resuscitate the *Consejo* by creating the *Consejo Reunido*—a reunion of the *Consejo Real* with all the other wrecks of the ancient royal councils. Thus the Junta spontaneously created for the counter-revolution a central power, which, rivaling their own power, never ceased to harass and counteract them with its intrigues and conspiracies, seeking to drive them to the most unpopular steps, and then, with a show of virtuous indignation to denounce them to the impassioned contempt of the people. It hardly need be mentioned that, having first acknowledged and then re-established the *Consejo Real*, the Central Junta was unable to reform anything, either in the organization of Spanish tribunals, or in their most vicious civil and criminal legislation.

That, notwithstanding the predominance in the Spanish rising of the national and religious elements, there existed, in the two first years, a most decided tendency to social and political reforms, is proved by all the manifestations of the provincial juntas of that time, which, though composed as they mostly were of the privileged classes, never neglected to denounce the ancient *régime* and to hold out promises of radical reform. The fact is further proved by the manifestoes of the Central Junta. In their first address to the nation, dated 26th October, 1808, they say:

"A tyranny of twenty years, exercised by the most incapable hands, had brought them to the very brink of perdition; the nation was alienated from its Government

---

[a] See this volume, p. 401.—*Ed.*

by hatred and contest. A little time only has passed since, oppressed and degraded, ignorant of their own strength, and finding no protection against the governmental evils, either in the institutions or in the laws, they had even regarded foreign dominion [as] less hateful than the wasting tyranny which consumed them. The dominion of a will always capricious, and most often unjust, had lasted too long; their patience, their love of order, their generous loyalty had too long been abused; it was time that law founded on general utility should commence its reign. Reform, therefore, was necessary throughout all branches. The Junta would form different committees, each entrusted with a particular department to whom all writings on matters of Government and Administration might be addressed."[a]

In their address dated Seville, 28th October, 1809, they say:

"An imbecile and decrepit despotism prepared the way for French tyranny. To leave the state sunk in old abuses would be a crime as enormous as to deliver you into the hands of Bonaparte."[b]

There seems to have existed in the Central Junta a most original division of labor—the Jovellanos party being allowed to proclaim and to protocol the revolutionary aspirations of the nation, and the Floridablanca party reserving to themselves the pleasure of giving them the lie direct, and of opposing to revolutionary fiction counter-revolutionary fact. For us, however, the important point is to prove from the very confessions of the provincial juntas deposited with the Central, the often-denied fact of the existence of revolutionary aspirations at the epoch of the first Spanish rising.

The manner in which the Central Junta made use of the opportunities for reforms afforded by the good will of the nation, the pressure of events, and the presence of immediate danger, may be inferred from the influence exercised by their Commissioners in the several provinces they were sent to. One Spanish author[c] candidly tells us that the Central Junta, not overflowing with capacities, took good care to retain the eminent members at the center, and to dispatch those who were good for nothing to the circumference. These Commissioners were invested with the power of presiding over the provincial juntas, and of representing the Central in the plenitude of its attributes. To quote only some instances of their doings: General Romana, whom the Spanish soldiers used to call Marquis de las Romerias,[d] from his perpetual

---

[a] Proclamation issued by the Central Junta of Spain to the Spanish Nation. Aranjuez, October 26, 1808.—*Ed.*

[b] Quoted from R. Southey, op. cit., Vol. II, pp. 497-98.—*Ed.*

[c] J. M. Toreno, op. cit., T. I, p. 374.—*Ed.*

[d] Literally "Marquis of the pilgrimages" from the Spanish *romero* (pilgrim), *romeria* (pilgrimage).—*Ed.*

marches and counter-marches—fighting never taking place except
when he happened to be out of the way—this Romana, when
beaten by Soult out of Galicia, entered Asturias, and as a
Commissioner of the Central. His first business was to pick a
quarrel with the provincial junta of Oviedo, whose energetic and
revolutionary measures had drawn down upon them the hatred of
the privileged classes. He went the length of dissolving and
replacing it by persons of his own invention. General Ney,
informed of these dissensions, in a province where the resistance
against the French had been general and unanimous, instantly
marched his forces into Asturias, expelled the Marquis de las
Romerias, entered Oviedo and sacked it during three days. The
French having evacuated Galicia at the end of 1809, our Marquis
and Commissioner of the Central Junta entered Coruña, united in
his person all public authority, suppressed the district juntas,
which had multiplied with the insurrection, and in their places
appointed military governors, threatening the members of those
juntas with persecution, actually persecuting the patriots, affecting
a supreme benignity toward all who had embraced the cause of
the invader, and proving in all other respects a mischievous,
impotent, capricious blockhead. And what had been the shortcomings of the district and provincial juntas of Galicia? They had
ordered a general recruitment without exemption of classes or
persons; they had levied taxes upon the capitalists and proprietors; they had lowered the salaries of public functionaries; they
had commanded the ecclesiastical corporations to keep at their
disposition the revenues existing in their chests. In one word, they
had taken revolutionary measures. From the time of the glorious
Marquis de las Romerias, Asturias and Galicia, the two provinces
most distinguished by their general resistance to the French,
withheld from partaking in the war of independence, whenever
released from immediate danger of invasion.

In Valencia, where new prospects appeared to open as long as
the people were left to themselves and to chiefs of their own
choosing, the revolutionary spirit was broken down by the
influence of the Central Government. Not contented to place that
province under the generalship of one Don José Caro, the Central
Junta dispatched as "their own" Commissioner, the Baron
Labazora. This Baron found fault with the provincial junta
because it had resisted certain superior orders, and cancelled their
decree by which the appointments to vacant canonship, ecclesiastical benefices, and commandries had been judiciously suspended
and the revenues destined for the benefit of the military hospitals.

Hence bitter contests between the Central Junta and that of Valencia; hence, at a later epoch, the sleep of Valencia under the liberal administration of Marshal Suchet; hence its eagerness to proclaim Ferdinand VII on his return against the then revolutionary Government.

At Cadiz, the most revolutionary place in Spain at the epoch, the presence of a Commissioner of the Central Junta, the stupid and conceited Marquis de Villel, caused an insurrection to break out on the 22d and 23d of February, 1809, which, if not timely shifted to the war of independence, would have had the most disastrous consequences.

There exists no better sample of the discretion exhibited by the Central Junta in the appointment of their own Commissioners, than that of the delegate to Wellington, Señor Lozano de Torres, who, while humbling himself in servile adulation before the English General, secretly informed the Junta that the General's complaints on his want of provisions were altogether groundless. Wellington, having found out the double-tongued wretch, chased him ignominiously from his camp.

The Central Junta were placed in the most fortunate circumstances for realizing what they had proclaimed in one of their addresses to the Spanish nation.

"It has seemed good to Providence that in this terrible crisis you should not be able to advance one step toward independence without advancing one likewise toward liberty." [a]

At the commencement of their reign the French had not yet obtained possession of one-third of Spain. The ancient authorities they found either absent or prostrated by their connivance with the intruder, or dispersed at his bidding. There was no measure of social reform, transferring property and influence from the Church and the aristocracy to the middle class and the peasants, which the cause of defending the common country could not have enabled them to carry. They had the same good luck as the French *Comité du salut public*[315]—that the convulsion within was backed by the necessities of defense against aggressions from without; moreover they had before them the example of the bold initiative which certain provinces had already been forced into by the pressure of circumstances. But not satisfied with hanging as a dead-weight on the Spanish revolution they actually worked in the sense of the counter-revolution, by re-establishing the ancient

---

[a] R. Southey, op. cit., Vol. II, pp. 497-98.—*Ed.*

authorities, by forging anew the chains which had been broken, by stifling the revolutionary fire wherever it broke out, by themselves doing nothing and by preventing others from doing anything. During their stay at Seville, on July 20, 1809, even the English Tory Government thought necessary to address them a note strongly protesting against their counter-revolutionary course "apprehending that they were likely to suffocate the public enthusiasm." [a] It has been remarked somewhere that Spain endured all the evils of revolution without acquiring revolutionary strength. If there be any truth in this remark, it is a sweeping condemnation passed upon the Central Junta.

We have thought it the more necessary to dwell upon this point, as its decisive importance has never been understood by any European historian. Exclusively under the reign of the Central Junta, it was possible to blend with the actualities and exigencies of national defense the transformation of Spanish society, and the emancipation of the native spirit, without which any political constitution must dissolve like a phantom at the slightest combat with real life. The Cortes were placed in quite opposite circumstances—they themselves driven back to an insulated spot of the Peninsula, cut off from the main body of the monarchy during two years by a besieging French army, and representing ideal Spain while real Spain was conquered or fighting. At the time of the Cortes Spain was divided into two parts. At the Isla de Leon, ideas without action—in the rest of Spain, action without ideas. At the time of the Central Junta, on the contrary, particular weakness, incapacity and ill will were required on the part of the Supreme Government to draw a line of distinction between the Spanish war and the Spanish revolution. The Cortes, therefore, failed, not, as French and English writers assert, because they were revolutionists, but because their predecessors had been reactionists and had missed the proper season of revolutionary action. Modern Spanish writers, offended by the Anglo-French critics, have nevertheless proved unable to refute them, and still wince under the *bon mot*[b] of the Abbé de Pradt[c]: "The Spanish people resemble the wife of Sganarelle who wanted to be beaten." [d]

---

[a] J. M. Toreno, op. cit., T. II, p. 3.—*Ed.*
[b] Witticisms.—*Ed.*
[c] D. Pradt, op. cit., p. 224.—*Ed.*
[d] Allusion to the words of Martine, wife of Sganarelle, principal character in Molière's *Le Médecin malgré lui* (Act I, Scene 2).—*Ed.*

V

The Central Junta failed in the defense of their country, because they failed in their revolutionary mission. Conscious of their own weakness, of the unstable tenor of their power, and of their extreme unpopularity, how could they have attempted to answer the rivalries, jealousies, and overbearing pretensions of their generals common to all revolutionary epochs, but by unworthy tricks and petty intrigues? Kept, as they were, in constant fear and suspicion of their own military chiefs, we may give full credit to Wellington when writing to his brother, the Marquis of Wellesley, on September 1, 1809:

"I am much afraid, from what I have seen of the proceedings of the Central Junta, that in the distribution of their forces, they did not consider military defense and military operations so much as they do political intrigue and the attainment of trifling political objects." [a]

In revolutionary times, when all ties of subordination are loosened, military discipline can only be restored by civil discipline sternly weighing upon the generals. As the Central Junta, from its incongruous complexion, never succeeded in controlling the generals, the generals always failed in controlling the soldiers, and to the end of the war the Spanish army never reached an average degree of discipline and subordination. This insubordination was kept up by the want of food, clothing, and all the other material requisites of an army—for the morale of an army, as Napoleon called it, depends altogether on its material condition. The Central

---

[a] W. Napier, *History of the War in the Peninsula and the South of France*, Vol. II, p. 437.—*Ed.*

Junta was unable regularly to provide for the army, because the poor poet Quintana's manifestoes would not do in this instance, and to add coercion to their decrees they must have recurred to the same revolutionary measures which they had condemned in the provinces. Even the general enlistment without respect to privilege and exemptions, and the facility granted to all Spaniards to obtain every grade in the army, was the work of the provincial juntas, and not of the Central Junta. If the defeats of the Spanish armies were thus produced by the counter-revolutionary in-capacities of the Central Junta, these disasters in their turn still more depressed that Government, and by making it the object of popular contempt and suspicion, increased its dependence upon presumptuous but incapable military chiefs.

The Spanish standing army, if everywhere defeated, neverthe-less presented itself at all points. More than twenty times dispersed, it was always ready again to show front to the enemy, and frequently reappeared with increased strength after a defeat. It was of no use to beat them, because, quick to flee, their loss in men was generally small, and as to the loss of the field, they did not care about it. Retiring disorderly to the sierras, they were sure to reassemble and reappear when least expected, strengthened by new reinforcements, and able, if not to resist the French armies, at least to keep them in continual movement, and to oblige them to scatter their forces. More fortunate than the Russians, they did not even need to die in order to rise from the dead.

The disastrous battle at Ocaña, November 19, 1809, was the last great pitched battle which the Spaniards fought; from that time they confined themselves to guerrilla warfare. The mere fact of the abandonment of regular warfare proves the disappearance of the national before the local centers of Government. When the disasters of the standing army became regular, the rising of the guerrillas became general, and the body of the people, hardly thinking of the national defeats, exulted in the local successes of their heroes. In this point at least the Central Junta shared the popular delusion. "Fuller accounts were given in the *Gaceta* of an affair of guerrillas than of the battle of Ocaña."

As Don Quixote had protested with his lance against gunpow-der, so the guerrillas protested against Napoleon, only with different success.

"These guerrillas," says the *Austrian Military Journal*[a] (Vol. I, 1821), "carried

---

[a] *Oesterreichische militärische Zeitschrift.—Ed.*

their basis in themselves, as it were, and every operation against them terminated in the disappearance of its object."

There are three periods to be distinguished in the history of the guerrilla warfare. In the first period the population of whole provinces took up arms and made a partisan warfare, as in Galicia and Asturias. In the second period, guerrilla bands formed of the wrecks of the Spanish armies, of Spanish deserters from the French armies, of smugglers, etc., carried on the war as their own cause, independently of all foreign influence and agreeably to their immediate interest. Fortunate events and circumstances frequently brought whole districts under their colors. As long as the guerrillas were thus constituted, they made no formidable appearance as a body, but were nevertheless extremely dangerous to the French. They formed the basis of an actual armament of the people. As soon as an opportunity for a capture offered itself, or a combined enterprise was meditated, the most active and daring among the people came out and joined the guerrillas. They rushed with the utmost rapidity upon their booty, or placed themselves in order of battle, according to the object of their undertaking. It was not uncommon to see them standing out a whole day in sight of a vigilant enemy, in order to intercept a carrier or to capture supplies. It was in this way that the younger Mina captured the Viceroy of Navarra, appointed by Joseph Bonaparte, and that Julian made a prisoner of the Commandant of Ciudad Rodrigo. As soon as the enterprise was completed, everybody went his own way, and armed men were seen scattering in all directions; but the associated peasants quietly returned to their common occupation without "as much as their absence having been noticed." Thus the communication on all the roads was closed. Thousands of enemies were on the spot, though not one could be discovered. No courier could be dispatched without being taken; no supplies could set out without being intercepted; in short, no movement could be effected without being observed by a hundred eyes. At the same time, there existed no means of striking at the root of a combination of this kind. The French were obliged to be constantly armed against an enemy who, continually flying, always reappeared, and was everywhere without being actually seen, the mountains serving as so many curtains.

"It was," says the Abbé de Pradt, "neither battles nor engagements which exhausted the French forces, but the incessant molestations of an invisible enemy, who, if pursued, became lost among the people, out of which he reappeared immediately afterward with renewed strength. The lion in the fable tormented to death by a gnat[a] gives a true picture of the French army."[b]

In their third period, the guerrillas aped the regularity of the standing army, swelled their corps to the number of from 3,000 to 6,000 men, ceased to be the concern of whole districts, and fell into the hands of a few leaders, who made such use of them as best suited their own purposes. This change in the system of the guerrillas gave the French, in their contests with them, considerable advantage. Rendered incapable by their great numbers to conceal themselves, and to suddenly disappear without being forced into battle, as they had formerly done, the guerrilleros were now frequently overtaken, defeated, dispersed, and disabled for a length of time from offering any further molestation.

By comparing the three periods of guerrilla warfare with the political history of Spain, it is found that they represent the respective degrees into which the counter-revolutionary spirit of the Government had succeeded in cooling the spirit of the people. Beginning with the rise of whole populations, the partisan war was next carried on by guerrilla bands, of which whole districts formed the reserve and terminated in *corps francs* continually on the point of dwindling into banditti, or sinking down to the level of standing regiments.

Estrangement from the Supreme Government, relaxed discipline, continual disasters, constant formation, decomposition, and recomposition during six years of the *cadrez* must have necessarily stamped upon the body of the Spanish army the character of praetorianism, making them equally ready to become the tools or the scourges of their chiefs. The generals themselves had necessarily participated in, quarrelled with, or conspired against the Central Government, and always thrown the weight of their sword into the political balance. Thus Cuesta, who afterwards seemed to win the confidence of the Central Junta at the same rate that he lost the battles of the country, had begun by conspiring with the *Consejo Real* and by arresting the Leonese deputies to the Central Junta. General Morla himself, a member of the Central Junta, went over into the Bonapartist camp, after he had surrendered Madrid to the French. The coxcombical Marquis de las Romerias, also a member of the Junta, conspired with the vainglorious Francisco Palafox, the wretched Montijo, and

---

[a] Aesop, "The Lion and the Gnat".— *Ed.*
[b] D. Pradt, op. cit., pp. 202-03.— *Ed.*

the turbulent Junta of Seville against it. The Generals Castaños, Blake, La Bisbal (an O'Donnell) figured and intrigued successively at the times of the Cortes as regents, and the Captain-General of Valencia, Don Javier Elío, surrendered Spain finally to the mercies of Ferdinand VII. The praetorian element was certainly more developed with the generals than with their troops.

On the other hand, the army and guerrilleros—which received during the war part of their chiefs, like Porlier, Lacy, Eroles and Villacampa, from the ranks of distinguished officers of the line, while the line in its turn afterward received guerrilla chiefs, like Mina, Empecinado, etc.—were the most revolutionized portion of Spanish society, recruited as they were from all ranks, including the whole of the fiery, aspiring and patriotic youth, inaccessible to the soporific influence of the Central Government; emancipated from the shackles of the ancient regime; part of them, like Riego, ieturning after some years' captivity in France. We are, then, not to be surprised at the influence exercised by the Spanish army in subsequent commotions; neither when taking the revolutionary initiative, nor when spoiling the revolution by praetorianism.

As to the guerrillas, it is evident that, having for some years figured upon the theater of sanguinary contests, taken to roving habits, freely indulged all their passions of hatred, revenge, and love of plunder, they must, in times of peace, form a most dangerous mob, always ready at a nod, in the name of any party or principle, to step forward for him who is able to give them good pay or to afford them a pretext for plundering excursions.

VI

On September 24, 1810, the Extraordinary Cortes assembled on the Island of Leon; on February 20, 1811, they removed their sittings thence to Cadiz; on March 19, 1812, they promulgated the new Constitution; and on September 20, 1813, they closed their sittings, three years from the period of their opening.

The circumstances under which this Congress met are without parallel in history. While no legislative body had ever before gathered its members from such various parts of the globe, or pretended to control such immense territories in Europe, America and Asia, such a diversity of races and such a complexity of interests—nearly the whole of Spain was occupied by the French, and the Congress itself, actually cut off from Spain by hostile armies, and relegated to a small neck of land, had to legislate in the sight of a surrounding and besieging army. From the remote angle of the *Isla Gaditana*[a] they undertook to lay the foundation of a new Spain, as their forefathers had done from the mountains of Covadonga and Sobrarbe.[316] How are we to account for the curious phenomenon of the Constitution of 1812, afterward branded by the crowned heads of Europe, assembled at Verona, as the most incendiary invention of Jacobinism, having sprung up from the head of old monastic and absolutionist Spain at the very epoch when she seemed totally absorbed in waging a holy war against the Revolution? How, on the other hand, are we to account for the sudden disappearance of this same Constitution, vanishing like a shadow—like "la sombra de un sueño,"[b] say the

---

[a] Cadiz.—*Ed.*
[b] The shadow of a dream.—*Ed.*

Spanish historians—when brought into contact with a living Bourbon[a]? If the birth of that Constitution is a riddle, its death is no less so. To solve the enigma, we propose to commence with a short review of this same Constitution of 1812, which the Spaniards tried again to realize at two subsequent epochs, first during the period from 1820-23, and then in 1836.

The Constitution of 1812[317] consists of 384 articles and comprehends the following 10 divisions: 1. On the Spanish nation and the Spaniards. 2. On the territory of Spain; its religion, government, and on Spanish citizens. 3. On the Cortes. 4. On the King. 5. On the tribunals and administration of justice in civil and criminal matters. 6. On the interior government of the provinces and communes. 7. On the taxes. 8. On the national military forces. 9. On public education. 10. On the observance of the Constitution, and mode of proceeding to make alterations therein.

Proceeding from the principle that

"the sovereignty resides essentially in the nation, to which, therefore, alone belongs exclusively the right of establishing fundamental laws,"

the Constitution, nevertheless, proclaims a division of powers, according to which:

"the legislative power is placed in the Cortes jointly with the King;" "the execution of the laws is confided to the King," "the application of the laws in civil and criminal affairs belongs exclusively to the tribunals, neither the Cortes nor the King being in any case empowered to exercise judicial authority, advocate pending cases, or command the revisal of concluded judgment."

The basis of the national representation is mere population, one deputy for every 70,000 souls. The Cortes consists of one house, viz: the commons, the election of the deputies being by universal suffrage. The elective franchise is enjoyed by all Spaniards, with the exception of menial servants, bankrupts and criminals. After the year 1830, no citizen can enjoy this right who cannot read and write. The election is, however, indirect, having to pass through the three degrees of parochial, district and provincial elections. There is no defined property qualification for a deputy. It is true that according to Art. 92, "it is necessary, in order to be eligible as a deputy to the Cortes, to possess a proportionate annual income, proceeding from real personal property," but Art. 93 suspends the preceding article, until the Cortes in their future meetings declare the period to have arrived in which it shall take effect. The King has neither the right to dissolve nor prorogue the

---

[a] Ferdinand VII.—*Ed.*

Cortes, who annually meet at the capital on the first of March, without being convoked, and sit at least three months consecutively.

A new Cortes is elected every second year, and no deputy can sit in two Cortes consecutively; i.e., one can only be re-elected after an intervening Cortes of two years. No deputy can ask or accept rewards, pensions, or honors from the King. The secretaries of state, the councilors of state, and those fulfilling offices of the royal household, are ineligible as deputies to the Cortes. No public officer employed by Government shall be elected deputy to the Cortes from the province in which he discharges his trust. To indemnify the deputies for their expenses, the respective provinces shall contribute such daily allowances as the Cortes, in the second year of every general deputation, shall point out for the deputation that is to succeed it. The Cortes cannot deliberate in the presence of the King. In those cases where the ministers have any communication to make to the Cortes in the name of the King, they may attend the debates when, and in such manner as, the Cortes may think fit, and may speak therein, but they cannot be present at a vote. The King, the Prince of Asturias, and the Regents have to swear to the Constitution before the Cortes, who determine any question of fact or right that may occur in the order of the succession to the Crown, and elect a Regency if necessary. The Cortes are to approve, previous to ratification, all treaties of offensive alliances, or of subsidies and commerce, to permit or refuse the admission of foreign troops into the kingdom, to decree the creation and suppression of offices in the tribunals established by the Constitution, and also the creation or abolition of public offices; to determine every year, at the recommendation of the King, the land and sea forces in peace and in war, to issue ordinances to the army, the fleet, and the national militia, in all their branches; to fix the expenses of the public administration; to establish annually the taxes, to take property on loan, in cases of necessity, upon the credit of the public funds, to decide on all matters respecting money, weights and measures; to establish a general plan of public education, to protect the political liberty of the press, to render real and effective the responsibility of the ministers, etc. The King enjoys only a suspensive veto, which he may exercise during two consecutive sessions, but if the same project of new law should be proposed a third time, and approved by the Cortes of the following year, the King is understood to have given his assent, and has actually to give it. Before the Cortes terminate a session, they appoint a permanent committee, consisting of seven of their members, sitting in the capital until the meeting of the next Cortes, endowed with powers to watch over the strict observance of the Constitution and administration of the laws; reporting to the next Cortes any infraction it may have observed, and empowered to convoke an extraordinary Cortes in critical times. The King cannot quit the kingdom without the consent of the Cortes. He requires the consent of the Cortes for contracting a marriage. The Cortes fix the annual revenue of the King's household.

The only Privy Council of the King is the Council of State, in which the ministers have no seat, and which consists of forty persons, four ecclesiastics, four grandees of Spain, and the rest formed by distinguished administrators, all of them chosen by the King from a list of one hundred and twenty persons [a] nominated by the Cortes; but no actual deputy can be a councilor, and no councilor can accept offices, honors, or employment from the King. The councilors of state cannot be removed without sufficient reasons, proved before the Supreme Court of Justice. The Cortes fix the salary of these councilors whose opinion the King will hear upon all important matters, and who nominate the candidates for ecclesiastical and judicial places. In the sections respecting the judicature, all the old *consejos*[b] are abolished, a new organization of tribunals is introduced, a Supreme Court of Justice is established to try the ministers when impeached, to take cognizance of all cases of dismissal and suspension from office of councilors of state, and the officers of courts of justice, etc. Without proof that reconciliation has been attempted, no law-suit can be commenced. Torture, compulsion, confiscation of property are suppressed. All exceptional tribunals are abolished but the military and ecclesiastic, against the decisions of which appeals to the Supreme Court are however permitted.

For the interior government of towns and communes (communes, where they do not exist, to be formed from districts with a population of 1,000 souls), *Ayuntamientos*[318] shall be formed of one or more magistrates, aldermen and public councilors, to be presided over by the political chief (*corregidor*) and to be chosen by general election. No public officer actually employed and appointed by the King can be eligible as a magistrate, alderman or public councilor. The municipal employments shall be public duty, from which no person can be exempt without lawful reason. The

---

[a] The figure 120 is omitted in Article 234 of the Constitution.— *Ed.*
[b] Councils.— *Ed.*

municipal corporations shall discharge all their duties under the inspection of the provincial deputation.

The political government of the provinces shall be placed in the governor (*jefe politico*) appointed by the King. This governor is connected with a deputation, over which he presides, and which is elected by the districts when assembled for the general election of the members for a new Cortes. These provincial deputations consist of seven members, assisted by a secretary paid by the Cortes. These deputations shall hold sessions for ninety days at most in every year. From the powers and duties assigned to them, they may be considered as permanent committees of the Cortes. All members of the *Ayuntamientos* and provincial deputations, in entering office, swear fidelity to the Constitution. With regard to the taxes, all Spaniards are bound, without any distinction whatever, to contribute, in proportion to their means, to the expenses of the State. All custom-houses shall be suppressed, except in the seaports and on the frontier. All Spaniards are likewise bound to military service, and, beside the standing army, there shall be formed corps of national militia in each province, consisting of the inhabitants of the same, in proportion to its population and circumstances. Lastly, the Constitution of 1812 cannot be altered, augmented, or corrected in any of its details, until eight years have elapsed after its having been carried into practice.

When the Cortes drew up this new plan of the Spanish State, they were of course aware that such a modern political Constitution would be altogether incompatible with the old social system, and consequently, they promulgated a series of decrees, with a view to organic changes in civil society. Thus they abolished the Inquisition. They suppressed the seignorial jurisdictions; with their exclusive, prohibitive, and privative feudal privileges, i.e., those of the chase, fishery, forests, mills, etc., excepting such as had been acquired on an onerous title, and which were to be reimbursed. They abolished the tithes throughout the monarchy, suspended the nominations to all ecclesiastic prebends not necessary for the performance of divine service, and took steps for the suppression of the monasteries and the sequestration of their property.

They intended to transform the immense wastelands, royal domains and commons of Spain into private property, by selling one half of them for the extinction of the public debt, distributing another part by lot as a patriotic remuneration for the disbanded soldiers of the war of independence and granting a third part, gratuitously, and also by lot, to the poor peasantry who should desire to possess but not be able to buy them. They allowed the inclosure of pastures and other real property, formerly forbidden. They repealed the absurd laws which prevented pastures from being converted into arable land or arable land converted into pasture, and generally freed agriculture from the old arbitrary and ridiculous rules. They revoked all feudal laws with respect to farming contracts, and the law according to which the successor of an entailed estate was not obliged to confirm the leases granted by his predecessor, the leases expiring with him who had granted them. They abolished the *voto de Santiago*, under which name was understood an ancient tribute of a certain measure of the best bread and the best wine to be paid by the laborers of certain provinces principally for the maintenance of the Archbishop and Chapter of Santiago.[a] They decreed the introduction of a large progressive tax, etc.

It being one of their principal aims to hold possession of the American colonies, which had already begun to revolt, they acknowledged the full political equality of the American and European Spaniards, proclaimed a general amnesty without any exception, issued decrees against the oppression weighing upon the original natives of America and Asia, cancelled the *mitas*, the *repartimientos*,[319] etc., abolished the monopoly of quicksilver, and took the lead of Europe in suppressing the slave-trade.

The Constitution of 1812 has been accused on the one hand—for instance, by Ferdinand VII himself (see his decree of May 4, 1814)—of being a mere imitation of the French Constitution of 1791,[320] transplanted on the Spanish soil by visionaries, regardless of the historical traditions of Spain. On the other hand, it has been contended—for instance, by the Abbé de Pradt (*De la Révolution actuelle de l'Espagne*)—that the Cortes unreasonably clung to antiquated formulas, borrowed from the ancient *fueros*,[321] and belonging to feudal times, when the royal authority was checked by the exorbitant privileges of the grandees.

The truth is that the Constitution of 1812 is a reproduction of the ancient Fueros, but read in the light of the French Revolution, and adapted to the wants of modern society. The right of insurrection, for instance, is generally regarded as one of the boldest innovations of the Jacobin Constitution of 1793,[322] but you meet this same right in the ancient Fueros of Sobrarbe, where it is

---

[a] Santiago de Compastela—a city in north-west Spain, the seat of an archbishopric, a famous place of pilgrimage.— *Ed.*

called the *Privilegio de la Union*. You find it also in the ancient Constitution of Castile. According to the Fueros of Sobrarbe, the King cannot make peace nor declare war, nor conclude treaties, without the previous consent of the Cortes. The Permanent Committee, consisting of seven members of the Cortes, who are to watch over the strict observance of the Constitution during the prorogation of the legislative body, was of old established in Aragon, and was introduced into Castile at the time when the principal Cortes of the monarchy were united in one single body. To the period of the French invasion a similar institution still existed in the kingdom of Navarre. Touching the formation of a State Council from a list of 120 persons presented to the King by the Cortes and paid by them—this singular creation of the Constitution of 1812 was suggested by the remembrance of the fatal influence exercised by the camarillas at all epochs of the Spanish monarchy. The State Council was intended to supersede the camarilla. Besides, there existed analogous institutions in the past. At the time of Ferdinand IV, for instance, the King was always surrounded by twelve commoners, designated by the cities of Castile, to serve as his privy councilors; and, in 1419, the delegates of the cities complained that their commissioners were no longer admitted into the King's Council. The exclusion of the highest functionaries and the members of the King's household from the Cortes, as well as the prohibition to the deputies to accept honors or offices on the part of the King, seems, at first view, to be borrowed from the Constitution of 1791, and naturally to flow from the modern division of powers, sanctioned by the Constitution of 1812. But, in fact, we meet not only in the ancient Constitution of Castile with precedents, but we know that the people, at different times, rose and assassinated the deputies who had accepted honors or offices from the Crown. As to the right of the Cortes to appoint regencies in case of minority, it had continually been exercised by the ancient Cortes of Castile during the long minorities of the fourteenth century.

It is true that the Cadiz Cortes deprived the King of the power he had always exercised of convoking, dissolving, or proroguing the Cortes; but as the Cortes had fallen into disuse by the very manner in which the Kings improved their privileges, there was nothing more evident than the necessity of cancelling it. The alleged facts may suffice to show that the anxious limitation of the royal power—the most striking feature of the Constitution of 1812—otherwise fully explained by the recent and revolting *souvenirs* of Godoy's contemptible despotism, derived its origin from the ancient Fueros of Spain. The Cadiz Cortes but transferred the control from the privileged *estates* to the national representation. How much the Spanish kings stood in awe of the ancient Fueros may be seen from the fact that when a new collection of the Spanish laws had become necessary, in 1805, a royal ordinance ordered the removal from it of all the remains of feudalism contained in the last collection of laws, and belonging to a time when the weakness of the monarchy forced the kings to enter with their vassals into compromises derogatory to the sovereign power.

If the election of the deputies by general suffrage was an innovation, it must not be forgotten that the Cortes of 1812 were themselves elected by general suffrage, that all the juntas had been elected by it; that a limitation of it would, therefore, have been an infraction of a right already conquered by the people; and, lastly, that a property qualification, at a time when almost all the real property of Spain was locked up in mortmain, would have excluded the greater part of the population.

The meeting of the representatives in one single house was by no means copied from the French Constitution of 1791, as the morose English Tories will have it. Our readers know already[a] that since Charles I (the Emperor Charles V) the aristocracy and the clergy had lost their seats in the Cortes of Castile. But even at the time when the Cortes were divided into *brazos* (arms, branches), representing the different estates, they assembled in one single hall, separated only by their seats, and voting in common. From the provinces, in which alone the Cortes still possessed real power at the epoch of the French invasion, Navarre continued the old custom of convoking the Cortes by *estates;* but in the Vascongadas the altogether democratic assemblies admitted not even the clergy. Besides, if the clergy and aristocracy had saved their obnoxious privileges, they had long since ceased to form independent political bodies, the existence of which constituted the basis of the composition of the ancient Cortes.

The separation of the judiciary from the executive power, decreed by the Cadiz Cortes, was demanded as early as the eighteenth century, by the most enlightened statesmen of Spain; and the general odium which the *Consejo Real,* from the beginning of the revolution, had concentrated upon itself, made the necessity of reducing the tribunals to their proper sphere of action universally felt.

---

[a] See this volume, pp. 394-95.—*Ed.*

The section of the Constitution which refers to the municipal government of the communes, is a genuine Spanish offspring, as we have shown in a former article. The Cortes only re-established the old municipal system, while they stripped off its medieval character. As to the provincial deputations, invested with the same powers for the internal government of the provinces as the *ayuntamientos* for the administration of the communes, the Cortes modelled them in imitation of similar institutions still existing at the time of the invasion in Navarre, Biscay and Asturias. In abolishing the exemptions from the military service, the Cortes sanctioned only what had become the general practice during the war of independence. The abolition of the Inquisition was also but the sanction of a fact, as the Holy Office, although re-established by the Central Junta, had not dared to resume its functions, its holy members being content with pocketing their salaries, and prudently waiting for better times. As to the suppression of feudal abuses, the Cortes went not even the length of the reforms insisted upon in the famous memorial of Jovellanos, presented in 1795 to the *Consejo Real* in the name of the economical society of Madrid.[a]

The ministers of the enlightened despotism of the latter part of the eighteenth century, Floridablanca and Campomanes, had already begun to take steps in this direction. Besides, it must not be forgotten that simultaneously with the Cortes, there sat a French Government at Madrid, which, in all the provinces overrun by the armies of Napoleon, had swept away from the soil all monastic and feudal institutions, and introduced the modern system of administration. The Bonapartist papers denounced the insurrection as entirely produced by the artifices and bribes of England, assisted by the monks and the Inquisition. How far the rivalry with the intruding government must have exercised a salutary influence upon the decisions of the Cortes, may be inferred from the fact that the Central Junta itself, in its decree dated September, 1809, wherein the convocation of the Cortes is announced, addressed the Spaniards in the following terms:

"Our detractors say that we are fighting to defend old abuses and the inveterate vices of our corrupted government. Let them know that your struggle is for the happiness as well as the independence of your country; that you will not depend henceforward on the uncertain will or the various temper of a single man," etc.[b]

---

[a] G. M. Jovellanos, op. cit.—*Ed.*
[b] The reference is to the initial draft of the decree which was rejected at the insistence of the British envoy. R. Southey, op. cit., Vol. II, p. 482.—*Ed.*

On the other hand, we may trace in the Constitution of 1812 symptoms not to be mistaken of a compromise entered into between the liberal ideas of the eighteenth century and the dark traditions of priestcraft. It suffices to quote Art. 12, according to which

"the religion of the Spanish nation is and shall be perpetually Catholic, Apostolic, and Roman, the only true religion. The nation protects it by wise and just laws, and prohibits the exercise of any other whatever";

or Art. 173, ordering the King to take, on his accession to the throne, the following oath before the Cortes:

"N., by the grace of God and the Constitution of the Spanish Monarchy, King of Spain, I swear by the Almighty and the Holy Evangelists, that I will defend and preserve the Catholic, Roman, and Apostolic religion, without tolerating any other in the kingdom."

On a closer analysis, then, of the Constitution of 1812, we arrive at the conclusion that, so far from being a servile copy of the French Constitution of 1791, it was a genuine and original offspring of Spanish intellectual life, regenerating the ancient and national institutions, introducing the measures of reform loudly demanded by the most celebrated authors and statesmen of the eighteenth century, making inevitable concessions to popular prejudice.

VII

There were some circumstances favorable to the assembling at Cadiz of the most progressive men of Spain. When the elections took place, the movement had not yet subsided, and the very disfavor which the Central Junta had incurred recommended its antagonists, who, to a great extent, belonged to the revolutionary minority of the nation. At the first meeting of the Cortes, the most democratic provinces, Catalonia and Galicia, were almost exclusively represented; the deputies from Leon, Valencia, Murcia and the Islas Baleares, not arriving till three months later. The most reactionary provinces, those of the interior, were not allowed, except in some few localities, to proceed with the elections for the Cortes. For the different kingdoms, cities and towns of old Spain, which the French armies prevented from choosing deputies, as well as for the ultramarine provinces of New Spain, whose deputies could not arrive in due time, supplementary representatives were elected from the many individuals whom the troubles of the war had driven from the provinces to Cadiz, and the numerous South Americans, merchants, natives and others, whose curiosity or the state of affairs had likewise assembled at that place. Thus it happened that those provinces were represented by men more fond of innovation, and more impregnated with the ideas of the eighteenth century, than would have been the case if they had been enabled to choose for themselves. Lastly, the circumstance of the Cortes meeting at Cadiz was of decisive influence, that city being then known as the most radical of the kingdom, more resembling an American than a Spanish town. Its population filled the galleries in the Hall of the Cortes and domineered the reactionists, when their opposition grew too obnoxious, by a system of intimidation and pressure from without.

It would, however, be a great mistake to suppose that the majority of the Cortes consisted of reformers. The Cortes were divided into three parties—the *Serviles*, the *Liberales* (these party denominations spread from Spain through the whole of Europe), and the *Americanos*, the latter voting alternately with the one or the other party, according to their particular interests.[323] The Serviles, far superior in numbers, were carried away by the activity, zeal and enthusiasm of the Liberal minority. The ecclesiastic deputies, who formed the majority of the Servile party, were always ready to sacrifice the royal prerogative, partly from the remembrance of the antagonism of the Church to the State, partly with a view to courting popularity, in order thus to save the privileges and abuses of their caste. During the debates on the general suffrage, the one-chamber system, the no-property qualification and the suspensive veto the ecclesiastic party always combined with the more democratic part of the Liberals against the partisans of the English Constitution. One of them, the Canon Cañedo, afterward Archbishop of Burgos, and an implacable persecutor of the Liberals, addressed Señor Muñoz Torrero, also a Canon, but belonging to the Liberal party, in these terms:

"You suffer the King to remain excessively powerful, but as a priest you ought to plead the cause of the Church, rather than that of the King."[a]

Into these compromises with the Church party the Liberals were forced to enter, as we have already seen from some articles of the Constitution of 1812. When the liberty of the press was discussed, the parsons denounced it as "contrary to religion." After the most stormy debates, and after having declared that all persons were at liberty to publish their sentiments without special license, the Cortes unanimously admitted an amendment, which, by inserting the word *political*, curtailed this liberty of half its extent, and left all writings upon religious matters subject to the censure of the ecclesiastic authorities, according to the decrees of the Council of Trent.[324] On August 18, 1813, after a decree passed against all who should conspire against the Constitution, another decree was passed, declaring that whoever should conspire to make the Spanish nation cease to profess the Catholic Roman religion should be prosecuted as a traitor, and suffer death.[b] When the *Voto de Santiago* was abolished, a compensatory

---

[a] Marliani, *Historia política de la España moderna.—Ed.*

[b] The decree on the freedom of the press adopted by the Cortes on November 10, 1810, and also the decrees of August 18, 1813 on the protection of the

resolution was carried, declaring Saint Teresa de Jesus the patro-
ness of Spain. The Liberals also took care not to propose and
carry the decrees about the abolition of the Inquisition, the tithes,
the monasteries, etc., till after the Constitution had been proclaimed. But from that very moment the opposition of the Serviles
within the Cortes, and the clergy without, became inexorable.

Having now explained the circumstances which account for the
origin and the characteristic features of the Constitution of 1812,
there still remains the problem to be solved of its sudden and
resistless disappearance at the return of Ferdinand VII. A more
humiliating spectacle has seldom been witnessed by the world.
When Ferdinand entered Valencia, on April 16, 1814,

> "the joyous people yoked themselves to his carriage, and testified by every
> possible expression of word and deed their desire of taking the old yoke upon
> themselves, shouting, 'Long live the absolute King!' 'Down with the Constitution!'"

In all the large towns, the Plaza Mayor, or Great Square, had
been named Plaza de la Constitución, and a stone with these words
engraved on it, erected there. In Valencia this stone was removed,
and a "provisional" stone of wood set up in its place with the
inscription: *Real Plaza de Fernando VII.* The populace of Seville
deposed all the existing authorities, elected others in their stead to
all the offices which had existed under the old regime, and then
required those authorities to re-establish the Inquisition. From
Aranjuez to Madrid Ferdinand's carriage was drawn by the
people. When the King alighted, the mob took him up in their
arms, triumphantly showed him to the immense concourse
assembled in front of the palace, and in their arms conveyed him
to his apartments. The word Liberty appeared in large bronze
letters over the entrance of the Hall of the Cortes in Madrid; the
rabble hurried thither to remove it; they set up ladders, forced out
letter by letter from the stone, and as each was thrown into the
street, the spectators renewed their shouts of exultation. They
collected as many of the journals of the Cortes and of the papers
and pamphlets of the Liberals as could be got together, formed a
procession in which the religious fraternities and the clergy,
regular and secular, took the lead, piled up these papers in one of
the public squares, and sacrificed them there as a political
auto-da-fe, after which high mass was performed and the Te

Constitution and the Catholic religion are given according to R. Southey, op. cit.,
Vol. III, p. 899. The decrees mentioned below were published in *Colección de los
decretos y órdenes que han expedido las Cortes generales y extraordinarias.—Ed.*

Deum sung as a thanksgiving for their triumph. More important perhaps—since these shameless demonstrations of the town mob, partly paid for their performances, and like the Lazzaroni of Naples, [325] preferring the wanton rule of kings and monks to the sober regime of the middle classes—is the fact that the second general elections resulted in a decisive victory of the Serviles; the Constituent Cortes being replaced by the ordinary Cortes on September 20, 1813, who transferred their sittings from Cadiz to Madrid on January 15, 1814.

We have shown in former articles how the revolutionary party itself had participated in rousing and strengthening the old popular prejudices, with a view to turn them into so many weapons against Napoleon. [a] We have then seen how the Central Junta, at the only period when social changes were to be blended with measures of national defense, did all in their power to prevent them, and to suppress the revolutionary aspirations of the provinces. [b] The Cadiz Cortes, on the contrary, cut off, during the greater part of their existence, from all connection with Spain, were not even enabled to make their Constitution and their organic decrees known, except as the French armies retired. The Cortes arrived, as it were, *post factum.* They found society fatigued, exhausted, suffering; the necessary product of so protracted a war, entirely carried on upon the Spanish soil; a war in which the armies, being always on the move, the Government of today was seldom that of tomorrow, while bloodshed did not cease one single day during almost six years throughout the whole surface of Spain, from Cadiz to Pamplona, and from Granada to Salamanca. It was not to be expected that such a society should be very sensible of the abstract beauties of any political constitution whatever. Nevertheless, when the Constitution was first proclaimed at Madrid, and the other provinces evacuated by the French, it was received with "exultant delight," the masses being generally expecting a sudden disappearance of their social sufferings from mere change of Government. When they discovered that the Constitution was not possessed of such miraculous powers, the very overstrained expectations which had welcomed it turned into disappointment, and with these passionate Southern peoples there is but one step from disappointment to hatred.

There were some particular circumstances which principally contributed to estrange the popular sympathies from the constitu-

---

[a] See this volume, pp. 403-04.—*Ed.*
[b] Ibid., pp. 414-18.—*Ed.*

tional regime. The Cortes had published the severest decrees against the *Afrancesados* or the *Josephites*.[a] The Cortes were partly driven to these decrees by the vindictive clamor of the populace and the reactionists, who at once turned against the Cortes as soon as the decrees they had wrung from them were put to execution. Upwards of 10,000 families became thus exiled. A lot of petty tyrants let loose on the provinces evacuated by the French, established their proconsular authority, and began by inquiries, prosecution, prison, inquisitorial proceedings against those compromised through adherence to the French, by having accepted offices from them, bought national property from them, etc. The Regency, instead of trying to effect the transition from the French to the national regime in a conciliatory and discreet way, did all in their power to aggravate the evils and exasperate the passions, inseparable from such changes of dominion. But why did they do so? In order to be able to ask from the Cortes a suspension of the Constitution of 1812, which, they told them, worked so very offensively. Be it remarked, *en passant*, that all the Regencies, these supreme executive authorities appointed by the Cortes, were regularly composed of the most decided enemies of the Cortes and their Constitution. This curious fact is simply explained by the Americans always combining with the Serviles in the appointment of the executive power, the weakening of which they considered necessary for the attainment of American independence from the mother country, since they were sure that an executive simply at variance with the sovereign Cortes would prove insufficient. The introduction by the Cortes of a single direct tax upon the rental of land, as well as upon industrial and commercial produce, excited also great discontent among the people, and still more so the absurd decrees forbidding the circulation of all Spanish specie coined by Joseph Bonaparte, and ordering its possessors to exchange it for national coin,[b] simultaneously interdicting the circulation of French money, and proclaiming a tariff at which it was to be exchanged at the national mint. As this tariff greatly differed from that proclaimed by the French in 1808, for the relative value of French and Spanish coins, many private individuals were involved in great losses. This absurd measure also contributed to raise the price of the first necessaries, already highly above the average rates.

---

[a] Supporters of the French influence, or adherents of Joseph Bonaparte.— *Ed.*

[b] Orden para que se indemnice en la Casa de Moneda a los tenedores de la del Rey intruso (Cádiz 4 de Abril de 1811) in: *Colección de los decretos y órdenes que han expedido las Cortes generales y extraordinarias* ..., T. I, p. 123.— *Ed.*

The classes most interested in the overthrow of the Constitution of 1812 and the restoration of the old regime—the grandees, the clergy, the friars and the lawyers—did not fail to excite to the highest pitch the popular discontent created by the unfortunate circumstances which had marked the introduction on the Spanish soil of the constitutional regime. Hence the victory of the Serviles in the general elections of 1813.

Only on the part of the army could the King apprehend any serious resistance, but General Elío and his officers, breaking the oath they had sworn to the Constitution, proclaimed Ferdinand VII at Valencia, without mentioning the Constitution. Elío was soon followed by the other military chiefs.

In his decree, dated May 4, 1814, in which Ferdinand VII dissolved the Madrid Cortes and cancelled the Constitution of 1812, he simultaneously proclaimed his hatred of despotism, promised to convene the Cortes under the old legal forms, to establish a rational liberty of the press, etc. He redeemed his pledge in the only manner which the reception he had met on the part of the Spanish people deserved—by rescinding all the acts emanating from the Cortes, by restoring everything to its ancient footing, by re-establishing the Holy Inquisition, by recalling the Jesuits banished by his grandsire,[a] by consigning the most prominent members of the juntas, the Cortes and their adherents to the galleys, African prisons, or to exile; and, finally, by ordering the most illustrious guerrilla chiefs, Porlier and de Lacy, to be shot.

---

[a] Charles III.— *Ed.*

VIII

During the year 1819 an expeditionary army was assembled in the environs of Cadiz for the purpose of reconquering the revolted American colonies. Enrique O'Donnell, Count La Bisbal, the uncle of Leopoldo O'Donnell, the present Spanish Minister, was intrusted with the command. The former expeditions against Spanish America having swallowed up 14,000 men since 1814, and being carried out in the most disgusting and reckless manner, had grown most odious to the army, and were generally considered a malicious means of getting rid of the dissatisfied regiments. Several officers, among them Quiroga, López Baños, San Miguel (the present Spanish La Fayette), O'Daly, and Arco Agüero, determined to improve the discontent of the soldiers, to shake off the yoke, and to proclaim the Constitution of 1812. La Bisbal, when initiated into the plot, promised to put himself at the head of the movement. The chiefs of the conspiracy, in conjunction with him, fixed on July 9, 1819, as the day on which a general review of the expeditionary troops was to take place, in the midst of which act the grand blow was to be struck. At the hour of the review La Bisbal appeared, indeed, but instead of keeping his word, ordered the conspiring regiments to be disarmed, sent Quiroga and the other chiefs to prison, and dispatched a courier to Madrid, boasting that he had prevented the most alarming of catastrophes. He was rewarded with promotion and decorations, but the Court having obtained more accurate information, afterward deprived him of his command, and ordered him to withdraw to the capital. This is the same La Bisbal who, in 1814, at the time of the King's return to Spain, sent an officer of his staff with two letters to Ferdinand. Too great a distance from the spot rendering it impossible for him to observe the King's movements, and to regulate his conduct according to that of the Monarch—in one letter La Bisbal made a pompous eulogy of the Constitution of 1812, on the supposition that the King would take the oath to support it. In the other, on the contrary, he represented the constitutional system as a scheme of anarchy and confusion, congratulated Ferdinand on his exterminating it, and offered himself and his army to oppose the rebels, demagogues, and enemies of the throne and altar. The officer delivered this second dispatch, which was cordially received by the Bourbon.

Notwithstanding the symptoms of rebellion which had shown themselves among the expeditionary army, the Madrid Government, at the head of which was placed the Duke of San Fernando, then Foreign Minister and President of the Cabinet, persisted in a state of inexplicable apathy and inactivity, and did nothing to accelerate the expedition, or to scatter the army in different seaport towns. Meanwhile a simultaneous movement was agreed upon between Don Rafael de Riego, commanding the second battalion of Asturias, then stationed at Las Cabezas de San Juan, and Quiroga, San Miguel, and other military chiefs of the Isla de Leon, who had contrived to get out of prison. Riego's position was far the most difficult. The commune of Las Cabezas was in the center of three of the headquarters of the expeditionary army— that of the cavalry at Utrera, the second division of infantry at Lebrija, and a battalion of guides at Arcos, where the commander-in-chief [a] and the staff were established. He nevertheless succeeded, on January 1, 1820, in surprising and capturing the commander and the staff, although the battalion cantoned at Arcos was double the strength of that of Asturias. On the same day he proclaimed in that very commune the Constitution of 1812, elected a provisional *alcalde*, and, not content with having executed the task devolved upon him, seduced the guides to his cause, surprised the battalion of Aragon lying at Bornos, marched from Bornos on Jerez, and from Jerez on Port St. Marie, [b] everywhere proclaiming the Constitution, till he reached the Isla de Leon, on the 7th January, where he deposited the military prisoners he had made in the fort of St. Petri. [c] Contrary to their previous agreement Quiroga and his followers had not possessed them-

---

[a] Calleja del Rey.—*Ed.*
[b] Puerto de Santa Maria.— *Ed.*
[c] San Pedro.— *Ed.*

selves by a *coup de main* of the bridge of Suazo, and then of the
Isla de Leon, but remained tranquil to the 2d of January, after
Oltra, Riego's messenger, had conveyed to them official intelli-
gence of the surprise of Arcos and the capture of the staff.

The whole forces of the revolutionary army, the supreme
command of which was given to Quiroga, did not exceed 5,000
men, and their attacks upon the gates of Cadiz having been
repulsed, they were themselves shut up in the Isla de Leon.

"Our situation," says San Miguel, "was extraordinary; the revolution, stationary
twenty-five days without losing or gaining an inch of ground, presented one of the
most singular phenomena in politics." [326]

The provinces seemed rocked into lethargic slumber. During the
whole month of January, at the end of which Riego, apprehending
the flame of revolution might be extinguished in the Isla de Leon,
formed, against the counsels of Quiroga and the other chiefs, a
movable column of 1,500 men, and marched over a part of
Andalusia, in presence of and pursued by a ten times stronger force
than his own, proclaiming the Constitution at Algeciras, Ronda,
Malaga, Cordova, etc., everywhere received by the inhabitants in a
friendly way, but nowhere provoking a serious pronunciamento.
Meanwhile his pursuers, consuming a whole month in fruitless
marches and countermarches, seemed to desire nothing but to
avoid, as much as possible, coming to close quarters with his little
army. The conduct of the Government troops was altogether
inexplicable. Riego's expedition, which began on January 27, 1820,
terminated on March 11, he being then forced to disband the few
men that still followed him. His small corps was not dispersed
through a decisive battle, but disappeared from fatigue, from
continual petty encounters with the enemy, from sickness and
desertion. Meanwhile the situation of the insurrectionists in the
Isla was by no means promising. They continued to be blocked up
by sea and land, and within the town of Cadiz every declaration
for their cause was suppressed by the garrison. How, then, did it
happen that, Riego having disbanded in the Sierra Morena the
constitutional troops on the 11th of March, Ferdinand VII was
forced to swear to the Constitution, at Madrid, on the 9th of
March, so that Riego really gained his end just two days before he
finally despaired of his cause?

The march of Riego's column had riveted anew the general
attention; the provinces were all expectation, and eagerly watched
every movement. Men's minds, struck by the boldness of Riego's
sally, the rapidity of his march, his vigorous repulses of the

enemy, imagined triumphs never gained, and aggregations and re-enforcements never obtained. When the tidings of Riego's enterprise reached the more distant provinces, they were magnified in no small degree, and those most remote from the spot were the first to declare themselves for the Constitution of 1812. So far was Spain matured for a revolution, that even false news sufficed to produce it. So, too, it was false news that produced the hurricane of 1848.

In Galicia, Valencia, Saragossa, Barcelona and Pamplona, successive insurrections broke out. Enrique O'Donnell, alias the Count La Bisbal, being summoned by the King to oppose the expedition of Riego, not only offered to take arms against him, but to annihilate his little army and seize on his person. He only demanded the command of the troops cantoned in the Province of La Mancha, and money for his personal necessities. The King himself gave him a purse of gold and the requisite orders for the troops of La Mancha. But on his arrival at Ocaña, La Bisbal put himself at the head of the troops and proclaimed the Constitution of 1812. The news of this defection roused the public spirit of Madrid where the revolution · burst forth immediately on the intelligence of this event. The Government began then to negotiate with the revolution. In a decree, dated March 6,[327] the King offered to convoke the *ancient* Cortes, assembled in *Estamentos* (Estates), a decree suiting no party, neither that of the old monarchy nor that of the revolution. On his return from France, he had held out the same promise and failed to redeem his pledge. During the night of the 7th, revolutionary demonstrations having taken place in Madrid, the *Gaceta* of the 8th published a decree by which Ferdinand VII promised to swear to the Constitution of 1812.

"Let all of us," he said, in that decree, "and myself first, fairly enter upon the path of the Constitution."

The people having got possession of the palace on the 9th, he saved himself only by reestablishing the Madrid *Ayuntamiento* of 1814, before which he swore to the Constitution. He, for his part, did not care for false oaths, having always at hand a confessor ready to grant him full remission of all possible sins. Simultaneously a consultative junta was established, the first decree of which set free the political prisoners and recalled the political refugees. The prisons, now opened, sent the first constitutional Ministry to the royal palace. Castro, Herreros, and A. Argüelles—who formed the first Ministry—were martyrs of 1814, and deputies of 1812.[328]

The true source of the enthusiasm which had appeared on the accession of Ferdinand to the throne, was joy at the removal of Charles IV, his father. And thus the source of the general exultation at the proclamation of the Constitution of 1812, was joy at the removal of Ferdinand VII. As to the Constitution itself, we know that, when finished, there were no territories in which to proclaim it. For the majority of the Spanish people, it was like the unknown god worshipped by the ancient Athenians.

In our days it has been affirmed by English writers, with an express allusion to the present Spanish revolution, on the one hand that the movement of 1820 was but a military conspiracy, and on the other that it was but a Russian intrigue. [329] Both assertions are equally ridiculous. As to the military insurrection, we have seen that, notwithstanding its failure, the revolution proved victorious; and, besides, the riddle to be solved would not be conspiracy of 5,000 soldiers, but the sanction of that conspiracy by an army of 35,000 men, and by a most loyal nation of twelve millions. That the revolution first acted through the ranks of the army is easily explained by the fact that, of all the bodies of the Spanish monarchy, the army was the only one thoroughly transformed and revolutionized during the war of independence. As to Russian intrigue, it is not to be denied that Russia had her hands in the business of the Spanish revolution; that, of all the European powers, Russia first acknowledged the Constitution of 1812, by the treaty concluded in Veliki Luki, on July 20, 1812[330]; that she first kindled the revolution of 1820, first denounced it to Ferdinand VII, first lighted the torch of counter-revolution on several points of the Peninsula, first solemnly protested against it before Europe, and finally forced France into an armed intervention against it. Monsieur de Tatischeff, the Russian Embassador, was certainly the most prominent character at the Court of Madrid—the invisible head of the camarilla. He had succeeded in introducing Antonio Ugarte, a wretch of low station, at Court, and making him the head of the friars and footmen who, in their back-staircase council, swayed the scepter in the name of Ferdinand VII. By Tatischeff, Ugarte was made Director-General of the expeditions against South America, and by Ugarte the Duke of San Fernando was appointed Foreign Minister and President of the Cabinet. Ugarte effected from Russia the purchase of rotten ships, destined for the South American Expedition, for which the order of St. Ann was bestowed upon him. Ugarte prevented Ferdinand and his brother Don Carlos from presenting themselves to the army at the first moment of the crisis. He was the mysterious author of the Duke of San Fernando's unaccountable apathy, and of the measures which led a Spanish Liberal to say at Paris in 1836:

"One can hardly resist the conviction that the Government was rendering itself the means for the overthrow of the existing order of things." [a]

If we add the curious fact that the President of the United States [b] praised Russia in his message for her having promised him not to suffer Spain to meddle with the South American colonies, [c] there can remain but little doubt as to the part acted by Russia in the Spanish revolution. But what does all this prove? That Russia produced the revolution of 1820? By no means, but only that she prevented the Spanish Government from resisting it. That the revolution would have earlier or later overturned the absolute and monastic monarchy of Ferdinand VII is proved: 1. By the series of conspiracies which since 1814 had followed each other; 2. By the testimony of M. de Martignac, the French Commissary who accompanied the Duke of Angoulême at the time of the Legitimist invasion of Spain; 3. By testimony not to be rejected—that of Ferdinand himself.

In 1814 Mina intended a rising in Navarre, gave the first signal for resistance by an appeal to arms, entered the fortress of Pamplona, but distrusting his own followers, fled to France. In 1815 General Porlier, one of the most renowned guerrilleros of the War of Independence, proclaimed the Constitution at Coruña. He was beheaded. In 1816, Richard intended capturing the King at Madrid. He was hanged. In 1817, Navarro, a lawyer, with four of his accomplices, expired on the scaffold at Valencia for having proclaimed the Constitution of 1812. In the same year the intrepid General Lacy was shot at Majorca for having committed the same crime. In 1818, Colonel Vidal, Captain Sola, and others, who had proclaimed the Constitution at Valencia, were defeated and put to the sword. The Isla de Leon conspiracy then was but the last link in a chain formed by the bloody heads of so many valiant men from 1808 to 1814. [331]

M. de Martignac who, in 1832, shortly before his death, published his work: *L'Espagne et ses Révolutions*, makes the following statement:

---

[a] Miraflores, *Essais historiques et critiques pour servir à l'histoire d'Espagne de 1820 à 1823*, T. I, p. XII.—*Ed.*

[b] James Monroe.—*Ed.*

[c] This data is taken from D. Urquhart, *Progress of Russia*, p. 33.—*Ed.*

"Two years had passed away since Ferdinand VII had resumed his absolute power, and there continued still the proscriptions, proceeding from a camarilla recruited from the dregs of mankind. The whole State machinery was turned upside down; there reigned nothing but disorder, languor and confusion—taxes most unequally distributed—the state of the finances was abominable—there were loans without credit, impossibility of meeting the most urgent wants of the State, an army not paid, magistrates indemnifying themselves by bribery, a corrupt and do-nothing Administration, unable to ameliorate anything, or even to preserve anything. Hence the general discontent of the people. The new constitutional system was received with enthusiasm by the great towns, the commercial and industrial classes, liberal professions, army and proletariat. It was resisted by the monks, and it stupefied the country people."

Such are the confessions of a dying man who was mainly instrumental in subverting that new system. Ferdinand VII, in his decrees of June 1, 1817, March 1, 1817, April 11, 1817, November 24, 1819, etc., literally confirms the assertions of M. de Martignac, and resumes his lamentations in these words:

"The miseries that resound in the ears of our Majesty, on the part of the complaining people, overset one another."

This shows that no Tatischeff was needed to bring about a Spanish revolution.

Karl Marx

THE REACTION IN SPAIN [332]

London, Friday, September 1, 1854

The entrance into Madrid of the Vicálvaro regiments has encouraged the Government to greater counter-revolutionary activity. The revival of the restrictive press-law of 1837, adorned with all the rigors of the supplementary law of 1842, [333] has killed all the "incendiary" portion of the press which was unable to offer the required *cautionnement*.[a] On the 24th the last number was given out of *El Clamor de las Barricadas* with the title of *Ultimas Barricadas*, the two editors having been arrested. Its place was taken on the same day by a new reactionary paper called *Las Cortes*.

"His Excellency, the Captain-General, Don San Miguel," says the program of the last-mentioned paper, "who honors us with his friendship, has offered to this journal the favor of his collaboration. His articles will be signed with his initials. The men at the head of this enterprise will defend with energy that revolution which vanquished the abuses and excesses of a corrupt power, but it is in the *enceinte* of the Constituent Assembly that they will plant their banner. It is there that the great battle must be fought."[b]

The great battle is for Isabella II, and Espartero. You will remember that this same San Miguel, at the banquet of the press, declared that the press had no other corrective but itself, common sense and public education, that it was an institution which neither sword nor transportation, nor exile, nor any power in the world could crush. On the very day on which he offers himself as a

---

[a] Caution money.—*Ed.*

[b] The quotation from *Las Cortes* is probably taken from *L'Indépendance belge*, No. 244, September 1, 1854.—*Ed.*

contributor to the press, he has not a word against the decree confiscating his beloved liberty of the press.

The suppression of the liberty of the press has been closely followed by the suppression of the right of meeting, also by royal decree. The clubs have been dissolved at Madrid, and in the provinces the juntas and committees of Public Safety, with the exception of those acknowledged by the Ministry as "deputations." The Club of the Union [334] was shut up in consequence of a decree of the whole Ministry, notwithstanding that Espartero had only a few days previously accepted its honorary Presidency, a fact which *The London Times* vainly labors to deny.[a] This club had sent a deputation to the Minister of the Interior,[b] insisting on the dismissal of Señor Sagasti, the *Jefe Politico* of Madrid, charging him with having violated the liberty of the press and the right of meeting. Señor Santa Cruz answered that he could not blame a public functionary for taking measures approved by the Council of Ministers. The consequence was that a serious trouble arose; but the *Plaza de la Constitución* was occupied by the National Guard, and nothing further occurred. The petty journals had scarcely been suppressed when the greater ones that had hitherto granted their protection to Sagasti, found occasion to quarrel with him. In order to silence *El Clamor Público*, its chief editor, Señor Corradi, was appointed Minister. But this step will not be sufficient, as all editors cannot be attached to the Ministry.

The boldest stroke of the counter-revolution, however, was the permission for Queen Cristina's departure for Lisbon, after the Council of Ministers had engaged to keep her at the disposal of the Constituent Cortes—a breach of faith which they have tried to cover by an anticipated confiscation of Cristina's estates in Spain, notoriously the least considerable portion of her wealth. Thus Cristina had a cheap escape, and now we hear that San Luis, too, has safely arrived at Bayonne. The most curious part of the transaction is the manner in which the decree alluded to was obtained. On the 26th some patriots and National Guards assembled to consider the safety of the public cause, blaming the Government on account of its vacillation and half and half measures, and agreeing to send a deputation to the Ministry calling upon them to remove Cristina from the Palace, where she was plotting liberticide projects. There was a very suspicious

---

[a] Report of the Madrid correspondent of August 23, 1854. *The Times*, No. 21832, August 29, 1854.—*Ed.*

[b] Rios y Rosas.—*Ed.*

circumstance in the adhesion of two aides-de-camp of Espartero with Sagasti himself, to this proposition. The result was that the Ministry met in council, and the upshot of their meeting was the elopement of Cristina.

On the 25th the Queen appeared for the first time in public, on the promenade of the Prado,[a] attended by what is called her husband,[b] and by the Prince of Asturias.[335] But her reception appears to have been extremely cold.

The committee appointed to report on the state of the finances at the epoch of the fall of the Sartorius Ministry has published its report in the *Gaceta*, where it is preceded by an *exposé* by Señor Collado, the Minister of Finance.[c] According to this the floating debt of Spain now amounts to $33,000,000, and the total deficit to $50,000,000. It appears that even the extraordinary resources of the Government were anticipated for years and squandered. The revenues of Havana and the Philippines were anticipated for two years and a half. The yield of the forced loan had disappeared without leaving a trace. The Almadén quick-silver mines were engaged for years. The balance in hand due to the *Caja*[d] of deposits did not exist. Not did the fund for military substitution. 7,485,692 reals were due for the purchase of tobacco obtained, but not paid for. Ditto 5,505,000 reals for bills on account of public works. According to the statement of Señor Collado the amount of obligations of the most pressing nature is 252,980,253 reals. The measures proposed by him for the covering of this deficit are those of a true banker, viz: to return to quiet and order, to continue to levy all the old taxes, and to contract new loans. In compliance with this advice Espartero has obtained from the principal Madrid bankers $2,500,000 on a promise of a pure *Moderado* policy. How willing he is to keep this promise is proved by his last measures.

It must not be imagined that these reactionary measures have remained altogether unresisted by the people. When the departure of Cristina became known, on the 28th August, barricades were erected again; but, if we are to believe a telegraphic dispatch from Bayonne, published by the French *Moniteur*,

---

[a] A boulevard in Madrid.— *Ed.*

[b] Francisco de Asis.— *Ed.*

[c] The committee's findings on the state of the finances in Spain and the account addressed by the Minister of Finance to the Crown (August 25, 1854) from the Spanish *Gaceta* are probably taken from a report from Madrid of August 26 published in *The Times*, No. 21836, September 2, 1854.— *Ed.*

[d] Bank.— *Ed.*

"the troops, united to the National Guard, carried the barricades and put down the movement."[a]

This is the *cercle vicieux*[b] in which abortive revolutionary governments are condemned to move. They recognize the debts contracted by their counter-revolutionary predecessors as national obligations. In order to be able to pay them they must continue their old taxes and contract new debts. To be able to contract new loans they must give guaranties of "*order*," that is, take counter-revolutionary measures themselves. Thus the new popular Government is at once transformed into the handmaid of the great capitalists, and an oppressor of the people. In exactly the same manner was the Provisional Government of France in 1848 driven to the notorious measure of the 45 centimes,[336] and the confiscation of the savings banks' funds in order to pay their interest to the capitalists.

"The revolutionary governments of Spain," says the English author of the *Revelations on Spain*,[c] "are at least not sunk so deep as to adopt the infamous doctrine of repudiation as practiced in the United States."

The fact is that if any former Spanish revolution had once practiced repudiation, the infamous Government of San Luis would not have found any banker willing to oblige it with advances. But perhaps our author holds the view that it is the privilege of the counter-revolution to contract, as it is the privilege of revolution to pay debts.

It appears that Saragossa, Valencia and Algeciras do not concur in this view, as they have abrogated all taxes obnoxious to them.

Not content with sending Bravo Murillo as Embassador to Constantinople, the Government has dispatched González Bravo in the same capacity to Vienna.

On Sunday, 27th August, the electoral reunions of the District of Madrid assembled in order to appoint, by general suffrage, the Commissioners charged with the superintendence of the election at the capital. There exist two Electoral Committees at Madrid—the Liberal Union, and the Unión del Comercio.

The symptoms of reaction above collected appear less formidable to persons acquainted with the history of Spanish revolutions than they must to the superficial observer—since Spanish revolu-

---

[a] Telegram from Paris of August 30, 1854. *L'Indépendance belge*, No. 243, August 31, 1854.— *Ed.*

[b] Vicious circle.— *Ed.*

[c] Probably [Hughes,] *Revelations of Spain in 1845.—Ed.*

tions generally only date from the meeting of the Cortes, usually the signal for the dissolution of Government. At Madrid, besides, there are only a few troops, and at the highest 20,000 National Guards. But of the latter only about one half are properly armed, while the people are known to have disobeyed the call to deliver up their arms.

Notwithstanding the tears of the Queen, O'Donnell has dissolved her bodyguard,[a] the regular army being jealous of the privileges of this *corps,* from whose ranks a Godoy, noticed as a good player upon the guitar and a singer of *seguidillas graciosas y picantes,* could raise himself to become the husband of the King's niece,[b] and a Muñoz, only known for his private advantages, become the husband of a Queen Mother.

At Madrid a portion of the republicans have circulated the following *Constitution of a Federal Iberian Republic:*

TITULO I. *Organization of the Federal Iberian Republic.*

Art. 1. Spain and its isles and Portugal will be united and form the Federal Iberian Republic. The colors of the banner will be a union of the two actual banners of Spain and Portugal. Its device will be Liberty, Equality, Fraternity.

Art. 2. The sovereignty resides in the universality of the citizens. It is inalienable and imprescriptible. No individual, no fraction of the people can usurp its exercise.

Art. 3. The law is the expression of the national will. The judges are appointed by the people through universal suffrage.

Art. 4. All citizens of 21 years of age and enjoying their civil rights to be electors.

Art. 5. The punishment of death is abolished, both for political and common crimes. The jury is to judge in all cases.

Art. 6. Property is sacred. The estates taken from political emigrants are restored to them.

Art. 7. The contributions will be paid in proportion to incomes. There will be one tax only, direct and general. All indirect contributions, *octroi,* and on consumption are abolished. Likewise abolished are the Government monopolies of salt and tobacco, the stamps, the patent dues, and the conscription.[337]

Art. 8. The liberty of the press, of meeting, of association, of domicile, of education, of commerce, and of conscience, is granted. *Every religion will have to pay for its own ministers.*

Art. 13. The administration of the republic is to be federal, provincial and municipal.

TITULO II. *Federal Administration.*

Art. 14. It will be intrusted to an Executive Council appointed and revocable by the Central Federal Congress.

---

[a] Isabella II. Royal decree of August 25, 1854, countersigned by Leopoldo O'Donnell, *Le Moniteur universel,* No. 245, September 2, 1854.—*Ed.*

[b] María Teresa de Borbón.—*Ed.*

Art. 15. The international and commercial relations, the uniformity of measures, weights and coins, the Post-Office, and the armed force are the domain of the Federal Administration.

Art. 16. The Central Federal Congress will be composed of nine Deputies for every province, elected by universal suffrage and bound by their instructions.

Art. 17. The Central Federal Congress is in permanency.

Art. 20. Whenever a law is to be enacted, the Administration thinking it necessary will bring the project under the cognizance of the confederation six months before if it be for the Congress, and three months if it be for the Provincial Legislation.

Art. 21. Any Deputy of the people failing to adhere to his instructions is handed over to justice.

Titulo III refers to the Provincial and Municipal Administration, and confirms similar principles. The last article of this chapter says:

There are to be no longer any colonies; they will be changed into provinces and administered on provincial principles. *Slavery shall be abolished.*

TITULO IV. *The Army.*

Art. 34. The whole people will be armed and organized in a National Guard, one portion to be *mobile* and the other sedentary.

Art. 35. The mobile guard to consist of the *solteros* between the ages of 21 and 35; their officers to be chosen in the military schools by election.

Art. 36. The sedentary militia consists of all citizens between 35 and 56 years; officers to be appointed by election. Their service is the defense of the communities.

Art. 38. The corps of artillery and engineers are recruited by voluntary enlistment, permanent, and garrisoning the fortresses on the coast of the frontiers. No fortresses shall be suffered in the interior.

Art. 39, alluding to the marine, contains similar provisions.

Art. 40. The staffs of the provinces and captain-generalcies[338] are suppressed.

Art. 42. The Iberian Republic renounces all wars of conquest, and will submit its quarrels to the arbitration of Governments disinterested in the question.

Art. 43. There shall be no standing armies.

Written on September 1 and 2, 1854

First published in the *New-York Daily Tribune*, No. 4185, September 16; reprinted in the *New-York Semi-Weekly Tribune*, No. 972, September 19 and the *New-York Weekly Tribune*, No. 680, September 23, 1854

Signed: *Karl Marx*

Reproduced from the *New-York Daily Tribune*

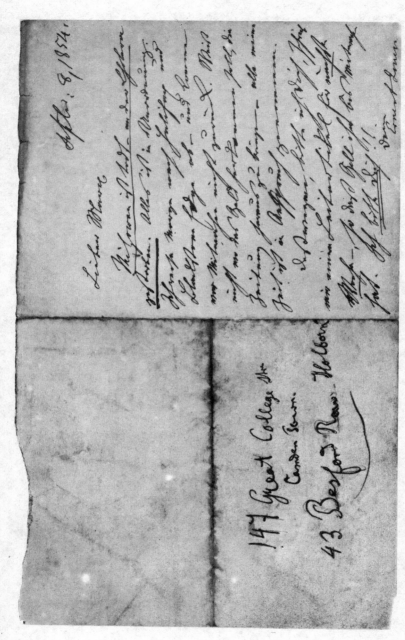

Ernest Jones' letter of September 8, 1854 to Marx asking him to write a leader for *The People's Paper*. The address is in Marx's handwriting

Karl Marx

[THE RUMOURS ABOUT MAZZINI'S ARREST.— THE AUSTRIAN COMPULSORY LOAN.— SPAIN.—THE SITUATION IN WALLACHIA][339]

London, Tuesday, Sept. 12, 1854

The papers contain diverse rumors about Mazzini's arrest at Bâle. I have received the following information from a friend: Mazzini was really arrested by two gendarmes at Zurich, but only for a few hours, after which he escaped. This escape was facilitated by another Italian causing himself to be arrested simultaneously at another place by pretending to be Mazzini. By this *coup* the authorities were misled, and M. Druey himself telegraphed from Berne to Geneva, that no further investigations would be required, as Mazzini was in prison. It is supposed that the person arrested in Mazzini's stead is Saffi, while some say it is a Hungarian officer of the name of Türr.

The *Milan Gazette*[a] of the 31st August takes pleasure in announcing that the municipal council of Pavia have resolved in their sitting of the 28th August, to participate in the national loan by subscribing for 200,000 florins. In contrast to this statement a non-official paper publishes the following as the real resolution of the Council in question:

"The Municipality of Pavia subscribes for the quota *imposed on and fixed* for the town of Pavia; but it does so neither as Representative of the Commune, nor in their quality as contributors, but only as an organ of Government, and as dependent on the executive power to which it is bound by the circular of 1830 to absolute obedience, as well as in execution of the orders transmitted to it by the Lieutenant-General[b] on Aug. 7."

At Treviso also the voluntary loan has only been subscribed to in consequence of direct menace. From the statement of the

---

[a] *Gazzetta Ufficiale di Milano.—Ed.*
[b] Radetzky.— *Ed.*

Trieste Council, it appears that even in that arch-Austrian loyal city the loan is neither voluntary nor so very generally taken as represented by the Austrian journals:

"Our commune has subscribed for another million of the national loan. The Magistrates hereby announce that this sum will be distributed among the contributors who have taken no part hitherto in the loan or not in proportion to their fortune. The 6th of September is, at the same time, fixed as the last term for voluntary subscriptions. The Council hope that everybody will hasten to profit by the advantages held out by the loan, the more so as, after the above term, the Council will be under the grievous necessity of proceeding by force."

The reactionary press is not yet satisfied with the late measures of the Spanish Government; they grumble at the fact that a new compromise had been entered into with the revolution. Thus we read in the *Journal des Débats*:

"It was only on the 7th August when Espartero declared 'that in conformity with the wishes of the people of Madrid, the Duchess of Riánsares[a] should not leave the capital, either by day or night, or in any furtive manner.' It is only on the 28th August that Queen Cristina, after a detention of twenty-one days, is allowed to depart in broad day, with a sort of ostentation. But the Government has been weak enough to order, simultaneously, the confiscation of her estates."[b]

The *Débats* now hopes that this order will be cancelled. But the hopes of the *Débats* are, perhaps, in this instance, even more doomed to disappointment than when it uttered faint hopes that confiscation of the Orleans estates[340] would not be carried out by Bonaparte. The *Jefe Político* of Oviedo has already proceeded to sequestrate the coal mines possessed by Cristina in the Province of Asturias. The directors of the mines of Siero, Langreo, and Piero Corril have received orders to make a statement and to place their administration under the Government.

With regard to the "broad day" in which the *Débats* effects the departure of Cristina, they are very wrongly informed. Queen Cristina on leaving her apartments, crossed the corridors in dead silence—everybody being studiously kept out of the way. The National Guard occupying the barracks in the court of the Palace were not aware of her departure. So secretly was the whole plan arranged that even Garrigó, who was to have charge of her escort, only received his orders on the moment of starting. The escort only learned the mission with which they were intrusted at a distance of twelve miles from Madrid, when Garrigó had all sorts of difficulties in preventing his men from either insulting Cristina

---

[a] María Cristina.— *Ed.*
[b] *Journal des Débats*, September 12, 1854.— *Ed.*

or returning direct to Madrid. The chiefs of the National Guard did not learn anything of the affair until two hours after the departure of Mme. Muñoz. According to the statement of the *España* she reached the Portuguese frontier on the morning of the 3d September. She is said to have been in very good spirits on the journey, but her Duke was somewhat *triste*.[a] The relations of Cristina and this same Muñoz can only be understood from the answer given by Don Quixote to Sancho Panza's question why he was in love with such a low country wench as his Dulcinea, when he could have princesses at his feet:

"A lady," answered the worthy knight, "surrounded by a host of high-bred, rich, and witty followers, was asked why she took for her lover a simple peasant. 'You must know,' said the lady, 'that for the office I use him he possesses more philosophy than Aristotle himself.'"[b]

The view taken by the reactionary press in general on Spanish affairs may be judged of by some extracts from the *Kölnische Zeitung* and the *Indépendance belge*:

"According to a well-informed and trustworthy correspondent, himself an adherent of O'Donnell and the Moderado party,—says the former,—the position of affairs is grievous, a deep conflict continuing to exist among parties. The working classes are in a state of permanent excitement, being worked upon by the agitators."

"The future of the Spanish monarchy," says the *Indépendance*, "is exposed to great dangers. All true Spanish patriots are unanimous on the necessity of putting down the revolutionary orgies. The rage of the libelers and of the constructors of barricades is let loose against Espartero and his Government with the same vehemence as against San Luis and the banker Salamanca. But, in truth, this chivalrous nation cannot be held responsible for such excesses. The people of Madrid must not be confounded with the mob that vociferated 'Death to Cristina,' nor for the infamous libels launched among the population, under the title of 'Robberies of San Luis, Cristina and the Acolytes.' The 1,800 barricades of Madrid and the ultra Communist manifestations of Barcelona bespeak the intermeddling of foreign Democracy with the Spanish Saturnalia. So much is certain, that a great number of the refugees of France, Germany and Italy have participated in the deplorable events now agitating the Peninsula. So much is certain, that Spain is on the brink of a social conflagration; the more immediate consequences will be the loss of the Pearl of the Antilles, the rich Island of Cuba, because it places Spain in the impossibility to combat American ambition, or the patriotism of a Soulé or Saunders. It is time that Spain should open her eyes, and that all honest men of civilized Europe should combine in giving the alarm."[c]

It certainly requires no intervention of foreign democracy to stir up the population of Madrid when they see their Government

---

[a] Sad.— *Ed.*

[b] Cervantes, *Don Quixote,* T. I, Ch. 25.— *Ed.*

[c] Report of the Paris correspondent of September 3. *L'Indépendance belge,* No. 247, September 4, 1854.— *Ed.*

break on the 28th the word given on the 7th; suspend the right of freely assembling, and restore the press-law of 1837, requiring a *cautionnement*[a] of 40,000 reals and 300 reals of direct taxes on the part of every editor.[341] If the provinces remain agitated by uncertain and undecided movements, what other reason are we to find for this fact, but the absence of a center for revolutionary action? Not a single decree beneficent to the provinces has appeared since the so-called revolutionary government fell into the hands of Espartero. The provinces behold it surrounded by the same sycophancy, intrigues, and place hunting that had subsisted under San Luis. The same swarm hangs about the Government— the plague which has infested Spain since the age of the Philips.[342]

Let us just cast a glance at the last number of the Madrid *Gaceta* of the 6th September.[b] There is a report of O'Donnell announcing a superabundance of military places and honors to such a degree that out of every three generals only one can be employed on active service. It is the very evil which has cursed Spain since 1823—this superincumbrance of generals. One would fancy that a decree was to follow abating the nuisance. Nothing of the sort. The decree following the report convokes a consultative junta of war, composed of a certain number of generals, appointed by the Government from generals holding at present no commission in the army. Besides their ordinary pay these men are to receive: each Lieutenant-General 5,000 reals, and each Maréchal-de-Camp 6,000 reals. General Manuel de la Concha has been named President of this military sinecurist junta. The same number of the *Gaceta* presents another harvest of decorations, appointments, etc., as if the first great distribution had failed to do its work. San Miguel and Dulce have received the grand-cross of the order of Charles III; all the recompenses and provisional honors decreed by the junta òf Saragossa are confirmed and enlarged. But the most remarkable portion of this number of the *Gaceta* is the announcement that the payment of the public creditors will be resumed on the 11th inst. Incredible folly of the Spanish people not to be satisfied with these achievements of their revolutionary government!

Travellers who have recently arrived from Wallachia give a very distressing account of the state of that Principality. It[a]is known

_____

[a] Caution money.— *Ed.*

[b] The review of the Madrid *Gaceta* for September 6 is given according to a reprint in *Le Moniteur universel*, No. 255, September 12, 1854.— *Ed.*

that Russia saddled the Principalities with a debt of 14,000,000 francs, on account of the occupation in 1848-49. This sum has been raised by the Russian generals during the late occupation. The Russians retreat after having emptied all the chests—the vestry chests, the central chests of the monasteries, the municipal chests—'and it is with the contents of these that they have paid the supplies contracted for with the Wallachian proprietors and peasants. But the transports, which make a very important item in an agricultural country, wood, coals, straw, etc., were not paid at all, but simply foraged. The treasury of the Principalities accordingly is so much exhausted that the vestries are expected to become bankrupt. All this without taking into account the use of the houses transformed into hospitals, and the thousands of property intrusted to Russian hands from the fear of the boyards of Turkish robbery.

We read in a letter from Athens, dated 29th August:

"The King continues to refuse any indemnity to Turkey. The hatred against the Occidental troops increases, and already several French soldiers have been ill-treated by the people."

It would be a curious history to expose to your readers how the Greek communities have been dissolved by British influence—how Capo d'Istria was imposed upon them, and how the whole of this people has been demoralized by the agency of Lord Palmerston. The honest intentions of the British Government even at this moment of their intervention in Greece, are sufficiently betrayed by the support it gives to General Kalergis, a man, like Capo d'Istria, born, bred and domiciliated in Russia.

Lord Stratford de Redcliffe and the British Government have at length obtained what they have labored to bring about—a revolution in Turkey, if not in Europe, at least in Anatolia. We knew already by reports from Rhodes, that on the coast opposite this island, the Zeybeks, a warlike Ottoman mountain-tribe, had revolted. The *Journal de Constantinople* of 20th Aug. now announces that anarchy in those parts is daily increasing. The rebels, in the absence of the regular army, constantly descend from the mountains, invade the villages, raise the tithes, plunder the inhabitants and caravans, violate the women, and murder every one that resists. Their excesses are gravest in the province of Mestescak. From Aiden the Governor has been obliged to flee to Thira. Denissli is in their hands, and the mufti Sahib Effendi, who went to inform the Governor-General, has been seized and beheaded with his followers. Their strength amounts to thousands. The source of these disturbances are the Bashi-Bazouks returning from Kars and Bayazid, who denounce the Porte for its oppression toward the Turks and its submission toward Russia.

If we cast a look at Europe, we meet with symptoms of revolution in Spain, Italy, Denmark, the Danubian Principalities, Greece, Asiatic Turkey; and even in the ranks of the French army at Varna, the cry has resounded, "À bas les singes!" [343]

Written on September 12, 1854

First published in the *New-York Daily Tribune*, No. 4197, September 30; reprinted in the *New-York Semi-Weekly Tribune*, No. 976, October 3, 1854

Signed: *Karl Marx*

Reproduced from the *New-York Daily Tribune*

Karl Marx

[THE ACTIONS OF THE ALLIED FLEET.— THE SITUATION IN THE DANUBIAN PRINCIPALITIES.—SPAIN.— BRITISH FOREIGN TRADE][344]

London, Friday, Sept. 15, 1854

We read in yesterday's *Moniteur* the following telegraphic dispatch:

"*Therapia*, Sept. 7.—The French and the Turks left Varna on the 5th. The English fleet was to join them at the Island of the Serpents. The weather is beautiful."[a]

The delay in the departure of this first portion of the expeditionary army was caused by the violent storms which visited the Bosphorus up to the 27th of August. The wind having come round from the north-east on the 27th, the fleet of transports was enabled to leave Constantinople for the Black Sea. The Isle of the Serpents (Ilade Adessi) is a little rocky islet at some distance from the Bessarabian coast, and nearly opposite the mouth of the Danube. Its circumference is not more than three English miles. The departure not having been effected until the 5th, the disembarkation of the troops cannot have taken place before the 9th of September.

A curious passage occurs in an article published by the *Moniteur*, in which the chances of the expedition are discussed.

"If," says the *Moniteur*, "*if* the number of the Russian troops stationed in the Crimea should be found to be more *considerable* than we are led to believe by the previous reports; if the force of Sevastopol should offer a *protracted defense*; if obstacles should be afforded by the *season*; if, finally, an important Russian army should succeed in reenforcing the Crimea, we should be quits for this time with a simple reembarkation, and the attack of Sevastopol would be resumed in the spring."[b]

---

[a] *Le Moniteur universel*, No. 257, September 14, 1854.— *Ed.*

[b] Report from Constantinople. *Le Moniteur universel*, No. 254, September 11, 1854.— *Ed.*

In one word, if any serious difficulties should be encountered by that "powerful armada, with its thousand of agencies of destruction," it will quickly return to the Bosphorus. At all events, it will not be their fault if such difficulties should not be met with, due notice of the expedition having been given to the Czar months ago, and it having been delayed up to the very last days of the season. The confidence felt by the French mariners in their commander may be judged of by the following extract of a letter from Constantinople, published by the *Augsburger Zeitung*:

"In the fleet St. Arnaud is generally called Florival, the name under which he made his début at the *Ambigu Comique* at Paris."[345]

According to the latest dispatches from Hamburg and Copenhagen, part of the French fleet, transports and soldiers, have passed through the Belt on their return to France. A Bonapartist paper, the *Constitutionnel*, makes a revelation on the Bomarsund affair:

"His majesty the Emperor Napoleon III did *not wish* that the devotion of the navy should be deprived of the *recompense* merited by it after such a prolonged and painful cruise in the Baltic."[a]

Bomarsund, then, was only bombarded for the amusement of the fleet, and as a concession to the impatience and ennui of the officers. Those two laconic allusions of the *Moniteur* and *Constitutionnel* contain more in qualification of the character of the war than all the swaggering leading articles of the ministerial English press.

The Czar has ordered the arrest of all the engineers who were engaged in the construction of the forts of Bomarsund. They are to be put on their trial. One of the charges raised against them is that the fortifications should have been constructed entirely of blocks of pure granite, while it has been proved since their fall that the interior of the walls was simply filled with sand and rough stones. All the commanders of the different fortresses along the Gulf of Finland have received orders from St. Petersburg to inquire into the most minute details of their construction, and to report on this subject without delay. It is now ascertained that Fort Gustavsvärn at Hango Head was blown up by the Russians themselves, at the moment when Baraguay d'Hilliers and General Jones appeared before it on their reconnoitering expedition. The Russians feared an attack on Abo, and in order to make the troops

---

[a] Quoted from a reprint in *L'Indépendance belge*, No. 255, September 12, 1854.— *Ed.*

of Fort Gustavsvärn disposable for the defense of that town the fort was destroyed.

Being still in the Baltic I may as well give a place here to the following piece of news contained in the *Aftonbladet.*

"A correspondent from Copenhagen announces as certain that the Danish Government authorized on Aug. 16, Mr. T. P. Shaffner to establish a line of electric telegraph extending from North America through Greenland, Iceland, the Faroe Islands and Norway to Copenhagen. On the 26th a line was opened from Stockholm to Malmö. The extent of this line is 68,670 yards."

Some of the London papers to-day give telegraphic news of a victory gained by Shamyl somewhere in the neighborhood of Tiflis. The French and German papers contain no mention of this fact. On September 4 the Turks crossed the Danube near Matchin, and occupied the island situated between that fortress and Ibraila. A great portion of the Turkish flotilla of the Danube has also cast anchor off Matchin. The occupation of Ibraila by the Turks was to take place on the 5th inst. You will notice the proclamation of General Krusenstern, posted up on the walls of Odessa on the 30th August, in which the inhabitants are warned, under heavy penalties, not to oppose the setting fire to the city should this act be deemed necessary by the troops for the defense of the country. The Russians have also given orders in all the districts of Bessarabia to burn towns and villages at the approach of the enemy. The order is the more ludicrous as the Russians are well aware that the Roumans of Bessarabia would no more regret their withdrawal than the Roumans of Wallachia and Moldavia.

I have described the circumstances accompanying the enrolment in the Russian service of the Wallachian and Moldavian militia.[a] From the English papers of to-day you will learn the details of the scenes which took place on the 28th August, between M. de Budberg and the officers of the Rouman militia, scenes which ended in Captain Phillippescu telling the Russian general to his face that the Wallachians considered the Sultan as their only suzerain. He was, of course, placed under arrest, in company with two brother officers who had indulged in similar remonstrances. The following account of the events which occurred on the 29th, the day on which the Russian campaign in the Principalities was brought to such a glorious conclusion, is from the Paris *Presse* of to-day:

---

[a] Marx probably refers to his article "Evacuation of the Danubian Principalities.—The Events in Spain.—A New Danish Constitution.—The Chartists" (see this volume, p. 351).— *Ed.*

"The arrest of Captain Phillippescu and two other officers, who dared to set at defiance the injunctions of General Budberg, had caused a great irritation in the ranks of the Moldavian militia, and augmented its reluctance to serve in the Russian army. On the 29th, shortly before the hour fixed for their review, the Hetman Maurocordatos repaired to the barracks of the cavalry, situated opposite the Administrative Palace. Great was his consternation at finding it completely deserted. The soldiers, instead of saddling their horses for the review, had contrived to make their escape from the stables, abandoning their arms and baggage. The unfortunate Hetman hastened to the barracks of the artillery to meet with a new surprise. The cannon were in their places in the Court, but the men had disappeared. Maurocordatos, in despair, fancied himself already on the road to Siberia. But he succeeded in reuniting about 30 men. Trembling with rage and fear, he ordered them to put the horses to the guns and to march out to the place of the review. 'Let us be carried away by force,' they shouted. 'We receive no orders from the Russians.' With these words they shut up the gates of the barracks. At that moment drums resounded in the place. It was the whole division of Osten-Sacken, composed of twelve battalions, one regiment of dragoons, and three battalions of artillery, which, after intercepting the communications, formed up on the place and completely blocked up both the Administrative Palace and the barracks of the Moldavian cavalry. Sixty Moldavian horsemen who had been brought back were drawn up before the barracks. Opposite to them were 12,000 Russians—infantry, cavalry and artillery. Osten-Sacken arrived, followed by General Budberg and a numerous staff. The Muscovite troops deployed in columns, and defiled before their generals, with bayonets fixed, shouting their hurrahs. They next formed in squares at a distance of 150 yards from the Moldavian horsemen. They received the command to load. The Russian soldiers after having made the sign of the cross, executed the order. Aim was taken at the sixty horsemen. This being done, Osten-Sacken advanced with his staff toward the little body of Moldavian militia-men, and summoned them to follow his army with the threat of having them all shot in case of refusal. A silence of several minutes followed his injunction. A terrible emotion seizes upon the crowd who had assembled on the place. Then one of the Moldavians steps from the ranks and in a calm voice addresses the Russian General. 'We are Moldavian soldiers, and our duty is to defend our country, not to fight for the foreigner. Do with us as you please. We shall not march with you.' 'You may murder us, but we shall not march with you,' repeat the sixty soldiers with one voice. On hearing this bold answer, Osten-Sacken ordered them to dismount from their horses and to lay down their arms, as though for immediate execution. They obey, prepared to die. In a moment thousands of soldiers surround them, rush upon them, and take them prisoners. This great feat of arms accomplished, the Muscovites advance to the Moldavian artillery barracks where the thirty men continue to keep the gates closed. The gates having been forced, they penetrate into the interior; a struggle takes place, and the artillerists also, overwhelmed by superior numbers, are taken prisoners. They are hurried away in the midst of insults and menaces of death. They remain impassible. Only one, a young cornet of 22 years, his eyes kindled with rage, advances toward General Wrangel, and uncovering his breast, exclaims: 'There is my breast, pierce it with your balls if you dare.' The General did not dare. The cornet and his comrades disarmed, were conducted between two rows of bayonets and brought to the camp of Osten-Sacken, outside the gates of Jassy. What has become of them, nobody knows. As to the three officers arrested on the evening before, it is generally feared that they will be shot. On the same evening the Russians surrounded the place where the regiment of Moldavian infantry was encamped. But they found only 150 men, the rest having escaped. The population of Jassy uttered loud execrations against their protectors. Sixty horsemen, thirty artillerists, and one hundred and fifty infantry captured and disarmed by 12,000 Russians with three batteries. This is the only victory, the laurels of which the Russians carry home from their campaign in the Principalities."

In a former letter I mentioned the order given by Omer Pasha to suppress the publication of the Austrian manifesto of General Hess.[346] We are now informed on what grounds this order was given, viz.: because the said proclamation called upon the Wallachian authorities to apply exclusively to the Austrian commander in all affairs. Omer Pasha sent word to General Hess that he had better abstain from intermeddling with the civil Administration of Wallachia, which belonged to his (Omer Pasha's) province. Having only intended his proclamation as a feeler how far he might go, General Hess apologised for the objectionable passage, and in order to convince Omer Pasha that it was all a mistake, he communicated to him the original German text, where the Wallachian authorities are only invited to apply to his Aide-de-Camp in such matters as are connected with the Austrian troops. The Austrian General Popovitch, who had entered Bucharest with the Austrian vanguard on the 3d September, and immediately commenced to play the part of Haynau, was likewise checked by Omer Pasha. How welcome the Austrian occupation is to the Wallachians in general may be understood from an extract from to-day's *Daily News*:

"Many of the villages on the road by which the Austrians advanced, have been deserted by their inhabitants, carrying with them all their worldly goods, fearing that they would be obliged to supply provisions or means of transport in return for paper money, worth exactly half its nominal value. The consequence is, that bread for the Austrian troops must be forwarded from Bucharest, twenty and even thirty miles distant."

It is certainly with respect to the infamies committed in the Principalities—*the consequences of English diplomacy*—that the sober *Economist*, alluding to some comparatively very slight faults of American diplomacy in Europe, draws the following line of distinction between English and American diplomacy:

"Now, we have no doubt that men of gentlemanly feeling, of deep sense of decorum, of a clear perception of what is due to others, abound in America as well as here. The difference between us, and the misfortune of our cousins, are these: that such men do not at the other side of the Atlantic either elect a government or give the tone to the nation, *or guide the language of the press*. With us the educated and *the upper classes* have the power in their own hands. In the United States it is the mass who govern; it is the populace who usurp the name and title of the nation; it is they who dictate what shall be done or said; it is they who elect the government and whom the government must serve; it is they who support the press and whom the press must please; in fact, it is they who have to be acted down to and written down to."[a]

Thus speaks the servant of the English stockjobbers, as if English diplomacy were not an identical term with infamy, and as if the "gentlemen" appointed by Mr. Wilson, the editor of *The Economist*, and Mr. Gladstone, his superior, had not been convicted before Parliament of swindling, gambling and larceny.

From Spain news is scarce. On the 8th inst. the Consultative Junta of Madrid definitively dissolved itself. The Junta of Seville only dissolved after a strong protest against the reactionary course of the Central Government. The Democrats of Catalonia have published a manifesto against General Prim, who had sent in his adhesion to the present Government from Turkey, in order not to be excluded from a share in the spoils. He contracted the hatred of the Catalonians by the investment of the Castle of Figueras in 1843, marked by the most shocking barbarities, committed from pure rage at the brave defense of the place by a comparatively small force under the command of Ametller. This Prim was characterized at that time as "a person of ridiculous vanity, whose head had been turned by fortuitous success and by being made a count and a lieutenant-general."

We read in the *Época* that on the 7th a small battle was fought at Aranjuez between the National Guard and a band of which it is not yet known whether it was composed of Carlists or Republicans. Quick and certain as the success of the reaction seems to be, the counter-revolutionary journals do not cease to give vent to their apprehensiveness that matters may not even yet be settled in Spain.

From the accounts of trade and navigation just issued I extract the following statement:

Total declared Value of the Exports of British and Irish Produce and Manufactures in each of the following years[b]:

	FOREIGN		
	1831	1842	1853
Russia, northern ports and Black Sea	£1,195,565	£1,885,953	£1,228,400
Sweden and Norway	115,707	334,017	556,183
Denmark	92,294	194,304	569,733
Prussia	192,816	376,651	579,588

---

[a] "American Diplomatic Taste and Morality." *The Economist*, No. 576, September 9, 1854.— *Ed.*

[b] *The Economist*, No. 576, September 9, 1854.— *Ed.*

[Continued]

Hanover & Hanseatic towns	3,642,952	6,202,700	7,565,493
Holland and		H. 3,573,362	4,482,955
Belgium .... }	2,082,536	B. 1,099,490	1,371,867
France	602,688	3,193,939	2,636,330
Portugal	975,991	947,855	1,210,481
Azores and Madeira	80,698	64,909	124,971
Spain and Balearic Isles...	597,848	322,614	1,360,719
Canary Islands	33,282	54,564	107,638
Italy—			
Sardinian Territories...... }	....	....	1,112,447
Duchy of Tuscany	....	....	639,794
Papal Territories .... }	2,490,376	2,494,197	207,491
Naples and Sicily	....	....	639,544
Austrian Territories....... }	....	....	637,353
Greece.................................. }	....	....	135,315
Turkey	899,100	1,489,826	2,029,305
Wallachia and Moldavia.... }	....	....	179,510
Syria and Palestine	....	375,551	306,580
Egypt	122,832	221,003	787,111
Morocco	426	41,952	75,257
French Possessions in Sene-gambia	....	....	1,725
West Coast of Africa....... .	234,768	459,685	617,764
Java and Sumatra	285,296	306,132	558,212
Philippines	39,513	47,019	386,552
China	519,443	969,381	1,373,689
Cuba	663,531	711,938	1,124,864
Hayti	376,103	141,896	133,804
United States and Califor-nia	9,053,583	3,535,381	23,658,427
Mexico	728,858	374,969	791,940
New-Granada .... }	248,250	231,711	450,804
Venezuela .... }			248,190
Brazile	1,238,371	1,756,805	3,186,407
Uruguay .... }	339,870	969,791	529,883
Buenos Ayres .... }			551,035
Chili	654,617	950,466	1,264,942
Peru	409,003	684,013	1,246,730
Other Countries	215	7,223	912,662
Total of foreign countries	£26,909,432	£34,119,587	£65,551,579

[Continued]
BRITISH POSSESSIONS

Channel Islands	£324,634	£364,359	£470,107
Gibraltar	367,285	937,719	670,840
Malta	134,519	289,304	297,906
Ionian Islands	50,883	83,600	116,567
South Africa	257,245	369,076	1,212,630
Mauritius	148,475	244,922	385,879
East Indies	3,857,969	5,169,888	8,185,695
Hong Kong	....	....	357,908
Australia	403,223	998,952	14,513,700
North American Colonies	2,089,327	2,333,525	4,898,544
West Indies	2,581,949	2,591,425	1,906,689
Other Possessions	39,431	18,675	347,787
Total to British possessions	£10,254,940	£13,261,436	£33,382,202
Total of British & Foreign	£37,164,372	£47,381,023	£98,933,781

The Economist selects the year of 1842, in order to exhibit the advantages of free trade since that period,[347] forgetting, with its usual candour, that 1842 was a year of commercial depression, and 1853 a year of the greatest prosperity. If the progress of English exports were produced by the magic of free trade, it would have been better proved by comparison of the relative exports to countries maintaining a strict protectionist system, Russia and France for instance; the former of these countries being moreover that from which imports have most increased, and which had been most subject to the influence of British free trade. Now we find that the exports to both these countries have declined.

The export to Russia having been	£1,106,767
While in 1831 it was	1,195,565
And the export to France having been in 1853	2,636,330
While in 1842 it was	3,193,939

The aggregate value of British exports in the seven months ending 5th August, 1854, compared with those during the corresponding months of 1853, shows an increase, in consequence of the metals having increased in value; but in the other ruling products of British industry we find a marked decline, as shown by the following table:

	1853	1854
Linen manufactures	£2,650,050	£2,456,953
Linen yarn	646,578	581,752
Silk manufactures	965,345	834,275
Silk, thrown	132,689	120,890
Wool manufactures	3,741,261	3,731,453
Cotton manufactures	15,515,224	14,762,981
Cotton yarn	3,897,080	3,838,393

The decline in cotton appears still more striking since the quantity of exports has increased, while the value realised has decreased. In 1854 there were exported 981,994,130 yards of cotton manufactures, exclusive of lace and patent net, while in 1853 there were only exported 969,293,663 yards.

Written on September 15, 1854

First published in the *New-York Daily Tribune*, No. 4198, October 2; reprinted in the *New-York Semi-Weekly Tribune*, No. 976, October 3 and partly in the *New-York Weekly Tribune*, No. 682, October 7, 1854

Signed: *Karl Marx*

Reproduced from the *New-York Daily Tribune*

Frederick Engels

THE ATTACK ON SEVASTOPOL[348]

At last it seems possible that the French and English may strike a serious blow at the power and prestige of Russia, and we in this country are accordingly looking with renewed interest to the movement against Sevastopol, the latest intelligence from which is detailed in another column.[349] As a matter of course, the British and French journals make a great parade about this undertaking, and if we can believe them, nothing grander was ever heard of in military history; but those who look at the facts in the case—at the inexplicable delays and senseless apologies attending the setting out of the expedition, and all the circumstances preceding and attending it—will refuse to be imposed upon. The termination of the enterprise may be glorious, but its origin would rather seem to be disgraceful.

Look at the past history of the allied armies in Turkey. At first these very heroic, but also exceedingly cautious warriors intended to land at Enos, on this side of the Dardanelles, and to approach that peninsula[a] only after everything should have turned out to be quite safe. Before this daring feat, however, was accomplished, they stretched their courage to an unexpected extent, and risked a landing on the Thracian Chersonesus at Gallipoli. But this was merely done in order to have the defensive works across the peninsula completed in less time, thus securing to themselves that most essential of all requisites, a base of operations. All the while the Turks on the Danube were facing those formidable opponents

---

[a] Gallipoli.— Ed.

whose presence in Wallachia was the pretext for those learned maneuvers of the allies; and they were facing them, too, with considerable success. But as more ships and more troops arrived, it was found out that the Dardanelles and peninsula cannot harbor them all. Thus another hole is made in the scientific arrangements agreed upon between Paris and London. A portion of the troops had actually to endure the dangers and risks of a landing at that very exposed spot, Constantinople! To remedy this, the fortification of this town was at once taken in hand. Fortunately, a good deal of time was spent in all these operations, and thus the main object was secured—not to gain time, but to lose it. Then it was ascertained that a division might, with little risk, be sent to Varna, to garrison that important place, for surely the Turks, who so gloriously defended it in 1828, had since then made such progress in European discipline, that the defense of such a post could no longer be entrusted to them. The division was sent accordingly, and one or two divisions more. When finely every pretext for keeping the troops in the Bosphorus was fairly worn out, the grand combined army was very leisurely concentrated at Varna. This was done at the same time when an Austrian army appeared like a menacing thunder cloud on the flank and rear of the Russians, and when thus, by political combinations, the base of the allied operations was at once transferred, for the moment, from Constantinople to Transylvania and Galicia. Without this, there is every reason to believe there would never have been an allied army in Bulgaria. The proof of it is in their behavior during the siege of Silistria. Everybody knows that there was the turning point of the campaign, and that in such an emergency, when both parties have been straining their powers to the utmost, the smallest extra weight added on one side, will in nine cases out of ten, turn the balance in its favor. Yet, during this decisive siege, there were 20,000 English and 30,000 French soldiers, "the flower of the two armies," smoking their pipes, and very quietly getting themselves in trim for the cholera at a very few days' march from the fortress. And, but for the havoc made by disease among the Russians, and for the unaccountable bravery of a handful of Arnauts ensconced in a ditch plowed by shells in every direction, Silistria would have fallen into the hands of the enemy. There is no instance in the history of war of an army within easy reach, thus cowardly leaving its allies to shift for themselves. No expedition to the Crimea, and no victory will ever clear away that stain from the honor of the French and English commanders. Where would the British have been at Waterloo if old Blücher, after his defeat at Ligny, two days before, had thus conscientiously acted in the manner of Raglan and St. Arnaud?[350]

The handful of Arnauts in the skirmishing ditch of Arab Tabiassi proved a match for the skill, intellect and military strength of Russia. No relieving army drove the Russians across the Danube; their own foolishness, the valor of the defenders, the marsh fever, the passive weight of the Austrians on the Dniester and of the allies on the Devna (for who could think they would act as they did?) made them finally abandon the siege, and give up both the campaign, the Principalities and the Dobrodja. After this great success, the allied generals of course thought of following it up—always according to the rules of that strategic system which they had hitherto applied with so much effect. Consequently, Lord Cardigan led the British cavalry to the Danube, on a reconnoitering expedition, in which they saw no Russians, lost many horses, and earned nothing but sickness and ridicule; while General Espinasse, mainly known by his betrayal of the National Assembly on December 2, 1851,[351] led his division into the Dobrodja for no other purpose than having a couple of fine regiments half destroyed by cholera, and bringing the germ of that epidemic into the allied camp. The great invasion of cholera which ensued among the allies at Varna was thus the well earned result of their fine strategic combinations. The soldiers fell off by thousands before they had even seen an enemy; they died like flies in a camp where, unattacked and undisturbed, they were enabled to live in comparative luxury. Discouragement, distrust in their commanders, disorganization ensued, not so much among the English, who suffered less and who have more power of endurance, as among the French, whose national character is more apt to give way to such influences, especially while their commanders hold them in a state of inactivity. But there was visible in the riots that actually broke out among the French troops, the natural effect of the abnormal state in which they have existed since 1849. The French soldier has been taught by the Bourgeoisie he rescued from the terrors of the revolution, to look upon himself as the savior of his country and of society at large. He has been petted by Louis Bonaparte as the instrument that restored the Empire. He was treated all the while in a way which taught him to command and made him forget to obey. Superior as he was instructed to consider himself to civilians, he very soon got a notion that he was at least equal to his commanders. Every effort was used to make him a pretorian, and all history shows that pretorians are but degenerate soldiers. They begin by commanding to the civilians, they next proceed to dictating to their generals, and they end by being thoroughly thrashed.

Now look at what occurred at Varna. When whole battalions dropped down on the burning sands, writhing in the agonies of cholera, the old soldiers began to compare the adventurers who now are at their head, with the old commanders that led them successfully through those very African campaigns which the heroes of the modern Lower Empire affect so much to disdain.[352] Africa was a hotter country than Bulgaria, and the Sahara is a good deal less pleasant than even the Dobrodja; but no such mortalities ever marked the paths of African conquest as attended the repose of Devna, and the easy reconnoitering marches around Kustendje. Cavaignac, Bedeau, Changarnier, Lamoricière led them through greater dangers, with far less loss, at a time when Espinasse and Leroy St. Arnaud were still buried in the obscurity from which political infamies only could raise them. Accordingly the Zouaves, the men who had done most work and smelt most powder, the best representatives of the African army, rose in a body and shouted: "*À bas les singes! Il nous faut Lamoricière!*"[353] Down with the apes! give us Lamoricière! His Imperial Majesty, Napoleon III, the head and soul of this actual official apery of a great past, must have felt, when this came to his knowledge that the cry of the Zouaves was for him "the beginning of the end." At Varna, it had a magic effect. We may say it was the chief cause of the expedition to the Crimea.

After the experience of this summer's campaigning, or rather promenading, from Gallipoli to Scutari, from Scutari to Varna, from Varna to Devna, Aladyn and back again, nobody will expect us to treat seriously the pretexts put forth by the allied commanders, why the expedition, after being so long delayed, was finally so hurriedly undertaken. One instance will sufficiently show what their arguments are worth. The delay was owing, it was said, to the French siege artillery not having arrived. Well, when the cholera riots occurred, and Leroy St. Arnaud saw that he must now play his best card and that without delay, he sent to Constantinople for Turkish siege artillery and ammunition, and it was got ready and embarked in a very short time; and if the French siege train had not arrived in the meantime, they would have sailed without it. But the Turkish siege artillery was ready many a month before, and thus all the delays that had occurred are proved to have been needless.

Thus we see that this grandiloquent expedition to the Crimea, with six hundred ships and sixty thousand soldiers, with three siege-trains and nobody knows how many field-pieces, instead of being the deliberate result of skilful movements, prepared scientifically long beforehand, is nothing but a hurried *coup de tête*,[a] undertaken to save Leroy St. Arnaud from being massacred by his own soldiers; poor old soft Lord Raglan not being the man to resist, especially as any longer delay would bring his army down to the same state of discipline and despondency which has already seized the French troops.

The *irony of events*, as a German writer has it, is still at work in contemporary as much as in past history, and poor Lord Raglan is its present victim. As to Leroy St. Arnaud, nobody ever treated him as a commander. He is a member of the swell mob of too long standing—this notorious old companion of female thieves and swindlers—this worthy acolyte of the man whom "Debt, not Destiny," hurried on to the expedition of Boulogne.[354] In spite of the censorship, his character and antecedents are known well enough in gossiping Paris. The twice cashiered Lieutenant—the Captain who robbed the regimental cash-box when Paymaster in Africa, is known well enough, and whatever he may accomplish in the Crimea, his successful expedition to a London pawn-shop with his landlady's blankets, followed up by his well-executed retreat to Paris, will still form his chief title to military glory. But poor Raglan, the Duke of Wellington's Adjutant-General, a man grown hoary among the theoretical labors and minute details of a staff-command, no doubt actually believes in the motives he gives for his actions. And upon him falls the full weight of the curious fact that the whole of the campaign has been so scientifically planned, so skilfully executed, that ten thousand men, or about one in seven, died before they saw an enemy, and that the whole of these elaborate proceedings have served only to bring about a helter skelter expedition into the Crimea at the close of the season. There is nothing so pungent as this very "irony of events."

For all that the expedition may be successful. The allies almost deserve it, for nothing would hold up to greater contempt the way in which they have previously carried on the campaign. So much fuss, such an expenditure of caution, such a profusion of science, against an enemy who succumbs to an undertaking which has for its end, not his destruction, but the preservation of their own army; this would be the greatest condemnation the allies could pass upon themselves. But then, they are not yet in Sevastopol.

---

[a] Impulsive act.— *Ed.*

They have landed at Eupatoria and at Staroye Ukreplienie.[a] Thence they have respectively fifty and twenty miles march to Sevastopol. Their heavy artillery is to be landed close to the latter place, to save the trouble of land-carriage; the landing then is far from completed. The force of the Russians is not exactly known, but there is no doubt it is large enough to allow them to be stronger than the allies on most points in the immediate vicinity of Sevastopol. The hilly ground and the bay cutting into the land some ten miles deep, will force the allies to expand on a very long line as soon as they attempt to invest the fortress. To break their line cannot, with a determined commander, be a matter of great difficulty. We do not of course know what the land-defenses of the place are; but what we know of old Menchikoff, leads us to presume that he will not have lost his time.

The first attack, we are led to believe from statements in the British journals, and from the line of operations chosen by the allies, will be the fort commanding the town from a hill on the north side. This is called by the Russians Severnaya Krepost, the Northern Fort. If this fort is anything like solidly constructed, it is capable of lengthy resistance. It is a large square redoubt, constructed upon Montalembert's polygonal, or *caponnière,* system, the flanking defense being formed by a low casemated work lying at the bottom of the ditch in the middle of each side of the square, and sweeping the ditch both right and left. These works have the advantage of not being exposed to the direct fire of the enemy until he has come with his works to the very brink of the ditch. The proximity of this work to the main fortress allows it to be made use of offensively as a support and base for strong sorties, and altogether its presence must force the allies to confine their main operations to the northern shore of the bay.

But the experience of Bomarsund has taught us that nothing certain can be said about Russian fortifications until they are actually put to the test. The chances of success for the Crimean expedition cannot, therefore, now be ascertained with any probability. But this much is pretty certain, that if the operation should be of a protracted character, if the setting in of winter should cause a fresh irruption of sickness, if the troops should be wasted in hurried and unprepared attacks, like those of the Russians against Silistria, the French army, and most likely the Turkish army, will relapse into that state of dissolution which the former underwent at Varna, and the latter has more than once

---

[a] Stary Fort (Old Fort).— *Ed.*

exhibited in Asia. The English are sure to hold together longer; but there is a point at which even the best disciplined troops give way. This is the real danger for the allies, and if the Russian resistance brings this state of things about, it must make a reembarkation before a victorious enemy a very hazardous thing. The expedition may very likely prove successful; but on the other hand, it may turn out a second Walcheren.[355]

Written on September 25, 1854   Reproduced from the newspaper

First published in the *New-York Daily Tribune*, No. 4209, October 14, 1854 as a leader

Frederick Engels

THE NEWS FROM THE CRIMEA[356]

Our columns this morning are filled with the stirring news of sanguinary battles in the Crimea, including the capture of Sevastopol, the destruction of its principal forts and of a great part of the Russian fleet, and the final surrender of Prince Menchikoff, and the remains of his defeated and more than decimated forces as prisoners of war. If these reports are strictly correct, for nearly forty years the world has witnessed no such gigantic bloodshed, nor any martial event pregnant with consequences so momentous. As to the correctness of the news, that is a point on which some light may perhaps be thrown by carefully separating what we know officially and positively from what we have only from vague and uncertain sources.

We must, then, distinguish the statements into two classes— those relating to the battle of the Alma, fought on Sept. 20, and those announcing the capture of Sevastopol itself. According to the dispatches of Lord Raglan and Marshal St. Arnaud, the allied armies on the 20th stormed the Russian intrenched camp on the hights to the south of the river Alma, and forced the Russians to retreat. The British took two guns. The French, in their dispatch, mention no trophies at all. The French loss was about 1,400; British the same. The Russians were estimated at 45,000 to 50,000 men; their loss at 4,000 to 6,000. These dispatches are evidently written in the full flush of a maiden victory. The 50,000 Russians present on the Alma contrast very strongly with the 45,000 troops which were said to be the maximum of what was spread over the length and breadth of the Crimea. The two guns taken in an intrenched camp, defended by a "numerous heavy artillery," look like very insignificant trophies when it is considered that it is almost impossible to save guns out of field-fortifications when once carried. Still more ominous is Marshal St. Arnaud's silence about the taking of guns by the French.

Supposing Menchikoff had actually concentrated 45,000 to 50,000 men in the intrenched camp on the Alma, what would it prove? Either that he had far more troops than was expected, being able to bring so many to the open field, or that the fortifications of Sevastopol were so weak on the land side that he could not hold the place, except by defeating the allies in the open field; or, thirdly, that he made a tremendous mistake in exposing his troops to an open battle, and to the demoralisation consequent upon a decisive defeat.

If we are to trust the earlier reports the Russian camp on the Alma mustered not more than 10,000 men. These might have been reenforced, but to bring them up even to 25,000 or 30,000 men the Russians must have made considerable effort. With 50,000 men within easy reach of the Alma, or within fifteen miles of the place of landing, how are we to account for their not having pounced upon the allies in the very act of debarkation?

The country between the Old Fort, where the allies landed, and Sevastopol is intersected by three watercourses, forming, by their deep ravines, as many military positions. The one nearest to Sevastopol is the Chornaya, emptying itself into the eastern end of the bay of Sevastopol. While Fort Severnaya defends the northern shore of this bay, that rivulet, or rather its deeply-cut valley forms a sort of natural ditch on the east of the town. There, then, is naturally the last important position for the defense. The next river is the Kacha, running east and west a few miles to the north of Severnaya; and again about twelve miles to the northward runs the Alma. Of the three lines of defense, in spite of tactical advantages which may exist, and which cannot be judged at this distance, it is hardly to be supposed that the Russians should have chosen the first and the remotest for a pitched battle in which the fate of Sevastopol could have been decided. The absence of the main body of the allied cavalry, however, might have encouraged the Russians to send a strong corps into the intrenchments of the Alma, as their own momentary superiority in that arm would secure them against flank movements of the hostile horse. The impossibility of making use of this arm when once cooped up in Sevastopol may have acted as an inducement.

The Russian defeat on the Alma becomes still more reduced in its tactical extent when more closely examined. The Russians are not fond of intrenching themselves in open walls. They prefer, wherever they have time and intend furious resistance, closed square redoubts. To save the artillery from such redoubts is impossible, as soon as the assault is actually carried through. But even from that class of works, technically known as lunettes, open at the gorge, there is almost no chance of saving artillery in the face of a storming enemy. For, if the guns be withdrawn at the very moment of the assault, the defense deprives itself of its own weapon; the ditch once crossed, who is to drag the guns from the embankments or the platform, who to re-limber them and drive off under the close fire of the enemy?

"Guns in intrenchments must be considered as lost when the intrenchments themselves can no longer be held; the only thing you can do is to sell them as dearly as possible,"

says General Dufour in his Manual of Field Fortifications.[a] The fact that the Russians lost but two guns is a proof that the camp was not defended to the last extremity, and that, perhaps, only one or two intrenchments were actually taken at the point of the bayonet. The remainder cannot have been defended with that arm, but must have been all but abandoned, before the storming column were in the ditch. The retreat of the Russians appears to have been executed in good order; their cavalry would protect them, and the impossibility of bodies of allied cavalry rapidly crossing the Alma and ravine would give them an advantage. But then, the saving of almost all their artillery is a sufficient proof that they broke off the battle before any great blow had thrown them into disorder.

This is all we know about the victory on the hights to the south of the Alma which was announced in England on the 1st inst. by the thunder of cannon and the ringing of bells, proclaimed at the Royal Exchange on Saturday evening, Sept. 30, at 10 o'clock by the Lord Mayor, preceded by a trumpeter sounding his bugle; cheered at the theaters, and registered by *The London Times* as the anticipated effect of the Archbishop of Canterbury's[b] thanksgivings prayer.[c] Correspondents announce that Marshal St. Arnaud had been unable to mount on horseback. Historians relate the same of Napoleon at the battle of Waterloo. The victory of the Alma was perhaps due to the same circumstance as the defeat of Waterloo.

---

[a] G. H. Dufour, *De la fortification permanente*, p. 309.— *Ed.*
[b] J. Sumner.— *Ed.*
[c] *The Times*, No. 21861, October 2, 1854, leader.— *Ed.*

We come now to the class of more startling news referring to the capture of Sevastopol.[a] The first announcement of this event reached London from Bucharest by telegraph, is dated from the latter town Sept. 28. It stated that Sevastopol had fallen into the hands of the allies after a combined attack by sea and by land. It purported to be derived in the first place from a French steamer dispatched from Sevastopol to Constantinople with this intelligence, which steamer was fallen in with by another French steamer en route for Varna. If the capture of the fortresses took place on the 25th, as is asserted, the news could have reached Varna in the night from the 26th to the 27th, and could have been conveyed to Bucharest by noon on the 28th—the distance between Varna and Bucharest being somewhat more than 100 miles and generally traversed by couriers in 24 hours. This was the news on which Bonaparte founded his address to the camp of Boulogne, which will be found in another column.[357] But it turns out that no courier arrived at Bucharest before September 30. The second news of the fall of Sevastopol, which is at least within topographical probability, is only dated from Bucharest at the very day on which Bonaparte made his announcement. This telegraphic dispatch, received by the Austrian Government at 6 p.m. on Oct. 1, and communicated to *The Times* by the Austrian Minister at London[b] on the 3d, is published by the *Moniteur* of the same day, with the remark that

"it had been forwarded to the French Government by M. de Buol, who had commanded M. de Hübner to congratulate the French Emperor, in the name of the Emperor of Austria, on the glorious success which had attended the French arms in the Crimea."[c]

It should be observed that the value of this intelligence entirely rests upon the verbal statement of the courier sent from Constantinople to Omer Pasha, which courier, not finding Omer Pasha at Bucharest, started again for Silistria, where Omer Pasha then had his quarters. According to the statement of this courier, Sevastopol had been taken, 18,000 Russians killed, 22,000 made prisoners, Fort Constantine destroyed, the other forts with 800 guns captured, six Russian ships-of-war sunk, and Prince Menchikoff retired to the head of the bay, with the remainder of the

---

[a] The telegrams here analysed were published in *The Times,* No. 21861, October 2, 1854.— *Ed.*

[b] Fr. Colloredo-Waldsee.— *Ed.*

[c] Telegram from Vienna of October 2, 1854. *Le Moniteur universel,* No. 276, October 3, 1854.— *Ed.*

squadron, declaring that he would blow them up rather than make an unconditional surrender. The allies had allowed him six hours for consideration. Constantinople was to be illuminated for ten days.

After what we have witnessed of Russian fortifications at Aland,[a] and after the success of the allies on the Alma, a surrender of Sevastopol within something like a fortnight offered strong probabilities. But who can think of an army of 50,000 men having had the good fortune to save almost all its artillery out of a lost battle, commanded by the most daring officer[b] who has yet appeared on the Russian side during this campaign, who can think of such an army laying down their arms after the first attack on the town? Nevertheless, this war has already offered such improbabilities and extraordinary features that we must not be reluctant to "march from surprise to surprise," as Napoleon did at the receipt of Sebastiani's dispatches from Constantinople in 1807.[358] The allies have done everything throughout the war to meet with an unprecedented disaster. Why should it not have pleased fortune to force upon them a triumph without comparison? History, never without a grain of irony, perhaps desired to reserve to the world the curious treat of lodging in a modest tower of the Bosphorus that old Muscovite Rodomonte who but a year ago left the capital of the dying man with the proud threat of swallowing up his empire. What a bitter punishment for the proud and arrogant Menchikoff, the fomenter and beginner of the war, to return to Constantinople a prisoner!

If this courier spoke truth, the history of the Crimean campaign may be resumed in a very few words: On the 14th and 16th the army landed at Old Fort without meeting resistance; on the 19th it marched; on the 20th it won the battle of the Alma, and on the 25th captured Sevastopol.

The next steamer due from Liverpool is the *Africa*, which comes directly to this port, and does not touch at Halifax. We can hardly expect her to arrive before Friday, till when we cannot hope for absolute certainty on this most interesting question.[359] Meanwhile it will probably be most fashionable to believe implicitly the whole story of this Turkish courier, and we hope that those who thus receive it may not be taken down as much as our friend Louis Bonaparte was at Boulogne on the same subject. That imperial gentleman, as our readers may see by referring to another part of

---

[a] See this volume, pp. 384-88.— *Ed.*
[b] Presumably Liprandi.— *Ed.*

this paper, proclaimed the intelligence at a review the other morning, in a rather melodramatic style, in the clear and positive words *Sébastopol est pris*.[a] As he said this he, perhaps, appeared to himself a real Napoleon announcing a great victory to his troops. Unfortunately for the nephew, the uncle never stood in need of announcing a victory: he fought his own battles, and his soldiers, who saw the enemy fly, required no confirmation. More unfortunately, the announcement which Louis Bonaparte could not withhold had to be qualified in the evening by the sous-préfet[b] of Boulogne, who placarded a statement that some dispatch had arrived stating the capture of Sevastopol, but that its correctness could not be vouched for. The Emperor of the French was thus corrected by his own sous-préfet of Boulogne! It is a striking circumstance, also, that the official journal of the French Government[c] of October 3, the latest date, contains no confirmation of the reported great event. Still it may all prove true enough, and we wait with intense interest for positive intelligence.

Written on October 2 and 3, 1854

First published in the *New-York Daily Tribune*, No. 4211, October 17 and the *New-York Semi-Weekly Tribune*, No. 980, October 17; reprinted in the *New-York Weekly Tribune*, No. 684, October 21, 1854 as a leader

Reproduced from the *New-York Daily Tribune*

---

[a] "Sevastopol is taken." This report of October 1 from Vienna was published together with the speech of Napoleon III made in Boulogne on September 30, 1854, in *Le Moniteur universel*, No. 275, October 2, 1854.— *Ed.*

[b] Sub-prefect.— *Ed.*

[c] *Le Moniteur universel.*— *Ed.*

Karl Marx and Frederick Engels

THE SEVASTOPOL HOAX [360]

"Catch a Tartar," is an English proverb. It happens that not only the English, but the French and Austrians as well, have been caught by a Tartar.[a] We may, perhaps, be pardoned for expressing a little satisfaction that *The Tribune* and those of its readers who carefully follow the course of the present campaign in the Crimea were not caught with the rest.

When the extraordinary story of the capture of Sevastopol first reached us, we endeavored to show,[b] by an examination of the alleged channels of the intelligence, as well as on critical military grounds, that the victory of the Alma, however decisive it might have been, could scarcely have been followed in so close succession by the surrender of the object of the campaign. But we think we established, at the same time, the fact that no very decisive victory had been gained at all by the allies, the Russians having retired in good order with all their guns. Lastly, we took particular care to point out how the whole statement, in so far as it exceeded the limits of the official report on the battle of the Alma, rested exclusively on the verbal relation of a Tartar sent to Omer Pasha with sealed dispatches. Thus we were fully prepared for receiving the news that the tremendous "Fall of Sevastopol" was nothing

---

[a] Here Marx and Engels pun on the word "Tartar". The Tartars were famous for their fast horses and were employed by the Turks as couriers. In the nineteenth century the word "Tartar" was used in the European languages as a synonym for *courier*, and it was so used in the news on the capture of Sevastopol printed in the European papers, *The Times* and *Le Moniteur universel* of October 3, 1854 in particular.— *Ed.*

[b] See this volume, pp. 477-82.— *Ed.*

but an imaginary exaggeration of the victory of the Alma, reported by a jocose Tartar at Bucharest, announced by the melodramatic Louis Napoleon at Boulogne, and implicitly believed by that excellent specimen of humanity, the English shopkeeper. The English press in general has proved a worthy representative of that class, and it would seem that the very name of Sevastopol need only be pronounced in England to put everybody in a fool's paradise. Perhaps our readers will recollect that at the close of the last Parliamentary session the destruction of Sevastopol was announced by Lord John Russell to be in the plans of the English Government, which announcement, though in the same sitting duly recanted, kept the honorable members five hours in a fool's paradise—to use the words of Mr. Disraeli, uttered on that occasion.[a] *The London Times* has now written no less than nine leaders, by actual count, all conceived, *bona fide* or *mala fide*,[b] in this identical fool's paradise; all, as it would appear, only with a view to entrap Sir Charles Napier into a headlong attack upon Kronstadt or Sveaborg. Affecting to be drunk with glory and flushed with success, that journal even proceeded to bombard—in imagination of course—the Prussian coasts on the Baltic, as well as King Bomba at Naples, and the Grand Duke of Tuscany,[c] at Leghorn. In fact it was ready to make war on all the world, not omitting "the rest of mankind,"[d] of course.

The actual state of the land fortifications of Sevastopol is too little known to admit of any positive prognostication as to how long that fortress may be able to hold out. The success on the Alma is an almost certain indication that the place will be taken, as it must have raised the courage and spirit of the allied troops, and will prove a powerful preventive against sickness—the most dangerous enemy they have to deal with in the Crimea, and one which is reported to be already at work. But it is foolish to expect that the allies should walk into Sevastopol as they would into a coffee-house.

After the great mystification of the conquest of the place, with its 30,000 killed and wounded and 22,000 prisoners—a mystification whose like was never known in all the history of hoaxes—it would be natural to expect that the real official documents would at least possess the merit of affording clear and positive

---

[a] See this volume, p. 326.— *Ed.*
[b] In good or bad faith.— *Ed.*
[c] Ferdinand II and Leopold II.— *Ed.*
[d] *The Times*, No. 21864, October 5, 1854, leader.— *Ed.*

information as far as they go. Still the report published in London on the 5th of October in an extraordinary number of *The Gazette*, and copied in our columns this morning,[361] is, after all, not free from ambiguous expressions. Indeed, it is most open to criticism— a circumstance which must be ascribed to its proceeding from Lord Stratford de Redcliffe, one of the Palmerston school of diplomacy. This dispatch, in the first place, purports to have been sent to England from Bucharest on the 30th of September at $3^1/_2$ p.m., while Lord Redcliffe dates it from Constantinople on the 30th at $9^1/_2$ p.m.; so that the dispatch purports to have been actually received at Bucharest six hours before it was sent off from Constantinople. In the second place, the dispatch omits all mention of what passed in the Crimea between the 20th and 28th of September, telling us that

"the allied armies established their basis of operations at Balaklava on the morning of the 28th, and were preparing to march without delay to Sevastopol. The *Agamemnon*"

(with Admiral Lyons)

"and other vessels of war were in the Bay of Balaklava. There were facilities there for disembarking the battering train."

Assuming this dispatch to be exact, the English press has naturally concluded that the allied armies had passed the Belbek and Severnaya, forced the hights at the back of the Bay of Sevastopol, and penetrated in a straight line to the Bay of Balaklava. We have here to observe that, on military grounds, it is inconceivable that an army in possession of the hights command-ing Sevastopol should quietly descend from them on the other side, in order to march to a bay eleven miles distant, for no other purpose than to "establish a base of operations." On the other hand, it is quite conceivable that Admiral Lyons should go around Cape Chersonesus with a portion of the fleet for the purpose of securing a harbor of refuge, at once close to Sevastopol and adapted to the debarkation of the siege artillery, which, we have always contended,[a] had not before been landed. The guns, of course, would not be landed without a protecting force, which may have been either detached from the main body of the army after landing at Old Fort, or may consist of a portion of the reserve shipped from Constantinople and Varna.

---

[a] See this volume, p. 475.— *Ed.*

17*

The new dispatch further states that

"Prince Menchikoff was in the field at the head of 20,000 men, expecting reenforcements."

Hence the English papers conclude that the Russians must have lost 25,000 to 30,000 men in the combats between September 20 and 28, assuming with Lord Raglan that they were from 45,000 to 50,000 strong in the battle of the Alma. We have previously stated[a] our *prima facie*[b] disbelief in these numbers, and have never allowed more than about 25,000 men to Prince Menchikoff, disposable for field operations, and in this it turns out that we were within the mark of the Russian statements.[c]

The dispatch next proceeds to state that

"the fortified place of Anapa has been burned by the Russians. Its garrison was marching to the scene of action."

We cannot believe this news to be true. If Prince Menchikoff expects any reenforcements at all to reach him in time, they can do so much better from Perekop than from Anapa, which is nearly two hundred miles distant; if none could be expected by him from the former place, it would have been most foolish, by calling up the garrison of Anapa, on the other side of the Black Sea, to sacrifice in addition to Sevastopol the last stronghold upon the Caucasus. It will be seen, then, that with all the "information" of this official dispatch, we are still sent back to the battle of the Alma as the chief event whose authenticity must be admitted. Of this event, however, the details are also still wanting, and the Duke of Newcastle has now warned the British public that they must not expect to receive them before Monday, October 9. All that we have learned, in addition to the official report by telegraph from Lord Raglan, amounts to this: That the hero of the London pawnshop, Marshal St. Arnaud, was "indisposed" on the day of battle—(who ever heard the like of other heroes?)—that Lord Raglan had the chief command, that the English loss was not 1,400 but 2,000, including 96 officers, and that already six steamers with wounded had arrived at Constantinople.

The movements of Omer Pasha's army, which is directed from Bucharest and Wallachia, by way of Rustchuk, Silistria and Oltenitza, to the coast of the Black Sea, appear to confirm the

---

[a] See this volume, pp. 477-78.— *Ed.*
[b] Based on the first impression.— *Ed.*
[c] These figures are given in a telegram from Vienna of October 4, published in *The Times*, No. 21864, October 5, 1854.— *Ed.*

report that the allied commanders in the Crimea have asked for reenforcements. But this retreat of the Turks from Wallachia may also be attributed to Austria's desire to keep them from every road in the direction of Bessarabia, except the impracticable one through the Dobrodja.

In the enormous credulity of which the English public have given us such imposing proofs, it deserves to be noted that the London Exchange was very little caught by the general enthusiasm, the rise in the funds having never exceeded $^5/_8$ per cent. At Paris, however, the rentes rose immediately $1^1/_2$ per cent., a rise which, after all, is insignificant when compared with the rise of 10 per cent. after the defeat of Waterloo. Thus the hoax, if, as is possible, it was invented for commercial purposes, has altogether failed to realize the great results its authors must have counted on.

Written on October 5 and 6, 1854   Reproduced from the newspaper

First published in the *New-York Daily Tribune*, No. 4215, October 21, 1854 as a leader

Karl Marx and Frederick Engels

THE SEVASTOPOL HOAX.—GENERAL NEWS

London, Friday, Oct. 6, 1854

It is impossible to describe the excitement and suspense of the English during the week. On Saturday last the dispatch about the victory of the Alma was proclaimed by the Lord Mayor[a] before the Exchange, with the sound of the trumpet; but the unauthenticated news of the fall of Sevastopol spread all over the country. All the world was taken in. Napoleon announced it to his army at Boulogne, the English and French papers contained leaders on the happy event, the Emperor of Austria congratulated the Emperor and the Queen upon their success, but cautiously did not mention Sevastopol; bonfires were lighted, and the cannon boomed. We soon obtained the dispatch which originated all this joy and exultation; and indeed it proved to proceed from a very suspicious source. A Tartar—that is to say, a Turkish postman—has arrived at Bucharest with dispatches from Constantinople for Omer Pasha, which, as the General was absent, had to be sent to him unopened—therefore we don't know their contents. But the postman related that at his departure from Constantinople the town was illuminated, and that orders were given to continue the illumination for ten days. He concluded, therefore, that Sevastopol was taken, and gave just such details as a Turkish or London postboy could give in a pothouse. He mentioned 18,000 Russians killed, but only 200 guns taken, though the forts contain above 500 guns; 22,000 Russians were of course prisoners, since it was known that the garrison amounted to about 40,000. The fleet was first taken; then again a portion of it was destroyed, and Prince

---

[a] Sidney.— *Ed.*

Menchikoff was on the point of blowing himself up with the remainder, &c., &c.

But it remained rather curious that such an important event had not been communicated by Lord Redcliffe to the Consul at Bucharest,[a] and that no dispatch had reached the French Government. Still, the news was too good not to be believed, and accordingly it was believed. Next day, it is true, there arrived a report from St. Petersburg mentioning a dispatch of Prince Menchikoff of the 26th, which showed that after the battle of the Alma he was retreating toward Simferopol. Still the papers believed that it was a misprint, and that the real date of the dispatch was the 20th, rather than to give up the agreeable delusion of the fall of Sevastopol at the first onset. To-day, however, has brought the English public to reason; the miraculous capture of a great fortress without a siege proves to have been a cruel hoax, which will make the papers more cautious in future.

In Spain disturbances have taken place not only in Malaga, where the Republican party, as I remarked in my last letter, is very strong,[362] but even in Logroño, where Espartero resided for many years; and in Jaen, the telegraph adds that a Republican conspiracy has been discovered, and that the Infant Don Enrique, the brother of the idiotic husband[b] of the Queen,[c] has been exiled to the Balearic Islands. Still the excitement about Sevastopol is so great that nobody pays attention to Spain.

In Denmark the Diet was opened on the 2d. The royal speech from the throne[d] breathes defiance to the Assembly. It was received by hisses and by hearty cheers for the Constitution. The *Frankfort Journal*[e] reiterates the statement that the allied powers have resolved to reconsider the famous treaty of the 8th of May, 1852,[363] by which the succession to the Danish throne was eventually made over to the Emperor of Russia. Urquhart has not ceased to bring this discreditable piece of European diplomacy before the public over and over again, and his endeavors seem now at last to have succeeded.[f] The object of this movement, if there be anything in the rumor, is simply by reopening the question to get Prussia, who dissented from that protocol, to ally

---

[a] Colquhoun.— *Ed.*
[b] Francisco de Asis.— *Ed.*
[c] Isabella II.— *Ed.*
[d] Reference to the speech made by Frederick VII.— *Ed.*
[e] *Frankfurter Journal.— Ed.*
[f] The reference is to Chapter IV ("Treaty of the 8th of May, 1852") in: D. Urquhart, *Progress of Russia.— Ed.*

herself with the western powers. It is worthy of note that Palmerston called the protocol, like the treaty of 1840, measures against Russia, while its suspension is now to be considered as an act of hostility toward Russia.

Austria is reported to have sent a note to St. Petersburg, offering once more the four conditions as the basis of peace,[a] and declaring that the refusal of the Czar to accept them will be taken for a *casus belli* by Francis Joseph. This is one of the results of the victories in the Crimea.

The following observations on a recent article in *The Economist* are taken from the trade circular of Messrs. Smith & Charles:

"Of all the announcements or intimations that have appeared since the war began, that put forth on Saturday last by *The Economist* is by far the most important in a Russo-commercial point of view. *It must be borne in mind that this weekly journal is the property of one of the Secretaries to the Treasury* (Mr. Wilson) *and hence the remarks to which we are about to draw attention may be regarded as semi-official.* Having explained the course of exchange in Petersburg, and shown that, as a consequence of our trade with Prussia, British gold must necessarily be furnished by this country to Russia for its belligerent purposes; having stated that this was all foreseen by our Government, but that they considered such a state of things the lesser of two evils, *The Economist* proceeds to say, that after the fall of Sevastopol 'we shall be in undisturbed possession of the Black Sea and its shores, and masters of the Danube. But in the meantime Russia may take a posture which we can never by our arms reach, in the hope of wearying the patience of England, as in such a posture Russia can only be reached by her trade, and it may become a question whether our national interests will not dictate before long a different policy from that we have hitherto followed. We shall find that we blockade the ports in vain, so long as our produce finds a ready market through neighboring countries; so long as we permit Prussia to profit so much by being the medium through which our blockade of Russian shores can be so easily evaded, &c.... If, therefore, considerations of general policy shall render it needful again to consider the question of the extent to which the blockade shall be enforced and the trade restricted by land as well as by sea,' &c. *The Economist* concludes with a most solemn warning, saying: 'It will be well for those who are disposed to engage in such hazardous undertakings (as supplying the Russians with capital to purchase goods in the winter, to be forwarded to this country next year) to consider that it may be found needful to pursue a very different policy in the second year of a Russian campaign, from that which was wisest and best in the first.' We need hardly point out that the upshot of all this (and we strongly recommend our friends carefully to consider the entire article) is, that the Allied Powers have determined—as the only way of bringing the war to a close—to prohibit the overland traffic next year; and to prevent capitalists from embarking in a trade which will then be prohibited, the Government has very considerately allowed one of the Secretaries of the Treasury to make known their intentions in sufficient time to prevent the serious consequences to our merchants which would otherwise ensue. On Saturday the tallow market was quiet, at a shade under Friday's prices. It is probable that but for the article in *The Economist*, to which we have drawn attention, our market would

---

[a] See this volume, pp. 579-84.—*Ed.*

have declined to-day in consequence of the news from Sevastopol, there being an opinion that the fall of this important fortress is likely to bring the Emperor to terms. Our opinion is the very reverse, and that the catastrophe in question is calculated only to excite the exasperation of the Czar, and to lead him to seek revenge in some other direction. It is quite certain that until he is compelled to fly from his own great cities he may consider himself not utterly beaten, and he has too much at stake to give in until he is driven to the utmost extremity. We therefore look on this war as one which may be protracted through many years, unless the course intimated by *The Economist* as likely to be adopted by the allies is actually put in force."[a]

The *Moniteur* of the 5th October announces that *Barbès*, for the last three years a prisoner at Belle-île, has been set at liberty without condition by order of Bonaparte on account of a letter in which he expresses anxious feelings of hope for the success of Decembrist civilization against Muscovite civilization,[364] the former of which, by the way, has recently manifested itself at Athens by reproducing the days of June, 1849[365]—the French *Soldateska* there seizing an "obnoxious" newspaper editor, burning his books and letters, and throwing him into prison. From this moment Barbès has ceased to be one of the revolutionary chiefs of France. By declaring his sympathies for the French arms in whatever cause, and under whatever command they may be employed, he has irretrievably associated himself with the Muscovites themselves, sharing their indifference as to the object of their campaigns. Barbès and Blanqui have long shared the real supremacy of revolutionary France. Barbès never ceased to calumniate and throw suspicion upon Blanqui as in connivance with the Government. The fact of his letter and of Bonaparte's order decides the question as to who is the man of the Revolution and who not.

Written on October 5 and 6, 1854   Reproduced from the newspaper

First published in the *New-York Daily Tribune*, No. 4215, October 21, 1854

---

[a] "Money Market and City News", *The Morning Post*, No. 25195, October 3, 1854.— *Ed.*

Frederick Engels

THE BATTLE OF THE ALMA[366]

The official accounts of the battle of the Alma have finally
arrived, and the dispatches of the commanders, the reports of
English journalists who were present, and of several naval officers,
are given at great length in our columns this morning,[367] confirming in every important respect the conclusions we drew from
the first telegraphic reports of the action.[a] The following are the
facts as they appear to have occurred:

About three miles from the coast, the river Alma makes a bend
so as to form a crescent, the two horns of which point toward the
North. The southern side of the river, generally formed by cliffs
about 300 feet high, here offers an amphitheater sloping down,
more or less gently, toward the stream. This slope, supported on
the right and left by abrupt high cliffs forming the edges of the
plateau, was selected by the Russians as their position. If repulsed,
their superior cavalry could always cover the retreat on the level
ground of the plateau, which also offered almost everywhere
facilities for carrying off the artillery. On a sort of terrace midway
between the plateau and the valley of the river, the Russians had
placed their main body of infantry, protected, on the left, by the
steep cliffs, considered impracticable, and on the right by equally
steep cliffs, by a redoubt on the terrace, and a heavy enfilading
battery on the commanding hights. Admiral Hamelin maintains
that this battery was mounted with twelve 32-pounders, but how
such heavy ordnance could have been carried off during the
retreat, as it most assuredly was, remains a secret to be explained

---

[a] See this volume, pp. 477-82.— Ed.

by that officer. The ground in front of the Russian position, intersected by vineyards and rocks, was favorable to the defense, and rendered still more difficult by *abattis* and other artificial obstacles, which, however, from the want of wood in the country, cannot have been very formidable. On the high plateau, behind and on both flanks of the Russians, were placed their reserves and cavalry. In front, their skirmishers extended beyond the river Alma, occupying the villages of Alma and Bourliouk.

Against this strong position the allies advanced on the 20th; the French had the right, the English the left wing. Early in the morning the French sent General Bosquet's division (the 2d) with eight Turkish battalions along the sea-shore to climb the cliffs on that side, under the protection of the guns of the steamers, and thus to turn the Russian left. The English were to execute a similar movement against the enemy's right. They, however, could not be protected by ships, and had the principal mass of the enemy's cavalry against them on the plateau, so that this part of the plan of attack was not executed. The French, under Bosquet, in the meantime succeeded in climbing the rocky edge of the plateau, and while the Russian troops on this elevation were shelled by the heavy guns of the steamers, the third French division under Prince Napoleon advanced in front against the Russian left. Further off, the Russian center and right were attacked by the English. Next to Prince Napoleon's came the second English division under Sir De Lacy Evans, the commander of the British Legion in Spain during the Carlist War.[368] He was supported by General England (3d division), while the extreme left wing of the allies was formed by the British light division under Sir G. Brown, supported by the division of Guards under the Duke of Cambridge. The reserve (4th division, Sir G. Cathcart, and cavalry division, Earl of Lucan) maneuvered in the rear of the left to prevent any outflanking attempts of the enemy.

The battle appears to have been distinguished by the feature, that its first phase—that of skirmishing along the whole line, while the real decisive maneuvers are carried on behind this covering curtain—was very much shortened. The position of the Russians was, indeed, so clearly defined, and their powerful artillery so placed, that any lengthened skirmishing would have not only been useless to the allies but positively damaging. The French appear to have had to expose themselves for a while to this galling fire, the English being the last in line; but, this once carried out, the French columns and the English extended line advanced steadily into the difficult ground before them, dislodged the Russians from the villages of Alma and Bourliouk (the latter of which was burned by the retreating force, so as to prevent its being used as shelter by the allies); passed the river and pressed up the hights without any unnecessary formalities. Here the combat on many points of the ground, in the vineyards, among the rocks and abattis, partook of the character of the battles between Verona and Castiglione in 1848.[369] No regular advance was possible; a thick, irregular cloud of skirmishers, mostly acting independently, worked their way up to the first terrace, where the Russian lines awaited them. In the meantime, General Bosquet succeeded in establishing one of his brigades on the plateau, whence he menaced the Russian left; a brigade of the fourth division (Forey's) was sent to his assistance, while Forey's second brigade supported Napoleon's division. Thus the French made good a position by which the Russian left was seriously compromised. On the Russian right, Sir George Brown took the Russian redoubt—the key of that part of their position on the terrace; and though an advance of the Russian reserve from the hights for a moment dislodged him, an attack of the Highlanders (Cambridge's division) finally secured the possession of this work. Thus the left wing of the Russians was turned, and their right wing was broken. The center, completely engaged along its front, could only beat a retreat up the slope toward the plateau, which, once reached, they found themselves secure from any serious attack by the presence of their cavalry and horse-artillery, in a country eminently adapted for the employment of these two arms. Nevertheless, some disorder must have reigned for a while on their left when outflanked by Bosquet; the French reports are unanimous as to that point, and the fact that Menchikoff's carriage here fell into the hands of the French, fully proves it. On the other hand, the carrying off of all their artillery, even of the heavy siege-guns in the battery on the right (the French took no guns, the English but three, and those probably dismounted), proves the great order in which the retreat, generally speaking, was executed, as well as the wise resolution of Menchikoff, to break off the struggle as soon as the scales had turned against him.

The bravery of the allied troops appears to have been very great. There are few examples of a battle consisting, like this, of an almost uninterrupted, slow but steady advance, and offering none of the vicissitudes and incidents which give such a dramatic interest to most other great battles. This single fact is sufficient to prove at least a considerable numerical superiority on the part of the allies, and to show that the allied generals in their reports have far overrated the strength of the Russians. We shall recur to this presently.

The generalship of the allies was good, but shows more confidence in the valor of their troops and the assistance of the fleet than in the inventive capacities of the generals themselves. It was, so to say, a plain, homely sort of battle, of a purely tactical nature, destitute in a rare degree of all strategical features. The flank maneuver of Bosquet was a very natural conception, and well executed by the African soldiers, who had been taught how to do such work in the defiles of the Atlas. The British broke the Russian right by unsophisticated hard fighting, facilitated, very likely, by good regimental and brigade maneuvering; but the monotony of the British advance in two successive long lines was broken by the obstacles of the ground alone, not by grand maneuvers intended to mislead or surprise the enemy.

Prince Menchikoff had well selected his position. He does not, however, appear to have made all the use of his cavalry he might have done. Why was there no cavalry on the left, to precipitate Bosquet's isolated brigade down the cliffs again as soon as it attempted to form? The breaking off of the battle, the disengaging [of] his troops from fire, the carrying off of his artillery, and the retreat in general, appear to have been carried out in a highly creditable style, and do more honor to his generalship than the victory does to that of the allied generals.

As to the forces engaged, the allies had under fire three French and four English divisions, besides their artillery, leaving one French and one English division, and all the cavalry, in reserve, besides eight Turkish battalions, which were sent to support Bosquet, but arrived after the close of the action. Now, the French having left stronger detachments and suffered greater losses at Varna than the British, the divisions may be considered almost equal on the day of the battle—the French about 6,000, the British about 5,500 strong, each. This would give an infantry force actually engaged of 40,000 infantry, with a reserve of about 16,000 men, including the Turks, which appears to agree with the statements as to the force of the expedition, deducting for the sick and for detachments. The Russians are stated by Marshal St. Arnaud to have mustered two divisions of the line, the 16th and 17th, with two brigades of reserve (soldiers on furlough, recalled to duty), the 14th and 15th, besides the 6th battalion of rifles. This force would comprise forty-nine battalions if the brigades had the full number of battalions. Every battalion counting 700 men (they have never mustered stronger in this war, although in the Hungarian war they were fifty men stronger) would give a total of 34,300 men. But the above are about as many regular land troops as we knew to be in and about Sevastopol, and it is most likely that five or six battalions at least were left behind as a garrison in that fortress. This would bring the Russians to a strength of 30,000 infantry, which may have been about the correct number. Their cavalry is said to have mustered 6,000 sabres, but of course a good number of them were mere Cossacks. This marked superiority of the allies deprives the victory of that excessive glory which, as our readers will see in our extracts from the English papers,[370] it is attempted to attach to it. The bravery appears to have been equal on both sides; and certainly the allied generals, were they ever so flushed with victory, never thought of marching into Sevastopol after their success, without any further delay or opposition, banners flying and bands playing.

The result of the battle, though morally great for the allies, can hardly produce any profound dejection in the Russian army. It is a retreat like that of Lützen or Bautzen; and if Menchikoff, from his flanking position at Bakshiserai, understands as well how to draw the allies after him as Blücher did before the battle of the Katzbach,[371] they may yet learn that such fruitless victories are of no great use to the gainer. Menchikoff is yet in force at their rear, and till they have defeated him a second time and entirely driven him away, he will still be formidable. Almost everything now will depend upon the arrival of reenforcements of the allied reserve on one hand, and of the Russian troops from Perekop, Kerch and Anapa on the other. Whoever is *first* the stronger, may strike a great blow. But Menchikoff has this advantage that he can at any time elude an attack by falling back, while the allies are tied to the spot where their dépôts, camps and parks are.

For the moment, Sevastopol, though invested on one side, appears safe, the superiority of the allies not being marked enough to make front in two directions. But should their reserve of 20,000 men arrive sooner than Menchikoff's support,—as appears almost certain from our dispatch by the *Niagara*, received last night by telegraph from Halifax[372]—a few days may decide much. A place like Sevastopol, if once seriously and vigorously attacked, cannot be expected to hold out a fortnight against open trenches. The reserve had all sailed from Varna and should have arrived by the 4th or 5th, though our Halifax dispatch does not mention their arrival; at any rate before the 16th or 18th, therefore, Sevastopol can hardly be expected to fall. There are chances that an active campaign in the open field might prolong its holding out for some time longer; but unless Menchikoff, with his moveable army in the rear of the allies, should gain some important advantage in the field, or unless sickness decimates the allied troops, it must certainly fall. But we may be sure, from the preparations and temper of the Russians that it will not be taken without desperate resistance, and terrible bloodshed; the sanguinary details of the battle on the Alma will certainly be exceeded in their kind by those of the storm and capture of Sevastopol.

Written on October 9, 1854

First published in the *New-York Daily Tribune*, No. 4219, October 26; reprinted in the *New-York Semi-Weekly Tribune*, No. 983, October 27 and the *New-York Weekly Tribune*, No. 685, October 28, 1854 as a leader·

Reproduced from the *New-York Daily Tribune*

Frederick Engels

THE MILITARY POWER OF RUSSIA [373]

We may safely leave John Bull and Jacques Bonhomme,[374] for a while, to their rejoicings at the "glorious victory" of the Alma and their anticipations of the fall of Sevastopol. The war on the Danube and in the Crimea, whatever importance it may have in the eyes of the allies and of the united Middle Class Liberalism of Europe, has very little weight, as far as Russia is concerned. The center of gravity of that country is in no wise affected by its possible results; while a defeat in the Crimea and forced retreat of the allies would cripple their land operations for a considerable time, and give them a moral check to recover from which would require their utmost exertions.

Some authentic reports of the distribution and late movements of the Russian forces have lately come to hand, and it may be well to sum them up in order to show how little, comparatively speaking, of the Russian force is as yet engaged, and what the remainder is expected to perform.

As is well known, the Russian army consists, as nearly as can be stated, of the following bodies:

I. THE GRAND ACTIVE ARMY—
  2 corps of *élite*, Guards and Grenadiers, containing 76 battalions, 92 squadrons, 228 guns.
  6 corps of the line, —"—, 300 battalions, 192 squadrons, 672 guns.
  3 Cavalry corps, —"—, 176 squadrons, 96 guns.
  Total, 376 battalions, 460 squadrons, 996 guns.

II. SPECIAL CORPS—
  Finland corps, 12 battalions.
  Orenburg corps, 10 battalions.
  Siberian corps, 15 battalions.

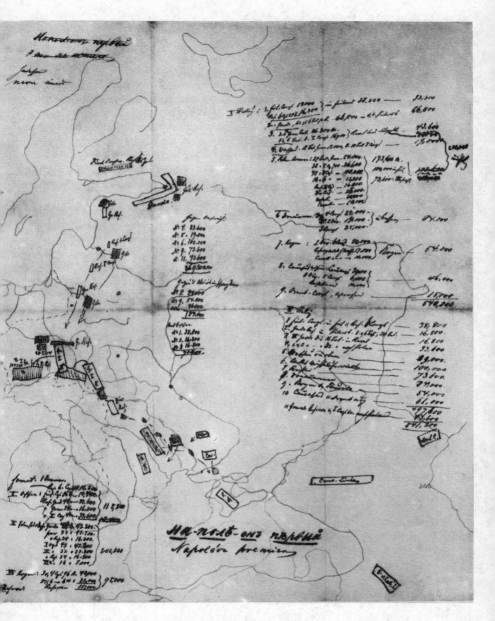

A page from Engels' preparatory material for the article
"The Military Power of Russia"

Caucasian corps, 55 battalions, 10 squadrons, 180 guns.
Reserve Caucasian corps, 36 battalions, 2 squadrons,—guns.
Caucasian line, 47 battalions,—squadrons,—guns.
Total, 175 battalions, 12 squadrons, 180 guns.

III. COSSACKS AND OTHER IRREGULARS—
About 700 squadrons, 32 battalions, and 224 guns.

IV. RESERVES—

1. About 50 battalions of Interior Guards, besides invalids, penal companies, 77.
2. Reserve of the grand army, or 4th, 5th and 6th battalions of Guards and Grenadiers, 5th and 6th battalions of the line, viz: three battalions for 24 regiments, and two battalions each for 72 regiments, or in all, 216 battalions.

As all the reserves are called in and fully organized, so far that *the formation of the 7th and 8th battalions* of each regiment has been commenced out of the lately decreed levy of 300,000 men, the above 216 battalions may be comprised in the grand total, which would give 726 battalions, 472 squadrons of regular, 700 squadrons of irregular cavalry, and considerably above a thousand guns. The organization of the reserves for cavalry and artillery not being well known out of Russia, they are not included in the above.

This array, fortunately, looks more formidable than it really is. From it we must deduct, to arrive at the number of troops actually available for a European war, the Siberian corps, the Internal Guard, and at least one-half of the Cossacks; thus leaving available about 650 battalions, 472 squadrons of regular and 350 squadrons of irregular cavalry, with about 1,200 guns. These troops may be estimated, at a very low figure, at 520,000 infantry, 62,000 cavalry, and 30,000 Cossacks, or rather more than 600,000 together, spread on the long line from the Caspian along the Black Sea and Baltic to the White Sea.

Since the beginning of the war with Turkey, the following troops have been successively engaged against the allies on the southern frontier of the empire:

1. The 3d, 4th and 5th corps of the line, with some of their reserves, which are, however, mostly still on the march.
2. The whole of the three Caucasian corps.
3. The two divisions (two-thirds) of the first corps of the line, without reserves.
4. A portion of the third cavalry corps (dragoons) in the Crimea.

This makes a total of about 240,000 men, *before* entering on the campaign, but now reduced to 184,000 men at the outside, of whom 84,000 may be taken as the strength of the army in Bessarabia, 54,000 in the Crimea, or marching toward it, and 46,000 in the Caucasus.

On the Baltic there were, up to the end of August:

	Men
In Finland, the reserve of the 6th Corps	16,800
The Finnish Corps	12,000
The Guards and their reserves	66,800
Of the Grenadier Corps at Revel	10,000
Total	105,600

There were in Poland, or marching for it:

	Men
The remainder of the Grenadiers and their reserves	55,000
The 1st and 2d Corps and their reserves	120,000
Cossacks and cavalry of different corps	30,000
Various reserves	25,000
Total	230,000

Making all together about 575,000 men, which, with the Orenburg Corps (at Astrakhan), the Reserve Cavalry Corps, and the detachments of the White Sea and others, comes up to the number stated before of the grand total. Of the troops in Poland, about 30,000 were on the march, about 20,000 garrisoned Warsaw, about 100,000 occupied the right bank of the Vistula, in the late Kingdom of Poland, and about 80,000 remained as a reserve in Volhynia and Podolia, on the Bug and Dniester. Thus the main bulk of the Russian army, and among them the crack regiments of Guards and Grenadiers, was concentrated on a line from St. Petersburg to Chotin, or along the western frontier of the Empire. But these positions did not appear significant enough. The Grenadiers left Revel, to be replaced by a division of Guards, and with the other two divisions of Guards marched off to Poland, the latter four battalions or regiments strong, leaving only the 5th and 6th battalions in Petersburg. Thus the army of the West was increased to above 270,000 men, and the greater portion of the three Reserve Cavalry Corps, *which have as yet not been engaged at all,* are marched off to join them; this will bring the army of the West to some 300,000 men.

Now the positions are changed. The 100,000 men, occupying the south-eastern portion of the Kingdom of Poland, have crossed the Vistula and taken up a position along the Austrian frontier. The 80,000 men have advanced from Volhynia into Poland, and continue the line along that frontier. Guards, Grenadiers— possibly the cavalry corps, when they arrive—take a central position to the rear. During the winter more troops can be spared from the ice-bound Baltic. By May the new levies, forming the 7th and 8th or new battalions of the different regiments, or 192 battalions in all (130,000 to 140,000 men), will be so far drilled as to replace them.

There is no doubt, then, that Nicholas cares comparatively little what happens to the south of his Empire, so long as he can concentrate above 300,000 men in the splendid strategical position of Poland. And a splendid position it is. Driven in like a wedge between Prussia and Austria, it outflanks both, while it is protected by the strongest means of resistance which art and nature combined can produce. Napoleon knew the military importance of the country inclosed by the Vistula and its affluents. He made it his base of operations for the campaign of 1807, until he took Danzig. But he neglected permanently to fortify it, and paid dearly for it after the retreat of 1812. The Russians, especially since 1831, have done what their predecessors in power omitted to do. Modlin, (Novo-Georgievsk), Warsaw, Ivangorod, Brzesc Litewski form a system of fortifications stronger, in its strategical combination, than any other in the world. This system offers a position in which a beaten army may defy double its numbers as long as it has plenty to eat; and to cut off a whole country from all communications is a thing that has not yet been attempted. This whole complex system of fortresses, says a German military writer who knows the country, indicates even more an aggressive than a defensive spirit. It is planned not so much to maintain the ground on which it stands as to serve as a base for offensive attacks toward the west.

And there are people who believe that Nicholas will sue for peace if Sevastopol be taken! Why, Russia has not played one-third of her trumps yet, and the momentary loss of Sevastopol and of the fleet is hardly felt at all by the giant to whom Sevastopol and the fleet were but a plaything. Russia knows full well that her decisive action does not lie along the sea shores or within reach of debarking troops; but on the contrary, on the broad interior of the Continent, where massive armies can be brought to act concentrated on one spot, without frittering away their forces in a fruitless coast defense against evanescent enemies. Russia may lose the Crimea, the Caucasus, Finland, St. Petersburg and all such appendages; but as long as her body, with Moscow for its heart, and fortified Poland for its sword-arm, is untouched, she need not give in an iota.

The grand actions of 1854 are, we dare say, but the petty preludes of the battles of nations which will mark the annals of 1855. It is not until the great Russian army of the West, and the Austrian army come into play, no matter whether against each other or with each other, that we shall see real war on a large scale, something like the grand wars of Napoleon. And, perhaps, these battles may be the preludes merely of other battles far more fierce, far more decisive—the battles of the European peoples against the now victorious and secure European despots.

Written on October 16, 1854

First published in the *New-York Daily Tribune*, No. 4223, October 31; reprinted in the *New-York Semi-Weekly Tribune*, No. 985, November 3 and the *New-York Weekly Tribune*, No. 686, November 4, 1854 as a leader

Reproduced from the *New-York Daily Tribune*

Frederick Engels

THE SIEGE OF SEVASTOPOL[375]

Next to the battle of the Alma, the principal achievement of the allies in the Crimea has been Lord Raglan's famous flank march from the Alma to Balaklava, by which he changed the apparent object of the campaign from the capture and occupation of Sevastopol to a *coup de main*[a] against a portion,— and the weaker portion, too,— of the fortifications, including, of course, the destruction of the Russian fleet, dockyards and arsenals, but involving the withdrawal of the allied forces as soon as this object should be attained. That such must be the case, was plain, from the entire movement in question. It was an abandonment of the idea of attacking the northern front of the fortress, which is the commanding front, where alone an attack could really be decisive; and thus it was a patent confession of incompetence on the part of the expedition to accomplish what was laid down in its program,— the complete capture and occupation of the place. Nevertheless, as we said,[b] this very march has been glorified as a most brilliant stroke of generalship through columns on columns of high-sounding phrases and rhetorical gibberish; and even the great journals of London, with their correspondents on the spot, did not discover the truth till a month afterward, when the Government seems to have given them a hint of it. Thus, *The London Times* of October 28, for the first time opening its eyes to the true state of the case, gently indicates that the minor object of the campaign may be the only one accomplished, and that the forts on the north

---

[a] Sudden attack in force.— *Ed.*
[b] See this volume, p. 485.— *Ed.*

side of the bay, if they do not voluntarily surrender, can hardly be taken. But *The Times* hopes they will behave respectably, and surrender, inasmuch as all dependent fortifications ought to give in when once the main body of the place is taken.[a] But the truth is that it is not the North Fort which depends upon the town of Sevastopol, but the town of Sevastopol which depends upon the North Fort, and we fear the argument of our cotemporary will hardly suffice to take so strong a fortress.

It is true that since the "glorious march" in question nothing has been done by the allies of which anybody could boast much, and, therefore, our transatlantic cotemporaries are not to blame for making the most of it.[376] As for the siege itself so far as it has proceeded, it is one of those things of which they may well think that the less said the better. But as we are bound to nothing but impartiality in the premises, we shall not be so delicate. The truth is that the war in general being an exceedingly curious war, this siege is one of its most curious points. The great feature of the war appears to be a belief that fieldworks are impregnable. First at Oltenitza, the old-fashioned way of cannonading was employed for a couple of hours and then the works were stormed but without success. At Kalafat the Russians did not even dare to make an attack. At Silistria a mere earthwork bore the brunt of the battle, and held out, even when almost leveled, against the frantic onslaught of the enemy. Now at Sevastopol a simple line of fieldworks is honored with more extensive breaching batteries, and with far heavier artillery, than were ever brought to bear against the most regular fortress. This siege is a striking proof of the fact that in the same proportion as the *materiel* of warfare has, by industrial progress, advanced during the long peace, in the same proportion has the *art* of war degenerated. A Napoleon, on seeing the batteries before Sevastopol, bristling with eight- and ten-inch guns, would burst out in a fit of irresistible laughter. But this is not the whole story by a great deal.

About the 1st of October, the allies were in position, but it was not till the 8th or 9th that the first ground was broken, and fire was not opened till the 17th. The reason of this delay was that the guns could not be brought up sooner. There were only four or five miles of ground to go over—all good, hard soil, with little undulation, and part of it a passable road. But they had no draught cattle. No draught cattle in the Crimea—the richest country for cattle in the whole world! Why, there were more

---

[a] *The Times*, No. 21884, October 28, 1854, leader.— *Ed.*

bullocks in the valley of Baidar, within sight from the hights off the Chernaya, than would have been required to drag all the united fleet across the hills. But the valley of Baidar was open to the Cossacks, and the allied cavalry, in protecting a razzia, might be exposed to these formidable opponents. Besides, the allies must keep on good terms with the inhabitants, and not seize their property. With such excuses, our English cotemporaries seek to hide the truth that Raglan and Canrobert, while blockading Sevastopol on the south, are themselves blockaded by Menchikoff's outposts on the Chernaya.[377] And yet, that they are so is proved by the simple fact that the allied soldiers, up to the latest report, were compelled to live upon salt meat, no fresh meat being at hand.

On the 3d of October five Russian battalions crossed the Chernaya near Inkerman, and were allowed to enter the fortress from the south, as "this could but be favorable to the allies." An original mode of making war! The enemy, represented as beaten, demoralized, dejected, sends 3,000 men into Sevastopol, under the very nose of the allies. He must have had a reason for doing so. But if he has reasons for sending them, Raglan has his reasons for bowing them in. He supposes the place to be overcrowded, though upon what grounds, is not clear. At all events, beside the four square miles inclosed within the Russian lines, there is the whole of the north shore and all the country lying behind it, to which any excess of troops may be sent in ten minutes. To represent a place as overcrowded, which is blockaded on one side only, is certainly the hight of absurdity.

When the landing was first reported, we said that disease would be the worst enemy of the allies if the campaign should be lengthened.[a] Disease is there in its worst forms, coupled, at least as far as the British are concerned, with the very worst sort of attendance. Indeed, to such an extent have the sick been neglected from this cause, that Lord Raglan has been obliged to issue a very peremptory reprimand to the medical staff. But this is not all. The doctors are at Constantinople, the medical stores at Varna, and the sick at Balaklava. Is not this a splendid illustration of the new military doctrine lately held forth by Louis Bonaparte at Boulogne, that every army, to have a good position, must be placed in a triangle?[b] The sickness increases with the roughness of the season, the regiments dwindle down—a British regiment, sent

---

[a] See this volume, pp. 475-76.— Ed.

[b] Speech of Napoleon III before the troops at Boulogne on September 2, 1854. Le Moniteur universel, No. 248, September 5, 1854.— Ed.

out 1,000 strong, now cannot count more than 600 men under arms—and the slowness of operations goes on its even course. The routine of the Horse Guards,[378] the fruit of forty years' peaceful schooling, is not to be upset by trifles of that sort. Perish the army, but let Sevastopol be taken according to Her Majesty's regulations!

In common sieges the besiegers usually try to place their first batteries as near as possible to the enemy's works, and six or seven hundred yards is considered a great distance. But in a grand siege like this, particularly if against mere fieldworks, just the reverse should be done, according to Raglan. The enemy allows us to come within seven hundred yards, but we must never do what the enemy wants us to do. So says Raglan, and opens his batteries at 2,500 and 3,000 yards distance—a fact we could not believe did the reports leave it possible to doubt. Next he comes down to 1,500 and 1,200 yards, and then states, as a reason for not opening fire, that breaching batteries, to be effective, must be within three or four hundred yards from the works to be breached! The distant batteries are to have Lancaster[379] and long-range ten-inch guns, since it seems the British artillerists are of opinion that these guns are like telescopes, only good at a great distance. Indeed, this long-range question, which is perfectly in its place for naval armaments, has caused more confusion and humbug than real good when applied to land artillery; we have an example of it in these ridiculous batteries.

The landward fortifications of Sevastopol, which have provoked all these outbursts of genius and perspicacity, are as follows: On the western side (attacked by the French) one or two faces of the Quarantine Fort are exposed. Behind this is a loopholed wall running up toward the head of the Quarantine Bay, and ending on a hill, in a round tower which forms a *reduit* for an earthwork constructed around it. Thence a wall of three feet average thickness is continued to the upper end of the harbor, thus inclosing Sevastopol on the south-west. This wall is said to be incapable of any defense, although it might easily have been made so; it is, therefore, protected by small earthworks lying in front of it. From the end of the harbor eastward to the Careening Bay (the British front of attack) there are no regular defenses whatever, except two towers surrounded and sheltered by lunettes, in a similar manner with the one described above. There are besides some earthworks of irregular form, the whole forming an entrenched camp of no great pretensions, if we are to believe the published plans of Captain Biddulph, sketched on the spot. At all events they show only one line of defenses, consisting of works open in the rear; there are no closed redoubts, of which as a general thing the Russians are so exceedingly fond. But we cannot believe that this is the case; if this was the only line to take, the British ought long since to have taken it with the bayonet. There must be a second line of redoubts behind it.

The whole of the Russian works have been armed with heavy guns from the fleet—the best use the Russians could make of them. Yet their practice with them is despicable. They fire away whole days and nights at the enemy, and make one hit for a hundred rounds. Perhaps it was this very bad practice which induced Lord Raglan to open his trenches at the safe distance of 3,000 yards. After three days' bombardment by the allied fleets and armies, it is stated that the British, on their side, had made one breach, while the French had not yet completed theirs.[a] As soon as this was completed, the assault was to take place. That it should take 200 guns of immense caliber three or four days to breach such defenses would be incredible, had we not very good authority for the respectful distance at which the allied batteries had been constructed. So much for the results already achieved; but whatever event may crown the operations, it is certain that the siege of Sevastopol will stand unparalleled in military history.

Written on October 30, 1854

First published in the *New-York Daily Tribune*, No. 4236, November 15; reprinted in the *New-York Semi-Weekly Tribune*, No. 989, November 17, 1854 as a leader

Reproduced from the *New-York Daily Tribune*

---

[a] General Canrobert to Drouyn de Lhuys, October 13, 1854. *The Times*, No. 21885, October 30, 1854.— *Ed.*

Frederick Engels

THE CAMPAIGN IN THE CRIMEA[380]

Our readers cannot but be struck with the novel spirit breathing through the intelligence from the seat of war in the Crimea, received by the *Baltic* yesterday, and published in our columns this morning. Hitherto an overweening and arrogant confidence has distinguished the comments of the British press, and the reports of British and French correspondents concerning the movements and prospects of the war. But now this has given way to a feeling of anxiety and even of alarm. It is confessed on all hands that there is no such superiority as has been claimed on the part of the allied armies over their antagonists. That Sevastopol is stronger, Menchikoff an abler General, and his army far more formidable than was supposed; and that instead of certain and decisive victory, the French and English now stand exposed to possible failure and disgrace. Such is the feeling expressed by our correspondent at Liverpool, himself an Englishman, alive to all the patriotic impulses and prejudices of his country[a]; and this feeling is equally manifested by the very energetic action of both the French and English Governments. Desperate efforts are made to hurry reenforcements to Sevastopol; the United Kingdom is drained of its last soldier; many steamships are taken up as transports; and 50,000 French troops are sent forward, all in the hope of arriving at the scene of action before it shall be too late to take part in the final, decisive struggle.

We published on Saturday a copious quantity of documents, relating principally to the earlier stages of the siege, and the

---

[a] Report of the Liverpool correspondent. *New-York Daily Tribune*, No. 4246, November 27, 1854.— *Ed.*

partially effective but yet disastrous cooperation of the fleets[a]; and we now add the official reports concerning Liprandi's murderous attack on the allies near Balaklava, with other accounts of the subsequent progress of operations, all of them, we must say, quite unfavorable to the allies.[b] From a careful examination of these documents we conclude that though the position is, as we have often stated,[c] a difficult and even precarious one, it is hardly so bad as is implied by our Liverpool correspondent. We do not think that they are in danger of any worse disaster than a compulsory retreat and embarkation. And, on the other hand, there is still the possibility of their carrying the town by a desperate and sanguinary assault. But however this may be, it must, we think, be decided long before the reenforcements leaving France and England can reach the Crimea. The campaign is evidently near its turning point; the movements, the errors and the omissions which have shaped its character and generated its results, are made; we are in possession of authentic and indisputable information as to the principal facts; and we accordingly propose succinctly and briefly to review the course of the contest.

It is now established that when the allies landed at Old Fort, Menchikoff had under his command in the field only forty-two battalions and two regiments of cavalry, besides some Cossacks, while Sevastopol was garrisoned by the marines and sailors of the fleet. These forty-two battalions were of the 12th, 16th and 17th divisions of infantry; and supposing each battalion to have had its full complement of 700 men, there were in all 29,400 men of infantry; with 2,000 Hussars, the Cossacks, artillery, sappers and miners; in all some 32,000 men in the field. With these he could not oppose the landing of the allies, as by so doing he would have exposed his troops, without a sufficient reserve, to the fire of the allied fleets. A powerful army, which could afford to have sacrificed a part of its strength, might have detached a force to open a petty war of surprises and night attacks against the invaders while landing; the Russians, in this instance, required every man for the great battle to come; besides, the Russian foot soldier is the clumsiest fellow alive for petty war operations; his forte is action in column by close order. As to the Cossacks, on the other

---

[a] *New-York Daily Tribune*, No. 4245, November 25, 1854.— *Ed.*

[b] "Reported Battle on Fourth of November, etc.", *New-York Daily Tribune*, No. 4246, November 27, 1854.— *Ed.*

[c] See this volume, pp. 496-97.— *Ed.*

hand, their mode of warfare is too petty, and is effective in proportion only as the chance of plunder increases. Besides, the campaign of the Crimea seems to prove that the regularization of the Cossacks, which has been gradually carried out for the last thirty years, has broken their individual spirit of enterprise, and reduced them to a subdued condition, in which they are spoiled for irregular and not yet fit for regular service. They seem incapable now either of outpost and detached duty, or of charging an enemy in line. The Russians, then, were quite right in reserving every sabre and bayonet for the battle of the Alma.

On the banks of this river, the 32,000 Russians were attacked by 55,000 allies. The proportion was almost one to two. When about 30,000 allies had been engaged, Menchikoff ordered the retreat. Of the Russians, up to then, not more than 20,000 were engaged; a further attempt to hold the position would have converted the Russian retreat into a complete rout, for it would have required the engaging of the whole Russian reserve in the battle. The success of the allies, with their tremendous numerical superiority, being established beyond doubt, Menchikoff broke off the battle, covered his retreat by his reserves, and after overcoming the first disorder created on his left by Bosquet's flank movement retired unpursued and unmolested, "in proud order," from the field. The allies say they had no cavalry for the pursuit; but since we know that the Russians had but two regiments of Hussars—less, if anything, than the allies—this excuse falls to the ground. As at Zorndorf, at Eylau, at Borodino,[381] the Russian infantry, though beaten, behaved up to the character given them by General Cathcart, who commanded a division against them, and who pronounced them "incapable of panic!"

But if the Russian infantry remained cool and unterrified, Menchikoff himself was panic-struck. The great numerical force of the allies, coupled with their unexpected decision and impetuosity in the attack, deranged, for a moment, his plans. He abandoned the idea of retreating into the interior of the Crimea, and marched to the south of Sevastopol, in order to hold the line of the Chernaya. This was a great and unpardonable mistake. Overlooking, from the hights of the Alma, the whole allied position, he must have been able to make out the strength of his opponents within 5,000 men. He must have known that, whatever was their relative superiority over his own forces, they were not strong enough to leave an army to observe Sevastopol while following him into the interior. He must have known that if the allies were two to one against him on the sea-shore, he could bring two against their one at Simferopol. And yet he marched, as he himself confesses, to the south side of Sevastopol. But, after this retreat had been effected, without any molestation from the allies, and his troops had rested a day or two on the hills behind the Chernaya, then Menchikoff resolved to redress his mistake. He did this by a perilous flank movement from the Chernaya to Bakshiserai. It was contrary to one of the first rules of strategy; yet it promised great results. When a blunder is once committed in strategy, you can seldom get over its consequences. The question then merely is, whether it is less disadvantageous to abide by them or to get over them by a second, but intentional, erroneous movement. In this case we think Menchikoff was perfectly right in risking a flank-march within reach of the enemy, in order to get out of his absurdly "concentrated" position around Sevastopol.

But in this contest between strategical mediocrities and routine generals, the movements of hostile armies assumed forms hitherto unknown in warfare. The fancy for flank-marches, like the cholera, was epidemic in both camps. At the same time that Menchikoff resolved on a flank-march from Sevastopol to Bakshiserai, Saint Arnaud and Raglan took it into their heads to move from the Kacha to Balaklava. The rear of the Russians and the van of the British met at Mackenzie's farm (so called from a Scotchman, later an admiral in the Russian service), and, as a matter of course, the van beat the rear. The general strategical character of the flank-march of the allies having already been criticised in *The Tribune*,[a] we need not now revert to it.

On the 2d or 3d of October Sevastopol was invested, and the allies took up that very position from which Menchikoff had just extricated himself. From that moment the memorable siege of Sevastopol began, and at the same time a new era in the campaign. Hitherto the allies, by their uncontested superiority, had it all their own way. Their fleets, commanding the sea, insured their landing. Once landed, their superior numbers, and certainly also their superior storming qualities, insured the victory at the Alma. But now the equilibrium of forces, which sooner or later is sure to be brought about in operations distant from their base and in an enemy's country, began to develop itself. Menchikoff's army, it is true, did not show itself yet; but it made necessary the placing of a reserve on the Chernaya, fronting to the east. Thus the actual besieging army was seriously weakened, and

---

[a] See this volume, pp. 505-06.— *Ed.*

reduced to numbers not much superior to those of the garrison.

Want of energy, want of system, especially in the cooperation of the different departments of the British land and sea forces, difficulties of ground, and, above all, an invincible spirit of routine, inherent, it appears, in the British administrative and scientific departments, delayed the commencement of actual siege operations to the 9th of October. At last the trenches were opened on that day, at the enormous distance of from 1,500 to 2,500 yards from the Russian works. Such a thing was never seen nor heard of in any previous siege. It proves that the Russians were still able to dispute the ground around the fortress, to the distance of at least a mile; and they actually held it up to the 17th. On the morning of that day the siege-works were far enough advanced to allow the allies to open their fire. Probably this would have been delayed a few days longer, as the allies were by no means in a fit position to do so with success on that day, had it not been for the arrival of the glorious news that all England and France were rejoicing at the capture of Sevastopol on the 25th of October. This news, of course, exasperated the armies, and, in order to tranquilize them, the fire had to be opened. But it turns out that the allies brought 126 guns against 200 or 250. Now, the great axiom of Vauban, which has been again and again used by the Anglo-French to keep public opinion quiet, viz:

"that a siege is an operation of mathematical certainty and success, a mere matter of time, unless interrupted from without."

This great axiom is based upon that other axiom of the same engineer that

"in a siege the fire of the attack can be made superior to that of the defense."

Now, here at Sevastopol, we have exactly the reverse; the fire of the attack, when opened, was decidedly inferior to that of the defense. The consequences were very soon made apparent. In a couple of hours the Russians silenced the fire of the French batteries and kept up an almost equal contest, throughout the day, with the English. To create a diversion, a naval attack was made. But it was neither better conducted nor more successful. The French ships, attacking the Quarantine Fort and Fort Alexander, supported the land attack upon these forts; and had it not been for their aid, there is no doubt the French would have been far more roughly handled. The English ships attacked the north side of the harbor, including Fort Constantine and the Telegraph Battery, as well as a temporary battery constructed to the north-east of Constantine. That cautious man, Admiral Dundas, had ordered his ships to anchor at 1,200 yards from the forts—he ⁻is evidently a friend of the long-range system. Now it is an old established fact that in a combat between ships and batteries on shore, the ships are beat unless they can close up within 200 yards or less to the batteries, so that their shot is certain to tell, and with the greater effect. Consequently, Dundas got his ships knocked about in a terrible manner and would have suffered a glorious defeat, had it not been for Sir Edmund Lyons, who, it appears, almost in defiance of orders, got three ships-of-the-line as close as he could to Fort Constantine and did it some damage in exchange for what he received. As, however, the British and French Admirals' reports have not yet said a single word about the actual damage done to the forts, we must conclude that here, as well as [at] Bomarsund, Montalembert Coast—forts and casemated batteries—proved a match for twice their number of guns on board ship. This is the more remarkable, as it is now pretty certain that the exposed masonry of these forts, as was already partially proved at Bomarsund, cannot withstand the breaching fire of heavy ship guns, established on shore, for more than twenty-four hours.

The French were almost silent for a couple of days afterward. The English, having established their batteries at a greater distance from the Russian lines, and mounting heavier calibers than their allies, were enabled to maintain their fire and to silence the upper tier of guns in a masonry redoubt. The naval attack was not renewed—the best proof of the respect inspired by the casemated forts. The Russians made a defense which very much undeceived the conquerors of the Alma. For every dismounted gun a fresh one was brought up. Every embrasure destroyed during the day by the enemy's fire was restored during the night. Earthworks against earthworks, the contest was very nearly equal, until measures were taken to give the allies the superiority. Lord Raglan's ridiculous order "to spare the town" was revoked, and a bombardment opened which, by its concentric effect upon crowded masses of troops, and by its harassing nature, must have done the garrison great harm. Skirmishers were, besides, sent out in advance of the batteries, to pick off, from any covered position they could find, the Russian gunners. As at Bomarsund, the Minié rifle did its work well. In a few days, what with the heavy guns and the Minié rifles, the Russian artillerymen were mostly put *hors de combat*.[a] So were the sailors from the fleet, the portion of the

---

[a] Out of action.— *Ed.*

garrison best instructed in the use of heavy guns. The usual
resource of besieged garrisons had then to be resorted to: the
infantry were commanded to serve the guns, under the superintendence of the remaining artillerymen. But their fire, as may be
imagined, was almost without effect, and thus the besiegers were
enabled to push their trenches nearer and nearer the place. They
have opened, it is stated, their third parallel at 300 yards from the
outworks. We do not know yet what batteries they have erected in
this third parallel; we can only say that a *third* parallel, in regular
sieges, is always made at the foot of the glacis of the works
attacked, that is, about 50 or 60 yards from the ditch. If this
distance has been exceeded before Sevastopol, we can but see in
this fact a confirmation of a report contained in several British
papers, that the irregularity of the lines of defense, instead of
giving the British engineers fresh scope for their inventive
capacities, has but disconcerted these gentlemen who can demolish, upon the most approved principle, a regular bastioned front,
but who seem to be badly off as soon as the enemy deviates from
the rule prescribed by the best authorities on the subject.

The southern attack once decided upon, the parallel and its
batteries should have been directed against one, or at most two
well-defined fronts of the defenses. Two of the outer forts next to
each other—or, at the very outside, three—should have been
attacked with concentrated forces; and, once demolished, then all
the other outworks would have been useless. In this way, the allies,
by bringing all their artillery to bear upon one point, could have
easily established at once a great superiority of fire, and shortened
the siege considerably. As far as can be judged from plans and
maps, the front, from the Quarantine Fort to the upper end of
the inner harbor, or the front against which the French now direct
their efforts, would have been the best to attack, as its demolition
would lay the town itself completely open. The one hundred and
thirty guns of the allies would have at once insured them a
superiority of fire on this limited front. Instead of this, the desire
to let each army act independently of the other produced this
unprecedented mode of siege, in which the whole of the ramparts,
extending over a length of three miles, is simultaneously
cannonaded on its whole extent. Such a thing has never been seen
before. Who ever heard of an attack which allowed the defense to
bring into play at once, from plain bastioned works and lunettes
the enormous mass of two hundred and fifty guns? A single
bastioned front can hardly mount twenty guns; and in an ordinary
siege no more than three or four fronts can contribute to the

defense. Unless the allied engineers can show, hereafter, very substantial reasons for their curious proceedings, we must conclude that they were unable to find out the weakest points of the defenses, and, therefore, in order not to miss them, fired upon every portion of the line.

In the meantime, reenforcements arrive to both parties. Liprandi's harassing and partially successful attacks on the allied outposts have shown the presence of a stronger Russian force than Menchikoff had led to Bakshiserai. As yet, he does not, however, appear strong enough for a relieving battle. Considering the progress made by the besiegers, considering that the damage done to the defense increases in a geometrical ratio as the besiegers approach the ramparts, considering that the outworks still hold out, but that the inner wall appears to be weak, we may expect that something decisive will have occurred from the 9th to the 15th of November; that either the south side of the town has fallen, or that the allies have suffered a decisive defeat and been obliged to raise the siege. But it must be recollected that all such predictions depend upon circumstances which cannot be fully known beforehand at such a distance from the spot.

Written on November 9, 1854

First published in the *New-York Daily Tribune*, No. 4246, November 27; reprinted in the *New-York Semi-Weekly Tribune*, No. 992, November 28 and the *New-York Weekly Tribune*, No. 690, December 2, 1854 as a leader

Reproduced from the *New-York Daily Tribune*

Frederick Engels

THE WAR IN THE EAST [382]

The arrival of the *Africa* has put us in possession of three days later dates from Europe, but nothing of additional interest from the seat of war beyond an infernal episode describing the roasting alive of a vast number of sick and wounded in hospital, and accounts of sufferings that render language a pauper in attempting to portray them. Of the bloody and undecisive battle of the 5th November, brief intelligence of which was brought by the *Baltic*, we have now Lord Raglan's curt dispatch,[a] but not yet the customary voluminous and exciting details by correspondents, whether actors or lookers-on. Much anxiety—much more than appears on the surface of things—exists in England as well as in France in regard to the increased and increasing difficulties of the war; and the stubborn refusal of Sevastopol to fall before the allies, those rivals in courage and sacrifices, is most ominously viewed. The extracts in another column of this journal,[383] from *The London Times*, exhibit an altered temper, and a spirit of doubt which may be mistaken by some for approaching despair. In the absence of details respecting the battle of the 5th sufficiently coherent to base remarks upon, we shall now offer some on the operations of the siege just previous to that time.

The 25th of October was the day on which the slow monotony of the siege of Sevastopol was first interrupted by a dramatic incident. The Russians, on that day, attacked the allied position covering the siege, and the advantages being more equally

---

[a] Lord Raglan's telegraphic dispatch to the Duke of Newcastle of November 6, 1854. *The Times*, No. 21900, November 16, 1854.— *Ed.*

Engels' rough draft of the article "The War in the East"
with a sketch of the battle

Baleclava

distributed, this time, to either side, the result was very different from that of the battle of the Alma. This action, in fact, was the very counterpart of that of the Alma: it was a cavalry fight almost exclusively, while at the Alma no cavalry was engaged; and instead of occupying a defensive position, the Russians were the assailants, while the advantages of strong positions were with the allies. It was, indeed, a drawn battle as nearly as that of the Alma, but this time the advantages remained to the Russians.

The Heracleatic Chersonese, the peninsula south of the Bay of Sevastopol, borders toward the main land of the Crimea by a range of hights running from the mouth of the Chernaya, or the head of the Bay of Sevastopol, to the south-west. This range slopes down gradually on its north-west side toward Sevastopol, while it is generally steep and bold toward the south-east, facing Balaklava. The allies occupying the Heracleatic Chersonese, this range was their natural defensive position against any Russian army trying to raise the siege. But unfortunately, Balaklava was the "base of operations" of the British, the chief harbor for their fleet, the grand dépôt for their stores; and Balaklava lay about three miles to the south-east of this range of hills. It was, therefore, necessary to include Balaklava in the system of defense. The country about Balaklava is formed by a group of very irregular hights, running from the southern extremity of the aforesaid range, nearly due east and west along the coast, and like all hills in the Crimea, sloping gently toward the north-west, but steep and craggy toward the south-east. Thus an angle formed between these two groups of hights is filled up by an undulating plain, rising gradually toward the east, until it ends in a steep descent toward the valley of the Chernaya.

The most remarkable feature of this plain is a range of hillocks and of slightly elevated ground running north-west and south-east, uniting what we call the Heracleatic range with the mountains on the south coast. It was on this elevation, about three miles east and north-east of Balaklava, that the allies had thrown up their first line of defenses, consisting of four redoubts, defending the roads from Bakshiserai and from the Upper Chernaya. These redoubts were garrisoned by Turks. A second line of fieldworks was erected immediately in front of Balaklava, and continued up to the apex of the angle formed by the coast hights and the Heracleatic range, which latter were fortified by the French division of General Bosquet, stationed there. Thus, while the second line, defended by English soldiers, marines and sailors, was continued and flanked by the French line of redoubts, the first or Turkish line, nearly two miles in advance, not only was completely unsupported, but strange to say, instead of forming a line perpendicular to the road on which the enemy could come, it was constructed almost in the prolongation of that line, so that the Russians might first take one, then the second, then the third and finally the fourth redoubt, gaining ground each time, and without the possibility of one redoubt much supporting the other.

The allied position was occupied: toward Balaklava, by the Turks in the redoubts, or first line; by British marines, on the hights, in the immediate vicinity of Balaklava; by the 93d Highlanders, and some convalescents in the valley north of Balaklava. Further north was the camp of the British cavalry; and on the Heracleatic hights, that of the advance guard of Bosquet's division.

At 6 o'clock on the morning of the 25th, General Liprandi led the Russians to the attack of this position. He had under him a combined division consisting of six regiments of infantry (Dnieper, Azoff, Ukraine, Odessa, Vladimir, Suzdal, the 6th battalion Rifles, and one battalion Tchornomorski Cossacks, or 25 battalions in all); three regiments of cavalry (the 11th and 12th Hussars, and a combined regiment of Lancers, or 24 to 26 squadrons), about two regiments of Cossacks, and 70 guns, of which 30 were 12-pounders.

He sent General Gribbe by a defile on his left to occupy, with three battalions Dnieper Infantry, the village of Kamara, in front of which the first and strongest redoubt is situated. General Gribbe occupied the village, and his three battalions appear to have spent the day there very quietly, as they have never been named during the fight which followed.

The main column, following first the course of the Chernaya, and then a by-road, gained the high-road from Bakshiserai to Balaklava. Here they met the redoubts, manned by Turks. The first redoubt being pretty strong, Liprandi had a fire of artillery opened upon it, and then sent the storming parties forward. A line of skirmishers hid the first, second and third battalion. Azoff, advancing in columns of companies, which were again supported behind either wing, by the fourth battalion Azoff and one battalion Dnieper, in close attacking columns. The redoubt, after a lively resistance, was taken; the 170 dead and wounded the Turks *left* in it show that, in spite of the invidious assertions of the British press, this redoubt was valiantly defended. The second, third, and fourth redoubts, however, being hastily constructed, were taken by the Russians almost without resistance, and by seven o'clock in the

morning, the first line of defense of the allies was completely in
their hands.

The abandonment of these redoubts by the Turks may have the
good effect of dispelling the monstrous superstitions regarding
Turkish bravery which have been commonly adopted since
Oltenitza and Silistria, yet the British generals and press play a
very shabby part in turning, all at once, upon the Turks on this
occasion. It is not so much the Turks who should be blamed, but
the engineers who contrived to shape their line of defense in such
a faulty manner, and who neglected to finish it in time, as well as
the commanders, who exposed the first line to an overwhelming
shock of the enemy without any support being at hand.

The 93d Highlanders, steady and slow, as it behoves Scotchmen,
got in line by-and-by, and then advanced up the hights toward the
redoubts, but not before they were taken. The fugitive Turks,
decimated by Russian cavalry, at last formed again on the flanks of
the Highlanders. These, in order to shelter themselves from the
Russian fire, laid down behind the crest of an undulation of
ground, in advance of all the positions still held by the allies, and
supported by the cavalry division only to their left. In the
meantime the Russians had formed their line of battle on the
hights where the redoubts were situated—on their left flank
Azoff, next to the right the Ukraine, next the Odessa infantry.
These three regiments filled up the space between the redoubts,
and occupied what had been the first line of the allies. Further on,
to the right of the Odessa regiment, the undulating plain formed
a favorable theater for cavalry movements. Thither the two Hussar
regiments were sent and they found themselves directly opposed
to the British cavalry, which was drawn up about two miles distant.
The regiments of Suzdal and Vladimir, part of the artillery and
the Lancers, which were just coming up, remained in reserve.

When the 93d Highlanders, reenforced by the convalescent
battalion and the Turks, made a stand against the Russians, the
Hussars were launched against them. But before they could come
up, the British heavy brigade of cavalry charged them. The seven
or eight hundred British heavy dragoons dashed at the Russians
and dispersed them in one of the most brilliant and successful
charges on record, considering their far inferior numbers. The
Russian Hussars, twice as numerous, were scattered in a moment.
The few Russian squadrons which had charged the 93d Highlanders were received with a quiet Scotch volley at fifteen yards from
the infantry, and reeled back as well as they could.

If the Turks had run away, the English, up to this time, had earned nothing but glory. The daring of the Highlanders who received cavalry in line, without deigning to form squares, the dashing attack of the heavy cavalry, were certainly things to boast of, especially as they were performed before any reenforcements came up. But now the First (Duke of Cambridge's) and Fourth (Cathcart's) Divisions, as well as Bosquet's French Division and the brigade of Chasseurs d'Afrique (cavalry) came up. The line of battle was formed, and only now could it be said that there were two armies in presence. The French of Bosquet forming upon the Heracleatic hights, Liprandi sent the regiments of Vladimir and Suzdal to form the extreme right wing on the hights beyond the position of the cavalry.

Then, the fire having almost ceased, because the armies were out of range of each other, a misunderstanding, which is not cleared up, caused a charge of the British light cavalry—a charge which had no object and ended in defeat. An order arrived to advance, and, in a few moments, the Earl of Cardigan led his light brigade up a valley opposite his position—a valley flanked by covering hights, crowned by batteries, concentrating their fire on the lower ground below. The whole brigade amounted but to 700 sabres; when within range of grape, they were received by the fire of the artillery and of the rifles stationed on the slopes; they charged the battery at the upper end of the valley, received fire at twenty yards, rode down the gunners, dispersed the Russian Hussars, who made a second but wavering charge, and were on the point of turning back when the Russian Lancers took them in flank. They had just come up, and fell at once upon the panting horses of the British. This time, in spite of partial successes, the British had to turn back, and were fairly defeated by the Russians, but, it must be said, by far superior numbers, and by the aid of a mistake, which sent them, without an object, right against the cross-fire of a numerous artillery. Of the 700 men that advanced, not 200 came back in a fighting condition. The light cavalry brigade may be considered destroyed, until re-formed by fresh arrivals.

This disaster to the British would have been far greater, and hardly a man would have come back, had it not been for two movements made on either flank of the charging light horse. On their right, Lord Lucan ordered the heavy brigade to demonstrate against the Russian batteries in front of them. They maneuvered forward during a few minutes, lost about ten men by the Russian fire and galloped back. On the left, however, the French Chasseurs d'Afrique, two of the finest cavalry regiments in the world, on seeing their allies broken, rushed forward to disengage them. They charged the battery which took the British light horse in flank, and which was placed higher up the hill, in front of the infantry regiments of Vladimir, were within the line of guns in a moment, sabred the gunners, and then retreated, having accomplished their object—which, too, they would have done, even without the advance the Vladimir infantry instantly made on them.

Here was another instance of the British system of warfare as manifested in this campaign, such as, more than once, we have had occasion to point out. They first made a blunder, and then recoiled from the untactical movement which could have alone averted its consequences. But the French Chasseurs instantly felt what was to be done. On *their* side of the cavalry action no flank attack of Russian horse took place, because their dash prevented it: while the cautious "heavies" of Brigadier Scarlett merely demonstrated, and that, of course, was not enough to prevent the Russian Lancers from falling on the flank of the Hussars. Had they charged, like the French, the Russian Lancers would have turned tail very soon. But while their fellow-brigade was ordered to be over-daring, they were ordered to be over-cautious, and the result was the ruin of the light brigade.

After this the action ceased. The Russians demolished the two redoubts nearest the allies, and kept the two others strongly occupied. They maintained the conquered ground, and Lord Raglan, not venturing to attack them, ordered the second line of redoubts to be strengthened, and confined himself to its defense. The first line was given up.

In this action the behavior of the 93d Highlanders is beyond all praise. To receive cavalry in line in the way they did, merely wheeling backward one company on their right flank *en potence*,[a] to hold back their fire to the decisive moment, and then deliver it with such deadly steadiness, is a feat which very few troops can perform, and which shows in them the highest qualities required in the infantry soldier. The Austrians and the British may be considered the only troops with whom such an experiment can be pretty safely tried; perhaps, also, with *some* Russian troops, for their length of service qualifies them for such a task, although we do not recollect them having ever been put to the test and stood it.

The superiority of the British and French cavalry over the Russian is incontestably proved by this action. The three brigades

---

[a] T-shaped.— *Ed.*

of the allies were about the same strength as the three regiments of the Russians; and had they been sent to the charge simultaneously instead of one after the other, and supported by artillery driving up, and the whole line of infantry moving onward, Liprandi and his troops were in great danger of being thrown down the steep descent toward the Chernaya, and meeting with the fate Blücher prepared for the French at the Katzbach.[384]

The strength of the two armies may be thus computed: The Russians had 25 battalions, which mostly had been engaged at the Alma, cannot have counted more than 14,000 men at the very outside. Cavalry, 24 squadrons, having mostly marched all the way from Moscow and Kaluga, certainly not above 2,400 men; besides about 1,000 Cossacks. Artillery, 70 guns.

The allies had of infantry the greater part of the first and fourth British divisions, and of Bosquet's French division; besides them an uncertain number of Turks, which we can only come at by computing the number of Turkish battalions landed. There were ten Turkish battalions with the expedition from the first, and according to Lord Raglan's dispatch of 18th October, six more battalions were landed at Balaklava.[a] As they were not employed on the siege, nor moved far from Balaklava, all these Turks must have been present there; although, after their retreat from the redoubts, they were no longer mentioned in the dispatches and not considered worth mentioning. Thus we shall be pretty near the fact, if we take the British at about 6,500, the French at about 3,500, and the Turks at 6,000 at least. Besides, there were about 1,000 British marines and sailors in the redoubts around Balaklava. Total infantry, 17,000; or, if the Turks count for nothing, 11,000. Of cavalry, the two British brigades amounted to about 1,400 (in the British reports rank and file only are counted); the Chasseurs d'Afrique at least 800; total, 2,200. Artillery, unknown, but inferior to the Russian in number, though far superior in quality.

Take it all in all, we consider that on this occasion the allies were at least as strong as the Russians, had the advantage of strong positions to fall back upon, and might have, by a bold attack, cavalry and infantry combined, gained a decisive victory—not like the one of the Alma, which had no results, but a victory which would have saved them the trouble of fighting that murderous battle on the 5th of November. As it was, they did not even retrieve the disadvantages which they had suffered, and by that

---

[a] *The Times*, No. 21897, November 13, 1854.—*Ed.*

curious mixture of over-daring and over-caution, of misplaced dash and misplaced timidity, of military fury not heeding the rules of the art, and of scientific disquisitions, letting slip the moment for action—by that singular way of doing always the wrong thing at the wrong moment, which has signalized all the doings of the allies, the battle of Balaklava was fairly lost to them.

From the battle of the 5th November, we can up to the present only draw the conclusion that it was the beginning of that crisis which we thought would occur from the 5th to the 10th. As we said long since,[a] as *The London Times* now says too[b]—it is merely a question of supplies and reenforcements.

Written on November 16, 1854

First published in the *New-York Daily Tribune*, No. 4249, November 30; reprinted in the *New-York Semi-Weekly Tribune*, No. 993, December 1 and the *New-York Weekly Tribune*, No. 691, December 9, 1854 as a leader

Reproduced from the *New-York Daily Tribune*

---

[a] See this volume, p. 496.— *Ed.*
[b] *The Times*, No. 21900, November 16, 1854, leader.— *Ed.*

Frederick Engels

THE BATTLE OF INKERMAN[385]

This sanguinary battle took place on the 5th of November, and yet it was not till the 23d that the reports of the allied commanders and of the correspondents of the leading journals reached London. Very brief accounts of the affair were brought to this country by the two recent steamers, but nothing in sufficient detail to enable us to foɪm any satisfactory judgment on the features of the struggle. To-day, however, the mails of the *Pacific* enable us to furnish the most complete accounts of the whole, including the dispatches of Raglan, Canrobert and Menchikoff, with the very excellent and spirited letters of the special correspondents of *The London Times*[a] and *The Morning Herald,* both of which journals are served on the spot by writers of distinguished ability. With all these, and other documents at hand, we proceed to analyze the story of the battle, with a view to enable our readers to arrive at an impartial and intelligent opinion concerning it.

Like the Prussians at Jena,[386] the British forces facing toward Inkerman were stationed on a range of hights accessible in front by a few defiles only. Like the Prussians, the British had altogether neglected to occupy an elevation on their extreme left, on which, like Napoleon at Jena, Menchikoff threw a portion of his army—there establishing himself upon the flank of the enemy before daybreak. The intention of the Russians was evidently to profit by this circumstance in order to bring the mass of their troops to bear upon the flank of the British, to deploy upon the

---

[a] *The Times,* Nos. 21906 and 21907, November 23 and 24, 1854.— *Ed.*

CRIMEAN THEATRE OF WAR, 1854

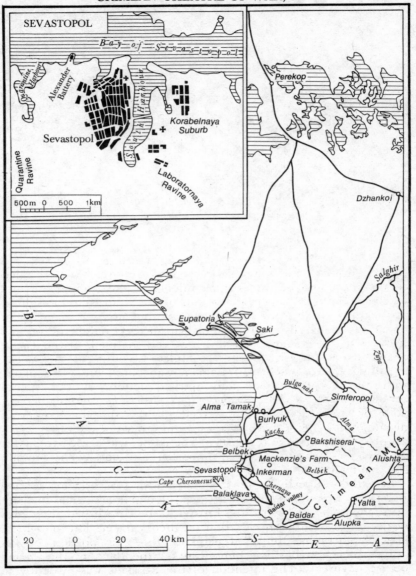

SEVASTOPOL

Bay of Sevastopol

Alexander Battery

Sevastopol

Korabelnaya Suburb

South Harbour

Quarantine Harbour

Quarantine Ravine

Laboratornaya Ravine

500m 0   500   1km

Perekop

Dzhankoi

Salghir

Eupatoria

Saki

Zuya

Bulganak

Simferopol

Alma Tamak

Burlyuk

Alma

Kacha

Bakshiserai

Belbek

Mackenzie's Farm

Belbek

Alushta

Sevastopol

Inkerman

Chernaya

Cape Chersonesus

Balaklava

Baidar valley

Yalta

Baidar

Alupka

Crimean Mts.

B L A C K

S E A

20   0   20   40km

hights thus secured, and crush the British divisions as they came up singly during the fatal but inevitable maneuver of changing their front, or to "roll them up," as it is technically called. To this maneuver Napoleon owed his brilliant success over an army which, though clumsy, slow, and badly commanded, was yet at that time the best of the old continental armies. The rapidity of his movements, executed with troops versed in the new mode of warfare introduced by the American war of independence, by the French revolutionary wars, and by Napoleon himself, favored this bold stroke. Here, at Inkerman, it was with slow and clumsy troops that Menchikoff attempted this same surprise upon the active and quick-moving troops of the British and French; and the result was accordingly the opposite of that at Jena.

The negligence shown by the British in the manner of occupying their positions is utterly disgraceful to their commander. There is no excuse, either for the non-occupation of the knoll on the south side of [the] Chernaya, or for the absence of field-works in this important position, for the attack of which, as he well knew, many thousand Russians were concentrating. The Russians, as we have said, profited by this neglect at once, by occupying the knoll on the north end of the range, forcing the British position with heavy field artillery. The British papers say the Russians had 24- and 32-pounders in the field, but this only shows their utter ignorance of artillery matters. The transport of their own artillery from Balaklava to the trenches should have shown them that 24- and 32-pounders cannot be taken into the field, much less into a night surprise. The fact is, what they call 24- and 32-pounders were howitzers, having a caliber similar to that of the 24- and 32-pound gun, but in fact light field guns, not heavier than the British field-howitzers. The howitzer, throwing a hollow projectile with a small charge, and obtaining range by elevation chiefly, can be made of a larger bore than the cannon for solid shot. The 24-pound howitzer corresponds in weight and effect to the 6-pound gun, and the so-called 32-pound (about 6-inch) howitzers to 12-pounders; these howitzers are attached in the Russian service to the batteries of these calibers. This shows how ignorance and national vanity unite in manufacturing heroes and enhancing the glory of a nation's arms.

So far, everything went in favor of the Russians. Their generalship had proved far superior to that of Lord Raglan. Their plan was excellent, and in a fair way of execution. A pivot had been secured, and the enemy's flank was turned. Immense superiority of numbers, ready to attack the long and weak line of the British at its weakest point, appeared to be a guarantee of final success. But the Russians did not yet fully know the soldiers they had to deal with. The British, surprised as they were, coolly changed their front from east to north, and met the assailing columns with a deadly fire. And now a fight began such as has not occurred in Europe since the day of Albuera,[387] as at Albuera the stubborn bravery of the British troops had to regain, with the blood of three-fourths of their number, a battle already lost by the presumptuous stupidity of their commander.[a] It is a fact that at Inkerman there was more actual bayonet-fighting than in the whole Peninsular war, where the two bravest armies of their time combated each other for six years. From half-past six to half-past nine about 8,000 British stood the shock of a Russian army, which, according to the Russians' own statement, had at least 30,000 men engaged. The firmness with which they again and again repulsed the Russian attacks, made often with fresh troops, is above all praise, and it is doubtful whether any other troops in Europe, except the best battalions of Radetzky's army, could have done the same. This bravery, it must be said, was aided by the nature of the position. The front, toward the east, was established on hights so abrupt that they could not be forced. The knoll to the north, occupied by the Russians, was also separated from these hights by a couple of ravines, forming so many defiles leading to the English position. Every advancing column of the Russians was, therefore, exposed to the full plowing fire of the British artillery, and had to advance in close order up to the top of the hights before it could deploy. Weakened by the fire of the artillery, and, when nearer, of the musketry, the Russian columns arrived on the crest, and, before they could deploy into line, a discharge and a rush with the bayonet threw them down again. It was found, in this fight, that, at close distances, the Minié bullet has an immense superiority over the common musket bullet, whose force of penetration is barely sufficient to kill one man, while a Minié bullet often killed four or five, and had a telling effect upon the deep Russian columns.

As the British divisions came up, the fight became general, and extended upon a longer front. The Russians, unable to make much headway, attacked the original front of the British position with their left, while their right tried to penetrate toward Sevastopol. They succeeded, partly, in establishing themselves on the British hights, without, however, being able to form a regular

---

[a] Beresford.— *Ed.*

line of battle. They tried to surround, and cut up, one by one, the separate small bodies of British troops. Though the struggle was hard, and the British fought wonderfully, yet they would have been crushed in this unequal contest, had not the French division of Bosquet come up. The Zouaves and the Foreign Legion charged the Russian left flank, and completely rolled it up, while the Chasseurs d'Afrique found an occasion to charge, and the Russian infantry had to retire. Thus, fourteen thousand allies, with a loss of one-third of their number, defeated thirty thousand Russians, and yet it is acknowledged that the Russians, individually, fought very well, while we have seen that their generalship, as far as the plan of attack was concerned, was far superior to that of the allies.

How, then, were they beaten? It must be said that most of the troops engaged were the broken and dispirited remnants of the besiegers of Silistria, and it is certain that Dannenberg's corps, next to Osten-Sacken's late corps, is at present the worst in the Russian army. But this was not the decisive circumstance. The battle was lost, next to the bravery of the English, through the essentially Russian way in which it was conducted. It is Russian warfare which has succumbed to European warfare. And this is the characteristic feature of the battle.

The Russian commander[a] begins by drawing up a very good plan of attack, borrowed from one of Napoleon's most celebrated battles (for no Russian General ever had an original thought, not even Suvoroff, whose only originality was that of direct advance). He follows this up by setting about its execution in the very best manner possible. He establishes himself on the enemy's flank. The strategical movement is completed; the tactical performance begins. And here, all at once, the scientific and learned mode of warfare, the work of western civilization, is thrown away, and the pure barbarism breaks forth. This splendid army, with its old troops, many of whom had been twenty-five years under arms, this model of parade-drill, is so clumsy, so incapable of skirmishing and fighting in small bodies, that its officers can do nothing with it but throw its heavy bulk in a single mass upon the enemy. All idea of tactical maneuvering is abandoned; advance, advance, advance, is the only thing that can be done. This dense mass of living flesh was, of course, by its very compactness, the best mark an artilleryman could wish for; and while the thin British lines, lying down behind the crest of the hill, were protected from fire,

---

[a] Menshikov.— *Ed.*

they plowed up the deep columns with round shot, killing them by thirties and forties at a discharge, and rained a storm of Minié bullets upon them hardly one of which could miss a target of such extent. The mere brute pressure, the weight of this mass was to break the allied lines. But here they found an opponent accustomed to that style of warfare. The British, in their Indian wars, have learned to withstand the shock of dense masses, even if of superior numbers. And, if the Russians are far above the Sikhs or Beloodshis,[a] yet the troops which were accustomed to beat six or eight times their number of Sikhs or Beloodshis might well stand the attack of three times their number of Russians, as soon as the Russians adopted the tactics of the Sikhs. The Russian column, when they arrived on the top of the hill, were already broken and disordered by the fire, and another volley at fifty yards and a charge with the bayonet was sufficient to break them. Afterward, as the Russians came up more numerously, the British, like Napoleon's squares among the Mamelukes, at the Pyramids,[388] stood among the flood of Russians surrounding them. The steadiness of forces having that full confidence in themselves which only the men of a highly civilized nation can possess, and the superiority of the armament and fire of the British, did the rest. The Russians are the worst shots of all known troops, and they showed it here, else they must have laid low every Englishman present.

,   This was the character, and this is the significance of the battle of Inkerman. It shows that the glories of the Russian infantry are passing away. It shows that whatever progress Russia may make, the West advances at twice her rate, and that she can have no chance with western troops in an even fight, nor even with such odds as she had at Inkerman. But for the disastrous loss of the allied transports in the Black Sea we should say that this battle would be sufficient, without very gross blunders on the part of the English and French generals, to render their final success in the Crimea beyond a doubt. Of that heavy calamity we have as yet no details beyond those of a telegraphic dispatch, from London, received by our agent at Liverpool just before the *Pacific* sailed[389]; we do not know whether the last vessels carried troops or only victuals and munitions, and from the silence of the telegraph we infer that they did not carry troops; but, if the large bodies of troops destined for the Crimea were lost in this storm, then, indeed, the allies have suffered a harder blow from the elements

---

[a] Baluchis.— *Ed.*

than from the enemy, and their forces before Sevastopol may be destroyed, by disease and harassing attacks, before it can be possible to send them new reenforcements. Another and a no less serious danger menaces them in the very attitude of the German powers. Austria now for the first time seems really inclined to break with the western powers and join the Czar, and all Germany will go with her. At any rate, it cannot be doubted that the moment for the war to swell into more gigantic and terrible proportions, and to wrap all Europe in its flames, is now close at hand.

Written on November 27, 1854

First published in the *New-York Daily Tribune*, No. 4261, December 14; reprinted in the *New-York Semi-Weekly Tribune*, No. 997, December 15 and the *New-York Weekly Tribune*, No, 692, December 16, 1854 as a leader

Reproduced from the *New-York Daily Tribune*

Frederick Engels

THE CRIMEAN CAMPAIGN[390]

Since the desperate and sanguinary day of Inkerman, the campaign in the Crimea has been marked by no military event of any importance; but, the advent of winter without the capture of Sevastopol having given a new character to the enterprise, it becomes proper to review the course of events since the landing of the Expedition, in order to determine what are the circumstances and chances amid which it enters upon the new developments that now await it. First, however, we must add a few words to our former observations upon the last memorable battle.[a] With regard to this event, extraordinary confusion and want of perspicacity characterizes the official reports, all of which we have published.[391] Lord Raglan's dispatch was evidently written in a great hurry.[b] Confounding that front of his army toward the Chernaya with that toward Sevastopol, he calls the same flank of his position sometimes the right, sometimes the left, in the same dispatch, so that it is impossible to get a clear idea of the events from this source. Canrobert's dispatch[c] is as diffuse and indefinite as it is short, and therefore quite useless; and whoever compares the so-called Menchikoff dispatch of the *Russian Invalid*[d] with the

---

[a] See this volume, pp. 528-35.— *Ed.*

[b] Lord Raglan's dispatch of November 8, 1854. *The Times*, No. 21906, November 23, 1854.— *Ed.*

[c] Canrobert's dispatch of November 7, 1854. *Le Moniteur universel*, No. 326, November 22, 1854.— *Ed.*

[d] Menshikov's dispatch on the battle of Inkerman dated November 6, 1854 and published in the *Russian Invalid* (Русский инвалид) is given according to *The Times*, No. 21906, November 23, 1854.— *Ed.*

former reports of Prince Menchikoff, must see at a glance that this was not penned by the same man. Nicholas, evidently, has found that he has allowed quite enough of the liberty of the press, and since telling the truth like a gentleman does not prevent his troops from getting beaten, he considers it quite as well to return to the old system of lying. By his Imperial will, the ordinary course of events is altered after the fact, and a defeated attack from his relieving army against the besiegers is changed to a victorious sally from within the town. The reason is evident: The sallying force necessarily retires into its fortifications so soon as the object of the sally is obtained; the retreat thus is explained and made a matter of course; while, if the facts were stated as they actually occurred, the disgrace of the defeat could not be hidden.

And well might Nicholas do his best to hide the circumstances of this battle from his people. Never since the battle of Narva has such ·disgrace been heaped upon the Russian arms. And, considering the tremendous difference between the Russians of Narva and the Russians of Inkerman, the undrilled hordes of 1700, and the well-drilled army of 1854, the day of Narva must, in comparison, be considered a bright one in Russian military history. Narva was the first grand disaster of a rising nation, whose determined spirit learnt how to conquer by defeat itself. Inkerman almost appears a certain indication of the decay of that hot-house development which Russia has experienced since Peter the Great. The artificial growth and the mere effort to keep up, with a barbarian material, a splendid show of civilization, appears already to have exhausted the nation and inflicted a sort of pulmonary consumption upon it. In all the battles of the present century, from Austerlitz and Eylau [392] down to Silistria, the Russians had shown themselves excellent soldiers. Their defeats, wherever they occurred, could be explained; they left no stain upon the honor of the army, if they did upon the reputation of its generals. But now the matter is completely changed. If Balaklava showed the superiority of the allied cavalry, if the whole of the siege of Sevastopol shows the enormous superiority of the allied artillery over the Russian, still the Russian infantry remained in possession of its high reputation. *Inkerman has settled this point too.* Strange to say, the Russian infantry has forfeited its renown in a battle, in which, perhaps, the individual Russian foot-soldier fought more bravely than ever. The sovereign mediocrity which has been the chief characteristic of all military operations in this war, both on the Russian and the allied side, has never been made more apparent. Every movement, and every step taken, has produced a result exactly the opposite of what was intended. A *coup de main*[a] is undertaken, and it turns out to involve a campaign—a winter campaign even. A battle is fought, but its gain is only momentary, vanishing in less than a week from the hands of the victors. An open town is assailed with heavy siege artillery; but, before the siege train is brought up, the open town is changed into a fortified camp of the first order. A siege is undertaken; and, when at the point of being successful, it has to be given up, because a relieving army comes up, and is—not victorious, but defeated. A strong position taken up against the relieving army becomes, by the very shortness of its front, the means in the hands of the relieving army to turn the besiegers into the besieged! Thus ten weeks are occupied with a series of efforts, combats, trench-works, plans and counter-plans; winter sets in, and finds both armies—but especially the allies—quite unprepared for the season; and all this with no result but a tremendous loss on both sides, leaving a decision of the campaign as remote and unlikely as ever.

The forces which the allies brought into the Crimea, from the first invasion to the 5th of November, did not exceed 25,000 British, 35,000 French, and 10,000 to 15,000 Turks, or from 70,000 to 75,000 altogether. When the expedition was undertaken, no more reenforcements from England or France were expected; a few battalions and squadrons were on the road, but they are comprised in the above estimate. All the additional forces they might have been able to bring up, at a short notice, must have been Turks; and, in spite of Chetatea and Silistria, neither the allied commanders nor the allied troops have ever shown any confidence in them. The 60,000 French and English were, then, the actually reliable portion of the expedition, and they alone can be counted as really effective. Now, this army was too small for a campaign, and too large for a *coup de main.* It could not be embarked with rapidity; the months employed in preparation were sufficient to put the Russians on their guard; and, if the presence of the Austrians guaranteed the Principalities and Bulgaria from Russian attacks, it also guaranteed Bessarabia and Odessa from *any* serious danger; for, the position of the Austrians being on the flank and rear of either line of operations, neither army could have marched forward without being at their mercy. Thus, the Russians must have been certain that all these preparations were directed against Sevastopol; beside which, the ports of Kherson and Nikolayev, the dock-yards of the Russian fleet, were the only

---

[a] Sudden attack in force.—*Ed.*

points in any way seriously menaced. Russian preparation in the Crimea was, therefore, sure to follow, step by step, the preparations of the allies. And so they did, until, at last, the contemplated *coup de main* was converted into a regular campaign, conducted, however — as was clear from the way it was commenced — in the most irregular manner.

When, at the Alma, the allies had to allow the Russians to withdraw in perfect order from the field of battle, although attacked by far superior numbers, the first glimpse of the truth burst upon them; the original plan was upset, the *coup* had failed, a new set of eventualities had to be provided for. Vacillation followed; days were lost; the march to Balaklava was at last resolved upon, and the advantages of a strong defensive position overruled the chance of soon obtaining possession of the north side of Sevastopol which commanded the town, and was, therefore, the decisive point. At the same time Menchikoff made similar mistakes by his hasty march to Sevastopol, and his equally hasty counter-march to Bakshiserai. Then followed the siege. Nineteen days elapsed before the batteries of the first parallel could open their fire, and then the advantages remained pretty equally divided. The siege went on with enormous slowness, but not very surely for all that. Hard work in the trenches, arduous outpost duty acting upon men weakened by a climate to which they were not bred, and by a fearful epidemic, thinned the ranks of the allies wonderfully. Their commanders had scarcely reckoned upon the common wear and tear of a campaign — they were taken quite unawares by such extraordinary losses. And the medical and commissariat departments, especially with the British, were totally out of order. Within sight lay the rich valley of Baidar, full of all the supplies most wanted; yet they could not venture into it! They had no hopes of early reenforcements; yet the Russians were coming up from all sides. Then came the affair of the 25th October.[a] The Russians gained the advantage, and one third of the allied cavalry was annihilated. Next followed the battle of the 5th November,[b] where the Russians suffered a repulse, but at a loss to the allies which they could not for a second time afford. Since then, both the Russian relieving army and the allied besiegers have been quiet. The siege of Sevastopol, if carried on at all, is carried on *pro forma*. Nobody will pretend that the lazy, desultory fire which the allies have kept up since the 5th of

---

[a] The battle of Balaklava, see this volume, pp. 518-27.— *Ed.*
[b] The battle of Inkerman, see this volume, pp. 528-35.— *Ed.*

November can do any harm to the defenses of the place, or even prevent the Russians from repairing the damage done up to that time. There is no doubt that the siege, if taken up again, will have to be done over afresh, with the only difference that, perhaps, the attacking batteries are brought some hundred yards nearer the place than they were at the first beginning, unless the fire from the town, supported by continuous attacks from Inkerman, should prove superior to that of the allies, and destroy the more advanced batteries.

Here, then, are the allies, in the beginning of December, in a country with cold winters, badly provided with clothing and other materials to enable them to get through the bad season in a passable manner; weak in spite of all reenforcements, arrived or on the way; having lost a vast number of men; entangled in the pursuit of objects and in modes of action which they never intended nor prepared for, and having gained nothing, absolutely nothing, but a consciousness of their individual and tactical superiority over their opponents. Twenty thousand men, chiefly French, must by this time have reenforced them, and more are expected; but if we recollect the difficulties and delays which accompanied the first allied expedition to Turkey — if we recollect, moreover, that almost all the transports used for carrying the first army have been kept back, and that new ships must be found for the divisions now under orders for the East, we must conclude that the army of the Crimea will remain without material increase of strength, for some time after the arrival of the 20,000 men above alluded to. Thus their strength may now be something like 55,000 to 60,000 men, one-third of whom come fresh from comfortable garrison life, and will have to suffer heavily before being inured to the hardships of a winter bivouac under a Crimean sky. In truth, these very reenforcements may prove an incumbrance, instead of an increase of strength, after the disasters encountered by the French and English transports, in the furious tempest of November 13. These disasters, however, cannot be said to belong to that order of fatal and overwhelming accidents, which the best contrived plans are unable to foresee or prevent. The storm of November 13th was a seasonable storm, and seasonable were the disasters that befell the allied fleets. The very date on which the Crimean expedition started, after three months of tedious and inexplicable delays, foreboded storms and wrecks, with losses of ships, crews, men and supplies. The framers of this extraordinary campaign were, moreover, again and again forewarned as to the incidents inseparable from Black Sea navigation at so advanced a period of the year. They, then, are responsible, even for the misfortunes of November 13, which threaten the allied forces with the fate of Napoleon's army during the Muscovite campaign. *The London Times* estimates the total loss of men, incurred on the 13th, at the various stations of the Crimea, at a thousand, "besides those that have fallen into the hands of the Cossacks." [a] The same journal also tells us that

"the *Prince*, a magnificent new screw steamer, of 2,700 tuns, carried out the other day to Balaklava the 46th Regiment, all the winter clothing for the troops engaged in the siege, including 40,000 great-coats, flannel suits, under-clothing, socks and gloves, beef, pork and other provisions; hospital stores for Scutari; and a vast quantity of shot and shell to carry on the siege. These are wholly lost. The *Resolute*, with 900 tuns of gunpowder, also went to the bottom. Thus, it seems, all the materials for carrying on the siege and providing against the severity of the winter, have been carried off at one fell swoop; and, even if we think to content ourselves with merely maintaining our position on the hights before Sevastopol, it is evident that we are not in condition to stand our worst foe — the coming winter." [b]

Though the Crimea is an almost insulated portion of the Russian Empire, and though the troops brought up against the allies have not been able to dislodge them when only 35,000 strong, yet nobody will venture to say that these 60,000 allies are strong enough to resist all the troops Russia may bring up. The Russians have six divisions of infantry and one reserved division in the Crimea, or about 100 battalions (besides marines and seamen, whom we have not counted on either side). These 100 battalions, one-half of which have made a murderous campaign of eighteen months on the Danube, cannot muster more than 50,000 to 60,000 men; including cavalry, field artillery and Cossacks, the whole Russian force in the field will exceed that of the allies by barely 10,000 to 15,000 men. But if it is true that Lüders's corps, or another 49 battalions of about 20,000 to 25,000 men (for they, too, have left one-third of their number on the Danube), is on the march to Perekop, if some more reserves of the new formations are concentrating in the same direction the opportunity may very soon present itself to the Russians to strike a grand blow; and as superiority, moral, physical, and tactical, only goes a certain way when opposed to superior numbers and about equal generalship, the result may well be considered doubtful. At the same time, if an extraordinarily severe winter should interrupt all operations, the allied armies are avowedly not in a condition to stand it.

---

[a] *The Times*, No. 21916, December 5, 1854, leader.— *Ed.*
[b] Ibid.— *Ed.*

This view of the state of things in the Crimea only justifies the
doubt and hesitation with which we have received the announcement that Austria has joined the western powers.[393] Certainly, the
circumstances we have detailed are not such as would be likely to
seduce the Cabinet of Vienna out of its wonted indecision, while
the precarious position of the British Ministry, and the urgent
necessity of covering this immense failure in the East by the show
of something considerable gained elsewhere, affords an ample
reason for exaggerating a small treaty into a grand offensive and
defensive alliance. We may be quite wrong in this; but our readers
know the reasons for our opinion,[a] and time will show whether
this vaunted accession of Austria to the allies is a reality, or a trick
specially designed for use at the meeting of Parliament.

Written on December 4, 1854

First published in the *New-York Daily
Tribune*, No. 4272, December 27; re-
printed in the *New-York Semi-Weekly
Tribune*, No. 1001, December 29 and the
New-York Weekly Tribune, No. 694, De-
cember 30, 1854 as a leader

Reproduced from the *New-York
Daily Tribune*

---

[a] See this volume, pp. 268-71 and 323-25.— *Ed.*

Karl Marx and Frederick Engels

PROGRESS OF THE WAR[394]

The sun of Austerlitz[a] has melted in water. A great battle, as was confidentially announced and believed in Paris, was to be fought before Sevastopol in celebration of the Second of December[395]; but from a dispatch of General Canrobert, of the 3d of December, it appears that

"rain was falling in torrents, the roads were cut up, the trenches filled with water, and the siege operations—as well as all the works—put in a state of suspense."[b]

The Russians hitherto had the offensive, the Allies the defensive, superiority on the Chernaya; at the walls of Sevastopol it was the reverse. In other words, the Russians were strong enough on the Chernaya to hold the field, but the Allies were not, though able to keep their position; while at Sevastopol the Allies, strong enough to carry on the siege, were so nearly equally matched by the garrison, that the operations, though not stopped from without, yet proceeded with hardly any visible effect. The proportions of force seem about to change, and the Allies appear on the point of becoming strong enough to repulse the Russians from the Chernaya. In that case the Russians can act in two ways, after having lost their position above Inkerman. Either they can go round and take up the intrenched camp about the North Fort, or they can with their main body retreat into the interior, where the Allies cannot follow them far. The Allies can hardly be strong enough before February either to invest the northern camp or

---

[a] An allusion to Napoleon I's words before the battle of Borodino: "This is the sun of Austerlitz."— *Ed.*

[b] *Le Moniteur universel*, No. 346, December 12, 1854.— *Ed.*

follow a retreating army much further than Bakshiserai. They could scarcely fight a second battle against an army intrenched somewhere about Simferopol. In either case, they would have to fall back on the Chernaya, and thus this game of alternate advance and retreat is likely to be played all the winter over, unless, indeed, Sevastopol, on the south side, succumbs to an assault. But as the news, which we receive by the *Atlantic*,[396] respecting the siege is very meager, we cannot say more on this point than that it is not at all likely. We are, indeed, aware that, according to a dispatch of December 7th, published in the Paris *Moniteur*, and reprinted in the London papers, the allied armies had all of a sudden got the upper hand, and only two days after the deluge, "almost completed the investment of the town."[a] This spurious dispatch was evidently concocted with a view to make amends for the baffled 2d of December prophecy.

A short time ago we gave a statement of the sum total of the Russian army, together with its disposal.[b] We then showed that of these nearly three-quarters of a million soldiers, up to the present time, hardly one-third had been engaged in active operations, and that the far greater portion of the remaining two-thirds were employed to menace Austria. In spite of the reenforcements sent to the Crimea, matters have not been much altered since then; for Dannenberg's corps, the 4th, which marched to the relief of Sevastopol, was withdrawn from the army of the Danube, where it had been previously reenforced. The only essential change in the position of the great Western Army of Russia, as we may call the corps of some 300,000 men concentrated on the Austrian frontier, is a slight extension of its left wing towards Bessarabia, and the Middle Dniester, in which position it is enabled, in case of need, to receive the remnants of the army of the Danube in case of their retreat from Bessarabia. The great Western Army may, besides, have detached a couple of divisions to the Crimea, and a few reenforcements to the Danube, but in the whole its strength is unimpaired, and the march of the 3d division of the Guards from Revel, and of some more reserves, will have made up for these detachments.

The Danubian army, however, may be considered as entirely broken up, and reduced to a mere corps of demonstration, placed in Bessarabia to keep up the appearance of a Russian occupation

---

[a] Report from Bucharest of December 11, 1854. *Le Moniteur universel*, No. 347, December 13, 1854, reprinted in *The Times*, No. 21924, December 14, 1854.— *Ed.*
[b] See this volume, pp. 498-504.— *Ed.*

as long as possible. By Liprandi's and afterwards Dannenberg's departure, that army was deprived of the whole of the 4th corps (10th, 11th and 12th Divisions), deducting from the remaining five divisions, the 7th, 8th, 9th, 14th, and 15th, the troops necessary for the occupation of the coast, and the garrisons of the fortresses from Bender and Ismail, to Kherson and Nikolayev, and, considering the enormous losses of the two Danubian campaigns, these five divisions could not muster for field operations more than 15,000 men. They are placed near the coast, and wherever there is coast, the Russian defensive, so efficient in the heart of the continent, is lame in the extreme. It has to guard numerous fortresses and dépôts against the attacks of the hostile fleet, and thus it is explained, that of the 30,000 or 35,000 men composing these five divisions not one-half is disposable for the field.

The dissolution of the army of the Danube, like most of the great strategical measures taken by Russia (for the blunders generally commence with the *execution* of them), is a very well-chosen step. Since the Anglo-French have engaged themselves over head and ears in the Crimea, no enemy opposes the Russians on the Danube. Omer Pasha's army, hardly amounting to some 40,000 men after the wear and tear of two campaigns, never made up for, has, by the aid of western diplomacy, been so broken up, as to leave it scarcely sufficient to invest Ismail, much less to detach a corps to cover the siege, or to repel the Russians in the field. Besides, an attack upon Bessarabia, which would have afforded a powerful diversion some months ago, would now lack a definite military object, and, consequently, Omer Pasha's army is now sent to the Crimea. The only force, then, purporting to menace the Russians on the south-west, is now the Austrian army, which, in a force of some 270,000, occupies Galicia, Transylvania and Moldavia. This force must, above all things, be held in check. For, should it declare itself hostile to Russia, Bessarabia, and even the country up to the Bug, would have to be abandoned, and operations have to be conducted either from the offensive basis of the Polish fortresses, or from the defensive basis of Kiev and the Dnieper. In both cases a Danubian army would be cut off, and have to find a base of its own somewhere in the steppes of the South, which is no easy matter, in a country which feeds many horses and sheep, but very few men. On the other hand, should Austria declare for Russia, or turn the points of her neutral bayonets towards the Alps and the Rhine, then the Polish army might either march into Germany as a reserve to the Austrians, after sending a strong corps toward the Danube, or the Austrians pour in a mass upon the Danube and risk a march to Constantinople. In either case, a separate army on the Danube, stronger than a demonstration corps, was superfluous.

As to the cooperation of Austria in this war, we can, of course, only speak in an altogether hypothetical way. The noisily trumpeted Treaty of Alliance said to have been concluded by her with France and England on the 2d of December, turns out to be but a snare laid for Parliament, as we warned our readers immediately on the announcement of the Treaty.[a]

In the Queen's speech the Treaty is alluded to in these words:

"It is with satisfaction I inform you that, together with the Emperor of the French, I have concluded a treaty with the Emperor of Austria, from which I anticipate important advantages to the common cause;"[b]

but, being hardly pressed by Lord Derby, Aberdeen went the length of declaring:

"We propose only that the House should learn with satisfaction that Her Majesty has made a treaty from which she (viz. old Aberdeen) anticipates important advantages."[c]

This is all the satisfaction he gave. Lord John Russell, in the Lower House, was forced by Mr. Disraeli to advance a step further, and plainly to confess that the boasted Treaty of Alliance means neither a treaty nor an alliance. He avows that it binds Austria to nothing at all, while it forces the Western Powers into an alliance offensive and defensive with Austria, *if* she should choose to declare war on Russia, and obliges them besides to propose to Russia, before the end of the year, conditions of peace on the basis of the famous four points.[d] After all, Austria might then, "without a breach of faith," release herself from the alliance by saying, "at the last moment," she did not concur in the interpretation put on the four points by the Western Powers. The result of Lord John Russell's explanation of the glorious treaty of December 2, was an immediate fall of the funds, both at London and at Paris.

A year ago, the coalition pretended to have allowed the massacre of Sinope to take place in order to obtain the alliance of

---

[a] See this volume, p. 542.— *Ed.*

[b] Victoria R. Speech at the opening of Parliament on December 12, 1854. *The Times*, No. 21923, December 13, 1854.— *Ed.*

[c] The Earl of Aberdeen's speech in the House of Lords on December 12, 1854. *The Times*, No. 21923, December 13, 1854.— *Ed.*

[d] Lord John Russell's speech in the House of Commons on December 12, 1854. *The Times*, No. 21923, December 13, 1854.— *Ed.*

the German powers. Now, a sham treaty with one of these powers is held out as the equivalent for the loss not of a Turkish fleet, but of a British army. We are even assured by the latest German papers that the opening of the British Parliament has given the signal for the reappearance of the specter of the Vienna Conference, which was about once more to set its cumbrous machinery at work.[397]

However, as Austria, according to Lord John Russell, declares it possible that she may be driven to war with Russia, and as the position taken by the Russian army on the Austrian frontier indicates the same thing, we may suppose, for a moment, that Austria and the rest of Germany, even including Prussia, are to join the Western Powers. How far would Russia be prepared to meet such an eventuality?

If in 1812 the Continental force launched against Russia was far weaker than that which she may perhaps see on her frontiers in April or May; if then England was her ally instead of her foe, Russia may console herself with the reflection that the more numerous the armies are which penetrate into her interior, the more chance is there of their speedy destruction, and that, on the other hand, she has now three times the troops under arms which she had then.

Not that we think "Holy Russia" unassailable. On the contrary, Austria alone we consider fully her equal as to military resources, while Austria and Prussia united, are quite able, if merely military chances are taken into account, to force her to an ignominious peace. Any forty millions of men, concentrated upon a country of the size of Germany proper, will be able to cope successfully with the scattered sixty millions of Russian subjects. The strategy of an attack upon Russia from the west has been clearly enough defined by Napoleon, and had he not been forced by circumstances of a non-strategic nature to deviate from his plan, Russia's supremacy and integrity were seriously menaced in 1812. That plan was to advance to the Dvina and the Dnieper, to organize a defensive position, both as to fortifications, dépôts and communications, to take her fortresses on the Dvina, and to delay the march to Moscow, until the spring of 1813. He was induced to abandon this plan, late in the season, from political reasons, from the outcry of his officers against winter quarters in Lithuania, and from a blind faith in his invincibility. He marched to Moscow, and the result is known. The disaster was immensely aggravated by the mal-administration of the French Commissariat, and by the want of warm clothing for the soldiers. Had these things been better

attended to, Napoleon, on his retreat, might have found himself
at Wilna at the head of an army twice in numbers that which
Russia could oppose to him. His errors are before us; they are
none of them of a nature irremediable: the fact of his penetrating
to Moscow, the march of Charles XII to Poltava, prove that the
country is accessible, though difficult of access; and as to
maintaining a victorious army in its heart, that all depends upon
the length of the line of operations, on the distance and the
security of the bases. Napoleon's line of operations from the Rhine
to Aylau and Friedland, if we consider long lines of operations in
their capacity of drawbacks upon the active force of an army, will
be about equal to a line of operations from Brest Litovski
(supposing the Polish fortresses to be taken in the first year) to
Moscow. And in this supposition no account is taken of the
circumstance that the immediate base of operations would have
been advanced to Vitebsk, Mogilev and Smolensk, without which
preparatory act a march on Moscow would certainly be hazardous.

Russia is certainly thinly populated; but we must not forget that
the central provinces—the very heart of Russian nationality and
strength—have a population equal to that of central Europe. In
Poland—that is, the five governments constituting the Russian
kingdom of Poland—the average is about the same. The most
populous districts of Russia—Moscow, Tula, Riasan, Nijni-
Novgorod, Kaluga, Yaroslaf, Smolensk, &c.—are the very heart of
Great Russia, and form a compact body; they are continued, in the
south, by the equally populous Little Russian Provinces of Kiev,
Poltava, Chernigov, Voronezh, &c. There are, in all, 29 Provinces
or Governments, in which the population is quite half as dense as
that of Germany. It is only the eastern and northern Provinces,
and the steppes of the south, where population is very thin; partly
also the formerly Polish Provinces of the west—Minsk, Mogilev
and Grodno—on account of extensive swamps between the
(Polish) Bug and Dniester. But an advancing army, having in its
rear the corn-producing plains of Poland, Volhynia and Podolia,
and in front, and for its theater of operations, those of Central
Russia, need not be afraid of its subsistence, if it manages the
matter anything like well, and if it learns from the Russians
themselves how to employ the means of transport of the country.
As for a devastation of all resources by the retreating army, as in
1812, such a thing is only possible on one line of operations, and
in its immediate vicinity; and if Napoleon had not, by his hurried
advance from Smolensk, tied himself down to a very short time in
which to complete his campaign, he would have found plenty of

resources around him. But being in a hurry, he could not forage out the country at a short distance from his line of march, and his foraging parties, at that time, appear actually to have been afraid of penetrating far into the immense pine forests which separate village from village. An army which can detach strong cavalry parties to hunt up provisions, and the numerous carts and wagons of the country, can easily provide itself with everything necessary in the shape of food; and it is not likely that Moscow will burn down a second time. But even in that case, a retreat to Smolensk cannot be prevented, and there the army would find its well-prepared base of operation provided with every necessary.

But not only military questions are to be decided. Such a war must be brought to a close by political action too. It is possible that the declaration of Germany against Russia would be the signal for the restoration of Poland by Russia herself. Nicholas would certainly not part with the Lithuanian and other West-Russian provinces; but the kingdom of Poland, Galicia, Posen, and perhaps West and East Prussia, would form a pretty good-sized kingdom. Whether such a revival of Poland would be durable, who can tell? One thing is certain: it would put an end to what is hollow in the enthusiasm for Poland, which, for the last forty years, has been affected by everybody and anybody calling himself liberal or progressive. A Russian appeal to Hungary would be sure to follow; and, if the Magyars should demur, we must not forget that two-thirds of the population of Hungary consists of Slavs, who consider the Magyars as a ruling and intruding aristocracy. On the other hand, Austria would, in such a case, not hesitate to restore the ancient Hungarian Constitution, thus aiming to blot Hungary out of the map of revolutionary Europe.

This suffices to show what a wide perspective of military and political interest would be opened by the accession of Austria to the western alliance, and a chance of a war of all Europe against Russia. On the contrary supposition, the spring is likely to see a million and a half of soldiers arrayed against the Western Powers, and an Austro-Prussian army marching on the French frontiers. And then the management of the war is sure to be taken out of the hands of its present leaders.

Written on December 14 and 15, 1854

First published in the New-York Daily Tribune, No. 4276, January 1; reprinted in the New-York Semi-Weekly Tribune. No. 1002, January 2, 1855 as a leader

Reproduced from the New-York Daily Tribune

Frederick Engels

THE MILITARY POWER OF AUSTRIA[398]

It is a curious fact that the English press, which, for the last six months, has busied itself with nothing but the position of Austria, should never have given us any positive information about the real military force which Austria can throw into the scale the moment she may choose to follow a definite line of policy. The London daily journals have been divided upon the question whether the Austrian alliance or an open rupture with Austria was the preferable thing. But these journals, which represent the public opinion of a nation priding itself upon being the most businesslike in the world, have never condescended to enter into those details and statistics which, not only in trade and political economy, but also in national policy, form the ground-work of every measure intelligently adopted. In truth, the British press would seem to be conducted by gentlemen who are as ignorant in their line of business as those British officers who think they are doing all their duty when they buy a commission.[a] One paper says the Austrian alliance must be cultivated at all hazards and under all circumstances, because Austria is an immense military power. Another says the Austrian alliance is worse than useless, because all her energies are required to keep in check Hungary, Poland and Italy. What the real military forces of Austria are, neither the one nor the other ever trouble themselves to know.

The Austrian army, though managed up to 1849 according to a cumbrous and old-fashioned system, was entirely remodeled in that year. The defeats in Hungary had as great a part in it as the victories in Italy. The Administration was freed from old traditional hindrances. The army, employed in a country where

---

[a] See this volume, p. 210.— *Ed.*

revolution in the capital and civil war in the provinces had only just been subdued, was organized on a regular war footing. The distribution of the army into permanent brigades, divisions, and corps, as it existed under Napoleon, and as it exists now in the Russian active army, was introduced with success. The 77 regiments of infantry, beside riflemen, and 40 regiments of cavalry, which had been split up during both the Italian and Hungarian campaigns, not only battalions of the same regiment, but even companies of the same battalions being employed partly in Hungary and partly in Italy at the same time—were now reunited and brigaded in such a manner as to prevent any similar disorder and to insure the regular course of regimental administration. According to this new plan, the Austrian force is divided into four armies, composed of twelve corps d'armée and two corps of cavalry. Every army is not only complete in the three arms, but provided with a perfectly independent administrative staff, and the material to insure its immediate readiness for action. The first army—1st, 2d, and 9th army corps—generally occupies the German provinces of the Empire; the second army—5th, 6th, 7th and 8th army corps, and 2d cavalry corps, and the third army—10th, 11th and 12th army-corps, and 1st cavalry corps— generally occupy the Hungarian and Slavonic provinces; while the fourth army, consisting only of the 4th army corps, occupies Italy.

Every army corps consists of from two to three divisions of infantry, one or two brigades of cavalry, four batteries of reserve artillery, and the necessary detachments of pontoniers, train-commissariat, and medical officers. A cavalry corps consists of two divisions, equal to four brigades, or eight regiments of cavalry, with a corresponding number of light batteries. An infantry division consists of two brigades of five battalions, with one foot battery each, and from two to four squadrons of cavalry.

The whole force thus distributed consists, as we have stated above, of seventy-seven regiments of infantry, beside riflemen, forty regiments of cavalry, and fourteen regiments of field-artillery, beside garrison-artillery, engineers, sappers, etc. The infantry is composed of sixty-two regiments of the line, fourteen regiments of frontier infantry, and one regiment and twenty-five battalions of riflemen. A regiment of the line consists of five active and one dépôt battalions, or of twenty-eight active and four dépôt companies. The active company numbers two hundred and twenty men, the dépôt company one hundred and thirty. A regiment of the line, consequently, is expected to number, in its five active battalions, 5,964 men, or, for 62 regiments, inclusive of dépôts,

369,800 men. The frontier infantry, counting fourteen regiments, has two active and one reserve battalions to each regiment, equal to twelve active and four reserve companies. The active company has the strength of 242 men, inclusive of 22 riflemen. A frontier regiment, therefore, numbers 3,850 men, and the whole of the fourteen regiments numbers 55,200. The rifle-force, or Jägers, consists of one regiment of seven battalions—32 companies, inclusive of dépôt; and 25 battalions—125 companies, inclusive of dépôts; every company numbering 202 men, making the entire rifle-force 32,500. The total is thus 470,000 men.

The Austrian cavalry consists of 16 heavy regiments (8 cuirassiers and 8 dragoons) and 24 light regiments (12 hussars and 12 lancers). In the arm of cavalry, the different nationalities composing the Austrian Empire have each been used, very properly, according to their distinctive capabilities. The cuirassiers and dragoons are almost exclusively Germans and Bohemians; the hussars are all Hungarians, and the lancers are all Poles. In the infantry a similar distinction could hardly be kept up with any profit. As a general rule, the Germans and Hungarians form the élite battalions of grenadiers, while the Tyrolese (German and Italian) and the Styrians generally furnish the riflemen; and the great majority of the frontier infantry is composed of Croats and Servians, who are equally well adapted to the duties of light infantry.

The heavy cavalry counts six active squadrons and one dépôt squadron to each regiment—the squadron numbering 194 men. The light cavalry counts eight active and one dépôt squadron to each regiment, with 227 men to each squadron. The entire active cavalry force is 62,500, without dépôts, and 67,000 men, including dépôts.

The artillery consists of twelve field regiments, one coast regiment, and one rocket regiment. The Austrians have no horse-artillery. In what they call cavalry-artillery, the men serving the guns are transported on the carriages. Every field regiment has four cavalry batteries (six-pounders) and seven foot batteries (four six-pounders and three twelve-pounders), beside reserve companies. Every battery has eight guns. The coast regiment has no permanent batteries, but is only divided into battalions and companies, and employed for garrisoning the coast defenses. The rocket regiment has 18 batteries, of eight tubes each. The total of Austrian artillery is thus seen to be 1,056 guns and 144 rocket-tubes. The artillery has, besides, eight battalions of garrison artillery, of about 10,400 men, with technical detachments consisting of 4,500 men. The engineering troops number about 16,700 men.

Beside these active, reserve and garrison troops, Austria possesses separate corps organized for special service, who, although not available as active combatants, prevent a reduction of the active force by those drafts of men which very often reduce battalions to companies, and regiments of cavalry to squadrons. There are three sanitary battalions, train-troops, and with every army corps a detachment of cavalry to do duty as orderlies. The latter institution has just been introduced into the English army, by the formation of the Mounted Staff Corps. The whole Austrian army counts altogether something like 476,000 men, and 1,140 guns of active troops; including dépôts, technical troops, staff, garrison and police troops (gendarmes), they count about 620,000.

The Austrian soldier serves eight years, remaining for two years more in the reserve. By this arrangement a reserve is kept available, which, in the case of war, can be called out to the strength of about 120,000 men. In the military frontier every Grenzer[399] has to serve from his twentieth to his fiftieth year. Thus the active force of 55,000 frontier infantry can be increased up to 150,000 or 200,000 men. During the year of 1849 there were at least 150,000 of them under arms. But at that time the military frontier was so deserted that the women had to do all the work of husbandry.

The sum total of these details, for the correctness of which we can vouch, shows that the military organization of Austria allows her to take the field, at once, with a force of 600,000 men, of whom 300,000, at the utmost, may be made available on any given point; and, at the same time, a reserve of about 200,000 veteran soldiers may be called out, without the necessity of any extra recruiting, or extra strain upon the productive forces of the country.

The Russian army is organized upon a footing which allows of far greater numbers being admitted into its framework. The population of Russia is 60,000,000 to Austria's 40,000,000; yet, we have seen that Austria, by merely calling in the reserves, can increase her army beyond 800,000; while Russia, in order to attain the same number, has been obliged not only to call in the reserves, but also to recruit fresh troops, at a ratio equal to four years' regular conscription.

Written on December 21, 1854

First published in the *New-York Daily Tribune*, No. 4281, January 8; reprinted in the *New-York Semi-Weekly Tribune*, No. 1008, January 23 and the *New-York Weekly Tribune*, No. 697, January 27, 1855 as a leader

Reproduced from the *New-York Daily Tribune*

Karl Marx

IN RETROSPECT[400]

I

London, December 29.

"The meeting between Count Buol, M. de Bourqueney and Prince Gorchakov at the home of the Earl of Westmorland, the English Ambassador in Vienna, was solely intended to give the Emperor of Russia the *desired* information as to the meaning of the Triple Alliance of December 2,[401] and as to the conditions under which the three big powers would be ready to open peace negotiations on the basis of the Four Points.[a] Prince Gorchakov immediately reported to Petersburg on the information received. The Tsar must accept or reject the preliminary conditions within the next few days. A decisive turning-point will mark the beginning of the new year."

Thus *The Morning Post*, Lord Palmerston's private *moniteur*,

"The Viennese negotiations," says the Tory *Press*, "are designed to give Austria a new opportunity to postpone its definitive statement to the Western powers on the date fixed in the Agreement of December 2."

It may be a decisive fact that, while politicians are discussing the new Vienna Conference[402] with ponderous political wisdom in the leading articles of both daily and weekly press, businessmen are bluntly calling it a "farce" in the stock-exchange columns of the same papers. Thus, for instance, the businessman in the money article[b] of today's *Morning Post*. Indeed the event at Vienna seemed to be a matter of such indifference to the London Stock Exchange that its publication gave neither bears nor bulls,[403] neither pessimists nor optimists of the stock exchange[b] cause for any action of the least significance. Minor fluctuations in quotations of Government securities during the past three days

---

[a] See this volume, pp. 579-84.— *Ed.*
[b] Marx used the English term.— *Ed.*

were connected not with Vienna diplomacy but with the Paris budget. It is supposed that English capitalists will have a share in the new Paris loan of 500 million francs, and will thus bring about a contraction of the money market which, moreover, looks increasingly dubious, as a result of the repercussions of the North American crisis (*a crisis more important in dimension than that of 1837*), the latest unfavourable business news from East India, the rising prices of grain, and several unexpectedly heavy bankruptcies in London and Liverpool. Illusions of peace prevail, in any case, on the part of the English Ministry, if not of the Tsar of Russia. It was the oligarchy that led the English people into the great war with France which began in the last century. It was the people that forced the English oligarchy into the current war with Russia. The reluctance of the oligarchy to conduct this war, which was forced upon it, is clearly visible in all its diplomatic, military and financial operations. Even the latest measure of the Ministry—the law concerning the recruiting of a foreign legion[404]—was, above all, designed to make the English "*dislike*" the war. There can be no question of the recruiting pool being exhausted in a country from where more than 100,000 able-bodied men emigrate annually without that emigration having a more than temporary effect on the wage level. And there was just as little question of providing an exceptional and sudden supply of auxiliary troops, since the ministerial measure is not calculated to help either suddenly or by way of exception. The Militia Bill passed in May empowered the Ministry to call up 80,000 soldiers in England and Wales alone, and the result has shown that a full quarter of the volunteers in all regiments called up in the spring opted for active service, yet up to the beginning of this month the Government had mobilised only eighteen militia regiments (approximately 13,500 men). It is well known that Englishmen have always protested against the introduction of foreign mercenaries into Great Britain—they have done so at the time of Charles I, under William III, under the early Georges,[a] and finally, during the great anti-Jacobin war. But it is new and unheard-of in English history for the use of foreign mercenaries outside English territory to arouse a storm of indignation. This very fact proves how *wholly different the character* of the present war is from all former English wars, as far as they belong to modern times. The ruling aristocracy is therefore deliberately conjuring up the spectre of the past, the long-standing practice of its agents, whereby soldiers would be bought in the

---

[a] George I and George II.— *Ed.*

cheapest market. It does this—as Sidney Herbert *admitted* in the House of Commons—without being in any way convinced of the *success* of the proposed measure.[a] It does this therefore not to wage war, but to prepare for peace. Today, in order to create an adequate *English* army, the Government would be compelled to increase pay, abolish corporal punishment, hold out the prospect of advancement from the ranks, in brief, to democratise the army and to transform it from its own property into the property of the nation. Up to now, says today's *Times*,

"in war, and in peace, the army is only a Government organ for the advancement of the aristocracy and the support of the Ministry."[b]

And here we come to the crucial point. For the English aristocracy *war with Russia* is equivalent to the *loss of its monopoly of government*. Forced since 1830 to conduct its internal policy exclusively in the interests of the industrial and commercial middle classes, the English aristocracy has nevertheless retained possession of all government posts, because it has retained the monopoly of *foreign* policy and of the army.

This monopoly, however, has remained secure only as long as there was no people's war—and such a war was possible *only against Russia*—which would make foreign policy the concern of the people. The whole of English diplomacy from 1830 to 1854, therefore, can be reduced to the one principle: to avoid war with Russia at *all* costs. Hence the continual concessions which have been made to Russia in Turkey, in Persia, in Afghanistan, in Denmark, and, indeed, everywhere in the world, for the past twenty-four years. That the aristocracy has calculated correctly is proved by the actual facts. War with Russia has hardly broken out when even *The Times* declares:

"The aristocracy is incapable of conducting our wars. The oligarchic state machinery stands in the sharpest contradiction to our social machinery."

II

London, January 1.

"Under the pressure of the present war our military departments [...] have completely broken down."[c]

---

[a] Sidney Herbert's speech in the House of Commons on December 19, 1854. *The Times*, No. 21929, December 20, 1854.— *Ed.*

[b] *The Times*, No. 21938, December 30, 1854, leader.— *Ed.*

[c] *The Times*, No. 21939, January 1, 1855, leader.— *Ed.*

Thus today's *Times*. Indeed, if one considers the organisation of the military administration, or any other official administration in this country, it would seem as though it had been intended to serve as a concrete example of the so-called principle of the constitutional balance of power. The different authorities have been co-ordinated in such a way that they keep each other completely in check, and the entire machinery is therefore bound to grind to a halt. That is why, during the present war, it was possible for the wounded soldiers to be at Balaklava, the military surgeons at Constantinople and medical supplies at Scutari. Hence the revolt of the Crimean army against a system which sacrifices it; for must we not call it a revolt when all ranks, from colonel down to private, commit breaches of discipline, writing thousands of letters to the London press every week and appealing to public opinion against their superiors? However, Lord Raglan is unjustly made responsible for a state of affairs which is conditioned by the system. What he is responsible for is military leadership.

Casting a retrospective glance at the Crimean campaign, we find that Lord Raglan made his first mistake during the battle of the Alma by ordering that the Russian army's left wing, which was covered by the sea, should be outflanked instead of its right. By the latter operation, one section of the Russians would have been pushed towards the sea and the other towards the North Fort, whereas now they have, in fact, been flung on Simferopol, i.e. on the line of retreat most favourable to them. While during the battle of the Alma the Allies took the bull by the horns to no purpose whatever, they shrank from taking that step when circumstances demanded it. The famous "outflanking march to Balaklava" was the abandonment of an attack on the northern front of the fortress; this front, however, is the commanding, and therefore the crucial, point; the North Fort is the key to Sevastopol. Thus the Allies gave up the bolder, and therefore in fact the safer, offensive in order to secure a strong defensive position.

The same mistake was made by Omer Pasha when he entrenched himself near Kalafat instead of marching from Oltenitza on Bucharest, breaking through the enemy's extended lines. Then came the siege of Sevastopol, proving, at any rate, that as a result of a long peace the art of war has deteriorated to the same degree as, thanks to industrial development, war materials have improved. Never before has there been a war where simple earthworks have played so important a role. It was at Oltenitza that the Russians first had recourse, albeit unsuccessfully, to the old system of bombarding them for several hours before making an assault. At Kalafat, earthworks which they did not dare attack kept the Russians in check. At Silistria, a half-demolished earthwork frustrated all the efforts of the Russian army, and now, at Sevastopol, a line of earthworks was favoured by more extensive assault batteries and heavy artillery than had ever before been used against a regular fortress. However, even before the siege-train had been set up, the open city had been transformed into a first-rate fortified camp. It is known that in the battle of Balaklava, on October 25, the English cavalry had been sacrificed against all rhyme and reason and contrary to all accepted rules. Finally, we come to the battle of Inkerman, the most important military event of this campaign. Like the Prussians at Jena, British troops before Inkerman were drawn up on a number of hillocks which, at the front, were accessible only through a few defiles. Like the Prussians, the British had neglected to occupy a hillock on their extreme left wing, and it was there that, like Napoleon at Jena,[405] Menshikov at Inkerman flung a part of his army, thus establishing himself in the enemy flank before daybreak. The Russians, never given to original ideas, borrowed Napoleon's plan of operation, but, as soon as the strategic movement was completed and the tactical performance had to begin, the mask of Western civilisation was dropped and the Tartar emerged. This magnificent Russian army with its old soldiers—many of them of twenty-five years' standing—these models of parade-ground drill, shows itself so clumsy, so ponderous, so incapable of skirmishing and fighting in small units, that its officers can think of nothing better to do with it than to fling its heavy mass at the enemy in one fell swoop. The sheer brutal pressure of this mass was meant to break the thin ranks of the British, while on the one hand these deep columns of human flesh ensured the unfailing and devastating effect of the English rifles[a] and artillery, and on the other hand, where an overwhelming number of Russians made bayonet attacks, the British received them with the same superiority as Napoleon's squares received the Mamelukes in the battle of the Pyramids.[406] Fourteen thousand Allied soldiers, with a loss of one-third of their total strength, defeated 30,000 Russians, although it is acknowledged that individually the Russians fought valiantly, and that their plan of attack was superior to that of the Allies. Never since the battle of Narva has such a disaster befallen Russian arms. And if we consider the extraordinary difference

---

[a] Marx used the English word.— *Ed.*

between the Russians of Narva and the Russians of Inkerman, between the half-savage hordes of 1700 and the well-drilled army of 1854, the day of Narva seems brilliant compared to that of Inkerman. Narva was the first great disaster of a rising nation which knew how to turn even defeats into means of victory. Inkerman appears almost as the certain indication of a decline in that hot-house development which Russia had undergone since Peter the Great. The artificially accelerated growth, and the tremendous effort of maintaining with semi-barbaric means the semblance of a brilliant civilisation seem to have already exhausted the nation and to have inflicted upon it some kind of consumption. The battle of Inkerman is for the Russian infantry what the battle of Rocroi was for the Spanish infantry.[407]

Written on December 29, 1854 and January 1, 1855

Printed according to the newspaper

First published in the *Neue Oder-Zeitung*. Nos. 1 and 5, January 2 and 4, 1855

Published in English for the first time

Karl Marx

THE PRESS AND THE MILITARY SYSTEM

London, January 3. A correspondent of *The Times* writes from the encampment at Sevastopol:

"It is said that the Emperor Nicholas engages to send all that are left of us in the spring away in a *single* line-of-battle ship."[a]

There follows a graphic description of the mortality, distress, disorder and disintegration prevailing in the English camp. Today this state of affairs provides almost the exclusive subject for the leading articles in London's daily press.

"The British army," says *The Times,* "is found to be no army at all in the general military sense of the word. It is a mob of brave men, not more than a mob, and rather less, inasmuch as it is evidently commanded by those who should not command it, and so deprived of its rude natural efficiency.... The command of the British army before Sevastopol is worse than a mere name... it is deliberately asserted by officers of distinction that the army might just as well be commanded by its sergeants as by the men who pretend to command it. We are aware that it is a painful act to supersede brave and loyal men, full of honours and years."[b]

However, *à la guerre comme à la guerre.*

"If there ever was a Ministry that had its path open for such a measure it is the present."

Why?

"Because it put off the war as long as it could," that is why the "Government surely has the game in its own hands, and is bound by no respect of persons."

---

[a] Letter of a British army officer from the encampment at Sevastopol dated December 12, 1854. *The Times,* No. 21941, January 3, 1855.— *Ed.*

[b] *The Times,* No. 21941, January 3, 1855, leader.— *Ed.*

Well roared, lion![a] It is because the present Ministry is conducting the war with Russia against its own will that mistakes in the conduct of the war cannot be ascribed to it, but must be blamed on the commanding general, and the public must understand that it is not the Ministry that stands in Lord Raglan's way, but Lord Raglan who stands in the way of the Ministry.

While *The Times* thus attacks Lord Raglan in order to shield the Ministry, *The Morning Chronicle*, the Peelite organ, attacks *The Times*, ostensibly to defend Lord Raglan, but really so as gratefully to accept *The Times* admission of the Ministry's innocence, to exploit it, and, at the same time, to create a diversion by a sham fight between two ministerial organs.

According to the worthy *Chronicle*:

"The despondency which has enveloped public opinion for the last few days, must, we regret to write it, be attributed to the sole influence of *The Times*. Events have been blackened, disasters exaggerated, the well-earned reputations of our general officers aspersed, and the Briton's proverbial generosity towards the absent disdained, with the sole view of causing a sensation—of creating an effect. It is, however, on the head of Field-Marshal Lord Raglan that the rancour and venom of these attacks have been accumulated.... The distress to which the army in the Crimea was reduced from the commencement of December until the last accounts, which are more favourable, must chiefly be attributed to the terrible hurricane of the 13th of November...."[b]

And the Ministry is magnanimous enough not to blame Lord Raglan for the hurricane of November 13. So all that is left is the claptrap of *The Times*.

Now we come to that section of the London press which represents certain *special* interests *within* the Ministry, that is, *The Daily News*, for some time *Palmerston's* secret organ, and *The Morning Post* which, for years, has been his official organ.

"Our administrative systems," says *The Daily News*, "are nearly as unchangeable as if they had been contrived by the Medes and Persians. [...] let an unforeseen crisis impend—and they utterly and disastrously break down. Yet in face of the most appalling sacrifices of life and property they are seldom so changed or modified as to enable them to meet similar catastrophes in future.... It is nearly the same now with the War Department. It was hoped that, when a Minister of War[c] was appointed, all the active business of the army would be concentrated under his responsible management.... Up to this day not a single abuse has it reformed, not [...] a particle of improvement has it effected.... Shall we blame the Duke of Newcastle? or shall we not rather strike at a deeper root, and aim the axe of Reform at the paralysing system, [...] a system that confines the functions of the state to the [...] 'cold shade of aristocracy'? ... In truth, whatever the merits of the Duke of Newcastle may be, he is not the *official Hercules* to be able to extinguish

---

[a] Shakespeare, *A Midsummer Night's Dream*, Act V, Scene 1.— Ed.
[b] *The Morning Chronicle*, No. 27464, January 3, 1855, leader.— Ed.
[c] The Duke of Newcastle.— Ed.

the system... but what he cannot do, the [...] people of England will insist upon having done."[a]

The Daily News is still new in its ministerial role. Besides, it has to take into account its bourgeois public. Nevertheless, one realises at first sight that the point of the article is the "official Hercules" who is needed. And who is this official Hercules? And how is one to come by him? *The Morning Post* provides the answer. It says:

"To begin by attacking Lord Raglan is certainly commencing at the wrong end, [...] Lord Raglan is" *above* the attacks of *The Times*.... But, "there can be no doubt about the shortcomings of the Government at home.... Take simply the War Department, is it to be conducted throughout in the spirit and after the model of the last nine months?... Let it be remembered that the army abroad is entirely at the mercy of the Administration at home.... Of what terrible importance is it, then, that the head of this department have a master mind, and work like a master.... *The old system*, it is said, stands in the way. But the master mind would, ere this, have kicked the system to the winds on his own responsibility.... The secret is, that the head of the Government is a dead weight upon Departmental exertion. The slow movement of the *Aberdeen* pulse communicates itself to every member of the Administration and gives its tone and time to the whole system.... The whole be re-cast, and a real and vigorous head put upon its shoulders."[b]

In other words: make Palmerston Prime Minister. He is the *official Hercules* of whom *The Daily News* has been dreaming, the same Palmerston whom Lord Melbourne, at the suggestion of the Russian Princess Lieven, appointed Foreign Secretary in 1830; who, in the Afghan war,[408] had sacrificed a British army in so mysterious a manner that Sir Robert Peel, in a public session of the House of Commons, threatened him with "revelations"[c] if he [Lord Palmerston] continued to provoke him with his boasting: the same Palmerston who was able to steer the offensive alliance *against Russia* proposed by France in 1839 and apparently already operative so adroitly that one fine day in 1840 it had been transformed into an Anglo-Russian alliance *against France*.[409] Although Palmerston is the *most influential* member of the present Administration, who acts, and *must* act, as its champion in all parliamentary circles, he continually summons up all his diplomatic skill to appear in the press as the determined opponent of Aberdeen and thus to preserve his popularity should the Coalition be wrecked. At the same time, the opposition is kept *from* taking decisive steps and kept *in* a state of futile tension about the internal quarrels of the Ministry. For instance, today, for the

---

[a] *The Daily News*, No. 2691, January 3, 1855.— *Ed.*

[b] *The Morning Post*, No. 25274, January 3, 1855, leader.— *Ed.*

[c] Sir Peel's speech in the House of Commons on August 10, 1842. *Hansard's Parliamentary Debates*, third series, Vol. 65, London, 1842, pp. 1268-90.— *Ed.*

hundredth time the Tory *Morning Herald* has fallen into the trap by declaring the breaking up of the Coalition to be final and talking at great length about the patriotic indignation of Palmerston and Russell against Aberdeen, Newcastle and Gladstone.[a] Ad vocem[b] *Gladstone*, it should be noted that, according to a leading article about the French loan in today's *Chronicle*,[c] Gladstone does not intend resorting to loans, but is determined to conduct the war through direct taxation, that is to say, in the most unpopular, oppressive and uneconomical form.

Written on January 3, 1855

First published in the *Neue Oder-Zeitung*, No. 9, January 6, 1855

Printed according to the newspaper

Published in English for the first time

---

[a] *The Morning Herald*, No. 22319, January 3, 1855, leader.— *Ed.*
[b] With regard to.— *Ed.*
[c] *The Morning Chronicle*, No. 27464, January 3, 1855, leader.— *Ed.*

Frederick Engels

BRITISH DISASTER IN THE CRIMEA[410]

The entire British public, starting from the recent vehement leaders of *The London Times*,[a] seems to be in a state of great anxiety and excitement respecting the condition of the forces in the Crimea. Indeed, it is impossible longer to deny or palliate the fact that, through unparalleled mismanagement in every branch of the service, the British army is rapidly approaching a state of dissolution. Exposed to the hardships of a winter campaign, suffering cold and wet, with the most harassing and uninterrupted field duty without clothing, food, tents, or housing, the veterans who braved the burning sun of India and the furious charges of the Beloodshis and Afghan, die away by hundreds daily, and as fast as reenforcements arrive, they are eaten up by the ravages of disease. To the question who is to blame for this state of things the reply just now most popular in England is that it is Lord Raglan, but this is not just. We are no admirers of his Lordship's military conduct, and have criticised his blunders with freedom,[b] but truth requires us to say that the terrible evils amid which the soldiers in the Crimea are perishing are not his fault, but that of the system on which the British war establishment is adminis-tered.

The British Army has a Commander-in-Chief, a personage dispensed with in almost all other civilized armies. But it would be a mistake to suppose that this commander-in-chief really com-

---

[a] *The Times*, No. 21941, January 3, 1855, leader.— *Ed.*
[b] See this volume, pp. 474 and 507-08.— *Ed.*

mands anything. If he has some control over the infantry and cavalry, the artillery, engineers, sappers and miners are entirely beyond his sphere. If he has any authority over trowsers, coatees, and socks, all great-coats are exempt from his influence. If he can make every foot-soldier carry two cartridge-pouches, he cannot find him a single musket. If he can have all his men tried by court-martial and well flogged, he cannot make them stir a single inch. Marching is beyond his competency, and as to feeding his troops, that is a thing which does not concern him at all.

Then there is the Master-General of the Ordnance. This person, a lamentable relic of the times when science was considered unsoldierlike, and when all scientific corps, artillery and engineers, were not soldiers, but a sort of nondescript body, half savants, half handicraftsmen, and united in a separate guild or corporation, under the command of such a Master-General. This Master-General of the Ordnance, beside artillery and engineers, has under him all the great-coats and small-arms of the army. To any military operation, of whatever nature, he must, therefore, be a party.

Next comes the Secretary at War. If the two preceding characters were already of comparative nullity, he is beyond nullity. The Secretary at War can give no order to any part of the army, but he can prevent any portion of the army from doing anything. As he is the chief of the military finances, and as every military act costs money, his refusal to grant funds is equivalent to an absolute veto upon all operations. But, willing as he may be to grant the funds, he is still a nullity, for he cannot feed the army; that is beyond his sphere. In addition to all this, the Commissariat, which really feeds the army, and, in case of any movement, is supposed to find it means of transport, is placed under the control of the Treasury. Thus, the Prime Minister, the first lord of the Treasury, has a direct hand in the getting up of every military operation, and can at his pleasure either push it, retard it, or stop it. Everybody knows that the Commissariat is almost a more important portion of the army than the soldiers themselves; and for this very reason, the collective wisdom of Great Britain has thought proper to make it quite independent of the army, and to place it under the control of an essentially different Department. Finally, the army, formerly put in motion by the Colonial Secretary, is now subject to the orders of the new War-Minister.[a]

---

[a] See this volume, pp. 227-28.— *Ed.*

He dislocates the troops, from England to China, and from India to Canada. But, as we have seen, his authority, taken singly, is as ineffectual as that of any of the four preceding military powers; the cooperation of all the five being required, in order to bring about the least movement.

It was under the auspices of this wonderful system that the present war began. The British troops, well fed and well cared for at home, in consequence of a forty years' peace, went out in high condition, persuaded that whatever the enemy might do, England would not let her gallant lads want for anything. But scarcely had they landed at their first stage, at Gallipoli, when the comparison with the French army showed the ludicrous inferiority of all British arrangements, and the pitiable helplessness of every British official. Although it was here comparatively easy to provide for everything, although sufficient notice had been given, and a very small body of troops only was sent out, everything went wrong. Everybody made himself very busy, and yet nobody would perform duties that had not fallen to his lot at home in time of peace, so that not a man was to be found to do that business which was created by the very war itself. Thus shiploads of stores were left to rot on the shore where they were first landed, and troops had to be sent on to Scutari for want of room. Chaotic disorder announced itself in unmistakable signs, but as it was the beginning of the war, an improvement was expected from growing experience.

The troops went to Varna. Their distance from home increased, their number increased, the disorder in the administration increased. The independent working of the five departments composing that administration, each of them responsible to a different Minister at home, here first resulted in open and unmistakable clashing. Want reigned in the camp, while the garrison of Varna had the best of comforts. The Commissariat, lazily indeed, got together some means of transport from the country; but as the General-in-Chief[a] did not appoint any escort wagons, the Bulgarian drivers disappeared again as fast as they had been brought together. A central dépôt was formed at Constantinople—a sort of first base of operations; but it served no purpose except to create a fresh center of difficulties, delays, questions of competency, quarrels between the army, the Ordnance, the paying staff, the Commissariat, and the War Office.

---

[a] Hardinge.— Ed.

Wherever anything was to be done, everybody tried to shove it off his own shoulders upon those of somebody else. The avoiding of all responsibility was the general aim. The consequence was that everything went wrong, and that nothing whatever was done. Disgust at these proceedings, and the certainty of seeing his army rot in inactivity, may have had some influence in determining Lord Raglan to risk the expedition to the Crimea.

This expedition crowned the success of John Bull's military organization. There, in the Crimea, came the "decided hit." So long as the army was, in point of fact, in a state of peace, as at Gallipoli, Scutari and Varna, the magnitude of the disorder, the complicity of the confusion, could hardly be expected fully to develop itself. But now, in the face of the enemy, during the course of an actual siege, the case was different. The resistance of the Russians gave full scope to the British officials for the exercise of their business-like habits. And it must be confessed, never was the business of destroying an army done more effectually than by these gentlemen. Of more than 60,000 men sent to the East since February last, not more than 17,000 are now fit for duty; and of these, some 60 or 80 die daily, and about 200 or 250 are every day disabled by sickness, while of those that fall sick, hardly any recover. And out of the 43,000 dead or sick, not 7,000 have been disabled by the direct action of the enemy!

When it first was reported in England that the army in the Crimea wanted food, clothing, housing, everything; that neither medical nor surgical stores were on the spot; that the sick and wounded had either to lie on the cold, wet ground, exposed to the weather, or to be crowded on board ships moored in an open roadstead, without attendance, or the simplest requisites for medical treatment; when it was reported that hundreds were dying for want of the first necessaries; everybody believed that the Government had neglected to send proper supplies to the scene of action. But soon enough, it became known, that if this had been partially the case in the beginning, it was not so now. Everything had been sent there even in profusion; but, unfortunately, nothing ever happened to be where it was wanted. The medical stores were at Varna, while the sick and wounded were either in the Crimea or at Scutari; the clothing and provisions arrived in sight of the Crimea, but there was nobody to land them. Whatever by chance got landed, was left to rot on the beach. The necessary cooperation of the naval force brought a fresh element of dissension to bear upon the already distracted councils of the Departments whose conflicts were to insure triumph to the British army. Incapacity, sheltered by regulations made for peace, reigned supreme; in one of the richest countries of Europe, on the sheltered coast of which hundreds of transports laden with stores lay at anchor, the British army lived upon half-rations; surrounded by numberless herds of cattle, they had to suffer from scurvy, in consequence of being restricted to salt meat; with plenty of wood and coal on board ship, they had so little of it on shore that they had to eat their meat *raw*, and could never dry the clothes which the rain had drenched. Think of serving out the coffee, not only unground, but even unroasted. There were stores of food, of drink, of clothing, of tents, of ammunition, by tuns and hundreds of tuns, stowed away on board the ships, whose masts almost touched the tops of the cliffs, where the camp was placed; and yet, Tantalus-like, the British troops could not get at them. Everybody felt the evil, everybody ran about, cursing and blaming everybody else for neglect of duty, but nobody knew, to use the vernacular expression, "which was which;" for everybody had his own set of regulations carefully drawn up, sanctioned by the competent authority, and showing that the very thing wanted was no part of *his* duty, and that *he*, for one, had no power to set the matter right.

Now, add to this state of things the increasing inclemency of the season, the heavy rains setting in and transforming the whole Heracleatic Chersonese into one uninterrupted pool of mud and slush, knee-deep if not more; imagine the soldiers, two nights at least out of four in the trenches, the other two sleeping, drenched and dirty, in the slush, without boards under them, and with hardly any tents over them; the constant alarms completing the impossibility of anything like proper rest and adequate sleep; the cramps, diarrhea and other maladies arising from constant wet and cold; the dispersion of the medical staff, weak though it was from the beginning, over the camp; the hospital-tents, with 3,000 sick almost in the open air and lying on the wet earth, and it will be easily believed that the British army in the Crimea is in a state of complete disorganization—reduced to "a mob of brave men," as *The London Times* says,[a] and that the soldiers may well welcome the Russian bullet which frees them from all their miseries.

But what is to be done? Why, unless you prefer waiting till half a dozen acts of Parliament are, after due consideration by the

---

[a] *The Times*, No. 21941, January 3, 1855, leader.— *Ed.*

Crown lawyers, discussed, amended, voted on and enacted—till, by this means, the whole business connected with the army is concentrated in the hands of a real War Minister—till this new Minister—supposing him to be the right man—has organized the service of his office, and issued fresh regulations—in other words, unless you wait till the last vestige of the Crimean army has disappeared, there is only one remedy. This is the assumption by the General-in-Chief of the expedition[a] upon his own authority, and his own responsibility, of that dictatorship over all the conflicting and contending departments of the military administration which every other General-in-Chief possesses, and without which he cannot bring the enterprise to any end but ruin. That would soon make matters smooth; but where is the British General who would be prepared to act in this Roman manner, and on his trial defend himself, like the Roman, with the words, "Yes, I plead guilty to having saved my country?"[b]

Finally, we must inquire who is the founder and preserver of this beautiful system of administration? Nobody but the old Duke of Wellington. He stuck to every detail of it as if he was personally interested in making it as difficult as possible to his successors to rival him in warlike glory. Wellington, a man of eminent common sense, but of no genius whatever, was the more sensible of his own deficiencies in this respect, from being the cotemporary and opponent of the eminent genius of Napoleon. Wellington, therefore, was full of envy for the success of others. His meanness in disparaging the merits of his auxiliaries and allies is well known; he never forgave Blücher for saving him at Waterloo. Wellington

---

[a] Raglan.— *Ed.*

[b] In the *Neue Oder-Zeitung* the next paragraph reads as follows: "The *origin* of this system lies apparently in constitutional precautions against a standing army. Instead of a *division of labour*, which would have given the army the greatest elasticity, a *division of authority*, which reduces its mobility to a minimum. Yet the system was by no means maintained for parliamentary or constitutional considerations, but because the influence of the oligarchy would be broken at least in this field, simultaneously with a timely reform of military administration. In the preceding session of Parliament, the Ministers had refused to allow any innovation except the separation of the Ministry of War from the Ministry of the Colonies. Wellington obstinately maintained the system from 1815 until his death, although he knew very well that *with* the system he would never have brought the Spanish war to a successful close had not his brother, the Marquis of Wellesley, by chance been the Minister. In 1832 and 1836, before the commissions instituted by Parliament for a reform of the old system, Wellington defended the old system to its full extent. Was he afraid to make it easier for his successors to gain fame?"— *Ed.*

knew full well that had not his brother[a] been Minister during the Spanish war, he never could have brought it to a successful close. Was Wellington afraid that future exploits would place him in the shade, and did he therefore preserve to its full extent this machinery so well adapted to fetter generals and to ruin armies?

Written on January 4, 1855

First published in the *Neue Oder-Zeitung*, Nos. 11 and 13, January 8 and 9 and in the *New-York Daily Tribune*, No. 4293, January 22; reprinted in the *New-York Weekly Tribune*, No. 698, January 27, 1855 as a leader

Reproduced from the *New-York Daily Tribune* checked with the *Neue Oder-Zeitung*

---

[a] Richard Wellesley.— *Ed.*

Karl Marx

[THE CRISIS IN TRADE AND INDUSTRY][411]

I

London, January 8. While clubs and newspapers here are fully occupied with self-important gossip about "ministerial crises", they have no time to realise the far more important fact that *once again one of the great British crises in trade and industry has broken out*, and in more calamitous dimensions than in 1847 and 1836. At long last this realisation—which had not been produced even by the bankruptcies which have been breaking out sporadically for the past three months and recently increased in number and intensity—has become unavoidable as a result of the publication of the annual trade reports and of the tables issued by the Board of Trade[a] which give the export and import figures for the past eleven months.[b] It follows from these figures that exports have decreased by £1,710,677, if compared with the corresponding eleven months of the year 1853, and by £1,856,988 when only the last month of both years—November 5 to December 5—is compared. From the export figures we have taken the following details which show a decline in some of the most important branches of industry:

---

[a] Marx used the English term.— *Ed.*

[b] "Accounts Relating to Trade and Navigation for the Eleven Months Ended 5th December 1854. III. Exports of British and Irish Produce and Manufactures from the United Kingdom", *The Economist*, No. 593, January 6, 1855.— *Ed.*

	1853 £	1854 £
Cotton manufacture	23,757,155	22,877,050
Cotton yarn	6,322,639	6,055,640
Linen manufacture	4,379,732	3,735,221
Linen yarn	1,069,812	852,763
Wool manufacture	9,470,413	8,566,723
Silk manufacture	1,492,785	1,144,506
Export of machinery	1,368,027	1,271,503

In the *trade reports* an attempt is of course made to blame the war for the crisis of 1854, just as the revolution of 1848 was blamed for a crisis which had already broken out in 1847. However, this time even the London *Economist*—which, as a matter of principle, tends to explain all crises as due to accidental circumstances, extraneous to trade and industry—has been forced to admit that the commercial misfortunes and losses of 1854 are the beginning of a natural reaction against the "convulsive prosperity" of 1853. In other words, the commercial cycle has again reached the point where overproduction and over-speculation turn into a crisis. Most effective proof: *the United States of North America*, which were affected by the oriental war [412] only insofar as it gave an unheard-of impetus to shipbuilding and shipping trade, and created markets for many American raw products formerly supplied exclusively by Russia. In the United States the crisis has already lasted more than four months and is still growing steadily, although already 109 of 4,208 banks, or about $2^1/_2$ per cent, have gone bankrupt; moreover, there has been such a stagnation of industry combined with such a depression of wages in the industrial states of the East that last month more than 4,000 European immigrants *"migrated back" to Europe*. The American crisis of 1837 *followed* on the British crisis of 1836. This time the course is reversed. America has taken the initiative in the matter of bankruptcies. The United States and Australia are equally flooded with British products. How important this is for British trade can be seen from the fact that out of approximately £100 million which Great Britain exported in the form of goods in 1853, £25 million went to the United States and £15 million to Australia. After the United States and Australia, the East Indies were the most important export market. However, even in 1852 the East Indies were so glutted that only by an entirely new expansion of trade across the Punjab and Sind to Bokhara, Afghanistan and Baluchistan and from there, on the one hand, to Central Asia, and on the other hand to Persia, could exports with difficulty be kept at the old level of £8 million. Now even in those areas all outlets are so congested that, a short while ago, goods were shipped from Hindustan to Australia, thus "carrying coals to Newcastle". The only market which, due to the oriental war, was for a time supplied "cautiously", was the *Levantine* market. However, it is an open secret in the City that, since the crisis in the United States and stagnation in Australia forced the commercial world to look out anxiously for any markets not yet glutted, Constantinople has become the store-house for all goods requiring buyers, and it, too, must now be considered as "closed". Similarly, the most recent movement in Spain has been used to smuggle in as much British merchandise as the country can hold. The last attempt of this kind is now being made in South American countries whose very small consumer capacity requires no proof.

In view of the vital importance of the British crisis for the social and political state of the whole world, it will be necessary to return at greater length and in more detail to the history of British trade before 1854.

II

London, January 9. The increase of British trade and of British industry in the period 1849 to 1853 may be judged by the following figures. In 1846 the tonnage of ships carrying goods from and into British seaports amounted to 9,499,000, in 1850 this had increased to 12,020,000 tons, and in 1853 to no less than 15,381,000, exactly double the tonnage of 1843. In 1846 the value of exported British manufactured goods and raw materials was £57,786,000, in 1850 £71,367,000, and in 1853 more than £98,000,000, that is to say, more than double the total exports of 1842. What part is played by the United States of North America and by Australia in this increase in exports? In 1842, the value of British exports to Australia amounted to less than £1,000,000, in 1850 they reached almost three million, and in 1853 as much as £14,513,000. In 1842, exports to the United States amounted to £3,582,000, in 1850 to almost 15 million, and in 1853 to no less than £23,658,000.

From these figures it follows, first of all, that the year 1854 represents a turning-point in the history of modern trade, analogous to the years 1825, 1836 and 1847; secondly, that the crisis in the United States is only a factor of the British crisis, and finally that the war of 1854—called, most aptly, *une guerre pacifique* by the *Pays, Journal de l'Empire*—has exercised no influence whatever on this social catastrophe, or, if any influence at all, it has been restricting and inhibiting. Individual branches of industry, e.g. the manufacture of leather, iron and woollen goods, as well as ship-building, have actually been helped by the demand created by the war. For a short time, the consternation caused by a declaration of war after forty years of peace, paralysed the flight of speculation. The loans of various European countries brought about by the war kept interest rates at a level which prevented rash industrial undertakings and thus retarded the crisis. However, says the Peace Society,[a][413] has not the war raised corn prices? Is not the rising of corn prices tantamount to a decline in domestic trade,[a] i.e. in British consumption of industrial products? And is not this contraction of the *home* market the main element of the crisis?—To begin with, it must be remembered that the year of greatest British prosperity—1853—was a year of *high* corn prices, and that corn prices of 1854 range, on average, *below* those of 1853, so that neither the prosperity of 1853 nor the crisis symptoms of 1854 can be explained from the level of corn prices. However, leaving aside the influence of corn prices on industry for the time being: what influence has the war had on corn prices? In other words: have corn prices risen, because supplies from Russia have dropped? Of the total corn and flour which Great Britain imports, Russia's share is about 19 per cent, and as total imports satisfy only about 20 per cent of national consumption, Russia supplies some $2^1/_2$ per cent of national consumption.

The *latest official* report on the comparative corn and flour imports from different continents and countries to Great Britain was published at the beginning of November 1854,[b] giving a comparative table for the first nine months of 1853 and 1854. According to this, in 1853 the total imports of wheat amounted to 3,770,921 quarters, of which 773,507 came from Russia and 209,000 quarters from Moldavia and Wallachia. Total imports of flour amounted to 3,800,746 hundredweights, of which Russia supplied 64 and the Danubian Principalities none at all. In the war year 1854, Great Britain received 505,000 quarters of wheat from Russia and 118,000 quarters from Moldavia and Wallachia. No one would wish to claim that *this* reduction (which, moreover, was

---

[a] Marx used the English phrase.— *Ed.*
[b] "The Supplies of Wheat, Home and Foreign", *The Economist*, No. 584, November 4, 1854.— *Ed.*

offset by larger imports of flour from other countries) has pushed up the prices of the *excellent* harvest of 1854 to approximately the level of the *bad* years, 1852 and 1853. On the contrary. Even a *total* cessation of Russian grain imports would not have had that effect. What remains enigmatic—although *unimportant* as far as the economic question is concerned—is the reduction of supplies from the *Danubian Principalities*. The solution of the riddle is simple. Though *nominally* the Coalition has blockaded the *Russian* Black Sea ports, *in fact,* however, it has blockaded first the Bosphorus and later the mouth of the Danube; instead of Russia, it blockaded Turkey and the Danubian Principalities. The Russian crusades against the Crescent—of 1812, 1828, 1848 (at that time reputedly against the *rebels* of Jassy and Bucharest) and 1854— were, as everyone knows, partly determined by trade competition of the southern Russian provinces against the Danubian Principalities and, incidentally, against the Danube trade of Bosnia, Serbia and Bulgaria. What a *stroke of genius*, therefore, on the part of an *English* Ministry to punish Russia by leaving her trade at Odessa and Taganrog free, but suppressing, blockading the trade of *Russia's competitors* on the Danube, thus cutting off their own [i.e. England's] supplies.

III

London, January 16. With reference to the present crisis in trade and industry, the London *Economist* remarks:

"Whatever may be the falling off in the export of other articles, there is none in machinery. The value in 1854 exceeds the value in 1853. Other countries, therefore, are now taking into use our machinery. We have no longer any advantage of this kind over them. France, Germany, Belgium, Holland, Switzerland, and the United States are all now great manufacturing countries; and some of them have advantages over us. We have a race to run, and we cannot succeed if we tie our legs. [...] Experience has satisfied every person that the restrictions imposed for the benefit of the landlord injured him, that restrictions imposed for the benefit of the master manufacturers injured them; and by and by the factory workers will find out that the restriction imposed for their benefit will injure them. It is to be hoped, however, that they will find it out before the countries before mentioned have made such progress as to supersede England in their own and third markets, and have reduced the factory hands to destitution."[a]

Mr. *Wilson,* editor of *The Economist* and factotum in the Ministry of Finance of the anointed and unctuous Mr. Gladstone, apostle of freedom and place-hunter rolled into one, a man who in one

---

[a] "Exports.—The Factory Act", *The Economist*, No. 594, January 13, 1855.— *Ed.*

column of his paper denies the necessity of the state in general and in another proves the indispensability of the coalition government in particular—Mr. Wilson, then, begins his homily with a deliberately distorted fact. The export tables for 1854[a] contain two columns on the export of machinery. The first, relating to railway locomotives, shows that in 1853 exports amounted to £443,254, but in 1854 to £525,702 which is undoubtedly an increase of £82,448. The second column, however, which includes all machines used in factories, i.e. every kind of machinery except locomotives, shows £1,368,027 for 1853, as against £1,271,503 for 1854, or a decrease of £96,524. If both columns are taken together, they reveal a decrease of £14,076. This detail is characteristic of the gentlemen of the Manchester school. They consider the present moment opportune for the abolition of "restrictions" benefiting industrial workers, that is the legal limitation of the working hours of young people under 18, of women, and of children under 12. To achieve so lofty a purpose, the falsification of a few figures may surely be permitted. But, according to the *Manchester Examiner*, the special organ of the Quaker Bright, and to every trade circular in the factory districts, the foreign markets, those traditional outlets for our surplus manufactures, are groaning under the weight of our over-production and over-speculation.

If such glutting of the world market has been achieved in spite of the improvisation of two new golden markets—Australia and California, in spite of the electric telegraph which has transformed the whole of Europe into one big commodity exchange, in spite of railways and steamships which have improved communication, and therefore commerce, to an incredible degree,—how long would it have taken for the crisis to come if the factory owner had been at liberty to order his workers to work eighteen hours instead of eleven? The arithmetical problem is too simple to require a solution. However, the relative acceleration of the crisis would not have been the only difference. A whole generation of workers would have forfeited 50 per cent of their physical strength, spiritual development and vitality. The same Manchester school which will answer our misgivings with the words:

> [why] should this distress distress us,
> since it increases our pleasures? [b]

---

[a] "Accounts Relating to Trade and Navigation...", *The Economist*, No. 593, January 6, 1855.— *Ed.*

[b] Goethe, "An Suleika", from *West-östlicher Divan.— Ed.*

deafens England with sentimental lamentations about the human sacrifice which is the price of her war with Russia, the price of any war! In a few days we shall hear Mr. Cobden at Leeds, protesting against the mutual slaughter of Christians. In a few weeks we shall hear him in Parliament, protesting against the "restrictions" which impede the too rapid consumption of human beings in the factories. Does he, of all heroic deeds, consider only one to be justified, that of Herod?

We agree with the Manchester school that compulsory legal restrictions of working hours do not exactly indicate a high level of social development. But we find the fault not in the laws, but in the conditions which make them necessary.

IV

London, January 22. It is well known that the Chancellor of the Exchequer, Mr. Robinson, opened the Parliament of 1825 with a dithyramb on the unprecedented boom in trade and industry.[a] Some weeks later, the Bank of England was on the point of suspending cash payments. Since then Mr. Robinson has kept the nickname of "Prosperity[b]-Robinson", given him by Cobbett. As the English are fond of historical precedents, it was inevitable that Prosperity-Robinson should have successors. The Queen's Speech which inaugurated the last extraordinary session of Parliament,[c] congratulated the country on the exceptional state of prosperity in agriculture, manufacture and trade. And yet, by then even the *semblance* of prosperity which might possibly have deceived Mr. Robinson had vanished. Ministerial congratulations seem to be part of the ceremonial with which, in England, disasters affecting the world market are suitably announced. Even stranger than the language of Ministers is the silence of the press at this moment. Does it believe it will be able to burke[b] the trade crisis, in the same way as in the literary coteries of Paris unpopular books are burked—by a conspiracy of silence? However, price lists talk, the lists of bankruptcies in the *Gazette* talk, and the letters of "business friends" talk. Soon, too, the newspapers will talk. Last week, very

---

[a] F. Robinson's speech in the House of Commons on February 28, 1825. *Hansard's Parliamentary Debates*, new series, Vol. 12, pp. 719-44.— *Ed.*

[b] Marx used the English word.— *Ed.*

[c] Queen Victoria's speech in Parliament on December 12, 1854. *The Times*, No. 21923, December 13, 1854.— *Ed.*

significant suspensions of payment occurred in the City, among the most important being that of Messrs Lonergan & Co., in the Spanish and West Indian trade; that of Messrs Rogers, Lowrey, trading with Manchester and the surrounding factory districts; that of Messrs Kotherington & Co., in the American trade; and finally that of the Auberten brothers, an old and respected firm. The liabilities of these various firms are said to amount to an average of £100,000 to £150,000. For the current week, new suspensions of payment by at least seven important City firms are expected.

From a business letter of January 20, from Birmingham, we have extracted the following details concerning the situation of industry in South Staffordshire:

"With the exception of firms in iron manufacture which are producing war materials for the Government, only very few have any orders at all, and those in hand are at extremely reduced prices. At present, £8 10s. will buy a ton of bar-iron, which in mid-summer was quoted at £12, but even at these reduced prices it is scarcely possible to make a sale, so that production has to be restricted. There are few of the important interests of the United States of North America which have suffered more on account of the trade crisis there than heavy industry. Nearly all the great iron works in the United States in which enormous sums have been invested, have turned their workers out into the street without any chance of early re-engagement. America's consumption of iron must therefore be regarded as almost completely suspended, and we may expect no further orders from there.

"Last Saturday many workers from the tin factories" (of Birmingham) "were sacked and many more will follow tonight" (January 20). "Ore and brass workers are no better off, since most of the big works here are on short time.

"Orders in hand for fashion articles are very scarce, and commercial travellers seeking spring orders in this branch are sending home very discouraging reports.

"The situation in the money market continues to have a disrupting effect on all branches of trade. The banks are raising their rate of interest in a most detrimental way, and at this moment only one business is doing well—that of the money-lender. Clients are flocking to the small pawnbrokers' shops, and discount houses are reaping a rich harvest."

Written between January 8 and 22, 1855

First published in the *Neue Oder-Zeitung*, Nos. 17, 19, 33 and 41, January 11, 12, 20 and 25, 1855

Printed according to the newspaper

Published in English for the first time

Karl Marx

[THE FOUR POINTS]

I

London, January 9. The telegram from Vienna[a] concerning the acceptance of the Four Points[414] on the part of Russia produced, on the one hand, a rise in Consols on the London Stock Exchange—for one moment [they were] $2^1/_2$ per cent above Saturday's[b] rate; on the other hand, a veritable panic in the tallow, oil and seed markets, where an early conclusion of peace would be the signal for large-scale bankruptcies. Today the excitement among City men has subsided, and, with a fair amount of agreement, they regard negotiations on the Four Points as a second edition of negotiations on the "Vienna Note".[415] According to the thoroughly ministerial *Morning Chronicle,* it was *premature* to speak of an actual acceptance by Russia of the guarantees demanded.[c] Russia had merely declared herself ready to negotiate on their basis, as interpreted jointly by the three powers. *The Times* believes that a victory of Western policy may legitimately be celebrated and declares on this occasion:

"We cannot too strongly repudiate the assumption, [...] that this war is to bring about what is called a revision of the map of Europe, by means of conquests or revolutions in which this country, at least, has no sort of interest."[d]

"The Allies," says *The Morning Post,* "have done enough to be able to withdraw from the theatre of war with honour, if their terms are accepted."[e]

---

[a] The telegram from Vienna of January 7, 1855. *The Times,* No. 21945, January 8, 1855.— *Ed.*

[b] January 6, 1855.— *Ed.*

[c] *The Morning Chronicle,* No. 27469, January 9, 1855, leader.— *Ed.*

[d] *The Times,* No. 21946, January 9, 1855, leader.— *Ed.*

[e] *The Morning Post,* No. 25279, January 9, 1855, leader.— *Ed.*

According to *The Daily News*, by resuming negotiations Russia intends to strengthen Prussia's belief in her moderation, to sow discord between the German powers, and to loosen the relationship between the Western powers and Austria. The only important aspect of the Four Points was the extra clause, according to which the Dardanelles Agreement of July 13, 1841 was to be revised "in the sense of a limitation of Russian naval power in the Black Sea". It was rumoured in the City that the Ministry was prepared to drop this extra clause. Lastly, *The Morning Advertiser* declares that the final Russian step had been agreed upon with Austria so as to give the latter an opportunity of getting rid of her obligations towards the Western powers. According to a newly arrived dispatch it has been stipulated that the negotiations must not interrupt war operations.

II

London, January 12. The unconditional acceptance of the "Four Points"—that is to say of the "Four" Points in the sense of the "three" powers—by Russia has turned out to be a hoax [a] of *The Morning Post* and *The Times*. We were the more inclined to believe in the hoax, as we know from Pozzo di Borgo's secret dispatches [416] (which, however, had become known following the Warsaw insurrection) that this master of diplomacy has laid down the principle that "in all cases of conflict Russia should induce the great European powers to *force her own conditions upon her*".

And in the "Four" Points we can see only "four" Russian *points*. If Russia, for the time being, does not accept them, we shall find the explanation once more with master Pozzo di Borgo. Russia, he declares, ought to make such apparent concessions to the West only from a victorious army camp. [417] This would be necessary to maintain the "prestige" on which her power was based. And so far, Russia, it is true, has got an "army camp", but she has not yet managed to gain the "victory". If Silistria had fallen, the "Four Points" would have been established long ago. According to *The Times* and *The Morning Post*, [b] the "Four Points" in the sense of the "three powers" had been adopted as basis for negotiations in order to start from them as a minimum. Now it

---

[a] Marx used the English word.— *Ed.*

[b] *The Times*, No. 21946, January 9, 1855, leader; *The Morning Post*, No. 25282, January 12, 1855, leader.— *Ed.*

turns out that Prince Gorchakov sees them as a problematical maximum from which to bargain down, or which are in effect intended only to furnish a pretext for another "Vienna Conference". Today, *The Morning Post,* in a self-important, diplomatically oracular leader,[a] confides that the provisional meetings of diplomats at Vienna are merely a preliminary to the actual conference which would not assemble until February 1 and which would not fail to surprise the world to a greater or lesser degree.

Yesterday the following announcement by the Admiralty was displayed at Lloyd's[b]:

"With reference to the last paragraph of my letter of the 8th November" (1854), "stating that the French and English Admirals in the Black Sea have received orders from their respective Governments to extend the blockade of the mouths of the Danube to all the ports in the Black Sea, and in the Sea of Azoff, which still remain in the possession of the enemy, I am commanded by my Lords Commissioners of the Admiralty to acquaint you, in order that the same may be made known to the mercantile community, that the Governments of England and France have further decided that the blockade in question shall take place on and after the 1st of February" (1855) "and that due notice will be given in the *London Gazette* of the blockade of the particular ports so soon as the same shall have been effected.

"I am etc.
"*W. A. B. Hamilton*"[c]

Here, then, it is openly admitted that up to now the allied fleets have blockaded only their own allies on the Danube estuary, but neither Russian ports in the Black Sea nor in the Sea of Azov. Nevertheless the Ministry has repeatedly declared in Parliament—in April, August and October—that it had issued the "strictest orders" for the blockade of Russian ports and coasts. As late as December 21, Lord Granville, in the name of the Ministry, announced to the House of Lords that

"Odessa was blockaded by five warships which have been constantly cruising in front of [Odessa]; reports have been constantly sent to [Her Majesty's] government ...."[d]

In a letter addressed to a daily paper, a well-known English pamphleteer sums up the consequences of the blockade measures taken, or rather *not* taken, by the Coalition, as follows:

---

[a] Marx used the English word.— *Ed.*
[b] Lloyd's offices located in the Royal Exchange, London.— *Ed.*
[c] *The Times,* No. 21948, January 11, 1855.— *Ed.*
[d] G. Granville's speech in the House of Lords on December 21, 1854. *The Times,* No. 21934, December 22, 1854.— *Ed.*

"(1) The English Government supplies England's enemy with money from England so that enemy may continue the war against her. (2) The Danube is blockaded in order to impoverish the Principalities and to cut off our own corn supplies. (3) Odessa, Taganrog, Kerch, etc., remain unmolested so that they may supply reinforcements, ammunition and provisions to the Russian troops in the Crimea. (4) The mock blockade is ruining our merchants while it enriches Greek, Russian and Austrian merchants."

The Times too takes the occasion of Mr. Hamilton's announcement to launch violent attacks on the Ministry's "blockade diplomacy".[a] It is characteristic of the Thunderer of Printing House Square that his thunderclaps have always been flung post festum. From March 26, 1854 till today *The Times* has defended "blockade diplomacy". Today when its rumblings obstruct no ministerial measures but may well gain it popularity, it suddenly turns into a clairvoyant.

The naval minister, or, as he is called here, the First Lord of the Admiralty, Sir *James Graham*, is sufficiently well known on the Continent on account of that magnificent achievement in black cabinet which led the Bandiera brothers to the scaffold.[418] It may be a less well known fact that in 1844, when Tsar Nicholas landed on the English coast, Sir James Graham did not dare to shake the proferred Imperial hand, but only to kiss it. (See *The Portfolio*, second series, 1844.[b])

III

London, January 15. As for the meaning of the Four Points:

"Nothing can be done in the way of further diplomacy till the first day of February." (Till February 5 or 6, says the Vienna correspondent of *The Times*.) "Meantime, the Czar has a clear month to move his forces where he will.[...] A month's time gained by acceptance of the four points may be lengthened to two months, by disputing the subsequent terms step by step, as the Envoy of Russia will probably be instructed to do; while it is far from improbable that strenuous efforts will be made to attract Austria into contentment with terms short of those which would be acceptable to England and France. To divide the three Powers would be the obvious thing to aim at...."[c]

Thus *The Morning Post*.

More important than the bandying of words in the English press

---

[a] *The Times*, No. 21949, January 12, 1855, leader.— *Ed.*

[b] Presumably reference to the article "The Visit of the Emperor", *The Portfolio*, London [1844], Vol. III, No. XII.— *Ed.*

[c] *The Morning Post*, No. 25284, January 15, 1855, leader.— *Ed.*

about Russia's secret intentions is its open confession (with the
exception, of course, of the ministerial organs) that the basis of
negotiations, the Four Points, are not worth negotiating for.

"The World, when the struggle commenced, was artfully made to believe,"
wrote *The Sunday Times*, "that the object to be secured by it was the breaking up of
the Russian empire, or, at least, the extorting from her of material guarantees for
the preservation of the peace of Europe. Towards accomplishing either of these
ends nothing has been done, and nothing will be done should peace be concluded
upon the basis of what are called the '*Four Points*'. If there be any triumph in the
matter, it will be a triumph achieved by Russia." [a]

"The Ministry of all the Incapacities," says *The Leader*, "cannot get beyond the
Four Points: it may go down to posterity as the Ministry of the Four Points. No
more of this dull comedy of war without a purpose." [...] Peace on the basis of the
Four Points could only be concluded because "they fear that in the tumult of war,
the peoples may become too important [...] and possibly to prevent Englishmen
from regaining those rights which Cromwell won for them. [...] That might be the
motive for patching up the conspiracy with Russia, and for restoring to her the
permission of renewing her encroachments upon Europe under the cover of a flag
of truce." [b]

The Examiner which incontestably commands the first position
among middle-class weeklies carries a detailed account of the
"basis" of peace negotiations, the essential points of which are
summarised below.

"...if such concessions as even the most rigid construction of the Four Points can
alone be held to involve, are to be considered equivalents for all the treasure that
has been lavished and all the blood·that has been shed by Englishmen in this
contest,—then the Emperor of Russia" in starting this war has shown that he is a
great statesman.... "She [Russia] is not even to be mulcted of the large sum she
annually receives from us for not observing the treaty of Vienna. The mouth of the
Danube, which, according to the correspondence recently published, she had
laboured most earnestly to close against English commerce, is to be left in her
hands. This latter point [...] would simply amount practically to the *status quo*, for
Russia never denied that the provisions relating to the navigation of rivers which
are contained in the treaty were applicable to the Danube." The abrogation of the
treaties of Kainardji and Adrianople[419] is of little singificance, for it is that these
treaties do not justify the claims Russia has made upon Turkey; "and when we
consider that Russia is to be one of the five powers which are to exercise a joint
protectorate over the Principalities and the Christian subjects of the Sultan ... we
believe that the benefits expected from the change will prove altogether illusory,
whilst it will be attended with the enormous disadvantage of giving a *legal* character
to the machinations of Russia for the *dismemberment of Turkey*. [...] We shall of
course be reminded that the Four Points include stipulations for a revision of the
Treaty of 1841 in the interest of the balance of power. The expression is vague
and mysterious enough, and we are not at all satisfied, from recent indications, that

---

[a] *The Sunday Times*, No. 1684, January 14, 1855.— *Ed.*
[b] "The Coming Peace" and "Russia Winning the Game", *The Leader*, No. 251,
January 13, 1855.— *Ed.*

the change contemplated under it may not be far more menacing to the independence of our ally" (Turkey) "than to the predominance of our enemy.... We should have rejected as utterly incredible any such possibility as we assume to be now under discussion at Vienna, but for that speech of Lord John's, in answer to Mr. Cobden, to the effect that the Government had no wish to deprive Russia of any of her territories."[a]

The last point is indeed crucial since, for instance, even the freedom of navigation on the Danube could only be secured if Russia were to lose the "territory" in the Danube estuaries which she seized, partly through the Treaty of Adrianople, in violation of the Treaty of London of 1827, and partly through a ukase of February 1836, in violation of the Treaty of Adrianople.[420] The point which *The Examiner* fails to emphasise refers to the Treaty of the Dardanelles of 1841. This treaty differs from the treaty concluded by Lord Palmerston in 1840[421] only insofar as *France* joined as a contracting party. The contents are identical. Only a few months ago, Lord Palmerston declared the Treaty of 1840, and thus also the Treaty of the Dardanelles of 1841, to be a victory by Britain over Russia, and himself the *originator* of that treaty. Why, then, should the *cancellation* of a treaty which was a victory by Britain over Russia, suddenly become a defeat of Russia by Britain? Or, if at the time, Britain had been deceived by her own Ministers, believing herself to be acting *against* Russia, while, in fact, she was acting *for* her, why not now? Disraeli, during the last extraordinary session of Parliament, cried: "No Four Points."[b] From the above extracts it can be seen that he has found an echo in the liberal press. Surprise at Russia's having accepted the Four Points, with or without reservations, is beginning to give way to surprise at Britain's having suggested them.

Written between January 9 and 15, 1855

First published in the *Neue Oder-Zeitung*, Nos. 20, 23 and 29; January 13, 15 and 18, 1855

Printed according to the newspaper

Published in English for the first time

---

[a] "Terms of Peace and Causes of War", *The Examiner*, No. 2450, January 13, 1855.— *Ed.*

[b] B. Disraeli's speech in the House of Commons on December 12, 1854. *The Times*, No. 21923, December 13, 1854.— *Ed.*

Karl Marx

THE COMMERCIAL CRISIS IN BRITAIN[422]

The English commercial crisis, whose premonitory symptoms were long ago chronicled in our columns,[a] is a fact now loudly proclaimed by the highest authorities in this matter—the annual circulars issued from the British Chambers of Commerce, and the leading commercial firms of the kingdom, along with extensive bankruptcies, mills running short-time, and stinted export tables, which speak to the same effect. According to the latest official "accounts relating to trade and navigation," the declared value of enumerated articles of export in the month ending Dec. 5, was:

	1852	1853	1854
	£6,033,030	£7,628,760	£5,771,772
Decrease in 1854		£261,258	£1,856,988

One cannot be astonished at the endeavor of the professional free-traders of Great Britain to show that the present crisis, instead of flowing from the natural working of the modern English system, and being altogether akin to the crises experienced at periodical intervals almost since the end of the 18th century, must, on the contrary, proceed from accidental and exceptional circumstances. According to the tenets of their school, commercial crises were out of the question after the corn laws were abrogated,[423] and free-trade principles adopted by the British legislature. Now they not only have high prices of corn with an abundant harvest, but also a commercial crisis. California and Australia added to the markets of the world and pouring forth

---

[a] See present edition, Vol. 12, pp. 95-96, 249 and 304-05 and this volume, pp. 468-69.—Ed.

their golden streams, with electric telegraphs transforming the whole of Europe in one single Stock Exchange, and with railways and steamers centuplicating the means of communication and of exchange. If their panacea had to be put to the test, they could not have expected to do it under circumstances more favorable than those which signalize the period from 1849 to 1854 in the history of trade and commerce.

They have failed to realize their promises, and naturally enough the war is now to be made the scapegoat of free-trade, just as the revolution in 1848 was. They cannot deny, however, that to a certain extent, the Oriental complication has delayed the revulsion, by acting as a check on the spirit of reckless enterprise, and turning part of the surplus capital to the loans recently contracted by most of the European powers; that some trades, like the iron trade, the leather trade and wool trade, have received some support from the extraordinary demand the war has created for these products; and, lastly, that in other trades, like the shipping, the woad trade, etc., where exaggerated notions as to the effects of the war fostered over-speculation on both sides of the Atlantic, only a partial outlet has been furnished to the already ruling and universal tendency to over-trading. However, their principal argument amounts to this, that the war has produced high prices for all sorts of grain, which high prices have engendered the crisis.

Now, it will be recollected that the average prices of corn ruled higher in 1853 than in 1854. If, then, these high prices are not to account for the unprecedented prosperity of 1853, they can as little account for the revulsion of 1854. The year 1836 was marked by commercial revulsion, notwithstanding its low corn prices; 1824 as well as 1853 were years of exceptional prosperity, notwithstanding the high prices that ruled in all sorts of provisions. The truth is, that although high corn prices may cripple industrial and commercial prosperity by contracting the home market, the home market in a country like Great Britain will never turn the balance, unless all foreign markets be already hopelessly overstocked. High corn prices must, therefore, in such a country, aggravate and prolong the revulsion; which, however, they are unable to create. Besides, it must not be forgotten that, conforming to the true doctrine of the Manchester School, high corn prices, if produced by the regular course of nature, instead of by the working of protection, prohibitive laws and sliding scales, altogether lose their fatal influence, and may even work advantageously by benefiting the farmers. As the two very deficient harvests of 1852 and 1853 cannot be denied to have been natural events, the free-traders turn around upon the year 1854, and affirm that the Oriental war, working like a protective duty, has produced high prices notwithstanding a plentiful harvest. Putting aside, then, the general influence of the prices of breadstuffs upon industry, the question arises as to the influence exerted by the present war upon these prices.

The Russian importation of wheat and flour constitutes about 19 per cent. of the entire importation of the United Kingdom, and its whole importations forming but about 20 per cent. of its aggregate consumption, Russia affords but little more than $2^{1}/_{2}$ per cent. of the whole. According to the latest official returns which do not extend over the first nine months of 1853, the entire imports of wheat into Great Britain were 3,770,921 qrs., of which 773,507 were from Russia, and 209,000 from Wallachia and Moldavia. Of flour, the entire imports amounted to 3,800,746 cwts., of which 64 were supplied from Russia, and none at all from the Principalities. Such was the case before the war broke out. During the corresponding months of 1854, the importation of wheat from Russian ports direct was 505,000 qrs., against 773,507 in 1853, and from the Danubian Principalities 118,000 against 209,000; being a deficiency of 359,507 qrs. If it be considered that the harvest of 1854 was a superior, and that of 1853 a very bad one, nobody will affirm that such a deficiency could have exerted any perceptible influence on prices. We see, on the contrary, from the official returns of the weekly sales in the English market of home-grown wheat—these returns representing but a small portion of the entire sales of the country—that in the months of October and November, 1854, 1,109,148 qrs. were sold, against 758,061 qrs. in the corresponding months of 1853—more than making up for the deficiency said to have been caused by the Russian war. We may remark, also, that had the English Cabinet not caused large stores of Turkish wheat to rot in the granaries of the Principalities by stupidly or treacherously blockading the Sulina, mouth of the Danube, and thus cutting off their own supplies, the war with Russia would not have stinted the importation of wheat even to the small amount it has done. Nearly two-thirds of the London imports of foreign flour being derived from the United States, it must be admitted that the failure of the American supply in the last quarter of 1854 was a much more important event for the provision trade than the Russian war.[424]

If we are asked how to explain the high prices of corn in Great Britain in the face of an abundant harvest, we shall state that more than once during the course of 1853, the fact was pointed at in

The Tribune,[a] that the free-trade delusions had caused the greatest possible irregularities and errors to take place in the operations of the British corn-trade, by depressing prices in the summer months below their natural level, when their advance alone should have secured the necessary supplies and sufficient orders for future purchases. Thus it happened that the imports in the months of July, August, September and October, 1854, reached but 750,000 qrs. against 2,132,000 qrs. in the corresponding months of 1853. Besides, it can hardly be doubted that consequent upon the repeal of the corn laws such large tracts of arable land were transformed into pasture in Britain, as to make even an abundant harvest, under the new regime, relatively defective.

"Consequently," to quote a circular of the Hull Chamber of Commerce, "the United Kingdom commences the year 1855 with very small stocks of foreign wheat, and with prices almost as high as in the beginning of 1854, while depending almost entirely on its own farmers' supplies until spring."

The reason of the English commercial revulsion of 1854, which is not likely to assume its true dimensions before the spring of the present year, is contained in the following few arithmetical characters: The exports of British produce and manufactures having amounted, in 1846, to £57,786,000, reached, in 1853, the enormous value of £98,000,000. Of those £98,000,000 of 1853, Australia, which, in 1842, had taken off less than one million, and in 1850, about three millions, absorbed near fifteen millions; while the United States, which, in 1842, had only consumed £3,582,000, and, in 1850, somewhat less than £15,000,000, now took the enormous amount of £24,000,000. The necessary reaction upon the English trade of the American crisis, and the hopelessly glutted Australian markets, need no further explanation. In 1837 the American crisis followed at the heels of the English crisis of 1836, while now the English crisis follows in the tracks of the American one; but, in both instances, the crisis may be traced to the same source—the fatal working of the English industrial system which leads to over-production in Great Britain, and to over-speculation in all other countries. The Australian and the United States markets, so far from forming exceptions, are only the highest expressions of the general condition of the markets of the world, both being about equally dependent upon England.

"We have the facts staring us in the face of glutted foreign markets and unprofitable returns, with few exceptions," exclaims a Manchester circular, relating to the cotton trade. "Most of the foreign markets," says another circular, relating

---

. [a] See present edition, Vol. 12, pp. 306-07, 326 and 440.— *Ed.*

to the silk trade, "usual vents for our surplus manufactures, have been groaning under the effects of overtrading." "Production was enormously increased," we are told by an account of the Bradford Worsted trade, "and the goods, for a time, found an outlet in foreign markets. Much irregular business has been done in reckless consignments of goods abroad, and we need scarcely remark that the results generally have been of the most unsatisfactory character."[a]

And so we might quote from a score of leading commercial circulars that reached us by the *Pacific*.[425]

The Spanish Revolution and the consequent activity of smuggling in that quarter, has created an exceptional market for British produce. The Levant market, consequent upon the apprehensions arising from the Oriental war, seems to be the only one which had not been overdone, but some three months since, as we learn, Lancashire set about retrieving what had been neglected in that quarter, and at this very moment we are told that Constantinople is also groaning under the overwhelming masses of cottons, woolens, hardware, cutlery, and all sorts of British merchandise. China is the only country where it can be pretended that political events have exerted a perceptible influence on the development of the commercial revulsion.

"The hopes entertained about the gradual increase in our export trade with China," says a Manchester house, "have been almost entirely dispelled, and the rebellion spreading at present, in that country, at first considered as favorable to foreign intercourse, seems now to be organized for the depredation of the country and the total ruin of trade. The export trade with China, which once was expected to increase greatly, has almost entirely ceased."[b]

Our readers will perhaps remember that when the Chinese revolution[426] first assumed anything like serious dimensions, we predicted the disastrous consequences[c] now complained of by the English exporting houses.

While denying all connection between the war and the commercial crisis, the symptoms of which had become apparent before the war was ever thought of, we are of course aware that the latter may dangerously aggravate the severe ordeal Great Britain will now have to pass through. The continuance of the war is tantamount to an increase of taxation, and increased taxes are certainly no cure for diminished incomes.

Written on January 11, 1855   Reproduced from the newspaper

First published in the *New-York Daily Tribune*, No. 4294, January 26, 1855 as a leader

---

[a] "Trade of 1854", *The Economist*, No. 593, January 6, 1855.— *Ed.*
[b] Ibid.— *Ed.*
[c] See present edition, Vol. 12, pp. 97-98.— *Ed.*

Karl Marx

SUNDAY OBSERVANCE AND THE PUBLICANS.— CLANRICARDE

London, January 19. In *The Morning Advertiser,* a lively discussion is taking place at this moment as to whether the accusation of "stupidity" levelled against the Coalition Ministry is just. From his point of view which presupposes a secret agreement of the Ministry with Russia, Urquhart has successfully defended the Ministry against the accusation of incompetence.

The Morning Advertiser is a peculiar phenomenon of the London press. Owned by the "Society of Licensed Victuallers", founded for charitable purposes, namely for the support of orphans, veterans and bankrupt members of the trade, it unquestionably enjoys the widest circulation among London dailies, after *The Times.* This is certainly not because of its editorial board, which is directed by a certain *Grant,* formerly a shorthand writer. This Grant married the daughter of Homer, the most influential man in the Society of Licensed Victuallers, that is the great Homer, as the united publicans call him, and the great Homer has made his little son-in-law chief editor of *The Morning Advertiser.* Since the Society had it in its power to push the *Advertiser* into every pub and even into most parlours,[a] the material foundations for the prosperity of the paper were laid. However, it owes its influence to the fact that it is *not* edited, but rather offers a forum where any member of the public may join in the discussion. Not admitted to the meetings of "respectable" London journalists because it is considered inferior, it takes its revenge on the fraternity by

---

[a] Marx used the English word.— *Ed.*

opening its columns, not only to the general public, but from time to time also to important writers who have not sold themselves to any party.

It is but a short step from *The Morning Advertiser* to *beer* and the latest *Beer Acts* of Mr. Wilson-Patten. This latest *ecclesiastical coup d'état* has caused much mirth and has proved that Shakespearean prototypes, etc., still flourish in the second half of the nineteenth century. The serious aspect, though, is the *surprise* of the masses at the presumption of the Church in meddling in an interfering and regulating manner in the lives of the citizens. The masses have become alienated from the Church to such a degree that its attempted encroachments are looked upon merely as practical jokes[a] which are rebuffed when they become tedious. Last night at Nottingham the ecclesiastical party, unaware of its position, had the effrontery to hold a public meeting during which it proposed that Parliament be petitioned for the closing of all public houses, not only during the times of day recently laid down by Wilson-Patten, but during the whole of Sunday. There was a huge audience of workers, and after a stormy session the following amendment was proposed by a factory worker, called Halton, and passed by a large majority

"that Parliament be petitioned to close all churches and chapels on Sundays."

We are assured that shortly after the opening of Parliament, Lord Lyndhurst, in the House of Lords, is going to summarise all the points of accusation against the Ministry. Everyone knows that during the session of 1853/54 the Marquess of Clanricarde was the would-be[a] leader of the anti-Russian opposition among the Peers. Of course, the letters which he and his son, Lord Dunkellin, sent to Tsar Nicholas[b]—on the occasion of Lord Dunkellin's release from Russian imprisonment—make it impossible for him to play this role any longer. With reference to Dunkellin's letter, the well-known humorist, Douglas Jerrold, remarks in *Lloyd's Paper*:

According to Lord Dunkellin, "Nicholas is 'a really great man;' for this tremendous reason—he liberated Lord Dunkellin! 'Great let me call him, for he conquered me!' Says the giantess of Tom Thumb; but here it is the dwarf that glorifies the ogre!"[c]

---

[a] Marx used the English words.—*Ed.*

[b] Clanricarde's letter to the Russian War Minister, Prince Dolgorukov, of November 18, 1854; and Dunkellin's letter to the Kaluga Governor, Count Tolstoi, of November 10, 1854. *The Times*, No. 21946, January 9, 1855.—*Ed.*

[c] *Lloyd's Weekly London Newspaper*, No. 634, January 14, 1855.—*Ed.*

Anyone who has studied the Blue Books[a] published in 1841 on Turko-Egyptian affairs,[b] and has gathered from their contents what position the Marquess of Clanricarde was accorded when British Ambassador at the Court of St. Petersburg, will also have realised that the Marquess' anti-Russian tirades in the House of Lords belonged exclusively to the category of opposition which every true Whig practises as a matter of principle whenever God does not give him an office.

Written on January 19, 1855

First published in the *Neue Oder-Zeitung*, No. 35, January 22, 1855

Printed according to the newspaper

Published in English for the first time

---

[a] Marx used the English title.— *Ed.*
[b] *Correspondence, 1839-41, relative to the Affairs of the East, and the Conflict between Egypt and Turkey*, 4 parts.— *Ed.*

Frederick Engels

CRITICAL OBSERVATIONS ON THE SIEGE OF SEVASTOPOL[427]

London, January 19. Sir Howard Douglas has added a critical appendix on the events of the recent war to a new edition of his famous work on *Naval Gunnery*.[a] Among other things, he proves, from most recent experience and on the basis of official material at his sole disposal, that fleets are inadequate against casemated forts if the latter are correctly constructed and properly defended; the uselessness of bombs against solid masonry; and finally, that it is possible to make a breach in towers and casemated forts, such as the ones at Bomarsund and Sevastopol, only with heavy siege-guns—32-pounders at least—and that, moreover, in the old manner, because the unsteady aim from a ship would never cause a breach without exposing the ship to certain destruction. As to the Crimean campaign in particular, Douglas, in spite of his partisanship for the commanders in the Crimea, and with all due semi-official consideration for his official position, comes to the conclusion that ultimately the Crimean expedition will prove a failure. But has not the Thunderer of *The Times* imparted the great news that Sevastopol was to be taken by *storm* after a forty-eight-hour cannonade! It had this, said *The Times,* from a reliable source, and it was solely to withhold its information from the Russians that it did not reveal all concerning an event which would definitely take place within the next few days (see *The Times* from December 26 to 31). There was no doubting it: Sevastopol was to be taken within the next few days.[b]

---

[a] Engels gives the title in English.— *Ed.*

[b] *The Times,* No. 21942, January 4, 1855, leader.— *Ed.*

This is what happened. As everyone knows, *The Times* displayed furious opposition to the Foreign Legion Bill, because it learned about this measure only when the rest of the general public did. Then it began to fret and fume and to grumble at the Ministry. To keep the paper quiet, the latter was cowardly enough to fling it a bit of news—the storming of Sevastopol, in doing which the Ministry transformed a design, considered by the generals for use in certain contingencies and under certain conditions, into a positive plan of campaign. That French papers—that is to say, semi-official organs—made similar reports is not surprising, for the loan of five hundred millions was near at hand.[428] That *The Times* was duped is equally obvious. It believes every news item which it receives twenty-four hours earlier than any other paper.

The situation in the Crimea has slightly improved. While the French suffer comparatively few losses from illness, their cavalry being well mounted and their infantry lively and active, the British continue daily to send 150 men into hospital and to bring out forty to fifty dead. Their artillery has no horses and their cavalry has to dismount, so that their horses may wear themselves out in hauling up the heavy cannon from Balaklava. Every two to three days the weather alternates between rain and light frost, so that there has been no decrease at all in the expanse of mud. Since almost all means of transport are occupied in supplying provisions for the army, the procuring of which remains the foremost necessity, neither cannon nor ammunition can be brought up. In the meantime, trenches have been dug close to the enemy positions, and a third parallel has been constructed which, although it cannot be provided with arms, must nevertheless be defended against sorties. It is impossible to say how close these trenches are to the nearest points under attack, since reports are contradictory and, of course, not published officially. Some say 140 or 150 yards, while, according to a French report, the nearest point is still 240 yards away. In the meantime, French batteries, now completed and mounted, must wait because the desultory and utterly ineffectual November cannonade has reduced supplies of ammunition, and a repetition of so desultory a fire would be inept. Thus the Russians have had, and still have, sufficient time, not only to repair any damage suffered through earlier attacks, but to raise new works, and they are doing this with so much enthusiasm that at present Sevastopol is stronger than ever before. Any decisive *storm* is quite outside the realm of possibility, as there are several lines of defence one behind another, and as the large stone buildings in the town behind the last circular wall have been transformed into as many redoubts. Whenever the siege recommences, everything will have to start again from the beginning, but with the difference that the batteries have come considerably closer to the town and hence are more effective. But at what a price has this advantage been bought! It was precisely the task of guarding these extended communication trenches which caused most of the cases of sickness in the British army by depriving the soldiers of their sleep to an excessive degree. Besides, the Russians were active enough in making sorties which, although not always successful, served to exhaust an already overworked enemy.

In the meantime, the Turkish army has gradually arrived in Eupatoria whence it will have to operate against Simferopol and, simultaneously, watch the northern side of Sevastopol. This operation which completely divides the Turks from the Anglo-French army, thus forming two quite separate armies, is another strategic blunder which invites the Russians to defeat each one separately. However, it was unavoidable. It would have been an even greater mistake to accumulate yet more troops on the small Heracleatic Chersonese.

This is how the results of the famous Balaklava "flank march" are developing.

Written on January 19, 1855

First published in the *Neue Oder-Zeitung*, No. 37, January 23, 1855

Printed according to the newspaper

Published in English for the first time

Frederick Engels

THE CRIMEAN CAMPAIGN [429]

The reason for this appears to be the knocking up of the horses in dragging heavy guns and provisions from Balaklava, both the artillery and commissariat being destitute of draught animals. The mud, however, is so deep that the transportation of cannon and ammunition had ceased, and a supply of food, such as it was, was all that was being brought up. The average number of daily admissions to the hospitals was 150, and of deaths about 50. In the meantime the trenches have been brought up nearer the enemy's works, and a third parallel constructed, which cannot be armed yet, though it must be defended against sorties. How near the trenches are now to the nearest attacked points, it is impossible to say, as reports are so contradictory, while nothing official, of course, is published; some say 140 or 150 yards, but a French report states that the nearest point is as far distant as 240 yards. The French batteries, which are completed and armed, have to wait, because the desultory, and as now appears, perfectly useless cannonade of November has reduced the stores of ammunition, and a repetition of such desultory firing would be equally useless. Thus the Russians have had ample time not only to repair all the damage done by the former attack, but to construct new works, and they have done so with such application, that Sevastopol is now stronger than ever. A decisive assault is entirely out of the question, where several succeeding lines of defense have to be taken in succession, and where, behind the last enceinte, the large stone buildings of the scattered town have been turned into as many redoubts.

The siege, whenever it is recommenced, will have to be done over again, with the only difference that the batteries are considerably more advanced toward the town, and consequently more efficient. But at the price of how many lives, lost by the hand of the enemy or by sickness, has this advantage been bought! It is the very work of guarding these extensive trenches which, by depriving the men of sleep, has produced many of the casualties by sickness in the British army. And the Russians have been active enough in sorties, which, if not always successful, have had their full effect as far as harassing an already overworked enemy is concerned.

It appears, too, that the reenforcements of the British and French have nearly all arrived, and unless fresh regiments are ordered for embarkation, very small additions will be made to the strength of either army in the Crimea. The Turkish army is getting very leisurely transported to Eupatoria, whence it is to operate toward Simferopol, observing, at the same time, the north side of Sevastopol. This operation, by entirely separating the Turks from their Allies, and forming two distinct armies, is another strategic blunder, inviting the Russians to defeat each army separately. But it could not be avoided; it would have been still worse to collect more troops on the little Heracleatic Chersonese. Thus, we see, the consequences of the celebrated flank march to Balaklava are developing themselves again and again in fresh false moves. That the Turks will get well beaten is very likely; they are no longer the army of Kalafat and Silistria. Disorganization, neglect, and want of everything have transformed that army, and Turkey has no second to replace it. Under these circumstances, nothing is so improbable as that the negotiations for peace should be disturbed by the fall of Sevastopol. There has been no time since the Allies landed when that event was not more likely than at present. It is not too much to say that in all military history there is no more signal failure than this Crimean campaign.

Written on January 19, 1855

First published in the *New-York Daily Tribune*, No. 4304, February 3; reprinted in the *New-York Semi-Weekly Tribune*, No. 1012, February 6, 1855 as a leader

Reproduced from the *New-York Daily Tribune*

Karl Marx

THE AIMS OF THE NEGOTIATIONS.—
POLEMIC AGAINST PRUSSIA.—
A SNOWBALL RIOT

London, January 23. The Western powers have declared that negotiations at Vienna must not for one moment interrupt their military operations. What *immediate military advantage* could Russia therefore gain by sham negotiations? This question, raised by the *Sun,* permits of a very positive answer. The sixth and part of the fifth (Russian) army corps formed the original garrison of the Crimea. The fourth corps arrived a few days before the battle of Balaklava; at this moment, the third corps is in the peninsula; the eighth division arrived at Bakshiserai on December 18, and the seventh and eighth divisions, together with the first division of Dragoons and about 240 cannon and four Cossack regiments are drawn up at Perekop. The Light Cavalry division, part of the third army corps, has been thrown out towards Eupatoria, which it is observing. Thus about half of the *active* Russian army (not counting reserves) is either in the Crimea or in garrison at Odessa, Kherson and Nikolayev, and sections of the second corps (Panyutin) are to march up to support them. It cannot, of course, be determined how great is the actual strength of these twelve infantry and six cavalry divisions following on the losses of an unsuccessful campaign and enormous marches, since we do not know whether the losses have been made good by fresh reinforcements. But, in any case, they must number at least 100,000 troops fit for active service, not counting the soldiers, marines and sailors there may be at Sevastopol. This great troop concentration in the Crimea, which absorbs at least a quarter of the entire Russian striking force, shows how important it is for Tsar Nicholas to involve Austria in renewed negotiations until the gaps in his Volhynian and Podolian armies, caused by the latest movements, have again been filled.

On the eve of the regular parliamentary session, the publication of the latest Prussian, Austrian and French dispatches is being exploited just as the treaty of December 2 [430] had been on the eve of special parliamentary session. It is very convenient for pro-government newspapers to reply to attacks on the English conduct of the war by attacks on Prussian diplomacy. The *Globe* and *The Morning Chronicle*, the two papers with the strongest pro-government bias, adopt the most violent tone in the polemic against Prussia.

A snowball riot which took place here last Sunday supplies new proof of how the importunate presumption of the ecclesiastical party and the Bill for the stricter observance of Sunday it smuggled through Parliament have only provoked the English people to hold somewhat rough, high-spirited and facetious demonstrations. Last Sunday, during morning service, a crowd of about 1,500 people assembled in Trafalgar Square near St. Martin's[in-the-Field], where they amused themselves by bombarding buses, cabs and pedestrians with snowballs. Because of the noise outside the church doors, the service had to be discontinued. As soon as the police intervened, they became the main object of attack, and within a few minutes, some constables were unable to look either left or right because of the piles of snow which had collected on their shoulders, helmets, etc. Soldiers who wanted to return to their barracks from church, were definitely forced to retreat, and their English phlegm was put to a severe test. About 100 special constables had to be sent to the scene of battle. Eventually the police made use of their truncheons, and fierce fighting ensued. Four ringleaders were captured and dragged to the police station in spite of several attempts in Chandos Street and Russell Street to free them from the arm of the law. Yesterday these gentlemen appeared before the police magistrate at Bow Street. The churchwardens of St. Martin's appeared also, to give evidence against them. Each hero was sentenced to forty shillings, or fourteen days' imprisonment, and here end the records of the snowball riot. At any rate it has served to refute the Prince de Ligne who, at the time of the revolt in the Netherlands [431] against Joseph II, refused his assistance because it was winter, snow and insurrection being mutually exclusive.

Written on January 23, 1855

First published in the *Neue Oder-Zeitung*, No. 43, January 26, 1855

Printed according to the newspaper

Published in English for the first time

Karl Marx

THE OPENING OF PARLIAMENT

London, January 24. The parliamentary session was opened yesterday. In the House of Lords, Lord Ellenborough gave notice that on Thursday, February 1, he would move for an official account of the number of troops—infantry, cavalry and sailors—sent out to the Crimea, and also the number of killed, wounded, sick and otherwise disabled.[a] The Duke of Richmond asked the Secretary *for* War why those who fought at Balaklava had been passed over in the awarding of medals. Not only those who fought at Balaklava would receive medals, but also all the sailors in the Black Sea area who had not been in combat, thus the Duke of Newcastle, the Secretary for War, trumped the Duke of Richmond. The Duke of Richmond, on the other hand, together with Lords Ellenborough and Hardwicke, asserted the truth of the proposition advanced long ago by Adam Smith that the value of fancy goods, hence of medals too, is in inverse proportion to their quantity.[b] After this important debate, which lasted about half an hour, the Lords adjourned.

The House of Commons was crowded. But the proceedings did not come up to expectations. Disraeli was not present, and Sir Benjamin Hall spoke. Having begun at a quarter to four, the sitting was over by 6 p.m. The Roman Senate has been admired for the dignified tranquility with which it received the news of the

---

[a] The debates in the House of Lords and the House of Commons on January 23 are given according to *The Times*, No. 21959, January 24, 1855.— *Ed.*

[b] Adam Smith has: "All sorts of luxuries and curiosities" (*An Inquiry into the Nature and Causes of the Wealth of Nations*, Vol. I, p. 354).— *Ed.*

defeat at Cannae.[432] The *patres conscripti*[a] of Rome have now been surpassed by the Commons of England. It was impossible to see these faces and to believe in the destruction of the British armies in the Crimea. The state of health of the Crimean army seems to have prompted Sir Benjamin Hall to introduce two Bills to improve the running of the health inspectorate in England. Sir Benjamin Hall is one of the so-called Radicals, of the same type as Sir William Molesworth, Osborne and Co. The radicalism of these gentlemen lies in their demanding ministerial posts even though they neither belong to the oligarchy nor possess plebeian talent. But their mere presence in the Ministry is a radical fact. So say their friends. Hence, when cholera was raging with great virulence in England in the summer of 1854 and the Board of Health, until then under the control of Palmerston, the Home Secretary, proved as incompetent as the medical department of the camp outside Sevastopol, the Coalition considered it a suitable time to create a new ministerial post, an independent President of the Board of Health, and to strengthen itself by making the "Radical" Sir Benjamin Hall a member of the Government. So Sir Benjamin Hall became Minister of Health. Cholera, it is true, did not disappear from London as soon as his appointment appeared in the *Gazette,* but a certain Taylor disappeared from *Punch,* where he had been poking fun at the Coalition and the Emperor of Russia. For Sir Benjamin Hall appointed him Secretary of the Board of Health at a salary of £1,000. As a Radical, Sir Benjamin Hall loves radical cures. As for the merits of his Bills, there will be time enough to discuss them when they are introduced. Yesterday they merely served to give him the opportunity of making his ministerial début in the House of Commons.

In answer to Layard's question,

"whether the Ministry has any objection to lay on the table of the House the correspondence that has taken place with foreign Powers with regard to the treaty of the 2d of December, 1854, and especially any document communicated to the Russian Government containing the interpretation put by the British and French governments on the Four Points,[b] not for negotiation but for acceptance",

Lord John Russell stated that he could not say if it would be possible to lay on the table any of the documents in question. Such a thing was not parliamentary. With reference to the history of the Four Points, however, he was able to tell his honourable friend, quite in general, the following: At the end of November Russia, through Gorchakov, had declared her acceptance of what is

---

[a] Honorary title of the ancient Roman senator.— *Ed.*
[b] See this volume, pp. 579-84.— *Ed.*

known as the Four Points; then came the treaty of December 2; then on December 28 a meeting in Vienna between Gorchakov and the ambassadors of England, France and Austria. The French Ambassador had, in the name of the Allies, read out a document in which they gave their interpretation of the Four Points—an interpretation which was to be considered as the basis of negotiations. In the third point it was proposed to put an end to Russia's preponderance in the Black Sea. Gorchakov did not accept this interpretation, he said however that he wanted to contact his Government for instructions. Ten days later he informed Count Buol that he had received these instructions. On January 7 or 8 another meeting was held in the offices of the Austrian Foreign Minister. Gorchakov read out a memorandum containing the views of his Government. Count Buol, Lord Westmorland and Baron de Bourqueney declared that they had no authority to accept the memorandum. The basis of negotiations had to be acceptance of the interpretation of the Four Points. Gorchakov then withdrew his memorandum and accepted the interpretation as the basis of negotiations. Russell added that despite her acceptance of this "basis" Russia had the right to dispute "every point" of the same as soon as it was definitely formulated. (A preliminary draft existed already.) The British Government stated that it was ready to open negotiations on the aforementioned basis. "But hitherto it has not yet given its ambassador any authorisation to negotiate." The last sentence is the only new piece of information Russell conceded to the Commons. The most important moment of the sitting was Roebuck's announcement that

"on Thursday next he should move for a select committee to inquire into the numbers and condition of our army before Sevastopol, and into the conduct of those departments of the Government whose duty it was to administer to the wants of that army".

The Times "implores" Roebuck to "cry aloud and spare not".[a] The imploring of The Times and the past of Mr. Roebuck are neither of them likely to remove entirely the suspicion that Roebuck will cry, or rather croak, to prevent others from speaking. Thersites, as far as we know, was never used by Ulysses, but Roebuck is certainly being used by the Whigs, who in their own way are as cunning as Ulysses.

Written on January 24, 1855

First published in the Neue Oder-Zeitung, No. 45, January 27, 1855

Printed according to the newspaper

Published in English for the first time

[a] The Times, No. 21959, January 24, 1855, leader.— Ed.

Karl Marx

COMMENTS ON THE CABINET CRISIS

London, January 26. When an envoy of Sultan Malik-Shah came to Alamut and called on Hasan-i Sabbah to surrender, the "old man of the mountains", instead of answering, beckoned to one of his fidawis,[433] commanding him to kill himself. At once the youth plunged his dagger into his breast and fell to the floor, a lifeless corpse. In the same way the "old man" of the Coalition[a] had ordered his Lord John Russell to commit suicide on his behalf in the House of Commons. Russell, the old parliamentary philanthropist, who always interpreted the commandment "Love thy neighbour as thyself" to mean that every man is his own neighbour, has preferred to kill the "old man" instead. We were not mistaken about Roebuck. His motion was arranged with Russell in order to salvage the "better part"—the Whigs—from the shipwreck.

Indeed! This motion is not directed against the Ministry but against the "departments" that are directly responsible for the conduct of the war, i.e., against the *Peelites*. Furthermore, it was obvious that at the opening of Parliament he had good reasons for making the declaration that the basis for negotiations was no basis insofar as Russia reserved the right to dispute each of the Four Points—and, that the negotiations were likewise no negotiations insofar as the English Cabinet had still not appointed a negotiator. Scarcely had Roebuck proposed his motion—on Tuesday—when Russell writes the same evening to the "old man" that this motion amounts to a vote of censure against the War Office (the Peelites),

---

[a] Aberdeen.— *Ed.*

and that *he* must therefore tender his resignation.[a] Aberdeen goes to the Queen at Windsor Castle and advises her to accept his [Russell's] resignation, which is what happens. The courage of the "old man" is understandable when one learns that Palmerston has *not* handed in his resignation.

At the Thursday sitting the House of Commons is informed of these important events. It adjourns its sitting (and Roebuck his motion) until this evening.[b] Now the whole of the House of Commons rushes into the House of Lords where clarification is expected of Aberdeen, but Aberdeen is clever enough to be absent—reportedly back in Windsor—and the Duke of Newcastle recounts the same tale in the Lords as Palmerston has told in the Commons. In the meanwhile the Whigs of the Commons are appalled to discover in the House of Lords that their plan has been seen through and their retreat cut off. The Tories, not at all eager to re-install the Whigs, at the expense of the Peelites, in their old privilege as "divinely-appointed tenants of the British Empire", have prevailed on Lord Lyndhurst to propose a motion which, in contrast to Roebuck's motion, does not merely censure— *à la* Roebuck—individual departments of the Government but puts the entire Government formally in the dock. Lord Lyndhurst's motion reads as follows:

"I shall move on Friday, February 2, that in the opinion of this House the expedition to the Crimea was undertaken by Her Majesty's Government with very inadequate means and without due caution or sufficient inquiry into the nature and extent of the resistance to be expected from the enemy: and that the neglect and mismanagement of the Government in the conduct of the enterprise have led to the most disastrous results."

There is no mistaking it: Lyndhurst's motion is aimed at the Whigs just as Roebuck's is aimed at the Aberdeenites. An incidental observation: Lord John Russell has informed the Commons through Hayter that he will explain the reasons for his resignation at the earliest opportunity, that is tonight. "He who expects nothing will not be disappointed."[434]

Written on January 26, 1855

First published in the *Neue Oder-Zeitung*, No. 47, January 29, 1855

Printed according to the newspaper

Published in English for the first time

---

[a] *The Times*, No. 21961, January 26, 1855, leader.— *Ed.*

[b] Speeches of Roebuck, Palmerston and Hayter in the House of Commons and of the Duke of Newcastle and Lord Lyndhurst in the House of Lords on January 25, 1855 were published in *The Times*, No. 21961, January 26, 1855.— *Ed.*

Karl Marx

PARLIAMENTARY NEWS

London, January 27. The tone and physiognomy of yesterday's Commons sitting showed precisely to what level the British Parliament has sunk.[a]

At the opening of the sitting, at about 4 p.m., the House was packed because a scene was expected, a scandal: Lord Russell's explanation of his resignation. As soon as the personal debate was over and the proper parliamentary debate, of Roebuck's motion, began the indignant patriots hurried off to dinner; the House thinned out and several voices shouted, "Divide, divide!" A considerable pause ensued until the Secretary at War, Sidney Herbert, rose and directed a long and well-worded speech at empty benches. Then the sated Members gradually strolled back to their seats. When Layard began his speech at about 9.30 p.m. there were some 150 Members present. When he concluded about an hour before the House adjourned, it was full again. The rest of the sitting, however, strongly resembled a parliamentary siesta.

Lord John Russell—all of whose merits can be reduced to one: expertise in parliamentary tactics—did not make his speech from the Speaker's table, as is customary on such occasions, but from the third bench behind the ministerial seats, where the discontented Whigs are installed. He spoke in a low, hoarse voice, drawling, mistreating English pronunciation as always, and frequently at odds with the rules of syntax. (Nota bene: One must on no account confuse the speeches as they are presented in the

---

[a] Parliamentary debates on January 26, 1855 were published in *The Times*, No. 21962, January 27, 1855.— *Ed.*

newspapers with the speeches as they are delivered.) While
ordinary orators make up for poor content by good delivery,
Russell sought to excuse poor content by means of even worse
delivery. The way in which he spoke was, as it were, an apology
for what he said.

And an apology was certainly necessary! The previous Monday
he had still not thought of resigning, he said, but on Tuesday, as
soon as Roebuck had tabled his motion,[a] he had found it
unavoidable. This reminds one of the lackey who was by no means
averse to telling a lie but whose conscience was troubled as soon as
the lie was discovered. From what point of view should he oppose
the request for a parliamentary inquiry, as his duty as ministerial
Leader of the House required! Because the evils were not great
enough to call for an inquiry! Nobody, he said, could deny the
melancholy state of the army at Sevastopol. It was not only painful
but shocking and heart-rending. Or ought he to have maintained
before the House that its committee of inquiry was pointless as
better arrangements to remedy the evils were in progress? Russell
is on slippery ground when raising this question for he was
directly responsible for adopting such arrangements, not only as a
member of the Ministry but especially as Lord President of the
Privy Council.[b] He admits that he consented to the appointment of
the Duke of Newcastle as "supreme" War Minister. He cannot
deny that precautionary measures to ensure provisions, clothing
and medical care for the army should have been taken by August
and September at the latest. What did he do, on his own
admission, during this critical period? He was travelling about the
country giving small talks to "literary institutions" and editing the
correspondence of Charles James Fox. While he was travelling
about in England, Aberdeen was travelling in Scotland, and there
was no Cabinet meeting from August until October 17. At this
meeting, Lord John, according to his own account, made no
proposals worth informing Parliament of. Lord John then takes
another whole month to think things over and then, on November
17, sends a letter to Aberdeen suggesting to him the amalgamation
of the office of Secretary of State *for* War with that of Secretary *at*
War and the appointment of Palmerston to fill them both—in
other words, the dismissal of the Duke of Newcastle. Aberdeen
rejects this. Russell writes to him again on November 28 in the
same spirit. On November 30 Aberdeen replies to him quite

---

[a] See this volume, p. 602.— *Ed.*
[b] Marx used the English term.— *Ed.*

correctly that his whole proposal amounts to the replacement of one man by another, of Newcastle by Palmerston.[a] But when the Colonial Office had been separated from the War Office, he said, Russell had readily consented to Newcastle taking over the latter, in order to bring one of his Whigs, Sir George Grey, into the Colonial Office.[b] Aberdeen then asked Russell himself whether he wanted to put his proposal to the Cabinet. Russell declined to do this, as he said, "so as *not* to cause the break-up of the Ministry". Hence, the Ministry first, then the army in the Crimea.

No measures had been taken to remedy the evils, confesses Russell. All reform of the management of the war was limited to the placing of the Commissariat under the Secretary of State *for* War. Nevertheless, although *no* remedial measures are taken, Russell calmly remains in the Government, making no further suggestions from November 30, 1854 until January 20, 1855. On this day—last Saturday—Aberdeen informs Russell of certain proposals for reforms in the management of the war; these are found unsatisfactory by the latter, who submits counter-proposals of his own in writing. Not until three days later does he deem it necessary to hand in his resignation, because Roebuck has tabled his motion and Russell is not inclined to share responsibility with a Cabinet with which he has shared office and actions. He had heard—declares Russell—that Aberdeen was never resolved to appoint Palmerston dictator in the War Office. If this were the case he—Curtius—congratulated himself on not having leapt in vain from the firm ground of the Ministry into the hollow tomb of the Opposition. After rolling thus far down his precipitous path our Lord John then destroys the last ostensible pretext for his resignation, declaring: 1. that the prospects for the war are by no means such as to give rise to the prevailing depression; 2. that Aberdeen is a great Minister, Clarendon a great diplomat, and Gladstone a great financier; 3. that the Whig Party does not consist of office-seekers but of fervent patriots, and finally that he, Russell, would abstain from voting on Roebuck's motion, although he is supposed to have resigned because a patriot can have *no* objection to Roebuck's motion. Russell's speech was received even more coldly than it was delivered.

Palmerston gets up on behalf of the Ministry. His situation is rather strange. Curtius Russell resigns because Aberdeen is

---

[a] These facts are cited according to Lord Russell's speech in the House of Commons on January 26, 1855. *The Times*, No. 21962, January 27, 1855.— *Ed.*

[b] See this volume, p. 228.— *Ed.*

unwilling to appoint Palmerston dictator over the war. Brutus Palmerston attacks Russell for leaving Aberdeen in the lurch in the moment of danger. Palmerston was quite pleased with this bizarre situation. It enabled him, as he usually does in critical moments, to laugh off the seriousness of the situation and transform it into a farce. When he rebuked Russell for not taking his heroic decision back in December, Disraeli—who at least does not conceal his joy at the demise of the Venetian Constitution— laughed out loud, and Gladstone, who makes seriousness his speciality, was evidently murmuring all the Puseyite[435] prayers he knew to stop himself from exploding. Palmerston declared that if the Roebuck motion were passed it would mean the fall of the Ministry. If it were defeated the Cabinet would meet to discuss its own reorganisation (including Palmerston's dictatorship).

A great magician this Palmerston! With one foot in the grave he can make England believe that he is a *homo novus,* and that his career is only just beginning. *Twenty years* Secretary at War, and as such known only for his systematic defence of flogging and of the purchase of commissions in the Army,[436] he ventures to pass himself off as the man whose mere name is enough to eliminate the faults in the system. Of all the English Ministers the only one to have been repeatedly denounced in Parliament, especially in 1848, as a *Russian agent,* he is able to make himself out to be the only man in a position to lead England in the war against Russia. A great man, this Palmerston!

About the debate on Roebuck's motion, which has been adjourned until Monday evening, next time. So cleverly is the latter formulated that the opponents of the Ministry declared that they would vote for it despite its insipidness, and the supporters of the Ministry declared that they would speak in favour of it, although they would vote against it. The Lords sitting contained nothing of interest. Aberdeen added nothing to Russell's explanation, except his surprise: Russell had surprised the whole Cabinet.

Written on January 27, 1855

First published in the *Neue Oder-Zeitung,* No. 49, January 30, 1855

Printed according to the newspaper

Published in English for the first time

Frederick Engels

THE EUROPEAN WAR [437]

As the term approaches for the opening of the new Conference at Vienna, the probability of any concessions on the part of Russia dwindles away into misty and most uncertain tenuity. The brilliant success of that great diplomatic *coup*,[a] the prompt acceptance by the Czar of the proposed basis of negotiations, puts him, for the moment at least, in a commanding position, and renders it certain that, under whatever appearances he may agree to proposals for peace, the only real basis on which he will now consent to arrange the quarrel is substantially that of the *status quo*. By accepting the Four Points[b] he has thrown Austria back into a doubtful position, while he retains Prussia in his leading strings, and gains time to bring all his reserves and new formations of troops to the frontier before hostilities can begin.

The very fact of negotiations having been agreed upon, sets free at once as many Russian soldiers of the army of observation on the Austrian frontier as can be replaced in two months or ten weeks—that is, at least sixty to eighty thousand men. As the whole of the late Danubian army has ceased to exist as such, the fourth corps having been in the Crimea since the end of October, the third corps having arrived there in the latter part of December, and the rest of the fifth corps, beside cavalry and reserves now being on the way thither, these troops must be replaced on the Bug and Dniester by fresh men, to be taken from the western army in Poland, Volhynia and Podolia. Accordingly, if the war is to be transferred to the center of the Continent, two or three

---

[a] Move.— *Ed.*
[b] See this volume, pp. 579-84.— *Ed.*

months' time is of the utmost importance to Russia; for, at the
present moment, the forces she has scattered on the long line
from Kalish to Ismail are no longer sufficient, without reenforcements, to withstand the increasing number of Austrian troops
opposed to them. That time she has now gained, and we proceed
to show what is the present state of her military preparations.

We have, on former occasions, given an outline of the Russian
military organization.[a] In the great active army, the one destined
to act against the South and West of Europe, there were originally
six army-corps, of forty-eight battalions each; two corps of selected
troops, of thirty-six battalions each, beside a comparatively strong
force of cavalry, regular and irregular, with artillery. As we have
before stated, the Government has not only called in the reserves
to form the fourth, fifth and sixth battalions of the selected troops,
and the fifth and sixth of the other six army-corps; but even the
seventh and eighth battalions of each regiment had been formed by
new levies, so that the number of battalions has been doubled for the
six corps of the line, and more then doubled for the selected troops
(Guards and Grenadiers). These forces may now be approximately
estimated as follows:

Guards and Grenadiers—the first four battalions per regiment	96 bats. at 900 men	86,400
Guards and Grenadiers—the last four battalions per regiment	96 bats. at 700 men	67,200
First and Second Corps (not yet engaged)—the first, or active, four battalions per regiment	96 bats. at 900 men	86,400
First and Second Corps—the last four battalions per regiment	96 bats. at 700 men	67,200
Third, Fourth, Fifth, Sixth Corps—the active battalions	192 bats. at 500 men	96,000
Third, Fourth, Fifth, Sixth Corps—the last four battalions per regiment	192 bats. at 700 men	134,400
Corps of Finland	16 bats. at 900 men	14,400
Total 784		552,000
Add: Cavalry, regular		80,000
Cavalry, irregular		46,000
Artillery		80,000
Total		758,000

---

[a] See this volume, pp. 498-504.— *Ed.*

A part of these estimates may appear high, but in reality they are not so. The enormous recruiting which has taken place since the war began, should have swelled the ranks of the army higher than this, in spite of the losses sustained, which, all of them, fell upon the 96 active battalions of the third, fourth, fifth and sixth corps; but we have allowed amply for the many recruits who die before they reach their regiments. Besides, for cavalry our estimate is very low.

Of the above troops, 8,000 men (one division of the fifth corps) are in the Caucasus, and must, therefore, be deducted; for we leave unnoticed here the forces employed out of Europe. The remaining 750,000 troops are distributed nearly as follows: On the shores of the Baltic, the Baltic Army, under General Sievers, consisting of the Finland corps, and reserves of the Guards, Grenadiers, and sixth corps, amounting, with cavalry and artillery, to about 135,000 men, part of whom, however, may be considered as raw recruits and battalions hardly organized. In Poland and on the frontier of Galicia, from Kalish to Kamenicz, the Guards, the Grenadiers, the first corps, one division of the sixth corps, and some reserves of the Grenadiers and first corps, with cavalry and artillery, about 235,000 men. This army is the finest part of the Russian troops; it contains the select troops, and the best of the reserves. In Bessarabia, and between the Dniester and Bug, are two divisions of the second corps, and part of its reserves, about 60,000 men. These formed part of the army of the West, but upon the army of the Danube being sent to the Crimea, they were detached to take its place. They now oppose the Austrian troops in the Principalities, and are commanded by General Panyutin. For the defense of the Crimea are destined the third and fourth corps, one division of the fifth corps, two divisions of the 6th, and some reserves already there, beside one division each of the second and fifth corps on the march, the whole composing, with cavalry and artillery, a force which can hardly be estimated at less than 170,000 men, under Menchikoff. The remainder of the reserves and new formations, especially of the first, second, third, fourth and fifth corps, are now being organized into a grand army of reserve by General Cheodayeff. They are concentrating in the interior, and must count about 150,000 men. How many of them are on the march to Poland or the South, is, of course, impossible to tell.

Thus the Emperor Nicholas, who, last summer, had less than 500,000 troops on the western frontier of his Empire, from Finland to the Crimea, now has 600,000 men placed there, beside a reserve forming in the interior to the number of 150,000. For all that, he is weaker now against Austria than he was then. In August or September there were in Poland and Podolia 270,000 Russians, and on the Pruth and Dniester the army of the Danube, counting about 80,000 men; for this latter was also kept there more for the sake of the Austrians than for anything else. This made a total of 350,000 men who might have operated against Austria. Now there are, as we have seen, only 295,000 men concentrated along the Austrian line of outposts, while Austria must by this time have 320,000 men directly opposed to them, and 70,000 to 80,000 men in Bohemia and Moravia to support these. This momentary inferiority of numbers on the Russian side, and the great uncertainty as to the time of arrival of fresh formations from the interior, in the present season, and in a country where the whole administration is corrupt, are quite sufficient causes to make the Russian Government try to gain as much time as possible. Such an inferiority of numbers disables the Russians for offensive operations; and in an open country like Poland, with no great river-lines between the two armies, this means the necessity of a retreat, on the first encounter, to a tenable position. In this especial case it means the cutting of the Russian army in two portions, one of which would have to retreat upon Warsaw, and the other upon Kiev; and between these two halves would there lie the impassable Polesian moors, extending from the Bug (tributary to the Vistula, not the Southern Bug), to the Dnieper. In fact, it would be better luck than the Russians generally have on such occasions, if large numbers escaped being driven into these morasses. Thus, even without a battle, the greater part of Southern Poland, Volhynia, Podolia, Bessarabia, the country from Warsaw to Kiev and Kherson would have to be evacuated. On the other hand, a superior Russian army could quite as easily drive the opposing Austrians, without their risking a decisive battle, out of Galicia and Moldavia, and force the passes into Hungary, and the consequences of such a result can easily be imagined. Indeed, in such a war between Austria and Russia, the first successful offensive movement is of the highest importance to either party; and either will do the utmost to establish itself first on the other's territory.

We have often said that this war would not have that military interest which properly attaches to European wars, until Austria should declare herself against Russia.[a] Even the efforts in the

---

[a] See this volume, pp. 543-49.— Ed.

Crimea are nothing but a great war upon a small scale. The enormous marches of the Russians, the sufferings of the Allies, have hitherto reduced the contending armies to such numbers that no really great battle has been fought. What are fights where but from fifteen to twenty-five thousand men on a side are engaged? What strategical operations of really scientific interest can occur within the small space from Cape Chersonesus to Bakshiserai? And even there, whatever occurs, there are never troops enough to occupy the whole line. The interest consists more in what is not done, than in what is done. For the rest, it is anecdote, instead of history, that is performed.

But it will be a different thing should the two grand armies, now facing each other on the Galician frontier, come into play. Whatever the intentions and capabilities of the commanders may be, the very magnitude of the armies and the nature of the ground admit of no sham war and of no indecision. Rapid concentrations, forced marches, stratagems and outflankings of the largest kind, changing bases and lines of operation—in fact, maneuvering and fighting on a grand scale, and according to real military principles, here become a necessity and a matter of course; and then the chief who is influenced by political considerations or who acts with a want of resolution must lose his army. War on such a scale and in such a country takes a serious and a business-like turn at once; and it is this which will make the Austro-Russian war, if it does break out, one of the most interesting events since 1815.

As to the prospect of peace, that is by no means so clear as it seemed a few weeks since. If the Allies are willing to put an end to the struggle on the terms, substantially, of the *status quo*, it may be done; but how little hope there is of that, our readers cannot require to be informed. Certainly, with half of Germany acting, morally at least, in her favor, and after having put on foot the enormous armies whose strength we have above exhibited, we cannot expect Russia to agree to any terms which France and England are likely to propose or consent to. The almost uninterrupted series of profitable treaties of peace, from Peter the Great to the peace of Adrianople, will hardly now be followed by a treaty surrendering the dominion of the Black Sea, before Sevastopol is taken, and when only one-third of the Russian forces have as yet been engaged. But if peace cannot be concluded before the fate of Sevastopol or of the allied expedition is fully developed, it will be less probable after this Crimean campaign is decided. If Sevastopol falls, the honor of Russia—if the Allies are

21*

defeated and driven into the sea, their honor—will not admit of a settlement until more decisive results are obtained. Had the preparations for the Conference been attended by an armistice, as we intimated on hearing of the Czar's acceptance of the Four Points, there would have been reason for continuing to entertain hopes of peace; but, under present circumstances, we are compelled to admit that a great European war is much more probable.

Written about January 29, 1855

First published in the *New-York Daily Tribune*, No. 4316, February 17; reprinted in the *New-York Semi-Weekly Tribune*, No. 1016, February 20 and the *New-York Weekly Tribune*, No. 702, February 24, 1855 as a leader

Reproduced from the *New-York Daily Tribune*

Karl Marx and Frederick Engels

FROM PARLIAMENT.—
FROM THE THEATRE OF WAR

London, January 29. Our judgment of the English Parliament[a] has been corroborated today by the English press.

"The Parliament of England," says *The Morning Advertiser,* "has met, and ... separated on the first night, in laughter more unseemly than the jesting of an idiot over his father's burial."[b]

The Times, too, cannot help remarking:

"There are few, we apprehend, who will rise from the perusal of Friday night's debate without a melancholy feeling, which they may not perhaps be able at once to define or analyse, but which, when examined, resolves itself into a conviction that our legislature, called together on a most urgent occasion to a consideration of the gravest nature, postpones primary to secondary objects, and gives up to party and personal considerations those hours which ought now to be exclusively devoted to the desperate situation of our army in the Crimea."[c]

In this situation, *The Times* proceeds to recommend making Palmerston prime minister because he is "too old" to be Secretary for War. It was *The Times* that recommended undertaking the Crimean expedition at such a time of the year and with such forces that almost certainly ensured failure, according to the testimony of Sir Howard Douglas, the greatest military critic of England.

Let us add a brief postscript to the account of Friday's sitting. Although Roebuck was forced by his old chronic ailment to break

---

[a] See this volume, pp. 600-01.— *Ed.*
[b] *The Morning Advertiser,* No. 19846, January 29, 1855, leader.— *Ed.*
[c] *The Times,* No. 21963, January 29, 1855, leader.— *Ed.*

off his speech after ten minutes and abruptly propose his motion, he did have time to formulate the fatal question: We have sent out 54,000 well-equipped troops to the East. Of these 14,000 still exist. What has become of the 40,000 who *are missing*? And what was the answer of the Secretary at War, Sidney Herbert, the great patron of the English Pietists, the Tractarians[438]? He said the system was no good.[a] But when the separation of the War Office from the Colonial Office was carried out a few months ago, who resisted every thorough-going reform of the system?[b] Sidney Herbert and his colleagues. Sidney Herbert, not content with hiding behind "the system", accuses the commanders of the brigades and regiments of total incompetence. Anyone who knows the system also knows that these commanders have nothing to do with administration, nor, consequently, with the maladministration which it is admitted has now sacrificed a model army. But the pious Herbert is not satisfied with confessing the sins of *other people*. The English soldiers, he claims, are inept. They are unable to take care of themselves. They are indeed gallant but stupid.

> "At fighting they are respectable,
> When it comes to thinking—miserable."[c]

He, Sidney Herbert, and his colleagues are all misunderstood geniuses. Is it any wonder that Herbert's sermon appealed to that eccentric Drummond and put the question in his mouth whether it were not time to suspend the constitution and appoint a dictator for England.[d] Vernon Smith, the former Whig Minister, eventually gave the general confusion a classic expression, declaring that he knew not what the intention of the motion was, nor what he should do himself, nor whether a new ministry was in the making, nor if the old one had ever existed, and therefore he would not vote for the motion.[e] *The Times* believes, however, that the motion will be passed this evening.[f] On January 26, 1810, as we recall, resistance was mounted in the English Parliament against Lord Porchester's proposal to establish a committee of inquiry into the

---

[a] S. Herbert's speech in the House of Commons on January 26, 1855. *The Times*, No. 21962, January 27, 1855.— *Ed.*

[b] See this volume, pp. 220 and 228.— *Ed.*

[c] Paraphrase of a couplet from Goethe's *Sprichwörtlich.— Ed.*

[d] H. Drummond's speech in the House of Commons on January 26, 1855. *The Times*, No. 21962, January 27, 1855.— *Ed.*

[e] V. Smith's speech in the House of Commons on January 26, 1855. *The Times*, No. 21962, January 27, 1855.— *Ed.*

[f] *The Times*, No. 21963, January 29, 1855, leader.— *Ed.*

Walcheren Expedition.[439] Similar resistance occurred on January 26, 1855. On January 29, 1810 the motion was passed, and England is a country of historical precedents.

The mere acceptance of peace negotiations allowed Russia to withdraw as many troops from the observation army on the Austrian border as can be replaced in two months or ten weeks, i.e. at least 60,000-80,000. We now know that the entire former (Russian) Danube army has ceased to exist as such, as the 4th Corps has been in the Crimea since the end of October, the 3rd arrived there in the final days of December and the rest of the 5th Corps, together with the cavalry and reserves, are at present marching thither. The new distribution of these troops, who have to be replaced on the Bug and Dniester by troops from the Western Army (stationed in Poland, Volhynia and Podolia), and the fact that in addition parts of the 2nd Corps and the reserve cavalry are likewise heading for the Crimea, are sufficient explanation, even disregarding all the other secondary diplomatic aims involved, why Russia did not hesitate a moment to resume negotiation on the so-called "basis". A period of two to three months is of decisive importance for her, because her army, spread out on the long line from Kalish to Ismail, is without reinforcements no longer capable of resisting the growing numbers of the Austrian army confronting it. In order to prove this in more detail we present here a survey, emanating from the best possible sources—and *over*estimating, rather than *under*estimating, the strength of the Russian forces—of the strength and position of the large Russian army on active service, which is to operate against the South and West of Europe. Initially it consisted of six army corps, each of 48 battalions, two corps of picked troops (Guards and Grenadiers), each 36 battalions strong, together with a relatively large number of cavalry, regular and irregular, and artillery. The Russian Government then called up reserves in order to form the 4th, 5th and 6th battalions of picked troops, and the 5th and 6th battalions of the other army corps. By raising more new troops it soon afterwards added a 7th battalion and 8th to each regiment, thus doubling the number of battalions in the line corps and more than doubling them for the picked troops.

These forces may be approximately estimated as follows: *Guards and Grenadiers*—the first four battalions of each regiment=96 battalions of 900 men=86,400 men, ditto the last four battalions of each regiment, ditto of 700 men=67,200 men. The *1st* and *2nd Corps* (not yet engaged)—the first four battalions of each regiment=96 battalions of 900 men=86,400 men. The last four battalions of each regiment=96 battalions of 700 men=67,200 men. The *3rd, 4th, 5th* and *6th Corps*—the first four battalions of each regiment=192 battalions of 500 men=96,000 men; the last four battalions of each regiment=192 battalions of 700 men=134,400 men. The *Finland Corps*—14,400 men. [Total]=784 battalions comprising 552,000 men. *Cavalry* (regular)—80,000 men. *Cavalry* (irregular)—46,000 men. *Artillery*—80,000 men. Total 758,000 men. Casualties have hitherto affected only the 96 active battalions of the 3rd, 4th, 5th and 6th Corps.

After deducting the 1st Division of the 5th Corps, which is at the Caucasus, there remain 750,000 men, that are now distributed as follows: On the shores of the Baltic Sea the Baltic Army under General Sievers, consisting of the Finnish Corps and the reserves of the Guards, Grenadiers and the 6th Corps, together with cavalry, etc., approximately 135,000 men, of which a proportion are raw recruits and recently organised battalions. In Poland and on the Galician border, from Kalish to Kamenez, the Guards, the Grenadiers, the 1st Corps, the 2nd Division of the 6th Corps, some of the reserves of the Grenadiers and of the 1st Corps, plus cavalry and artillery, approximately 235,000 men. The crack troops of the Russian Army are commanded by Gorchakov. In Bessarabia and between the Dniester and the Bug, there are two divisions of the 2nd Corps and a part of the reserves, approximately 60,000 men. These formed a part of the army of the West. But when the Danube army was sent to the Crimea they were detached from the Western army in order to take the place of the Danube army and, under the command of General Panyutin, they are now confronting the Austrian army in the Principalities. Intended for the defence of the Crimea: the 3rd and 4th Corps, two divisions of the 6th Corps and reserves, as well as one division of both the 2nd and 5th Army Corps on the march, together with cavalry they amount to some 170,000 men under Menshikov. The rest of the reserves and newly formed battalions, particularly of the 1st, 2nd, 3rd, 4th and 5th Corps, are being reorganised as the great reserve army under General Cheodayev. This reserve army, numbering about 150,000 is concentrated in the interior of Russia. How many of them are marching towards Poland or southward is unknown.

Thus while at the end of last summer Russia could muster less than 500,000 men on the western borders of her empire, from Finland to the Crimea, she now has 600,000 men, besides a reserve army of 150,000. Nevertheless she is weaker vis-à-vis

Austria than at that time. Then, in August and September, there were 270,000 Russians in Poland and Podolia, while the army on the Pruth, Dniester and Danube amounted to roughly 80,000 men, making a total of 350,000 men capable of operating together against Austria. Now—there remain only 295,000 men, while Austria has 320,000 directly confronting them and can support them with another 70,000-80,000 in Bohemia and Moravia. Therefore Russia cannot risk an offensive operation *at the present moment.* In an open country like Poland, without any big river lines between the two armies, this is synonymous with the necessity of retiring to a tenable position. If Austria attacked now the Russian army would have to split up into two halves, one withdrawing towards Warsaw, the other towards Kiev, separated by the inaccessible marshlands of Polesye, which extend from the Bug to the Dnieper. Therefore *at the present moment* it is essential for Russia to gain time. Hence her "diplomatic considerations".

Written on January 29, 1855

First published in the *Neue Oder-Zeitung*, No. 53, February 1, 1855

Printed according to the newspaper

Published in English for the first time

Karl Marx and Frederick Engels

THE LATE BRITISH GOVERNMENT [440]

In recording the advent of Lord Palmerston's Government to what we are confident must prove a brief and not very brilliant career, it seems not improper to cast a glance at the history of its predecessor, of which it is hard to say whether the splendor of its opening pretensions, the momentous nature of the events in which it participated, its unprecedented incapacity, or the ignominy of its downfall will the most distinguish the future record of its existence.

It will be remembered that Lord Aberdeen and his Coalition came into office through the vote which upset, on the 16th December, 1852, the Derby Administration. Disraeli, in a vote upon his budget, was left in a minority of nineteen, under the pretext that his extension of the house-tax and of the general area of direct taxation was not in harmony with Whig and Peelite principles of sound political economy. The vote, however, was in reality carried by the Irish Brigade,[441] whose motives, as is well known, are of a far less theoretical nature; and even the so-called Liberals and liberal Conservatives had to belie their words by their acts when they repeated in their own budget many of Disraeli's proposals and most of his arguments. At all events, the Tories were turned out, and, after some struggles and fruitless attempts, this Coalition was formed, by which, according to *The London Times*,[a] England had now arrived "at the commencement of the political millennium."[b] This millennium lasted exactly two years

---

[a] *The Times*, No. 21316, January 4, 1853, leader.— *Ed.*

[b] The thousand years during which holiness is to be triumphant throughout the world. Some believe that during this period Christ will reign on earth in person with his saints.— *Ed.*

and one month; it ended in universal defeat and disaster, amid the general indignation of the British people. The very *Times* which inaugurated the reign of "All the Talents" as a millennium, was, of all journals, the one which contributed most toward its downfall.

The Talents met Parliament on the 10th of February, 1853. They recited over again the identical Whig programme which Lord John Russell had already once inaugurated in 1850 and which had then very soon led to a ministerial turn-out. As to the main question, Parliamentary Reform, that was a matter which could not be thought of before "next session." For the present the country was to be satisfied with minor, but more plentiful and more practical administrative reforms, such as law-reform, railway-regulations, and improvements in education. The retirement of Lord John Russell from the Foreign office, where he was replaced by Lord Clarendon, was the first of the changes which characterize this talented administration, and which all ended in the institution of new places, new sinecures, new salaries for its faithful supporters. Russell was for a time a member of the Cabinet, without any function but that of Leader of the House of Commons, and without salary; but he very soon applied for the latter commodity, and finally was elevated to the style and title of President of the Council, with a good round sum per annum.

On the 24th of February Lord John brought in his bill for removal of Jewish Disabilities, which ended in nothing, being burked by the House of Lords. On the 4th of April, he followed it up by his Educational Reform bill. Both bills were as tame and innocuous as could be expected from a Do-Nothing Ministry. Meanwhile, Palmerston, in his position as Home Secretary, discovered the new gunpowder-plot, the great Kossuth-Hale rocket affair.[442] Palmerston, it will be recollected, had Mr. Hale's rocket factory searched, and a quantity of rockets and composition seized; the matter was made a great deal of, and when discussed in Parliament, on April 15, Palmerston gave it still greater importance by his mysterious language. But about one point he used no mystery; he declared himself the general informer of the Continental police, with regard to refugees, quite as openly as Sir James Graham had done in 1844, on the occasion of the opening of Mazzini's letters. At last, however, the affair had to be virtually abandoned by the noble informer, in as much as Mr. Hale could only be charged with having carried on a manufacture of explosive matter at an unlawful proximity to the suburbs of

London; and the great plot for blowing up all Europe was reduced to a simple, fineable contravention of police regulations!

It was now Russell's turn again. On May 31, in a speech in the House, he offended the Roman Catholics—the men who had put him in office—in such a manner that the Irish members of the Administration at once resigned. This was more than the "strong Government" could stand. The support of the Irish Brigade was the first condition of its existence, and, consequently, Aberdeen, in a letter to one of the Irish members, had to disavow his colleague, and Russell had to retract in Parliament.[a]

The main feature of this session was the East India bill, by which the Ministry proposed, without any material improvement of Indian government, to renew the East India Company's charter for twenty years. This was too bad, even for such a Parliament, and had to be abandoned. The charter was to be revocable by Parliament at a year's notice. Sir Charles Wood, the late bungling Chancellor of the Exchequer of the Russell Cabinet, now proved his capabilities in the Board of Control, or Indian Board. The whole of the reforms proposed were confined to a few petty alterations of doubtful effect in the judicial system, and the throwing open of civil employments and the scientific military service to public competition. But these reforms were merely pretexts; the real gist of the bill was this: Sir Charles Wood got his salary as President of the Board of Control raised from £1,200 to £5,000; instead of 24 India Directors elected by the Company, there were to be only 18, six of whom were in the gift of Government, an accession of patronage which was the less despicable as the Directors' salaries were raised from £300 to £500, while the Chairman and Deputy-Chairman received £1,000. Not satisfied with this waste of public money, the Governor-General of India, formerly at the same time Governor of Bengal, was now to have a separate Governor of that Presidency under him, while a new Presidency, with a new Governor, was to be created on the Indus. Every one of these Governors must, of course, have his Council, and overpaid and luxurious sinecures the seats in these Councils are. How happy India should be, governed as it is, at last, according to unsophisticated Whig principles!

Then came the Budget. This splendid financial combination, along with Mr. Gladstone's scheme for doing away with the

---

[a] Aberdeen to Monsell, June 3, 1853. *The Times*, No. 21447, June 6, 1853; Lord John Russell's speech in the House of Commons on June 6, 1853. *The Times*, No. 21448, June 7, 1853.— *Ed.*

national debt, has been so fully illustrated in *The Tribune*[a] that it is needless to recount its features. Many of them were taken from Disraeli's budget, which had so much roused the virtuous indignation of Gladstone; nevertheless the reduction of the tea duty, and the extension of direct taxation, were common to both budgets. Some of its most important measures were forced upon the great financier after his opposition against them had been repeatedly voted down in Parliament; thus the repeal of the Advertisement duty, and the extension of the Succession duty to landed property. The reform of the Licensing system, several times remodeled pending the discussion, had to be dropped. The budget, brought out with pretensions to a complete system, transformed itself during the debate into a confused *mixtum compositum*[b] of unconnected little items, hardly worth a hundredth part of the talk they occasioned.

As to the reduction of the national debt, Gladstone broke down still more completely. This scheme, brought forward with still greater pretensions than the budget, resulted in creating $2^1/_2$ per cent. Exchequer bonds, instead 1 per cent. Exchequer bills, the public thus losing $1^1/_2$ per cent. on the whole amount; in the necessity for the repayment, at the greatest public inconvenience, of the whole amount of the Exchequer bills, as well as of 8 millions of South Sea[443] stock; and in the total failure of his Exchequer bonds, which nobody would take. By this wonderful arrangement, Mr. Gladstone had the satisfaction of seeing the balance in the Exchequer diminished, on the 1st April 1854, from £7,800,000 which it was a year before, to £2,800,000, thus reducing, on the very eve of a war, the available funds of the public treasury by five millions. All this in the face of the secret correspondence of Sir H. Seymour, by which the Government must have known a year beforehand that a war with Russia was inevitable.

The new Irish Landlords and Tenants' bill,[444] brought in under Lord Derby, by the Tory Napier,[c] passed the Commons with at least some show of consent on the part of the Ministry; the Lords threw it out, and Aberdeen stated, on the 9th of August, his satisfaction at this result. The Transportation bill,[445] Navigation bill, and others which passed into law, had been inherited from the Derby Cabinet. The bills on Parliamentary Reform, National

---

[a] See present edition, Vol. 12, pp. 44 and 66 and this volume, pp. 117-18 and 184-88.— *Ed.*

[b] Mixture.— *Ed.*

[c] Joseph Napier.— *Ed.*

Education Reform, and almost all bills on Law Reform, had to be postponed. The British Whigs seem to consider it a misfortune that any of their measures should escape this fate. The only bill which passed, and which may be considered as the rightful property of this Ministry, is the Great Cab Act, which had to be reformed the day after its passage, in consequence of a general rebellion of the cabmen. Not even a set of regulations for cabs could All the Talents bring into successful existence.

On the 20th of August, 1853, Palmerston dismissed Parliament with the assurance that the people might be tranquil as to the Eastern difficulties; the evacuation of the Principalities was guaranteed by "his confidence in the honor and character of the Russian Emperor, which would move him to withdraw his troops from the Principalities!" On the 3d December, the Turkish fleet was destroyed by the Russians at Sinope. On the 12th, the Four Powers sent a note to Constantinople, in which, in reality, far more concessions were asked from the Porte than even in the preceding note of the Vienna Conference.[446] On the 14th, the British Ministry telegraphed to Vienna that the Sinope affair was not considered an obstacle to the continuation of the negotiations. Palmerston consented expressly to this; but on the next day he resigned—ostensibly for some difference respecting Russell's Reform bill, in reality, in order to make the public believe that he had resigned on grounds of foreign and war-policy. His purpose being obtained, he re-entered the Cabinet after a few days and thus avoided all unpleasant explanations in Parliament.

In 1854, the performance opened with the resignation of one of the junior Lords of the Treasury, Mr. Sadleir, who also was the Ministerial broker of the Irish brigade. Scandalous disclosures in an Irish Court of law, deprived the Administration of his talents. Afterward fresh scandalous matter came forward. Mr. Gladstone, the virtuous Gladstone, attempted to procure the governorship of Australia for one of his relations, his own secretary, a certain Lawley, known only as a betting-man and a jobber on the Stock Exchange; but, fortunately, the matter crept out too soon. In the same way, the same Gladstone was unpleasantly connected with vice by the absconding with a considerable amount of public money, of one O'Flaherty, a man employed under him and placed in his post by him. Another individual, of the name of Hayward, wrote a voluminous pamphlet of no literary or scientific value against Disraeli, and was rewarded by Gladstone with an office in the Poor-Law Board.

Parliament met in the beginning of February. On the 6th Palmerston gave notice of a bill for the organization of the militia in Ireland and Scotland; but, as war was actually declared on the 27th March, he considered it his duty not to bring it forward before the end of June. On the 13th Russell brought in his Reform bill, only to withdraw it ten weeks later, "with tears in his eyes," also because war had been declared.[a] In March, Gladstone comes forward with his budget, asking merely "for the sum which would be necessary to *bring back* the 25,000 men about to leave the British shores."[b] Thanks to his colleagues, he is now saved that trouble. In the meantime the Czar, by the publication of the secret correspondence, forced the French and English Cabinets to declare war. This secret correspondence, beginning with one of Russell's dispatches of the 11th January, 1853,[c] proved that at that time the British Ministers were fully aware of the aggressive intentions of Russia. All their assertions about the honor and character of Nicholas, and the pacific and moderate attitude of Russia, now looked like so many barefaced untruths, invented merely to humbug John Bull.

On the 7th of April, Lord Grey, feeling a strong vocation for the post of Minister of War, in order to ruin discipline in the army as he had ruined allegiance in almost every British Colony during his former Colonial administration—Lord Grey launched a philippic against the present organization of the War Department. He asked for a consolidation of all its offices under one War Minister. This speech gave Ministers an opportunity to create, in June, a new Secretaryship *for* War, by separating the War Department from the Colonial Department. Thus everything was left as defective as heretofore, while merely a new office with a new salary was created. The whole of that session of Parliament may be summed up thus: seven principal bills were brought in; of these, the bills for the change of the Law of Settlement,[447] for Public Education in Scotland, and for the reconstruction of Parliamentary oaths[448]—another shape of the Jews bill—were defeated; three others, the Bribery Prevention bill, the Civil Service Reorganization bill, and the Reform bill, were withdrawn; one bill, the Oxford University Reform bill, passed, but in a dreadfully mutilated state.

---

[a] Lord John Russell's speech in the House of Commons on April 11, 1854. *The Times*, No. 21713, April 12, 1854.— *Ed.*

[b] Mr. Gladstone's speech in the House of Commons on March 6, 1854. *The Times*, No. 21682, March 7, 1854.— *Ed.*

[c] Reference to Seymour's dispatch to Lord Russell of January 11, 1853.— *Ed.*

The conduct of the war, the diplomatic efforts of the Coalition need not here be alluded to. They are fresh in the memory of everybody. Parliament, prorogued on the 12th of August last, met again in December to pass hurriedly two measures of the utmost urgency; the Foreign Legion bill, and the bill permitting the Militia, as such, to volunteer for service abroad. Both of them have remained, to this day, a dead letter. In the mean time the news of the disastrous state of the British army in the Crimea arrived. The public indignation was roused; the facts were glaring and undeniable; Ministers had to think of retreat. Parliament met in January, Roebuck gave notice of his motion, Lord J. Russell at once disappeared, and a defeat unparalleled in Parliamentary history upset All the Talents after but a few days' debate.

Great Britain has had many a seedy administration to boast of, but a Cabinet so seedy, needy and greedy, and at the same time so presumptuous as All the Talents, never existed. They began with unbounded boasting, lived upon hair-splitting and defeat, and ended in disgrace as complete as it is possible for man to attain.

Written on February 1, 1855

First published in the *New-York Daily Tribune*, No. 4321, February 23; reprinted in the *New-York Semi-Weekly Tribune*, No. 1018, February 27, 1855 as a leader

Reproduced from the *New-York Daily Tribune*

Karl Marx

ON THE MINISTERIAL CRISIS

London, February 2. Yesterday evening the House of Commons again adjourned after Palmerston had made the official announcement of the resignation of the Ministry.

In the House of Lords, Aberdeen gave the funeral oration of the "Cabinet of all the Talents".[a] He said that he had opposed Roebuck's motion not because his Administration wished to avoid an inquiry but because the motion was unconstitutional. Aberdeen avoided, however, giving any historical illustration of this in the manner of his friend Sidney Herbert, who asked the Commons if it was of a mind to imitate the French Directory (founded 1795), which sent out commissars to arrest Dumouriez—commissars who, as everybody knows, were extradited to Austria by Dumouriez in 1793.[449] Such learning is shunned by our Scottish thane. His Cabinet, he assures us, would only stand to gain by a committee of inquiry. He goes even further. He anticipates the outcome of the inquiry in a panegyric over himself and his colleagues, firstly the Secretary for War, then the Chancellor of the Exchequer, then the First Lord of the Admiralty and finally the Foreign Secretary. Each is claimed to have been a great man in his job—a talent. As far as England's military situation is concerned, the position of the Crimean army is, he admits, vexatious, but Bonaparte has told Europe that the French army comprises 581,000 men; in addition he is said to have ordered a new levy of 140,000. Sardinia had placed 15,000 splendid troops at the disposal of Lord Raglan. If

---

[a] Speeches by Aberdeen, Derby and Newcastle in the House of Lords on February 1, 1855 were published in *The Times*, No. 21967, February 2, 1855.— *Ed.*

the peace negotiations in Vienna should break down then they were assured of the aid of a great military power with an army of 500,000 men.

At any rate our Scottish thane does not suffer from the same fault as the great economist and historian Sismondi, who, as he relates himself, saw everything in black with one eye. Aberdeen sees rosy colours with both eyes. Thus he now discovers thriving prosperity in all districts of England, while businessmen, manufacturers and workers allege that they are suffering from a major trade crisis. His antagonist Lord Derby is sprinkled by him with a measure of the Attic salt that Lord Byron long ago lauded in the Scottish thane.[a]

My lords, the present need of the country is a strong Administration. How that is to be formed it was not for him to say. Rumour has asserted very confidently that Lord Derby has been commanded by Her Majesty to undertake the formation of an Administration. But seeing him in his place, he presumes that this was not the case and that public rumour errs.

In order to grasp the Attic subtlety of this statement it is necessary to compare it with Lord Derby's reply:

"The noble earl Aberdeen has certainly underrated the source of his information, because not only may general rumour have informed him on the subject, but previously to entering into this House he (Derby) had, under his own hand, given the noble earl information as to the result of this command received from the Queen. Consequently, the general rumour which led the noble earl to believe it might be possible that he (Derby) had had some communication with Her Majesty are phrases which must have been employed by the noble earl in his usual care to guard against exaggeration and to avoid overstating any part of his case."

In this situation Derby then declared that the state of the parties at the moment and the present position in the House of Commons did not permit him to undertake the formation of an Administration.

For the audience in the House of Lords, and for the noble peers themselves, the elucidations of the War Secretary, the Duke of Newcastle, and the picture that he painted of the interior of the "harmonious family" not only supplanted all interest in the Crimean army but even in the ministerial crisis. Lord John Russell's declaration in the Commons obliged him—said the Duke of Newcastle—to make a statement about his personal position in the defeated Cabinet. Russell's version of the story had been neither complete nor faithful. In the matter of the separation of the War Office from the Colonial Office he had insinuated that he

---

[a] Byron, *English Bards and Scotch Reviewers.—Ed.*

had only reluctantly given way to Newcastle's "strong wish" when he consented to the bestowal of the War Office on the Duke. Rather, when this separation was decided by the Cabinet he (Newcastle) had stated that "as far as he personally was concerned he was quite prepared to assume either or neither of the two departments". He could not, he said, remember Russell ever having expressed the desire to give the. War Office to Palmerston, but recollected that Russell himself once wished to take it over. He (Newcastle) had never thought of putting obstacles in his path. He had accepted the War Office, he said, in the full awareness that in the eventuality of success he would not receive the credit for it, and, in the eventuality of failure, all blame would be thrust on him. But he had deemed it his duty not to desert in the face of the danger and difficulties of this thankless post. This was, he went on, what some people had called his "arrogance", and Lord John Russell in his nobly patronising fashion had termed his "commendable ambition". Lord Russell, he claimed, had deliberately withheld from the House of Commons the following passage from a letter from Aberdeen to the noble Lord:

"I have shown your letter to the Duke of Newcastle. and Sidney Herbert. They both, as might have been expected, strongly urged me to adopt any such arrangement with respect to their offices as should be thought most conducive to the public service."

At this juncture he (Newcastle) had declared verbally to Aberdeen:

"Do not give Lord Russell any pretext for quitting the Government. On no account resist his wishes to remove me from office. Do with me whatever is best for the public service."

Lord John Russell, he said, had referred mysteriously in the Commons to the errors which he had denounced in writing to Aberdeen. He had taken good care not to read out the relevant passages. The first concerned the failure to send the 97th Regiment from Athens to the Crimea, but the Foreign Secretary had declared the withdrawal of English troops from Athens to be impermissible and dangerous. As regards his second error, that he failed to send out 3,000 recruits, Lord Raglan had protested against the further supply of such young and undisciplined soldiers. Moreover, he said, at that time there had been no transport ships available. These two alleged errors were all that Russell had managed to concoct, relaxing with his colleagues in bathing resorts while he (Newcastle) had remained at his post toiling away throughout the year 1854. Incidentally, Russell himself had finally written to him on October 8 regarding the "errors":

"You have done all that could be done and I am sanguine of success."

Moreover, he went on, Aberdeen had put Russell's proposal concerning changes in personnel before the whole Cabinet. It had been unanimously rejected. On December 13 he (Newcastle) had defended his management of affairs in a detailed speech in the House of Lords; on December 16 Russell told Aberdeen that he had changed his mind and had given up his wishes regarding the change in posts. Russell, he continued, had never taken any measures or made any proposals as to the reform of the War Administration, with two exceptions. Three days before his resignation and, Roebuck's motion there had been a Cabinet meeting. Russell suggested giving the meetings of the heads of all the military departments, which had been taking place at the offices of the Secretary for War, a formal and official character. Russell's proposal was accepted. Shortly afterwards, Russell had sent in a written proposal, which, apart from the innovation already approved by the Cabinet, contained only two suggestions: 1. the creation of a supreme board headed by the Secretary of State for War to absorb the Board of Ordnance and control the entire civil administration of the army; 2. the appointment of two senior officers, apart from the heads of the war departments hitherto involved, to this supreme board. Russell declared in the Commons that he had had good reason to believe that his "written proposals" would be rejected. This was untrue. Suggestion No. 1 was accepted by Newcastle; suggestion No. 2 was rejected, among other reasons because the "Commissary General" whom Russell wished to call in had for many years been a mythical person and no longer existed in the British army. Thus, he said, Russell had never made a proposal that had not been accepted. Moreover, he (Newcastle) had already informed Lord Aberdeen on January 23 that however Parliament might decide, whether for or against the Ministry, he would resign from the Ministry. He simply did not want to give the appearance of running away before Parliament had passed judgment.

Lord John Russell, whose whole life, as old Cobbett says, was just a series of "false pretexts for living", has, as Newcastle's speech shows, now died on false pretexts too.

Written on February 2, 1855   Printed according to the newspaper

First published in the *Neue Oder-Zeitung*,   Published in English for the first
No. 59, February 5, 1855   time

Karl Marx

FALL OF THE ABERDEEN MINISTRY

London, Friday, Feb. 2, 1855

Never in the whole annals of representative government has an administration been turned out half as ignominiously as the celebrated Cabinet of "all the Talents" in England. To be in a minority is a thing which may happen to anybody, but to be defeated by 305 against 148, by more than two to one, in an assembly like the Commons' House of Great Britain, that was a distinction reserved for the galaxy of genius commanded by *ce cher Aberdeen.*

There is no doubt the Cabinet considered its days as numbered as soon as Parliament met. The scandalous proceedings in the Crimea, the utter ruin of the army, the helplessness of all and every one connected with the administration of the war, the outcry in the country, fed by the diatribes of *The Times,* the evident determination of John Bull to know for once who was to blame, or at least to wreak his wrath upon some one or another—all this must have proved to the Cabinet that the time had arrived when they must put their house in order.

Notices of threatening questions and motions were given in abundance and at once; above all, the notice of Mr. Roebuck's threatening motion, for a committee to inquire into the conduct of the war, and of all parties who had any responsibility in its administration. This brought matters to an issue at once. Lord John Russell's political scent made it at once clear to him that this motion would be adopted in spite of minorities[450]; and a statesman like him, who boasts of more minorities than years, could not well afford to be again outvoted. Accordingly, Lord John Russell, with that spirit of pusillanimity and pettifogging meanness, which is visible during his entire career, through a cloak of important talkativity and constitutional precedentism, thought discretion the better part of valor,[a] and decamped from office without giving his colleagues even a moment's notice. Now, although he is a man who can hardly expect to be missed anywhere, yet it appears that "all the talents" were entirely upset by his sudden retreat. The press of Great Britain unanimously condemned the little statesman, but what of that? All the press and all its condemnations could not set the ministerial "higgledy piggledy" up again; and in this state of disorganization, with the Duke of Newcastle resigning the War Office, and Lord Palmerston not having taken possession of it, the Cabinet had to meet Mr. Roebuck's formidable motion.

Mr. Roebuck is a little lawyer, who would be just as funny a little Whig as Lord John Russell, and quite as inoffensive, had he only been more successful in his parliamentary career. But the ci-devant[b] briefless barrister, and present parliamentary spouter, has failed, with all his sharpness and activity, to amass any political capital worth speaking of. Though generally a sort of secret and confidential understrapper to any Whig Ministry, he never succeeded in reaching that position which insures Place, the great goal of all British Liberals. Our friend Roebuck, blighted in his blandest hopes, underestimated by his own party, ridiculed by his opponents, gradually felt the milk of human kindness turning sour within his bosom, and became, by and by, as invidious, unsociable, unpleasant, provoking a little cur as ever barked on the floor of a House of Parliament. In this capacity he has served, in turns, all men who knew how to handle him, without ever gaining claims upon the gratitude or consideration of any party; and nobody knew how to make a better use of him than our old friend Palmerston, whose game he again was made to play on the 26th ult.

Mr. Roebuck's motion, as it actually stood, could hardly have any sense in an assembly like the British House of Commons. Everybody knows what clumsy, lazy, time-killing things the Committees of the Commons are; an investigation of the conduct of this war by such a committee would be of no practical use whatever, for its results would come many a month too late to do any good—even if any good did result from the inquiry. It is only in a revolutionary, dictatorial assembly like the French National Convention of 1793 that such committees might do any good. But

---

[a] Shakespeare, *King Henry IV*, Part I, Act V, Scene 4.— *Ed.*
[b] Former.— *Ed.*

there the Government itself is nothing but such a committee—its agents are the commissioners of the assembly itself, and, therefore, in such an assembly similar motions would be superfluous. Yet, Mr. Sidney Herbert was not entirely wrong in pointing out that the motion (surely quite unintentionally on Mr. Roebuck's part) had a somewhat unconstitutional character, and in asking, with his usual historical accuracy, whether the House of Commons intended sending Commissioners to the Crimea, the same as the *Directory* (sic) did to General Dumouriez.[a] We may as well observe here that this same precious chronology which makes the Directory (instituted 1795) send Commissaries to Dumouriez, whom this latter General had arrested and delivered up to the Austrians as early as 1793—that this chronology is quite of a piece with the confusion of time and space reigning in all the operations of Mr. Sidney Herbert and colleagues. To return to Mr. Roebuck's motion, the informality alluded to served as a pretext to a great many candidates for place, not to vote for it, and thus to remain free to enter into any possible combination. And yet, the majority against Ministers was so crushing!

The debate itself was characterized particularly by the different departments of the Government quarreling among themselves. Each of them threw the blame upon the other. Sidney Herbert, Secretary at War, said it was all the fault of the transport service; Bernal Osborne,[b] Secretary of the Admiralty, said it was the viciously rotten system at the Horse Guards [451] which was at the bottom of all the mischief; Admiral Berkeley, one of the Lords of the Admiralty, pretty distinctly advised Mr. Herbert to pull his own nose, &c. Similar amenities passed in the House of Lords, at the same time, between the Duke of Newcastle, War Minister, and Viscount Hardinge, Commander-in-Chief.[c] Mr. Herbert's position, it is true, was rendered extremely difficult by Lord John Russell, who, in explanations respecting his resignation, confessed that all that the press had said on the state of the Crimean army was substantially correct, and that the condition of the troops was "horrid and heart-rending."[d] After this, Sidney Herbert could do

----

[a] See this volume, p. 627.— *Ed.*

[b] The speeches of Bernal Osborne and Berkeley in the House of Commons on January 29, 1855 were published in *The Times*, No. 21964, January 30, 1855.— *Ed.*

[c] The speeches of the Duke of Newcastle and Viscount Hardinge in the House of Lords on January 29, 1855 were published in *The Times*, No. 21964, January 30, 1855.— *Ed.*

[d] Lord John Russell's speech in the House of Commons on January 26, 1855. *The Times*, No. 21962, January 27, 1855.— *Ed.*

no better than to give in to the facts without a murmur, and to make a series of extremely lame and partly unfounded excuses. He had to confess, even more pointedly, the complete incapacity and disorganization of the War Administration. We have succeeded with comparative ease in bringing 240,000 tuns of stores of all descriptions, and a numerous army, after a 3,000 miles' journey, to Balaklava; and now follows a glowing account of all the clothing, the housing, the provisions, the luxuries even, sent in profusion to the army. But, alas! It was not at Balaklava they were wanted, but six miles higher up the country. Three thousand miles we can carry all the stores; but three thousand and six— impossible! The fact that they had to go six miles further has ruined everything!

For all that, his deprecating attitude might have aroused some pity for him, had it not been for the speeches of Layard, Stafford, and his own colleague, Gladstone.[a] The two former members had but lately returned from the East; they had been eye-witnesses to what they recounted. And far from merely repeating what the papers had already published, they gave instances of neglect, mismanagement and incapacity; they described scenes of horror far surpassing what had been known before. Horses, shipped on sailing transports from Varna to Balaklava without any provender to feed them; knapsacks made to journey five or six times from the Crimea to the Bosphorus, while the men were starving, and cold and wet for want of their clothes contained in them; "reconvalescents" sent back for active duty to the Crimea while too weak to stand on their legs; then the disgraceful state of neglect, of exposure, of filth, to which the sick and wounded were exposed in Scutari, as well as in Balaklava and on board the transports—all this formed a picture, compared to which the descriptions of "Our Own Correspondent," or of private letters from the East, were pale in the extreme.

To counteract the terrible effect of these descriptions, the sapient self-complacency of Mr. Gladstone had to take its stand on the breach; and, unfortunately for Sidney Herbert, he retracted all the confessions made by his colleagues on the first night of the debate. Herbert had been asked point-blank by Roebuck: You sent 54,000 men from this country; there are now only 14,000 under arms; what has become of the remaining 40,000? Herbert merely replied

---

[a] The speeches of Herbert and Layard in the House of Commons on January 26 and of Stafford and Gladstone on January 29, 1855 were published in *The Times*, Nos. 21962 and 21964, January 27 and 30, 1855.—*Ed.*

by reminding Roebuck that some of them had died already at Gallipoli and Varna; he never questioned the general correctness of the numbers quoted as lost or disabled. But Gladstone now turns out to be better informed than the Secretary at War, and actually makes the army number, not 14,000, but 28,200 men, besides from 3,000 to 4,000 marines and sailors serving on shore, "at the dates of the last returns which have reached us!" Of course, Gladstone takes good care not to say what these "dates of the last returns" are. But in view of the exemplary idleness displayed in all departments, and most particularly in the Brigade, Divisional and General Staffs, as evinced by the slow returns of casualties, we may be allowed to suppose that Mr. Gladstone's wonderful returns bear a date somewhere about the first of December, 1854, and include a great many men who were definitively knocked up by the six weeks bad weather and overwork following that date. Gladstone appears actually to have that blind faith in official documents which he on former occasions expected the public to have in his financial statements.

I will not enter into a more lengthened analysis of the debate. Beside a host of *dii minorum gentium*,[a] Disraeli spoke, also Walpole, the late Tory Home Secretary, and finally Palmerston, who "nobly" stood up for his calumniated colleagues.[b] Not a word had he said in the whole course of the debate, until he had ascertained its drift clearly. Then, and then only, he got up. The rumors brought up to the Treasury Bench by their understrappers, the general disposition of the House, made a defeat certain—a defeat which ruined his colleagues, but could not injure him. Though ostensibly turned out along with the remainder, he was so safe of his position, he was so sure to profit by their retirement, that it devolved upon him, almost as a duty of courtesy, to bow them out. And of this he acquitted himself by his speech just before the division.

Palmerston, indeed, has managed his resources well. Voted to be, on the Pacifico question, the "truly English Minister," [452] he has held that character ever since, to such an extent that in spite of all astounding revelations, John Bull always thought himself sold to some foreign power as soon as Palmerston left the Foreign Office. Ejected out of this office by Lord John Russell in a very

---

[a] Lesser gods, figuratively—second-rate magnitudes.— *Ed.*
[b] The speeches of Walpole in the House of Commons on January 26, of Disraeli and Palmerston on January 29, 1855 were published in *The Times,* Nos. 21962 and 21964, January 27 and 30, 1855.— *Ed.*

unceremonious way, he frightened that little man into silence respecting the causes of this ejection, and from that moment the "truly English Minister" excited a fresh interest as the innocent victim of ambitious and incapable colleagues, as the man whom the Whigs had betrayed. After the downfall of the Derby Ministry, he was put into the Home Office, a position which again made him appear the victim. They could not do without the great man whom they all hated, and as they would not put him into that position which belonged to him, they put him off with a place far too low for such a genius. So thought John Bull, and was prouder still of his Palmerston, when he saw how the truly English Minister bustled about in his subordinate place, meddling with Justices of the Peace, interfering with cabmen, reprimanding Boards of Sewerage, trying his powers of eloquence upon the licensing system, grappling with the great Smoke Question, attempting police centralization, and putting a barrier in the way of intramural interments. The truly English Minister! His rule of conduct, his source of information, his treasury of new measures and reforms, were the interminable letters of "Paterfamilias"[a] in *The Times*. Of course, nobody was better pleased than Paterfamilias, whose like form the majority of the voting middle classes of England, and Palmerston became their idol. "See what a great man can make of a little place! what former Home Secretary ever thought of removing such nuisances!" For all that, neither were cabs reformed, nor smoke suppressed, nor intramural church-yards done away with, nor the police centralized, nor any of these great reforms carried—but that was the fault of Palmerston's envious and thick-headed colleagues! By and by, this bustling, meddling propensity was considered as the proof of great energy and activity; and this unsteadiest of all English statesmen, who never could bring either a negotiation or a bill in Parliament to a satisfactory issue, this politician who stirs about for the fun of the thing, and whose measures all end in being allowed to go quietly to sleep—this same Palmerston was puffed up as the only man whom his country could count upon in great emergencies. The truth is, he contributed a great deal to this puffing himself. Not content with being co-proprietor of *The Morning Post*, where he was advertised every day as the future savior of his country, he hired fellows like the Chevalier Wykoff to spread his praise in France and America; he bribed, a few months ago, *The Daily News*, by communication of telegraphic dispatches and other

---

[a] Presumably, Martin Farquhar Tupper.— *Ed.*

useful hints; he had a hand in the management of almost every paper in London. The mismanagement of the war brought on that emergency in which he intended to rise great, unattained and unattainable, upon the ruins of the Coalition. In this decisive moment he procured the unreserved support of *The Times.* How he managed to bring this about, what contract he made with Mr. Delane, of course we cannot tell. Thus, the day after the vote, the whole daily press of London, *The Herald* only excepted, with one voice cried out for Palmerston as Premier; and we suppose he thought he had obtained the object of his wishes. Unfortunately, the Queen has seen too much of the truly English Minister, and will not submit to him, if she can help it.

Written on February 2, 1855

First published in the *New-York Daily Tribune,* No. 4316, February 17; reprinted in the *New-York Semi-Weekly Tribune,* No. 1016, February 20, 1855

Signed: *Karl Marx*

Reproduced from the *New-York Daily Tribune*

Karl Marx

THE DEFEATED GOVERNMENT

London, February 3. On December 16, 1852 the first point of Disraeli's budget—extension of direct taxation, initially house duty, was defeated by a majority of 19 votes. The Tory Government resigned. After ten days of intrigues the Coalition Government was formed. It consisted of a section of the Whig oligarchy—the Grey clan was excluded this time—of the Peelite bureaucracy, an admixture of so-called Mayfair Radicals, such as Molesworth and Osborne, and finally the brokers of the Irish Brigade who had decided the issue on December 16—Sadleir, Keogh, Monsell—and were accommodated in subordinate ministerial posts. The Ministry described itself as the "Cabinet of All the Talents". And in fact it did include nearly *all* the talents that had been relieving one another in government for thirty years and more. *The Times* proclaimed the "Cabinet of All the Talents" with the words: We have "now arrived at the commencement of the *political millennium.*" The "political millennium" had in fact dawned for the ruling classes the moment they discovered that their party formations had dissolved, that their internal contradictions were only due to personal whims and vanities, and that their reciprocal frictions could no longer grip the nation's interest. The Coalition Government represented no particular faction. It represented "all the Talents" of the class that has hitherto ruled England. It is therefore important to cast a glance in retrospect at its achievements.

After the fall of the Derby ministry Parliament adjourned for the Christmas recess. It then adjourned again for the Easter recess. Not until then did the real session of 1853 commence, almost completely taken up with the debates on Gladstone's budget, Sir Charles Wood's Bill on India and Young's Bill regulating the relations between landlords and tenant-farmers in Ireland.

Before introducing his budget Gladstone announced major operations to reduce the national debt—both floating and consolidated debts. The operation regarding the former consisted in a lowering of interest on Exchequer Bills from $1^1/_2$d. to 1d. per day, and that at a time when the market rate of interest was rising. The result was that first he had to redeem 3 million Exchequer Bills, and then he had to reissue them at a higher rate of interest. Even more significant was his experiment with that monster, the consolidated national debt. The ostensible aim was its reduction. He acted so skilfully that at the end of the financial year he had to buy back 8 million South Sea notes at par, though at the current stock exchange price they were only worth 85 per cent. At the same time he launched on to the stock exchange a new security invented by himself—Exchequer bonds. He had got Parliament to authorise him to issue £30 million worth of these securities. With some difficulty he got rid of £400,000 worth. In a word: his operations to reduce the national debt resulted in an increase of the capital of the consolidated debt, and an increase in the rate of interest of the floating debt.

His *budget*, the pride of the Coalition, consists of various heterogeneous elements. Parts of it, such as the reduction of tea tax, of excise duty (except that he reduced it on soap, and Disraeli on malt) and the increase in direct taxation, have been borrowed from the budget of his predecessor. The other and most important provisions such as imposition of death duty on land, the abolition of tax on newspaper advertisements, etc., were forced on him since he twice failed to get his counter-proposals approved by the House. Other constituents of his plan, such as the new regulation of the licensing system, he was obliged to withdraw entirely. What he brought to the House as an encyclopaedic system emerged as a mish-mash of heterogeneous and contradictory items. His only remaining original contribution is the passage in the budget in which *The Times* is exempted from paying £30,000-40,000 p.a. as a result of the abolition of stamp duty on the supplements that *The Times* is the only one of the newspapers to publish. He insisted all the more firmly—and thus gained the goodwill of *The Times* to that it will not want to miss him in a new Administration either—on the retention of stamp duty for the main part of the newspaper. Those were Gladstone's masterpieces from which the Coalition derived its sustenance throughout the whole of the 1853 session.

The charter of the *East India* Company expired on April 30, 1854. England's relations with India thus had to be regulated anew. The Coalition intended renewing the charter of the East India Company for another 20 years. It failed. India is not to be "leased out" to the Company again for decades. It now exists only by "proclamation", which Parliament can send it any day. This, the only significant feature of the India Bill, was passed *despite* the Government. With the exception of a few marginal reforms in the Indian judiciary and the opening of civil posts and scientific military posts to all qualified applicants, the actual kernel of the India Bill may be summarised as follows: the salary of the minister governing India from London (President of the Board of Control[a]) has been raised from £1,200 to £5,000 p.a. Of the 18 directors the government will henceforth elect six, and the meeting of share-holders of the East India Company only twelve. The salary of these directors has been raised from £300 to £900 and that of their two managers from £400 to £1,000. Moreover, the office of Governor of Bengal (together with his board of control) is in future to be separate from that of Governor General of India; a new President, plus board, is likewise to be created for the Indus district itself. The Indian reform of the Cabinet of All the Talents is limited to this raising of salaries and creating of new sinecures.

The Bills concerning relations between landlords and tenants in Ireland had been taken over by the Coalition Government from its Tory predecessors. It was not to be outdone by them. It adopted the Bills and carried them through the House of Commons shortly before the end of the session after a ten-month debate, or to be more accurate, allowed them to pass. In the House of Lords, on the other hand, Aberdeen consented to the rejection of the very same Bills—on the pretext of scrutinising them more closely and taking them up again in the next session.

The ministerial Bills for parliamentary reform, education, legal and judicial reforms were postponed by request of the Cabinet until the next session. The great work of "all the Talents"—the Bill regulating the cab-drivers of London—actually became law, but had scarcely crossed the threshold of Parliament before it had to return again to be refashioned. It had proved to be impracticable.

---

[a] Marx used the English term.— *Ed.*

Finally on August 20 Parliament adjourned. Palmerston sum-marised the foreign policy of the Ministry during this session when he dismissed Parliament with the words: It could adjourn without anxiety. He had full confidence in the honour and character of the Russian Emperor, who, he said, would evacuate the Danubian Principalities voluntarily.

Palmerston's public intervention in foreign policy was limited in the 1853 session to this declaration; to a parliamentary speech a few days before the adjournment of the House of Commons in which he treated the blocking of the Sulina estuary of the Danube by the Russians as a bad joke; and finally to the admission extracted from him in the sitting of April 15, 1853—on the occasion of the so-called Kossuth Powder Plot—that on behalf of continental courts he was employing the English police for the surveillance of political refugees.

Written on February 3, 1855

First published in the *Neue Oder-Zeitung*, No. 63, February 7, 1855

Printed according to the news-paper

Published in English for the first time

Karl Marx

THE PARTIES AND CLIQUES[453]

London, February 5. The duration of the present ministerial crisis is more or less normal, as such crises last on average nine to ten days in England. It is astonishing that in his famous work *The Abilities of Man*,[a] Quetelet manages to demonstrate that the annual total of accidents, crimes, etc., in civilised countries can be determined in advance with almost mathematical accuracy.[b] The normal duration of English ministerial crises in different periods of the nineteenth century is, on the other hand, nothing amazing, for—as is well known—there are always a given circle of combinations to be traversed, a given number of posts to be disposed of, and a given sum of intrigues have to paralyse one another. The only extraordinary thing is the character of the combinations which the dissolution of the old parties necessitates this time. The fact of this dissolution made the formation of the fallen Coalition Ministry possible and inevitable. The governing caste, which in England is by no means the same as the ruling class, will be driven from one coalition to another, until the proof is furnished exhaustively that it has lost its calling to govern. The Derbyites, it will be remembered, had objected most vehemently to the Coalition. The first step of Lord Derby, as soon as the Queen had charged him to form a new Cabinet, was to attempt a coalition, not only with Palmerston—to whom Disraeli had expressly declared during the Roebuck debate that the proposed vote of censure was no more directed against the Duke of

---

[a] A. Quetelet, *Sur l'homme et le développement de ses facultés, ou Essai de physique sociale.—Ed.*

[b] For details see present edition, Vol. 11, p. 497.—*Ed.*

Newcastle or Aberdeen than against him—but also with Gladstone and Sidney Herbert, that is with the Peelites, who are persecuted by the Tories with especial hatred as the immediate instruments of the disintegration of their party. When Russell in his turn is requested to form a Cabinet he attempts a coalition with the very same Peelites whose presence in the old Ministry he had taken as the pretext for his resignation, and who had given the lie to him in all the solemnity of a parliamentary sitting. Finally Palmerston, if he manages to form his Ministry, will merely present a second, little changed edition of the old Coalition Ministry. The Grey clan of Whigs will perhaps replace the Russell clan of Whigs, etc. The old parliamentary parties that had been entrusted with a monopoly of government now exist merely in the form of coteries; but the same causes that deprived these coteries of the strength to form parties, to differ from one another, deprive them of the strength to unite. No epoch in English parliamentary history, therefore, shows such disintegration into a mass of insignificant and fortuitous cliques as precisely the epoch of the Coalition Ministry. Only two of these cliques are numerically significant, the Derbyites and Russellites. In their train follows a highly ramified group of powerful old families with a numerous clientele. But it is precisely this numerical strength that constitutes the weakness both of the Derbyites and the Russellites. Too small to command an independent parliamentary majority, they are too large and have too many place-hunters to sustain in their own ranks to be able to buy sufficient support from outside by giving away important posts. The numerically weaker cliques of the Peelites, Greyites, Palmerstonians, etc., are therefore more suitable for forming coalition ministries. But the factor that enables them to form ministries—the weakness of each of these cliques—turns their parliamentary majority into a matter of chance, liable to be lost any day of the week whether by a combination of Derbyites and Russellites, or by a combination of the Manchester school, etc., with the Derbyites.

From another point of view the recently attempted combinations of Ministers are just as interesting. All of them contained members of the old Cabinet. The last is headed by the most important member of that Cabinet.[a] And did not the House of Commons, in passing the Roebuck motion against all members of the old Coalition—as Palmerston himself declared in his reply to Disraeli—not only announce a vote of censure but also a committee

---

[a] Palmerston.— Ed.

of inquiry? The committee is not yet appointed, the inquiry not yet opened, and the accused are again taking over the helm of State. But if Parliament possesses the power to topple the Ministry, the Ministry possesses the power to *dissolve* Parliament. What effect the prospect of dissolving the present Parliament must have may be gathered from the statement made by Sir John Trollope in the House of Commons on March 1, 1853:

> "There are," he observed, "already 14 committees sitting which the House has created out of its Members to investigate the cases of bribery which occurred at the last parliamentary elections. If we continue in the same fashion, the whole of Parliament will disintegrate into committees of inquiry. And furthermore, the number of Members accused is so overwhelming that the unsullied remainder will not suffice to try them, or even inquire into their misdemeanours."

It would be hard to lose the seats bought so dearly right at the beginning of the third legislature—out of patriotism.

Written on February 5, 1855

First published in the *Neue Oder-Zeitung*,
No. 65, February 8, 1855

Printed according to the newspaper

Karl Marx

TWO CRISES

London, February 6. Public opinion is at present absorbed by two crises: the crisis of the Crimean army and the ministerial crisis. The former occupies the people; the latter, the clubs and drawing-rooms. According to the latest letters from the Crimea, which paint a gloomy picture, the English forces have shrunk from 14,000 to 12,000 men and the early relief of the siege of Sevastopol may be expected. In the meanwhile the drawing-room intrigue is being debated in the House of Commons. Lord [John] Russell and Mr. Gladstone[a] once more fill a whole sitting with lengthy discourses on, for and against the resignation of the great Russell from a Cabinet that has ceased to exist. No new facts are advanced by either side but the old ones are ventilated. Lord John is his own advocate, Gladstone the advocate of the Duke of Newcastle. The profound probings into the fitness of the latter as Secretary of State for War are endowed with new lustre[b] by the circumstance of there being no more army needing to be administered. Even the House of Commons, however, gave vent to its displeasure with its well-known, traditional grunting when at the end of his well-turned speech Gladstone let fall the words: "he wished that the whole misunderstanding (between Russell and Newcastle) could be revoked".

Hence it was not the vote of no confidence in the House, even less the destruction of an English army that caused the ministerial

---

[a] The speeches of Lord John Russell and Mr. Gladstone in the House of Commons on February 5, 1855 were published in *The Times*, No. 21970, February 6, 1855.— *Ed.*

[b] Marx used the English word.— *Ed.*

crisis, but it simply amounts to a "misunderstanding" between an old lord and a young duke. The Crimea is merely an excuse for the drawing-room intrigue. The misunderstanding between Ministry and Commons does not even merit the honour of a mention. That was too strong even for this House of Commons. Russell was a flop, Gladstone was a flop, the whole sitting was a flop.

Both Houses were notified that Lord Palmerston had been charged with the formation of a Ministry. But he encountered unexpected obstacles. Lord Grey refused to assume the management of a war of which he disapproved from the outset and still disapproved. A stroke of luck, this, for the army, whose discipline he most surely would have broken, just as he had broken the discipline of the colonies in his time. But Gladstone, Sidney Herbert and Graham also proved to be intractable. They demanded the restoration of the Peelites, lock, stock and barrel. These statesmen are aware that they form only a small clique commanding about 32 votes in the Commons. Only if its "great" talents keep together can this little clique hope to preserve its independence. A section of the leading Peelites in the Cabinet and another *outside* of it—this would be synonymous with the disappearance of this excellent club for statesmen. In the meantime Palmerston is trying his hardest to dictate to Parliament, in which he has no party, in the same way that he dictated to the Queen. His Cabinet is still not formed and he is already threatening in *The Morning Post* to appeal from the legislature to the people.[a] He threatens to dissolve the House should it dare "not to bestow on him the esteem which he enjoys outside the Palace of Westminster, amongst the public". This "public" is restricted to the journals half or wholly belonging to him. Wherever the people has recently made itself heard, e.g. at the meeting in Newcastle-upon-Tyne—whence petitions were addressed to Parliament to impeach the Ministry—Palmerston was denounced most vehemently as the secret leader of the late Coalition.

Now some additional information to complete the obituary of the "Cabinet of All the Talents". On November 30, 1853 occurred the incident at Sinope; on December 3 it became known in Constantinople; on December 12 the representatives [of the Four Powers] handed the Porte a note demanding greater concessions to Russia than the notorious Vienna note. On December 14 the British Government telegraphed to Vienna that Sinope should not

---

[a] *The Morning Post*, No. 25303, February 6, 1855, leader.— *Ed.*

interrupt the Vienna peace conference. Lord Palmerston attended the Cabinet meeting at which this was decided. He approved this decision but resigned from the Cabinet the following day on the pretext that the Reform Bill proposed by Russell conflicted with his conservative views. The real point was to wash his hands of the Sinope incident in front of the public. As soon as he had achieved this end he readily rejoined the Cabinet.

At the beginning of February 1854 Parliament is re-opened. The diplomatic documents on the Eastern troubles are ostensibly submitted to it. The most important papers are missing. Instead of receiving them from the British Ministers Parliament receives them from Tsar Nicholas via Petersburg.[454] The "Secret and Confidential Correspondence" published there makes it as clear as day to an astonished Parliament that its Ministers have deliberately duped it over foreign policy throughout the entire sessions of 1853 and 1854. It [the Correspondence] compels the Ministers on March 27 to make a declaration of war. On February 6 Palmerston had announced that he would be introducing a Bill calling up the militia in Scotland and Ireland. But as soon as war is declared he postpones his Bill and does not introduce it until the end of June. On February 13 Russell introduces his Reform Bill, postpones the second reading until the end of April, withdraws it in March sobbing passionately and—hitherto having neither department nor salary—is rewarded for this sacrifice by his colleagues with a ministerial sinecure carrying a salary, being made Lord President of the Council, a minister extraordinary so to speak. On March 6 the great financier Gladstone presents his budget. He contents himself with doubling income tax for six months. He requests "only a sum which would be necessary to bring back the 25,000 men about to leave the British shores".

He has now been relieved of this worry by his colleague Newcastle. By May 8 he is already forced to present a second budget. On April 11 he declares himself opposed to any form of government loan; on April 21 he asks the House to sanction a loan of £6 million to meet the cost of his unfortunate conversion experiment with the national debt.[a] On April 7 Lord Grey makes his speech on the shortcomings of the English war administration. On June 2 the Ministry uses the proposed reform—just as it had used the Reform of India and the Cholera Reform—in order to create a new post. The War Office is separated from the Colonial Office. All else remains as before. The legislative achievements of

---

[a] *The Times*, No. 21722, April 22, 1854.— *Ed.*

the Ministry in this session may be summarised in this way: it introduces seven important Bills. It fails with three of them: the Settlement Bill, and the Bills for education in Scotland and for the alteration of the parliamentary oath. It withdraws three of them: the Bills for the prevention of electoral bribes, for the complete re-organisation of the Civil Service, and for the reform of Parliament. One Bill is passed, that for the reform of the University of Oxford, but so plastered with amendments that its original shape is no longer recognisable. The great diplomatic and military feats are fresh in everyone's memory. That was the "Cabinet of All the Talents".

Written on February 6, 1855

First published in the *Neue Oder-Zeitung*, No. 67, February 9, 1855

Printed according to the newspaper

Published in English for the first time

FROM THE PREPARATORY MATERIALS

Karl Marx

A CENTRAL JUNTA[455]

September 26, 1808 (Aranjuez)-January 29, 1810[a]

Madrid having been evacuated by the French, it was to be expected that Napoleon would soon re-appear at the head of a more powerful army. Measures of common defence became then inevitable, and it was generally felt that the Polyarchy of the Provincial Juntas, whose dissensions grew even more clamorous after the success at Beylen, must give way to some sort of Central Government. The juntas, however, anxious to retain their hold upon Power, resolved, upon the proposal of the Junta of Sevilla, to select each from their own body two deputies the reunion of whom was to constitute the Central Government, while the Provincial Juntas remained invested with the internal government of their respective government. Thus a Central Junta, composed of 34 deputies from the Provincial Juntas, met on September 26, 1808, at Aranjuez and remained at the head of affairs till January 29, 1810. This Central Junta was driven by the Invader from Madrid to Sevilla and from Sevilla to Cadiz. While they waged a war of edicts from the Royal Palace of Aranjuez, the pass of Samosierra was forced by the French, and while they amused the people with vigorous proclamations from Sevilla, the passes of the Sierra Morena were lost and Soult's army inundated Andalusia.

During the reign of the Central Junta, the Spanish armies disappeared from the soil, ignominious defeats overset each other, and the disastrous battle at Ocaña (November 19, 1809) was the last pitched battle which the Spaniards fought, from that time confining themselves to a Guerrilla warfare.

---

[a] Here Marx made a note in the manuscript "(January 1809, Florida Blanca)."— Ed.

When "His Majesty"—this was the title assumed by the
Junta—fled from Sevilla, Cadiz offered the only asylum, and if
the Duke of Albuquerque, instead of marching his corps upon
Cadiz, had in obedience to their orders proceeded to Cordova, his
own army would have been cut off, Cadiz must have surrendered
to the French, and there would have been an end of any Central
Power in Spain. Where heroic resistance is exceptionally met with,
it is not the regular armies, in the open field, but only on the part
of assieged towns as at Saragossa and Gerona.

These few reminiscences from the Spanish war of Independence
suffice to characterise the Central Junta. The expulsion of the
French army from the Spanish soil was the great object of their
installation and in that object they signally failed. Under revolutionary still more than under ordinary circumstances the successes
[of] armies reflect the character of the Central Government. The
mere fact of the abandonment of the regular warfare for Guerrilla
exploits proves the disappearance of the national centre before the
local centres of resistance. Whence this failure of the National
government?

The very composition of the Central Junta certainly not suited
the task imposed upon them. Being for a dictatorial power too
many and too fortuitously mixed together, they were too few to
pretend to the authority of a National Convention. The mere fact
of their power being delegated from the Provincial Juntas,
incapacitated them to overcome the self-governing propensities,
the bad will, and the capricious egotism of these Juntas. The two
most marked members of the Central Junta: Florida Blanca—the
octogenarian minister of the enlightened despotism of Charles
III—and Jovellanos, a well-intentioned reformer who from
overconscientious scruples as to the means never dared to
accomplish an end—were certainly no match for the terrible crisis
the country was placed in.

The sense of their own weakness and the unstable tenure of
their power with respect to the people kept them in constant fear
and suspicion of the generals to whom they were obliged to
entrust the military commands. General Morla, himself a member
of the Central Junta, went over into the Bonapartist Camp, after
he had surrendered Madrid to Napoleon. Cuesta, [who] had
begun with arresting the Leonese Deputies to the Central Junta
and with forging plans for the restoration of the old authority of
the Captains General[456] and the royal *audiencias*,[a] also seemed

---

[a] Supreme Courts of Appeal in Spain and Latin America.— *Ed.*

afterwards to win the confidence of the Government in the same measure as he lost the battles of the country. Their distrust in Generals la Romana and Castaños, the victor of Beylen, proved well founded by the open hostility the former shew them in his address to the nation, d[e] d[ato]: Sevilla, on October 4, 1809, and the other by his conduct towards them when he became a member of the Regency. The Duke of Albuquerque, who of all the Spanish generals of that epoch was perhaps the only man to conduct a great war, seemed to be singularly gifted with all the dangerous qualities of a military dictator, a reason quite sufficient to remove him from all important commands. We may then give full credit to the Duke of Wellington writing to his brother, the Marquis of Wellesley, on September 1, 1809:

> "I am much afraid, from what I have seen of the proceedings of the Central Junta, that in the distribution of their forces they did not consider military defence, and military operations, so much, as they do political intrigue, and the attainment of trifling political objects."

The first popular government of Spain seemed overawed by a presentiment of the prominent part military men were destined to act in internal commotions. Devoid as they were of all truly revolutionary force by their very composition, the Central Junta could not but resort to petty intrigues in order to check the ascendancy of their own generals. On the other hand, incapable to resist the pressure of popular clamour, they often forced the generals into precipitate actions where the success could only be expected from most cautious and protracting stay upon the defensive.

Written between September 5 and 22, 1854

Reprinted from the manuscript

First published in: Marx and Engels, *Works*, Second Russian Edition, Vol. 44, Moscow, 1977

Karl Marx

[UNPUBLISHED EXTRACT FROM A SERIES OF ARTICLES "REVOLUTIONARY SPAIN"] [457]

... banner of revolution, the army of Ballesteros, which, since the capitulation of his chief [was] still concentrated at Priego, 10 leagues north of Malaga. On this his second Cadiz expedition [458] he[a] was made prisoner by one of General Molitor's corps, surrendered to the apostolical band, and sent to Madrid there to be executed, on the 7th November, four days before Ferdinand's return to the capital.

> "Non por su culpa cajó Riego:
> Por traición
> De un vil Borbón."

("Not by his fault fell Riego but by the treason of a vile Bourbon.")

When Ferdinand on his arrival at Madrid was waited upon and congratulated by the officers of the bands of the Foi [459] they having withdrawn, he exclaimed in the midst of his court: "It is the same dogs but with different collars".

The number of friars who in 1822 had mustered 16,310, amounted in 1830 to 61,727, being an increase of 45,417[b] in the course of 8 years. From the Madrid *Gaceta* we see that in the single month from the 24th August to the 24th September 1824, 1,200 persons were shot, hanged, and quartered, and then the barbarous decree against Comuneros, [460] Freemasons, etc., had not

---

[a] Riego.— *Ed.*

[b] Here the words "professional beggars" are crossed out in the manuscript.— *Ed.*

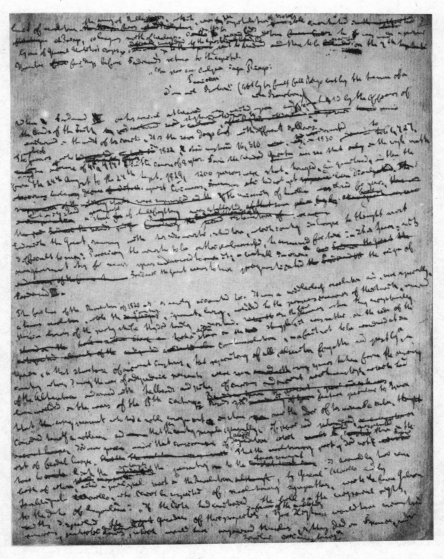

Original of unpublished extract from Marx's *Revolutionary Spain*

yet been divulgated.[a] The University of Sevilla was closed for years, but in its stead a governmental school of bullfighting was established.

Frederick the Great, conversing with his War Minister, asked him, which country in Europe he thought most difficult to ruin? Perceiving the minister to be rather embarrassed, he answered for him:

"It is Spain: as its own government has for many years endeavoured to ruin it—but all in vain."[b]

Frederick the Great seems to have prognosticated the reign of Ferdinand VII.

The failure of the Revolution of 1820-1823 is easily accounted for. It was a middle class revolution and, more especially, a town revolution, while the country, ignorant, lazy, wedded to the pompous ceremonies of the church, remained passive observers of the party strife they did hardly understand. In the few provinces where they exceptionally took an active share in the struggle, it was rather on the side of the counter-revolution,—a fact not to be wondered at in Spain, "that storehouse of ancient customs, that repository of all, elsewhere forgotten and past by", a country where, during the war of independence peasants were seen using spurs taken from the armoury of the Alhambra and armed with halberds and pikes of curious and ancient workmanship, which had been wielded in the wars of the 15th century. Besides it was a feature peculiar to Spain that every peasant who had a noble ensign cut in stone over the door of his miserable cabin, considered himself a nobleman and that thus the country people, generally, if poor and plundered, did never groan under that consciousness of abject degradation which exasperated them in the rest of feudal Europe. That the revolutionary party did not know how to link the interests of the peasantry to the town movement, is avowed by two men, both of whom acted a principal part in the Revolution, by General Morillo and by San Miguel. Morillo, who cannot be suspected of revolutionary sympathies, wrote from Galicia to the Duke of Angoulême:

"If the Cortes had sanctioned the bill on the seignorial rights, and thus despoiled the grandees of their properties in favour of the multitude, Your Highness would

---

[a] *Examen critique des la révolutions d'Espagne*. The decree mentioned by Marx was adopted on October 12, 1824.— *Ed.*

[b] John Bramsen, *Remark of the North of Spain*, p. 52.— *Ed.*

have encountered numerous, patriotic and formidable armies, which would have
organized themselves, as they did in France, under similar circumstances".

On the other hand San Miguel (see his *Civil War of Spain,*
Madrid. 1836) tells us:

"The greatest error of the liberals consisted in their not considering that by far the
majority of the nation were indifferent or hostile to the new laws. The numerous
decrees published by the Cortes with a view to ameliorating the material condition of
the people, were unable to produce so immediate results as were required by the
circumstances. Neither the abolition of half the tithes, nor the sale of the monastic
estates, contributed to ameliorating the material condition of the lower agricultural
classes. The last measure, on the contrary, by throwing the land out of the hands of
the indulgent monks into those of calculating capitalists, impaired the position of the
old farmers by causing higher rents to be imposed upon them, so that the superstition
of this numerous class, already wounded by the alienation of sanctified patrimony,
became exaggerated by the suggestions of material interests".

The revolutionary town population thus estranged from the
mass of the nation, were therefore forced, in their struggle with
the Grandees, the rural clergy, the monastic power, and the crown
which represented all these antiquated elements of society, to
depend altogether on the army and its chiefs. The *very* position
thus usurped by the army in the revolutionary camp, together
with its isolation from the masses, made it an instrument
dangerous for the hands that wielded it, but inoffensive to the
enemy it was to strike. Finally, the upper rank of the middle-class,
the so-called Moderados, became soon lukewarm and then traitors
to the Cause of the Revolution, lulling themselves, as they did, into
the hope of getting their reign established by means of a French
intervention and thus enjoying the fruits of a new society without
painstaking and without admitting the plebeians to participate in
them.

The positive result of the Revolution of 1820-1823 was not
limited to the great fermentation which expanded the minds and
renewed the character of some large classes of the nation. The
second restoration,[461] in which the antiquated elements of society
assumed such shapes as to become insupportable to, and
incompatible with the national existence of Spain, was itself a
product of the Revolution. Its principal work was to whet the
antagonism to such a point as to make all compromises impossible
and a war to the knife inevitable. According to Lord Liverpool
himself, there never was an extensive political change attended
with less violence or bloodshed than the Spanish Revolution

during 1820-1823.[a] When we behold, therefore, the civil war of 1833-1843[462] exterminating the antiquated elements of Spanish society,[b] with fire and sword and disgracing itself by acts of cannibalism, we must not attribute the savage inexorableness of that epoch to the peculiar character of the Spanish race, but to the same force of circumstances that imposed upon France the reign of terrorism. While the French centralised and, therefore, abbreviated the reign of terrorism, the Spaniards, true to their traditions, decentralised and, consequently, procrastinated it. Conforming to Spanish tradition, the revolutionary party was not likely to prove victorious by subverting the throne. With them, to be successful, the Revolution itself needed to appear as a competitor for the throne. The struggle of the two societies ought to assume the form of a struggle of opposite dynastic interests. The Spain of the 19th century did her revolution with ease; when she was allowed to give it the form of the civil wars of the XIVth century. It was Ferdinand the Seventh who gave to the Revolution a royal name—that of Isabella, while he leagued to the counter-revolution the Don Quixote of the Auto-da-fé, Don Carlos. Ferdinand VII proved true to his character to the [end].[c] If, during his whole life, he had cheated the liberals by false promises, should he not indulge the sport [when ch]eating the serviles on his death-bed?[463] As to religious matters, he had always been a sceptic. He was unable to [con]vince himself that any one—even the Holy Ghost—should be so silly as to speak the truth.

Written between November 14 and 21, 1854

Reproduced from the manuscript

First published in: Marx and Engels, *Works*, Second Russian Edition, Vol. 10, Moscow, 1958

---

[a] Lord Liverpool's speech in the House of Lords on February 4, 1823. *Hansard's Parliamentary Debates*, new series [2], Vol. 8, London, 1823, pp. 29-34.— *Ed.*
[b] The words "the feudal and monastic power" are crossed out here.— *Ed.*
[c] Here and below the manuscript is damaged. The words in square brackets are restored by the editors.— *Ed.*

APPENDIX

THE ENGLISH MIDDLE CLASS [464]

And as regards the journeyman of all descriptions, in what relation does he stand to his employer? All know with what opposition the employers met the "Ten Hours" bill. The Tories, out of spite for the recent loss of the Corn Laws, helped the working class to get it; but when passed, the reports of the district supervisors show with what shameless cunning and petty underhand treacheries it was evaded. Every subsequent attempt in Parliament to subject Labor to more humane conditions has been met by the middle class representatives with the catch-cry of Communism! Mr. Cobden has acted thus a score of times. Within the workshops for years the aim of the employers has been to prolong the hours of labor beyond human endurance, and by an unprincipled use of the contract system, by pitting one man against another, to cut down the earning of the skilled to that of the unskilled laborer. It was this system that at last drove the Amalgamated Engineers to revolt, and the brutality of the expressions that passed current among the masters at that time showed how little of refined or humane feeling was to be looked for from them. Their boorish ignorance was further displayed in the employment by the Masters' Association of a certain third-rate litterateur, Sidney Smith, to undertake their defense in the public press and to carry on the war of words with their revolted hands. The style of their hired writer well fitted the task he had to perform, and when the battle was over, the Masters, having no more need of literature or the press, gave their hireling his congé. Although the middle class do not aim at the learning of the old school, they do not for that cultivate either modern science or literature. The ledger, the desk, business, that is education sufficient. Their daughters, when expensively educated, are superficially endowed with a few "accomplishments;" but the real education of the mind and the storing it with knowledge is not even dreamed of.

The present splendid brotherhood of fiction-writers in England, whose graphic and eloquent pages have issued to the world more political and social truths than have been uttered by all the professional politicians, publicists and moralists put together, have described every section of the middle class from the "highly genteel" annuitant and Fundholder who looks upon all sorts of business as vulgar, to the little shopkeeper and lawyer's clerk. And how have Dickens and Thackeray, Miss Brontë and Mrs. Gaskell painted them? As full of presumption, affectation, petty tyranny and ignorance; and the civilized world has confirmed their verdict with the damning epigram that it has fixed to this class that "they are servile to those above, and tyrannical to those beneath them."

The cramped and narrow sphere in which they move is to a certain degree due to the social system of which they form a part. As the Russian nobility live uneasily betwixt the oppression of the Czar above them and the dread of the enslaved masses below them, so the English middle class are hemmed in by the aristocracy on the one hand and the working classes on the other. Since the peace of 1815, whenever the middle class have wished to take action against the aristocracy, they have told the working classes that their grievances were attributable to some aristocratic privilege and monopoly. By this means the middle class roused the working classes to help them in 1832 when they wanted the Reform Bill, and, having got a Reform Bill *for themselves,* have ever since refused one to the working classes—nay, in 1848, actually stood arrayed against them armed with special constable staves. Next, it was the repeal of the Corn Laws that would be the panacea for the working classes. Well, this was won from the aristocracy, but the "good time" was not yet come, and last year, as if to take away the last possibility of a similar policy for the future, the aristocracy were compelled to accede to a tax on the succession to real estate—a tax which the same aristocracy had selfishly exempted themselves from in 1793, while they imposed it on the succession to personal estate. With this rag of a grievance vanished the last chance of gulling the working classes into the belief that their hard lot was due solely to aristocratic legislation. The eyes of the working classes are now fully opened: they begin to cry: "Our St. Petersburg is at Preston!" Indeed, the last eight months have seen a strange spectacle in the town—a standing army of 14,000 men and women subsidized by the trades unions and workshops of all parts of the United Kingdom, to fight out a grand social battle for mastery with the capitalists, and the capitalists of Preston, on their side, held up by the capitalists of Lancashire.

Whatever other shapes this social struggle may hereafter assume, we have seen only the beginning of it. It seems destined to nationalize itself and present phases never before seen in history; for it must be borne in mind that though temporary defeat may await the working classes, great social and economical laws are in operation which must eventually insure their triumph. The same industrial wave which has borne the middle class up against the aristocracy, is now assisted as it is and will be by emigration bearing the working classes up against the middle classes. Just as the middle class inflict blows upon the aristocracy, so will they receive them from the working classes. It is the instinctive perception of this fact that already fetters the action of that class against the aristocracy. The recent political agitations of the working classes have taught the middle class to hate and fear overt political movements. In their cant, "respectable men don't join them, Sir". The higher middle classes ape the aristocracy in their modes of life, and endeavor to connect themselves with it. The consequence is that the feudalism of England will not perish beneath the scarcely perceptible dissolving processes of the middle class; the honor of such a victory is reserved for the working classes. When the time shall be ripe for their recognized entry upon the stage of political action, there will be within the lists three powerful classes confronting each other—the first representing the land; the second, money; the third, labor. And as the second is triumphing over the first, so, in its turn, it must yield before its successor in the field of political and social conflict.

First published in the *New-York Daily Tribune*, No. 4145, August 1, 1854 as a leader

Reproduced from the newspaper

NOTES
AND
INDEXES

NOTES

[1] When determining the authorship and the date of writing of the majority of the articles by Marx and Engels published in the *New-York Tribune* between February 13, 1854 and February 6, 1855 (which make up the bulk of this volume), great use was made of Marx's Notebook for 1850-54 and the letters of Marx and Engels to each other and to third persons. Important additional information was also obtained from the study of sources used by Marx and Engels for their reports, the schedules of transatlantic ships, and other indirect data.

Marx's wife, Jenny, and sometimes Marx himself entered in the Notebook the dates on which the articles were sent from London to New York—usually on Tuesdays and Fridays. This was necessary for the accounts with the *Tribune* and was done in the form of lists, each with its own numbering. There are eight lists in all for the period covered by this volume, and each includes eight to fourteen articles. Unfortunately, such entries were only made up to December 22, 1854 and there are none for the next two years (1855 and 1856). Apart from the dates, these entries often contained summaries of the articles. Usually Marx dictated his articles to his wife Jenny or to Wilhelm Pieper (a participant in the 1848-49 revolution and a Communist League member) on the day of their dispatch, and Engels used to write his the day before. Sometimes Marx added to the articles received from Engels the latest information from English and French morning newspapers on the day of their dispatch to America. From June 1854 Engels was too busy with office work and could write articles only on Saturday and Wednesday evenings. The study of the sources he used suggests that as early as September 1854 he resumed his previous custom of writing the articles on Mondays and Thursdays, on the eve of their dispatch to London.

The editors of the *Tribune* treated the articles at their discretion, dividing them and publishing the most important items as leaders in their own name. Marx repeatedly protested against such practice but his financial dependence on the newspaper compelled him in the end to comply with the editors' terms. From the middle of 1855 all Marx's and Engels' articles were published unsigned. As a rule, the editors reprinted these articles from the *New-York Daily Tribune* in the *New-York Semi-Weekly Tribune* and the *New-York Weekly Tribune*, generally using the same matrix. All such instances are indicated in this volume at the end of the articles.

Notes to some articles also indicate instances when they were reprinted in the collection: K. Marx, *The Eastern Question. A Reprint of Letters written 1853-1856 dealing with the events of the Crimean War*, edited by Eleanor Marx-Aveling and Edward Aveling, London, 1897.

The article "The War Question in Europe" was written by Engels at Marx's request and sent from Manchester to London on February 13. The article started with the words: "In the meantime, the armaments prepared..." (fourth paragraph). On February 14, Marx added to it an analysis of Napoleon III's letter to the Russian Tsar and also some information which he had probably received from Urquhart (see Note 4).

In the Notebook the dispatch of the article was entered as "Dienstag. 14. Februar. Rüstungen". The beginning of the first sentence, "Though the arrival of the *Nashville* puts us in possession of no decisive news from the seat of war" was inserted by the editors of the *Tribune*.   p. 3

[2] Napoleon III's letter (January 29, 1854) was published by the editors in the same issue of the *New-York Daily Tribune*. They inserted the words "which we copy in another place".   p. 3

[3] In 1853 and 1854 the Ambassadors of Britain, France and Prussia and the Austrian Foreign Minister Buol held a number of conferences in Vienna. The first, in July 1853, to which the Russian Ambassador was also invited but which he refused to attend, was officially aimed at mediation between Russia and Turkey in view of the worsening relations between them. The words "first Vienna Note" refer to the draft agreement between Russia and Turkey drawn up by Buol and concluded at the end of July 1853. It obliged the Sultan to abide by the Kuchuk-Kainardji (1774) (see Note 17) and the Adrianople (1829) (see Note 176) treaties on the rights and privileges of the Orthodox Church in the Ottoman Empire. The Turkish Sultan Abdul Mejid agreed to sign the Note but demanded a number of changes and reservations, which the Russian Government found unacceptable.   p. 4

[4] Probably Marx heard about this letter from David Urquhart with whom he had a meeting at the time (see Marx's letter to Engels of February 9, 1854, present edition, Vol. 39).   p. 4

[5] The phrase "by the steamer now due here, or at furthest within a few days" was inserted in Engels' text by the editors of the *New-York Daily Tribune*. They also added the following paragraph at the end of the article: "Our London correspondent in another column intimates his unwillingness to believe in such treachery, but facts are stubborn things, and the mind must at last be affected by their force. After having gone the desperate lengths they have avowedly done to avoid war, it is hard to think of anything they would shrink from." This is an allusion to an article by F. A. Pulszky, who was also a London correspondent of the newspaper at the time and signed his reports "A.P.C.". His article was published on p. 5 of the same issue of the *New-York Daily Tribune*.   p. 7

[6] This article is entered in the Notebook as "Freitag. 17. Februar. Germany News". Eleanor Marx included it under the title "Count Orloff's Proposals" in *The Eastern Question*, in which the first paragraph was mistakenly ascribed to the editors of the *New-York Daily Tribune*.   p. 8

[7] The reference is to Ferdinand Lassalle's letter to Marx dated February 10, 1854. It is published in Ferdinand Lassalle, *Nachgelassene Briefe und Schriften*. Herausgegeben von Gustav Mayer. 3. Band. Der Briefwechsel zwischen Lassalle und Marx, Stuttgart-Berlin, 1922, S. 66-70. p. 8

[8] The *German Confederation*—a union of German states formed by the Vienna Congress (see Note 112) on June 8, 1815. It initially included 34 absolutist feudal states and 4 free cities. The Confederation sanctioned the political and economic dismemberment of Germany and hindered the country's development. p. 8

[9] The Kingdom of Sardinia, which existed from 1720 to 1861 and played a considerable role in the unification of Italy, consisted of Piedmont, Sardinia, Savoy, Nice and Liguria (including Genoa). p. 8

[10] The article "Debates in Parliament" is dated February 21, 1854, which coincides with the date of its dispatch from London to New York entered in the Notebook.

Eleanor Marx included this article in an abridged form in *The Eastern Question*. p. 11

[11] The *British East India Company* was founded at the beginning of the seventeenth century. It enjoyed a monopoly of trade with the East Indies and played a decisive part in the establishment of the British colonial empire. p. 11

[12] In accordance with the procedure adopted in the British Parliament, when certain important questions are to be discussed the House of Commons declares itself a Committee of the whole House, which is tantamount to a closed sitting. The Chairman of the Committee at such sittings is one of a list of chairmen, and is specially appointed by the Speaker for the given sitting; when discussing important questions covering state expenditures the House of Commons assembles as the Committee of Ways and Means. p. 11

[13] In 1844, on the order of Sir James Graham, the British Home Secretary, the letters of the Bandiera brothers to Mazzini containing the plan of their expedition to Calabria were opened. The participants in the expedition were arrested, and the Bandieras executed. p. 13

[14] In May 1851 the French Ambassador Lavalette arrived in Constantinople and delivered to the Sultan the demands of the French President Louis Napoleon that all the rights and privileges of the Catholic Church in Jerusalem be observed. By his firman (edict) of February 9, 1852 the Sultan recognised France's rights to protect the Catholic Church as defined in a number of previous Franco-Turkish treaties. p. 13

[15] The *battle of Navarino* took place on October 20, 1827 between the Turko-Egyptian fleet and the British, French and Russian squadrons, under the English Vice-Admiral Edward Codrington, which were sent to the Greek waters by the European powers for the purpose of armed mediation in the war between Turkey and the Greek insurgents. The battle began when the Turkish command refused to stop the massacre of the Greek population; it ended in the

defeat of the Turko-Egyptian fleet and hastened the Russo-Turkish war of 1828-29, in which Russia was victorious.   p. 17

[16] The reference is to John Aberdeen's Coalition Ministry of 1852-55 (the Cabinet of All the Talents), which consisted of Whigs, Peelites and representatives of a faction of Irish Members.   p. 18

[17] The *treaty of Kuchuk-Kainardji* was concluded between Russia and Turkey on July 21, 1774. Russia got territories on the northern shore of the Black Sea between the South Bug and the Dnieper with the fortress of Kinburn, and also Azov, Kerch and Yenikale and secured recognition of the Crimea's independence. Russian merchantmen were granted the right of free passage through the Bosphorus and the Dardanelles. The treaty obliged the Sultan to grant a number of privileges to the Orthodox Church; Article 14 in particular provided for the building of an Orthodox Church in Constantinople.   p. 20

[18] The reference is to the documents sent by Colonel Rose to London and published in *Correspondence respecting the Rights and Privileges of the Latin and Greek Churches in Turkey. Presented to both Houses of Parliament by Command of Her Majesty,* London, 1854, Part I, pp. 112-15.   p. 23

[19] Disraeli's speech contained several inaccuracies, viz.: Count Nesselrode's dispatch to Brunnow was dated June 1 (May 20) and not June 20, 1853, its contents were communicated to Lord Clarendon on June 8; the quotation only partly coincides with the dispatch, and the end of it was apparently taken by Disraeli from Clarendon's letter to the English Ambassador to Vienna, the Earl of Westmorland, of July 4, 1853 (see *Correspondence...,* Part I, pp. 321-22).
                                          p. 23

[20] The reference is to Lord Clarendon's letters to the Earl of Westmorland of July 4 and to Lord Stratford de Redcliffe of July 28 (*The Times* mistakenly gives July 18), 1853. This quotation, from Disraeli's speech, which *The Times* of February 21, 1854 gave as an extract from Lord Clarendon's letter to Stratford de Redcliffe, was Disraeli's own conclusion (*Correspondence...,* Part I, pp. 320-21, 399-400).   p. 23

[21] This refers to the battle between the Russian and Turkish troops at Oltenitza on the left bank of the Danube on November 4, 1853 (see present edition, Vol. 12, pp. 516-22).   p. 24

[22] This article is dated February 24, 1854 which coincides with the date of its dispatch from London to New York as entered in the Notebook ("Freitag, 24. Februar. Pozzo di Borgo"). It was included in abridged form by Eleanor Marx in *The Eastern Question* under the title "Kossuth.—Disraeli and Hume.—United States.—France and England.—Greece".   p. 26

[23] The Crimean war aroused hopes among European emigrants for a new upsurge of revolutionary liberation activity in Poland, Italy and Hungary. Preparations for such action were made by Mazzini, Garibaldi and Kossuth. In the winter of 1853-54, Kossuth negotiated—unsuccessfully—with the USA and France for aid in arms and money for the Hungarian emigrants who wished to fight against Tsarist Russia on the side of Turkey. Kossuth hoped to organise a Hungarian Legion expecting that its arrival at the Danubian theatre of war

would spark off an uprising against Austrian rule in Hungary, where, on the basis of information received from his agents, he reckoned on the support of 130,000 Honveds. In the summer of 1853, Kossuth addressed a memorandum on the subject to the Turkish Government, but the latter, not wishing to enter into conflict with Austria, disapproved of all Kossuth's attempts to form a Hungarian Legion and only separate individuals got permission to enlist in the Turkish army on condition that they would embrace Islam. On January 7, 1854 Kossuth wrote to Gál, his agent in Constantinople, that Turkey had rejected the Hungarian proposal on the grounds that "as long as Turkey was on friendly terms with Austria contacts with the Hungarian emigrants were out of the question".

On the formation of the Polish Legion see Note 122. p. 26

[24] See Note 16. p. 26

[25] This refers to the secret agreement between Denmark and Sweden to observe neutrality in the event of a war in Europe. King Oskar of Sweden informed his Parliament of this on December 27, 1853. The text of the treaty was brought to the knowledge of the European governments by a special note. p. 28

[26] This refers to the dispatch of the Russian Ambassador in France Pozzo di Borgo to Chancellor Count Nesselrode dated October 16 (4), 1825 in reply to the latter's circular of August 18 (6), 1825 drawn up on instructions from Alexander I. The circular asked for the opinion of Russian Ambassadors abroad concerning the attitude of the Western powers to Russia in connection with the Eastern question and about the policy to be followed by Russia. Pozzo di Borgo recommended that Russia should resort to direct military action against Turkey. The dispatch was included in *Recueil des documents pour la plupart secrets et inédits et d'autres pièces historiques utiles à consulter dans la crise actuelle (juillet 1853)* published in Paris. Marx used the second edition of this book (1854). p. 28

[27] Карамзинъ, *Исторія Государства Россійскаго*, Т. XI, Спб., 1824, стр. 28 (Karamzin, *The History of the Russian State*, Vol. XI, St. Petersburg, 1824, p. 28). Where Marx took this quotation from is not established. p. 29

[28] In 1839 war broke out between Turkey and Egypt, aggravating the Eastern problem and the conflict between the Great Powers. The Western states were afraid that Russia would intervene separately in the Turko-Egyptian war and sent a collective note to the Sultan suggesting their collaboration. However, the struggle between Britain and France for spheres of influence in the Middle East, in Egypt in particular, led to the signing of the London Convention of July 15, 1840 on measures of military aid to the Sultan by Britain, Russia, Austria and Prussia without France. The last-named, relying on Mehemet Ali, was soon compelled to yield and leave Egypt to its fate. On July 13, 1841 the London Convention on the Black Sea Straits was signed by Russia, Britain, France, Austria and Prussia, on the one hand, and Turkey, on the other. The convention laid down that in peacetime the Bosphorus and Dardanelles would be closed to warships of all powers. Marx called this convention the treaty of the Dardanelles. p. 30

[29] Marx has in mind the following passages from James Graham's speech in the House of Commons on February 17, 1854: "We have also succeeded in

combining Austria and Prussia with us in many most important transactions"
and from Lord John Russell's speech on the same occasion: "My belief is,
therefore, although we have no engagement with them,—and I state it plainly
to the House, that they are not bound to us to resist in any manner the acts of
aggression on the part of Russia..." (*The Times,* No. 21668, February 18, 1854).

p. 31

[30] Apparently Marx got this information and the data given below from Urquhart
or his associates (see Note 4).   p. 31

[31] The insurrection of the Greek population of the Ottoman Empire which started
in January 1854 with the support of the Greek troops was suppressed by the
Turkish Government with the aid of Britain and France in June of the same
year.   p. 32

[32] When Marx wrote this article, he obtained his information on the contents of
these dispatches from Cobden's speech in the House of Commons on February
20, 1854, published in *The Times* on February 21, 1854. In March 1854 Marx
acquainted himself with the authentic documents relating to the origin of the
Eastern conflict of 1853 and devoted two special articles to their analysis (see
this volume, pp. 73-99).   p. 33

[33] During the Austro-Turkish war of 1788-90 Austrian troops occupied Serbia
(1789). In 1791, under pressure from Britain and Prussia, Austria concluded a
peace treaty with Turkey on condition of restoring the *status quo ante bellum.*
Austria got only Old Orsova without the right to fortify it.   p. 33

[34] The article "English and French War Plans.—Greek Insurrection.—Spain.—
China" was compiled by the editors of the *New-York Daily Tribune* from two
articles written by Marx on February 28 and March 3, 1854; the editors took
the first six paragraphs, up to the words "The Anglo-French expedition may be
set down...", from the article written by Marx on March 3 (the second half of
this article was published as a leader, without Marx's signature, under the title
"Austrian Bankruptcy", see Note 43). In the Notebook the second part of the
article is entered: "Dienstag. 28. Februar. Etwas Militaria. Spain. Dost
Mohammed etc., etc., etc.". It is probable that "Militaria" in this article was
written by Engels, but there are no direct proofs of this.
    The article "English and French War Plans.—Greek Insurrection.—Spain.—
China" was included in abridged form by Eleanor Marx in *The Eastern Question*
under the title "France and England.—The Greek Rising.—Asia".   p. 35

[35] Here Marx has in mind his article written on February 28 (see Note 34), but
the paragraph he mentions about Charles Napier was probably arbitrarily
omitted by the editors of the *Tribune.*
    On events of 1840, see Note 28.   p. 35

[36] Marx used Bonaparte's opening speech at a joint sitting of the Corps Legislatif
and the Senate on March 2, 1854 as published in *Le Moniteur universel,* March
3, 1854.
    The term *Entente cordiale* was used in the nineteenth century to denote the
rapprochement between France and Britain after the July revolution of 1830,
which was formalised by the Quadruple Alliance in April 1834 (see Note 39).

p. 35

[37] The reference is to Clause 2 of the treaty signed in Constantinople later, on March 12, and ratified on May 8, 1854 by Britain and France, on the one hand, and the Ottoman Empire, on the other. Marx's main source of information on this question were periodical publications.   p. 36

[38] In January 1854 it was announced in Constantinople that the police had discovered a conspiracy of the Greeks, and a Greek priest named Athanasius had been arrested in Vidin. According to the Western press, the conspiracy was headed by Baron Oelsner, ex-adjutant of General Lüders, and its aim was to incite the Greeks and Slavs living in Turkey to revolt.   p. 36

[39] The reference is to the Quadruple Alliance concluded in April 1834 between Britain, France, Spain and Portugal (see Note 36). Even at the time the treaty was concluded conflicts of interests appeared between Britain and France which later aggravated relations between the two countries. This treaty was formally directed against the absolutist "Northern powers" (Russia, Prussia and Austria), but in actual fact allowed Britain to strengthen her position in Spain and Portugal, under the pretext of rendering military assistance to both governments in their struggle against the pretenders to the throne, Don Carlos in Spain and Dom Miguel in Portugal (see notes 227 and 253).   p. 40

[40] The reference is to the marriage of Queen Isabella II of Spain to Don Francisco de Asis in 1846 (contrary to the wishes of the British ruling circles—see Note 277), and that of Infanta Maria Luisa Fernanda to the Duke of Montpensier, son of King Louis Philippe of France. If Isabella had no direct heirs, the Duke of Montpensier would have become one of the first pretenders to the Spanish throne. This victory of French diplomacy caused great dissatisfaction in Britain.   p. 40

[41] Here Marx refers to events of the first Anglo-Afghan war of 1838-42 in which the English army was defeated.   p. 41

[42] In 1850 popular disturbances occurred in a number of southern provinces of China and developed into a big peasant war. The rebels established a state of their own over a considerable part of China's territory. Its leaders put forward a utopian programme of transforming the Chinese feudal social system into a militarised patriarchal one based on the egalitarian principle in production and consumption. The movement, which was also anti-colonial, was weakened by inner dissensions and the rise of a local aristocracy among the Taipings. The rebellion was suppressed in 1864, mainly due to intervention by Britain, the USA and France.   p. 41

[43] In the Notebook the dispatch of this article under the title "Oesterreichs Finanzen" is dated March 3. The article dealt not only with the state of Austrian finances, but analysed Napoleon III's speech of March 2 and contained some other material which the *Tribune*· editors arbitrarily combined with Marx's previous report (see Note 34). The article on Austrian finances was published as a leader. As the editors were wont to pass off his articles for their own, Marx wrote to Engels on April 22, 1854: "Of late the *Tribune* has again been appropriating all my articles for its leaders and putting *my* name to nothing but rubbish. It has appropriated, for example, a detailed account of Austrian finances, articles on the Greek insurrection, etc. Not to speak of their

'congenital' habit of making a splash with your military stuff" (see present edition, Vol. 39).   p. 43

[44] The reference is to the *Société générale du Crédit Mobilier*—a big French joint-stock bank founded in 1852 by the Péreire brothers. The bank was closely connected with the Government of Napoleon III and, protected by it, engaged in speculation. It went bankrupt in 1867 and was liquidated in 1871. p. 43

[45] This patent, the instructions of the Austrian Government in the sphere of finances mentioned below as also the information on the Austrian budget are given by Marx according to *Der gegenwärtige Stand der Finanzen und des Geldumlaufs in Oesterreich. Von einem Unbetheiligten*, Leipzig, 1853. Marx was obviously also conversant with the books by Josef Ritter von Hauer, *Beiträge zur Geschichte der österreichischen Finanzen*, Vienna, 1848 and *Ueber Oesterreichs Staatsausgaben und Verwaltung in Hauptumrissen dargestellt*, Vienna, 1849, and other sources.   p. 45

[46] In February and March 1846, simultaneously with the national liberation insurrection in the free city of Cracow which had been under the joint control of Austria, Prussia and Russia since 1815, a big peasant uprising flared up in Galicia. Taking advantage of class contradictions, the Austrian authorities provoked clashes between insurgent Galician peasants and the Polish lesser nobility (szlachta) who strove to support Cracow. Having overwhelmed the insurgent szlachta, the Austrian Government also suppressed the peasant movement in Galicia.   p. 47

[47] The peace treaty between Austria and the Kingdom of Sardinia (Piedmont) (see Note 9) of August 6, 1849 obliged Piedmont to pay Austria an indemnity of 75 million florins.

In 1853 the Austrian Government confiscated in Lombardy and Venice the property of participants in the 1848-49 revolution who had subsequently emigrated.

The decree of the Austrian Imperial Diet dated August 31, 1848 abolished serfdom in Austria; after approval by the emperor on September 9 it acquired the force of law.   p. 47

[48] *Military Frontier* (or *Border*)—in the sixteenth-nineteenth centuries the southern regions of the Austrian Empire bordering on Turkey and having a military administration; their inhabitants (borderers) were allotted land in return for military service in the border regiments.   p. 48

[49] In 1789 a national rebellion, called the Brabant revolution, against Austrian rule took place in the Austrian Netherlands (Belgium). It was suppressed by Austrian troops in 1790 after the death of Joseph II.   p. 49

[50] This article is entered in the Notebook as "Dienstag. 7. March. Labour Parliament. Gladstone".   p. 50

[51] In 1853, with the growth of a massive strike movement of the English proletariat, a group of Chartists headed by Ernest Jones proposed to create a broad workers' organisation, The Mass Movement, which was to unite trade unions and unorganised workers with the primary aim of coordinating strikes in the various districts of the country. The organisation was to be headed by a regularly convened Labour Parliament consisting of delegates elected at

meetings of both unorganised workers and of the trade unions associated with The Mass Movement. The Labour Parliament assembled in Manchester on March 6, 1854 and was in session till March 18, 1854. It discussed and adopted the programme of The Mass Movement and set up an Executive of five members. Marx, elected honorary delegate to the Parliament, sent a letter to it (see this volume, pp. 57-59).

The attempt to found The Mass Movement failed, because the majority of the trade union leaders did not approve of associating the trade unions with the political struggle and did not support the idea of creating a single mass workers' organisation. By the summer of 1854 the strike movement had abated and this also cut short the participation of broad masses of workers in the movement. After March 1854 the Labour Parliament never met again.   p. 50

52 The reference is to the Government Commission on the Workers' Question which met at the Palais du Luxembourg and was presided over by Louis Blanc. The Commission was set up on February 28, 1848 by the Provisional Government of the French Republic under pressure from workers who demanded a Ministry of Labour. The Commission consisted of workers and employers and acted as mediator in labour conflicts, often taking the side of the employers. On the very next day after the mass actions of May 15, 1848, the Government disbanded the Luxembourg Commission.   p. 50

53 *Organisation of labour, organisers of labour*—an allusion to the utopian socialists (in particular Fourier and his followers) who put forward a plan for the peaceful transformation of society by means of association, that is by "organisation of labour", which they opposed to the anarchy of production under capitalism.

Some of these ideas were used by the French petty-bourgeois socialist Louis Blanc in his book *Organisation du travail* (Paris, 1839) in which he proposed that the bourgeois state should transform contemporary society into a socialist society.   p. 50

54 The *National Charter Association* was founded in July 1840. It was the first mass workers' organisation in the history of the working-class movement and counted up to 50,000 members when Chartism was at its peak. Its Executive—the leading body—was elected at congresses and conferences of delegates. After the defeat of the Chartists in 1848 and the ensuing split in their ranks, the Association lost its mass character. Nevertheless, in 1851 and 1852, led by Ernest Jones and other revolutionary Chartists, it fought for the revival of Chartism on a revolutionary basis, for the implementation of the People's Charter and the socialist principles proclaimed by the Chartist Convention in 1851. The Association ceased its activities in 1858.   p. 51

55 Marx quotes Article 14 of the law on the French Budget for 1854 passed in 1853 (Loi, portant fixation du budjet...). However, he changes the figure 150 million to 250 million in accordance with a special decree of 1854 (Décret imperial...), which he quotes below (see *Collection complète des lois, decrets, réglements et avis du Conseil d'Etat. Publiée sur les éditions officielles par J. B. Duvergier*, tome 53, Année 1853, p. 232; tome 54, Année 1854, p. 45). Marx probably obtained his information on the financial measures of the French Government from the Paris letter mentioned below and a report in *Le Moniteur universel* of March 7, 1854.   p. 51

23*

[56] An allusion to the participants in the Bonapartist coup d'état in France on December 2, 1851. p. 52

[57] This refers to the manifesto of Nicholas I of February 21 (9), 1854 breaking off diplomatic relations with France and Britain; in a letter to Napoleon III of February 9 (January 28), 1854 Nicholas I refused to compromise on the Eastern question. These documents were published in *The Times* of March 6, 1854 under the titles "Manifesto of the Emperor Nicholas" and "The Emperor of Russia and the Emperor Napoleon". p. 52

[58] The *South Sea Company* was founded in England about 1712, officially for trade with South America and the Pacific islands. The Company received from the Government a number of privileges and monopoly rights, in particular the right to issue securities, and plunged into large-scale speculation which led to its bankruptcy in 1720 and the growth of the national debt. In compliance with the draft financial reform of 1853 Gladstone proposed to reduce the interest on the Company's stocks from 3 to $2^3/_4$ per cent. p. 56

[59] Marx's letter to the Labour Parliament was read out by Jones at the evening sitting on March 10. Jones also declared that he was expecting Marx to come to Manchester the following week, obviously basing himself on Marx's promise given in a private letter to Jones (which has not been found). p. 57

[60] On Marx's election as an honorary delegate to the Labour Parliament, see Note 51. p. 57

[61] This article is entered in the Notebook as: "Freitag. 10 March. Labour Parliament". p. 61

[62] The plan of action for the Labour Parliament given below was published in *The People's Paper* only on March 11, 1854. When writing this article Marx presumably made use of a leaflet or a manuscript copy of the programme which had been sent to him together with an invitation to take part in the work of the Parliament (see Note 51). p. 62

[63] Engels wrote the article "Retreat of the Russians from Kalafat" on March 13 on Marx's request and it was mailed to New York on March 14, as is testified by the entry in the Notebook: "Dienstag. 14 March. Militaria. Kalafat." Before sending it off Marx added a review of Greek events (see Note 65) and other information taken from *The Times* of March 14, 1854. On March 18 Marx published this article in the Chartist *People's Paper*. The *New-York Daily Tribune* and the *New-York Weekly Tribune* carried it under the title "The Russian Retreat". It was included by Eleanor Marx in *The Eastern Question* under the same heading. In this edition the text is reproduced from *The People's Paper* and checked with that of the *New-York Daily Tribune*. Substantially different readings are given in footnotes. p. 65

[64] The camp at *Bunzelwitz* was fortified on the order of Frederick II of Prussia in 1761 during the Seven Years' War.

The *fortifications at Torres-Vedras* (in Portugal, between the Tagus River and the Atlantic coast) were built in 1810 on the order of Wellington to protect Lisbon from the French forces.

Entrenchments behind Verona were built not far from the town by the troops of the Archduke Charles of Austria during the war of the third coalition (1805) against Napoleonic France.

In all three instances the fortifications were not captured by the enemy.

p. 67

[65] The mailing of the article "The Greek Insurrection" to New York is not registered in the Notebook, but the fact that it is by Marx is established by his letters to Engels of April 22 (see Note 43) and May 3, 1854. This article, published by the editors of the *New-York Daily Tribune* as a leader, was presumably a part of the article mailed by Marx to New York on March 14 (see Note 63). It could not have been written before March 14 because it expounded Milnes' speech delivered in the House of Commons on the 13th and published in *The Times* on March 14, 1854.

p. 70

[66] In the spring of 1821 a national liberation movement started in Greece which ended after a long struggle in Greece winning independence. As a result of Russia's victory in the Russo-Turkish war of 1828-29, Turkey recognised Greece as an independent state. Forced by public pressure to give military aid to Greece, the ruling circles of the European powers imposed, however, a monarchist form of government on the country after its liberation. The final status of the Kingdom of Greece and its territory were determined by the protocols of March 22, 1829, February 3, 1830 and May 7, 1832 of the London Conference (1827-32). Greece included Morea, the Cyclades and the southern part of Greek mainland, between the mouths of the Spercheios and the Aspropotamo rivers.

p. 70

[67] See Note 38.

p. 71

[68] This article, dated March 21, 1854, is entered in the Notebook under the same date. It was reprinted by Eleanor Marx in *The Eastern Question*. In this and the next article "The Secret Diplomatic Correspondence" (see this volume, pp. 84-99) Marx analyses the secret correspondence (and other documents) of the British Ambassador to St. Petersburg, Hamilton Seymour, and the British Foreign Secretary concerning the negotiations between Seymour and Nicholas I on the Turkish question at the beginning of 1853, according to *Correspondence...* (Parts V and VI).

p. 73

[69] This refers to the article published in the *Journal de Saint-Pétersbourg* of February 18 (March 2), 1854 in connection with Lord Russell's speech in the House of Commons on February 17, 1854 (see this volume, pp. 13, 19 and 24). The article alluded to the existence of a conspiracy between the Russian and British governments on the Turkish question, and proved it from Hamilton Seymour's correspondence of 1853 and the memorandum of 1844.

p. 73

[70] In the articles published in the *New-York Daily Tribune* ("Russian Policy Against Turkey.—Chartism", "War in Burma.—The Russian Question.—Curious Diplomatic Correspondence", "Financial Failure of Government.—Cabs.—Ireland.—The Russian Question"—present edition, Vol. 12; "Parliamentary Debates of February 22.—Pozzo di Borgo's Dispatch.—The Policy of the Western Powers"—this volume, pp. 28-29) Marx repeatedly quoted Pozzo di Borgo's dispatches, but did not mention this statement by Nicholas I.

p. 78

[71] Marx takes the French expression "de leur échapper" (to escape from them) from Seymour's previous report of January 11, 1853 (*Correspondence...*, Part V,

p. 877) but in this document the expression "nous rester sur les bras" (remain on our hands) is used.   p. 78

[72] The treaty on the partition of the Spanish succession was signed by Louis XIV, King of the French, and William III, King of England, on March 3, 1700. It envisaged that, in the event of King of Spain Charles II of Habsburg dying childless, Spain, her colonies and the Spanish Netherlands would go to Archduke Charles, second son of Emperor Leopold I. For a number of reasons Charles II refused to accept the terms of this treaty and on October 2, 1700 made a will by which all the Spanish possessions went to the grandson of Louis XIV, Philip, Duke of Anjou. On November 1, 1700 Charles II died and Philip, Duke of Anjou, became King Philip V. By the will of Charles II, Philip V was independent of France, but Louis XIV violated this condition by making him his heir in 1701 and thus the danger arose that power in both Spain and France would be concentrated in the hands of one King. This led to the long war of the Spanish succession (1701-14) (referred to below) between France, on the one hand, and Britain, Holland and the Habsburg Empire, on the other.
                                                                                    p. 81

[73] The reference is to the family pact of 1731 concluded between King Philip V of Spain and the Grand Duke of Tuscany, Gian Gastone. It provided for the Duchy to go to the Spanish heir, Prince Charles (future King Charles III of Spain), after the death of the childless Gian Gastone.   p. 81

[74] Marx uses as a source Lassalle's letter of March 7, 1854 (see Ferdinand Lassalle, *Nachgelassene Briefe und Schriften*. Herausgegeben von Gustav Mayer. 3. Band, Der Briefwechsel zwischen Lassalle und Marx, Stuttgart-Berlin, 1922, S. 74-76).
                                                                                    p. 83

[75] Here Marx has in mind the fact that he was constantly shadowed by the Prussian Government. Among the organisers of this surveillance in the 1850s was Bunsen, the Prussian Ambassador to London, who received a certain assistance from the British authorities. In their correspondence Marx and Engels repeatedly mentioned that their letters had been opened.   p. 83

[76] This article is the continuation of the previous one (see Note 68) and is entered in the Notebook as "24. März. Blue Books. Secret Correspondence. 2. Teil." The article was reprinted abridged in *The Eastern Question*.   p. 84

[77] In the *New-York Daily Tribune* this article is erroneously datelined "London, Friday, March 24, 1854", the correct date was established on the basis of Marx's Notebook: "28. März. Geschichte des Protektors" and the sources of information used in the article.

The article was included in abridged form by Eleanor Marx in *The Eastern Question* under the title "War Declared—Mussulman and Christian".
                                                                                    p. 100

[78] Under the legislation in force in England from 1662 paupers who changed their place of residence or applied to a parish for alms could be returned to their former place of residence by court decision. On February 10, 1854 a Settlement and Removal Bill was introduced in the House of Commons envisaging prohibition of forced settlement of paupers in England and Wales. It was rejected by Parliament.   p. 101

79 On March 12, 1854 a treaty was concluded in Constantinople between France, Britain and Turkey. The Allies pledged to help Turkey with their naval and land forces, and Turkey pledged not to enter into peace negotiations with Russia and to conclude no peace without the consent of Britain and France.
p. 101

80 *Ulemas*—the highest social estate of theologians and jurists in the Moslem countries who kept in their hands the administration of justice and the management of all religious establishments and schools; the ulemas exerted a great influence on the political life of the Ottoman Empire.
Fetva—decision of the supreme Moslem priest in Oriental countries on the conformity of a measure or action to the norms of Islam.   p. 101

81 This refers to the dissensions among the Turkish ruling circles caused by the treaty of March 12, 1854 (see Note 79). Sheik ul-Islam Arif Hikmet Bey and the President of the State Council of Justice, Rifaat Pasha, opposed any compromise on the status of Christians in Turkey and were dismissed from their posts.   p. 101

82 The *Berber States*—the name used in the nineteenth century for the Moslem states in North Africa on the shore of the Mediterranean (Algeria, Tunis and Morocco).   p. 102

83 On the *Kainardji treaty*, see Note 17. The treaty between France and Turkey, referred to in the text, ended the Egyptian expedition of the French army (1798-1801). It was concluded on October 8, 1801 and finally signed in Paris on June 25, 1802.   p. 105

84 The manuscript "The Fortress of Kronstadt" is one of Engels' military articles intended for the London *Daily News* (see Note 95), but it was not published in his lifetime.
Sometimes the figures which Engels gives for the artillery in Kronstadt differ from those of the Russian command. This is explained by the lack of information to which Engels himself pointed.   p. 109

85 The dispatch of this article to New York is entered in the Notebook as "Freitag. 31. März. Allerlei, Income tax, Mr. Baines, Wash. Wilks. Preston". The *Tribune* editors omitted the part of Marx's article which contained a critical analysis of the book by a radical English author, Washington Wilks, *Palmerston in Three Epochs: a Comparison of Facts with Opinions,* London, 1854. An idea of Marx's critical remarks on this book can be formed from his letter to Engels dated April 4, 1854 (see present edition, Vol. 39).
The only available photocopy of the newspaper is very poor.   p. 117

86 The reference is to Gladstone's proposal to double the rate of income tax for six months in view of Britain's forthcoming entry into the Crimean war. On March 27, 1854 Britain declared war on Russia, and on March 30, after the third reading, the Income Tax Bill was passed.   p. 117

87 For a detailed description of the budget proposed by Gladstone on April 18, 1853 see Marx's articles "Feargus O'Connor.—Ministerial Defeats.—The Budget", "L.S.D., or Class Budgets, and Who's Relieved by Them", "Riot at Constantinople.—German Table Moving.—The Budget", "Soap for the People, a Sop for *The Times.*—The Coalition Budget" (present edition, Vol. 12).
p. 117

[88] Marx refers to Gladstone who adhered to *Puseyism*—a trend in the Anglican Church from the 1830s to the 1860s named after one of its founders, Edward Pusey, an Oxford University theologian. He advocated the restoration of Catholic rites and certain dogmas in the Anglican Church. Stressing Gladstone's sanctimoniousness and hypocrisy, Marx often called him "unctuous" (see, for instance, present edition, Vol. 12, p. 72). Below Marx quotes Gladstone according to Pakington (*The Times* of March 31, 1854).   p. 117

[89] Marx plays on the name "Doctor Subtilis" given to the medieval scholastic philosopher Duns Scotus.   p. 118

[90] See Note 58.   p. 118

[91] This refers to an event during one of the biggest strikes of English workers at the time. In August 1853 the weavers and spinners at the cotton mills in Preston and its environs went on strike demanding a 10 per cent wage increase. They were supported by workers of other trades. The Associated Masters responded with a lock-out in September 1853. About 25,000 out of the 30,000 Preston workers were out of work, but assistance by workers of other towns allowed the Preston workers to hold out for more than 36 weeks. The lock-out ended in February 1854, but the strike continued. To frustrate it the Associated Masters brought in workers from Ireland and from English workhouses. On the course and importance of the strike see present edition, Vol. 12, and this volume, pp. 200 and 664-65.

The strike ended in May 1854.   p. 120

[92] The *Associated Masters of Preston* binds each of its members by a bond to obey all orders passed by a majority of its members, failing in which an offending master is liable to a penalty of £5,000.   p. 120

[93] *Special constables*—volunteers who perform police duties in their spare time.
                                                                          p. 120

[94] The *Riot Act*—an act for preventing tumults and riotous assemblies, and for the more speedy and effectual punishing of the rioters. If an unlawful assembly of twelve or more persons was ordered by a magistrate to disperse and did not do so within one hour, the magistrate could give the order to open fire. It was introduced in Parliament in 1714 and passed in 1715.   p. 121

[95] With the outbreak of the Crimean war Engels offered his services as military commentator to the liberal London *Daily News* and sent to the editors his article "The Fortress of Kronstadt" (see Note 84) on March 30, and after April 3, 1854, on the request of the editors, the article "The Russian Army" which was to open a series of articles on the Russian land and naval forces. The article was set and Engels probably received the proofs on April 12, 1854 together with a letter by the editor H. J. Lincoln, who asked Engels about his terms. Engels pinned great hopes on this collaboration, believing that permanent work on the newspaper would enable him to give up his commercial activity and move to London. However, as can be judged from Engels' letter to Marx of April 20, 1854, Lincoln cancelled the previous contract when he found out about Engels' political views. Some of the propositions formulated in the article "The Russian Army" were elaborated in "The Military Power of Russia" (this volume, pp. 498-504) and "The Armies in Europe" (present edition, Vol. 14) published in the *New-York Daily Tribune* and *Putnam's Monthly*.   p. 123

[96] The proposal to partition Poland was made by Heinrich of Prussia in 1770 during a visit to St. Petersburg. Initially the tsarist government, wishing to retain its influence over the whole of Poland, opposed this plan, but when Prussia and Austria drew closer to each other, Catherine II was compelled in 1772 to conclude a convention with them on the partition of part of Polish territory between the three powers (the first partition of Poland).							p. 126

[97] This refers to the Russo-Turkish war of 1828-29.							p. 127

[98] This article by Marx and Engels was initially a part of "The War Debate in Parliament" (see Note 101) sent by Marx to New York on April 4, 1854. The editors of the *Tribune* extracted three paragraphs of this article and published them separately as a leader. The editors' interference with the original text of Marx and Engels can be easily traced:

The beginning of the article, up to the words "but this report our well-informed London correspondent pronounces a mere stock-jobbing invention", belongs to the editors. The greater part of the first paragraph, from the words "In fact, it seems perfectly clear..." up to the end, was written by Engels; textually it coincides with Engels' letter to Marx of April 3, 1854 (present edition, Vol. 39). The rest of the paragraph was written by Marx.

The editors similarly dealt with Marx's *second paragraph* as can be seen by comparing it with the fourth and fifth paragraphs of "The War Debate in Parliament"; it is more difficult to establish the degree of their interference here, though it is almost beyond doubt in the sentence: "Had these terms been openly proffered sooner they might have greatly diminished the chances of the war, as there is no doubt that the allies mean to procure just such an emancipation." The last sentence "on that head we shall doubtless have full information by the next steamer" also belongs to the editors.

The contents of the *third paragraph* in the main coincide with Marx's articles "The Greek Insurrection", "Declaration of War.— On the History of the Eastern Question" and also "Greece and Turkey.— Turkey and the Western Powers.— Falling Off in Wheat Sales in England" written later (see this volume, pp. 70-72, 100-08 and 159-62).							p. 129

[99] In March 1854 Frederick William IV of Prussia requested Nicholas I to withdraw his troops from the Danubian Principalities to avoid a conflict. Nicholas I consented on condition that the Western powers would guarantee emancipation of the Christians in Turkey and withdraw their fleets from the Black Sea. Marx got the information about these negotiations from material published in *The Times*, No. 21706, April 4, 1854.							p. 130

[100] See Note 81.							p. 130

[101] In Marx's Notebook the dispatch of this article is dated April 4, but its contents, in contrast to other entries, are not disclosed. The editors published a lesser part of this article as a leader (see Note 98) and the greater part as a separate article under the title "The War Debate in Parliament". The latter, like the rest of Marx's articles which the editors published over his signature, was preceded by "From Our Own Correspondent", but Marx's signature was omitted, presumably due to negligence.

"The War Debate in Parliament" was published in *Die Reform*, a German-language newspaper of American workers, between April 20 and 22, 1854 (the editors of this edition are not in possession of this text). Eleanor

Marx included it in abridged form in *The Eastern Question* under the title "The War with Russia".   p. 132

[102] See Note 16.   p. 135

[103] Marx made a detailed analysis of Lord Palmerston's foreign policy in his pamphlet *Lord Palmerston* written between October and early December 1853 (see present edition, Vol. 12, pp. 341-406).   p. 141

[104] This article is entered in Marx's Notebook as "Freitag. 7. April. Notenwechsel, Oesterreich und Preussen. Kölnische Zeitung". In the abbreviated version of the article published by the *Tribune* the editors omitted the part on the *Kölnische Zeitung*. A fragment of the article was included in the leader published in the same issue of the newspaper. Here is this fragment: "Our correspondent at Vienna announces the conclusion of an alliance between the German powers, by which the entire Confederation, including Austria and Prussia of course, undertakes to maintain neutrality through the war. Whether they can succeed in keeping out of the quarrel for so long a time is a question on which a positive opinion cannot be formed at present. The new complications which may arise, and the new interests which may be developed in the course of the struggle, may very easily render nugatory the most exact calculations that can now be made. Certain it is that but for dread of revolution, against which Russia is supposed to offer a protection, the German powers, and especially the German people, must all desire the humiliation of the Czar, whose preponderant influence they hate, and whose aggrandizement they spontaneously incline to resist. But on the other side, such is their pecuniary weakness, and so entire is their doubt of the loyalty of their subjects, that they must regard the risk of permanent Russian supremacy as far less formidable than that of engaging in a universal war with the revolution lying in ambush behind the eventualities of the contest. So they will remain neutral as long as they can, and will hold themselves ready, when they finally decide to go into the fight, to embrace whichever side offers them the greater advantages. We do not believe they will be led either way by any other motives than regard for their own interest. All the gratitude Austria owes Russia will indeed only prove a reason for her to attack the Czar, should other causes seem to render it the more profitable course; and the same is true of all Germany as well."

The article was reprinted in the *New-York Weekly Tribune*, No. 659, April 29, 1854, but the first and last paragraphs and also Marx's signature were omitted. The article was published in *The Eastern Question* under the title "Russia and the German Powers".   p. 143

[105] When forming his Coalition Ministry (see Note 16) in December 1852 the Prime Minister Lord Aberdeen gave ministerial posts to three members of the Irish Brigade (see Note 441), Keogh, Sadleir and Monsell, thus provoking a strong protest on the part of several Irish deputies which led to a split in the Brigade. The pro-Government Irish deputies were backed by the higher Catholic clergy, Irish bourgeoisie and landlords, who feared the growing national liberation movement in Ireland. The other part of the Brigade (the so-called Independent opposition) headed by Duffy relied on a section of rich Irish leaseholders who wanted the Government to pass a new lease law in Ireland.   p. 144

[106] The reference is to one of the stages in the work of the Vienna conferences (see Note 3). The conferences dealt with in this article ended with the signing of a protocol between England, France, Austria and Prussia on April 9, 1854. It

demanded that Russia immediately evacuate the Danubian Principalities and guaranteed the preservation of the Ottoman Empire.   p. 148

[107] The article "Position of the Armies in Turkey" was written and sent by Engels to Marx in London on April 13; in the Notebook it is entered as "Freitag. 14. April. Militaria".   p. 150

[108] This article is entered in the Notebook as "Dienstag. 18. April. Note Reschid Pasches. Italienische Zeitung benutzt". The article was included in abridged form by Eleanor Marx in *The Eastern Question* under the title "Turkey and Greece.—Italy".   p. 154

[109] See Note 15.   p. 154

[110] At the beginning of 1853 the Austrian Government expelled from Lombardy over 5,000 natives of the Ticino Canton (Switzerland) on the ground that the uprising in Milan in February 1853 had been prepared by Italian revolutionary emigrants residing in Ticino. Only in March 1855, after long diplomatic negotiations, did the Austrian Government permit the expelled Ticinese to return.   p. 155

[111] Here Marx has in mind the Liberal Party (the so-called *moderatti*) headed by Cavour; this party voiced the interests of liberal-monarchist big bourgeoisie and bourgeoisified nobility who strove to unite Italy from above, under the aegis of the Savoy dynasty; fearing the mass revolutionary movement, they based their tactics on use of the favourable international situation and assistance from other states. In 1853-54 this party tried to bring Piedmont into the Crimean war on the side of Britain and France, hoping in this way to secure the support of these powers for the unification of Italy. Piedmont entered the war in 1855.
                                                                             p. 156

[112] The reference is to a system of treaties concluded by the participants in the Vienna Congress of the European monarchs and their Ministers (September 1814-June 1815). It established the boundaries and status of the European states after the victory over Napoleonic France, sanctioned the reshaping of the political map of Europe and the restoration of the "legitimate" dynasties, overthrown as a result of the French Revolution and the Napoleonic wars.
                                                                             p. 157

[113] See Note 17.   p. 157

[114] This refers to the treaty of March 12, 1854 (see Note 79).   p. 157

[115] On the formation of the *Kingdom of Greece* see Note 66.
    The *conquest of Algeria*, which in the eighteenth century was already a military feudal state independent of the Ottoman Empire, began in 1830. It met fierce armed resistance on the part of the Algerian population. By 1842 most of Algeria was conquered, but the Algerian people continued their struggle for independence.
    A *half-independence of Egypt*—the so-called Egyptian crises (1831-33 and 1839-41)—conflicts between Mehemet Ali of Egypt and the Ottoman Empire, with the European powers actively interfering. They ended with the introduction of a new statute for Egypt which remained dependent on the Turkish Sultan.
    Aden was seized by England in 1839 and turned into a military naval base.

The Englishmen who covet Egypt—the reference is to the concession which the English obtained for the construction of the railway line from Alexandria to Suez and Cairo and to the plans for building the Suez canal (opened for navigation in 1869).   p. 158

[116] This article was entered in the Notebook as "Freitag. 21. April. Allerlei. Mark Lane".

It was included by Eleanor Marx in *The Eastern Question* abridged under the title "Austria and Servia.—Greece and Turkey.—Turkey and the Western Powers".

p. 159

[117] *Pera*—a district in Istanbul (Constantinople).   p. 160

[118] By the treaty of Ninfeo (1261) between the Nicaean Empire and Genoa, the latter obtained strongholds in Asia Minor, on the Straits and in the Crimea, thus establishing its domination on the shores of the Aegean and Black seas.

p. 160

[119] This article was written by Engels on April 24, 1854. The authorship is established on the basis of Engels' letter to Marx of April 21, 1854 (see present edition, Vol. 39 and the entry in the Notebook on its dispatch to New York: "Dienstag. 25. April. Militaria"). It was sent by the steamer *Washington* which left Southampton on April 26 and arrived in New York with considerable delay on May 14. The newspaper editors interested in Engels' military reviews published the material as a leader. At the same time they made it appear to have been written on the basis of later information received with the *Atlantic*, which left Europe a week later, on May 3, 1854. For this purpose they added the first paragraph with a survey of the news of the bombardment of Odessa by the allied fleet, published in the same issue of the *New-York Daily Tribune* in the section "The War". The ironical appraisal of Admiral Dundas' bravery may have been taken by the *Tribune* editors from Marx's article "The Bombardment of Odessa.— Greece.— Proclamation of Prince Daniel of Montenegro.— Manteuffel's Speech" published in the same issue (this volume, pp. 173-80). The first paragraph was as follows:

"The *Atlantic* arrived yesterday, bringing intelligence of the first actual attack on the Russians by the British and French fleet in the Black Sea. It seems that the British war-steamer *Furious* went to Odessa with a flag of truce to bring away the British and French Consuls, from that place, and that after having got them on board, she was fired at from the shore. The British represent this act as a wanton violation of the rights of the flag of truce, for which summary vengeance must be taken. The Russians on the other hand say that after the Consuls were embarked, the ship remained in the harbor to enable the officers to take sketches of the fortifications, and that she was fired at simply to put an end to such impropriety. However this may be, the British and French Admirals agreed that something must be done, and accordingly a large force was sent to bombard the place. This operation does not seem to have been accomplished in a very brilliant way, for though the official details have not yet reached us, there is a report that several British ships were badly damaged in process of silencing the shore batteries, burning a few merchant ships in port, and knocking to pieces a palace belonging to Prince Woronzoff, not far from the water's edge. The town of Odessa they did not harm, as it is situated on the top of a hill comparatively out of the way. Having thus taken vengeance, they sailed away again. Admiral Dundas has apparently adopted for his rule of action the advice of a letter from one of his officers, which has been published at London, and means to take anything easy, but to leave difficult and dangerous enterprises alone."   p. 163

[120] The reference is to the Russo-Turkish war of 1828-29.   p. 163

[121] The Notebook gives only the date when this article was mailed ("Freitag. 28. April") but does not disclose its contents. Judging by the reference to *Le Moniteur universel* of April 26, 1854, Marx started to write the article on April 27 and finished it on the day of its dispatch to New York, April 28, 1854. It was included in abridged form in *The Eastern Question* under the title "The Greek Insurrection.—Alliance Between Prussia and Austria.—Russian Armaments".

p. 166

[122] General Zamoiski was permitted to form the Polish Legion at the beginning of 1854. It included supporters of Prince Czartoryski; General Wysocki, protected by Joseph Charles Paul Bonaparte (1822-1891), tried to form a legion of Polish democratic emigrants. But by the summer of 1854 it became clear that his plan had failed and Wysocki left Istanbul. During the Crimean war the Polish emigrants also fought in the ranks of the Cossack formations of Sadyk Pasha (Chaikovsky).   p. 167

[123] See notes 3 and 106.   p. 169

[124] This article was entered in the Notebook as "2. Mai. Dienstag. Militaria". It was sent from Liverpool on May 3 by the steamer *Atlantic*. Before mailing it to Liverpool in the morning of May 3, Marx added information from the morning issue of *The Times* for May 3. It was included by Eleanor Marx in *The Eastern Question* abridged under the title "Bombardment of Odessa.—Austria and Russia.—The Greek Insurrection.—Montenegro.—Manteuffel".   p. 173

[125] During the events described here the acting Governor-General of Novorossia and Bessarabia, P. I. Fyodorov, left for the Caucasus (in March), and N. N. Annenkov, appointed to replace him, arrived in Odessa only on the night of April 9 (21), 1854. During that time the defence of Odessa was led by D. Y. Osten-Sacken.   p. 173

[126] Probably Marx drew this information from a number of papers, in particular *The Times* of April 26, 1854, which published all sorts of rumours about the Russian Government buying back grain from foreign merchants in Odessa.

p. 175

[127] The editors of this edition are not in possession of this issue of *La Presse*. The passage quoted by Marx was obviously published in the newspaper on May 2, for Marx wrote to Engels on May 3: "*Metaxas*, who was Greek Ambassador in Constantinople where he engaged in plotting—the Paris *Presse* published a pretty account of this Russo-Greek Bangyanade—was the principal tool of the infamous Capodistria" (see present edition, Vol. 39). Probably Marx read about this in *L'Indépendance belge*, No. 123, May 3, 1854.   p. 176

[128] Representatives of Prussia and Austria and the Russian Ambassador to Vienna, Meyendorff, acting as a mediator, met in Olmütz on November 29, 1850. The meeting ended with the signing of an agreement by which Prussia consented to restore the German Confederation (see Note 8) and to give Austrian troops passage to Hesse-Cassel and Holstein in order to suppress revolutionary movements there.

The Olmütz agreement was the last victory scored by Austrian diplomacy in the struggle against Prussia.   p. 176

[129] The reference is to the decisions of the London Conference of 1827-32 (see Note 66). The material from the *Nouvelliste de Marseille* is given as published in *L'Indépendance belge*, No. 121, May 1, 1854.   p. 177

[130] The reference is to the national liberation struggle of the German people against French domination which started after the defeat of Napoleon's army in Russia. The ruling circles and governing dynasties tried to use the popular struggle for consolidating the reactionary feudal system in Germany.

Treubund (the Union of the Loyal)—a Prussian monarchist society founded in Berlin at the end of 1848. Late in 1849 it split into ultra-royalists and constitutional monarchists.   p. 178

[131] The authorship of this article was established on the basis of Engels' letters to Marx of May 1, 6 and 9, 1854, the entry in the Notebook ("5. Mai. Freitag. Militaria") and comparison of its text with the reports in *The Times* which Engels used as a source for describing military operations on the Danube front. There are signs of the *Tribune* editors' interference with Engels' text.
                                                                               p. 181

[132] Engels' doubts as to the authenticity of the information about "a decisive victory" gained by Omer Pasha at Chernavoda were fully confirmed. On May 9, 1854, *The Times* carried an article by its own Vienna correspondent who regarded this event as an ordinary encounter with enemy troops and the data on Russian casualties as highly exaggerated.   p. 181

[133] This sentence was inserted in Engels' text by the editors of the *New-York Daily Tribune*.   p. 182

[134] These words are added to Engels' text by the editors of the *New-York Daily Tribune* and refer to the article "The Greek Insurrection" printed in the same issue of the newspaper.   p. 182

[135] See Note 38.   p. 182

[136] Engels refers to Marx's articles "Parliamentary Debates of February 22.—Pozzo di Borgo's Dispatch.—The Policy of the Western Powers", "English and French War Plans.—Greek Insurrection.—Spain.—China", "The Secret Diplomatic Correspondence" (this volume, pp. 26-34, 35-42 and 84-99) and in part to his own article "The Turkish Question" (present edition, Vol. 12). This reference corresponds to Engels' intention about which he wrote to Marx on May 1, 1854: "It is time we harked back to our first articles on the subject, including the political aspect. Here, too, we have been splendidly vindicated by circumstances" (present edition, Vol. 39).   p. 183

[137] The article "British Finances" is entered in the Notebook as "9. Mai. Dienstag. *Financial*". The material was also used for a leader in the *New-York Times*, as is seen from a letter of Cluss to Marx, dated May 25, 1854.   p. 184

[138] *Whitehall*—a street in London named after the Whitehall Palace where in the mid-nineteenth century the following government offices were located: the Admiralty, the Treasury, the Home Office, the Foreign Office, etc.

Somerset House—a palace near the Strand (London) built by the Duke of Somerset in 1549. After its reconstruction in 1776-86, it accommodated such government offices as the Office of the Inspector General of Naval Hospitals and Fleets, the Office of the Registrar General of Births, Deaths and Marriages, and the Audit Office.   p. 188

[139] The reference is to agreement signed by Russia, Britain and the Netherlands in London on May 19 (7), 1815 to defray Russia's war expenses incurred in driving out Napoleon's army from the Dutch and Belgian provinces. The governments of Britain and the Netherlands undertook to pay in compensation part of Russian debts to the Dutch bankers Hope and Co. (25 million Dutch guldens each). A special article of the agreement stipulated that payments would be suspended if the Belgian provinces separated from the Netherlands. After the revolution of 1830, when an independent Belgian state was formed, the Netherlands Government ceased payments. Palmerston signed, on behalf of the British Government, a new agreement with Russia on November 16 (4), 1831 confirming Britain's former financial obligations.   p. 190

[140] This article was written by Engels on May 15, 1854 at Jenny Marx's request. Its dispatch was entered in the Notebook on May 16 under the title "Militaria". The appraisal of the Odessa events here is completely identical with that given by Engels in his letter to Marx of May 9, 1854 (see present edition, Vol. 39).
p. 192

[141] Engels is inaccurate here. It was the same Russian general, Dmitry Yerofeyevich Osten-Sacken, who from December 1853 commanded the troops on the Black Sea coast from the Bug to the Danube, and his headquarters was in Odessa.   p. 192

[142] See Note 125.
p. 192

[143] The *battle at Eckernförde* on April 5, 1849—an operation during the Schleswig-Holstein war between Denmark and Prussia in 1848-50.   p. 194

[144] Engels may have obtained the information about the battle from the Imperial ukase conferring the Order of St. Andrew on Osten-Sacken, which was reprinted by *The Times* on May 15, 1854 from the *Russky Invalid* of May 5, 1854.
p. 194

[145] As a source for this article Marx used the article "Barbarians in Briton" by Ernest Jones published in *The People's Paper* on May 13, 1854. It is entered in the Notebook as "19. Mai. Freitag. Auszug aus Jones". The first paragraph, which bears signs of interference by the *Tribune* editors, was presumably either written entirely by Engels or drawn up by Marx on the basis of Engels' views expressed in "A Famous Victory" (this volume, p. 195).   p. 196

[146] See Note 94.
p. 199

[147] On the Preston strike see Note 91. Marx took the material on the attempt to close the case against the abuses on the part of the Preston magistrates from "Abandonment of the Preston Prosecution", published in *The People's Paper* on May 13, 1854.
p. 200

[148] This article was written by Engels and published by Marx in *The People's Paper*, and also in the *New-York Daily Tribune* under the title "The Exploits in the Baltic and Black Seas.—Anglo-French System of Operations". In the Notebook the date of mailing to New York and the fact of its being printed in *The People's*

Paper are entered as "23. Mai. Dienstag. Militaria (abgedruckt in P[eople's] Paper)".

In *The People's Paper* the article was preceded by an editorial text: "In order to make room for the following able letter, written by a celebrated continental politician, now in England, we are compelled to withdraw our usual summary."

The article was included by Eleanor Marx in *The Eastern Question* under the title "The Exploits in the Baltic and Black Seas.—Anglo-French System of Operations".

In this volume the article is reproduced from *The People's Paper;* readings differing from the *New-York Daily Tribune* are given in footnotes.   p. 201

149 Engels presumably alludes to the victory of the English squadron under Nelson over the Franco-Spanish squadron at Trafalgar on October 21, 1805. The battle was fought when a superior Franco-Spanish squadron attempted to break through the blockade by Nelson's ships in Cadiz harbour.   p. 204

150 On the fulfilment of Marx's intention see notes 165 and 169.   p. 206

151 This article was written by Engels on May 25, 1854 at the request of Marx and his wife in view of Marx's illness. The article was mailed to New York on May 26, 1854 as is testified by the entry in the Notebook: "26. Mai. Freitag. Abuses in the Army. Wellington." The *New-York Semi-Weekly Tribune* reprinted it without any title.   p. 208

152 *Horse Guards*—an old building in London erected in the mid-eighteenth century in the district of government offices between St. James' Park and Whitehall; general headquarters of the English army at that time.   p. 209

153 The reference is to the army camp and military manoeuvres at Chobham, near London, from June 21 to August 20, 1853 in connection with preparations for the war against Russia.   p. 210

154 Inaccuracy in the text: from 1852 to 1858 Ralph Bernal Osborne was Secretary of the Admiralty first in the Aberdeen Coalition Ministry and then in the Palmerston Ministry.   p. 213

155 *The Mayfair Radicals*, nickname given to a section of English aristocracy (Molesworth, Bernal Osborne, and others) who made advances to democratic circles. Mayfair is a former aristocratic district east of Hyde Park.   p. 213

156 The mailing of this article to New York was registered in the Notebook in Marx's own hand as "30. Mai. Dienstag. Russische Seemacht in Baltic. Disraeli und Russell. Quadrprotokoll".   p. 215

157 See Note 56.   p. 215

158 The reference is to the protocol of the current Vienna conference (see notes 3 and 106) signed on May 23, 1854.   p. 215

159 Here Marx cites the treaty of April 20, 1854 between Austria and Prussia according to Blackett's speech, which does not coincide with the authentic text of the treaty analysed by Marx in his article "The Greek Insurrection.—The Polish Emigration.—The Austro-Prussian Treaty.—Russian Documents" (this volume, p. 168).   p. 215

160 See Note 78.   p. 218

[161] The reference is to Russell's motion for "the removal of some disabilities of Her Majesty's Jewish subjects" made in the House of Commons in February 1853 with a view to admitting Jews to the Commons. Russell's Bill was adopted in the House of Commons, but was not passed by the House of Lords. Marx describes this Bill in the article "Parliamentary Debates.—The Clergy Against Socialism.—Starvation" (present edition, Vol. 11). p. 218

[162] The mailing of this article is entered in the Notebook as "2. Juni. Kriegsplan in Varna. (Times), Fabel aus der 'Biene'. Mark Lane. Gladstone and Archangel", which fits in with the following lines in Marx's letter to Engels dated June 3, 1854: "I wrote an article yesterday deriding the plan of campaign published in Thursday's Times" (see present edition, Vol. 39).

The article was published in abridged form by Eleanor Marx in The Eastern Question under the title "Delay on the Danube". p. 220

[163] Presumably Marx has in mind information contained in one of Engels' letters to him which is not available (Engels' letters to Marx written between May 9 and June 10, 1854 have not been found). p. 225

[164] Sir James Graham made this statement not on Monday, May 29, 1854 as erroneously stated in the text, but on Thursday, June 1. It was published in The Times on June 2, 1854. p. 226

[165] This article is entered in the Notebook as "9. Juni. Kriegsministerium Gover. Varna Powers. Handel. Getreide. St. Arnaud". The New-York Weekly Tribune, No. 668 of June 1, 1854 only published the first paragraph of the article. The article was printed in abridged form in The Eastern Question under the title "Speeches. St. Arnaud." p. 227

[166] The reference is to the rout of the Turkish army at Vienna on September 12, 1683 by Austrian, German and Polish troops, with the Polish army under Jan Sobieski playing the decisive role. This battle stopped the advance of the Turks into Central Europe. p. 227

[167] The Peelites—a group of moderate Tories who rallied around Sir Robert Peel and supported his policy of concessions to the commercial and industrial bourgeoisie in the economic sphere while preserving the political domination of the big landlords and financiers. In 1846, in the interests of the industrial bourgeoisie, Peel repealed the Corn Laws. This caused great dissatisfaction among the Tory protectionists, led to a split in the Tory party and the secession of the Peelites. After Peel's death in 1850, the Peelites formed a political group without any definite programme, they participated in the Aberdeen Coalition Ministry (1852-55) and merged with the Liberal Party in the late 1850s and early 1860s. p. 228

[168] The reference is to the demands for the immediate evacuation of the Danubian Principalities and other territories occupied by the Russian troops made by Austria and Prussia to Chancellor Nesselrode after the signing of the treaty on April 20, 1854 (on the treaty, see this volume, p. 168). p. 228

[169] The first half of the article about Saint-Arnaud was written by Marx on June 6, 1854 as entered in the Notebook: "6. Juni. St. Arnaud." The article has not been found in the issues of the New-York Daily Tribune, the New-York Semi-Weekly Tribune, and the New-York Weekly Tribune available to the editors of this edition. p. 230

[170] This refers to the July 1830 bourgeois revolution in France.   p. 230

[171] *Aide-toi, le ciel t'aidera* (Help yourself, heaven will help you)—a political society of a moderate liberal trend formed in France in 1827 with the help of a few future members of the July monarchy (Guizot, Barrot, Lafayette, etc.). It also included a group of bourgeois republicans (Flocon, Godefroy Cavaignac and others).

The society *"dix-mille"* ("ten thousand")—an ironical name given by Marx to the secret Bonapartist Society of December 10. It was formed in 1849 and included mainly declassed elements. Marx described this society in detail in his *The Eighteenth Brumaire of Louis Bonaparte* (present edition, Vol. 11, pp. 148-51).

The words "ten thousand" (ten thousand Persian archers) belong to Agesilaus II, King of Sparta. In 394 B.C., during the Corinthian war (395-387 B.C.) between the Peloponnesian Alliance headed by Sparta and the coalition of Greek states headed by Athens, Agesilaus II had to interrupt his successful military operations against Persia in Asia Minor and return to Greece. He declared that he had been driven from Asia by "ten thousand Persian archers" thus hinting that Persia was subsidising Athens in this war (archers were depicted on Persian gold coins).   p. 230

[172] In calling the famous improviser Eugène de Pradel the teacher of Saint-Arnaud, Marx alludes to an episode in the life of the Commander-in-Chief of the French army in the Crimea: during the Restoration Jacques Leroy (Saint-Arnaud) played in the Paris theatre Gaieté under the stage name of Florival.   p. 231

[173] In 1832, when the royalist coup against Louis Philippe failed, the Duchess of Berry, mother of the Duke of Chambord who was a legitimist pretender to the French throne, was imprisoned in the castle of Blaye, and in 1833 sent to Italy to Duke Luccheri-Palli to whom she had been secretly married.   p. 231

[174] The mailing of this article to New York written by Engels in the evening of June 10 is entered in the Notebook as "*13. Juni.* Belagerung von Silistria".   p. 234

[175] The reference is to an episode in the Danish-Prussian war of 1848-50.   p. 237

[176] The *peace treaty of Adrianople* was concluded by Turkey and Russia in September 1829, at the end of the war of 1828-29. Under it Russia obtained the islands in the mouth of the Danube and a considerable part of the eastern coast of the Black Sea south of the Kuban estuary. Turkey was obliged to recognise the autonomy of the Danubian Principalities, Moldavia and Wallachia and grant them the right to elect hospodars (rulers) independently. Russia was to guarantee this autonomy, which was tantamount to establishing a Russian protectorate over the Principalities. The Turkish Government also pledged to guarantee the autonomy of Greece and Serbia.   p. 240

[177] *Bashi Buzouks*—irregular detachments of the Turkish army in the eighteenth and nineteenth centuries; the name was also given to troops noted for cruelty, plunder and lack of discipline.   p. 243

[178] This information did not prove true. Count Nikolai Alexeyevich Orlov, who stormed Silistria, remained alive.   p. 243

[179] The article "State of the Russian War" by Marx and Engels, and the one following it, "The Russian Retreat", were arbitrarily compiled by the *Tribune*

editors from two works: Marx's article dispatched to New York on June 16 (it is entered in Marx's Notebook as "16. *Juni*. St. Arnaud (Schluß). *Dänemark*. Einfluss der Verteidigung von Silistria auf den Kriegsplan v.d. *Times* (sieh. 9)") and Engels' and Marx's article written on June 19 and 23 respectively (this joint article is entered in the Notebook as "23. Juni. Freitag"). The first article was probably delivered to New York by the steamer *Washington* on July 5, and the second to Halifax by the *America* on July 5, 1854. The editors omitted from the first article the passage concerning Saint-Arnaud and Denmark and added from the second article some details about military operations at Silistria.

The article "State of the Russian War" was included by Eleanor Marx in *The Eastern Question*. The first paragraph was left out. p. 246

[180] The reference is to the Austro-Turkish treaty signed in Constantinople on June 14, 1854. It provided for immediate occupation of the Danubian Principalities by Austria, after the withdrawal of the Russian troops. p. 246

[181] Paskievich's official report on the siege of Silistria by the Russian troops was published in *The Times* on June 24, 1854; Marx may have used some other source. p. 246

[182] An allusion to the participation of Tsarist troops in suppressing the Hungarian revolution of 1849. p. 248

[183] Marx presumably refers to a number of reports from Wallachia and one from Dobrudja which were published anonymously in the *Wiener medizinische Wochenschrift* in the first half of 1854. p. 249

[184] The words "of which we give a full report in this paper" were inserted in Marx's and Engels' text by the *Tribune* editors, and the words "a full report" refer to Marx's article "The War.—Debate in Parliament" (this volume, pp. 258-66). p. 256

[185] The date on which this article was written is corroborated by the entry in the Notebook ("Dienstag, 27. Juni") and Marx's letter to Engels of June 27, 1854. Eleanor Marx published an abridged version of this article in *The Eastern Question*. p. 258

[186] Presumably a misprint. Marx had in mind the following report in *Le Moniteur universel*, No. 177, June 26, 1854.

"Report from Belgrade, June 25, noon. According to a telegraphic dispatch of June 23 from Bucharest, the siege of Silistria has been lifted by order of superior command, the Russians have evacuated Giurgevo and the whole army of the Muscovites will withdraw beyond the Pruth." p. 258

[187] The third edition of *The Times* is not available; the material from it was partly published on the next day in the morning issue of the newspaper (No. 21778, June 27, 1854). p. 258

[188] Marx quotes this document according to a copy of a dispatch from Prince Lieven and Count Matuszcewicz to Count Nesselrode, dated London 1st (13th) June, 1829, published by David Urquhart in: *The Portfolio. Diplomatic Review.* New Series, London, 1843, Vol. I, No. 1. p. 261

[189] On the *Adrianople treaty*, see Note 176.

The *Unkiar-Skelessi treaty* of defensive alliance was concluded by Russia and Turkey on July 8 (June 26), 1833. It provided for mutual aid in the event of war with a third power. A secret article of the treaty freed Turkey from the obligation to give military aid to Russia in return for an undertaking to close the Straits to all foreign warships on Russia's demand.   p. 263

[190] The reference is to the conference of the Turkish Foreign Minister Pertev Pasha, the English Ambassador Gordon, the French Ambassador Guilleminot and the Prussian envoy Royer on September 7, 1829. They discussed the Russian project of a treaty and drew up Turkish proposals. The Ambassadors promised Pertev Pasha to mediate in the negotiations with the Russians.
p. 265

[191] See Note 39.   p. 265

[192] This article is registered in the Notebook as "Dienstag. 4. Juli. *Moldau und Walachei*". It was published in abridged form by Eleanor Marx in *The Eastern Question* under the title "Russia, Austria, Turkey, Wallachia, and Redcliffe".
p. 267

[193] This refers to a military coup (*pronunciamento*) in Madrid on June 28, 1854. Since the spring of 1854 the Spanish people's dissatisfaction with their great economic hardships and with their reactionary government had been growing stronger; it intensified especially after the dissolution of the Cortes which tried to oppose the government decree that taxes must be paid six months in advance. The leaders of the *pronunciamento*, generals O'Donnell and Dulce, who pursued personal aims in the overthrow of the Sartorius dictatorship in Spain, were compelled to promise certain bourgeois tax reforms. They also promised to do away with the camarilla, to convene the Cortes, form a national militia and introduce other changes. Participation of the popular masses in the struggle led to the bourgeois revolution of 1854-56, which in 1854 again brought to power the Progresista Party headed by Espartero (see Note 210). Frightened by the activity of the broad masses, however, the bourgeoisie sided with the counter-revolution, and in 1856 extreme reactionaries returned to power.   p. 267

[194] Marx presumably has in mind the revolt of the Saragossa garrison in February 1854.   p. 267

[195] The *remarkable affair at Bronzell*—an ironical description of an insignificant clash between Prussian and Austrian detachments on November 8, 1850 in the electorate of Hesse-Cassel (Kurhessen). Prussia and Austria, contending for supremacy in Germany, claimed the right to interfere in the internal affairs of Hesse-Cassel to suppress the mounting constitutional movement against the elector Frederick William I and his reactionary ministers. In this conflict with Austria, which received diplomatic support from the Russian Emperor, Nicholas I, Prussia had to yield and allow Austria to carry out a punitive expedition in Hesse-Cassel (see also Note 266).   p. 269

[196] See Note 3.   p. 270

[197] Marx quotes the treaty of 1393 according to D. Bratiano's *Documents Concerning the Question of the Danubian Principalities*; the text of the treaty is also given by Marx in the synopsis of the anonymous book, *The Russians in Moldavia and Wallachia*, London, 1849, which he made in September 1853. Marx may have used this synopsis too when writing this article. Marx's notebook with excerpts, dated January-April and July 1854, contains an outline of part of this article on Moldavia and Wallachia.   p. 271

[198] Marx may here be quoting the treaty of 1460 between Wallachia and Turkey according to D. Bratiano's *Documents Concerning the Question of the Danubian Principalities.*   p. 271

[199] On the *Adrianople treaty,* see Note 176.
Article V of the treaty is given by Marx according to *The Russians in Moldavia and Wallachia.*   p. 272

[200] The revolutionary events of 1848 in Moldavia and Wallachia are described by Marx mainly on the basis of the books: *The Russians in Moldavia and Wallachia* (see Note 197) and J. Héliade Radulesco's *Mémoires sur l'Histoire de la Régénération roumaine ou sur les Événements de 1848 accomplis en Valachie,* Paris, 1851. The author of the second book, J. Héliade Radulesco, took part in the events, was a member of the provisional government known for his pro-Turkish leanings, and during the revolution pursued a compromise policy in respect of the Turkish Government and the Wallachian boyars.   p. 272

[201] Under Article V of the Adrianople treaty (see Note 199) Moldavia and Wallachia were to be occupied by the Russian troops until Turkey paid indemnities (the troops were withdrawn in 1834). Turkey pledged to recognise the autonomy of the Danubian Principalities and grant them the right to elect hospodars (rulers) independently. In 1831-32, on the basis of a project drafted by the Tsarist Government, the assemblies of boyars and clergy in Wallachia and Moldavia adopted "organic regulations" which granted legislative powers in each principality to an assembly elected by big landowners and executive powers to hospodars elected for life by representatives of the landowners, clergy and towns. The "regulations" planned a number of bourgeois reforms: annulled internal customs, introduced free trade, separated judiciary from administrative power, allowed the transfer of peasants to new owners, and prohibited torture. But the preservation of the former feudal order, including serfdom, and the concentration of political power in the Principalities in the hands of the big landowners and boyars, led the progressive sections to regard the "regulations" as a symbol of feudal stagnation.   p. 273

[202] In speaking about the Constitution, Marx had in mind the Izlaz programme, Point 13 of which provided for the abolition of feudal duties of the peasants. The programme was adopted in the village of Izlaz on June 9 (21), 1848. In the book by Radulesco it was entitled "Au nom du Peuple roumain".

p. 273

[203] Marx obtained this information from *The Russians in Moldavia and Wallachia;* the reference is presumably to "Circulaire adressée par le comte de Nesselrode, ministre des affaires étrangères de l'Empereur de toutes les Russies, aux Missions de Russie près les cours d'Europe. En date de St.-Pétersbourg 19 juillet/1 août 1848." ·   p. 273

[204] The *Balta Liman treaty* (convention) was concluded by Russia and Turkey on May 1 (April 19), 1849 in view of the presence of their troops in Moldavia and Wallachia where they had been sent to suppress the revolutionary movement. According to the Convention the occupying regime was to continue until the danger of revolution was completely removed (foreign troops were withdrawn from the Principalities in 1851); provisionally hospodars were to be appointed by the Sultan in concert with the Tsar, and a number of measures were envisaged in the event of a new revolution. "Organic regulations" were re-introduced (see Note 201).   p. 274

[205] On September 28 (October 10), 1848, on the occasion of the Wallachian revolutionary troops being disbanded, their commander Georgiu Magheru (Maghiero) wrote three documents: *Réponse à la lettre du consul anglais; Protestation de Maghiero adressée aux représentants des puissances de l'Europe; La Lettre à Fuad-Effendi.* The texts of these documents are given in the book by Radulesco; the quotation cited by Marx partly conveys their contents.

                                                                                    p. 275

[206] Marx received this article from Engels on July 7 and sent it off to New York on July 11, 1854, as is seen from his entry in the Notebook: "*Dienstag, 11, Juli. Belagerung von Silistria (Schluß).*" Before dispatching the article to New York he made several additions to it from the latest issues of newspapers. The article was published in *The Eastern Question* with some abbreviations, under the title "The Siege of Silistria".   p. 276

[207] The words "having received by the *Pacific*" were inserted in Engels' text by the *Tribune* editors.   p. 277

[208] This article is entered in the Notebook as "*Freitag. 7. Juli (Spanische Revolution)*"; part of the article under the title "Austria" was reproduced by Eleanor Marx in *The Eastern Question.*   p. 282

[209] This refers to the old royal palace *Buen Retiro* built in the seventeenth century for Philip IV. It was turned into artillery barracks in the nineteenth century. The palace was situated in the Retiro Park, in which there were some other government buildings, palaces, an art gallery, observatory, etc.   p. 284

[210] The liberal-bourgeois Progresista party was formed in the 1830s. The Progresistas found support among the urban middle and petty bourgeoisie, intellectuals and some officers. Their principal demand was restriction of the power of the monarchy (see also Note 193).   p. 285

[211] The reference is to the Spanish government decree of May 19, 1854 on payment of land and industrial taxes six months in advance.   p. 286

[212] This article was written by Marx on July 13-14, 1854; it is entered in the Notebook as "Freitag. 14 July. Rückzug von Cronstadt. Schiessen gegen Sebastopol. Geschichten in der Walachei. Angebliches Bombardement von Sulina. Gezwungene Verhältnisse von Bukarest, St. Arnaud. Vorschiebung in der Zahl der Truppen von Calais. Italien. Espagne. Russische Note aus der Indépendence. Oesterreich. Preussen. Protest der Serben. Schweden, Dänemark, Holland. Case of Peithman". The article was included in abridged form in *The Eastern Question* under the title "The Theatre of War.—The Russian Note to the German Powers.—Servia and Austria".   p. 291

[213] There are inaccuracies in the appraisal of the proclamations of O'Donnell (the so-called Manzanares Manifesto adopted in Manzanares, La Mancha, on July 7, 1854) and of Dulce. This is presumably because Marx did not have the texts of the proclamations when he wrote the article. The proclamations were published in the *Journal des Débats* only on July 17, 1854 (see this volume, p. 305).

On June 18, 1837, during the Spanish revolution of 1834-43, a new Constitution was adopted. Being a compromise between some bourgeois liberals and the liberal nobility, the 1837 Constitution gave the Cortes the right of free convocation, the king retaining the right to veto and dissolve the Cortes. Qualifications for election to the Lower Chamber were reduced; its deputies were elected by direct vote, the Senate was appointed by the king from a list submitted to him by special electoral collegiums. Catholicism was recognised as the state religion. The 1837 Constitution remained in force till 1845. p. 294

[214] This refers to Count Nesselrode's dispatch to Prince Gorchakov, the Russian representative in Vienna, of June 29 (17), 1854, which contained the Russian Government's reply to Austria's categorical demand for the Russian evacuation of the Danubian Principalities, which were to be occupied by Austrian troops under the treaty concluded by Austria and Turkey on June 14, 1854. Marx used a report on the dispatch (which had not yet been published) which appeared in *L'Indépendance belge* on July 11, 1854.   p. 294

[215] See Note 106.   p. 295

[216] See Note 195.   p. 296

[217] On the *German Confederation*, see Note 8. Besides the German states the Confederation included the duchies of Holstein, which belonged to the Danish Crown, and of Luxemburg, a possession of the King of the Netherlands. The King of Denmark, as Duke of Holstein, and the King of the Netherlands, as the Grand Duke of Luxemburg, were members of the Federal Diet of the Confederation.   p. 298

[218] This article is entered in the Notebook as "*Dienstag*. 18. Juli. Österreich. Türkei. Spanien. Ministerkrisis. Peithman". The analysis of the sources used in the article allows us to assume that it was heavily edited by the *Tribune* editors who presumably arbitrarily combined the material of this article and of the subsequent one: "The Spanish Revolution.—Greece and Turkey". Both articles, dispatched to America by the steamships *Alps* and *Canada* on July 19 and 22 respectively, arrived in New York almost at the same time and were published on August 3 and 4, 1854. The article "A Congress at Vienna" was included by Eleanor Marx in *The Eastern Question*.   p. 301

[219] See notes 3, 106 and 158.   p. 301

[220] Marx has in mind representatives of several German states (Bavaria, Saxony, Hanover, Württemberg, Baden, Hesse-Cassel, Hesse-Darmstadt and Nassau) which met at a conference at Bamberg in May-June 1854 and decided to adhere to the Austro-Prussian treaty of April 20, 1854 (see this volume, pp. 167-68).   p. 301

[221] See Note 106.   p. 301

[222] *Peterhoff*—summer residence of the Russian emperors.   p. 302

[223] This article is entered in the Notebook as "*Freitag*. 21 *July. Spain*". Presumably, part of the material of this article was included by the editors of the *Tribune* in the preceding one (see Note 218).   p. 309

[224] The *pronunciamentos of 1843*—a counter-revolutionary military mutiny organised in May by generals Narváez, Concha and others against the dictatorship of Espartero, leader of the Progresistas (see Note 210). Some of the Progresistas, dissatisfied with the dictator's policy, supported the mutiny. On July 30, 1843, Espartero fled from the country, General Narváez, a leader of the Moderados, who found support among the big landowners, became the dictator. Thus the

third Spanish revolution (1834-43) came to an end and reaction set in till the fourth revolution (1854-56).   p. 309

[225] The *Peninsular war* or *Spanish war* (1808-14)—a war fought by Britain against France on Spanish and Portuguese territory. Simultaneously with it, the Spanish and Portuguese peoples waged a war of independence against France (see this volume, pp. 400-23).   p. 309

[226] Marx has in mind the 1812 Cadiz Constitution adopted during the first Spanish bourgeois revolution (see this volume, pp. 424-33) and events of the second Spanish bourgeois revolution (1820-23) which reached its peak in 1822. After the defeat of the monarchist conspiracy in the summer of 1822, representatives of the Left wing of the revolutionary movement—the *exaltados*, with Riego as one of their leaders, came to power. They were supported by democratic officers, urban middle and petty bourgeoisie, artisans and workers.   p. 309

[227] The *Carlists*—a reactionary clerico-absolutist group in Spain consisting of adherents of the pretender to the Spanish throne Don Carlos, the brother of Ferdinand VII. Relying on the military and the Catholic clergy, and also making use of the support of the backward peasants in some regions of Spain, the Carlists launched in 1833 a civil war which in fact turned into a struggle between the feudal-Catholic and liberal-bourgeois elements and led to the third bourgeois revolution (1834-43).   p. 310

[228] On the *Progresistas*, see Note 210.
On the *Constitution of 1837*, see Note 213.   p. 310

[229] On December 2, 1851 Louis Bonaparte made a coup d'état by dissolving the Legislative Assembly; "the hands of the Second of December" means Napoleon III's Government.   p. 312

[230] In March 1848 the Provisional Government of the French Republic, in which the party of moderate bourgeois republicans grouped around the newspaper *Le National* played the leading part, organised national workshops in Paris in the hope of using those employed there in their own struggle against the revolutionary proletariat. This attempt to split the working class was a failure; the workers of these workshops formed the core of the June 1848 insurrection.
                                              p. 313

[231] This article is entered in the Notebook as "*Dienstag. 25 July.* Debatte". It was reprinted by Eleanor Marx in *The Eastern Question* under the title "Another War Debate".   p. 316

[232] See Note 176.   p. 317

[233] See notes 3, 106 and 158.   p. 318

[234] See Note 106.   p. 320

[235] This refers to the battle of Sinope, between Russian and Turkish naval squadrons on November 30 (18), 1853, during the Crimean war. It ended in a defeat for the Turks.   p. 321

[236] The words in parentheses were inserted by the *Tribune* editors. The text of Disraeli's speech was printed on p. 7 of the same issue of the *Tribune* in the section "Great Britain. The War Debate in the Commons".   p. 322

[237] This article was entered in the Notebook as "Freitag. 28 July. Treaty vom 14. Juni. Oesterreich. Walachei. Serbien. Italien. Sitzung Parl. Montag, Dienstag, Mittwoch, Dr. Peithman". It was included in abridged form by Eleanor Marx in *The Eastern Question.*   p. 323

[238] As a result of the uprisings of 1804-13 and 1815 and support by Russia, Serbia under the treaty of Akkerman of 1826, subsequently confirmed by the treaty of Adrianople in 1829 (see Note 176), was proclaimed an autonomous principality under Turkish supremacy. The Serbs were granted the right to maintain their own army, courts and schools.   p. 325

[239] Marx, who was present at the debates on the war and the military budget in the House of Commons on July 24 and 25, gives an account of the speech by Lord John Russell on July 24, 1854. In the text of John Russell's speech published by *The Times*, No. 21802 on July 25, 1854 the most glaring contradictions and false assertions about the capture of Sevastopol by the Allies were omitted.
                                                                             p. 326

[240] The British steam frigate *Tiger* ran aground near Odessa on May 12, 1854; it was bombarded by an artillery battery and seriously damaged; the crew was compelled to surrender, and the frigate was burnt.   p. 328

[241] The reference is to an unsuccessful attempt by the British to capture some Russian ships in the Baltic which ended in the loss of a British ship.
                                                                             p. 328

[242] An allusion to Palmerston's position in the Anglo-Greek conflict of 1850 concerning the Portuguese merchant Pacifico, who was a British subject. Using as a pretext the setting on fire of the latter's house in Athens, Palmerston, then Foreign Secretary, presented Greece with an ultimatum and sent ships there. In his speech in Parliament Palmerston justified his actions by the need to safeguard the prestige of British subjects and drew an analogy between them and Roman citizens (*The Times*, No. 20525, June 26, 1850). The Latin "civis romanus sum" (I am a Roman citizen) meant the high status and privileges of Roman citizenship.   p. 332

[243] Thomas Paine's book: *Rights of Man, being an Answer to Mr. Burke's Attack on the French Revolution*, London, 1791-92, in which the author defended the French Revolution, was prohibited in Britain; Paine was persecuted and was compelled to emigrate to France.   p. 332

[244] See Note 139.   p. 333

[245] This article is entered in the Notebook as "*Dienstag*. 1. August. Krieg gegen Spain". It was reprinted by Eleanor Marx in *The Eastern Question*. Engels' authorship is also confirmed by Marx's letter to Engels of July 27, 1854.
                                                                             p. 334

[246] See Note 115.   p. 337

[247] The *Sikhs*—a religious sect which appeared in the Punjab (North-West India) in the sixteenth century. Their teaching on equality of people was used by the peasants who fought against the Hindu feudal lords and the Afghan invaders at the end of the seventeenth century. Subsequently a local aristocracy emerged among the Sikhs and its representatives ruled the Sikh state, which in the early nineteenth century included the Punjab and some border regions. In 1845-46

and 1848-49 Britain waged aggressive wars against the Sikhs which ended with the subjugation of the Punjab. The conquest of the Punjab completed the British colonisation of India.

The Kaffirs—an obsolete name of the South-African people (Xhosas) against whom Britain waged wars in the eighteenth and nineteenth centuries (Kaffir wars). Under the 1853 treaty the Xhosas were compelled to cede part of their lands to Britain.   p. 337

248 See Frederick Engels, "The Movements of 1847", present edition, Vol. 6, pp. 520-29.   p. 338

249 The reference is to the uprising of the Paris proletariat of June 23-26, 1848, which was brutally suppressed by the French bourgeoisie. The defeat of the June uprising was a signal for a counter-revolutionary offensive in European countries.   p. 338

250 This article is entered in the Notebook as "*Freitag.* 5. August. Espartero" (actually the first Friday of August 1854 was August 4). The article was heavily edited by the newspaper editors as is seen from Marx's letter to Engels of October 10, 1854: "By the by, they [the *Tribune* editors— *Ed.*] had deleted every one of my jokes about *constitutional* heroes *en général,* suspecting that, lurking behind the 'Monk-Lafayette-Espartero' trio, were certain sarcasms aimed at the noble 'Washington'" (see present edition, Vol. 39). Besides, the editors added the following sentence at the end: "Our readers can judge whether the Spanish Revolution is likely to have any useful result or not." Marx described this sentence as "silly".   p. 340

251 See Note 210.   p. 340

252 The *battle at Ayacucho* (Peru)—the last major battle in the war of the Spanish colonies in America for independence (1810-26) took place on December 9, 1824.   p. 341

253 On the *Carlist war,* see Note 227.
      On August 31, 1839 an agreement was signed in Vergara between the Carlist General Maroto and Espartero, the commander of the royal army, ending the civil war in Spain. The Carlist forces were disbanded and Don Carlos emigrated to France on September 14, 1839. General Cabrera's attempt to continue the struggle ended in the utter defeat of the Carlists in July 1840.
                                                                             p. 341

254 Marx has in mind Señor de Marliani's book: *Historia politica de la España moderna,* Barcelona, 1849. In the summer of 1854 (presumably in July) Marx started making notes from this edition of Marliani's book. Further excerpts from it were contained in three other notebooks for 1854.   p. 341

255 *Moderados*—a party advocating a constitutional monarchy and representing the interests of the big bourgeoisie and liberal nobility, was organised at the beginning of the bourgeois revolution of 1820-23. In the 1840s and 1850s one of its leaders was General Narváez—an organiser of the counter-revolutionary mutiny in 1843 (see Note 224)—who later became virtual dictator over Spain. During the fourth bourgeois revolution (1854-56) the Moderados opposed all bourgeois reforms and entered into agreement with the most reactionary forces.   p. 342

256 [M. A. Principe, R. Giron, R. Satorres, A. Ribot,] *Espartero: su pasado, su*

presente, su porvenir, Madrid, 1848. The synopsis of this book made by Marx in the summer of 1854 (presumably in July) is extant.   p. 344

[257] The reference is to the divorce case in 1820 between George IV of England and Queen Caroline. The king accused the queen of adultery.   p. 346

[258] This article by Engels was included by Marx, as is seen from his letter to Engels of August 8, 1854, in his own article: "Evacuation of the Danubian Principalities.—The Events in Spain.—A New Danish Constitution.—The Chartists" (see this volume, pp. 350-56). This composite article was entered in the Notebook as "*Dienstag. 8. August. Sebastopol. Alandsinseln. Russian Retreat—Espartero Recit—Danish coup d'état—Jones Rede in Bacup*". The *Tribune* editors cut up Engels' war review and published it as a leader. Marx's article was published in the same issue of the newspaper. The title of Engels' article, "The Attack on the Russian Forts", was presumably given by the *Tribune* editors.   p. 347

[259] This sentence was added by the *Tribune* editors.   p. 347

[260] This article is part of Marx and Engels' joint article (see Note 258). The first section of the article, devoted to the movement of troops in the Danubian Principalities, was written by Marx with Engels' assistance, as can be seen from Marx's letter to Engels of July 22, 1854. Part of the article was included in *The Eastern Question* under the title "The Russian Retreat.—Denmark."   p. 350

[261] The reference is to the Pacheco Ministry (March-August 1847), one of the numerous ministries during the reactionary dictatorship of General Narváez (1843-54).   p. 351

[262] In the article cited by Marx below Ernest Jones developed the ideas on cooperation he had expounded earlier in his articles on cooperation written with the direct participation of Marx (see present edition, Vol. 11, Appendices).   p. 354

[263] This article is entered in the Notebook as "*Freitag. 11. August. Oesterreich, Walachei. Russischer Rückzug. Weisser See. Sulina. Sebastopol Expedition. Polen. Dänemark—Wladimir—Vertagung des Parlaments—Spanien*". The article was included in abridged form in *The Eastern Question* under the title "The Evacuation".   p. 357

[264] See Note 180.   p. 358

[265] The "*potato war*"—an ironical name given to the Austro-Prussian war of the Bavarian succession (1778-79). Here Marx alludes to a conflict which arose between Austria and Prussia in the autumn of 1850 (see notes 195 and 266).   p. 359

[266] In May and October 1850 conferences in which Austria, Prussia and Russia took part were held in Warsaw on the initiative of the Russian Emperor. They were called in connection with the growing tension in the struggle between Austria and Prussia over supremacy in Germany. Acting as arbiter, the Russian Emperor made Prussia renounce her intention of achieving political unification of the German states under her aegis. The protocol mentioned by Marx is: "Procès-verbal des conférences tenues à Varsovie entre les ministres présidents d'Autriche et de Prusse pour arriver à l'amiable à une solution de la question

de la constitution allemande. Signé à Varsovie, le 28 octobre 1850." In 1851 this protocol was published by the Prussian Government in the pamphlet *Von Warschau bis Olmütz*.   p. 359

267 Early in August 1854 the Russian warship *Vladimir*, on its way from Sevastopol to the Bosphorus, attacked the British *Cyclops*, sank several Turkish ships, and returned unharmed to Sevastopol without meeting any resistance from the Anglo French fleet.   p. 361

268 The *Kingdom of Poland*—the name given to the part of Poland which was ceded to Russia by decision of the 1815 Vienna Congress and given the status of a constitutional monarchy united to Russia in the person of the emperor. After the suppression of the 1830-31 insurrection the autonomy of the Kingdom of Poland was abolished. The "organic statute" of 1832 was not implemented.   p. 361

269 Marx has in mind Russia's *Declaration of armed neutrality* of March 11 (February 28), 1780. It was directed against Britain, whose ships attacked ships of neutral states during the American War of Independence (1775-83). The declaration proclaimed the right of neutral states to trade with the belligerent powers; goods of the belligerent states carried by neutral ships were declared inviolable; a port was considered blockaded if its approaches were guarded by ships of the attacking power. This declaration provided a basis for agreements between Russia and Denmark (June 28, 1780) and between Russia and Sweden (July 21, 1780). In 1780-83 they were joined by Holland, Prussia, Austria, Portugal and the Kingdom of the Two Sicilies.   p. 362

270 In 1845 the Cortes adopted a law revising the Constitution of 1837 (see Note 213). The new law raised the electoral qualifications, gave the king the exclusive right to appoint senators, abolished the right of the Cortes to convene without special permission of the monarch, and reserved to the Crown the right to define the range of questions for discussion by the Cortes.   p. 363

271 The concordat between Pope Pius IX and Queen Isabella II of Spain was concluded on March 16, 1851 and approved by the Cortes in October 1851. Under it the Spanish Crown was obliged to pay the Catholic Church from the treasury, to stop confiscating church lands and to return to the monasteries the land confiscated during the third bourgeois revolution (1834-43) which had not yet been sold.   p. 363

272 This article is entered in the Notebook as "Dienstag. 15. August. Dänemark und U.St.—Bundestags Gesetz-[gebung]—Serbische Antwort an die Pforte wegen der Entwaffnun [illegible] Österreichs [illegible] Frage der Wiener Konferenz—Clarendons Revelation in H[ouse] etc.—Spanien". The first part of the article under the title "Servia—England, France and Constantinople" was published in *The Eastern Question*.   p. 364

273 The so-called "Berlin revolutionist conspiracy" was a police provocation (see present edition, Vol. 12, pp. 28-31).   p. 364

274 The *Cologne Communist Trial* (October 4-November 12, 1852) was a trial of a group of Communist League members charged with "conspiracy bearing the character of high treason". The trial was rigged by the Prussian police on the basis of forged documents and fabricated evidence, which were used not only against the accused but also to discredit the whole proletarian organisation.

Such evidence included, for instance, the "Genuine Minute-book" of the Communist League Central Authority meetings and other documents forged by police agents, as well as genuine documents of the adventurist Willich-Schapper faction which was responsible for the split in the Communist League. Seven of the twelve accused were sentenced to imprisonment for terms of three to six years. Marx directed the defence from London, sending material revealing the provocative methods of the prosecution, and after the trial he exposed its organisers (see Marx's pamphlet *Revelations Concerning the Communist Trial in Cologne* and Engels' article "The Late Trial at Cologne", published in the *New-York Daily Tribune*, present edition, Vol. 11).   p. 365

275 See notes 3, 106 and 158.   p. 365

276 The reference is to the London Convention on the Black Sea Straits of July 13, 1841 (see Note 28). The convention annulled the Unkiar-Skelessi treaty which had been very advantageous for Russia (see Note 189).   p. 366

277 An allusion to the marriage planned in 1845 of Prince Leopold Saxe-Coburg-Gotha—a cousin of the English Queen's husband, Prince Albert, and Queen Isabella II of Spain which would have led to a strengthening of Britain's position in the Peninsula. Palmerston, who became Foreign Secretary in 1846, vigorously supported this plan. It was not put into effect (see Note 40).
                                                                                 p. 367

278 The *Congress of Verona* of the Holy Alliance was held from October to December 1822. It adopted the decision on France's armed intervention against revolutionary Spain, and on continuance of Austria's occupation of the kingdoms of Naples and Sardinia, and condemned the national liberation uprising of the Greek people against the Turkish yoke.   p. 367

279 Marx alludes to the editorial of *The Times* of August 14 which contained the following passage: "It is notorious that on the occurrence of this revolution—and, indeed, for some time before—the signal had been given throughout Europe for the disbanded soldiers of sedition to repair to Madrid, and that several hundred of the disciples of the French Red Republic are at present in that capital, assisting the insurrection, teaching the noble art of street fighting, and endeavouring to exasperate the Spanish people to the last extremities against the Court."

Insurrectionists of June—participants in the June 1848 uprising of the Paris proletariat.   p. 368

280 The Manchester textile manufacturer Richard Cobden was one of the Free Trade leaders who demanded, in the interests of English industrial bourgeoisie, a reduction in expenses on the state administration. Among these they listed expenses connected with conquest of colonies and their administration. Cobden, Bright and others considered that Britain, being the most developed industrial power, could conquer any market, ousting her rivals by means of cheaper industrial goods. The centre of Free Trade agitation was Manchester, hence the name of the Manchester School, denoting the Free Trade trend in English economic thinking.   p. 369

281 Under the Cadiz Constitution of 1812 (see this volume, pp. 424-33) the population of the Spanish colonies, excluding the Negroes, received Spanish citizenship and equal political rights with the population of Spain proper,

including the right to elect their representatives to the Cortes. By creating a semblance of equality between colonies and the mother country the Spanish liberals who drafted the Constitution tried to prevent the war for independence which was developing at the time in the Spanish colonies in America.

p. 369

[282] See notes 213 and 270.   p. 371

[283] On the *exaltados*, see Note 226. Marx used this term to characterise the Spanish republicans during the fourth revolution in Spain (1854-56).   p. 371

[284] This article is entered in the Notebook as "*Freitag.* 18. August. Spanien— Aland.—Schweden—Preussen, Anatolien—Dänemark—[illegible] Omer Pasha. Refugees. Austria. Prussia". When it was published in the *Tribune* it was mistakenly dated August 21 (London, Friday, August 21, 1854). The last part of the article was included by Eleanor Marx in *The Eastern Question* under the title "The Capture of Bomarsund".   p. 372

[285] The *Union Club*—one of more democratic of the organisations which appeared at the beginning of the 1854-56 bourgeois revolution in Spain. Its members included republicans and also the utopian socialists Figueras, Pi y Margall, Orense and others. The organisation demanded universal suffrage, freedom of conscience, of the press, assembly and petition, abolition of indirect taxes and capital punishment, and also the arming of the people. At the same time it completely ignored the agrarian question. The club was closed at the end of 1854 (see this volume, p. 448).   p. 372

[286] See Note 213.   p. 372

[287] On April 7, 1823, in accordance with the decision of the Congress of Verona (see Note 278), the French army invaded Spain to suppress the Spanish revolution of 1820-23; the "royalists", who advocated restoration of the absolute monarchy, actively assisted the intervention.

In the course of the war the *Carlists* (see Note 227) resorted to guerrilla tactics.   p. 374

[288] During the 1820-23 bourgeois revolution, besides democratic clubs, numerous secret societies were formed in Spain. They were connected with Left-wing freemasons and included urban bourgeoisie, officers and representatives of the lower urban sections. Being organised with great secrecy and having branches in different regions of the country, these societies had a considerable influence on the policy of the government and of the Cortes. Most prominent among their leaders were Riego, San Miguel and Alpuente.   p. 375

[289] The *Coburg-Braganza* (more correctly *Braganza-Coburg*)—the junior branch of the Braganza royal dynasty in Portugal.

By the *Unionist party* are meant the adherents of a united monarchy in the Iberian Peninsula.   p. 375

[290] See Note 211.   p. 376

[291] This refers to the declaration of neutrality by Sweden and Denmark in 1853 which reflected their hostile attitude towards Russia. Simultaneously, Sweden started negotiations with Britain and France on entering the war on the Allies' side. The negotiations broke down and Sweden did not take part in the Crimean war.   p. 377

292 The two articles by Engels on the capture of Bomarsund which were published in the *New-York Daily Tribune* as leaders are directly connected with the previous one, "The Revolution in Spain.—Bomarsund" written by Marx. The first article is entered in the Notebook as "*Dienstag. 22. August. Bomarsund*". Both articles were published under the same title. Subtitles were provided by the editors of the present edition.   p. 379

293 This article is a continuation of Engels' first article on Bomarsund and only partly corresponds to the entry in the Notebook: "*Dienstag. 29. August. Bomarsund. Einrücken der Oesterreicher in die Walachei. Zustand des Heeres zu Varna.*" The second part of the article dispatched to New York on August 29, 1854, was written by Marx. The article was heavily edited by the newspaper editors, who published the part concerning Bomarsund as a leader. From the rest of the article they took several sentences concerning the entry of the Austrian troops into Wallachia and included them in the review of the news brought by the steamboat *St. Louis*: "From the war there is nothing of great moment except it be the continued entry of the Austrians into the Principalities. We do not hear, however, that the Russians have ceased diplomatic relations at Vienna, though warlike preparations continue there on a large scale." It may also be assumed that material from the item "Zustand des Heerés zu Varna" was included as a separate paragraph in Pulszky's article published in the same number: "The news from the seat of war is very unsatisfactory. The cholera at the camp of Varna has demoralized the Anglo-French army, and though the sailing of the expedition to the Crimea or some other point was to have taken place on the 15th, it has been postponed—first to the 20th and then to the beginning of September. The French do not like the plan of the campaign, which was devised by the English, but still they have accepted it. As to the Turkish defeat at Kars, or according to other Petersburg dispatches at Bayazid we have now reliable information of a late date from the Turkish camp, and can positively assure you that no battle had taken place in July nor in the first days of August, and that, therefore, the defeat over and over reported in *The Times* is a fabrication in order to influence the exchange; indeed, the Turkish scrip, which was already at 7 per cent premium declined to six in consequence of the rumour, and even the English funds were heavy for a day. General Klapka is said to have been sent to the army of Kars; if such be the case, he will soon be in opposition with Guyon." It is not only the above-mentioned entry in the Notebook which gives ground to assume that this paragraph belonged to Marx, but also Marx's letter to Engels of September 2, 1854: "I am in a fix because in one of my latest articles I stated that the report of the Turkish defeat at Kars was an invention of Vienna." (The telegramme on the defeat of the Turkish army at Kars published in *The Times* on August 25, 1854 was dated from Vienna.) See also Marx's letter to Engels of August 26, 1854: "So far as I can gather from the papers, the Polish and Hungarian émigrés in the Turkish Asiatic army do nothing but engage in mischief, place-seeking and intrigues" (present edition, Vol. 39). It is impossible to ascertain to what extent the *Tribune* editors interfered with Marx's original text of these two paragraphs as the manuscript is not extant.   p. 384

294 The series of articles *Revolutionary Spain* was written by Marx for the *New-York Daily Tribune* between August and November 1854. Marx observed all the symptoms of the revolutionary movement in Europe and paid much attention to the revolutionary events in the summer of 1854 in Spain. He held that the

revolutionary struggle there could provide a stimulus for the development of the revolutionary movement in other European countries. In 1854 Marx made a thorough study of the events of the Spanish revolutions of the first half of the nineteenth century so as to improve his understanding of the specific character and features of the new Spanish revolution; Marx's five notebooks of excerpts from the English, French and Spanish authors are extant. We can judge from Marx's Notebook that he sent nine articles to the *New-York Daily Tribune* relating to the first (1808-14), second (1820-23) and partly third (1834-43) Spanish bourgeois revolutions, of which only the first six were published (the articles of September 29 and October 20 were printed in four issues of the newspaper)—thus eight articles in all. The remaining three were not published and the manuscripts have not been found (see Note 457). It is possible that the ninth article did not complete the series, because the extant extract of the manuscript on the causes of the second bourgeois revolution and the nature of the Carlist wars (see this volume, pp. 654-59) exceeds the range of the ninth article as outlined by Marx in his Notebook ("Freitag, 8. December, Spain—1833").

When the editors of the *New-York Daily Tribune* published Marx's articles they treated them arbitrarily.

The first article of the series was published in the newspaper under the title: "Spanish Revolutions", the rest under the title "Revolutionary Spain". Articles were published in part also in the *New-York Semi-Weekly Tribune*, Nos. 970, 975, 984, 986, 996, September 12 and 29, October 31, November 7 and December 12 respectively and in the *New-York Weekly Tribune*, Nos. 679, 682, 685, 686, 687, September 16, October 7 and 28, November 4 and 11, 1854.

Marx's series of articles "Revolutionary Spain" was reproduced in English in 1939 by Lawrence & Wishart Ltd. and also by the International Publishers: Marx and Engels, *Revolution in Spain*.   p. 389

[295] This sentence was presumably written entirely by the *Tribune* editors who mention in it the article by their London correspondent Pulszky of August 25, 1854 published in the *New-York Daily Tribune*, No. 4178, September 8, 1854 in the column "The State of Europe".   p. 391

[296] An allusion to the 1848 February revolution.   p. 391

[297] From 1581 to 1640 Portugal was ruled by the Spanish kings who appointed viceroys to administer it. The arbitrary rule of vice-queen Margaret of Savoy and her favourite Miguel de Vasconcellos led to an uprising in 1640 as a result of which Spanish rule was overthrown and the Braganza dynasty came to power (see Note 289).   p. 392

[298] The *war of the Holy League*—an insurrection of the Castilian towns (*comuneros*) in 1520-22 against the absolute power of Charles I.   p. 392

[299] *Ayuntamientos*—organs of local government in Spain which played a great political role in the period of the Reconquest, or struggle for Spain's liberation from the Arab yoke (eighth-fifteenth centuries). After the suppression of the *comunero* uprising in the sixteenth century which is described in this article, the *Ayuntamientos* were in the main liquidated. Re-establishment of the *Ayuntamientos* was one of the democratic demands made during the bourgeois revolutions at the beginning of the nineteenth century.   p. 393

[300] *States-General*—a body representing the estates in medieval France. It consisted of representatives of the clergy, nobles and burghers. It met in May 1789, after a 175-year interval, at the time of the maturing bourgeois revolution, and on June 17 was transformed by a decision of the deputies of the third estate into the National Assembly, which proclaimed itself the Constituent Assembly on July 9 and became the supreme organ of revolutionary France.   p. 393

[301] The reference is to the Castile Cortes which met in Valladolid in January-February 1518 with the purpose of taking the oath of allegiance to King Charles I and to receive his oath to observe the *fueros* (see Note 321).

There is a slip on Marx's part here; the Cortes met before Charles I of Spain was made Holy Roman Emperor (1519) and before he went to Germany for coronation (1520).   p. 394

[302] *The Holy Brotherhood,* or the *Santa Hermandad,* was a union of Spanish towns formed at the end of the fifteenth century with the approbation of the King, who sought to make use of the bourgeoisie in the struggle between absolutism and the big feudal lords. From the mid-sixteenth century the armed forces of the *Santa Hermandad* performed police functions.   p. 394

[303] *Auto-da-fé* (in Spanish and Portuguese, literally an act of faith)—the solemn announcement of sentences by the High Court of Inquisition in Spain, Portugal and their colonies, the name was also given to the burning of the victims at the stake. The last auto-da-fé took place in Valencia in 1826.   p. 395

[304] The term "*civil society*" (bürgerliche Gesellschaft) is used by Marx and Engels in two different senses: 1) to denote the economic system of class society irrespective of the historical stage of development, the sum total of material relations which determine the political institutions and ideological forms and 2) to denote the material relations of bourgeois society (or society as a whole) under capitalism.   p. 395

[305] The Constitution worked out by Napoleon I for Spain was adopted at the conference of the Spanish nobles in the French town of Bayonne (the Bayonne Cortes) in July 1808. It vested the King (Joseph Bonaparte) with almost unrestricted power. He appointed nobles to the Senate which was to be established and about half of the deputies to the Cortes. The Constitution introduced public legal proceedings, abolished torture and did away with inland customs. The Catholic religion became the only state religion.   p. 399

[306] There is one more sentence in the *New-York Daily Tribune* here ("Let us hope that the additions now being made to their annals by the Spanish people may prove neither unworthy nor fruitless of good to themselves and to the world") which was inserted by the newspaper editors judging from Marx's letter to Engels of October 10, 1854 (see present edition, Vol. 39).   p. 399

[307] *Mémoires et correspondance politique et militaire du roi Joseph,* T. I-X, Paris, 1853-54. The text of a secret treaty allegedly concluded between Alexander I and Napoleon I in Tilsit is given in the comments to the fourth volume of the memoirs (pp. 246-48), purportedly according to the Madrid *Gaceta* of August 25, 1812. The author of the comments was the publisher of the memoirs A. du Casse, aide-de-camp of Joseph Bonaparte. This text was reproduced by Marx in the summary of the memoirs he made in August 1854 during his work on the series of articles "Revolutionary Spain".

708 Notes

There is no mention of such points either in the Tilsit treaty signed by Russia and France on July 7 (June 25), 1807 or in the secret convention supplementing the treaty. p. 400

308 An allusion to Spain's participation in the first coalition against republican France (1793-97). After temporary success in 1793 the Spanish troops were utterly defeated, and Spain was compelled to conclude a separate peace with France in Basle in July 1795. p. 401

309 A popular insurrection in Bilbao against the French invaders took place in August 1808. It was brutally suppressed by General Merlin whose troops stormed the town. p. 407

310 The negotiations between Napoleon I and Alexander I took place in Erfurt from September 27 to October 14, 1808. Festivities which accompanied the event were attended by the kings of Bavaria, Saxony and Württemberg and by a number of other German princes. p. 408

311 Marx has in mind a representative assembly similar to the National Convention formed during the French revolution as a result of the popular uprising of August 10, 1792. p. 408

312 The Jesuits were expelled from Spain in 1767; this was done at the suggestion of Floridablanca, then prosecutor of the Royal Council of Spain. p. 410

313 Reference to the reign of the Castilian kings in the fourteenth-fifteenth centuries: Enrique II (1369-79), Juan I (1379-90), Enrique III (1390-1406) and Juan II (1406-54). p. 413

314 Marx has in mind a regulation in Las Siete Partidas—Spanish code of laws—drawn up in the kingdom of Castile and León in the thirteenth century but actually introduced only after 1348. The *Partidas* functioned parallel with the *fueros* (see Note 321) and gradually became predominant in the legal proceedings only in the sixteenth and seventeenth centuries. p. 414

315 *Le Comité du salut public* (The Committee of Public Safety) established by the Convention on April 6, 1793 during the Jacobin dictatorship (June 2, 1793-July 27, 1794) was the leading revolutionary government body in France. It lasted till October 26, 1795. p. 417

316 At Covadonga (in the Asturian mountains) the Spanish troops defeated the Arabs in 718. This victory promoted the establishment of a small independent state in the mountainous regions of Asturia which became a bulwark of struggle against the Arab invaders (the beginning of the Reconquest).
Another centre of resistance to the Arab invaders arose somewhat later in Sobrarbe, a small territory in Northern Aragon. p.424

317 The summary of the Cadiz Constitution which Marx made in August 1854 from the book: *The Political Constitution of the Spanish Monarchy. Proclaimed in Cadix, 19 March 1812*, London, 1813 is extant. Below Marx quotes articles of the Constitution from this edition. p. 425

318 See Note 299. p. 427

319 *Mita*—here the compulsory assignment of Indians, by drawing lots, to work in the gold and silver mines, at manufactories and construction sites in Spanish colonies in America.

Repartimiento—here the right of a white person to employ as many aliens on his land as he is able to feed. p. 429

320 The *Constitution of 1791*, approved by the Constituent Assembly, established a constitutional monarchy in France, giving the king full executive powers and the right of veto. This Constitution was annulled as a result of the popular uprising of August 10, 1792, which brought about the fall of the monarchy. After the Girondist government (the Girondists were the party of the big bourgeoisie) had been overthrown by the uprising of May 31-June 2, 1793 and the revolutionary dictatorship of the Jacobins established, the National Convention adopted a new democratic Constitution of the French Republic.
p. 429

321 *Fueros* here means the charters which, in medieval Spain, established the rights, privileges and duties of townspeople and members of village communities in matters of local government, jurisdiction, taxation, military service, etc.
p. 429

322 This refers to one of the main principles of the Declaration of the Rights of Man and the Citizen (*Déclaration des droits de l'homme et du citoyen*), a preamble to the Constitution adopted by the French Convention in 1793 during the revolutionary dictatorship of the Jacobins. The last article, the 35th, of the Declaration reads: "When the government violates the rights of the people, insurrection is the imprescriptible right and irremissible duty of the people as a whole and of each of its sections." p. 429

323 *Serviles*—the name given to a reactionary clerico-absolutist group during the first bourgeois revolution in Spain (1808-14); later the *serviles* formed the Court camarilla of Ferdinand VII, and during the last years of his life pinned their hopes on his brother Don Carlos.
Liberales, who expressed the interests of the bourgeoisie and liberal nobility, put forward as their programme the 1812 Constitution.
Americanos—the name given to small group in the Cortes representing the Spaniards living in the Spanish colonies in Latin America. They played no significant role. p. 435

324 The *Council of Trent* was a general council held by the Catholic Church in Tridentum (Trient) and Bologna from 1545 to 1563. It condemned Protestantism and adopted a number of decisions concerning the Catholic Church; in particular, it proclaimed the Pope's authority over the councils and strengthened the power of bishops. The main result of the Council of Trent was the persecution of heretics and free-thinkers, and intensification of Church censorship. From 1559 the *Index librorum prohibitorum* was published regularly and in 1571 the Congregation of the Index (an office in Vatican dealing with censorship) was set up; it remained till 1917. p. 435

325 *Lazzaroni*—the name of declassed, lumpenproletarian elements in Italy; they were repeatedly used by the reactionary monarchist circles in their struggle against the liberal and democratic movement. p. 437

326 Marx is presumably quoting from W. Walton, *The Revolutions of Spain, from 1808 to the end of 1836*, London, 1837 (Vol. I, p. 221), a summary of which he made during his work on the series of articles "Revolutionary Spain". During that time Marx also read San Miguel's *De la guerra civil en España*, Madrid, 1836 and *Memoria Sucinda sobre 10. Acaecido en la columna Movil de las Tropas Nacionales al Mando del comandante General de la Primera División Don Rafael del*

Riejo, desde su Salida de la Ciudad de San Fernando el 20 de Enero de 1820, hasta su total Disolucion en Bienvenida el 11 de Marzo del mismo año. Madrid, 1820; he made excerpts from the former in August, and from the latter in October 1854.   p. 442

[327] The decree of March 6, 1820 and the decrees mentioned by Marx below were published in Miraflores, *Essais historiques et critiques pour servir à l'histoire d'Espagne, de 1820 à 1823,* t. I, Paris, 1836, pp. 257, 261-62. It is probable that Marx's main source in describing these events were: Henry Davis, *The War of Ormuzd and Ahriman in the Nineteenth Century,* Baltimore, 1852; *La España. Bajo el Poder Arbitrario de la congregacion Apostólica o Apuntes Documentados para la Historia de este Pais desde 1820 a 1832.* Second edition, Paris, 1833 and M. de Chateaubriand, *Congrès de Vérone. Guerre d'Espagne. Negociations. Colonies espagnoles,* Brussels, 1838, t. 1, excerpts from which he made in October 1854.
                                                                                          p. 443

[328] After the return of Ferdinand VII, from May 1814 onwards reaction set in in Spain, destroying all the gains of the bourgeois revolution of 1808-14; the revolutionary leaders were imprisoned, some of them executed.   p. 443

[329] Marx polemises against the following works: *Last Days of Spain. By an Eye-Witness,* London, 1823; *The Holy Alliance versus Spain, etc. By a Constitutionalist,* London, 1823; Walton, *The Revolutions of Spain, from 1808 to the end of 1836,* and D. Urquhart, *Progress of Russia.* In the excerpts from these books he made in October 1854, Marx stressed the facts concerning Tatishchev's activity in Madrid.   p. 444

[330] On July 20 (8), 1812 the Russian Government and the representatives of the Cadiz Cortes concluded in Velikiye Luki a treaty establishing friendly relations between Russia and Spain in the war against Napoleonic France, and also reviving and developing trade between the two states. By signing this treaty Russia recognised the Cadiz Cortes and the Constitution drawn up by them. Marx cites this fact from Manuel de Marliani's *Historia politica de la España Moderna,* Barcelona, 1849, and also from *The Holy Alliance versus Spain; or, Notes and Declarations of the Allied Powers* published in the *Edinburgh Review* (v. XXXVIII for 1823, pp. 243-44), excerpts from which are in Marx's notebook of excerpts for November 1854.   p. 444

[331] Presumably a slip of the pen in the manuscript or a misprint in the newspaper; it should be 1814-20, the period between the first and the second Spanish bourgeois revolutions, and not 1808-14.   p. 445

[332] This article is entered in the Notebook as "*Freitag. 1. September.* Spanien Revolution. Constitutientwurf [?]". Marx seems to have finished the article in the morning of September 2, as he used information published in the September 2 morning issue of *The Times* and *Le Moniteur universel* of the same date. The title was probably supplied by the *Tribune* editors.   p. 447

[333] The press law promulgated in Spain on March 22, 1837 abolished preliminary censorship, but imposed high caution money and stipulated strict responsibility of authors and editors for the material published. Later several supplementary laws were passed making the prescriptions of the 1837 law more rigid; the most severe of them was the law of 1852, which reintroduced preliminary censorship. The reference is presumably to this law and not that of 1842.
                                                                                          p. 447

³³⁴ See Note 285. p. 448

³³⁵ The *Prince of Asturias*—a title bestowed on the Crown prince in Spain since 1850. If there were no male heirs the title was conferred on the eldest princess who lost it if a male heir was born. Here the reference is to Isabel Francisca de Asis de Borbón, Isabella II's eldest daughter. p. 449

³³⁶ The reference is to the 45-centime tax—an addition to the four direct taxes on landowners (land tax, real estate tax, window and door tax, patent dues) the burden of which fell mostly on the peasants. The decree introducing this addition was issued by the Provisional Government of the French Republic on March 16, 1848. p. 450

³³⁷ *Octrois*—tolls levied by a city on imported consumer goods, existed in France from the thirteenth century. It was repealed in 1791 during the French Revolution, but later reintroduced on some foodstuffs (salt, wine, fish, etc.).
The *conscription*—here a military tax on persons freed from military service. p. 451

³³⁸ The *captain-generalcies*—administrative areas established in Spain in the sixteenth century in which the supreme military and administrative authority belonged to captain-generals. p. 452

³³⁹ This article was entered in the Notebook as *"Dienstag. 12. September.* Spain. [illegible]". p. 455

³⁴⁰ The confiscation of the estates of the House of Orleans was decreed by Louis Bonaparte on January 22, 1852. p. 456

³⁴¹ See Note 333. p. 458

³⁴² By the age of the Philips, Marx means the reign of the Spanish kings Philip II (1556-98), Philip III (1598-1621) and Philip IV (1621-65). p. 458

³⁴³ Here a derogatory nickname for generals who supported Napoleon III. Marx informed Engels about this evidence of the growth of anti-Bonapartist sentiment in the French army on September 13, 1854. He wrote in greater detail about this on September 25 of the same year in his article for the *New-York Daily Tribune* (see this volume, p. 473). p. 460

³⁴⁴ This article is entered in the Notebook as *"Freitag. 15. September.* Sebastopol Bomarsund Expedition Moldau und [illegible] Oesterreicher in die Walachei. [illegible] Spain. Exports". p. 461

³⁴⁵ See Note 172. p. 462

³⁴⁶ This presumably refers to Marx's article, not yet found, which was entered in the Notebook as *"Freitag. 8 September.* Turkey. Russians Refusal. Prussia. Spain". Part of the material from Marx's article, particularly that concerning Spain, may have been included by the *Tribune* editors in Pulszky's report published in the newspaper on September 22, 1854. p. 465

³⁴⁷ The tariff reform of 1842 lowered customs duties on corn and other imported goods, but introduced income tax as a compensation for the treasury. p. 468

³⁴⁸ Engels wrote this article on September 25, drawing on the first reports of the allied landing at Eupatoria and at the Old Fort in the Crimea which were

published in *The Times* on September 21-25, 1854. The article was entered in Marx's Notebook as *"Dienstag. 26. September"*, then followed the word "Cars" which was changed to "Sev[astopol]". Marx presumably made this correction because he had mailed Engels' article on military actions in the Caucasus to New York on September 19. It was entered in Marx's Notebook as *"Dienstag. 19. September"*. Marx's letter to Engels of September 22 shows that Engels wrote such an article and that Marx had received it by Tuesday, September 19, 1854. In the entry in his Notebook Marx at first mistakenly wrote "Cars" in reference to a latter article and then changed it to Sev[astopol]. Engels' article on Cars written on September 19 has been lost, as the steamship *Arctic* which carried it sank in the Atlantic on September 27, 1854.

The article "The Attack on Sevastopol" was published by Eleanor Marx in *The Eastern Question.*   p. 470

[349] This sentence was changed by the *Tribune* editors. The reports on the movement of the allied troops to Sevastopol were printed on p. 6 of the same issue of the *New-York Daily Tribune.*   p. 470

[350] On June 16, 1815 a battle between Napoleon's army and the Prussian forces commanded by Field Marshal Blücher took place at Ligny. Despite the defeat of the Prussians, Blücher escaped with his army from pursuit by the French and joined the Anglo-Dutch armies at Waterloo, where they fought the main body of the French army. The French were defeated after the arrival of the Prussian troops.   p. 472

[351] On the night of December 1, 1851 a battalion from General Espinasse's regiment was ordered to guard the National Assembly; on December 2, General Espinasse, bribed by the Bonapartists, occupied with his troops the building where the Assembly was sitting, thus promoting the success of Louis Bonaparte's coup d'état.   p. 472

[352] *Lower Empire*—a term used in historical literature to denote the Byzantine Empire, and also the Roman Empire during its decline; it came to be used to describe a state at the period of its decline and disintegration.   p. 473

[353] See Note 343.   p. 473

[354] This refers to Louis Bonaparte's attempted coup d'état on August 6, 1840. Profiting by a certain revival of pro-Bonapartist sentiments in France, Louis Bonaparte landed with a handful of conspirators at Boulogne and tried to raise a mutiny among the local garrison. His attempt failed. He was sentenced to life imprisonment but escaped to England in 1846.   p. 474

[355] The reference is to the expedition of the English fleet to the Scheldt estuary in 1809 during the war of the fifth coalition against Napoleonic France. Though the English captured the isle of Walcheren, they did not develop military operations and were obliged to abandon the island after losing about ten thousand men out of the forty-thousand-strong force through famine and disease.   p. 476

[356] This article is entered in the Notebook as *"Dienstag. 3. Oktober. Sevastopol"*. When Marx prepared it for mailing to New York he added some facts from the reports published in the morning papers of October 3. The first sentence of the article bears signs of interference by the *Tribune* editors.   p. 477

[357] The words "which will be found in another column" were added by the *Tribune* editors and refer to the item entitled "The News of the Victory"

published in the same number. This item contained Napoleon III's address to the soldiers at the camp of Boulogne in connection with the news of the capture of Sevastopol by the allies, which later proved to be false.   p. 480

358 In 1806-07, during the reign of Selim III, the French ambassador Sebastiani succeeded in gaining exceptional influence over the Turkish Government. Napoleon I hoped to use the Turkish army as an ally in the war against Russia. However, in May 1807, there was a mutiny in Constantinople of Janissaries opposing the reforms being carried out in Turkey at the time, and on May 29, 1807, Selim III was dethroned.   p. 481

359 The first two sentences of this paragraph were added by the *Tribune* editors. There are signs of interference also in the fourth sentence.   p. 481

360 The article "The Sevastopol Hoax" and the following one, "The Sevastopol Hoax.—General News", were sent by Marx to New York as one article which was entered in the Notebook as "*Freitag, 6. October.* Renommage über *Sebastopol*". The editors divided it in two, and published them both in the same issue on October 21, 1854, one as a leader, the other unsigned but with the note usual for signed items: "Correspondence of the *New-York Tribune*". The beginning of the article "The Sevastopol Hoax" was reprinted in the *New-York Semi-Weekly Tribune*, No. 685, October 28, 1854.   p. 483

361 The words "and copied in our columns this morning" were added by the *Tribune* editors. This refers to the reprint: "From the London *Gazette* Extraordinary. War Department, Oct. 5" published in the *New-York Daily Tribune* on October 21, 1854. Reports on the events in the Crimea published in the same issue of the *Gazette* are analysed by Marx and Engels below.
    p. 485

362 Events in Malaga are not mentioned in Marx's article published in the *Tribune*. Marx presumably refers to his article written on September 8, 1854 which was not published by the *Tribune* editors (see Note 346). If this material was contained in some other article, the *Tribune* editors omitted it.   p. 489

363 The reference is to the London Protocol of May 8, 1852 recognising the integrity of the Danish monarchy, signed by Austria, Britain, France, Denmark, Prussia, Russia and Sweden. It established the indivisibility of the lands belonging to the Danish Crown, including the Duchy of Schleswig-Holstein. The Protocol mentioned the Russian Emperor among the lawful claimants to the Danish throne (as a descendant of Duke Charles Peter Ulrich of Holstein-Gottorp, who reigned in Russia as Peter III), who waived their rights in favour of Duke Christian of Glücksburg-Gottorp, who was proclaimed successor to King Frederick VII.   p. 489

364 The reference is to Napoleon III's order of October 3, 1854, by which Armand Barbès, sentenced to life imprisonment for participation in revolutionary actions of the Paris workers on May 15, 1848, was released from prison unconditionally. This order followed the interception of a private letter written by Barbès on September 18, 1854, in which he welcomed the war with Russia and wished the French troops success in "the name of civilisation". The order and an excerpt from the letter were published in *Le Moniteur universel* on October 5, 1854. After his release, on October 11, Barbès wrote a letter to the editors of the *Moniteur* acknowledging the authenticity of the letter and stating that "the greatness of France had always been his religion" but that he had always been and remained an enemy of the Bonapartist regime. The letter was

published in the democratic press; on October 18, 1854 it appeared in the weekly *L'Homme. Journal de la démocratie universelle* published in 1853-55 in Jersey, and subsequently in London by the petty-bourgeois emigrants.

p. 491

365 Marx has in mind the events of June 13, 1849 when a peaceful anti-government demonstration organised by the Montagnards was dispersed; the editorial offices of democratic and socialist papers were raided and the principal ones among them were banned.   p. 491

366 This article is entered in the Notebook as *"Dienstag. 10. Oktober.* Schlacht bei Alma". On that day Marx wrote to Engels: "First my compliments on your most glorious and sound criticism. It is pity that this *fait d'armes* [feat of arms] could not appear in the London press. Your position in this field would have been assured through such a move" (present edition, Vol. 39).   p. 492

367 The words: "and the dispatches of the commanders, the reports of English journalists who were present, and of several naval officers, are given at great length in our columns this morning" were added by the *Tribune* editors.

p. 492

368 The *British Legion in Spain* was a force recruited in England to support the Government of Maria Cristina during the Carlist war (see Note 227). This force of 10,000 men commanded by General Evans took part in military operations in 1835-37.   p. 493

369 This refers to a battle between the Piedmontese army and the Austrian troops in Northern Italy during the Austro-Italian war of 1848-49.   p. 494

370 The words "as our readers will see in our extracts from the English papers" were added by the *Tribune* editors.   p. 496

371 The *battle of Lützen* (Saxony) between Napoleon I's army and the Russian and Prussian forces took place on May 2, 1813; the battle between the allied army and the French at Bautzen (Saxony) took place on May 20-21 of the same year. In both cases Napoleon forced the allied troops to retreat though he sustained great losses; in both cases also the retreat was an orderly one.

The *battle of the Katzbach* between the French army and the allied troops took place on August 26, 1813. A successful manoeuvre allowed Blücher to inflict a serious defeat on the French.   p. 496

372 The words "as appears almost certain from our dispatch by the *Niagara,* received last night by telegraph from Halifax", and lower: "though our Halifax dispatch does not mention their arrival" were added by the *Tribune* editors.

p. 496

373 This article is entered in the Notebook as *"Dienstag. 17. Oktober.* Russische Kriegsmacht en général.—Belagerung von Sebastopol". Apparently, the *Tribune* editors omitted the part on the siege of Sevastopol.   p. 498

374 John Bull and Jacques Bonhomme were nicknames given to the English and French.   p. 498

375 This article is entered in the Notebook as *"Dienstag. 31. Oktober,* Belagerung von Sebastopol". Eleanor Marx included it in *The Eastern Question.*   p. 505

376 This sentence shows signs of interference by the *Tribune* editors.   p. 506

377 This sentence shows signs of interference by the *Tribune* editors.   p. 507

[378] See Note 152.   p. 508

[379] *Lancaster*—an eight-inch gun with an oval rifled bore named after its inventor and first used by the British during the Crimean war.   p. 508

[380] Engels' article, which was entered in the Notebook as "*Freitag. 10. November.* Übersicht der Crimean Campaign", was mailed to New York on November 11, 1854 by the *Canada.* It arrived in New York with delay because the *Canada* collided with another ship off the American coast, so the *Tribune* editors changed two first paragraphs in it using the November European press later reports.   p. 510

[381] Engels enumerates battles in which the Russian troops showed great courage and staunchness.

The *battle of Zorndorf,* which took place on August 25, 1758 between the Russian and the Prussian armies was one of the major battles in the Seven Years' War (1756-63). Repeated Prussian attacks were repulsed with great valour by the Russians who inflicted severe losses on the enemy by counter-attacks and artillery fire.

The *battle of Preussisch-Eylau* (Eastern Prussia) on February 7-8, 1807 between the French and Russian troops was one of the bloodiest during the war of the fourth coalition against France. Despite heavy losses Napoleon's army failed to achieve a decisive victory.

The *battle of Borodino* on September 7, 1812 was a major engagement in the Patriotic war against Napoleon in which the Russian troops displayed high fighting qualities and inflicted heavy losses on the French. The outcome of the battle changed the course of the war in Russia's favour and led to the defeat of Napoleon's army despite the forced but expedient evacuation of Moscow by the Russians.   p. 512

[382] This article was entered in the Notebook as "*Freitag. 17. November.* Schlacht vom 25. Oktober (Liprandi)." The *Tribune* published it under the title "The War in the East".   p. 518

[383] The first and second sentences and the reference to quotations from *The Times* were inserted by the *Tribune* editors. The material from *The Times* was printed in the *Tribune* under the heading "From *The London Times* of November 17".   p. 518

[384] See Note 371.   p. 526

[385] This article by Engels was entered in the Notebook as "*Dienstag. 28. November.* Schlacht von Inkerman". When he dispatched his article to London, Engels appears to have forgotten the first two pages of the article (see Marx's letter to Engels of November 30, 1854): "By some oversight the first two pages were omitted from your splendid article of Tuesday's date. However the substance was contained in the 5 following ones, so all that suffered was the style" (see present edition, Vol. 39). That is probably why the first introductory paragraph of the article was written by Marx; however, it was heavily edited by the *Tribune* editors.   p. 528

[386] This refers to the battle of Jena and Auerstadt fought by the French against Prussia and Saxony on October 14, 1806 during the war between Russia and Prussia on the one hand and France on the other (1806-07).   p. 528

[387] The *battle of Albuera* took place on May 16, 1811 between the allied army of Britain, Spain and Portugal, commanded by Beresford, which laid siege to the fortress of Badojos occupied by the French, and the French army under Marshal Soult marching to relieve the fortress.   p. 532

[388] The reference is to an incident during the Egyptian expedition of the French army in 1798-1801.   p. 534

[389] This sentence was inserted by the *Tribune* editors.   p. 534

[390] This article is entered in the Notebook as *"Dienstag. 5. Dezember.* Schlacht bei Inkerman. Relative Position der aliierten Armeen und der russischen bei Sebastopol. Der Seesturm und das Untergehn des Transports vom 13. Novemb. Der s.g. Vertrag von Oesterreich vom 2. Dezember und die Eröffnung des Parlaments". The last part of the article may have been abridged by the *Tribune* editors, as only one paragraph of it was left.   p. 536

[391] The words "all of which we have published" were added by the *Tribune* editors.   p. 536

[392] The *battle of Narva*—the first major battle during the Northern war (1700-21) fought by the Russian army of Peter the Great and the Swedish forces of Charles XII on November 30, 1700.
    The *battle of Austerlitz*, which took place on December 2, 1805 between the Russian and Austrian armies (third coalition) on the one hand and the French on the other, was won by Napoleon I.
    The *battle of Preussisch-Eylau*—see Note 381.   p. 537

[393] The reference is to a treaty concluded by Britain, France and Austria on December 2, 1854 undertaking to abstain from separate negotiations with Russia and prevent occupation of the Danubian Principalities by the Russians. Negotiations with Russia were to be conducted on the basis of the famous Four Points (see this volume, pp. 579-84).   p. 542

[394] This article was entered in the Notebook as *"Freitag. 15. December.* Strategisch-politische Betrachtungen über European War against Russia". The article was included by Eleanor Marx in *The Eastern Question.*   p. 543

[395] December 2, 1854 was the third anniversary of Louis Bonaparte's coup d'état and the second anniversary of his proclamation as Emperor, and also the anniversary of Napoleon Bonaparte's proclamation as Emperor of the French (December 2, 1804) and the battle of Austerlitz (December 2, 1805).   p. 543

[396] The words "which we receive by the *Atlantic*" were added by the *Tribune* editors.   p. 544

[397] See notes 3, 106 and 158.   p. 547

[398] This article was entered in the Notebook as *"Freitag. 22. December.* Oesterreich. Militärkraft".   p. 550

[399] *Grenzers*—inhabitants of the Military Border area (see Note 48).   p. 553

[400] This article was Marx's first contribution to the German democratic daily newspaper *Neue Oder-Zeitung* published in Breslau (Wrocław) from 1849 to 1855.

The paper was founded in March 1849 as a result of the split in the editorial board of the Catholic oppositional *Allgemeine Oder-Zeitung* which had been published since 1846. In the 1850s the *Neue Oder-Zeitung* was considered the most radical German newspaper and was persecuted by the government.

At that time the bourgeois democrats Temme, Stein and Elsner headed the editorial board. Its publisher, the German journalist Max Friedländer, Ferdinand Lassalle's cousin, invited Marx to contribute at the end of 1854. In 1855 Marx was the paper's London correspondent. He sent two or three articles a week, which were published unsigned, but marked "×". As there was practically no workers' press during the years of reaction, Marx and Engels considered it extremely important to use the bourgeois-democratic press for the struggle against reactionary forces. Marx's contributing to the *Neue Oder-Zeitung* made it possible to maintain ties with Germany and keep the German readers informed on the vital problems of international and domestic politics, the working-class and democratic movement, and economic development in the capitalist countries, primarily Britain and France. Marx regularly sent articles on military operations in the Crimean war, and often made use of entire reports by Engels for the *New-York Daily Tribune,* translating them into German; he also sent to the *Neue Oder-Zeitung* abridged versions of Engels' articles, with occasional changes and additions.

This volume contains fifteen articles written by Marx and Engels for the *Neue Oder-Zeitung,* but most are published in Volume 14 of this edition.

The article "In Retrospect" published in two issues of the *Neue Oder-Zeitung* presents a retrospective review of the events in the Crimean war in which Marx sums up his own views and those of Engels as set forth in their articles for the *New-York Daily Tribune.*   p. 554

[401] See Note 393.   p. 554

[402] After the Four Points (see Note 414) had been accepted by the tsarist government in November 1854, negotiations of the representatives of Britain, France, Austria and Russia (the so-called Vienna Conference, see notes 3, 106 and 158) were resumed in December that year.   p. 554

[403] The *bear*—a person who sells stocks and securities for future delivery in expectation of a fall in the market. The *bull*—a person who endeavours to raise the market price of stocks. The *bears* and *bulls* (the *Neue Oder-Zeitung* erroneously has bulldogs) of the Stock Exchange, whose interest it is, the one to depress, and the other to raise prices, are now said to be so called in allusion to the bear's habit of pulling down, and the bull's of tossing up.   p. 554

[404] The Enlistment of Foreigners Bill was introduced in Parliament by the War Secretary Newcastle with the aim of reinforcing the British army in the Crimea. The Bill was passed on December 22, 1854. However, a foreign legion was not formed because of the rising protest against the use of foreign mercenaries in the war.   p. 555

[405] See Note 386.   p. 558

[406] See Note 388.   p. 558

[407] In the *battle of Rocroi* (a French fortress near the Belgian frontier) during the Thirty Years' War (1618-48) the Spanish troops besieging the fortress were utterly defeated on May 19, 1643. The defeat of the Spanish infantry hitherto considered invincible marked a turn in the war.   p. 559

[408] The reference is to the Anglo-Afghan war of 1838-42 in which the British forces were utterly defeated.   p. 562

[409] The reference is to the London Convention of July 15, 1840 between Britain, Russia, Austria and Prussia on supporting the Turkish Sultan against the Egyptian ruler Mehemet Ali (see Note 28). France, who supported Mehemet Ali, did not participate. The threat of an anti-French coalition made France give up her support of the Egyptian ruler.   p. 562

[410] The authorship of the article "British Disaster in the Crimea" has been established on the basis of the coincidence of its main points with those in other articles by Engels. It was also translated by Marx into German for the *Neue Oder-Zeitung* and published in that newspaper as two separate articles on January 8 and 9, 1855 under the same title "Zum englischen Militärwesen". Marx rearranged the material in the article, abridged it and gave a new version of one paragraph which is given in this volume in the footnote.

The article "British Disaster in the Crimea" was published by Eleanor Marx in *The Eastern Question*.   p. 564

[411] The four articles of the series published below had the following titles in the original: 1—"Geschäfts-Krisis"; 2—"Die Zunahme des englischen Handels und der englischen Industrie in den Zeitraum von 1849 bis 1850"; 3 and 4—"Zur Handels-Krise".   p. 571

[412] The reference is to the Crimean war of 1853-56.   p. 572

[413] The *Peace Society*—a pacifist organisation founded in London in 1816 by the Quakers. It was actively supported by the Free Traders (see Note 280), who maintained that in peacetime Free Trade would allow England to make fuller use of her industrial supremacy and gain economic and political domination.
                                                                              p. 574

[414] The reference is to demands presented by the Western powers to Russia in a Note of August 8, 1854 as preliminary conditions for peace negotiations. Russia was to give up her protectorate of Moldavia, Wallachia and Serbia, which was to be replaced by a European guarantee; to allow free passage of ships on the Danube; to consent to the revision of the 1841 London Convention on the Straits (see Note 28) and to give up protection of Christian subjects in Turkey. At first the tsarist government rejected these Four Points but in November 1854 it was compelled to accept them as the basis of future peace negotiations.
                                                                              p. 579

[415] See Note 3.   p. 579

[416] During the 1830-31 insurrection Polish revolutionaries captured in Warsaw the archives of Grand Duke Constantine which contained secret diplomatic documents of the Tsarist Government. The reference here is presumably to a dispatch sent by Pozzo di Borgo on October 16 (4), 1825 and published in *Recueil de documents relatifs à la Russie pour la plupart secrets et inédits utiles à consulter dans la crise actuelle*, Paris, 1854.   p. 580

[417] This presumably refers to *Dispatch from Prince Lieven and Count Matusczewicz, addressed to Count Nesselrode*, dated London, 1st (13th) June, 1829 written on the occasion of the treaty of Adrianople (see Note 176): "It is in the midst of our camp that peace must be signed, and it is when it shall have been concluded

that Europe must know its conditions. Remonstrances will then be too late, and it will then patiently suffer what it can no longer prevent" (*Portfolio, Diplomatic Review (New Series)*, London, 1843, Vol. I, No. 1, p. 24).   p. 580

[418] See Note 13.   p. 582

[419] See notes 17 and 176.   p. 583

[420] Under Article V of the London Convention signed by Britain, France and Russia on July 6, 1827 in connection with the Greek war of liberation against the Turkish yoke, the contracting parties agreed not to seek expansion of their territories, exclusive influence or advantage in trade unless the same was granted to the other two parties.

Under the treaty of Adrianople of 1829 (see Note 176) Russia got islands in the Danube estuary, and free navigation on the Danube was guaranteed.

On March 2 (February 19), 1836 by a Tsarist government decree a quarantine post was set up at the Sulina mouth of the Danube which actually performed customs functions.   p. 584

[421] See Note 28.   p. 584

[422] Marx's article "The Commercial Crisis in Britain" is a variant of the article written by him in January 1855 for the *Neue Oder-Zeitung* (see this volume, pp. 571-78). The authorship and date of writing of the article "The Commercial Crisis in Britain" are also established on the basis of Marx's letter to Engels of January 12, 1855 and a rough draft of the article in one of Marx's notebooks of excerpts.   p. 585

[423] The Corn Laws were repealed in June 1846. The Corn Laws, introduced in the interests of the landowners, imposed high duties on imported corn with the aim of maintaining high prices on it on the home market. The repeal of the Corn Laws marked the victory of the industrial bourgeoisie whose motto was Free Trade.   p. 585

[424] A rough draft has here the following text which was not included in the final version: "It so happens that this time the greatest literary authority of English free-trade, the *London Economist*, quite untrue to his traditions, and in open contradiction to the Manchester school, not only avows that 'the war had little or no connection with the high price of grain', but also that the prosperity of 1853 was 'convulsive', that 'in 1853 there was a fever which has left to 1854 some of the debility consequent on disease', and that 'whether war had come or not, a commercial revulsion was at hand'."   p. 587

[425] This phrase was changed by the *Tribune* editors.   p. 589

[426] See Note 42.   p. 589

[427] This article by Engels is a German version of the article originally written for the *New-York Daily Tribune* (see Note 429). The translation was probably made by Marx.   p. 593

[428] The reference is to a decision adopted by the French Legislative Corps on December 30, 1854 to issue a loan of 500 million francs for the purpose of covering the cost of the war.   p. 594

[429] This article was written by Engels for the *New-York Daily Tribune* at Marx's request (see Marx's letters to Engels of January 12, 17 and 19, 1855).

The first paragraph and the first sentence of the second were added by the *New-York Daily Tribune.* They read as follows:

"A more gloomy picture of disaster and suffering, consequent on blundering and imbecile mismanagement, was never presented than in the letter of our correspondent at Constantinople, published in this morning's paper. It is true his account of the condition of the British army in the Crimea communicates no general facts with which we were not before acquainted, but some of his details are as new as they are painful, while he expresses the feelings of the army thus decimated, and of the English at Constantinople, with a freedom and vividness equaled by few English writers. The indignation at the Government and its agents, at the Field-Marshal commanding, the Commissariat, and the system under which affairs are thus frightfully misconducted, must, indeed, be deep and ardent. We are confident that it is not in the least exaggerated by our correspondent; as our readers will learn from one of our London letters, this feeling is shared by the people of England.

"We yesterday quoted *The London Times* to the effect that the British cavalry before Sevastopol had ceased to exist as a force."   p. 596

[430] See Note 393.   p. 599

[431] The reference is to the Brabant revolution of 1789-90 (see Note 49). p. 599

[432] On August 2, 216 B.C. a major battle of the Second Punic War took place at Cannae (south-eastern Italy), in which forty-eight thousand Romans were killed and ten thousand taken prisoner.   p. 601

[433] *Fidawis*—literally a man who sacrifices himself for an idea; in Persia, Syria and Lebanon—members of a secret order of Assassins (late eleventh-thirteenth centuries) founded to fight the Seljuk Turks and the Crusaders.   p. 603

[434] On the basis of telegraphic dispatches from London the editors of the *Neue Oder-Zeitung* added at the end of Marx's article the following paragraph omitted in the present edition:

"According to telegraphic dispatches from London dated January 26 and 27, Lord John Russell, in connection with the explanation given to Parliament on the causes of his resignation, submitted among other things correspondence exchanged between him and Lord Aberdeen in which he urges a change in the management of the affair. In his view the lamentable situation of the army before Sevastopol cannot be disputed and notwithstanding all his experience in the matter it is impossible for him to establish the causes of the misfortune. Lord Palmerston criticised the motives of John Russell's resignation, but nevertheless admitted that the war must be pursued with the greatest energy. He maintains that all the ships have been used as they should have been: to transport troops, clothing and provisions to the Crimea, and requested a formal vote of confidence or no confidence in the Government. Roebuck's speech was, despite the fact that the speaker was visibly suffering, repeatedly interrupted by applause from all parts of the House. In the Upper House the Earl of Aberdeen stated that the Ministers considered it their duty, despite the resignation of their influential colleague, to oppose the request for the appointment of a commission of inquiry."   p. 604

[435] See Note 88.   p. 608

[436] The system of sale and purchase of officers' commissions in the British army originated at the end of the seventeenth century. Lasting till 1871 it secured predominance of the aristocracy in the army. For details see Marx's article: "The Buying of Commissions.—News from Australia" (present edition, Vol. 14).   p. 608

[437] The authorship of this article was established on the basis of complete coincidence of a number of its propositions with those expounded in the article "From Parliament.—From the Theatre of War" (see this volume, pp. 615-19) published in the *Neue Oder-Zeitung* and marked with Marx's correspondent's sign. In the latter article the report on the parliamentary debate was written by Marx and "Militaria" was compiled and translated by Marx from this article written by Engels.   p. 609

[438] *Tractarianism* (Puseyism)—a system of High Anglican principles set forth in a series of ninety pamphlets issued at Oxford between 1833 and 1841 and called *Tracts for the Times*. (See also Note 88.)   p. 616

[439] See Note 355.   p. 617

[440] This article was written by Engels on the basis of Marx's letter of January 31, 1855 and earlier articles by Marx on Gladstone's budget published in the *New-York Daily Tribune*. Marx received Engels' article in London not later than Friday, February 2. He also used the material of this article in writing two short articles for the *Neue Oder-Zeitung*: "On the Ministerial Crisis" and "The Defeated Government" (see this volume, pp. 627-30 and 638-41).   p. 620

[441] The *Irish Brigade*—the Irish faction in the British Parliament from the 1830s to the 1850s. It was led until 1847 by Daniel O'Connell, who used the tactics of parliamentary manoeuvring to obtain concessions from the British Government to the Irish top bourgeoisie. In the early 1850s some MPs belonging to this faction entered into an alliance with the radical Irish Tenant-Right League and formed in the House of Commons the so-called Independent Opposition. However, the leaders of the Irish Brigade soon entered into an agreement with the British ruling circles and refused to support the League's demands. This led to the demoralisation and final dissolution of the Independent Opposition in 1859.   p. 620

[442] Marx describes as a Gunpowder plot (by analogy with the Gunpowder plot of the Catholics against James I in 1605) the accusation of conspiracy made by the British authorities in April 1853 against the owners of a rocket factory in Rotherhithe, with a view to start repressions against Kossuth and other political emigrants in England. On this see Marx's articles in Volume 12, pp. 82-84, 107.   p. 621

[443] See Note 58.   p. 623

[444] On Irish Landlords and Tenants' Bills introduced in Parliament in November 1852, see Marx's articles in Volume 12, pp. 157-62 and Volume 14, "From the Houses of Parliament.—Bulwer's Motion.—The Irish Question".   p. 623

[445] The *Transportation Bill*, which abolished deportation of criminals to penal colonies, was passed on August 12, 1853. After the preliminary detention the accused were given release certificates granting them the right to reside in Britain under police surveillance and they were used as cheaper labour for

public works. Marx assessed this Bill in his article: "The War Question.—
British Population and Trade Returns.—Doings of Parliament" (see Vol. 12).
p. 623

[446] See Note 3.   p. 624

[447] See Note 78.   p. 625

[448] Under the law in force in England since the early eighteenth century newly
elected MPs were to take an "oath of abdication" denying the right of any
heirs of James II to the throne; the oath contained expressions of loyalty to
Christianity. Refusal to take the oath deprived an MP of the right of active
participation in the work of Parliament.   p. 625

[449] Marx alludes here to the confusion of historical facts by Herbert, who ascribed
to the Directory, which was established in 1795, the actions which took place in
1793. On April 2, 1793 while revolutionary France was at war with the
European Coalition, commissars of the Convention and the War Minister were
sent to the headquarters of the commander-in-chief of the Northern Army,
General Dumouriez, with an order for him to present himself before the
Convention for interrogation on a charge of treason to the revolution. General
Dumouriez refused to obey, and instead arrested the commissars and the War
Minister and handed them over to the Austrians. Soon after he openly deserted
to the Austrians. The editors of the *Neue Oder-Zeitung* apparently changed
the text to tone down Marx's irony (cf. a similar passage in the article
"Fall of the Aberdeen Ministry", this volume, p. 633).   p. 627

[450] By the *minorities* Marx understood various small factions and groups in the
British Parliament. Marx characterised the parliamentary factions and groups
in his article "The Parties and Cliques" (see this volume, pp. 642-44). p. 631

[451] See Note 152.   p. 633

[452] See Note 242.   p. 635

[453] This article was first published in English in *Surveys from Exile Political Writings*,
Vol. 2. Edited and Introduced by David Fernbach, Penguin Books Ltd.,
London, pp. 279-81.   p. 642

[454] See Note 69.   p. 647

[455] This draft is apparently the initial version of the third article in the
Revolutionary Spain series (see this volume, pp. 407-12). It contains many
deletions which are not reproduced in this publication. The title of the draft
belongs to Marx.   p. 651

[456] See Note 338.   p. 652

[457] As can be judged from Marx's Notebook, he wrote and mailed to New York
three articles more of the *Revolutionary Spain* series which were entered in the
Notebook as "Dienstag. 14. November. Spain 1820-Juli 1822"; "Dienstag. 21.
November. Spain. [illegible] Intervention"; "Freitag. 8. December. Spain—
1833". None of the articles were printed in the newspaper; their manuscripts
have not been discovered. The rough draft published in this volume is
apparently part of the article mailed on November 21, 1854. The manuscript
contains many deletions only some of which are reproduced in this publication.
p. 654

[458] By the *second Cadiz expedition* Marx means Riego's campaign in 1823. In August 1823 Riego arrived in Malaga from Cadiz besieged by the French and tried to break through to Catalonia where General Mina was then engaged in fierce fighting with the interventionists. Riego's attempt to gain support from Ballesteros' army, which had ceased resistance, failed, and at the head of a small detachment he marched in the direction of Cartagena. At Jerez his detachment was defeated; on September 15, Riego was captured.

The *first Cadiz expedition* was Riego's campaign of 1820, which was the starting point of the revolution (see this volume, pp. 442-43).   p. 654

[459] Reference to the *army of faith*—the name of detachments formed by the Catholic absolutist group. In 1822 these detachments staged a mutiny against the revolutionary government in Catalonia, Navarre and Biscay; in 1823 they fought on the side of the French interventionists.   p. 654

[460] *Comuneros*—members of a secret political association, the Confederation of the Spanish *comuneros*, founded during the 1820-23 bourgeois revolution. The *comuneros* voiced the interests of the most democratic sections of the urban population: artisans, workers, sections of intellectuals and officers and the petty bourgeoisie. They numbered seventy thousand and most resolutely opposed the counter-revolution. After the suppression of the revolution the *comuneros* were severely persecuted and ceased their activities.   p. 654

[461] The reference is to the restoration in Spain of the absolutist regime of Ferdinand VII as a result of suppression of the 1820-23 revolution. The first restoration of Ferdinand VII was in 1814, after Napoleon's defeat.   p. 658

[462] The reference is to the Carlist war of 1833-40 and the bourgeois revolution in Spain (1834-43). See also notes 224, 227.   p. 659

[463] In September 1832, Ferdinand VII, then gravely ill, annulled his decree of 1830, by which his daughter Isabella, an infant at the time, was made heiress to the throne; when he recovered Ferdinand reinstated her, thus disappointing the hopes of the *serviles* (see Note 323) who supported his brother Don Carlos.
          p. 659

[464] The material published in the Appendix to this volume contains the second part of the article published in the *New-York Daily Tribune* under the title "The English Middle Class". This part is based on Marx's text, the beginning of the article was written by the editors and is not reproduced in this volume.
          p. 663

NAME INDEX

President of the military junta in 1854.—342, 375, 458

Joly—French police commissary.—232

Jones, Ernest Charles (1819-1869)—leading figure in the English labour movement, proletarian poet and journalist, Left Chartist leader; friend of Marx and Engels; editor of *The Northern Star, Notes to the People* and *The People's Paper;* initiator of the Labour Parliament convened in Manchester in 1854.—50, 51, 64, 354, 356

Jones, Sir Harry David (1791-1866)—English general, military engineer; fought in the Peninsular war against Napoleon in 1810-13; commander of an expeditionary force in the Baltic (1854) and of army engineers in the Crimea (1855).—382, 387, 462

Joseph II (1741-1790)—Emperor of the Holy Roman Empire (1765-90).—48, 49, 409, 599

Jovellanos y Ramirez, Gaspar Melchor de (1744-1811)—Spanish statesman, writer, lawyer and economist; follower of the French philosophers of the eighteenth-century Enlightenment; opposed the clerical and feudal regime in Spain; Minister of Justice (1797-98); leader of the Left minority in the Central Junta in 1808-10.—403, 409, 410, 415, 432, 652

Julián—see *Sánchez, Julián*

K

Kalergis, Demetrios (1803-1867)—Greek general and politician; took part in the liberation struggle of the Greek people against Turkish rule (1821-29); War Minister (1854-55).—459

Kalik, Anton (b. 1818)—Austrian army officer, was sent on a special mission to the Danubian Principalities in the summer of 1854.—365

Karamzin, Nikolai Mikhailovich (1766-1826)—Russian historian and writer.—29

Keogh, William Nicholas (1817-1878)—Irish lawyer and politician, a leader of the Irish Brigade in the British Parliament; repeatedly held high judicial posts in Ireland.—638

Khrulev, Stepan Alexandrovich (1807-1870)—Russian general, army commander on the Danube and in the Crimea during the Crimean war; took part in the defence of Sevastopol.—304

Kisseleff (Kiselyev), Nikolai Dmitrievich (1800-1869)—Russian diplomat, held high posts in the Russian embassy in Paris from 1841 onwards, envoy to Paris in 1853 and 1854.—3, 174

Kisseleff (Kiselyev), Pavel Dmitrievich, Count (1788-1872)—Russian statesman; fought in the Patriotic war against Napoleon in 1812; Minister of the Imperial Domains from 1837 to 1856; subsequently ambassador to Paris (1856-62).—171, 172

Knight, Frederick Winn (b. 1812)—English politician, M.P.—321

Kock, Charles Paul de (1793-1871)—French novelist and playwright.—92

Kossuth, Lajos (1802-1894)—leader of the Hungarian national liberation movement, head of the bourgeois democrats during the revolution of 1848-49 and of the Hungarian revolutionary government; emigrated to Turkey after the defeat of the revolution and later to England and America.—26, 90, 167, 227, 321, 621, 641

Kotzebue—Russian consul in Bucharest in 1848.—272

Kovalevsky, Yegor Petrovich (1811-1868)—Russian army officer, traveller, writer and diplomat; commissioner in Montenegro in 1853, then served at army headquarters on the Danube (1853-54) and in the Crimea (1854).—179

Krusenstern, Nikolai Ivanovich—Russian general, military governor of Odessa during the Crimean war.—463

Kurakin, Alexander Borisovich, Prince (1752-1818)—Russian diplomat, Vice-Chancellor (1796-98, 1801-02); took part in the signing of the Tilsit treaty between Russia and France in 1807; ambassador to Paris (1808-12).—400

L

Leopold II (1797-1870)—Grand Duke of Tuscany (1824-59).—484

Lieven, Darya (Dorothea) Khristoforovna, Princess (1785-1857)—wife of the Russian diplomat K. A. Lieven; was hostess of political salons in London and Paris.—562

Lieven, Khristofor Andreyevich, Prince (1774-1839)—Russian diplomat, envoy to Berlin (1810-12), ambassador to London (1812-34).—260-61

Ligier, Alphonse—French consul at Cartagena (Spain) in 1854.—311

Ligne, Charles Joseph, Prince de (1735-1814)—Austrian general, diplomat and writer, participant in the Seven Years' War (1756-63).—599

Linage, Francisco (1795-1847)—Spanish general, member of the Progresista Party, close friend of Espartero and his secretary from 1835; inspector general of infantry and militia in 1843; when the dictatorship of Espartero was overthrown, emigrated together with the latter to Britain.—342

Liprandi, Pavel Petrovich (1796-1864)—Russian general, commanded a division on the Danube (1853-54) and in the Crimea (1854-55).—268, 481, 511, 517, 522, 524, 526, 545

Liverpool, Robert Banks Jenkinson, Earl of (1770-1828)—English statesman, a Tory leader, held a number of ministerial posts, Prime Minister (1812-27).—658

López, Joaquín María (1798-1855)—Spanish lawyer, man of letters and politician, a Progresista Party leader, head of government in 1843.—342, 345

López Baños, Miguel—Spanish army officer, participated in the war of independence (1808-14) and the revolution of 1820-23.—440

Louis XI (1423-1483)—King of France (1461-83).—392

Louis XIV (1638-1715)—King of France (1643-1715).—81, 104

Louis Napoleon—see *Napoleon III*

Louis Philippe (1773-1850)—Duke of Orléans, King of the French (1830-

48).—30, 33, 35, 40, 132, 231, 342, 344, 370

Lozano de Torres, Juan Esteban—Spanish politician, Minister of Justice (1817-19).—417

Lucan, George Charles Bingham, Earl of (1800-1888)—English general, Tory, commanded a cavalry division in the Crimea (1854-early 1855).—493, 524

Lucullus (Lucius Licinius Lucullus) (c. 117-c. 56 B.C.)—Roman soldier, famous for his wealth and sumptuous banquets.—43

Lüders, Alexander Nikolayevich, Count (1790-1874)—Russian general, commanded a corps on the Danube (1853-54) and the Southern army (1855).—66, 129, 181, 247, 268, 292, 541

Luján, Francisco (1798-1867)—Spanish general, writer and scientist, a founder of the Spanish Academy of Sciences; a Cortes deputy from 1836, sided with the Moderado Party; Minister of Public Works (1854).—351, 375

Lukianovich, Nikolai Andreyevich (c. 1806-d. after 1855)—Russian army officer and military historian, took part in the Russo-Turkish war of 1828-29, and in suppressing the Decembrists' uprising (1825) and the Polish insurrection of 1830-31.—123

Luna, Alvaro de (1388-1453)—First Minister of Juan II, King of Castile and León.—391

Lyndhurst, John Singleton Copley, Baron of (1772-1863)—English statesman, lawyer, Tory; Lord Chancellor (1827-30, 1834-35 and 1841-46).—259, 262, 591, 604

Lyons, Edmund, Baron (1790-1858)—English admiral, minister at Athens (1835-49); second in command of the British fleet in the Black Sea under Admiral Dundas (1854).—35, 204, 304, 485, 515

M

Mackenzie, Foma Fomich (Thomas) (d. 1786)—Russian admiral, Scot by birth; commanded a squadron of the Black Sea fleet from 1783 to 1786.— 513

Madvig, Johan Nicolai (1804-1886)— Danish philologist and statesman, Minister of Public Worship (1848-51), President of the Rigsråd (1856-63).— 378

Magheru, Georgiu (1804-1880)— member of the Provisional Government and commander of the revolutionary army in Wallachia in 1848.—275

Mahmud II (1785-1839)—Turkish sultan (1808-39).—240

Malik-Shah (1055-1092)—ruler (sultan) of the Seljuk state (1072-92).—603

Malmesbury, James Howard Harris, Earl of (1807-1889)—British statesman, Tory, subsequently Conservative; Foreign Secretary (1852, 1858-59).— 133-35

Manners, John James Robert, Duke of Rutland (1818-1906)—British statesman, Tory, subsequently Conservative; member of the Young England group in the 1840s, M.P., held ministerial posts.— 15

Mansbach, Carl, von und zu (1790-1867)—Swedish general and diplomat, envoy to Vienna (1852-55) and Berlin (1855-58).—301

Manteuffel, Otto Theodor, Baron von (1805-1882)—Prussian statesman, Minister of the Interior (1848-50), Prime Minister and Foreign Minister (1850-58).—9, 83, 147, 149, 168, 170, 179, 180, 286

Marchesi y Oleaga, José María (1801-1879)—Spanish general, member of the Moderado Party, military governor of Barcelona (1853-54), War Minister (1864).—312

Margaret of Savoy, Duchess of Mantua (1589-1655)—Vice-Queen of Portugal prior to the 1640 insurrection after which Portugal won independence and ceded from Spain.—392

Maria Alexandrovna (1824-1880)—wife of Alexander II of Russia (from 1841).—87

María Anna of Neuburg (1667-1740)— Queen of Charles II of Spain (from 1689).—392

María Cristina de Borbón, senior (1806-1878)—Queen of Ferdinand VII of Spain; regent for her daughter Isabella II (1833-40); after the death of Ferdinand VII she secretly married Muñoz, who later received the title of Duke of Riánsares.—285, 305, 309, 312, 341, 342, 345, 351, 363, 370, 448, 449, 451, 456, 457

María Luisa Fernanda (1832-1897)— infanta of Spain, Isabella II's sister, wife of Duke of Montpensier.—52

María Luisa of Parma (1751-1819)— Queen of Charles IV of Spain (from 1788).—392, 399

María Teresa de Borbón, condessa de Chinchón—wife of Manuel de Godoy and Charles IV's cousin.—451

Maria Theresa (1717-1780)— Archduchess of Austria (1740-80), wife of the Holy Roman Emperor Francis I (1745-80).—45, 46

Marie Amélie Therese (1782-1866)— Queen of Louis Philippe, King of the French, (from 1809).—314

Marliani, Manuel de (d. 1873)—Spanish politician and historian, adherent of Espartero; lived in Spain up to 1859, then emigrated to Italy.—341, 368, 435

Marmont, Auguste Frédéric Louis Viesse de (1774-1852)—Marshal of France, took part in Napoleon I's campaigns; in April 1814 sided with the Bourbons, commanded Charles X's troops during the July 1830 revolution.—37

Maroto, Rafael (1783-1847)—Spanish general, appointed commander-in-chief of the Carlist army by Don Carlos in 1838.—341

Martignac, Jean Baptiste Sylvère Gay, vicomte de (1778-1832)—French lawyer and politician, royalist; in 1823 took part in suppressing the Spanish revolution; in 1828-29 Minister of the Interior, virtual head of the cabinet.—445, 446

Martínez de la Rosa Berdejo Gómez y Arroyo, Francisco de Paula (1787-1862)—Spanish writer and politician, a leader of the Moderados, head of government (1834-35).—306

Marx, Karl (1818-1883).—25, 33-35, 50, 59, 60, 78, 106, 118, 149, 177, 179, 185, 196, 197, 202, 226, 230, 267, 282, 286, 289, 295, 303, 304, 310, 311, 323-25, 329, 331, 365, 367, 377, 453, 462-64, 489, 635

Matusczewicz, Andrzej (Adam Faddeyevich), Count (1796-1842)—Russian diplomat, took part in the congresses of Troppau (1820) and Verona (1822) and in the London conference of 1830.—260

Maurocordatos, Alexander, Prince (1791-1865)—Greek statesman and diplomat; Prime Minister (1844, 1854-55).—217

Maurocordatos, Nicolas—hetman in Moldavia (1854).—464

Mazarin, Jules (Mazarini, Giulio) (1602-1661)—Italian-born French cardinal and statesman; Minister from 1643; virtual ruler of France till Louis XIV's maturity.—107

Mazarredo, Manuel de (1807-1857)—Spanish general, War Minister (1847), captain general of the Basque provinces (1852-54).—312

Mazzini, Giuseppe (1805-1872)—Italian revolutionary, a leader of the national liberation movement in Italy; head of the Provisional Government of the Roman Republic in 1849; an organiser of the Central Committee of European Democracy in London in 1850; sought support among the Bonapartists in the early 1850s, but later opposed them.—90, 167, 321, 455, 621

Mecklenburg-Strelitz, Georg, Duke of (1824-1876)—German aristocrat, general in the service of Russia.—144

Mehemet Ali Pasha (1807-1868)—Turkish statesman; Grand Vizier from 1852 to May 1853; subsequently War Minister (1853-January 1854).—32

Mehemet Kebresli Pasha (c. 1810-1871)—Turkish soldier and statesman; Capudan-Pasha (Minister of Marine) from January to May 1854; Grand

Vizier from May to November 1854.—32

Melbourne, William Lamb, Viscount (1779-1848)—British Whig statesman, Home Secretary (1830-34), Prime Minister (1834, 1835-41).—562

Melgar, Juan Tomás Enríquez Cabrera, conde de (1652-1705)—First Minister of King Charles II of Spain (1693-99); exiled from Spain after the 1699 popular uprising.—392

Menchikoff (Menshikov), Alexander Sergeyevich, Prince (1787-1869)—Russian general and statesman; was sent on an extraordinary mission to Constantinople (February to May 1853); commander-in-chief of the army and navy in the Crimea (1853-February 1855).—15, 21-23, 31, 87, 92, 94, 98, 99, 117, 139, 140, 475, 477, 478, 480, 481, 486, 489, 494-97, 507, 510-13, 517, 528, 531, 533, 536, 537, 539, 558, 611, 618

Mensdorff-Pouilly, Alexander, Count (1813-1871)—Austrian statesman, general; envoy to St. Petersburg (1852-54), minister of the Imperial Court and Foreign Minister (1864-66).—176

Merlin, Christophe Antoine, comte (1771-1839)—general of the French occupation army in Spain in 1808-14.—407

Meroni—Austrian consul in Belgrade in 1854.—159

Messina, Felix María de—Spanish general.—283

Metaxas, Andreas, Count (1786-1860)—Greek statesman and diplomat, Prime Minister (1843-44), ambassador to Constantinople (1850-54).—155, 159

Metternich-Winneburg, Clemens Wenzel Lothar, Prince von (1773-1859)—Austrian statesman and diplomat; Minister of Foreign Affairs (1809-21); Chancellor (1821-48); an organiser of the Holy Alliance.—29, 246, 259, 264

Meyendorf(f), Pyotr Kazimirovich, Baron von (1796-1863)—Russian diplomat,

1867)—Spanish general and politician, a leader of the Moderado Party; made attempts to use revolutionary crisis in the country to establish military dictatorship in 1854; as War Minister directed the suppression of the 1854-56 revolution; head of government (1856, 1858-63, 1865-66).—267, 282-84, 294, 305, 306, 310, 313, 342, 351, 362, 367, 375, 440, 451, 457, 458

O'Flaherty, Edmond—British Treasury official in charge of collecting taxes in Ireland in 1854.—624

Olózaga, Salustiano (1805-1873)—Spanish statesman and diplomat, a leader of the Progresista Party; head of government (1843); minister to Paris (1840-43 and 1854); participant in the 1854-56 revolution.—342, 345, 346, 370

Oltra—Spanish army officer, participant in the 1820-23 revolution.—442

Omer (Omar) Pasha (Michael Lattas) (1806-1871)—Turkish general of Croatian origin, commander-in-chief on the Danube (1853-54), in the Crimea (1855) and in the Caucasus (1855-56).—6, 7, 65, 67, 68, 151, 152, 164, 181, 221, 222, 223, 237, 243, 247, 254, 263, 274, 279, 280, 302, 303, 323, 329, 332, 335, 336, 350, 359, 360, 365, 366, 465, 480, 483, 486, 545, 557

Orléans—royal dynasty in France (1830-48).—40, 456

Orloff (Orlov), Alexei Fyodorovich, Count, from 1856 Prince (1786-1861)—Russian general and statesman, diplomat; signed the treaties of Adrianople (1829) and Unkiar-Skelessi (1833) with Turkey; headed the Russian delegation at the Paris Congress (1856).—8, 145, 177

Orloff (Orlov), Nikolai Alexeyevich, Count (1827-1885)—Russian colonel; was heavily wounded during the storm of Silistria in 1854.—243, 247

Oropesa, Emanuel Joaquín, conde de (1642-c. 1707)—head of the Spanish Government under Charles II (1685-

91 and 1698-99); banished from Spain after the popular uprising of 1699.—392

Orozco—Spanish army officer, participant in the 1854-56 revolution in Spain.—294

Oscar I (1799-1859)—King of Sweden and Norway (1844-59).—144, 362, 377, 387

Osten-Sacken, Dmitry Yerofeyevich, Count (1789-1881)—Russian general; during the Crimean war commander of a corps in the South of Russia (1853-54), and of the Sevastopol garrison (end of 1854 and 1855).—66, 192, 193, 464, 533

O'Sullivan de Grass, Alphonse Albert Henri, comte (1798-1866)—Belgian diplomat, envoy to Vienna from 1837 to 1866.—301

Otto I (1815-1867)—King of Greece (1832-62), member of the Bavarian ruling family of Wittelsbach.—31, 39, 130, 177, 196, 217, 459

Otway, Sir Arthur John, Baronet (1822-1912)—British M.P.; in the 1850s, Tory.—298, 307, 332

Oushakoff (Ushakov), Alexander Kleonakovich (1803-1877)—Russian general, commanded the Russian forces on the Danube in 1854 and in the Crimea in 1855.—129, 292

P

Pacheco, Juan, marqués de Villena (1419-1474)—Spanish statesman, favourite of King Henry IV of Castile.—391, 392

Pacheco y Gutiérrez Calderón, Joaquín Francisco (1808-1865) — Spanish lawyer, writer and politician; belonged to the Moderado Party; participant in the 1854-56 revolution, Foreign Minister (1854).—351

Pacifico, David (1784-1854)—British trader of Portuguese origin in Athens.—635

Padilla, Juan Lopez de (c. 1490-1521)—Spanish nobleman, a leader of the uprising of Castilian towns (*Com-*

Q

Quesada y Matheus, Jenaro, marqués de Miravalles (1818-1889)—Spanish general and statesman, military governor of Madrid in 1854.—283

Quetelet, Lambert Adolphe Jacques (1796-1874)—Belgian statistician, mathematician and astronomer.—642

Quintana, Manuel José (1772-1857)—Spanish poet and politician, follower of the French writers of the eighteenth-century Enlightenment, participant in the revolutions of 1808-14 and 1820-23; member of the Central Junta (1808-10).—411, 420

Quiroga, Antonio (1784-1841)—Spanish army officer, liberal, participant in the revolutions of 1808-14 and 1820-23.—440-42

R

Radetzky, Josef, Count of Radetz (1766-1858)—Austrian field marshal; commanded the Austrian forces in Northern Italy from 1831; suppressed the national liberation movement in Italy in 1848-49; governor-general of the Kingdom of Lombardy and Venice (1850-56).—152, 164, 287, 292, 455, 532

Raglan, Lord Fitzroy James Henry Somerset, Baron (1788-1855)—British general, field marshal from November 1854; Master-General of the Ordnance; commanded the British forces in the Crimea (1854-55).—182, 221, 247, 249, 327, 332, 335, 337, 360, 366, 472, 474, 477, 486, 505, 507-09, 513, 515, 518, 525, 526, 528, 531, 536, 557, 561, 562, 564, 569, 627, 629

Reshid Pasha, Mustafa Mehemed (1802-1858)—Turkish statesman, repeatedly held the post of Grand Vizier; Foreign Minister from May 1853 to May 1855 (with an interval).—32, 155, 167, 289, 291, 318, 323-25

Ribot, A.—Spanish journalist.—345

Richard, Vicente (d. 1816)—Spanish revolutionary, executed after an abortive attempt at an uprising against Ferdinand VII.—445

Richmond, Charles Gordon-Lennox, Duke of (1791-1860)—British Tory politician, protectionist.—600

Riego y Núñez, Rafael del (1785-1823)—Spanish army officer, participant in the war of independence (1808-14); prominent figure during the revolution of 1820-23; executed after its defeat.—423, 441-43, 657

Rifaat Pasha, Sadik (1798-1855)—Turkish statesman, Foreign Minister (from March to May 1853), President of the State Council of Justice (from May 1853 to March 1854).—130

Rios y Rosas, Antonio de los (1812-1873)—Spanish politician, belonged to the Moderado Party, deputy to the Cortes, Minister of the Interior (1854 and 1856).—370, 448

Riza Pasha (1809-1859)—Turkish general and statesman, Capudan Pasha (Naval Minister) from December 1853 to January 1854, Seraskier (War Minister) from January 1854 to June 1855.—32, 221

Robinson, Abraham—Chartist of the 1850s.—64

Robinson, Frederick John, Viscount Goderich, Earl of Ripon (1782-1859)—English statesman, Tory; Chancellor of the Exchequer (1823-27) and Prime Minister (1827-28).—577

Roebuck, John Arthur (1801-1879)—British politician and journalist, radical M.P.; in 1855 Chairman of the Select Committee of Inquiry into the Condition of the Army in the Crimea.—13, 602-08, 615, 626, 627; 630-33, 634, 635, 642

Romana, Pedro Caro y Sureda, marqués de la (1761-1811)—Spanish general, participant in the war of independence (1808-14); commissioner of the Central Junta in Asturia.—406, 415, 416, 422, 653

Romerias—see Romana, Pedro Caro y Sureda

Ros de Olano, Antonio (1808-1886)—Spanish general and politician, be-

INDEX OF LITERARY AND MYTHOLOGICAL NAMES

INDEX OF QUOTED
AND MENTIONED LITERATURE

WORKS BY KARL MARX AND FREDERICK ENGELS

Marx, Karl

Achievements of the Ministry (present edition, Vol. 12). In: *New-York Daily Tribune,* No. 3753, April 27, 1853.—185, 623

[*The Actions of the Allied Fleet.— The Situation in the Danubian Principalities.—Spain.— British Foreign Trade*] (this volume). In: *New-York Daily Tribune,* No. 4198, October 2, 1854.—585

Affairs in Holland.—Denmark.—Conversion of the British Debt.—India, Turkey and Russia (present edition, Vol. 12). In: *New-York Daily Tribune,* No. 3790, June 9, 1853.—15

Austrian Bankruptcy (this volume). In: *New-York Daily Tribune,* No. 4033, March 22, 1854.—288

British Finances (this volume). In: *New-York Daily Tribune,* No. 4086, May 23, 1854.—622-23

British Finances.—The Troubles at Preston (this volume). In: *New-York Semi-Weekly Tribune,* No. 929, April 21, 1854.—622-23

[*A Congress at Vienna.—The Austrian Loan.—Proclamations of Dulce and O'Donnell.— The Ministerial Crisis in Britain*] (this volume). In: *New-York Daily Tribune,* No. 4147, August 3, 1854.—310, 311, 315

[*Declaration of the Prussian Cabinet.—Napoleon's Plans.—Prussia's Policy*] (this volume). In: *New-York Daily Tribune,* No. 4022, March 9, 1854.—83

[*The Details of the Insurrection at Madrid.—The Austro-Prussian Summons.—The New Austrian Loan.—Wallachia*] (this volume). In: *New-York Daily Tribune,* No. 4136, July 21, 1854.—304-05, 326

The Documents on the Partition of Turkey (this volume). In: *New-York Daily Tribune,* No. 4045, April 5, 1854.—136

WORKS BY DIFFERENT AUTHORS

Ariosto, L. *L'Orlando furioso.*—326, 481

Arnold. *The Coming War.* In: *The Leader,* Vol. V, No. 200, January 21, 1854, pp. 59-60.—165

Beaumont, M. [Speech in the House of Lords on June 26, 1854.] In: *The Times,* No. 21778, June 27, 1854.—264

Berkeley, M. [Speeches in the House of Commons]
— July 25, 1854. In: *The Times,* No. 21803, July 26, 1854.—329-31
— January 29, 1855. In: *The Times,* No. 21964, January 30, 1855.—633

Bernal Osborne, R. [Speech in the House of Commons on January 29, 1855.] In: *The Times,* No. 21964, January 30, 1855.—633

Biddulph, M. A. *Sketches of the Assault of Sevastopol.* London, 1854.—508

Blackett, J. [Speech in the House of Commons on May 29, 1854.] In: *The Times,* No. 21754, May 30, 1854.—215

Bonaparte, Joseph. *Mémoires et correspondance politique et militaire du roi Joseph.* Publiés, annotés et mis en ordre par A. du Casse. Paris, 1853, T. IV, pp. 246-47, 290.—400-01

Bramsen, J. *Remark of the North of Spain.* London, 1823.—657

Bratiano, D. *Documents Concerning the Question of the Danubian Principalities. Dedicated to the English Parliament.* London, 1849, pp. 10-11, 26.—271, 274

Bright, J. [Speeches in the House of Commons]
— March 31, 1854. In: *The Times,* No. 21704, April 1, 1854.—141, 387
— May 29, 1854. In: *The Times,* No. 21754, May 30, 1854.—219

Brougham and Vaux, H. [Speeches in the House of Commons]
— March 31, 1854. In: *The Times,* No. 21704, April 1, 1854.—133
— June 26, 1854. In: *The Times,* No. 21778, June 27, 1854.—266

Butt, I. [Speeches in the House of Commons]
— February 20, 1854. In: *The Times,* No. 21670, February 21, 1854.—18
— July 21, 1854. In: *The Times,* No. 21800, July 22, 1854.—332-33

Бутурлинъ, Д. *Исторiя нашествiя императора Наполеона на Россiю въ 1812-мъ году.* Части первая-вторая. Санктпетербургъ, 1823-1824.—123-24

Byron, G. *English Bards and Scotch Reviewers.*—628

Calderón, P. de la Barca. *La puente de Mantible.*—411

Cardwell, E. [Speech in the House of Commons on May 4, 1854.] In: *The Times,* No. 21733, May 5, 1854.—190-91

Carnicero, J.C. *Historia razonada de los principales sucesos de la gloriosa revolución de España.* T. 1-4, Madrid, 1814-1815.—403
— *La Inquisición justamente restablecida e impugnación de la obra "Anales de la Inquisición en España" por Llorente.* T. 1-2, Madrid, 1816.—403
— *Napoleon ó El verdadero D. Quixote de la Europa, ó sean. Comentarios crítico-patriótico-burlescos a varios decretos de Napoleon y su hermano José, distribuidos en dos partes y cincuenta capítulos, y escritos por un español amante de su patria y rey desde primeros de febrero de 1809 hasta fines del mismo año.* T. I-VI, Madrid, 1813.—403

Cervantes Saavedra, M. de. *Vida y hechos del ingenioso hidalgo Don Quixote de la Mancha.*—457

Chambers, Th. [Speech in the House of Commons on February 28, 1854.] In: *The Times,* No. 21677, March 1, 1854.—119

Chateaubriand, F. R. *Congrès de Vérone. Guerre d'Espagne. Négociations. Colonies espagnoles.* T. I-II, Bruxelles, 1838.—40, 367

Clanricarde, U. J. [Speeches in the House of Lords]
— June 26, 1854. In: *The Times,* No. 21778, June 27, 1854.—260, 264-66
— July 24, 1854. In: *The Times,* No. 21802, July 25, 1854.—317-18
— [Letter to the Russian War Minister, Prince Dolgorukov, of November 18, 1854.] In: *The Times,* No. 21946, January 9, 1855.—591

Clarendon, G. W. [Speeches in the House of Lords]
— April 25, 1853. In: *The Times,* No. 21412, April 26, 1853.—24
— August 12, 1853. In: *The Times,* No. 21506, August 13, 1853.—98
— February 6, 1854. In: *The Times,* No. 21658, February 7, 1854.—265
— March 31, 1854. In: *The Times,* No. 21704, April 1, 1854.—132-33, 137
— April 6, 1854. In: *The Times,* No. 21709, April 7, 1854.—143
— July 24, 1854. In: *The Times,* No. 21802, July 25, 1854.—318
— August 10, 1854. In: *The Times,* No. 21817, August 11, 1854.—357-58, 366
— [Letter to Stratford de Redcliffe of June 24, 1853.] In: *The Times,* No. 21670, February 21, 1854.—14

Cobden, R. [Speeches in the House of Commons]
— February 20, 1854. In: *The Times,* No. 21670, February 21, 1854.—13-16
— July 24, 1854. In: *The Times,* No. 21802, July 25, 1854.—321

The Crisis of Spain. 2[d] ed., London, 1823, pp. 21-22.—403

Derby, E. G. [Speeches in the House of Lords]
— March 27, 1854. In: *The Times,* No. 21700, March 28, 1854.—101
— March 31, 1854. In: *The Times,* No. 21704, April 1, 1854.—132, 134, 136
— February 1, 1855. In: *The Times,* No. 21967, February 2, 1855.—628

Державин, Г. Р. *На взятие Варшавы.*—276

Dickens, Ch. *The Life and Adventures of Nicholas Nickleby.*—307

Disraeli, B. [Speeches in the House of Commons]
— February 17, 1854. In: *The Times,* No. 21668, February 18, 1854.—13
— February 20, 1854. In: *The Times,* No. 21670, February 21, 1854.—19, 21, 24, 26
— March 6, 1854. In: *The Times,* No. 21682, March 7, 1854.—56
— March 31, 1854. In: *The Times,* No. 21704, April 1, 1854.—137, 142
— May 29, 1854. In: *The Times,* No. 21754, May 30, 1854.—218-19
— July 20, 1854. In: *The Times,* No. 21799, July 21, 1854.—316
— July 21, 1854. In: *The Times,* No. 21800, July 22, 1854.—316, 321
— July 24, 1854. In: *The Times,* No. 21802, July 25, 1854.—321-22, 326, 331, 484
— December 12, 1854. In: *The Times,* No. 21923, December 13, 1854.—584
— January 29, 1855. In: *The Times,* No. 21964, January 30, 1855.—635

Donizetti, G. *Belisario.* Opera. Libretto S. Cammarano.— 170

Douglas, H. *A Treatise on Naval Gunnery.* London, 1820.—385

Douglas, H. *A Treatise on Naval Gunnery.* Fourth edition, revised. London, 1855. Appendix I. *On the Naval and Military Operations in the Black Sea.*—593

Drummond, H. [Speeches in the House of Commons]
— February 20, 1854. In: *The Times,* No. 21670, February 21, 1854.—17-18
— January 26, 1855. In: *The Times,* No. 21962, January 27, 1855.—616

Dufour, G. H. *De la fortification permanente,* Genève, 1822, p. 309.—479

Duncombe, Th. S. [Speech in the House of Commons on March 30, 1854.] In: *The Times,* No. 21703, March 31, 1854.—119

Dunkellin, U. C. [Letter to the Kaluga Governor, Count Tolstoi, dated November 10, 1854.] In: *The Times,* No. 21946, January 9, 1855.—591

Ellenborough, E. L. [Speeches in the House of Lords]
— July 24, 1854. In: *The Times,* No. 21802, July 25, 1854.—317
— January 23, 1855. In: *The Times,* No. 21959, January 24, 1855.—600

Examen critique des révolutions d'Espagne de 1820 à 1823 et de 1836. T. 1-2. Madrid, 1837.—657

Fallmerayer, J. Ph. *Fragmente aus dem Orient.* Bd. I-II, Stuttgart und Tübingen, 1845.—72

Famin, C. *Histoire de la rivalité et du protectorat des églises chrétiennes en Orient.* Paris, 1853, pp. 12, 13, 49, 50, 54-55.—102, 107-08

Fitzwilliam, Ch. W. [Speech in the House of Lords on July 24, 1854.] In: *The Times,* No. 21802, July 25, 1854.—317

Florez, J. S. *Espartero. Historia de su vida militar y politica y de los grandes sucesos contemporáneos.* Segunda edicion, T. I-IV. Madrid, 1844-1845.—341

[Fox, Ch.] *Memorials and Correspondence of Charles James Fox.* Ed. by Lord John Russell. Vols. 1-3. London, 1853-1854. (The last, fourth, volume came out in 1857.)—606

Gladstone, W. E. [Speeches in the House of Commons]
— April 18, 1853. In: *The Times,* No. 21406, April 19, 1853.—117, 185, 190
— March 6, 1854. In: *The Times,* No. 21682, March 7, 1854.—53-56; 186, 187, 190, 625, 647
— March 21, 1854. In: *The Times,* No. 21695, March 22, 1854.—186
— April 11, 1854. In: *The Times,* No. 21713, April 12, 1854.—186, 647
— May 8, 1854. In: *The Times,* No. 21736, May 9, 1854.—184, 647
— January 29, 1855. In: *The Times,* No. 21964, January 30, 1855.—634
— February 5, 1855. In: *The Times,* No. 21970, February 6, 1855.—645

Goethe, J. W. von. *An Suleika* (from *West-östlicher Divan*).—576
— *Sprichwörtlich.*—616

Graham, J. R. [Speeches in the House of Commons]
— February 17, 1854. In: *The Times,* No. 21668, February 18, 1854.—12-13, 27, 31, 365
— February 20, 1854. In: *The Times,* No. 21670, February 21, 1854.—25

— April 3, 1854. In: *The Times*, No. 21706, April 4, 1854.—142
— June 1, 1854. In: *The Times*, No. 21757, June 2, 1854.—225-26

Granville, G. [Speeches in the House of Lords]
— March 31, 1854. In: *The Times*, No. 21704, April 1, 1854.—134
— December 21, 1854. In: *The Times*, No. 21934, December 22, 1854.—581

Grey, H. G. [Speeches in the House of Lords]
— March 31, 1854. In: *The Times*, No. 21704, April 1, 1854.—133
— April 7, 1854. In: *The Times*, No. 21710, April 8, 1854.—625, 647

Hall, B. [Speech in the House of Commons on January 23, 1855.] In: *The Times*, No. 21959, January 24, 1855.—600

Hammer, J. von. *Geschichte des Osmanischen Reiches, grossentheils aus bisher unbenützten Handschriften und Archiven.* Bd. 1-10, Pest, 1827-1832.—227

Hardinge, H. [Speech in the House of Lords on January 29, 1855.] In: *The Times*, No. 21964, January 30, 1855.—633

Hardwicke, Ch. [Speeches in the House of Lords]
— March 31, 1854. In: *The Times*, No. 21704, April 1, 1854.—133
— July 24, 1854. In: *The Times*, No. 21802, July 25, 1854.—317
— January 23, 1855. In: *The Times*, No. 21959, January 24, 1855.—600

Hayter, W. G. [Speech in the House of Commons on January 25, 1855.] In: *The Times*, No. 21961, January 26, 1855.—604

Heine, H. *Atta Troll.*—83

Henley, J. W. [Speech in the House of Commons on July 26, 1854.] In: *The Times*, No. 21804, July 27, 1854.—332

Hennigsen, Ch. F. *Revelations of Russia.* Vols. I-II. London, 1844.—123

Herbert, S. [Speeches in the House of Commons]
— February 20, 1854. In: *The Times*, No. 21670, February 21, 1854.—18-20
— July 25, 1854. In: *The Times*, No. 21803, July 26, 1854.—327-30
— December 19, 1854. In: *The Times*, No. 21929, December 20, 1854.—556
— January 26, 1855. In: *The Times*, No. 21962, January 27, 1855.—605, 616, 627, 633-34

Hildyard, R. Ch. [Speech in the House of Commons on July 25, 1854.] In: *The Times*, No. 21803, July 26, 1854.—330

[Hobbes, Th.] *The English Works of Thomas Hobbes,... now first collected and edited by Sir William Molesworth...*, Vols. I-XI. London, 1839-1845.—213
— *Opera philosophica quae latine scripsit omnia, in unum corpus nunc primum collecta studio et labore Guilielmi Molesworth...*, T. I-V. Londini, 1839-1845.—213

The Holy Alliance versus Spain etc. By a Constitutionalist. London, 1823.—444

The Holy Alliance versus Spain; or, *Notes and Declarations of the Allied Powers.* In: *Edinburgh Review*, v. XXXVIII, 1823, pp. 241-64.—444

Horsfall, Th. B. [Speech in the House of Commons on February 21, 1854.] In: *The Times*, No. 21671, February 22, 1854.—28

Horsman, E. [Speech in the House of Commons on February 20, 1854.] In: *The Times*, No. 21670, February 21, 1854.—16-17

[Hughes, T. M.] *Revelations of Spain in 1845. By an English Resident* 2 vols. London, 1845.—341, 343, 346, 450

Hume, J. [Speech in the House of Commons on February 22, 1854.] In: *The Times,* No. 21672, February 23, 1854.—26-27

Jocelyn, R. [Speech in the House of Commons on February 17, 1854.] In: *The Times,* No. 21668, February 18, 1854.—13

Jones, E. *Barbarians in Briton.* In: *The People's Paper,* No. 106, May 13, 1854.—196-200
— *The Cotton Law of Preston.—Who Are the Real Conspirators?* In: *The People's Paper,* No. 99, March 25, 1854.—120-21
— [Speech at a meeting at Bacup on July 30, 1854.] In: *The People's Paper,* No. 118, August 5, 1854.—354-56

Jovellanos, G. M. de. *Informe de la Sociedad económica de esta corte al real y supremo consejo de Castilla, en el expediente de ley agraria.* Madrid, 1795.—404, 432

Карамзинъ, Н. М. *Исторія Государства Россійскаго.* Т. XI, Санктпетербургъ, 1824, стр. 28.—29

Kossuth, L. [Speech at a meeting in Sheffield on June 5, 1854.] In: *The Times,* No. 21761, June 7, 1854.—227

Lansdowne, H. [Speech in the House of Lords on March 31, 1854.] In: *The Times,* No. 21704, April 1, 1854.—133

Las Cases, E. *Mémorial de Sainte-Hélène.* T. 6, Paris, 1824, p. 186.—96

Last Days of Spain. By an Eye-witness. London, 1823.—444

Layard, A. H. *Nineveh and Its Remains: with an Account of a Visit to the Chaldaean Christians of Kurdistan, and the Yezidis, or Devil-worshippers; and an Enquiry into the Manners and Arts of the Ancient Assyrians.* 2 vols. London, 1849.—137
— [Speeches in the House of Commons]
— February 17, 1854. In: *The Times,* No. 21668, February 18, 1854.—11
— March 31, 1854. In: *The Times,* No. 21704, April 1, 1854.—137-41
— June 23, 1854. In: *The Times,* No. 21776, June 24, 1854.—259
— July 24, 1854. In: *The Times,* No. 21802, July 25, 1854.—321
— January 23, 1855. In: *The Times,* No. 21959, January 24, 1855.—601
— January 26, 1855. In: *The Times,* No. 21962, January 27, 1855.—605, 634

Liverpool, R. [Speech in the House of Lords on February 4, 1823.] In: *Hansard's Parliamentary Debates,* New Series [2], Vol. 8, London, 1823, pp. 29-34.—658-59

Лукьяновичъ [Н. А.] *Описаніе Турецкой войны 1828 и 1829 годовъ.* Части первая-четвертая. Санктпетербургъ, 1844-1847.—123-24

Lyndhurst, J. S. [Speeches in the House of Lords]
— June 19, 1854. In: *The Times,* No. 21772, June 20, 1854.—262
— January 25, 1855. In: *The Times,* No. 21961, January 26, 1855.—604

Malmesbury, J. H. [Speech in the House of Lords on March 31, 1854.] In: *The Times,* No. 21704, April 1, 1854.—133-35

Manners, J. J. [Speech in the House of Commons on February 20, 1854.] In: *The Times,* No. 21670, February 21, 1854.—15-16

Manteuffel, O. Th. [Speech in the Committee on Credits of the First Chamber of the Prussian Diet on April 22, 1854.] In: *Berlinische Nachrichten von Staats- und gelehrten Sachen*, Nr. 95, 23. April 1854.—168-71
— [Speech in the Chambers of the Prussian Diet on April 29, 1854.] In: *Königlich privilegirte Berlinische Zeitung von Staats- und gelehrten Sachen*, Nr. 101, 30. April 1854.—179

Marliani, M. de. *Historia política de la España moderna.* Barcelona, 1849.—341, 368, 435, 444

Marmont, A. F. L. *De l'esprit des institutions militaires.* Paris, 1845.—37

Martignac, J. B. S. *Essai historique sur la révolution d'Espagne et sur l'intervention de 1823.* T. I, Paris, 1832, pp. 160, 163-66, 202-03.—445-46

Михайловскій-Данилевскій, А. И. *Описаніе Отечественной войны въ 1812 году.* Санктпетербургъ, 1839.—123-24

Milnes, R. M. [Speeches in the House of Commons]
— March 13, 1854. In: *The Times*, No. 21688, March 14, 1854.—71
— May 29, 1854. In: *The Times*, No. 21754, May 30, 1854.—217

Miraflores, M. de. *Essais historiques et critiques pour servir à l'histoire d'Espagne, de 1820 à 1823.* T. I, Paris, 1836, pp. XII, 182-90, 257, 261-62.—443, 445

Mislin, J. *Les Saints Lieux, pèlerinage à Jérusalem, en passant par l'Autriche, la Hongrie, la Slavonie, les provinces danubiennes, Constantinople, l'Archipel, le Liban, la Syrie, Alexandrie, Malte, la Cicile et Marseille, par Mgr Mislin*, Bruxelles, 1852, Vol. II, p. 291.—107

Molière, J. B. *Le Médecin malgré lui.*—418

Moltke, H. K. B. von. *Der russisch-turkische Feldzug in der europäischen Türkei 1828 und 1829.* Berlin, 1845, S. 206.—241

Montalembert, M. R. *La Fortification perpendiculaire, ou Essai sur plusieurs manières de fortifier la ligne droite, le triangle, le quarré et tous les polygônes....* Paris. 5 Tomes en 3. vol. 1776-1784.—113, 347, 380-81

Mooney, J. [Speech at a meeting at Bacup on July 30, 1854.] In: *The People's Paper*, No. 118, August 5, 1854.—356

Moore, G. H. [Speech in the House of Commons on April 6, 1854.] In: *The Times*, No. 21709, April 7, 1854.—143-44

Napier, W. *History of the War in the Peninsula and in the South of France, from the Year 1807 to the Year 1814.* Vols. I-VI. London, 1828-1840.—124, 419

[Nasmyth, Ch.] *The Siege of Silistria.* In: *The Times*, No. 21762 and No. 21783, June 8 and July 3, 1854.—242, 277-78

Newcastle, H. [Speeches in the House of Lords]
— January 23, 1855. In: *The Times*, No. 21959, January 24, 1855.—600
— January 25, 1855. In: *The Times*, No. 21961, January 26, 1855.—604
— January 29, 1855. In: *The Times*, No. 21964, January 30, 1855.—633
— February 1, 1855. In: *The Times*, No. 21967, February 2, 1855.—628-29

Omer Pasha. [Letter to the Governor of Vidin, Sami Pasha, dated June 1854.] In: *Le Moniteur universel*, No. 190, 9 juillet 1854.—279-80

Otway, A. J. [Speeches in the House of Commons]
— July 14, 1854. In: *The Times*, No. 21794, July 15, 1854.—307
— July 26, 1854. In: *The Times*, No. 21804, July 27, 1854.—332

Paine, Th. *Rights of Man: being an Answer to Mr. Burke's Attack on the French Revolution.* 6th ed. London 1791.—332

Pakington, J. [Speech in the House of Commons on March 30, 1854.] In: *The Times*, No. 21703, March 31, 1854.—117-18

Palmerston, H. J. [Speeches in the House of Commons]
— June 1, 1829. In: *Hansard's Parliamentary Debates*. New Series [2], Vol. XXI. London, 1829, pp. 1643-70.—265
— April 15, 1853. In: *The Times*, No. 21404, April 16, 1853.—621, 641
— August 16, 1853. In: *The Times*, No. 21509, August 17, 1853.—641
— August 20, 1853. In: *The Times*, No. 21513, August 22, 1853.—24, 624, 641
— February 6, 1854. In: *The Times*, No. 21658, February 7, 1854.—625, 647
— February 20, 1854. In: *The Times*, No. 21670, February 21, 1854.—24-25, 265
— February 21, 1854. In: *The Times*, No. 21671, February 22, 1854.—28
— February 22, 1854. In: *The Times*, No. 21672, February 23, 1854.—26-27
— March 31, 1854. In: *The Times*, No. 21704, April 1, 1854.—141
— July 14, 1854. In: *The Times*, No. 21794, July 15, 1854.—307-08
— July 26, 1854. In: *The Times*, No. 21804, July 27, 1854.—332-33
— January 25, 1855. In: *The Times*, No. 21961, January 26, 1855.—604
— January 26, 1855. In: *The Times*, No. 21962, January 27, 1855.—607-08
— January 29, 1855. In: *The Times*, No. 21964, January 30, 1855.—635
— February 1, 1855. In: *The Times*, No. 21967, February 2, 1855.—627, 643

Peel, R. [Speech in the House of Commons on August 10, 1842.] In: *Hansard's Parliamentary Debates*. Third Series, Vol. 65, London, 1842, pp. 1268-90.—562

Percival. [Statement on Peitman's Case.] In: *The Morning Advertiser*, No. 19676, July 14, 1854.—299-300

Pradt, D. *Mémoires historiques sur la révolution d'Espagne.* Paris, 1816, pp. 202-03, 224, 360.—408, 418, 421-22
— *De la révolution actuelle de l'Espagne, et de ses suites.* Paris-Rouen, 1820, pp. 177-78.—429

[Principe, M. A., Giron, R., Satorres, R., Ribot, A.] *Espartero: su pasado, su presente, su porvenir.* Madrid, 1848, p. 58.—345

Quetelet, A. *Sur l'homme et le développement de ses facultés, ou Essai de physique sociale.* T. 1-2. Paris, 1835.—642

Radulesco, J. H. *Mémoires sur l'Histoire de la Régénération roumaine ou sur les Evénements de 1848 accomplis en Valachie.* Paris, 1851.—272-75

Richmond, Ch. [Speech in the House of Lords on January 23, 1855.] In: *The Times*, No. 21959, January 24, 1855.—600

Robinson, F. [Speech in the House of Commons on February 28, 1825.] In: *Hansard's Parliamentary Debates*. New Series, Vol. 12, London, 1825, pp. 719-44.—577

Roebuck, J. A. [Speeches in the House of Commons]
— February 17, 1854. In: *The Times*, No. 21668, February 18, 1854.—13

— January 23, 1855. In: *The Times*, No. 21959, January 24, 1855.—602-03, 606
— January 25, 1855. In: *The Times*, No. 21961, January 26, 1855.—604
— January 26, 1855. In: *The Times*, No. 21962, January 27, 1855.—605, 608, 615-16, 627, 631-32, 634, 642-43

Russell, J. [Speeches in the House of Commons]
— February 24, 1853. In: *The Times*, No. 21361, February 25, 1853.—621
— April 4, 1853. In: *The Times*, No. 21394, April 5, 1853.—621
— May 31, 1853. In: *The Times*, No. 21443, June 1, 1853.—622
— June 6, 1853. In: *The Times*, No. 21448, June 7, 1853.—622
— February 13, 1854. In: *The Times*, No. 21664, February 14, 1854.—625, 647
— February 17, 1854. In: *The Times*, No. 21668, February 18, 1854.—13, 19, 24, 31, 86
— February 23, 1854. In: *The Times*, No. 21673, February 24, 1854.—31
— March 3, 1854. In: *The Times*, No. 21680, March 4, 1854.—52
— March 17, 1854. In: *The Times*, No. 21692, March 18, 1854.—80
— March 31, 1854. In: *The Times*, No. 21704, April 1, 1854.—137
— April 6, 1854. In: *The Times*, No. 21709, April 7, 1854.—143
— April 11, 1854. In: *The Times*, No. 21713, April 12, 1854.—625
— May 5, 1854. In: *The Times*, No. 21734, May 6, 1854.—190
— May 29, 1854. In: *The Times*, No. 21754, May 30, 1854.—216-19
— June 8, 1854. In: *The Times*, No. 21763, June 9, 1854.—228
— June 26, 1854. In: *The Times*, No. 21778, June 27, 1854.—258
— July 17, 1854. In: *The Leader*, No. 226, July 22, 1854.—307
— July 20, 1854. In: *The Times*, No. 21799, July 21, 1854.—316
— July 24, 1854. In: *The Times*, No. 21802, July 25, 1854.—319-22, 326, 330, 484
— July 25, 1854. In: *The Times*, No. 21803, July 26, 1854.—327, 331
— December 12, 1854. In: *The Times*, No. 21923, December 13, 1854.—546
— January 23, 1855. In: *The Times*, No. 21959, January 24, 1855.—601-02
— January 26, 1855. In: *The Times*, No. 21962, January 27, 1855.—605-07, 628, 633
— February 5, 1855. In: *The Times*, No. 21970, February 6, 1855.—645
— [Letter to Aberdeen of November 17, 1854.] In: *The Times*, No. 21962, January 27, 1855.—606
— [Letter to Aberdeen of November 28, 1854.] In: *The Times*, No. 21962, January 27, 1855.—606

The Russians in Moldavia and Wallachia. London, 1849, pp. 5, 10, 16-18.—271-75

Sacy, S. de. [Account of current events.] In: *Journal des Débats*, 16 juillet 1854.—305
— [Review of current events.] In: *Journal des Débats*, 15 août 1854.—372
— [Review of current events.] In: *Journal des Débats*, 12 septembre 1854.—456

St.-Albin, A. de. *La révolution espagnole*. In: *L'Assemblée nationale*, No. 674, 14 août 1854.—372

San Miguel, E. *De la guerra civil en España*. Madrid, 1836.—442, 658
— [Speech at the banquet of the press in Madrid on August 14, 1854.] In: *Journal des Débats*, 21 août 1854.—447

Shaftesbury, A. [Speech in the House of Lords on March 10, 1854.] In: *The Times*, No. 21686, March 11, 1854.—71

Shakespeare, W. *Julius Caesar*.—86
— *King Henry IV*.—632

— *Love's Labour's Lost.*—213
— *A Midsummer Night's Dream*—26, 561
— *Troilus and Cressida.*—302

Sheridan, R. B. *The School for Scandal.*—346

Sismondi, J. C. L. Simonde de. *De la Littérature du Midi de l'Europe.* Paris, 1813, T. IV, pp. 259-60.—405

Smith, A. *An Inquiry into the Nature and Causes of the Wealth of Nations.* Edinburgh, 1828, Vol. I, p. 354.—600

Smith, V. [Speech in the House of Commons on January 26, 1855.] In: *The Times,* No. 21962, January 27, 1855.—616

Smitt, F. *Geschichte des polnischen Aufstandes und Krieges in den Jahren 1830 und 1831.* Theile I-III. Berlin, 1839-1848.—123-24

Soledad, F. B. de la. *Memorial historico y politico, que descubre las ideas del Christianissimo Luis XIV, para librar a España de los infortunios, que experimenta por medio de su legitimo Rey Don Carlos III.* Viena, 1703.—413

Southey, R. *History of the Peninsular War.* 3 vols, London, 1823-1832. Vol. I, pp. 301-05, 318-21; Vol. II, pp. 482, 497-98; Vol. III, p. 899.—401-02, 408, 415, 417, 432, 435-36

Stafford, G. [Speech in the House of Commons on January 29, 1855]. In: *The Times,* No. 21964, January 30, 1855.—634

Stuart, D. [Speeches in the House of Commons]
— February 17, 1854. In: *The Times,* No. 21668, February 18, 1854.—13
— July 24, 1854. In: *The Times,* No. 21802, July 25, 1854.—321-22, 329
— July 25, 1854. In: *The Times,* No. 21803, July 26, 1854.—327

Thousand and One Nights.—340

Tidd, W. *Practice of the Court of King's Bench in Personal Actions,* etc. London, Parts I-II, 1790-1794.—355

Tolstoy, J. *Relation des opérations de l'armée russe en Hongrie.* Paris, 1850.—123, 124

Toreno, J. M. *Historia del levantamiento, guerra y revolución de España.* 3 vols. Paris, 1838. T. I, pp. 278, 374; T. II, p. 3.—409, 415, 418

Les trois maréchaux, MM. Saint-Arnaud.—Magnan.—Castellanne. Bruxelles, 15 décembre 1852.—233

Trollope, J. [Speech in the House of Commons on March 1, 1853.] In: *The Times,* No. 21365, March 2, 1853.—644

Urquhart, D. *Progress of Russia in the West, North, and South.* London, 1853, pp. 31-35, 40-50.—367, 445, 489
— The Ministry of War. To the Editor of *The Morning Herald.* In: *The Morning Herald,* No. 22486, June 1, 1854.—220

Vauban, S. *Traité de l'Attaque et de la Défense des Places.* 2 v. Paris, 1739.—382

Virgil. *Aeneid* (II, 49).—387

The Visit of the Emperor. In: *The Portfolio.* London [1844]. Vol. III, No. XII.—582

Voltaire, F. M. A. *Dissertation sur la tragédie ancienne et moderne.* In: *La Tragédie de Sémiramis, et quelques autres piéces de littérature.* Paris, 1749.—132

Walpole, H. [Speech in the House of Commons on January 26, 1855.] In: *The Times,* No. 21962, January 27, 1855.—635

Walsh, J. B. [Speech in the House of Commons on February 23, 1854.] In: *The Times,* No. 21673, February 24, 1854.—31

Walton, W. *The Revolutions of Spain, from 1808 to the end of 1836.* 2 vols, London, 1837; Vol. I, pp. 221, 343-44.—442, 444

Wellington, A. [Letter to the Earl of Liverpool dated November 21, 1809.] In: Wellington, A. *Selections from the Dispatches and General Orders of Field Marshal the Duke of Wellington.* London, 1842, p. 319.—215
— [Letter to Marquis of Wellesley dated September 1, 1809.] In: Napier, W. *History of the War in the Peninsula and in the South of France, from the Year 1807 to the Year 1814.* Vols. I-VI. London, 1828-1840. Vol. II, p. 437.—419

Wilson, J. [Speech in the House of Commons on July 26, 1854.] In: *The Times,* No. 21804, July 27, 1854.—333

DOCUMENTS

Aberdeen, G. [Dispatch to Heytesbury, Ambassador to St. Petersburg, of October 31, 1829 respecting the signing of the Adrianople Peace Treaty.] In: *Le Moniteur universel,* No. 182, 1 juillet 1854.—259, 261-62, 264

Accounts relating to Trade and Navigation. III. Exports of British and Irish Produce and Manufactures from the United Kingdom. In: *The Economist,* No. 562, June 3, 1854.—229

Accounts relating to Trade and Navigation. III. Exports of British and Irish Produce and Manufactures. In: *The Economist,* No. 576, September 9, 1854.—466, 468

Accounts relating to Trade and Navigation for the eleven months ended 5th December 1854. III. Exports of British and Irish Produce and Manufactures from the United Kingdom. In: *The Economist,* No. 593, January 6, 1855.—571, 576

An act for preventing tumults and riotous assemblies, and for the more speedy and effectual punishing of the rioters (1715).—121

Acte constitutionnel présentée au peuple français par la convention nationale. 24 juin 1793. In: *Collection des constitutions, chartes et lois fondamentales des peuples de l'Europe et des deux Amériques.* Par MM. P.-A. Dufau; J.-B. Duvergier et J. Guadet. T. I. Paris 1823, pp. 135-48.—429

Blaser y San Martin. [Bulletin of July 15, 1854.] In: *Le Moniteur universel,* No. 201, 20 juillet 1854.—313

Budberg, A. I. [Proclamation of July 26 to the Wallachians.] In: *Le Moniteur universel,* No. 219, 7 août 1854.—351

Canrobert, C. [Letter to War Minister Drouyn de Lhuys dated October 13, 1854.] In: *The Times,* No. 21885, October 30, 1854.—509
— [Dispatch to the War Minister, Drouyn de Lhuys, of November 7, 1854.] In: *Le Moniteur universel,* No. 326, 22 novembre 1854.—536

— [Dispatch to the War Minister, Drouyn de Lhuys, of December 3, 1854.] In: *Le Moniteur universel*, No. 346, 12 décembre 1854.—543

Capitulations ou Traités anciens et nouveaux entre la cour de France et la Porte Ottomane, Renouvelés et augmentés l'an de J.C. 1740, et de l'hégire 1153; Traduits à Constantinople par le sieur Deval, secrétaire-interprète du roi et son premier drogman à la cour ottomane, 1761. In: Famin, C. *Histoire de la rivalité et du protectorat des églises chrétiennes en Orient.* Paris, 1853, pp. 475-514.—104

[Circular of Messrs. Smith and Charles. October 2, 1854.] In: *The Morning Post*, No. 25195, October 3, 1854.—490-91

Colección de los decretos y órdenes que han expedido las Cortes generales y extraordinarias. Tomo III.—436

Constitution décrétée par l'Assemblée Constituante. 3 septembre 1791. In: *Collection des constitutions, chartes et lois fondamentales des peuples de l'Europe et des deux Amériques.* Par MM. P.-A. Dufau; J.-B. Duvergier et J. Guadet. T. I. Paris, 1823, pp. 97-132.—429-31, 433

[Constitution of Spain, 1808 (Bayonne Constitution).]—399, 401

[Constitution of Spain. March 19, 1812.] In: *The Political Constitution of the Spanish Monarchy. Proclaimed in Cadix, 19 March, 1812.* London, 1813.—310, 367, 369, 404, 424-33, 435-45

[Constitution of Spain. 1837.]—294, 305, 310, 352, 363

[Constitution of the Danish Monarchy for Its Common Affairs. 1854.] In: *Le Moniteur universel*, No. 216, 4 août 1854.—353

Convention entre la Russie, et la Turquie relative aux Principautés danubiennes, signée à Balta-Liman, le 1 mai 1849.—274

Convention signée à Londres le 13 Juillet 1841 entre l'Autriche, la Grande-Bretagne, la Prusse et la Russie d'une part et la Porte Ottomane de l'autre part, dans le but de maintenir à l'avenir le principe que le passage des détroits des Dardanelles et du Bospore reste toujours fermé aux bâtimens de guerre étrangers, tant que la Porte se trouve en paix.—366

Correspondence Respecting the Rights and Privileges of the Latin and Greek Churches in Turkey. Presented to both Houses of Parliament by Command of Her Majesty. London, 1854 [published in several parts].—12-14, 19, 20, 23, 73, 85, 94-95, 100, 117, 136, 169, 623, 647

Part I

Seymour to Russell, January 7, 1853, p. 56.—77
Seymour to Russell, January 8, 1853, pp. 56-57.—21, 77
Nesselrode to Brunnow, January 14, 1853, pp. 61-65.—20
Russell to Cowley, January 28, 1853, pp. 67-68.—93
Clarendon to Stratford de Redcliffe, February 25, 1853, pp. 80-82.—84-85
Clarendon to Cowley, March 22, 1853, pp. 93-94.—22, 88
Clarendon to Seymour, March 23, 1853, pp. 94-95.—22, 94, 95
Clarendon to Cowley, March 29, 1853, p. 98.—88
Rose to Clarendon, April 1, 1853, pp. 112-14.—22, 23
Nesselrode to Brunnow, March 26/April 7, 1853, pp. 115-18.—23

Menchikoff to Rifaat Pasha. Pera, April 7/19, 1853. (Inclosure in the despatch of Stratford de Redcliffe to Clarendon. Constantinople, April 23, 1853), pp. 158-60.—98-99

Clarendon to Seymour, May 16, 1853, p. 163.—23

Nesselrode to Brunnow, June 1, 1853, pp. 238-45.—20, 23

Clarendon to Stratford de Redcliffe, July 28, 1853, pp. 399-400.—23

Clarendon to Westmorland, July 4, 1853 (I), pp. 320-21.—23

Clarendon to Westmorland, July 4, 1853 (II), pp. 321-22.—23

Part V *

Seymour to Russell, January 11, 1853, pp. 875-78.—76-78

Seymour to Russell, January 22, 1853, pp. 878-82.—78-79, 89, 95

Russell to Seymour, February 9, 1853, pp. 883-86.—79-82, 84-87, 89, 92

Seymour to Russell, February 21, 1853, pp. 886-87.—87-88

Seymour to Russell, February 22, 1853, pp. 887-92.—89-92, 95

Seymour to Nesselrode, February 24/March 8, 1853, p. 897.—92

Seymour to Clarendon, March 9, 1853, p. 892.—92, 93, 94

Memorandum [by the Russian Cabinet to the British Government of February 21, 1853]. (Inclosure in the despatch of Seymour to Clarendon, March 9, 1853), pp. 893-96.—89, 92-94, 98

Seymour to Clarendon, March 10, 1853, pp. 897-98.—93

Clarendon to Seymour, March 23, 1853, pp. 898-901.—94-98

Clarendon to Seymour, April 5, 1853, pp. 902-04.—97-98

Memorandum [by the Russian Cabinet to the British Government dated 3/15 April, 1853]. (Inclosure in the despatch of Seymour to Clarendon, April 21, 1853), pp. 907-08.—98

Part VI

Memorandum by Count Nesselrode, delivered to Her Majesty's Government, and founded on communications received from the Emperor of Russia subsequently to His Imperial Majesty's visit to England in June 1844, pp. 911-14.—73-76, 79, 99, 133-36

Correspondence 1839-1841, relative to the Affairs of the East, and the Conflict between Egypt and Turkey. 4 parts. [London, 1841.]—592

Danilo. [Proclamation to the Montenegrin chiefs dated March 16, 1854.] In: Journal des Débats, 2 mai 1854.—178

[Decree of the Spanish Government dated May 19, 1854 on the payment of taxes.] In: Le Moniteur universel, No. 148, 28 mai 1854.—286, 375-76

Décret impérial qui autorise le ministre des finances à porter à deux cent cinquante millions, pour le service de 1854, la somme des bons du trésor en circulation [1854]. In: Collection complète des lois, décrets, ordonnances, règlements et avis du Conseil d'Etat... Par J.B. Duvergier. T. 54. Année 1854. Paris, p. 45.—51

Decreto CLXXIV de 16 de Junio de 1812. Reglas para verificar la aplicacion de parte de los diezmos á las urgencias del Estado. In: Colección de los decretos y órdenes que han

---

* Pages of Parts V and VI are given according to the 1856 edition.

expedido las Cortes generales y extraordinarias. Tomo III, Madrid, 1813, pp. 26-28.—436

Decreto CLXXVI de 28 de Junio de 1812. Declaración del patronato de Santa Teresa de Jesus en favor de las Españas. In: *Colección de los decretos...* T. III. Madrid, 1813, p. 36.—436

Decreto CCIII de 14 de Octubre de 1812. Abolición del voto de Santiago. In: *Colección de los decretos...* T. III, p. 137.—435

Decreto CCXXIII de 22 de Febrero de 1813. Abolición de la Inquisición: establecimiento de los tribunales protectores de la fe. In: *Colección de los decretos...* T. III, pp. 215-18.—436

Dispatch of Baron von Manteuffel to Baron von Werther. June 12, 1854.—286

Drouyn de Lhuys, E. [Letter to Bourqueney dated July 22, 1854.] In: *Le Moniteur universel,* No. 223, 11 août 1854.—366

Ducos, Th. [Report on the equipment of the Baltic expedition.] In: *Le Moniteur universel,* No. 57, 26 février 1854.—202

Dulce, O'Donnell, Ros de Olano. [Proclamation of July 1, 1854, Aranjuez.] In: *Journal des Débats,* 17 juillet 1854.—294, 305

[Election law of 1837 in Spain.]—371, 372-73
[Election law of 1845 in Spain.]—363, 371-72

Erster Bericht der Kommission zur Vorprüfung der Gesetz-Entwürfe, betreffend die Kredit-Bewilligung und die Erhebung eines Zuschlages zur klassifizierten Einkommensteuer, zur Klassensteuer und zur Mahl- und Schlachtsteuer. In: *Stenographische Berichte über die Verhandlungen der durch die Allerhöchste Verordnung vom 29. Oktober 1853 einberufenen Kammern.* Zweite Kammer. Dritter Band. Anlagen zu den Verhandlungen der Zweiten Kammer. Nr. 1-140. Berlin, 1854, S. 398-406.—145-49

Ferdinand VII. [Decree of May 4, 1814.] In: Miraflores. *Essais historiques et critiques pour servir à l'histoire d'Espagne,* pp. 182-90.—429, 439
— [Decree of July 21, 1814 re-establishing the Holy Inquisition.] In: *Le Moniteur universel,* No. 214, 2 août 1814.—405

Francis I. [Patent of June 1, 1816 on the withdrawal of paper-money from circulation.] In: *Der gegenwärtige Stand der Finanzen und des Geldumlaufes in Oesterreich. Von einem Unbetheiligten.* Leipzig, 1853, S. 24.—46
— [Patent of December 23, 1817 on the land-tax.] In: *Der gegenwärtige Stand...,* S. 15.—48

Frederick VII. [Decree of August 26 on the convocation of the Rigsrad on September 1, 1854.] In: *Le Moniteur universel,* No. 216, 4 août 1854.—353
— [Decree of August 26, 1854 on nominations.] In: *Le Moniteur universel,* No. 216, 4 août 1854.—353

Habeas Corpus Act.—119

Hamelin, F. A. [Report to the Minister of the Marine of April 10, 1854.] In: *Le Moniteur universel,* No. 120, 30 avril 1854.—174
— [Reports of May 1-5, 1854 on the operations of the allied fleet in the Black Sea.] In: *Le Moniteur universel,* No. 141, 21 mai 1854.—204

Hess, H. [Manifesto to the inhabitants of Moldavia and Wallachia of August 18 (30).] In: *The Times,* No. 21844, September 12, 1854.—465

Isabella II. [Decree of August 1, 1854 sanctioning the existence of provincial juntas, countersigned by Espartero.] In: *Le Moniteur universel*, No. 220, 8 août 1854.— 352
— [Decree of August 11, 1854 for the convocation of the Cortes.] In: *Le Moniteur universel*, No. 230, 18 août 1854.— 372
— [Decree of August 25, 1854 on the dissolution of the bodyguard, counter-signed by L. O'Donnell.] In: *Le Moniteur universel*, No. 245, 2 septembre 1854.— 451

Krusenstern, N. I. *To the Inhabitants of Odessa.* (Proclamation.) In: *The Times*, No. 21847, September 15, 1854.— 463

Lara, J. de. [Proclamation of June 28, 1854.] In: *Le Moniteur universel*, No. 185, 4 juillet 1854.— 313
— [Account of the battle at Vicálvaro sent to the Minister of War on June 30, 1854.] In: *The Times*, No. 21787, July 7, 1854.— 283

[Lieven and Matuszczewicz.] *Copy of a Despatch from Prince Lieven, and Count Matusczewicz, addressed to Count Nesselrode, dated London 1st (13th) June, 1829.* In: *The Portfolio.* Diplomatic Review. New Series, London, 1843, Vol. I, No. 1. — 260-61

Loi portant fixation du budget général des dépenses et des recettes de l'exercice 1854 [1853] In: *Collection complète des lois, décrets, ordonnances, règlements et avis du Conseil d'Etat...* Par J. B. Duvergier. T. 53. Année 1853. Paris, pp. 230-42.— 51

Loi relative à la dotation de la caisse d'amortissement. In: *Collection complète des lois, décrets, ordonnances, règlements et avis du Conseil d'État...* Par J. B. Duvergier. T. 33. Année 1833. Paris, pp. 193-96.— 51

Memorandum of the Serbian Government to the Sublime Porte concerning the occupation of this Principality by Austrian Troops. [Belgrade, April 5/17, 1854.] In: *Correspondence, papers, treaties, etc., respecting the rights and privileges of the Latin and Greek churches in Turkey; Hostilities with Russia; Military Affairs in Asiatic Turkey, and the Re-establishment of Peace.* London 1856, pp. 271-75.— 296-97, 325

Menshikov, A. S. [Dispatch of November 6, 1854 on the battle of Inkerman.] In: *The Times*, No. 21906, November 23, 1854.— 528, 536

Napier, Ch. [Reports of August 1854 on the capture of Bomarsund.] In: *The Times*, Nos. 21827 and 21828, August 23 and 24, 1854.— 387

Napoleon III. [Letter to Nicholas I dated January 29, 1854.] In: *Le Moniteur universel*, No. 43, 14 février 1854.— 3
— [Speech at the Opening Session of Corps Législatif on March 2, 1854.] In: *Le Moniteur universel*, No. 62, 3 mars 1854.— 35
— [Message to the Senate and Corps Législatif.] In: *Le Moniteur universel*, No. 87, 28 mars 1854.— 100
— [Address to the soldiers in Boulogne on July 12, 1854.] In: *Le Moniteur universel*, No. 194, 13 juillet 1854.— 298
— [Speech before the troops at Boulogne on September 2, 1854.] In: *Le Moniteur universel*, No. 248, 5 septembre 1854.— 507
— [Speech before the troops at Boulogne on September 30, 1854.] In: *Le Moniteur universel*, No. 275, 2 octobre 1854.— 481-82

Nesselrode. [Dispatch to Gorchakov dated June 17/29, 1854.] In: *Le Moniteur universel*, No. 223, 11 août 1854.— 294, 295, 366

Stratford de Redcliffe. [Circular to the British Consuls in Turkey and Greece dated April 1, 1854.] In: *L'Indépendance belge*, No. 108, 18 avril 1854.—156

Treaties (chronologically)
— [The Treaty of 1393 between Wallachia and Turkey.] In: Bratiano, D. *Documents Concerning the Question of the Danubian Principalities. Dedicated to the English Parliament.* London, 1849, p. 26.—271
— [The Treaty of 1460 between Wallachia and Turkey.] Ibid.—271
— [The Treaty of 1511 between Moldavia and Turkey.] In: *The Russians in Moldavia and Wallachia.* London 1849, p. 6.—271-72
— *Traité de paix perpétuelle et d'amitié entre l'Empire de Russie et la Porte Ottomane, conclu le 10 juillet 1774...*—20, 105, 157
— *Traités secrets de Fontainebleau, entre la France et l'Espagne; signés le 27 octobre 1807.*—392, 399
— *Traité d'amitié et d'Alliance entre l'Espagne et la Russie, signé à Welliki-Louki le 8/20 juillet 1812.*—444
— *The general treaty signed at the Vienna Congress, 9 June 1815.*—190
— *Traité de paix entre la Russie et la Porte Ottomane, signé à Adrianople le 2/14 Septembre 1829.*—240, 259, 261-64, 272, 317
— *Traité d'Unkiar-Iskelessi entre la Russie et la Porte Ottomane, signé à Constantinople le 8 juillet 1833.*—263
— [The Treaty between Sweden and Denmark, 1853.]—28
— [The Treaty of alliance between France, England, and Turkey, signed at Constantinople on March 12, 1854.] In: *The Daily News*, No. 2459, April 7, 1854.—36, 39, 101, 144
— [The Treaty of alliance between Austria and Prussia, concluded April 20, 1854.] In: *Hannoversche Zeitung*, Nr. 187, 22. April 1854.—168, 215-16, 295
— [Treaty of alliance between France, England and Turkey, signed on May 23, 1854.] In: *The Times*, No. 21750, May 25, 1854.—215-16
— [The Treaty between Austria and Turkey, signed on June 14, 1854.] In: *The Times*, No. 21783, July 3, 1854.—246-47, 269-71, 318, 323-25, 358
— [The Treaty of alliance between England, Austria, and France, signed at Vienna December 2, 1854.] In: *The Times*, No. 21926, December 16, 1854.—542, 546, 554

Victoria, R. [The Royal message of March 27, 1854 declaring war on Russia.] In: *The Times*, No. 21700, March 28, 1854.—100-01, 132
— [Speech at the opening of Parliament on December 12, 1854.] In: *The Times*, No. 21923, December 13, 1854.—546, 577

ANONYMOUS ARTICLES AND REPORTS PUBLISHED
IN PERIODIC EDITIONS

Allgemeine Zeitung, Nr. 183, 2. Juli 1854, Beilage: *Die österreichische Nationalanleihe.*—288

Le Bulletin français, Brx., No. 5, le 29 janvier, 1852, p. 96: *Les Spoliateurs.*—233

The Daily News, No. 2597, September 15, 1854.—465
— No. 2691, January 3, 1855.—562

The Economist, No. 562, June 3, 1854: *Our Trade.*—229
— No. 576, September 9, 1854: *American Diplomatic Taste and Morality.*—465-66

— No. 576, September 9, 1854: *Our Exports. Eleven Years under Protection and Eleven Years under Free Trade.*—466-69
— No. 579, September 30, 1854.—490-91
— No. 584, November 4, 1854: *The Supplies of Wheat, Home and Foreign.*—574
— No. 593, January 6, 1855: *Trade of 1854.*—588-89
— No. 594, January 13, 1855: *Exports.—The Factory Act.*—575

The Examiner, No. 2450, January 13, 1855: *Terms of Peace and Causes of War.*—583-84

The Globe and Traveller, No. 17439, June 1, 1854.—223
— No. 17445, June 8, 1854.—228
— No. 17469, July 6, 1854.—288-89

L'Indépendance belge, No. 60, 1 mars 1854: [Report from Vienna.]—43-44
— No. 108, 18 avril 1854: [Reports from *L'Observateur d'Athènes.*]—154
— No. 121, 1 mai 1854.—174
— No. 121, 1 mai 1854: [Reports from *Nouvelliste de Marseille.*]—177
— No. 187, 6 juillet 1854: [Report from Madrid of July 1.]—284
— No. 187, 6 juillet 1854: [Reprint from *Der Lloyd.*]—287
— No. 188, 7 juillet 1854: [The Austro-Prussian summons dispatched on June 3, 1854.]—286
— No. 193, 12 juillet 1854: [Review of current events.]—295
— No. 194, 13 juillet 1854: [Reprint from the *Messager de Bayonne.*]—294
— No. 197 et 198, 16 et 17 juillet 1854: [Reprint from the *Neue Preußische Zeitung.*]—302
— No. 219, 7 août 1854: [Report from the Paris correspondent of August 6.]—352
— No. 221, 9 août 1854: [Reports from *El Clamor Público.*]—370
— No. 221, 9 août 1854: [The account from *El Tribuno.*]—363
— No. 222, 10 août 1854: [Report from the Paris correspondent of August 9.]—361
— No. 223, 11 août 1854: [Report from the Hamburg correspondent of August 8.]—362
— No. 223, 11 août 1854: [Reprint from the *Gazette du Midi.*]—361
— No. 230, 18 août 1854: [Report from Hamburg of August 13.]—377
— No. 230, 18 août 1854: [Report from Hamburg of August 14.]—377
— No. 243, 31 août 1854: [Telegram from Paris of August 30.]—450
— No. 244, 1 septembre 1854: [Quotation from *Las Cortes.*]—447
— No. 247, 4 septembre 1854: [Report from the Paris correspondent of September 3.]—457
— No. 255, 12 septembre 1854: [Reports from *Le Constitutionnel*].—462

Journal de Saint-Pétersbourg, 4me Série, No. 336, 18 février (2 mars), 1854: [On the Eastern Question.]—73, 99, 218
— 4me Série, No. 402, 11 (23) mai, 1854: [Review of war operations in the Black Sea.]—224

Journal des Débats, 29 juin 1854: [Reports from the *Ost-Deutsche Post.*]—268
— 6 juillet 1854: [Reprint from the *Oesterreichischer Soldatenfreund* of June 30.]—287
— 7 juillet 1854: [Reprint from the *Berlinische Nachrichten von Staats- und gelehrten Sachen.*]—288
— 17 juillet 1854: [Telegraphic dispatch from Vienna of July 15.]—303-04
— 18 juillet 1854: [Reprint from *Der Lloyd* of July 13.]—303
— 10 août 1854: [Dispatch from Constantinople of July 30.]—360
— 12 septembre 1854.—456

— No. 21676, February 28, 1854: *India and China.*—42
— No. 21677, March 1, 1854 (leader).—36
— No. 21686, March 11, 1854 (leader).—68, 80
— No. 21688, March 14, 1854: [Report from the Vienna correspondent of March 8.]—68
— No. 21693, March 20, 1854 (leader).—80
— No. 21694, March 21, 1854: *The Wages' Movement.*—121
— No. 21699, March 27, 1854 (leader).—100
— No. 21700, March 28, 1854 (leaders).—101
— No. 21705, April 3, 1854 (leader).—137
— No. 21706, April 4, 1854: [Telegraphic dispatch from Berlin of April 3.]—134
— No. 21709, April 7, 1854: [Report from the Vienna correspondent of April 2.]—143
— No. 21709, April 7, 1854: [Telegraphic dispatch from Berlin of April 5.]—145
— No. 21718, April 18, 1854: [Report from the Constantinople correspondent of April 3.]—156
— No. 21719, April 19, 1854 (leader).—161
— No. 21722, April 22, 1854: [Notice of the Exchequer.]—647
— No. 21723, April 24, 1854: *Sweden.*—175
— No. 21731, May 3, 1854: [Telegraphic dispatch from Odessa of April 26.]—173
— No. 21731, May 3, 1854: *Turkey and Russia.*—175
— No. 21731, May 3, 1854: [Report from the *Augsburger Zeitung.*]—177
— No. 21731, May 3, 1854: [Report from the *Agramer Zeitung.*]—179
— No. 21732, May 4, 1854: *Defeat of the Russians.*—181
— No. 21732, May 4, 1854: [Report from the *National Zeitung.*]—182
— No. 21747, May 22, 1854 (leader).—251
— No. 21751, May 26, 1854: [Report from Gothland of May 16.]—251
— No. 21753, May 29, 1854 (leaders).—215-16
— No. 21754, May 30, 1854 (leader).—217
— No. 21756, June 1, 1854: [Telegraphic dispatch from Paris.]—221
— No. 21756, June 1, 1854 (leader).—221
— No. 21757, June 2, 1854 (leader).—220
— No. 21762, June 8, 1854 (leader).—227
— No. 21774, June 22, 1854 (leader).—251
— No. 21787, July 7, 1854: [Telegraphic dispatch from Vienna of July 6.]—286
— No. 21790, July 11, 1854: [Telegraphic dispatch from Vienna of July 10.]—292
— No. 21791, July 12, 1854: [Telegraphic dispatch from Vienna of July 11.]—292
— No. 21792, July 13, 1854: *Naval and Military Intelligence.*—298
— No. 21793, July 14, 1854: [Report from the Vienna correspondent of July 9.]—296
— No. 21795, July 17, 1854: [Report from the Vienna correspondent.]—304
— No. 21796, July 18, 1854 (leader).—302
— No. 21798, July 20, 1854: [Report from the Vienna correspondent.]—304
— No. 21799, July 21, 1854: [Debates in Parliament.]—316
— No. 21799, July 21, 1854: [Report from the Vienna correspondent of July 17.]—302
— No. 21799, July 21, 1854: [Telegraphic dispatch from Paris of July 21.]—311

— No. 21799, July 21, 1854 (leader).—315
— No. 21800, July 22, 1854 (leader).—374
— No. 21802, July 25, 1854: [Debates in Parliament.]—316
— No. 21803, July 26, 1854: [Telegram from Vienna of July 25.]—325
— No. 21805, July 28, 1854: [Report from Varna of July 13.]—332
— No. 21807, July 31, 1854 (leader).—359
— No. 21814, August 8, 1854 (leader).—347
— No. 21815, August 9, 1854 (leader).—361
— No. 21816, August 10, 1854 (leader).—360
— No. 21816, August 10, 1854: [Telegraphic dispatch from Vienna of August 8.]—359
— No. 21817, August 11, 1854 (leader).—357
— No. 21819, August 14, 1854 (leader).—368, 372
— No. 21820, August 15, 1854: [Report from Vienna of August 10.]—366
— No. 21820, August 15, 1854 (leader).—369
— No. 21823, August 18, 1854 (leader).—373
— No. 21832, August 29, 1854: [Report from the Madrid correspondent of August 23.]—448
— No. 21836, September 2, 1854: [Report from Madrid of August 26.]—449
— No. 21861, October 2, 1854 (leader).—479
— No. 21861, October 2, 1854: [Telegraphic dispatch about the capture of Sevastopol.]—480
— No. 21864, October 5, 1854 (leaders).—484
— No. 21864, October 5, 1854: [Telegram from Vienna of October 4.]—486
— No. 21864, October 5, 1854: [Report from Vienna.]—490
— No. 21884, October 28, 1854 (leader).—505-06
— No. 21900, November 16, 1854 (leader).—527
— No. 21906, November 23, 1854: [Report from a special correspondent on the battle of Inkerman.]—528
— No. 21907, November 24, 1854: [Report from a special correspondent on the battle of Inkerman.]—528
— No. 21916, December 5, 1854 (leader).—541
— No. 21924, December 14, 1854: [Report from Bucharest of December 11.]—544
— No. 21938, December 30, 1854 (leader).—556
— No. 21939, January 1, 1855 (leader).—556
— No. 21941, January 3, 1855: [Letter of a British army officer from the encampment at Sevastopol dated December 12, 1854.]—560
— No. 21941, January 3, 1855 (leader).— 560, 564, 568
— No. 21942, January 4, 1855 (leader).—593
— No. 21945, January 8, 1855: [Telegram from Vienna of January 7.]—579
— No. 21946, January 9, 1855 (leader).—579-80
— No. 21948, January 11, 1855: [Announcement by the Admiralty.]—581
— No. 21949, January 12, 1855 (leader).—582
— No. 21959, January 24, 1855 (leader).—602
— No. 21961, January 26, 1855 (leader).—603-04
— No. 21963, January 29, 1855 (leader).—615-16

L'Unione, No. 138, 12 aprile 1854.—156-58
Wiener medizinische Wochenschrift, Nr. 1, 4, 9, 12, 14, 19, 22, 23; 7., 28. Januar; 4., 25. März; 8. April; 13. Mai; 3., 10. Juni, 1854: [Reports from Wallachia.]—249

INDEX OF PERIODICALS

SUBJECT INDEX

A

GLOSSARY OF GEOGRAPHICAL NAMES [a]

Abo	Turku	Gallipoli	Gelibolu
Adramyti	Edremit	Giurgevo	Giurgiu
Adrianople	Edirne	Hangö, Hango Udd	Hanko
Akkerman	Belgorod-Dnestrovsky	Helsingfors	Helsinki
		Hermannstadt	Sibiu
Aland	Ahvenanmaa	Isaktsha	Isaccea
Aluta	Olt or Oltul	Ivangorod	Deblin
Argish	Argeş	Kaffa	Feodosia
Austerlitz	Slavkov	Kalarash	Călăraşi
Aylau — see Preussisch Eylau		Kalugereni	Călugăreni
Bazardjik	Tolbukhin	Kamenicz	Kamenets Podolski
Botushani	Botoşani	Kamtchik	Kamčiya
Bourliouk	Burlyuk	Kara-su	Medgidia
Brailow (Ibraila)	Brăila	Katzbach	Kocaba
Brzesc Litewski	Brest	Kimpina	Câmpina
Buseo (Busau)	Buzău	Königsberg	Kaliningrad
Candia	Crete	Kruschevatz	Kruševac
Colberg	Kołobrzeg	Kustendje	Constanţa
Constantinople	Istanbul	Matchin	Maçin
Contessa, Gulf of	Rendina (Orfani)	Memeľ	Klaipeda
Czeraswitz	Chernovtsy	Mezzovo	Métsovon -
Danzig	Gdansk	Navarino	Pylos
Egripo	Euboea, Negropont (Euboia)	New Archangel	Sitka (city)
		Nissa	Niš
		Nixitshy	Nikšič
Euxine, the	Black Sea	Nizhni Novgorod	Gorky
Fokshani	Focşani	Olmütz	Olomouc
Friedland	Pravdinsk	Oltenitza	Olteniţa
Fünen	Fyn	Oranienbaum	Lomonosov
Galatch, Galatz	Galaţi	Petershoff	Petrodvorets

---

[a] This glossary includes geographical names occurring in Marx's and Engels' articles in the form customary in the press of the time but differing from the national names or from those given on modern maps. The left column gives geographical names as used in the original (when they differ from the national names of the time, the latter are given in brackets); the right column gives corresponding names as used on modern maps and in modern literature.— Ed.

Petersburg—see St. Petersburg
Plojesti .... Ploeşti
Posen .... Poznán
Preussisch Eylau .... Bagrationovsk
Rassova .... Raşova
Redut-Kaleh .... Kulevi
Revel .... Tallinn
Rotherthurm .... Turnu Roşu
Rustchuk..................... Ruse (Rusčuk)
St. Petersburg .... Leningrad
Salonica...................... Thessaloniki (Salonika)
Scutari....................... Usküdar
Serpents, Isle of the
    (Ilade Adessi) .... Serpent Island
Shumla...................... Shumen

Sitka (isl.) .... Baranof
Slobodzic.................... Slobodzia
Smyrna .... Izmir
Stettin .... Szczeciń
Sukhum-Kaleh .... Sukhumi
Sweaborg (Sveaborg). Suomenlinna
Swinemunde .... Swinoujscie
Tiflis .... Tbilisi
Tilsit .... Sovetsk
Tirgovest .... Târgovişte
Tultsha .... Tulcea
Tver .... Kalinin
Uleaborg .... Oulu
Vasa .... Vaasa
Wilna .... Vilnius